Income Property Valuation

Income Property Valuation

Jeffrey D. Fisher
Robert S. Martin

Dearborn™
Real Estate Education

While a great deal of care has been taken to provide accurate and current information, the ideas, suggestions, general principles, and conclusions presented in this text are subject to local, state, and federal laws and regulations, court cases, and any revision of same. The reader is thus urged to consult legal counsel regarding any points of law—this publication should not be used as a substitute for competent legal advice.

Publisher: Carol Luitjens
Development Editor: Robert A. Porché, Jr.
Project Editor: Debra M. Hall
Cover Design: Lucy Jenkins
Cover Photo: Brent Jones
Interior Design: Jim Buddenbaum

Published by Dearborn™ Real Estate Education
a division of Dearborn Financial Publishing, Inc.®
30 South Wacker Drive
Chicago, IL 60606-7481
(312) 836-4400
http://www.dearbornRE.com

Printed in the United States of America.

10 9 8 7

Library of Congress Cataloging-in-Publication Data

Fisher, Jeffrey D.
  Income property valuation / Jeffrey D. Fisher & Robert S. Martin.
    p. cm.
  Includes index.
  ISBN 0-88462-980-5
  1. Real property—Valuation.   2. Rental housing—Valuation.
  3. Commercial buildings—Valuation.   I. Martin, Robert S.
  II. Title.
    HD1387.F5298   1994
    333.33'2—dc20   93-42615
                                                          CIP

This book is dedicated to Gert Fisher, Greg Fisher, Jerry Fisher, Gretchen Fisher, Jason Fisher, Cary Martin, Robert Martin, Jr., Griffith Martin, Elizabeth Martin and Kristen Martin.

Contents

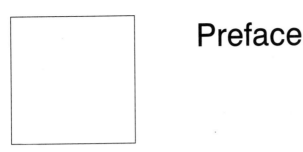

Preface

The purpose of this book is to provide a comprehensive coverage of the appraisal of real estate income property. Although many of the concepts apply to the appraisal of owner-occupied residential real estate, the focus is on properties that are purchased by investors because of income potential. There are no prerequisites to understanding the topics covered in this book. The book does not, however, replicate material that would be found in an introductory real estate text or a text that emphasizes the appraisal of residential real estate.

Because the focus of this text is the appraisal of income property, coverage of the three approaches to value is organized differently from its organization in traditional appraisal books. The income approach to value is covered *before* the other approaches to value are discussed. This is done for two reasons. First, the value of real estate income property obviously depends on its income potential. Thus, understanding how investors typically forecast income and analyze the investment potential of a property provides insight into the appraisal process used to value income property. Second, the other two approaches to estimating value often rely on the use of the income approach for some of the adjustments. Thus, the sales comparison and cost approaches can be better understood and applied to income property after coverage of the income approach.

The first chapter provides an introduction to the appraisal of real estate income property with emphasis on the nature of real estate as a unique asset to be valued in a dynamic market characterized by lack of frequent sales and incomplete information about market transactions. This provides a background to why there are three main approaches used in the appraisal process. Chapter 2 discusses the appraisal process with emphasis on applying that process to income property. Appraisal principles that provide the underlying theory behind the various approaches to value are emphasized and the concept of highest and best use is introduced. Because highest and best use analysis is so important to the appraisal process, an entire chapter is devoted to this topic near the end of the text after covering all three approaches to value. This allows students to see how the techniques taught throughout the text can be applied in various highest and best use analyses.

Because the value of real estate is very dependent on the market in which the property must compete, chapter 3 discusses how appraisers analyze the market area and neighborhood. The appendix to chapter 3 includes short case studies that apply market analysis to housing, office and retail markets.

Because the income will be received in the future, it is necessary to understand how to forecast future income and cash flows and discount that income to estimate the value of the property. These topics are covered in chapters 4 and 5. We believe that it is critical to understand investors' motivations for purchasing real estate income property in order to thoroughly understand the rationale behind the various approaches to estimating the value of income property. Thus, chapter 6 discusses how investors evaluate real estate income properties. Chapter 7 introduces the income approach to valuation. As noted above, this approach to estimating value is covered first in this book because investors in real estate income property obviously pay a price that reflects their expectations of receiving income from operation and resale of the property.

Chapter 8 discusses how the sales comparison approach can be applied to real estate income property. Emphasis is placed on knowing how to adjust comparable sales to obtain a reliable estimate of value. Chapter 9 emphasizes the importance of including a proper description and analysis of the site and improvements that are being valued. This provides a lead-in to chapter 10, which deals with valuation of the site using either the sales comparison approach or the income approach. This is especially necessary when the cost approach is used to value the improvements, the subject of chapter 11.

Real estate income property is frequently purchased subject to existing leases on the property. Chapter 12 deals with the effect of these leases on the value of the leased fee and leasehold estates that are created by the leases.

Because financing is so important in many real estate transactions, chapter 13 discusses how investors analyze the effect of financing on the expected cash flows and measures of investment performance. Financial leverage is examined on both a cash flow and a yield basis.

Techniques for valuing mortgage and equity interests in properties are discussed in chapter 14. This topic is first presented in a straightforward discounted cash-flow (DCF) analysis framework. Traditional mortgage equity techniques such as Ellwood and Akerson are then discussed as historical ways of solving DCF problems before the advent of handheld calculators and personal computers. Properties are frequently purchased with an existing mortgage on the property that may have terms that differ from those currently available in the market. Special financing also may be provided by the seller. Chapter 15 discusses how special financing affects the value of the property and the implications for determining the cash equivalent value of a comparable sale.

The price that investors are willing to pay for a property depends on the perceived riskiness of the property. Thus, chapter 16 contains a thorough discussion of risk analysis, including the effect of financial leverage on risk.

Chapter 17 introduces taxation of real estate income property with emphasis on knowing how federal income taxes affect the after-tax cash flow from a property and the relationship between the before-tax return and the after-tax return. Although real estate is usually appraised on a before-tax basis, the before tax return that investors are willing to accept may depend on the tax consequences of the investment. Thus, an introduction to income property taxation provides a better understanding of the valuation process and helps the appraiser select an appropriate discount rate when valuing a property.

Because selection of an appropriate discount rate is so important to the income approach, chapter 18 is dedicated to a discussion of the various ways of selecting and supporting a discount rate. This pulls together many of the concepts from previous chapters.

Chapter 19 provides an in-depth discussion of highest and best use analysis, with numerous examples to illustrate how to analyze the highest and best use of a vacant or an improved site. Because the income approach is covered before this chapter, the applications discussed in the chapter demonstrate highest and best use analysis in a more comprehensive manner than other appraisal texts. This helps the reader integrate many of the concepts that were discussed in earlier chapters of the book.

The concepts and techniques from the previous chapters are applied to the valuation of proposed projects in chapter 20 and to the valuation of distressed properties in chapter 21. These important topics are not adequately covered in other appraisal books. The book concludes with a case study of a sample appraisal that illustrates the application of all three approaches to estimate the value of an apartment building.

The authors would like to thank Paige Mosbaugh for carefully reviewing the manuscript for this text and checking all the calculations. She also helped us incorporate the suggestions of other reviewers into the final manuscript and assisted in the preparation of the glossary. Also thanks to Sherrie Henry, who assisted in the preparation of the glossary. We also thank Terry Vaughn Grissom, PhD, MAI, CRE, Price Waterhouse—Valuation/Research, Houston, Texas; Donald R. Epley, PhD, MAI, SRA, Mississippi State University; Val Pasquarella, Jr., SRA, ASA, Greater Philadelphia Realty Board School; William J. Pastuszek, Jr., MAI, SRA, MRA, Newton, Massachusetts; Mark T. Kenney, MAI, SRPA, Appraisal Affiliates, Inc., Warminster, Pennsylvania; and Judith Meadows for their reviews and comments on the preliminary draft of this book.

One of the authors is a full-time university professor and the other is a full-time appraiser. We believe that this combination results in a text that is practical yet theoretically sound. Both of us have jointly and independently developed and presented numerous courses and seminars for professional appraisal organizations. We have extensive experience valuing a variety of income property investments and have both served as expert witnesses in valuation litigation. We believe collective appraisal experience has been captured in this book.

Jeffrey D. Fisher, PhD

Robert S. Martin, MAI

About the Authors

Jeffrey D. Fisher, PhD is the Director of the Center for Real Estate Studies and Associate Professor of Finance and Real Estate at the Indiana University School of Business. He served as a trustee of the Appraisal Foundation from its formation in 1987 until 1993 and helped develop the content outline for the uniform national appraisal certification exam. He is a past president of the American Real Estate and Urban Economics Association (AREUEA) and past chairman of the Real Estate Center Directors and Chairholders Association. He currently serves on the board of director of the National Council of Real Estate Investment Fiduciaries (NCREIF) and is on the board of directors of MIG Residential Real Estate Investment Trust. He received the 1992 PREA/Graaskamp Award for Research Excellence from the Pension Real Estate Association. He serves on the board of directors of the Wimer School of Advanced Studies in Real Estate and Land Economics, Homer Hoyt Advanced Studies Institute and is a faculty associate with the Lincoln Institute of Land Policy in Cambridge, Massachussetts. He is the author of six other books, including *Real Estate Finance, Real Estate Appraisal, Questions and Answers to Help You Pass the Appraisal Certification Exam,* and *The Language of Real Estate Appraisal.* He also wrote a chapter on performance measurement for *The Office Building,* a joint publication of the Counselors of Real Estate, the Appraisal Institute and the Society of Industrial and Office REALTORS.® Dr. Fisher developed the "Computer-Assisted Investment Analysis" course and more recently the "Advanced Income Capitalization" course for the Appraisal Institute. He has also developed numerous seminars for the Appraisal Institute, The American Society of Appraisers and other appraisal organizations. He has also been a consultant to appraisers, attorneys, corporations, developers, financial institutions and other universities, and has served as an expert witness on several occasions.

Robert S. Martin, MAI, SREA, CRE is president of Martin and Associates of Winston-Salem, North Carolina. Martin and Associates is a real estate appraisal and consulting firm that specializes in the valuation and evaluation of income producing properties located primarily throughout the Southeastern United States. Typical properties appraised include apartments, office buildings, neighborhood shopping centers, regional malls, hotels, resort properties, golf courses, industrial buildings and subdivisions; and appraisals are prepared for financing decisions, bankruptcies, foreclosures, condemnation and property tax appeals. Mr. Martin is the author of three other books, including *Income Property Appraisal, The Language of Real Estate Appraisal* and *Subdivision Analysis.* He is the developer of numerous computer software programs for income property appraisal, including DCFast, DVM2 and Valucom. Mr. Martin developed the "Market and Investment Analysis" course for the former Society of Real Estate Appraisers and more recently the "Advanced Applications" course for the Appraisal Institute. He has also developed numerous seminars for the Appraisal Institute, including "Appraising Troubled Properties," "Condominium Analysis" and "Preparation of the UCIAR Appraisal Report Form." His clients include financial institutions, attorneys, governmental agencies, corporations, developers and accountants, and he has served as an expert witness on numerous occasions.

<table>
<tr><td>CHAPTER 1</td><td></td></tr>
</table>

| CHAPTER 1 | Introduction to Income Property Valuation |

INCOME PROPERTY INVESTMENTS

This book deals with the valuation of property that is typically purchased as an income-producing investment. The income potential of the property generally depends on the willingness of individuals or firms to pay for the use of space. As is the case in the market for other economic goods and services, the price that can be received for renting a particular income property depends on the supply of competing space as well as on the demand for that space by potential users. Property that is capable of producing income has a value to investors who are willing to purchase real estate in anticipation of a return on their investment. Real estate income property is owned by a variety of different types of investors, including individuals, partnerships, corporations, real estate investment trusts, insurance companies, pension funds, and state and local governments.

The discipline of real estate appraisal deals with the theory and techniques involved in estimating the value of property. Income property may be classified as either residential or nonresidential and may have a variety of characteristics. Figure 1.1 summarizes the main classifications of income property. *Residential* income property, in its simplest form, consists of a single-family rental property; in its most complex form it might consist of a high-rise apartment project in a downtown metropolitan area. In either case rented space is used as a residential dwelling for one or more individuals.

FIGURE 1.1 Classifications of Income Property

Residential	*1–4 family*	*Multifamily* Garden apartment Low rise High rise

Nonresidential	*Commercial*
	Office
	  High rise
	  Low rise
	  Single tenant
	  Medical
	Shopping centers
	  Superregional
	  Regional
	  Community
	  Neighborhood
	  Specialty
	Other retail stores
	Financial institutions
	Restaurants
		Industrial
		Manufacturing
		Warehouse
		Office warehouse
		Lofts
		Garage space
		Distribution
		Research and development

	Hotel Motel High rise Convention Resort	*Special purpose* Hospitals Nursing homes Marinas Shipping facilities Power plants Other

---

Nonresidential income-producing real estate includes commercial, industrial, hotels and other special purpose properties. Commercial space can be further divided into office buildings, shopping centers (superregional, regional, community, neighborhood and specialty), financial institutions, restaurants and other retail stores.

Office space can be classified as high-rise, low-rise, single tenant and medical space. Industrial property can be divided into manufacturing, warehouses, lofts, garage space, distribution, and research and development. Hotels can be classified as motels, high-rise, convention or resort properties. Special-use properties include hospitals, nursing homes, marinas, shipping facilities, power plants and so forth.

COMPONENTS OF PROPERTY VALUE

Real estate is a complex economic good that actually consists of various component parts that contribute to the value of a particular property. Figure 1.2

summarizes the major value components. Real estate has two major physical components: the land and the improvements that are added to the land. *Land* is defined as the earth's surface including land, water and anything attached to it; natural resources in their original state (e.g., mineral deposits, timber, soil). In law, land is considered to be the solid surface of the earth and does not include water. *Improvements* are structures or buildings that are permanently attached to the land.

A distinction is often made between the physical real estate and the legal property rights associated with the physical real estate. The legal rights are referred to as real property. *Real property* is defined as the interests, benefits and rights inherent in the ownership of real estate. *Real estate* is defined as an identified parcel or tract of land, including improvements, if any.[1] When appraising real estate, the appraiser must identify the physical real estate being appraised as well as determine what legal rights are associated with the property being appraised.

All rights to real property are referred to as the *bundle of rights* and are defined as follows: An ownership concept that describes real property by the legal rights associated with owning the property. It specifies rights such as the rights to sell, lease, use, occupy, mortgage and trade the property among others. These rights are typically purchased by the buyer in a sales transaction unless specifically noted or limited in the sale.

Ownership of the complete bundle of rights is referred to as the *fee simple estate* (or fee simple interest) and is defined as absolute ownership of real estate that is unencumbered by any other interest or estate and is subject to the limitations of eminent domain, escheat, police power and taxation. A fee simple estate can be valuated by the present value of the income generated by market rents.

An owner may convey all or part of the bundle of rights to another entity. For example, when a property is leased to an outside tenant under a written agreement or lease, the landlord has relinquished the right to occupy and use the property until the lease expires. The ownership interest that remains and is held by a landlord subject to the lease is referred to as the *leased fee*

FIGURE 1.2 Value Components

Physical real estate
   Land
   Improvements

Property rights
   Real property interests
   Nonrealty interests
     Personal property
     Intangible property
      Business value
      Financing premiums

Bundle of rights (estates)
   Fee simple
   Leased fee
   Leasehold

Financial
   Mortgage
   Equity

---

estate and is defined as an ownership interest in the real estate held by a landlord who has transferred the right of occupancy to a property through the execution of a lease. The leased fee estate can be valued as the present value of the lease income plus the right to the reversion at the end of the lease. The landlord retains the right to receive rental payment throughout the term of the lease and the right to possess the property at the termination of the lease.

Under a lease arrangement, the tenant holds the right to occupy and use the property as long as the terms of the lease are not violated. The lessee's right of occupancy is forfeited when the lease expires. This interest is known as the *leasehold estate* and is defined as an ownership interest in real estate held by a tenant during the term of a lease. The leasehold estate can be valued as the present value of the difference between the market rent and the rent specified by the lease. The tenant is given the right to use and occupy a property for a time and based on the restrictions contained in the lease.

Under certain circumstances, if the lease allows, the tenant may transfer the right to occupy and use the tenant space. If the lease terms created an advantage for a prospective tenant, the leasehold interest may have value and therefore could be sold for a profit.

A leasehold interest is also created when the land is leased. A developer may enter into a long-term *land lease* (ground lease) and construct the improvements. Under this circumstance, the tenant holds a leasehold interest in the land and owns the improvements until the land lease expires. The owner of the land has a leased fee interest in the land and a reversionary interest in the improvements at the expiration of the land lease. Either party has the right to sell, mortgage or trade the interest, but only the lessee of the land has the right to occupy and use the property. This right is lost when the land lease expires.

Real estate valuation assignments may involve the analysis of any or all of these real estate interests. The task is to identify and estimate the value of the interest.

NONREALTY INTERESTS

Due to the complex nature of many real estate appraisal assignments, non-realty interests may be involved. *Nonrealty interests* include personal property and intangible property such as business value and contractual arrangements.

Personal Property

The most obvious example of inclusion of a nonrealty interest is when tangible personal property is included. *Personal property* is defined as identifiable, portable and tangible objects that are considered by the general public as being "personal," e.g., furnishings, artwork, antiques, gems and jewelry, collectibles, machinery and equipment; all property that is not classified as real estate.

Examples of real estate projects where personal property may be included are (1) restaurant equipment in a restaurant setting, (2) machinery and equipment in an industrial plant and (3) furniture in a hotel. Personal property is not typically permanently attached to real estate. In some instances, the decision as to whether an item should be considered personal or real property is difficult, especially with regard to industrial property.

Although personal property has value, its value must be separated from that of the real property in an appraisal report. For example, the value of a hotel might include furniture, fixtures and equipment in the hotel that are considered personal property. The appraisal report would indicate the value of this property in addition to the value of the real property (land and improvements).

Business Value

Another nonrealty interest that is frequently part of a real estate transaction is business value. *Business value* is defined as the value resulting from business organization including such things as management skills, assembled work force, working capital, legal rights (trade names, business names, franchises, patents, trademarks, contracts, leases, operating agreements) that have been assembled to make the business a viable and valuable entity in its competitive market. Business value is often associated with properties such as hotels, nursing homes and regional shopping centers.

The term "going-concern value" refers to the total value of the property, including the real property, tangible personal property and the enhancement to value resulting from an operating business. Going-concern value assumes that the business operation will continue. For example, the appraiser may determine that a hotel has a going-concern value because of its national franchise and above-average management, which have allowed it to capture a higher percentage of the market than other hotels. Thus, in addition to the land, improvements and personal property, the appraiser may assign an additional value to the business enterprise. All of this would be included in the going-concern value of the hotel.

Tax Incentives

For certain property types, governmental agencies have created incentives through the granting of tax credits, depreciation deductions and/or property tax reductions to encourage the development or rehabilitation of certain property types. The value of these incentives would be classified as a nonrealty interest. Analysis of these interests involves a complex process that will not be considered in this book. The analyst should, however, be aware of the possibility that these interests may exist.

MORTGAGE AND EQUITY INTERESTS

Numerous real estate transactions are funded using debt financing. Once the debt is incurred, the lender receives a *mortgage interest* on the property. The owner's interest becomes an *equity interest*. The mortgage instrument creates a contractual relationship between the owner and borrower. The lender is free to sell his mortgage obligation to another lender. The borrower may or may not be able to sell the property and have the subsequent owner assume the loan at its original terms.

If the loan terms are below those typical of the market and the loan is assumable, a potential buyer may pay a premium amount for the right to assume the loan. This premium is referred to as a "financing premium" and would be a nonrealty interest. The additional price does not represent payment for the real property; in effect, a premium is paid for the equity interest in the property. However, because the loan terms are below those typical of the market, the existing mortgage interest in the property is worth less. Should the lender wish to sell the loan to another lender, if the contract terms are less favorable than typical terms, the loan may have a market value less than its current balance. In theory, the additional amount an equity investor would pay for the right to assume the below-market loan is offset by the lower amount the lender would receive if the mortgage interest were sold. Thus the sum of the mortgage and equity interests is still the same as the value of the real property with market financing. Chapter 14 discusses techniques for determining the value of financing premiums.

REAL ESTATE MARKET CHARACTERISTICS

Real estate appraisal differs in many ways from valuation techniques commonly applied to other investments such as stocks and bonds. In part, this is a result of the characteristics of real estate markets versus other capital markets.

A market for an item is created by the interaction of buyers and sellers, all seeking to exchange similar goods. In today's economy, the medium of exchange is typically monetary in nature. The remainder of this book deals with issues and methods used to analyze real estate markets and approaches to estimating the market value for various property types and interests. Following is a review of the various characteristics of the real estate market.

No Organized Market

Unlike the market for stocks and bonds, there is no centralized market for real estate transactions. Thus, it is difficult to know the price of a particular type of real estate at a given point in time.

Availability of Market Information

Information concerning sale prices, lease terms, financing and any other agreements that are part of a transaction may be confidential and unavailable to individuals who are not parties to the sale. There is no recognized source of published information that contains information in the detail needed to analyze a sale accurately. Negotiations for a specific property may involve extended periods of time because of the complexity of a transaction and the need to make judgments concerning construction quality, environmental issues, legal documents, past operating history, and so forth.

Because of the time necessary to complete transactions, available information about the transaction price could reflect terms that were agreed on at a point significantly earlier than the actual closing date. Sale prices also may have included consideration paid for interests other than the real estate itself.

Infrequent Trades of Property

Transactions for real estate investments are not continuous, making it difficult to know how prices are changing over time. Appraisers often must use information from property sales that occurred considerably earlier than the date the value is being estimated for the present property appraisal.

Immobility of Real Estate

Unlike many investment opportunities available to the investment community, real estate property is tied to a fixed location. The potential success or failure of a real estate project may be significantly affected by happenings and trends in the general and immediate geographic area that surrounds it. Stocks, bonds and commodities are not tied to a specific location. Even a business can generally be moved to another location if success is not expected at its current location. Real estate, however, is and always will remain a product that is heavily affected by its surroundings. Because the success of an income-producing property is so heavily dependent on the state of its environment, a real estate analyst must place heavy emphasis on an analysis of the area and neighborhood market conditions as well as of the property itself. Another variable factor is that market conditions are not stable and may, therefore, change significantly over time. The change may come abruptly and may have either a positive or a negative impact on the property. If a change is negative, actions to counteract the adverse condition may be physically, politically or financially beyond the capability of a property owner. The immobility of real estate is what makes real estate such a fascinating subject: Identical physical improvements on two lots of the same size may have significantly different market values because of each lot's unique location.

Each Parcel Is Unique

Because of the immobility of real estate we can say that no two parcels of real estate can ever be *exactly* alike. They will always be at different locations. Whether this difference has a significant impact on value is a different consideration. Because each parcel is unique, the price of one property may or may not be a good indication of the value of another property.

Segmented Markets

The real estate market is divided into numerous segments or submarkets that do not necessarily behave the same way. The division occurs not only by property type and market area but also within each segment itself. For example, the success of one type of building in a particular neighborhood does not automatically ensure that the same building type will be successful in another neighborhood. Construction costs of a Class A office building in Neighborhood X might be absorbed rapidly, and the building might command attractive tenants and rent levels. Because of an oversupply of Class A office space in Neighborhood Y, however, if the same Class A office building were to be constructed in this neighborhood, it might not achieve the same level of success. Technological advances may impact on market segments and change market perceptions. In other words, new segments might be created that would have an impact on existing market segments. For example, the recent rise of small specialty shopping centers has had a significant impact on the tenant mix of neighborhood and community centers. The notion that a neighborhood center cannot be successful without major tenants has disappeared.

Real estate markets may not only be segmented by user type and location but also by investor type. For example, major "investment grade" property may include a multitude of property types but be similar in location, size, effective age, construction quality and, therefore, perceived risk.

GOVERNMENT REGULATIONS

Real estate is heavily regulated and is subject to rules promulgated not only at the local level but also on the state and national levels. New construction must meet the strict requirements set forth in zoning restrictions, development requirements, environmental controls and building inspection requirements. Land use may be further controlled by other public programs. For example, incentives are available for low-income residential housing projects that meet predetermined guidelines. These guidelines are restrictions on the project in addition to the restrictions imposed by zoning, environmental rules and development requirements. It is important to realize that heavy government regulation is a major factor in the real estate market and that changes in rules and laws may significantly affect a real estate investment. In 1981 tax laws were changed to provide incentives to encourage construction of new projects during a period of high inflation and high interest rates. These incentives worked: Significant new construction occurred from 1982 to 1986 in many markets around the country. In 1986 the tax incentives were eliminated. Because the market for certain properties in several market areas had become out of balance, a severe slump in real estate values in oversupplied areas resulted in the late 1980s.

Local controls are emerging as significant factors in the marketplace today, evidenced by severe restrictions that may be placed on new construction. Laws governing such development factors as density, traffic patterns and control, and the impact of new construction on the capacity of public facilities are gradually becoming more restrictive. It appears a developer's options may be reduced even further in the future. Any analysis of the real estate market that does not seriously consider the effect of government controls would certainly be deficient.

MARKET TRENDS

Although there are numerous investment markets that are more volatile (commodities, for example), the real estate market is subject to significantly large shifts over time. Supply and demand for real estate are seldom in balance. Once demand exceeds supply, opportunistic developers typically enter the market and construct new facilities that may exceed the immediate demand. The lead time needed to construct new projects, the size of new projects, the lack of perfect market information and financing alternatives—all contribute to the cyclical nature of the real estate market. Economic factors such as employment, income levels, the level of business activity and the health of financial markets all affect real estate values and are therefore the driving forces behind the fluctuations in real estate markets. Because market information is imperfect, reading and assessing the impact of the cyclical nature of real estate is certainly difficult. A reasonable assessment of market information is obviously needed in an analysis of the real estate market.

Supply Adjusts Slowly

It takes time for the supply of real estate to change through development of new properties or even conversion from one use to another. This adds an additional complication to attempting to measure real estate values. For example, in "equilibrium," value might equal cost if both are accurately and appropriately measured. However, in the short run, value may differ considerably from cost.

Few Buyers and Sellers at One Time

Compared with some other markets, such as stocks and bonds, there are usually relatively few buyers and sellers in the market for a particular property at a particular time. This can result in transaction prices that differ from market value. It also means that in some cases a particular buyer can influence the price. Such a market differs from one characterized by perfect competition, where buyers are "price takers"; that is, a market in which individual buyers do not influence the price. In real estate markets prices are often influenced by a particular buyer who is willing to bid much more than another bidder. Consequently, some analysts question whether market value is being paid—especially when it is the "optimist" who ends up with the property!

THE ROLE OF CAPITAL MARKETS

We have discussed the characteristics of the market for real estate assets. This is the market in which interests in real property, that is, land and buildings, are traded. Real estate income property is often bought and sold by investors who are primarily interested in the rate of return that they expect to earn on the investment. (Rate of return measures are discussed in chapter 8.) These investors expect a rate of return commensurate with that available from other capital investments of similar risk. Furthermore, real estate investments are typically financed with mortgages that are obtained from various types of financial institutions, including banks, S&Ls, insurance companies and mortgage real estate investment trusts.

It should be clear that real estate values can be influenced by trends in the broader capital market. Thus, it is important for real estate appraisers to be aware of rates of return that are currently available for alternative investments and have a general understanding of the overall market for real estate capital.

The term *capital market* refers to the market for all the various sources of capital for either lending or investment, including government and corporate bonds, corporate stocks, as debt and equity capital for real estate.

Debt capital is used for construction loans and permanent financing in the form of long-term mortgages. Capital for construction has traditionally come from commercial banks and S&Ls. However, because of the problems experienced by the S&L industry during the late 1980s and early 1990s, it has become more difficult for developers to rely on these sources for construction and development loans. Capital for long-term mortgage loans on single-family residences and smaller residential and nonresidential income property investments typically comes from a bank, S&L or credit union. For larger residential or nonresidential income properties, the debt capital might come from an insurance company, a pension fund or a mortgage real estate investment trust (REIT).

The term *primary market* refers to the initial source of capital received by a user to fund a project. The initial supplier of capital may, in turn, sell the financial instrument that was created when the capital was supplied. For example, a home buyer might receive a loan from an S&L that results in the creation of a mortgage instrument that indicates the terms of the loan and makes the property collateral for the loan. The S&L might sell this mortgage in what is referred to as the "secondary market." The *secondary market* is the market for existing financial claims.

In the case of the secondary mortgage market, purchasers include such entities as the Federal National Mortgage Association (FNMA), referred to as "Fannie Mae," and the Federal Home Loan Mortgage Corporation (FHLMC), referred to as "Freddie Mac." These secondary market participants play an important role in capital markets by providing a source of liquidity for mortgage lenders, a provision that helps ensure the availability of mortgage capital for single-family residential properties.

Equity capital for real estate comes from a wide variety of sources, ranging from small individual investors to large institutional investors such as insurance companies and pension funds. These funds could be invested directly into the real estate project or through a financial intermediary, for example, an equity REIT or some type of syndication such as a public or private limited partnership. The nature of these intermediaries has changed significantly over time. In the early to middle 1980s, syndications were quite active because of their ability to pass the tax benefits associated with real estate through to the investors. With the reduction in tax incentives in 1986, these vehicles became much less attractive. At the same time, the role of pension funds as a source of real estate capital increased in significance. Although some pension funds invest directly in real estate, others prefer to invest through some type of intermediary that can provide expertise in selecting investments and managing the property. Many insurance companies and other money managers responded by establishing funds for pension fund investment. These funds received the capital from the pension fund and invested the money in real estate investments that were then managed by the funds.

TYPES OF REAL ESTATE STUDIES

Real estate studies may be classified in several different categories: market studies, marketability studies, investment analyses, feasibility studies, environmental impact studies, highest and best use analysis, cost-benefit studies, land utilization studies and real estate appraisals. Studies relevant to the preparation of a real estate appraisal include market studies, marketability studies, highest and best use analysis and feasibility studies. Results of each of these studies are vital inputs in an appraisal report. Each category of study is defined below.

Market Study

A thorough real estate analysis of the general market conditions affecting a property includes a *market study* of demographic, economic, political, and cultural trends and conditions that affect the current supply and demand for a particular property type.

Market studies focus specifically on the property *type*, not on the specific property itself. In this sense, market studies are the most general in nature. The other study types focus specifically on a certain property. Key data analyzed in a market study are the demographic and economic factors that affect the subject property as well as governmental policy and social trends.

Marketability Study

A *marketability study* is a real estate analysis that addresses the ability of a property to be absorbed, sold or leased under current and anticipated market conditions.

In contrast to market studies, marketability studies involve analysis of a specific property. Marketability study information is used to test whether current and foreseeable market forces will support development of a specific use and the rate at which absorption could take place. Marketability studies focus closely on competitive facilities to formulate three kinds of conclusions: the price at which a property will be sold or rented; the quantity likely to be sold or rented over the absorption period; and the conditions, marketing techniques and features that will enhance the success of the project.

Marketability study information is used to forecast various key inputs in an appraisal, including rent and expense estimates, the relative contribution of property attributes, absorption periods and absorption patterns. Rent estimates include not only the absolute rent levels but also typical terms: rental increase provisions, options, expense passthroughs, sales overage provisions and so forth.

Investment Analysis

According to the Uniform Standards of Professional Appraisal Practice, an *investment analysis* is a study that reflects the relationship between acquisition price and anticipated future benefits of a real estate investment.

The term "investment analysis" is also used as a general term to describe any of a number of studies that analyze expected future cash flows in relation to money or capital used to purchase an interest in a property. For example, analyses to decide whether to refinance or dispose of a property could be considered investment analyses.

Feasibility Study

According to the Uniform Standards of Professional Appraisal Practice, a *feasibility study* is a study of the cost-benefit relationship of an economic endeavor. It is an analysis of a real estate project that incorporates the results of market and marketability studies to determine whether a project will meet the economic return requirements of a specific market or investor.

The feasibility study focuses directly on the expected performance of the subject property in a real estate appraisal. In undertaking a feasibility study the appraiser takes information and judgments made based on data from market and marketability studies and applies the analytic techniques associated with investment analysis to calculate benchmarks of expected performance for the subject. If the expected levels of performance meet the standards of an investor for the property, the project passes the test of feasibility. The preparation of feasibility studies will be discussed in a later chapter after the appraiser has been exposed to the analytical techniques used to test the cash flow inputs forecast using market and marketability study information.

Highest and Best Use Analysis

A highest and best use (HBU) analysis is essentially a series of feasibility studies for different use scenarios for the subject property, both for the land as if vacant and for the property as if improved. The use for each that results in the highest value is the use assumed in the appraisal report. In essence, an HBU analysis uses the results of market studies, marketability studies and feasibility studies to arrive at a conclusion regarding the best use of the property.

The HBU is the reasonable and probable use that results in the highest present value of the land after considering all legally permissible, physically possible and economically feasible uses. Capitalization rates or discount rates for each feasible use should reflect typical returns expected in the market. Highest and best use is usually determined under two different premises, as if the site were

1. vacant and could be improved in the optimal manner; or
2. currently improved.

In the latter premise, the choices will be either to keep the existing building or to demolish the building and construct one that would fulfill the highest and best use of the site. In general, it is not feasible to demolish an existing building as long as it contributes value above that of the vacant site.

Environmental Impact Study

An *environmental impact study* is an analysis of the impact of a proposed land use on its environment, including the direct and indirect effects of the project during all phases of use and their long-run implications.

The National Environmental Policy Act of 1969 requires that every recommendation or report on proposals for legislation and other major federal actions significantly affecting the quality of the human environment must be filed with a detailed impact statement. The environmental impact study provides an analysis of any adverse environmental effects that cannot be avoided should the proposal be implemented, alternatives to the proposed action, the relationship between local short-term uses of the environment and the maintenance and enhancement of long-term productivity, and any irreversible and irretrievable commitments of resources that would be involved in the proposed action should it be implemented.

Cost-Benefit Study

A *cost-benefit study* is an analysis of the cost of creating an improvement versus the benefits that will be created by the improvement, including non-monetary issues.

A cost-benefit study is typically used by public agencies to make decisions concerning capital improvements. A cost-benefit ratio is typically developed through the analysis of a proposed project. The ratio equals the dollar amount of benefits generated by an improvement divided by the cost of that improvement. The ratio must exceed 1.00 for the improvement to be considered desirable.

Land Utilization Study

A *land utilization study* is an analysis of the potential uses of a parcel of land and a determination of the highest and best use for that parcel; a complete inventory of the parcels in a given community or other area classified by type of use, plus (in some cases) an analysis of the spatial patterns of use revealed by this inventory.

Land utilization studies do not embody the viewpoint of any particular investor nor do they focus on any one parcel. Furthermore, the consideration of markets and feasibility is not normally included.

Appraisal

According to the Uniform Standards of Professional Appraisal Practice, an *appraisal* is defined as (1) the act or process of estimating value; an estimate of value and (2) pertains to appraising and related functions, e.g., appraisal practice, appraisal services.

An appraisal provides an unbiased estimate of the value of an identified interest in real property, related personalty or intangible assets. The appraisal process involves undertaking selective research and analysis of pertinent market data, applying the appropriate analytical approaches, drawing from experience and academic skills, and applying judgment to arrive at an estimate of value. Ultimately, the results of all the key real estate studies are presented in an appraisal report as support for the final value estimate selected.

The three approaches to appraisal include:

1. the cost approach;
2. the direct sales comparison approach; and
3. the income capitalization approach.

This book illustrates the application of each approach to the appraisal of real estate income property.

NEED FOR AN APPRAISAL PROCESS

Real estate differs from other economic goods or investments in a number of ways. Its value depends on its physical, legal, social and economic characteristics as well as on the dynamics of the market in which it is bought and sold. The complexity of real estate as well as the lack of market information compared with many other economic goods must be reflected in the appraisal process used to estimate value. The validity of this process is important to market participants such as buyers, sellers, lenders and government agencies that rely on the appraiser's conclusions. The remainder of this book explores the appraisal process in more depth, with emphasis on the valuation of real estate income property.

SUMMARY

Income property can be classified as residential or nonresidential. Nonresidential property includes commercial, industrial, hotels and special purpose properties. Physical characteristics of real estate include land and improvements. The term real property refers to the legal rights associated with the real estate. A fee simple interest in the property owns the complete bundle of rights. When a property is leased, the lessor transfers some of the rights to the lessee. The lessor's interest is referred to as a leased fee interest, and the lessee's rights are referred to as the leasehold interest.

A property may include nonrealty interests in addition to real property. Examples include personal property and business value. When there is a business value, the going concern value of the property exceeds that of the real property and the personal property.

When a mortgage is used to finance a property, a mortgage interest and an equity interest are created. Mortgages that have favorable terms can result in a financing premium, which is an amount paid for the right to assume the mortgage. This premium does not add value to the real property.

Real estate markets are characterized by lack of an organized national market, difficulty in obtaining market information, infrequent sales and a small number of active buyers and sellers at a particular point in time. Real estate is also immobile and each parcel is unique. Markets tend to be segmented and real estate is subject to many government regulations.

A market study is an analysis of general market conditions, whereas a marketability study is an analysis of the ability of a specific property to be absorbed, sold or leased under current or anticipated market conditions. A feasibility study combines the results of the market and marketability studies to determine whether a project will meet the economic return requirements of a specific market or investor. A highest and best use analysis combines the results of market studies, marketability studies and feasibility studies to determine the use that results in the highest value. An appraisal is an unbiased estimate of the value of an identified interest in real property, related personal property and any intangible assets such as business interests and financing premiums. The need for an appraisal can arise from a variety of sources, including owners, sellers, buyers, lenders, insurance companies and government agencies.

The value of real estate is affected by local market trends, slow adjustments in supply and changes in the capital market. Because of the unique characteristics of real estate assets and the complexities of real estate markets, appraisers follow a well-defined process when estimating value. This process is the subject of the remainder of the text.

KEY TERMS

appraisal	land utilization study
bundle of rights	leased fee estate
business value	leasehold estate
capital market	marketability study
cost-benefit study	market study
environmental impact study	mortgage interest
equity interest	nonrealty interests
feasibility study	nonresidential property
fee simple estate	personal property
improvements	primary mortgage market
income	real estate
income property	real property
investment analysis	residential property
land	secondary mortgage market
land lease	segmented market

QUESTIONS

1. What are the ways of classifying income property?
2. What is the difference between real estate and real property?
3. What is meant by the term "bundle of rights"? How can these rights be separated?
4. What are the sources of nonrealty interests? Do nonrealty interests have value?
5. What interests are created when a property is financed with a mortgage?
6. What is meant by the term "appraisal"?
7. Why is it necessary to appraise real estate income property?
8. What distinguishes real estate markets from the market for other investments?
9. How could changes in the capital market affect the value of real estate income property?
10. What is the difference between a marketability study and a market study?
11. What is a highest and best use analysis?

END NOTE

1. In some jurisdictions, the terms "real estate" and "real property" have the same legal meaning. The separate definitions recognize the traditional distinction between the two concepts in appraisal theory.

| CHAPTER 2 | # Appraisal Principles and Highest and Best Use |

APPRAISAL PRINCIPLES

The theoretical framework of an appraisal is based on several basic principles of economic theory. These appraisal principles are the theories that attempt to explain the rationale of market behavior that influences value. The following principles form the basis for appraisal theory and govern the thought process used when preparing an appraisal report.

Anticipation

The principle of *anticipation* states that value is created by the expectation of benefits to be received in the future. Expectations for income-producing properties generally manifest themselves as anticipated income from the operation and the ultimate resale of the property in the future. In the appraisal of income properties, the principle of anticipation forms the foundation for the income capitalization approach to estimating value. Historical income for a property is relevant only if it is useful in projecting anticipated future income.

Change

The principle of *change* recognizes that a property and its environment are always in transition and are affected by economic and social forces that are constantly at work. Change is inevitable—it is certainly an important issue in the appraisal of real estate because of the cyclical nature of the real estate market. Consideration of changes in market conditions is a key element in any real estate analysis, especially in the appraisal of income-producing properties. Uncertainty due to unanticipated changes in factors that affect future benefits is reflected in the rate of return that investors expect when they purchase a property.

Supply and Demand

The principle of *supply and demand* applies to the real estate market in several ways. First, rental rates depend on the supply of competitive space, as well as on the demand for space by users. When the demand for space exceeds the supply, rental rates tend to rise and vacancy rates fall. This excess demand for space is the driving force behind construction of new buildings and demolition or conversion of old, outdated properties. When the supply of space exceeds the demand, rent levels tend to fall, vacancy rates rise and construction of new space becomes uneconomical.

Second, the value of a property depends on the supply of competitive real estate investments, as well as on the demand for real estate investments by investors. The desire of investors to own real estate depends on the perceived benefits of holding real estate versus other investments. This desire is affected by factors such as tax laws, interest rates and inflationary expectations. For example, during the early 1980s there was an increased demand for real estate investments because of the favorable tax environment. This led to an increase in the price of real estate investments, which, in turn, made it attractive for developers to construct new buildings. This ultimately led to an oversupply of buildings and falling rental rates during the late 1980s.

The supply and demand for space and the supply and demand for real estate investments are seldom in balance. To project changes in rental rates and real estate prices, changes in supply and demand must be considered.

Substitution

The principle of *substitution* states that a buyer will pay no more for a property than the cost of obtaining an equally desirable substitute. If several similar goods are supplied, the good with the lowest price will produce the greatest demand and quantity sold. This principle forms the basis for implementation of the direct sales comparison approach to estimating value because it assumes prices paid for comparable properties reflect the relative ranking of their attributes in the marketplace. This principle is also important to the cost approach, which assumes that an investor will not pay more than it would cost to develop substitute space. Finally, the principle applies to the income approach, which assumes that rental rates must compete with those of substitute space and that rates of return required by investors must be in line with those for alternative (substitute) investments.

Balance

The principle of *balance* is that value is maximized when contrasting or opposing market forces are in a state of equilibrium. That is, the various factors that contribute to the value of a property are being used in the proportions that are most economical. For example, value is maximized when there is a proper ratio of land to building. Higher ratios of building to land tend to be used in areas where land prices are high.

Conformity

Conformity refers to the relationship between a property and its surroundings. A property that conforms with its surroundings tends to be better accepted in the marketplace. Conformity can be controlled by market forces and/or governmental controls imposed by zoning ordinances and development restrictions.

Contribution

The principle of *contribution* states that the value of a particular component is measured by the marginal increase in value attributable to its existence. This increase in value is not necessarily equal to the cost of the component. Contribution is a key concept in appraisal theory and forms the theoretical basis for adjusting comparables in all three approaches to value.

Opportunity Cost

Opportunity costs are costs associated with sacrificing opportunities not taken. The opportunity cost concept is important in estimating value, because income-producing real estate competes in the market for investment funds. Real estate must offer competitive returns based on the relative degree of risk. Investors who select real estate have opportunity costs associated with alternative investments that they did not select.

Utility

Utility is the ability of a good to satisfy a need, want or desire. Because income-producing real estate theoretically satisfies the needs of the businesses or individuals who occupy the space, the functional utility of an income-producing property is one of the major elements that create value. Utility is the prime element of comparison between two competing properties.

THE FUNCTION OF REAL ESTATE APPRAISALS

The diversity of income-producing real estate property, the complexity of the legal issues involved and the immense dollar value and number of income properties in this country created a need for a segment of professionals schooled in the analysis and valuation of this class of asset. The real estate appraisal profession subsequently emerged as an important segment of the real estate community; it is becoming even more important today, with the introduction of state *certification* for real estate appraisers.

The need for real estate appraisals stems from the fact that the real estate market is imperfect; therefore, estimating and supporting the value estimate for an income-producing property can be complex and time consuming. Motivating factors for performing an appraisal are many and include:

- financing;
- determining a listing price;
- supporting a sales price;
- property taxation;
- condemnation appraisal;
- lease vs. buy decisions;
- new project feasibility;
- litigation of property rights and interests;
- project performance; and
- fire and casualty insurance.

Financing

Lenders usually require an appraisal as part of the underwriting process for a mortgage loan. They do not want the loan to exceed a certain percentage of the property value.

Determining a Listing Price

Once an owner decides to offer his property for sale, a real estate appraisal may be undertaken to estimate the most probable sales price, given existing and foreseeable market conditions.

Supporting a Sales Price

Contracts for the sale of income-producing properties frequently are entered into with the stipulation that the contract price not be greater than the appraised value of the property. An independent, unbiased analysis therefore is required to ascertain whether the sales price is reasonable, assuming current market conditions.

Property Taxation

Government authorities are granted powers of *taxation,* the power to tax real property in their jurisdictions. The amount of taxes typically is based on the assessed value assigned to a specific property. Periodically, the authorities reappraise each parcel to assure fairness in their taxing policy. To reflect fairness, the appraisal should be accomplished using appropriate techniques and unbiased judgment.

Condemnation Appraisal

As part of the governmental powers of *eminent domain,* a public agency may take real property to enhance the public welfare. In the process of *condemnation,* independent appraisals are prepared to estimate the loss in value a property owner suffers by the taking of property. Because the owner is entitled to *just compensation* for a loss, an unbiased and competent appraisal is necessary in this process.

Lease versus Buy Decisions

Frequently, a potential occupant of a tenant space faces the option of whether to purchase the real estate or enter into a lease contract and occupy the building as a tenant, rather than as an owner. Two key factors to be considered in this discussion are the price of the property and a reasonable rental rate. Both of these parameters are contained in a complete appraisal report.

New Project Feasibility

An appraisal of a proposed project addresses the feasibility of the development and typically contains estimates of the value of the project at several points in time. The key values are "as is value," or the value of what is currently in place, and *prospective value* upon completion of construction, or the value when the project is complete but prior to lease-up of the tenant space. A third estimate is the prospective value of the property when it reaches stabilized occupancy levels.

Litigation of Property Rights and Interests

Frequently, ownerships are split and/or contracts are contested that involve income-producing real estate, thus creating a need for real estate appraisals.

Partnership re-formation, deaths, divorces and gifts are all instances in which decisions are based on real estate value estimates determined by appraisers.

Project Performance

Pension funds typically have income-producing properties reappraised periodically to track the property's performance over time and therefore determine the real estate's contribution to the overall portfolio return.

Fire and Casualty Insurance

An appraisal may be undertaken to set benchmarks for insurance purposes. Under these circumstances several values may be estimated, depending on the needs and requirements of a particular insurance company. Market value, replacement cost, reproduction cost or cash value may be needed.

TYPES OF VALUE

An appraisal assignment may require the estimation of one or more values for an income-producing property. The various values represent estimates made assuming a set of assumptions determined by the ultimate use of the estimate. Most appraisals seek the market value of a property as of a specific date. A more meaningful number to an insurance company, however, might be the cost to replace a building, assuming it is damaged beyond repair. In this instance the market value of the property as a whole in today's market may be significantly different from the cost to replace the improvements (the "insurable value"). Following is a list of the types of value an appraiser may be asked to estimate:

- market value;
- market price;
- cost;
- investment value;
- value in use;
- assessed value;
- insurable value;
- going concern value;
- salvage value;
- book value;
- mortgage loan value; and
- liquidation value.

Market Value

Market value is a value estimate made as of a specific date that represents the most probable price that a seller could expect to command for a specific interest in real estate property, assuming a typical, knowledgeable investor, a reasonable marketing time, and a sale made in cash or its equivalent. A more detailed discussion of market value is included in the section on the appraisal process in this chapter. The important feature of the market value concept is that the value estimate is made assuming the property is offered for sale on the open market for a reasonable period of time and is subsequently purchased by a purchaser assumed to have the characteristics of a typical investor for the property being appraised.

Market Price

Market price is the price actually paid for an income-producing property. If the purchaser at this price has the characteristics of a typical investor, the price paid represents a market price; if only a real estate interest was purchased, the market price represents the market value of the real estate as of the date of the transaction.

Cost

Cost is the actual dollar amount needed on a specific date to replace improvements that are part of an income-producing property. When the dollar amount represents the cost to create an exact duplicate of the existing structure, the estimate is referred to as "reproduction cost new." If the estimate represents the cost to create improvements with the same functional utility as an existing structure, the estimate is referred to as the "replacement cost new." Either cost estimate may represent the market value of the improvements, if the improvements have not experienced any depreciation due to age, wear and tear, and/or functional or external obsolescence. It is rare that the market value and cost of real estate improvements are equal and such a balance only occurs when the new buildings represent the optimum improvement for the site.

Investment Value

Investment value is the value of an income-producing property to a specific investor. The value is found by employing an analytic model that uses the specific return requirements of an investor. If the return requirements of the investment mirror those of the typical buyer in the marketplace, investment value and market value are identical. Otherwise, there could be a significant difference in the two values.

Value in Use

Value in use is similar to investment value in that it reflects the requirements of a specific investor. Value in use differs from investment value, however, in representing the value of an income-producing property to its current user. The building may have attributes that benefit the existing tenant, which would add no value to the next tenant to occupy the space. This condition may occur when a current occupant uses the building for a special purpose or to create a unique product or service with limited demand in the market area. It also may occur if the building contains an outmoded or superadequate construction feature that benefits an existing user but would not be installed in the building if a new, more typical tenant occupied the space. The value in use is the present value of the future benefits that accrue to the existing tenant.

Assessed Value

Assessed value, or assessment value, is the value of the property used to calculate periodic ad valorem taxes. The assessed value may bear little resemblance to the market value of the property. The relationship depends on how often the property is reassessed, the legal definition governing the meaning of the assessed value, plus the data and methods used to calculate the value.

Insurable Value

Insurable value is the benchmark value used to calculate the fire and extended damage coverage insurance premiums for a property. This value may bear little resemblance to the market value, because typically the value of the vacant land is excluded and additional coverage may be needed to cover the possibility that the replacement may be greater than the contributing market value of the improvements.

Going-Concern Value

As discussed earlier, *going-concern value* is the total value of a business enterprise. In real estate, several types of projects may actually be viewed as business ventures, including hotels, shopping malls, healthcare facilities and restaurants. The market value of the going concern may be different from the market value of the real estate if nonrealty interests such as personal property, business value and beneficial contracts are included in the appraisal.

Salvage Value

Salvage value is the value of any improvements to an entity that moves the improvements off a specific site. The obvious case arises if the entire structure can be moved and placed on another site. Salvage value could also be created if components of an existing structure could be saved and used elsewhere.

Book Value

Book value is an accounting concept and is defined as the historical cost of improvements less any allowance for depreciation plus the cost of any capital improvements made in subsequent years. Market value and book value may have little relationship to each other.

Mortgage Loan Value

Mortgage loan value is the benchmark on which lenders base mortgage investments in real estate. Typically, market value and mortgage value are identical. A lender, however, may introduce restrictions in its underwriting policy that alter this relationship.

Liquidation Value

The *liquidation value* is the price that results from sale of the property without allowing for a reasonable time on the market. It may be less than market value, depending on the degree of interest in the property at the time it is liquidated.

An appraisal assignment may include the estimation of one or more of the above values (except, possibly, for book value or salvage value). The appraiser should recognize the differences and similarities in the methods used to estimate each.

MARKET VALUE VERSUS INVESTMENT VALUE AND VALUE IN USE

The income approach is a viable and often-used method of estimating *investment value* as well as *market value*. When estimating investment value, however, the investment measures and rates of return used in the analysis reflect those of a specific investor rather than a typical investor, as in the case of market value. Typically, the net operating income forecasts are the same for estimating either market value or investment value. However, the projected before-tax cash flow, after-tax cash flow and desired rate of return for investing in the property may differ from those of the typical investor. Before-tax cash flows (NOI less mortgage debt service) may differ because of access to special financing that is not available to the typical investor. After-tax cash flows may differ because of the investor's particular tax status.[1] Rate-of-return requirements can differ because of differences in the way different investors evaluate the riskiness of the investment. This risk is somewhat unique to the investor because it depends on how the investment fits into the investor's overall investment portfolio and investment strategy. For example, if a pension fund already had a significant investment in office buildings in Dallas it might view the risk of purchasing another office building in Dallas as much greater than would a pension fund that currently owned no office buildings in Dallas. The difference lies in the diversification benefits associated with the investment, which influences the perceived risk and required rate of return.

The income approach may also be used to estimate *value in use,* which is closely related to the concept of investment value. In this instance, the estimate would represent the value of a property to its current occupant and user. Investment value and value in use may be identical if the investor is also the occupant of the property. In estimating the value in use, the forecast cash flows represent the perceived benefits recognized by the current user, and the discount rate represents the required rate of the return of the user. The benefits of the user could be quantified as either opportunity costs or cost savings created by building features (location, size, shape, design features, accessory facilities) that enhance the operation of the existing user but apparently would not benefit the next "typical" user of the building.

THE APPRAISAL PROCESS AND HIGHEST AND BEST USE ANALYSIS

The purpose of a real estate appraisal is to estimate the value of an ownership interest in real estate and any related nonrealty interests. Appraisers follow a systematic process when conducting an appraisal assignment. This process is generally referred to as the appraisal process and is illustrated in Figure 2.1.[2]

Identification of the Appraisal Problem

When given an appraisal assignment, the appraiser first identifies the key issues that need to be addressed and plans a strategy for completing the assignment. It is critical to understand the appraisal problem by communicating with the client and ascertaining the objectives of the appraisal. Clients who are unfamiliar with the appraisal process may not truly understand the differences between the methodologies used to estimate values for different property types and may be unaware of the various ownership interests that potentially exist. The client and the appraiser must fully understand and reach agreement on the assignment before the analysis begins.

Part of the understanding process is to accurately identify the interest(s) to be appraised. As mentioned earlier, many ownership interests and potential values exist for an income-producing property. Typically, the value estimate is to reflect *market value,*[3] defined as the most probable price that a property should bring in a competitive and open market under all conditions requisite to a fair sale, the buyer and seller each acting prudently and knowledgeably, and assuming the price is not affected by undue stimulus. Implicit in this definition is consummation of a sale as of a specified date and the passing of title from seller to buyer under conditions whereby:

1. buyer and seller are typically motivated;
2. both parties are well-informed or well-advised, and acting in what they consider their best interests;

FIGURE 2.1   The Appraisal Process

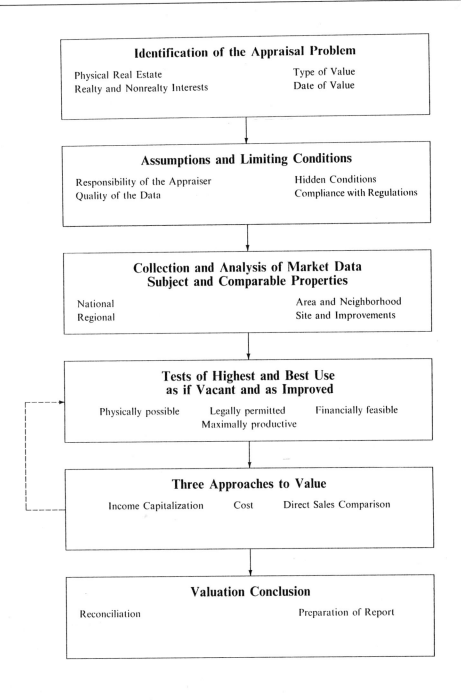

3. a reasonable time is allowed for exposure in the open market;
4. payment is made in terms of cash in United States dollars or in terms of financial arrangements comparable thereto; and
5. the price represents the normal consideration for the property sold unaffected by special or creative financing or sales concessions granted by anyone associated with the sale.

The key elements of this definition are that a reasonable time has been allowed for exposure in the open market and that typically well-informed buyers and sellers are involved in the transaction. The definition also emphasizes the importance of the price's being unaffected by special financing. As discussed in chapter 1, special financing does not affect the value of the real property.[4] This definition is somewhat idealistic, given the imperfect nature of the real estate market, but it serves as a theoretical basis for appraisal methodology.

In addition to the identification of the property rights appraised, the effective date of the appraisal must be selected. The *effective date* of the appraisal is the date for which the value is being estimated. The effective date of valuation is often the last date the property was physically inspected, not the date the appraisal report is being written. However, circumstances may exist that require an earlier or later effective date. For example, when doing property appraisals for estate purposes the effective date is a date prior to the date of property inspection. The importance of selecting a specific effective date is that unforeseen events may occur subsequent to the effective date that affect the value of the property. Identification of a specific date provides a point of reference from which the appraisal can be judged. The value of a property should be based on what was known to buyers and sellers at the effective date of the appraisal.

When estimating the value of proposed projects, the appraiser may be asked to estimate prospective values expected as of a future effective date. Key dates for this type of appraisal are the date construction is to be completed and the date the project is expected to reach stabilized occupancy levels. Proper identification of these key dates is vital in the appraisal process so that the value estimate will not be misleading.

Assumptions, Limiting Conditions and Certification

Along with identification of the rights appraised, the appraiser also must list any *assumptions* or *limiting conditions* that the value estimate is subject to. Limitations on the analysis time and the data used, as well as the source of the information used to prepare an appraisal, must be listed in detail. An appraiser does not have the expertise to verify all information (for example, to make an actual survey of the property boundary lines), but he or she must state the source of the information used in the report. Any assumptions should be realistic and not affect the integrity of the value conclusion. In addition to the assumptions and limiting conditions, the appraiser is asked to certify certain facts, including the unbiased nature of the analysis, as well as provide a statement that all relevant information has been included in the report. This issue will be covered in more detail in the chapter describing the typical elements to include in a report.

Collection and Analysis of Market Data

Once the appraisal problem has been identified and the property rights determined, the next step is to collect and analyze the data. The first step in gathering data is to inspect the subject property. Inspection includes determining construction type and quality, observing the physical condition of the property and the current level of occupancy, and making judgments concerning the functionality of the improvements.

The next step is to gather all market data needed to arrive at a logical and supportable conclusion. There are several means of collecting data, among which are a review of secondary data sources, interviews with market participants and solicitation of data from other real estate professionals, including appraisers. Some of the data will be area-specific, some neighborhood-basic, some property-specific. The data must be verified as to both their accuracy and their applicability to solving the appraisal problem.

Depending on the property type, data may be needed concerning national, regional and local economic trends, including an economic base analysis, which is a detailed study of the area employment trends. With regard to local, area and neighborhood information, key data include employment and population data, income levels, household size, housing statistics and studies of traffic patterns and location of support facilities such as shopping, schools, public utilities and transportation. The strategy implemented by the appraiser is, first, to arrive at conclusions concerning the current economic health of a community, compare the area's current condition and prognosis with that of the neighborhood and reconcile any differences in the expectations for each.

Once the area and neighborhood trends have been analyzed, the appraiser focuses attention on the subject property itself and the competitive market segment in which it is operating or will operate. Factors such as rent levels, operating expense projections, absorption rates, occupancy, construction quality and property condition are all considered in an appraisal report. The goals of the appraiser are to identify factors affecting the subject property, to select the profile of the typical investor for the property type being appraised and to apply appraisal methods that duplicate the current buying strategy and methodology of this particular investor. The market analysis should identify the factors that are the most important to the typical buyer, consider the relative strengths and weaknesses of the subject property with regard to these attributes and arrive at logical and supportable conclusions regarding the market value of the subject.

Tests of Highest and Best Use

When undertaking an appraisal assignment with the purpose of estimating market value, the primary concern governing the methodology and data used to estimate value is the concept of highest and best use (HBU). In appraisal practice, the concept of HBU represents the premise on which value is based.

Highest and best use is such an important issue that a complete chapter in this book has been devoted to explaining this concept. The theoretical basis for HBU is introduced in this chapter. The practical applications will be presented in the later chapter. This two-step approach to presenting HBU was selected by the authors because it is difficult to truly apply the principle of highest and best use without a complete understanding of all the basic valuation methods. This is why Figure 2.1 indicates a "feedback loop" from the three approaches to value to tests of HBU.[5]

Highest and best use is defined as the reasonable and probable use that results in the highest present value of the land after considering all legally permissible, physically possible and financially feasible uses.

This definition applies specifically to the HBU of land. It must be recognized that in cases where a site has already been improved, the HBU as improved may not coincide with the HBU of the land if it were vacant. The existing use will continue, however, until the difference between the land value based on its HBU and demolition costs exceeds the total value of the property (land and building) as currently improved. In equation form, the existing use will continue until

Value of Land *as if Vacant* − Demolition Costs >
Value of Property *as Improved.*[6]

The existing use may not be the HBU of a property as improved. That is, there may be a different use for the existing improvements that would result in a greater value of the property as improved. In some cases, this may involve some renovation costs. In this case the appraiser determines the value of the property as currently improved by considering its use after renovation and the renovation costs. Assuming renovation is feasible and results in the HBU of the site as improved, the value of the property as improved would be

Value of Property as Improved =
Value after Renovation − Renovation Costs

This assumes that the price a well-informed buyer would pay for the property is based on knowing that it can be renovated to achieve its HBU.

Typically, the appraiser applies *four* tests to a potential use of the property and improvements and gradually narrows down the potential options to the use that would result in the highest value of the property. The four tests include:

1. Is the use physically possible?
2. Is the use legally permitted?
3. Is the use financially feasible?
4. Is the use maximally productive?

The four tests of HBU must be applied first to the land "as if" it were vacant and then to the property as currently improved. As discussed earlier in this chapter, the HBU of the land may not be identical to the highest and best use of the property as improved. If this situation occurs, the HBU of the site as improved is referred to as the "highest and best interim use." *Interim use* is defined as a temporary use for a property when the highest and best use of the property is different from the highest and best use of the land "as if" vacant.

When the existing improvements do not represent the HBU of the vacant land, the result is a reduction in the remaining economic life of the improvements. The remaining economic life of the existing improvements becomes the time between the current date and the date when the value of the vacant land based on its HBU less demolition costs equals the value of the property as currently improved.

Appraisers frequently will reverse the order of the first two of the four tests to reduce the number of use options at the beginning of the analysis. It makes little difference whether the user begins with legally permissible uses or physically possible uses, because the use ultimately must pass both tests.

- *Physically Possible:* Unless prohibited by soil or subsoil problems or land size constraints, it is *physically possible* to place most potential improvements on the site. Usually this test, if performed first, will not significantly reduce the number of potential uses. It would be obvious, however, that a major hospital would not fit on a small fast-food site.
- *Legally Permissible:* Uses that are *legally permissible* are those allowed under current or likely zoning and those that could meet building codes. In addition, local communities may have restrictions on public utility loads, traffic creation, access restrictions and so on, all of which must be considered when selecting legally permissible uses. In practice a tract of land may not be zoned to allow for a use that would appear to be its most probable use. Sometimes it is reasonable and proper for an appraiser to conclude that a property could reasonably be expected to be rezoned. When arriving at this decision, however, the appraiser must have substantial evidence supporting this conclusion, including statements from public officials, support by recent zoning changes and/or definite emerging trends in use patterns in a neighborhood.
- *Financially Feasible:* Uses that are considered economically or *financially feasible* are those that potentially would logically produce net operating income and net resale price levels high enough to adequately support construction of the potential improvements and provide the investor with a reasonable profit. The appraiser should recognize that riskier projects require higher profit levels. This test is usually a very limiting test. There are typically only a few possible uses that will pass this requirement. Frequently, an appraiser may also discover that some uses that would be expected to be feasible are temporarily nonfeasible because of adverse market conditions.

- *Maximally Productive:* The final test performed is to ascertain which of the financially feasible uses would be *maximally productive,* that is, would result in the highest land value or value as improved, whichever case is being considered. As far as the land valuation approach, the land value is typically the value of the property as theoretically improved less the cost to construct the improvements. The "HBU as improved" would be the use that results in the "HBU as is." When considering the HBU as improved, the appraiser should be cognizant of the fact that it is possible to consider and assume rehabilitation of a property if the improvements will add value to the property by an amount greater than the rehabilitation costs.

Once the four tests have been applied, the HBUs for the vacant land and for the property as currently improved should be reasonably obvious. When estimating the HBU of the land, the best approach to take is to analyze different options, assuming the construction of an ideal improvement. When possible, the appraiser should report not only the use category but also the makeup of the improvements that have been assumed. For example, a vacant tract of multifamily land's HBU should not simply be reported as being for an apartment project. Rather, the HBU should be stated as, for example, for an apartment project with a density of 12 units per acre with an average unit size of 900 square feet. It is also possible that two different uses could represent the HBU of a property, that is, the residual land value would be virtually the same for either proposed use (for example, either a high-rise office or a high-rise hotel). In this case, both uses should be reported.

AUTHORS' NOTE: Some textbooks conclude that the HBU measure should be the use that produces the highest rate of return to the property. There are two problems that can arise when using this approach. First, the land value must be known before a rate of return can be calculated. Second, the uses may have different risks, so the use with the highest risk would always be chosen under this scenario.

The Three Approaches to Value

There are three traditional approaches to estimating the value of an income-producing property; the income capitalization approach, the sales comparison approach and the cost approach. Each views the valuation problem from different perspectives and considers data from different sources. When possible, the appraiser should use all three approaches to estimate the value of income-producing real estate. Value estimates by each approach should be arrived at independently and tested against each other in order to provide a cross-check. In some assignments, the data used in a particular approach may be more reliable, which would result in the estimate by that approach being the most logical and supportable. The strengths and weaknesses of each approach should be considered before selecting a final estimate of value for the subject property.

Income Capitalization Approach. The *income capitalization approach* is defined as one of the three traditional approaches to estimating value in appraisal where the value of the property is derived by converting the expected income generated from a property into a present value estimate using one of many income capitalization procedures.

In this approach a property is viewed through the eyes of a typical investor, whose primary objective is to earn a profit on the investment principally through the receipt of expected income generated from operations and the ultimate resale of the property at the end of a holding period. The theoretical basis for this approach comes from the principles of anticipation and substitution. The principle of anticipation applies because the value of a property is, in theory, the present value of expected future cash flow. The principle of substitution is also applicable, because rental rates for the subject property must be in line with those of competitive (substitute) space. Furthermore, the value estimated by the income capitalization approach assumes that investors will earn a rate of return consistent with that available for alternative investments of comparable risk. Generally, the value found by the income approach for an income-producing property is the most important approach used and is the one an appraiser may rely on most heavily in the final value conclusion. The reliability of this approach is, however, directly related to the quality of the data used and the proper application of income capitalization techniques. This approach will be considered first in this book because several of the adjustments that may be required in the direct sales comparison and cost approaches are estimated using the income capitalization approach.

Cost Approach. The *cost approach* is defined as one of the three traditional appraisal approaches to estimating value. In this approach, value is based on adding the contributing value of any improvements (after deduction for accrued depreciation) to the value of the land as if it were vacant based on its highest and best use. If the interest appraised is other than fee simple, additional adjustments may be necessary for nonrealty interest and/or the impact of existing leases or contracts.

In this approach the land value is based on its highest and best use "as if vacant." The land value is added to the contributing value of any existing improvements to arrive at an estimate of value for the subject property. The theoretical basis for this approach is found in the principles of substitution, contribution and utility. The reliability of this approach depends on the ability of the appraiser to estimate vacant land value and the cost new and the accrued depreciation for the improvements. When the existing improvements and land have the same highest and best use and the improvements have suffered little loss in value (depreciation) due to age, wear and tear, functional or external market problems, the cost approach is relatively reliable in estimating the value of an income-producing property. When the site and improvements have a different HBU, when the improvements are older or when market conditions are adverse, the cost approach would be suspect.

Sales Comparison Approach.   The *sales comparison approach* is defined as one of the three traditional appraisal approaches to estimating value; value is estimated by comparing similar properties that have sold recently to the subject property.

   This approach is sometimes referred to as the "direct sales comparison approach" and was also formerly referred to as the "market approach."[7] In this approach, the subject property is compared directly with other recent sales of similar properties in the marketplace. This comparison is typically accomplished by extracting "units of comparison," for example, price per square foot, and then adjusting these units of comparison for the comparable sales for differences between the subject and each comparable.[8] The theoretical basis for this approach lies in the principle of substitution, under which investors or owner-users are able to comparison-shop and set prices based on relative differences in properties. The reliability of an indication found by this method depends on the quality of the comparable data found in the marketplace and the ability of the appraiser to make reasonable and supportable adjustments. When recent sales of comparable properties are not available, the direct sales comparison approach may not result in a reliable indication of value. Sometimes listing prices are used when actual transactions are not available. However, this must be done with caution, because listing prices do not represent a meeting of the minds between buyers and sellers. Excessive listings may indicate an excess supply of properties for sale. In these situations the spread between listing prices and eventual transaction prices can be great. On the other hand, a shortage of listings sometimes results in properties selling for more than their listing price. This occurred to some extent with so-called showcase properties purchased by foreign investors during the mid-1980s.

Valuation Conclusion

After the appraiser has estimated value using one or more of the three approaches to value, conclusions must be made regarding the value of the property interest being estimated in the appraisal report. The appraisal process is only completed after the appraisal report is prepared. An *appraisal report* is defined as a report, written or oral, that relates the results of an appraisal. The standard report contains at a minimum the definition of the value estimated, the effective date of the value estimate, descriptions of the property and rights appraised, data supporting the value conclusions, the value conclusion itself, and all applicable certifications and limiting conditions.

   There are numerous formats for written appraisal reports, including letter, predesigned appraisal forms and narrative reports.

   The final value selection is made after consideration of the appropriateness of each approach. The appraiser need not select the indication from one approach; rather, a value may be selected from the range indicated by more than one approach if weight can be given to more than one approach. In other words, an appraiser may wish to give credence to the indication on the basis of more than one approach by selecting a value from the range supported by each. It is unlikely that the estimate from each approach will be the same value because of the imperfections in the market and lack of information, as discussed in chapter 1. Thus, the appraiser must draw a conclusion about the best estimate of the value for the property and explain why that particular choice was made. Because of the uncertainty associated with the quality of information and the fact that many judgments have to be made by the appraiser when interpreting market information, any single estimate of value should be viewed as being selected from a range of reasonable value estimates.[9] Analyzing and combining value estimates from each approach to arrive at a conclusion about the estimated value of the subject property is referred to as *reconciliation.* Often the appraiser has different degrees of confidence in the results from each of the approaches, depending on the data that were available for each and the nature of the property interest being appraised. More will be said about the reliability of each approach as it is discussed in the remainder of this text.

VALUE COMPONENT APPRAISED

The income approach may be used to estimate the worth of any of the value components discussed in chapter 1. For example, the appraiser can estimate the market value of a *fee simple interest* in the entire property (land and improvements), which represents the complete bundle of rights unencumbered by any existing leases or existing financing.[10] The appraiser also may be asked to estimate the value of separate components of the total property value. For example, the income approach can be used to estimate the value of a portion of the bundle of rights, such as the leased fee estate or leasehold estate. Or the appraiser may be asked to estimate the value of one of the physical components, such as the land or building. The appraiser may also be asked to include the value of nonrealty interests such as personal property and business value. (In this case it is important to indicate the value of the nonrealty component separately from the value of the realty component.)

The value of some combination of ownership rights can also be estimated using the income approach. For example, an investor might own a building on land that is being leased from another investor. The building might have existing leases to users of space in the building and there may be an existing mortgage on it. In this case the appraiser might be asked to estimate the value of the equity investors' interest, which would include a leased fee estate in the building and a leasehold interest in the land. There may also be a nonrealty value associated with the existing loan if it has a below-market interest rate and is assumable.

Value of a Fee Simple Interest

When estimating the value of the fee simple interest by the income approach, the annual operating income is forecast assuming market levels. The term "market levels" means that the income and expenses are set at levels considered suitable for the subject property after comparing it to similar properties under current market conditions. Rental rates are projected based on expected *market rents* and vacancy, and collection loss is based on what is typical in the market for properties renting at the market rate. A fee simple interest is assumed to be unencumbered by any existing leases that would result in a rental rate differing from the current market rate. Similarly, the estimate of resale proceeds at the end of the investment holding period assumes that the next buyer will receive market rental rates. The capitalization procedure used to estimate the value of a fee simple interest implicitly or explicitly assumes that investors will require a market rate of return on funds invested in the property.

Value of Leased Fee and Leasehold Interests

The income approach also may be used to estimate the market value of both the leased fee and leasehold ownership interests in an income-producing property. The value of a *leased fee interest* is the value of a property, assuming that all or a portion of the right to use and occupy the property has been granted to an outside entity by the execution of a lease contract. The value of the leased fee estate, therefore, is the value of the property subject to any existing leases. The value of the *leasehold estate* is the value of any beneficial interest in the lease contract itself. A lease may have value if the lease terms specified in the contract are better than market lease terms for the same space as of a specific date.

Leased Fee Interest.　In estimating the value of the leased fee interest, the cash flows used are those forecast after considering the impact of all existing leases. In other words, the incomes used are those specified in the existing leases, the vacancy and credit loss is allocated after considering the impact of the lease, and the operating expenses are those expected to be paid while the leases are in effect. If some of the leases expire before the property is sold, that space is assumed to be leased at the estimated market rate at that point in time. Estimated vacancy rates should also reflect the expiration of leases and any possibility of a higher vacancy rate until the space is re-leased.

The resale forecast must be made after considering the possible impact of any leases that may be in effect at the end of the holding period used in the valuation analysis. The rate of return used to discount the leased fee cash flows would be the "typical" leased fee rate required by "typical purchasers" of leased fee interests that are subject to similar leases. In other words, the leased fee discount rate applicable to one set of lease-affected cash flows may not be the same as a leased fee discount rate applicable to another series of lease-affected cash flows unless the existing lease structures and tenant quality are similar. A building leased at a fixed rate that is significantly below the market rate on a long-term basis to a high-credit tenant may have a lower applicable leased fee discount rate than a building with multiple short-term leases to medium-credit tenants at near market rates.

Leasehold Interest.   In estimating the value of a leasehold interest, the cash flows are typically the difference between *contract rent* and market rent, and generally no resale is involved unless the holding period selected is less than the actual lease term. The rate of return used to discount the rent benefits is the typical leasehold discount rate used by the typical investor in the market. Chapter 13 deals specifically with the valuation of leased fee and leasehold interests.

Nonrealty Interests

The income approach can be used to estimate the value of *nonrealty interests* such as personal property, financing premiums and business value. In fact, the income projected to be received by the owner of an income-producing real estate investment often already includes the income attributable to these components. The appraiser must, therefore, be careful to distinguish between what portion of the total income is attributable to the real property and what portion is attributable to the nonrealty components. For example, the appraisal of a hotel that is part of a national franchise may begin with potential gross income from all sources of the revenue that results from owning and operating the hotel (rental of rooms, restaurant, telephone services and so on). This income must cover all expenses of operating and managing the hotel, must cover payment of franchise fees and must provide a rate of return on capital invested in the physical real estate as well as the personal property. Furthermore, the hotel and restaurant may have an established clientele because of previous investments in marketing and training employees. In this case, the appraiser must determine how much of the net operating income represents income attributable to the real property versus the amount attributable to the "hotel business," which is a nonrealty interest.

As discussed previously, favorable financing can also result in a financing premium paid by equity investors. This is a nonrealty interest that does not change the total value of the real property. Techniques for dealing with below-market financing are discussed in chapter 14.

SUMMARY

Appraisal principles provide the theoretical framework for understanding and measuring the determinants of real estate value. Because real estate markets are imperfect and information is difficult to obtain, a professional real estate appraisal is often required to provide an estimate of the value of an interest in real property. The purpose of an appraisal is usually to estimate market value, although there are other types of value that might be estimated. Appraisers follow a systematic process to estimate the type of value required in a particular appraisal report. This process is known as the appraisal process.

The appraisal process begins with an identification of the exact nature of the appraisal problem. This includes specification of the property rights being appraised, the type of value being estimated and the effective date of the appraisal. The appraiser must also state any assumptions and limiting conditions that are important in interpreting the conclusions of the appraisal report. Data must then be collected to interpret trends in the market that could affect the value of the property being appraised. This may include national and regional data, as well as data on the local area and neighborhood in which the subject property is located. Market information such as rental rates and sale prices must also be collected from comparable properties.

A key part of the appraisal process is to determine the highest and best use of the site being appraised. This includes tests to determine whether the use is physically possible, legally permissible, economically feasible and maximally productive. The appraiser first determines the highest and best use for the site as if it were vacant and could be used in such a way as to maximize the value of the land. This determines the value of the land. If the existing improvements are not the same as the highest and best use as if vacant, the appraiser must determine whether the existing use is an interim use or whether the improvements should be demolished or renovated.

Appraisers use three different approaches to estimate the value of a property. These approaches are the cost approach, the direct sales comparison approach, and the income capitalization approach. Although the approaches are interrelated, in theory they provide independent estimates of value, and the values indicated by the three approaches will usually differ. Appraisers use a process of reconciliation to arrive at a final estimate of value after considering the reliability of the data available to estimate value with each of the three approaches.

KEY TERMS

anticipation	balance
appraisal report	book value
as if vacant	certification
as improved	change
assessed value	condemnation
assumptions	conformity

contribution	market price
cost	market value
cost approach	maximally productive
effective date	mortgage loan value
eminent domain	opportunity cost
financially feasible	physically possible
going-concern value	prospective value
highest and best use (HBU)	reconciliation
income capitalization approach	sales comparison approach
insurable value	salvage value
interim use	substitution
investment value	supply and demand
just compensation	taxation
legally permissible	utility
limiting conditions	value in use
liquidation value	

QUESTIONS

1. Why is the principle of anticipation fundamental to the income approach?
2. What is the relationship between the principle of change and the riskiness of real estate investments?
3. How might knowledge of excess demand for space affect projections of rental rates?
4. Why is the principle of substitution applicable to estimating rental rates for real estate income property?
5. What does the definition of market value assume about the time the property is on the market?
6. What could cause market value to differ from the price paid for a property or the cost of replacing the property?
7. What is the difference between market value and investment value?
8. What is meant by the term "prospective value"?
9. Under what conditions would the existing improvements on a site be demolished?
10. Under what conditions would the property be renovated?
11. What four tests are used to determine the highest and best use of a site? Should the tests be done in a specific order?
12. What is an "interim use"?
13. What is the basic premise of the income capitalization approach?
14. Can the cost approach be used for real estate income property?
15. What is the basic premise of the sales comparison approach?
16. Should all three approaches result in the same value estimate?
17. Why do appraisers usually follow an "appraisal process"?

END NOTES

1. The tax benefits associated with real estate income property can vary considerably for different investors depending on their other sources of taxable income.

2. Different authors tend to illustrate the steps in the appraisal process slightly differently. However, the common theme is to start with an identification of the objective of the particular appraisal assignment, then follow a logical sequence of steps that include data collection, analysis and application of appraisal techniques that lead to a conclusion about the value of the interests being appraised.

3. Definition taken from the *Uniform Standards of Professional Appraisal Practice.*

4. Chapter 15 discusses this issue in further detail and illustrates how the price of comparable sales that include financing premiums can be adjusted to obtain a "cash equivalent" value.

5. Appraisal texts have not traditionally shown this feedback in the appraisal process. However, it is important to realize that application of one or more of the three approaches to value is necessary before one can conclude that a particular use is the highest and best use of the site that maximizes the value of that site.

6. It might be noted that this is equivalent to saying that the existing use will continue until the value of the property (land and proposed improvements) based on the highest and best use as if vacant less any demolition costs and construction costs (for the proposed improvements) exceeds the value of the property (land and existing improvements) as currently improved. If the proposed improvements represent the highest and best use of the vacant site, then their value should equal their construction cost.

7. The term "market approach" is somewhat of a misnomer because all three approaches rely on market data although the cost and income approaches do not necessarily rely on comparable sales as does the sales comparison approach.

8. Common units of comparison for real estate income property are reviewed in chapter 18.

9. Statistically we might say that there is a confidence interval around the unobservable "true" value of the property. A single estimate of value made by any one appraiser could fall anywhere within that confidence interval. The size of the confidence interval depends on the amount and quality of data available for application of the three approaches.

10. Fee simple ownership is still subject to the governmental powers of taxation, escheat, police power and eminent domain.

<table>
<tr><td>

CHAPTER 3

</td><td>

Market Area and Neighborhood Analysis

</td></tr>
</table>

FUNCTION OF MARKET ANALYSIS

The purpose of a real estate appraisal is to estimate the value of a real estate ownership, assuming the motivations and purchasing strategies of a typical investor for the particular property type. The appraisal of an income property also requires a detailed forecast of expected future cash flows, as well as support for rates of return and trends assumed in the appraisal. The only reasonable method for an appraiser to identify and forecast the concerns of a typical investor and support forecasts and assumptions in an appraisal is a thorough analysis of the market for the property. A real estate appraiser therefore undertakes a selective search of relevant market data to identify the important issues affecting the real estate being appraised and makes judgments with regard to the important factors needed to arrive at a logical and supportable value estimate.

As discussed in chapter 1, different types of market analyses can be conducted for a variety of reasons and may even be reported independent of an appraisal. Generally the purpose of a market analysis is to analyze and make judgments concerning the future demand for a real estate product and to identify the present and anticipated supply of competitive facilities in a defined market area. The resulting supply and demand analysis becomes the basis for an appraiser's choice of rental ranges and absorption rates for the property being appraised.

Market analysis is the foundation for identifying the relationship between the different property types and market segments in the marketplace. In addition, market analysis helps an appraiser identify the demographic and economic factors that affect the subject property. Ultimately, the results of all the key real estate studies are presented in an appraisal report as support for the final value estimate selected.

THE MARKET ANALYSIS PROCESS

Identification of the Area To Be Analyzed

The first step in implementing a market study is to identify the area to be analyzed. This can be either the general market area or the neighborhood in which the property is located. The general market area is usually analyzed first. Then the trends and conditions identified for the general market area can be used as benchmarks for comparison with neighborhood trends. In a *neighborhood analysis,* the elements analyzed are basically the same as those analyzed for the market area: employment, population, income levels, housing, retail sales, new construction, occupancy trends, and so forth. The purpose of neighborhood studies is twofold. Such studies include

1. an independent identification of the trends and conditions in the neighborhood itself; and
2. a comparison of neighborhood trends with general market area trends to determine the neighborhood's relative condition.

If trends appear more positive for the neighborhood, it may be directly in the path of growth. If the relative neighborhood trends are negative, it may be in a period of decline. This comparison gives the appraiser an excellent idea of the stage of development of the neighborhood. Because the factors studied in the analyses of neighborhoods and general market areas are so similar, these analyses will be discussed simultaneously, although in practice they would be separate.

General Market Area.   The *general market area* is the area in which shifts in the general economic or demographic trends influence the performance of a subject property. It may cover a broad geographic area or only a small portion of a city. The area of influence is related directly to the size of the property, the market area it serves and the property type. The general market area for a major distribution center could be regional in nature; a small rural apartment complex might draw tenants from only a small portion of a county. The general market area can be delineated by geographic boundaries (streets, natural geographic features, government facilities), or it can be based on political divisions such as a township or zip code area. The general market area can contain a broad spectrum of complementary land uses.

Neighborhood.   The *neighborhood,* frequently referred to as the competitive market area, is defined as an area comprising a group of complementary land uses, in which changes would affect all of the properties in the area. It is typically delineated geographically but can also be delimited by political boundaries. In other words, a neighborhood is the geographic area in which the subject property and its major competitors would be directly affected in the same manner by changes in employment, population, income levels, new construction, transportation patterns, land-use controls and so on. Conversely, areas that would not be affected by new construction or other forces in the immediate area of the subject property would not be included as part of the neighborhood. Inhabitants of a neighborhood share a commonality of interests.

For example, the general market area for an office building might be a county, whereas the neighborhood would probably include all competing buildings of the same construction type and quality that are in close proximity to the subject and would compete for the same tenants. The tenants would be attracted by accessibility, proximity to other office facilities and supporting residential neighborhoods. Sometimes delineating a general market area and a neighborhood are difficult because of the property type. Typically, the general market area will be the smallest geographic area for which economic and demographic data are readily available, and the neighborhood will be the area encompassing the major competitors to the subject property.

Typically, the *neighborhood life cycle* includes four stages.

1. *Growth:* Once development is begun, an area experiences a period of rapid growth while the public recognizes and accepts the neighborhood. This period is characterized by significant new construction and rising prices. The growth at times may be erratic as supply and demand move in and out of balance, but the primary trend is upward.
2. *Stability:* Once a neighborhood is fully developed, it usually experiences a period of stability. This period is characterized by increasing prices, high occupancy rates and little new development. Depending on development trends in the general market area and physical characteristics of neighborhood, the stability period can exist for significantly varying lengths of time. A neighborhood comprising high-priced residential subdivisions and commercial properties in the vicinity of major traffic arteries will probably remain in this stable period for a long period of time. Lower-priced residential housing in close proximity to industrial facilities would probably remain in the stable phase for a much shorter period of time.
3. *Decline:* Once an area has become undesirable because of physical or environmental reasons or a change in the land-use demand pattern that results in a gradual transition in land use, the neighborhood enters a stage of decline. This period is characterized by decreasing property values and higher vacancy rates. The level of property maintenance declines, and the renter:owner occupancy ratio increases. If the decline

is caused by a transition in land use, vacant properties may sit in disrepair until they are ultimately demolished for new construction.

4. *Revitalization:* The final stage is, typically, revitalization. This period is generally characterized as a period of renewal, modernization and revitalization. Once prices have reached their lowest levels, it frequently becomes desirable either to demolish existing structures and build new improvements or to rehabilitate existing structures. The renewal period is similar to the growth period, except that major modernization replaces new construction. Theoretically, the pattern of revitalization is characterized first by fluctuating prices and later by increasing prices and high occupancy levels.

Data-Gathering Techniques

Before beginning a detailed analysis of a market area, data must be collected regarding different factors that may affect the subject property. Obviously, the quality and reliability of any real estate study, whether it be an investment analysis or an environmental impact study, depends on the quality and timeliness of the data used in arriving at conclusions. There are generally two types of data used in a real estate study: *primary data,* which are gathered by the appraiser and are not available in published sources, and *secondary data,* which are obtained from published sources and have not been collected by the appraiser; for example, census information, demographic information and published interest rates.

Primary Data.   Primary data are factual and numerical information obtained by the appraiser or an associate at first hand, using some form of survey technique. Typical basic survey techniques include personal or telephone interviews or surveys structured around mailed questionnaires. The source of the information is typically a participant in the activity being surveyed or a person who would reasonably be expected to have knowledge of the activity. Primary data are generally more accurate and reliable, because the party contacted is assumed to have direct knowledge of the information being solicited. Collecting data first hand, however, can be time consuming and, therefore, expensive, so care must be taken to ensure that the survey design is optimum.

There are several types of data that can be obtained from primary research.

- *Verification of Historical Fact:* Direct contact with participants in a transaction can not only lead to confirmation of information available in public records but may disclose information not otherwise known or available. In addition, some data may be found and confirmed only by the parties to a transaction. In this case, the only way to obtain accurate information is by personal interview.
- *Demographic and Socioeconomic Characteristics:* A typical appraisal requires up-to-date demographic data to support a conclusion. Frequently,

secondary data sources are not current, especially with regard to competitive market area (neighborhood) information. The only place to obtain these data, therefore, may be from a primary source.

- *Attitudes and Opinions:* Attitudes and opinions frequently influence market behavior. Information on attitudes and opinions is seldom available from secondary sources and, therefore, is generally tested using primary sources.
- *Awareness and Knowledge:* Awareness and knowledge refer to what people active in a real estate market know or do not know about factors affecting the market. Awareness can shape the delineation of a competitive market area as well as the ranking of competitors for the subject property.
- *Intentions:* Intentions influence future behavior and cannot be analyzed using secondary data. Intentions can greatly influence absorption of a proposed project, as well as occupancy levels for an existing project.
- *Behavior and Motivations:* Behavior patterns are observable trends, but the underlying force behind behavior is motivation. For example, understanding the motivations of a particular market segment may be essential to the selection of a project unit mix in an apartment project.

When undertaking a primary data search, an appraiser should be familiar with the two types of gathering data: communication and observation.

1. *Communication.* The data collected by communication can be gathered either orally or by written response. No matter whether the oral or the written strategy is selected, the survey should be designed to provide the pertinent information needed. In the appraisal profession, oral communication is used significantly more than written communication because

   - appraisers are typically dealing with small numbers of possible participants;
   - appraisers are typically not schooled in written questionnaire design; and
   - preparing a formal written questionnaire survey with a sample size large enough to provide an adequate level of response is generally extremely expensive.

   Oral communication is the most effective method of gathering data when the sample size is small, because the issues may be complex and reliability of the information gathered is essential.

2. *Observation.* Important information may be gathered by observing the behavior of market participants. Appraisers may observe the tenant mix in office buildings, and they certainly rely heavily on the observation method in physically inspecting subject buildings and comparable properties.

A primary data search can be as simple as soliciting comparable rental information from a leasing agent and as complicated as pretesting potential regional lot buyers for a proposed major resort.

Secondary Data. Secondary data are not gathered for a specific study at hand but are gathered by other sources and published typically on a periodic basis. A prime example of secondary data is U.S. Census data. Use of secondary data generally saves time, effort and money. Since secondary data are readily available, these sources are usually the first to be investigated by the appraiser. The reliability of secondary data depends on the age of the information, the care taken by those employed to gather the original data, any differences in the terminology or measurement unit used, and data grouping procedures. In general, secondary data sources are considered less reliable than primary sources, but information from many sources now receives a high level of acceptability in the marketplace. The chief advantages of secondary data are cost and time savings. The disadvantages are that measurements of units from one source may differ from those of another source. As a result, comparison of two sources may be difficult, the data may be old, and the definition and terminology used may be different. In addition, data-gathering techniques, data presentation, rounding and handling of nonresponses may differ from one source to another. Following is a partial list of secondary data sources:

- U.S. Census data;
- Employment Security Commission;
- Chambers of commerce;
- Federal Reserve Bulletin;
- Department of Housing and Urban Development;
- Local government agencies;
- County business patterns;
- Survey of Current Business; and
- Private publications.

In addition, several private companies offer services that supply historical, estimated current and projected future area-by-area forecasts based on all types of economic and demographic data. Several of the major firms include:

- CACI;
- "Survey of Buying Power," *Sales and Marketing Magazine;*
- National Decision Systems;
- Urban Decision Systems;
- Western Economic Research Company; and
- National Data Planning Board.

MARKET ANALYSIS

After identifying the area to be analyzed, an appraiser collects and analyzes pertinent market information to make judgments regarding the area's current economic condition and to formulate a prognosis for the foreseeable future of the area. Key information includes demographic and economic data, as well as supply and demand data for the property type and market segment data for the subject property.

Although market area data can be found, current data for a specific neighborhood may be difficult to obtain. Sources are available, though. Many private data companies such as CACI and National Decision Systems will supply data based on small geographic areas. These private companies can usually supply concentric circle data using a specific point of reference and census tract data; and, in some cases, they can supply forecasts, given specific geographic boundaries that do not correspond directly to political boundaries.

The Postal Service frequently undertakes housing studies for HUD that divide housing data by zip code. This information can be readily transformed into data applicable to the neighborhood. When the U.S. Census is taken every ten years, data are reported for most states, based on census tract. This information also can be adapted to neighborhoods. In the years immediately following the census, the data are timely. In later years, the appraiser must use various techniques to update the census data, using new housing construction, postal service statistics, and so forth.

Generally, the key elements to be analyzed in a market can be classified as physical (environmental), economic, governmental or social. These four forces interact in the marketplace to shape the climate of the area and the performance of the subject property.

Physical (Environmental) Factors

An area consists of numerous observable physical attributes, many of which have an impact on its real estate market. *Physical factors* include location, natural geographic boundaries, topography, soil conditions, climate, natural resources, water availability and transportation patterns. In fact, physical features may be the primary factor determining the characteristics of a community. For example, a community located on the ocean with a naturally protected harbor would be expected to have shipping as one of its major industries, with shipping-related jobs making up a significant portion of its basic employment. Conversely, relatively level inland areas, outside major metropolitan areas, with substantial rainfall and a long growing period would probably have agriculture as part of their economic base. Soil conditions may influence the size, shape and costs of new construction. Highway patterns influence access to employment, shopping, public facilities and public transportation. In areas with significantly varying elevations and wind patterns and with rugged topography, climatological patterns can affect the desirability of a neighborhood for residential or agricultural use. Additionally, wind patterns may affect the environment if adverse odors are periodically swept into a neighborhood.

An appraiser analyzing physical characteristics should consider each physical and environmental attribute and make judgments as to whether each will have a positive or negative impact on future growth. A city without adequate water resources for expansion will not be physically able to support rapid expansion, even if economic indicators are good. A city situated in the mountains may be rapidly running out of developable land. A community located in an attractive climate, however, may be a prime market for new retirement housing. Physical characteristics that both limit and encourage new development are key factors in the potential success of real estate development in all segments of the market.

In addition to the above factors, the physical features of a neighborhood may be analyzed in even more detail. Size and shape of the neighborhood, location of utilities and of support facilities are studied. The capacity of public utilities, including sewer, water, natural gas, telephone and electric service, influences new construction costs, project density and project design. In some instances, the lack of public utilities may prohibit the construction of an improvement. Because a neighborhood comprises a group of complementary land uses, the existence of an optimum mix of uses, including support facilities, is desirable. In a residential neighborhood this mix would include compatible residential uses, both single-family and multifamily, and adequate shopping, plus the existence of schools and recreational facilities. In the central business district, the mix would include office buildings, parking facilities and selected retail and public institutions. In an industrial neighborhood the mix could include manufacturing, warehousing, distribution centers, some retail, restaurants and possibly residential properties for the employees of local industries. These factors would have been considered in the original delineation of the neighborhood boundaries, because they all affect current condition and expectations for the area.

Economic Trends

An analysis of current economic conditions and trends in a general market is an essential ingredient of any appraisal report. *Economic trends* can be classified into international, national, regional and local. On an international level, factors such as balance of payments, exchange rates, interest rates, industrial production and inflation expectations can affect the market for various goods and, therefore, affect such segments of the real estate market as manufacturing plants, distribution facilities and retail outlets. Relative political stability can affect the flow of investment funds among countries of the world and, therefore, the sources of funds for real estate investment. The status of international economics, however, basically would have an indirect rather than a direct impact on most segments of the real estate market. As the world moves closer to becoming a single economy, the impact of economic shifts may be more direct in the future.

National and regional economic trends certainly have an impact on many segments of the real estate market, especially those that serve national and regional interests such as manufacturing plants and office buildings. Key factors providing indicators of the health of the national economy include income levels, the consumer price index, interest rates, new construction and employment. Analysis of national and regional indicators provides the appraiser with benchmarks by which to judge the health of the local economy.

The key local economic indicators include population, employment, households, housing, income levels, retail sales, and other demographic factors such as age profiles and marital status. These local factors are particularly scrutinized in the neighborhood analysis. All these factors, plus the key statistics for the property type and market segment being appraised, give indications of the status of supply and demand in the local market and help the appraiser forecast future supply and demand. Following is a brief discussion of several of these key factors.

Employment.   Probably the most important single aspect of any market study is an analysis of recent employment trends. Employment is the driving force behind population and income growth. It stimulates demand for new housing, office buildings, shopping centers and other real estate markets. If employment is declining, there are very few circumstances where an area's economy can be classified as healthy. Overall information on employment is generally readily available in a local market area. In addition to absolute growth in employment, shifts in employment type are key indicators of the makeup of the economic base of a community, and any analysis should be based not only on absolute levels but also on employment type. A shift in employment from manufacturing to service industries can have a negative effect on the demand for manufacturing space but a positive impact on the demand for new office space. Statistics on neighborhood employment by type, however, are generally available only every ten years from the U.S. Census.

The types of employment that dominate a local market form the *economic base* of an area, which usually remains relatively stable over time. The strength of this economic base is the driving force behind a community's growth. Generally, an employment segment is categorized as basic to an area if there is a higher percentage of that type of employment in that local area than what would be expected, based on the national average. Each local area has its own employment profile: In some areas, manufacturing employment may be the basic industry; in others, tourism. Identifying the industries that are considered basic to an area is important, especially when considering national and international employment trends. An economy based on textile manufacturing at a time when many firms are importing products from abroad may have a more questionable future than one whose primary employment is in higher education (a growing college town). Employees in classifications that experience rapid turnover may prefer rental housing, whereas administrative personnel (with higher incomes) may prefer owner-occupied single-family housing.

Demographic Data.   *Demographic data,* including population, households, household size, age profile and marital status, provide the appraiser with a profile of the inhabitants of the neighborhood and also provide support for forecasts of future trends. Because people need shelter and employment, population is a key statistic in the analysis of any market. Population change affects households, household size, age profiles and marital status, all key demographic information observable in the local market area. Population growth comes from an excess of births over deaths and greater movement into an area than out of it. Typically, population growth is fueled by employment growth. Household growth is the key factor in housing demand. Therefore, an appraisal of single-family or multifamily housing would place heavy emphasis on projected household growth. In some markets, such as the retirement centers in Florida and Arizona, population and household growth are not necessarily driven by employment growth. Age profile, therefore, can be a significant factor in an analysis of multifamily housing, especially in considering elderly housing. In addition, the markets for medical care and nursing home facilities would be influenced by age profile forecasts. Retail sales are certainly influenced by population growth, so such growth is a vital input in an analysis of retail space.

Information on all these demographic factors is readily available for most market areas. When analyzing a neighborhood, neighborhood trends should be compared to the trends identified for the general market area. This will give a good indication of the relative performance of the neighborhood. If the area and neighborhood trends and expectations do not correspond, an appraiser should identify the source of the difference to decide whether a continuation of the divergent patterns is reasonable and logical. If the neighborhood is not performing as well as the area, there must be an identifiable reason. If the neighborhood is performing better, is the trend expected to continue?

Income Levels.   Effective demand is a function not only of the size of a population but also of the purchasing power of that population. Change in income level, therefore, is vital data that must be considered in the analysis of a real estate market. Data pertaining to income levels, however, are reported in many formats, including household income, per capita income, effective buying income and disposable income. An appraiser must be careful when analyzing data from various sources to ensure that the income figures are based on the same definition.

Declining incomes could indicate problems in a neighborhood that arise from a shift from high-income to low-income employment. In neighborhoods with income levels below the average of the area, housing prices, rents and retail sales for certain types of goods would be expected to be below average. Income levels have a direct impact on housing affordability and are vital inputs needed to segregate the demand for housing by size, quality and price level. Neighborhoods with income levels above average could be more attractive to developers of single-family houses, specialty retail centers and suburban office buildings.

Retail Sales.   Information on total retail sales and retail sales by store group is readily available for most local areas and is an excellent indicator of local market conditions. However, information for retail sales segmented by neighborhood is difficult to obtain directly. In any case, per capita retail sales are usually directly related to per capita income. An appraiser can generally forecast per capita sales for a neighborhood, either by using a reasonable method to adjust average per capita sales for the area or by comparing the neighborhood income profile with those of similar areas for which per capita sales figures are available. When retail sales are compared with those of neighboring markets on a per capita basis, the appraiser should be able to ascertain whether the local market is the hub of significant retail activities or the inhabitants travel elsewhere to purchase major goods. A forecast of retail sales by store group is a vital input in estimating the demand for retail space in a neighborhood.

Housing.   Growth in housing, especially if viewed as a function of housing type (single-family, multifamily, condominiums and so on), is an excellent indicator of the condition of a local market. Additional housing information to consider includes occupancy trends, price ranges, multifamily unit share of the total housing stock, rent levels, pace of new construction and rental rates. The housing profile for the general market area, when compared subsequently to neighborhood profiles, gives an excellent indication of the relative condition of the neighborhood. Rising prices, falling vacancy rates and compatibility in improvement type in residential neighborhoods are certainly positive attributes.

New Construction.   New construction information can be gained from building permits, which provide an excellent indicator of past development trends and the desirability of a neighborhood. New construction is generally reported by the building inspections department as the number of building permits issued and dollar cost of new construction. The data are usually not reported for subareas in the marketplace, so appraisers may be required to undertake their own surveys of new construction in particular neighborhoods. When gathering new construction data, it is important that appraisers consider both the total square feet of actual building construction and the total area absorbed. In addition, appraisers should consider not only new construction information for the subject's property type but also that for other real estate segments. New construction is one of the key ingredients in a demand and supply analysis. After gathering economic data for the local market area, an appraiser develops an opinion concerning the current status of the area relative to past years and makes judgments concerning future market trends.

Government Regulations

Changes in government policy, whether they are in the area of land use control, taxation or location of public facilities, can have an impact on the economic health of an area. Because real estate is immobile, is owned and used by numerous individuals, and represents a significant portion of the national wealth, it is heavily regulated by many agencies of government. Local regulations can vary widely from one area to another; therefore, a detailed study of pertinent government regulations and tax policy is vital to any appraisal report. Government regulations are generally consistent throughout a general market area unless it crosses political jurisdictions, which suggests that the restrictions created by zoning ordinances, development restrictions and environmental controls would generally be the same for both the area and the neighborhood. This interrelationship could have a significant impact on the potential for new construction of certain property types in a neighborhood if rezoning is an issue in an appraisal assignment. For example, suppose the neighborhood under analysis appears to be an excellent location for additional apartment units. The general market area may contain an adequate supply of vacant multifamily land; however, all the multifamily land in the neighborhood being analyzed has been developed. Is the final conclusion that because of governmental restrictions, no new units can be built, or is the issue of zoning vacant land for apartments explored? If the demand is there and the vacant land is there, it would appear logical and reasonable to explore the rezoning issue.

Tax burden in the form of property taxes can vary from market area to neighborhood in two ways. Either the land value portion of a property assessment may differ or special taxing jurisdictions may cover only a portion of the general market area. Special school, utility and/or fire districts are often created for funding public projects or services, and these could include all or part of a neighborhood and place a disproportionate share of the tax burden on properties in these special districts. The decision on where to locate a new development could be affected by property tax rates that are out of proportion to those in competing areas. Following are brief discussions of several regulatory issues.

Zoning.   *Zoning* is a legal mechanism that enables a local government to regulate development of privately owned property. Most communities have established a pattern of allowable land uses by the creation of zoning ordinances. In areas that do not have established zoning districts, land use is controlled primarily through development restrictions and the interaction of supply and demand. Zoning ordinances can contain a variety of property use classifications. Frequently, overlap in property uses is allowed in zoning districts, which can make the job of estimating the impact of zoning even more confusing. In theory, zoning classifications are designed to promote compatibility in new development. In practice, however, zoning ordinances are only marginally successful in accomplishing this goal. Zoning restrictions can greatly influence property value, so political pressures to promote liberal interpretation of rules are generally strong. Zoning ordinances typically control not only property use but also development density, building height, parking requirements and so forth. The zoning for a local market area is usually uniform. Conflicts can arise, however, when a general market area encompasses more than one zoning jurisdiction.

Unusually restrictive laws can hinder new development and adversely affect market activity.

Development Requirements.   Through a series of approval processes, government agencies can affect the timing and cost of new construction by *development requirements*. Typically, a developer must gain prior approval from several sources, including land planners, mechanical inspectors, traffic and utility engineers, and so on, to construct a new building. The more cumbersome the process, the more restraint placed on market activity.

Environmental Controls.   *Environmental controls* are governmental standards to control adverse environmental conditions. As governments become more sensitive to potential environmental problems, including traffic volume and control, water runoff, noise and "visual" pollution, they require more detailed studies of environmental issues before they grant new construction permits. In addition, closer attention is being paid to the performances of existing properties, especially in the areas of emissions, job safety and pollution control. Policies developed in these areas may improve the quality of life for the current inhabitants but have a negative impact on new development. Real estate market segments such as manufacturing and utility companies have been significantly affected by new rules.

Social Factors

Social factors deal with the status, attitudes and behavior of the inhabitants of an area, all of which are generally qualitative rather than quantitative in nature. Because of their qualitative nature, these issues are difficult for an appraiser to assess by direct observation, but they are factors that may have significant bearing on a market. The effects of social factors may be evident in observable facts such as occupancy levels, tenant turnover, price levels, rent levels and property appearance.

The relative status of social factors in an area can sometimes be analyzed in terms of observable data: predominant employment type, relative income levels, population density, education levels, age profile, cultural origin, typical family size, marital status, predominate language spoken in the home, and the existence of community and neighborhood organizations, among others. Observable data are available from the U.S. Census. Generally, however, information concerning attitudes and behavior can be found only by observing the activities in the market and by communicating with participants in the market itself. Methods of gathering data concerning social attitudes will be discussed in the appendix to this chapter.

Conclusions

In addition to physical, economic, governmental and social factors, the appraiser should also gather data for the property type being appraised with regard to the current status of supply and demand, occupancy patterns and expectations of future absorption and new construction. When finally considered in combination, the appraiser should be able to arrive at reasonable conclusions concerning the current economic condition of the general market area, the state of demand and supply, and expectations for the foreseeable future. Remember that although forecasting the future is not an exact science, some conclusions are more logical than others when reached based on past trends and the current economic condition of the real estate market.

SUMMARY

To estimate the value of a real estate ownership, an appraiser must know the motivations and purchasing strategies of a typical investor. In addition, the appraisal of income properties requires a detailed forecast of expected future cash flows. Therefore, a thorough analysis of the market is necessary to identify the concerns of a typical investor and to support forecasts of future cash flows.

Typically both the general market area and the neighborhood in which a property is located are identified and studied. The general market area is the area in which shifts in the general economic or demographic trends would affect the performance of the subject property. The neighborhood is an area comprising a group of complementary land uses, changes in which would influence all of the properties in the area. Neighborhoods mature through a life cycle, which includes stages of growth, stability, decline and revitalization. A comparison of neighborhood trends with general market area trends can determine the neighborhood's relative condition and give a more detailed analysis of the area affecting the property.

Data collected for the study can be either primary (collected by the appraiser) or secondary (published sources collected by a third party). Key elements in a market study include physical (environmental) factors, economic trends, government regulations and social factors. Additional data should be collected on the current status of supply and demand, occupancy patterns, and expectations of future absorption and new construction for the subject property type. Combined with the above factors, reasonable conclusions can then be made about the current economic condition of the general market area and future trends in the appropriate real estate market.

The discussions in this chapter have been somewhat general in nature, partly because the factors that are important vary significantly across the broad spectrum of income-producing property types. An example of a market analysis is provided in the appendix to this chapter to provide a more in-depth view. In addition, more definitive statements concerning area and neighborhood issues for various property types will be presented later in this book.

KEY TERMS

demographic data

economic base

economic trends

environmental controls

general market area

government regulations

neighborhood

neighborhood analysis

neighborhood life cycle

physical factors

primary data

secondary data

social factors

zoning

QUESTIONS

1. Why is a market analysis conducted as part of an appraisal?
2. What is the difference between primary data and secondary data? What are the advantages and disadvantages of using primary versus secondary data?
3. What types of data can be collected through primary data research?
4. What is meant by the term "general market area"?
5. Why is the neighborhood analyzed in addition to analyzing the general market area?
6. Describe the stages of a neighborhood life cycle.
7. What are the key elements to be studied in a market analysis?
8. Describe how physical factors can affect the real estate market in a community.
9. What economic trends should be studied in a market analysis?
10. How can government regulations differ between general market areas and neighborhoods?
11. What is the purpose of zoning regulation and how can it affect property value?
12. What social factors should be considered in a market analysis?

CHAPTER 3 APPENDIX A: *Typical Market Study—Retail*

The following retail case study illustrates how market data may be used to support forecasts of market trends and absorption of proposed projects. Below is a brief description of a proposed retail drugstore that will be the subject of the case study.

Top Value Drugstore

Building size	10,500 square feet (sq. ft.)
Land size	45,000 sq. ft.
Construction type	Masonry
Parking spaces	58

COMMENTS: The project is located in the general market area identified as ABC County. The neighborhood is defined as Census Tracts 8, 9 and 10 in ABC County. The building is expected to be completed in 1992.

PURPOSE OF THE STUDY

The purpose of the study is to estimate whether there is a demand for a new drugstore in the neighborhood. The ingredients in estimating whether or not there is demand for construction of a retail store include

- population forecast for the neighborhood,
- total retail sales demand for a store group,

- total retail demand in square feet and
- comparison of current and proposed supply with demand.

General Market Area Analysis

The first table includes the population information for the general market area, ABC County.

Population—ABC County

Year	Source	State	MSA	ABC County
1980 (Act.)	U.S. Census	4,807,304	894,704	270,080
1990 (Act.)	U.S. Census	5,432,441	1,048,857	312,177
1992 (Est.)	Planning Dept.	5,489,400	1,093,600	330,500
1995 (Est.)	Planning Dept.	5,846,782	1,145,000	355,200

Conclusion.   Analysis of the annual growth rates for each area reveals the following:

Annual Popluation Growth Rate

Years	State	MSA	ABC County
1980–1990	1.23%	1.60%	1.46%
1990–1992	1.43	2.11	2.94
1992–1995	1.49	1.55	2.40

The county grew faster than the state but slightly slower than the Metropolitan Statistical Area (MSA). Expectations, however, are that the county has grown faster than either from 1990 to 1992 and that this growth is expected to continue.

The next information analyzed is the employment information.

Employment—ABC County

Type	1989	%	1990	%	1991	%	U.S.%
Total	152,473	100.0	159,210	100.0	164,821	100.0	100.0
Agriculture	602	0.4	590	0.4	611	0.4	0.5
Mining	40	0.1	50	0.1	126	0.1	1.3
Construction	8,916	5.8	7,429	4.7	8,406	5.1	5.2
Manufacturing	53,902	35.4	55,841	35.0	52,707	32.0	25.0
Transportation	9,807	6.4	10,667	6.7	11,804	7.1	6.2
Wholesale trade	14,947	9.8	15,829	9.9	16,241	9.8	7.0
Retail trade	28,446	18.6	30,861	19.4	31,471	19.1	20.9
Fin/Ins/RE	9,437	6.2	9,342	5.8	9,082	5.5	7.6
Service	26,200	17.2	28,372	17.9	33,730	20.5	25.8
Other	176	0.1	229	0.1	643	0.4	0.5
Unemployment	3.8%		4.1%		3.9%		

Conclusion. Following is a summary of the key employment trends in the county:

Employment Trends—ABC County

	1989–1990 Total Change	1989–1990 % Change	1990–1991 Total Change	1990–1991 % Change	1991 County%— US%
Total	6,737	+ 4.4	5,611	+ 3.5	—
Agriculture	– 12	– 2.0	21	+ 3.6	–0.1
Mining	10	+25.0	76	+152.0	–1.2
Construction	1,487	– 16.7	977	+ 13.2	–0.1
Manufacturing	1,939	+ 3.6	–3,134	– 5.6	+7.0
Transportation	860	+ 8.7	1,137	+ 10.6	+0.9
Wholesale trade	882	+ 5.9	412	+ 2.6	+2.8
Retail trade	2,415	+ 8.5	610	+ 2.0	– 1.8
Fin/Ins/RE	– 95	– 1.0	– 260	– 2.8	–2.1
Service	2,172	+ 8.3	5,358	+ 18.8	– 5.3
Other	53	+30.1	414	+180.8	+1.0

A review of the key employment information indicates that the economic base has been manufacturing. That base, however, appears to be changing. The pertinent categories that have shown significant growth include transportation, wholesale trade, retail and service industries. The county appears to be in transition from manufacturing to becoming a stronger distribution and service center. Construction has fluctuated significantly, which is not unusual. Overall employment has grown faster than the population. As of 1990, the employed work force represented 51 percent (159,210 ÷ 312,177) of the population.

The next statistics reviewed are household information. The number of households are important when analyzing housing demand and when addressing retail demand, if household rather than per capita income is used to estimate total purchasing potential.

Households—ABC County

Year	Source	ABC County	Annual % Change	Household Size
1980 (Act.)	U.S. Census	99,803	N/A	2.71
1990 (Act.)	U.S. Census	122,031	2.0	2.56
1992 (Est.)	Planning Dept.	130,200	3.3	2.54
1995 (Est.)	Planning Dept.	142,000	2.9	2.50

Conclusion. Households grew faster than the population from 1980 to 1990 because the average household size dropped from 2.71 to 2.56. The trend in the reduction in household size is projected to stabilize in the 2.50 to 2.55 range over the next five years, which would indicate that population growth and household size should grow at the same relative rate in the near future.

Household Income—ABC County

Year	Source	State	Income per Household MSA	ABC County
1980 (Act.)	U.S. Census	$18,421	$19,831	$20,814
1990 (Act.)	U.S. Census	26,321	27,461	28,421
1992 (Est.)	Planning Dept.	28,500	31,200	31,350
1995 (Est.)	Planning Dept.	32,000	34,000	33,800

Conclusion. The household income for the county is slightly higher than the MSA and state levels.

The next information analyzed is sales. Because the property being analyzed is a retail drugstore, a key factor considered in an analysis would obviously be retail drugstore sales, not only on a per capita basis but also on a per square foot of store area basis, which will be considered later in this analysis.

Retail Sales of Drugstores in ABC County

Year	Population	Drugstore Sales	Per Capita Drug Sales
1989	307,500 (Est.)	$45,347,000	$147.47
1990	312,177	48,890,500	156.61
1991	321,500 (Est.)	52,809,300	164.26

Conclusion. Retail drug sales have been rising in the county because of both an increase in population and an increase in per capita retail sales.

Neighborhood Market Studies

After gathering and analyzing data for the general market area, the next step is to gather neighborhood information. In this case, the neighborhood boundaries correspond to three census tracts (8, 9 and 10).

Neighborhood Population—U.S. Census Data

Year	Census Tract 8	Census Tract 9	Census Tract 10	Total
1980	8,217	6,448	5,926	20,591
1990	9,478	8,740	7,704	25,922
Change	+1,261	+2,292	+1,978	+5,331
Annual % change	1.44	3.1	2.7	2.3

Conclusion. The neighborhood grew substantially faster than the county as a whole from 1980 to 1990. Census tract 8 grew at approximately the same rate as the county but tracts 9 and 10 grew approximately twice as fast.

Neighborhood Households—U.S. Census Data

Year	Census Tract 8	Census Tract 9	Census Tract 10	Total
1980	3,065	2,488	2,370	7,923
1990	3,645	3,462	3,210	10,317
Change	+ 580	+ 974	+ 840	+ 2,394
Annual % change	1.70	3.40	3.10	2.70
Mean household size, 1990	2.60	2.52	2.40	2.52

Conclusion. The average household size in the neighborhood is slightly smaller than that in the county as a whole.

Neighborhood Household Income—U.S. Census Data

Year	Census Tract 8	Census Tract 9	Census Tract 10
1980	$20,873	$22,603	$18,941
1990	28,424	31,216	29,823
Change	+$7,551	+$8,613	+$10,882
Annual % change	3.1	3.3	4.6

Conclusion. The household income levels for the neighborhood are highly similar to countywide income levels. It appears, therefore, that the spending levels would also be near average levels.

Neighborhood Drugstores

	Size (sq. ft.)	Year Built	Retail Sales	Retail Sales per Sq. Ft.
1	5,500	1976	$ 612,300	$111.33
2	8,300	1982	1,401,700	$168.88
3	9,500	1988	1,788,500	$188.26
Total	23,300		$3,802,500	

Typical retail sales per square foot (Urban Land Institute) = $140.00.

Conclusion. Drugstore 1 is old and is not generating a reasonable sales volume. Stores 2 and 3 have above-average retail sales per square foot.

Results

The previous information indicates that all economic and demographic indicators are positive. The neighborhood appears to be performing better than the county as a whole. Population, household growth and income levels are better than average. First, retail sales demand is estimated by multiplying the estimated neighborhood population times per capita sales. Assuming recent trends, the population in the neighborhood for 1992 would be as follows:

1990 Population		*Annual Change*		*1992 Estimate*
25,922	×	$(1.023)^2$	=	27,128

Another approach is to use the same annual percentage change that was estimated by the planning department for the county.

1990 Population		*Annual Change*		*1992 Estimate*
25,922	×	$(1.0294)^2$	=	27,468

NOTE: Another method is to analyze new housing construction and occupancy patterns in the neighborhood and estimate new households in the neighborhood. A population estimate could then be found by multiplying this household increase estimate by an average household size.

The next step in estimating drugstore demand is to multiply the 1992 population estimate by the projected per capita retail drugstore sales to arrive at an estimate of the total dollars expected to be spent in retail drugstores in 1992.

1992 Estimate		*Projected per Capita Sales*		*Retail Sales*
27,500 (R)	×	$175.00	=	$4,812,500

The final step is to translate this dollar demand estimate into a square-foot estimate by dividing total retail demand by the typical sales volume expected on a square-foot basis for a drugstore.

Retail $ Demand		*Typical Sales per Sq. Ft.*		*Sq. ft. Demand*
$4,812,500	÷	$140.00	=	34,375

NOTE: The $140 per square foot (Urban Land Institute number) was used rather than the sales for one of the stores because there appears to be a shortage of stores, resulting in higher than typical sales volumes for stores 2 and 3.

The final step is to compare the square-foot demand figure with the existing supply.

Square-Foot Demand	34,375 sq. ft.
Less Current Supply	−23,300 sq. ft.
Excess Demand	11,075 sq. ft.

The demand is nearly equal to the size of the proposed building, so there appears to be a demand for a new drugstore. This assumes that no competitors are also planning to develop a new drugstore or that one of the existing stores plans to expand.

Although the above analysis was done in a market study format, the data could also have been used to conduct a marketability study. The first step in undertaking a marketability study is to thoroughly analyze the subject property. Factors such as size, shape, construction type, construction quality, amenities and design are important elements in identifying the property segment with which the subject property would compete. The second step is to identify the market segment itself by location, property use, property attributes, price levels, construction quality, design and tenant or consumer preferences. Sometimes the boundaries of a market segment are not clearly definable; for example, a 20-year-old, excellent quality office building may compete directly with new class B space because of rent levels, location and tenant mix, even though their appearances may be significantly different. The final step is to gather specific data from the market segment, compare the competitors with the subject and make judgments as to the relative strengths and weaknesses of each.

With regard to our sample case study, it was estimated that excess demand for 11,075 square feet of drugstore space should exist in 1992, which, on the surface, suggests a demand for the subject. Using the information from marketability studies, an appraiser would next be able to ascertain whether the proposed drugstore will have attributes other than size alone to satisfy the market. The attributes may include location, building design, construction quality and site improvements. In addition, the marketability study information should supply support for the market rent and estimates needed to estimate value by the income approach.

CHAPTER 3 APPENDIX B:
Typical Market Study—Residential

The following multifamily residential housing case study illustrates how market data may be used to support forecasts of market trends and absorption of proposed projects. Below is a brief description of a proposed apartment project that will be the subject of the case study.

Total Number of Units—100

Unit Mix

Building Size	85,000 Sq. Ft.
Land Size	8 acres
Construction Type	Frame

COMMENTS: The project is located in the general market area identified as ABC County. The neighborhood is defined as Census Tracts 1, 4 and 7 in ABC County. The building is expected to be completed in 1992.

PURPOSE OF THE STUDY

The purpose of the study is to estimate whether there is a demand for new apartments in the neighborhood. The ingredients in estimating whether there is demand for construction of a retail store include

- household demand forecast for the neighborhood,
- multifamily housing demand in the neighborhood,

- multifamily housing demand in the market segment and
- comparison of current and proposed supply with demand.

General Market Area Analysis

The first table includes the population information for the general market area, ABC County.

Population—ABC County

Year	Source	State	MSA	ABC County
1980 (Act.)	U.S. Census	4,807,304	894,704	270,080
1990 (Act.)	U.S. Census	5,432,441	1,048,857	312,177
1992 (Est.)	Planning Dept.	5,489,400	1,093,600	330,500
1995 (Est.)	Planning Dept.	5,846,782	1,145,000	355,200

Conclusion: Analysis of the annual growth rates for each area reveals the following:

Annual Population Growth Rate

Years	State	MSA	ABC County
1980–1990	1.23%	1.60%	1.46%
1990–1992	1.43	2.11	2.94
1992–1995	1.49	1.55	2.40

The county grew faster than the state but slightly slower than the Metropolitan Statistical Area (MSA) from 1980 to 1990. The county also has grown faster than either from 1990 to 1992, and this growth is expected to continue.

The next information analyzed is the employment information.

Employment—ABC County

Type	1989	%	1990	%	1991	%	U.S.%
Total	152,473	100.0	159,210	100.0	164,821	100.0	100.0
Agriculture	602	0.4	590	0.4	611	0.4	0.5
Mining	40	0.1	50	0.1	126	0.1	1.3
Construction	8,916	5.8	7,429	4.7	8,406	5.1	5.2
Manufacturing	53,902	35.4	55,841	35.0	52,707	32.0	25.0
Transportation	9,807	6.4	10,667	6.7	11,804	7.1	6.2
Wholesale trade	14,947	9.8	15,829	9.9	16,241	9.8	7.0
Retail trade	28,446	18.6	30,861	19.4	31,471	19.1	20.9
Fin/Ins/RE	9,437	6.2	9,342	5.8	9,082	5.5	7.6
Service	26,200	17.2	28,372	17.9	33,730	20.5	25.8
Other	176	0.1	229	0.1	643	0.4	0.5
Unemployment	3.8%		4.1%		3.9%		

Conclusion: Following is a summary of the key employment trends in the county.

Employment Trends—ABC County

| | 1989–1990 | | 1990–1991 | |
	Total Change	% Change	Total Change	% Change
Total	6,737	+ 4.4	−5,611	+ 3.5
Agriculture	−12	− 2.0	21	+ 3.6
Mining	10	+25.0	76	+152.0
Construction	1,487	−16.7	977	+ 13.2
Manufacturing	1,939	+ 3.6	−3,134	− 5.6
Transportation	860	+ 8.7	1,137	+ 10.6
Wholesale trade	882	+ 5.9	412	+ 2.6
Retail trade	2,415	+ 8.5	610	+ 2.0
Fin/Ins.RE	−95	− 1.0	−260	− 2.8
Service	2,172	+ 8.3	5,358	+ 18.8
Other	53	+30.1	414	+180.8

A review of the key employment information indicates that the economic base has been manufacturing, which is 32 percent of total employment in the county versus 25 percent for the U.S. That base, however, appears to be changing. The pertinent categories that have shown significant employment growth include transportation, wholesale trade, retail and service industries. The county appears to be in transition from manufacturing to becoming a stronger distribution and service center. Construction has fluctuated significantly, which is not unusual. Overall employment has grown faster than the population. As of 1990, the employed work force represented 51 percent (159,210 ÷ 312,177) of the population.

The next statistics reviewed are household information. The number of households and household income are important factors to consider when analyzing housing demand.

Households—ABC County

Year	Source	ABC County	Annual % Change	Household Size
1980 (Act.)	U.S. Census	99,803	N/A	2.71
1990 (Act.)	U.S. Census	122,031	2.0	2.56
1992 (Est.)	Planning Dept.	130,200	3.3	2.54
1995 (Est.)	Planning Dept.	142,000	2.9	2.50

Conclusion: Households grew faster than the population from 1980 to 1990 because the average household size dropped from 2.71 to 2.56. It is reasonable to assume that the trend in the reduction in household size will stabilize in the 2.50 to 2.55 range over the next 5 years, which would indicate that population growth and household size should grow at the same relative rate in the near future.

Household Income—ABC County

Year	Source	State	Income per Household MSA	ABC County
1980 (Act.)	U.S. Census	$18,421	$19,831	$20,814
1990 (Act.)	U.S. Census	26,321	27,461	28,421
1992 (Est.)	Planning Dept.	28,500	31,200	31,350
1995 (Est.)	Planning Dept.	32,000	34,000	33,800

Conclusion: The household income for the county is slightly higher than the MSA and State levels.

The next information analyzed is the housing profile in the county. Because the property being analyzed is an apartment project, the percentage of housing constructed as multifamily housing units is considered.

Housing Occupancy—ABC County

Year	Source	Total Units	Multifamily Units	% Multifamily
1980 (Act.)	U.S. Census	104,630	30,471	29.1
1990 (Act.)	U.S. Census	129,042	38,421	29.8
1992 (Est.)	Planning Dept.	138,300	41,627	30.0
1995 (Est.)	Planning Dept.	147,000	44,100	30.0

Conclusion: The percent of the housing stock that is multifamily has remained relatively constant over time.

Neighborhood Market Studies

After gathering and analyzing data for the general market area, the next step is to gather neighborhood information. In this case, the neighborhood boundaries correspond to three census tracts (1, 4 and 7).

Neighborhood Population—U.S. Census Data

Year	Census Tract 1	Census Tract 4	Census Tract 7	Total
1980	6,471	9,362	6,422	22,255
1990	7,547	12,340	7,905	27,792
Change	1,077	2,978	1,483	5,537
Annual % change	1.55	2.8	2.1	2.2

Conclusion: The neighborhood grew substantially faster than the county as a whole from 1980 to 1990. Census tract 1 grew at approximately the same rate as the county, but tracts 4 and 7 grew approximately twice as fast.

Neighborhood Households—U.S. Census Data

Year	Census Tract 1	Census Tract 4	Census Tract 7	Total
1980	2,311	3,404	2,335	8,050
1990	2,881	4,802	3,200	10,883
Change	+570	1,398	865	2,833
Annual % change	2.23	3.50	3.20	3.10
Mean household size, 1990	2.62	2.57	2.47	2.57

Conclusion: The average household size in the neighborhood is similar to that in the county as a whole.

Neighborhood Household Income—U.S. Census Data

Year	Census Tract 1	Census Tract 4	Census Tract 7
1980	20,920	24,000	20,450
1990	28,115	33,206	29,409
Change	7,195	9,206	8,959
Annual % change	3.0	3.3	3.7

Conclusion: The household income levels for the neighborhood are similar to countywide income levels. It appears, therefore, that the spending levels for housing would also be near average levels for the county as a whole.

The next information analyzed is the housing profile for the neighborhood.

Housing Occupancy—Neighborhood

Year	Source	Total Units	Multifamily Units	% Multifamily	Multifamily Vacancy
1980 (Act.)	U.S. Census	8,474	2,712	32.0	4.8%
1990 (Act.)	U.S. Census	11,524	3,630	31.5	6.1
1992 (Est.)	Planning Dept.	11,812	3,780	32.0	N/A
1995 (Est.)	Planning Dept.	12,534	4,011	32.0	N/A

Conclusion: The neighborhood has a slightly higher multifamily occupancy than the county as a whole.

Following is a survey of competitive projects in the neighborhood.

Project	Year Built	No. of Units	Occupied Units	Vacant Units	Vacancy, %
Quail Creek Apartments	1985	60	58	2	3.3
Inglewood Apartments	1986	105	100	5	4.8
Forest Oaks Apartments	1988	130	116	14	10.8
Bay Hill Apartments	1989	75	74	1	1.3
Northridge Apartments	1991	106	93	13	12.3
TOTALS		476	441	35	7.4
Silas Ridge Apartments (under construction)	1993	60	0	0	0

Based on the previous information, the competitive units are experiencing a 7.4 percent vacancy rate. Silas Ridge is a 60-unit project that is currently under construction and should be available for occupancy in the middle of 1993. Assume the optimal vacancy rate is 5 percent.* This means that there were $35 - 476 (0.05) = 11$ excess units available as of the effective date of this analysis.

---

*There is always some vacancy owing to people relocating and space built in anticipation of future demand.

Results

The previous information indicates that all economic and demographic indicators are positive. The neighborhood appears to be performing better than the county as a whole. Population, household growth and income levels are better than average.

First, neighborhood household growth resulted in total household growth for 1980 to 1990 to be 2,833, or 283 per year. With households expected to grow by 2.9 percent to 3.3 percent per year (say 3 percent), and with household size remaining relatively stable, neighborhood household growth could be expected to be (10,883 × 0.03) = 326 per year.

Next, assuming that the percentage of the households that would desire multifamily housing would remain at 32 percent, the expected annual growth in multifamily households would be (326 × 0.32) = 104.

Assuming optimal vacancy is 5 percent, the multifamily housing demand, based on expected household growth, would be 104/(1 − 0.05) = 109 units per year.

Since 441 competitive units have been absorbed in the neighborhood from 1985 to the present or 55 per year (441/8), about 50 percent of the multifamily absorption (55/109) has taken place in the competitive market segment. Assuming this trend continues, about 50 percent of the demand created by household growth could be expected in the market segment.

NOTE: Some replacement demand would typically occur in the low end of the multifamily housing market, but our project is to be good quality, so no additional demand for the subject could be expected from replacement.

The last step is to compare the demand with supply to estimate the absorption for the subject project. The time to construct the subject must be considered on the supply and demand analysis. It appears the earliest the subject could be expected to have units available is 1984.

Excess units	11
New units for rent, 1993	60
Total inventory	71
Unit absorption	55
Units remaining at end of 1993	16
Subject units complete	100
Total units	116
Unit absorption (subject)	55
Units remaining at end of 1994	61
Unit absorption (subject)	55
Units remaining at end of 1995	6

Based on the previous analysis, it appears that absorption of the subject could be expected over a 2-year period. It is essential, however, that the analyst consider the possibility of the construction of competitive units in the neighborhood in the future. If additional competition is expected, the absorption may extend over a 3- or 4-year period. In addition, relative qualitative factors may influence the capture rate.

CHAPTER 3 APPENDIX C:
Typical Market Study—Office

The following office case study illustrates how market data may be used to support forecasts of market trends and absorption of proposed projects. Below is a brief description of an office building that will be the subject of the case study.

Office Building

Building size	100,000 Sq. Ft.
Land size	120,000 Sq. Ft.
Construction type	Masonry—Class A

COMMENTS: The project is located in the general market area identified as XYZ County. The neighborhood is defined as the northwest suburban office market in XYZ County. The building is under construction and is expected to be completed early in 1993. There is an additional 165,000-square-foot office building under construction in the market segment that will be available for occupancy in 1993.

PURPOSE OF THE STUDY

The purpose of the study is to estimate whether there is demand for a new office building in the neighborhood. The ingredients in estimating whether there is demand for construction of an office building include

- population forecast for the neighborhood,
- employment forecast for the area and neighborhood,

- expected employment growth in office employment and
- comparison of current and proposed supply with demand.

General Market Area Analysis

The first table includes the population information for the general market area, XYZ County.

Population—XYZ County

Year	Source	State	MSA	XYZ County
1980 (Act.)	U.S.Census	4,807,304	894,704	295,081
1990 (Act.)	U.S. Census	5,432,441	1,048,857	344,144
1992 (Est.)	Planning Dept.	5,489,400	1,093,600	362,350
1995 (Est.)	Planning Dept.	5,846,782	1,145,000	388,500

Conclusion: Analysis of the annual growth rates for each area reveals the following:

Annual Population Growth Rate

Years	State	MSA	XYZ County
1980–1990	1.23%	1.60%	1.55%
1990–1992	1.43	2.11	2.61
1992–1995	1.49	1.55	2.35

The county grew faster than the state but slightly slower than the Metropolitan Statistical Area (MSA). Expectations, however, are that because the county has grown faster than either from 1990 to 1992, this growth is expected to continue.

The next information analyzed is the employment information.

Employment—XYZ County

Type	1990	%	1991	%	1992	%	U.S. %
Total	178,902	100.0	184,821	100.0	189,178	100.0	100.0
Agriculture	406	0.2	412	0.2	390	0.2	0.5
Mining	116	0.1	108	0.1	125	0.1	1.3
Construction	9,682	5.4	8,906	4.8	9,106	4.8	5.2
Manufacturing	56,892	31.8	57,936	31.4	56,426	29.8	25.0
Transportation	12,462	7.0	12,312	6.7	12,507	6.6	6.2
Wholesale trade	8,422	4.7	9,387	5.1	9,634	5.1	7.0
Retail trade	26,529	14.8	28,301	15.3	29,401	15.6	20.9
Fin/Ins/RE	17,982	10.1	18,306	9.9	19,006	10.1	7.6
Service	36,822	20.6	39,074	21.1	42,261	22.3	20.8
Government	9,326	5.2	9,804	5.3	10,106	5.3	5.0
Other	263	0.1	275	0.1	216	0.1	0.5
Unemployment	3.6%		3.1%		2.9%		

Following is a summary of the key employment trends in the county.

Employment Trends—XYZ County

	1990–1991		1991–1992		1992 County, % − U.S., %
	Total Change	% Change	Total Change	% Change	
Total	+5,919	+3.3	4,357	2.4	...
Agriculture	+6	+1.5	−22	−5.3	−0.3
Mining	−8	−6.9	+17	+13.6	−1.2
Construction	−776	−8.0	+200	+2.2	−0.4
Manufacturing	1,044	+1.8	−1,510	−2.6	+4.8
Transportation	−150	−1.2	+195	+1.6	+0.4
Wholesale trade	+965	+1.7	+247	+2.6	−1.9
Retail trade	1,172	+6.7	+1,100	+3.9	−4.3
Fin/Ins.RE	+324	+1.8	+700	+3.8	+2.5
Service	+2,252	+6.1	+3,187	+8.2	+1.5
Government	+478	+5.1	+302	+3.1	+0.3
Other	+12	+4.6	−59	−21.5	−0.4

Conclusion: Employment totaled 52 percent of the population in 1990 and 52.2 percent based on the 1992 population estimate. Employment has grown by approximately 4 percent per year over the last 2 years with the greater proportion of changes taking place in retail trade, finance/insurance/ real estate, service and government. The percentage of employment in manufacturing is gradually becoming a smaller percentage of total employment.

The first step is to translate total employment into office employment. Some employment types require significantly more office space than others. For example, agricultural companies generally have office space only for employees responsible for administration of agricultural programs. On the other hand, all employees engaged in finance, insurance and real estate would typically require office space. To estimate the percentage of office employment for each category, an analysis of each type based on SIC code was undertaken and the following percentages were developed by XYZ County:

Office Employment Percentages by Employment Type—XYZ County

Employment Type	% Office
Agricultural	10
Mining	0
Construction	5
Manufacturing	25[1]
Transportation	15
Wholesale trade	5
Retail trade	5
Finance/Insurance/Real Estate	100
Service	65[2]
Government	90
Other	10

[1]The manufacturing segment of the market reports 25 percent of employment is in administration.
[2]The service employment excludes employment in hotels, personal services, auto repair, miscellaneous repair services, motion pictures, recreation, hospitals and education.

NOTE: The percentages for a given market area may vary widely, depending on the profile of employment and its economic base. Employment trends are analyzed next.

Office Employment by Employment Type—XYZ County

	1990	Office Employees	1991	Office Employees	1992	Office Employees
Total	178,902	. . .	184,821	. . .	189,178	. . .
Agricultural	406	41	412	41	390	39
Mining	116	0	108	0	125	0
Construction	9,682	484	8,906	445	9,106	455
Manufacturing	56,892	11,387	57,936	11,587	56,426	11,285
Transportation	12,462	1,869	12,312	1,847	12,507	1,876
Wholesale trade	8,422	421	9,387	469	9,634	482
Retail trade	26,529	1,326	28,301	1,415	29,401	1,470
Finance/Insurance/ Real Estate	17,982	17,982	18,306	18,306	19,066	19,066
Service	36,822	23,934	39,074	25,398	42,261	27,470
Government	9,326	8,393	9,804	8,823	10,106	9,095
Other	263	26	275	27	216	21
TOTALS		65,863		68,358		71,259
% of Total		36.8		37.0		37.7
Annual Growth, %		N/A		3.8		4.2

NOTE: The office employment is estimated by multiplying the percentage of office by type, then multiplying by the total employment for each category.

Conclusion: Growth in office employment (3.8 percent and 4.2 percent) has taken place at a faster rate than population (2.6 percent) or total employment (3.3 percent and 2.4 percent), which suggests a shift toward employment requiring office space.

The next step is to gather information with regard to the supply and vacancy rates for office space in XYZ County and the northwest market segment.

Total Office Space Survey—XYZ County

Year	Beginning Inventory	Additions	Ending Inventory	Occupied Space	Space Absorbed	Vacant Space	Vacancy, %
1989	8,146,902	432,312	8,579,214	8,291,403	—	467,811	5.5%
1990	8,579,214	267,402	8,846,616	8,591,306	299,903	255,310	2.9%
1991	8,846,616	561,307	9,407,923	8,887,346	296,040	520,577	5.5%
1992	9,407,923	387,407	9,795,330	9,242,316	354,970	553,014	6.6%
Total		1,648,428					

Office Space Survey—Northwest Suburban Market

Year	Beginning Inventory	Additions	Ending Inventory	Occupied Space	Space Absorbed	Vacant Space	Vacancy, %
1989	2,247,300	247,216	2,494,516	2,261,420	—	233,096	9.3%
1990	2,494,516	86,402	2,580,092	2,416,402	154,982	163,690	6.3%
1991	2,580,092	112,216	2,692,308	2,597,413	181,011	94,895	3.5%
1992	2,692,308	143,216	2,835,524	2,687,318	89,905	148,206	5.2%
Total		589,050					

Office Market Profile

In 1989, 27.6 percent (2,247,300/8,146,902) of the office space in the county was located in the northwest suburban market. This percentage grew to 28.9 percent (2,835,524/9,795,330) by the end of 1992. In the 4-year period from 1989 to 1992, 1,648,828 square feet of office space was added to the inventory in the county (412,207 per year) and 589,050 square feet was added in the market segment (147,262 per year). Of the office space built, 35.7 percent was in the subject's market segment. During the 3-year period beginning at the end of 1989 and extending through the end of 1992, 950,913 square feet of office space was absorbed in the county (316,971 per year), and 425,898 square feet was absorbed in the market segment (141,966 per year). Therefore, 44.8 percent of the office absorption took place in the subject's market segment. The vacancy rate at the end of 1992 was 6.6 percent in the county and only 5.2 percent in the market segment. Based on the information, the northwest office market segment is absorbing space faster than the county as a whole. By the end of 1992, 29.1 percent of the occupied office space was in the subject's market segment. Based on a 5 percent stabilized vacancy rate (implied by the market data of the county, there is a 6,430-square-foot oversupply of office space in the market segment.

	Space, sq. ft.
1992 total space (market segment)	2,835,524
Vacancy, assuming 5 percent	− 141,776
1992 stabilized occupancy level	2,693,748
1992 occupied space	2,687,318
Difference = oversupply	6,430

Office Space—Employee Profile

Year	Occupied Office Space, sq. ft.	Office Employment	Average Office Space per Employee, sq. ft.
1990	8,591,306	65,863	130.4
1991	8,887,346	68,358	130.0
1992	9,242,316	71,259	129.7

Conclusion: The occupied office space per employee has remained relatively stable over the last three years.

Results

The previous information indicates that all economic and demographic indicators are positive. Employment and office space employment have grown steadily over the past few years. To estimate the expected absorption rate for the subject, the first step is to estimate the expected growth in office employment. Based on a historical growth rate of 3.8 percent and 4.2 percent, and assuming this trend will continue, a 4 percent growth rate would indicate 1993 office employment growth as follows:

1992 Office Employment		Annual Change		1993 Growth
71,259	×	.04	=	2,850

NOTE: Analysis of the economic conditions in the county would indicate whether the assumption of continue growth is warranted.

The next step is to estimate the office space that will be needed to serve the expected 2,850 in employment growth. Based on past trends, it appears reasonable to assume that the space per employee would be about 130 square feet.

Office Employee Growth		Office Space per Employee		Annual Office Space Demand
2,850	×	130 sq. ft.	=	370,500 sq. ft.

The next step is to estimate the capture rate for the northwest market segment. The segment represented 28.9 percent of the market inventory and 29.1 percent of the occupied space. However, 35.7 percent of the new office space was built in the market segment in the past four years and 44.8 percent of the absorption took place in this segment. Because absorption is the most important factor, the assumption will be made that 40 percent of new absorption could be expected in the subject's market segment, which results in the following absorption forecast:

Annual Office Absorption		Market Segment Capture Rate		Segment Absorption
370,500 sq. ft.	×	.40	=	148,200

NOTE: The appraiser should have strong support to assume the continuation of historical trends.

The final step is to estimate the absorption period for the subject.

New Construction—1993

	Sq. Ft.	% of Total
Subject	100,000	37.7
Competitor building A	165,000	62.3
Total expected additions	265,000	

Less: stabilized occupancy (5%)	– 13,250
New space available 1993	251,750
Plus: excess space	6,430
Total supply 1993	258,180
Less: absorption (148,200 sq. ft.)	
Subject, 37.7%	– 55,871
Building A, 62.3%	–102,295
Ending inventory, 1993	99,514

NOTE: By the end of 1993 the remaining unleased space in the subject is expected to be 39,129 sq. ft. (95,000 sq. ft. – 55,871). Without significant new construction it would appear reasonable to assume that this space could be absorbed within 9 months (no new construction), or 1 year if only one other building is expected to be constructed.

Conclusion: The space in the subject office building could be expected to be absorbed over a 21- to 24-month period.

<table>
<tr><td></td><td>
CHAPTER 4
</td><td>
Compound Interest and Discount Factors
</td></tr>
</table>

IMPORTANCE OF THE TIME VALUE OF MONEY

The income approach assumes that the value of a property equals the present value of anticipated future benefits. This chapter reviews the concepts of compound interest and discounting that form the foundation for converting estimated future income into a *present value.*

Someone unfamiliar with the concept of compound interest might believe that we could merely add up the anticipated future benefits, as demonstrated below.

Year	Annual Cash Flow
1	$ 10,000
2	10,000
3	12,000
4	12,000
5	130,000
Total	$174,000

If the present value of future benefits were calculated in this manner, and the investor paid $174,000 for the property, he or she would not earn a rate of return on the capital invested. The annual cash flow would be just sufficient to return the investor's initial investment in the property. This is not likely to occur for two reasons. First, investors must expect to receive a return of more than their original investment to be induced to invest money rather than spend it. Second, alternative investment opportunities of comparable risk are likely to be available that could be expected to give the investor an additional rate of return on capital invested. Thus there is an opportunity cost associated with making an investment that does not provide the same return for the same level of risk. This can be summarized by the financial principle of the *time value of money,* which is defined as a financial principle based on the assumption that a positive interest can be earned on an investment and therefore money received today is more valuable than money received in the future.

To properly capture the time value of money, *compound interest* theory was developed. Compound interest theory assumes periodic interest is earned on funds that have been deposited. It further assumes that interest for a specific period is also earned on the interest that has accumulated from prior periods.

A second theory was developed under which expected future cash flows could be reduced to a present value estimate by calculating what would be needed today to grow at compounded interest to the future expected value. This mathematical process is referred to as *discounting,* which is defined as the process of converting future income to a present value by mathematically reducing future cash flow by the implied interest that would have been earned assuming an initial investment, an interest rate and a specified time period.

The discounting process is used extensively by appraisers to estimate the present value of expected future cash flows.

VARIABLES IN THE DISCOUNTING PROCESS

Any problem involving calculations using the discounting process involves four variables:

1. the time period;
2. the interest rate;
3. the expected future cash flow (or cash flows); and
4. the present value.

Once any three of these variables are known, the fourth can usually be calculated by using published tables, a hand-held calculator or a computer.[1] The two variables most likely to be calculated by appraisers are the interest rate and the present value.

Interest Rate

If the present value is known or assumed to be known, along with the expected future cash flows over a specified time period (holding period), the *interest rate* can be calculated. For example, the present value might represent the price recently paid for a comparable property. If the appraiser knows what cash flows the buyer projected over time, the interest rate can be calculated. This interest rate represents the rate of return or *yield rate* (also referred to as an *internal rate of return*) that the investor would expect to earn.

Present Value

Appraising income property requires the appraiser to estimate the present value of anticipated future cash flows. Depending on the particular capitalization technique chosen, the appraiser may be required to forecast the expected cash flows over a specific time period and calculate the present value of those cash flows, using a specified interest rate as a *discount rate.* The interest rate selected as a discount rate should be the rate of return investors would require to invest in properties of comparable risk.

COMPOUND INTEREST AND DISCOUNT FACTORS

Before the invention of hand-held calculators, appraisers relied mainly on published tables of factors for specific interest rates and holding periods. These factors were precalculated for either a present value of one dollar or for periodic payments of one dollar. Most tables included six different columns of factors calculated on an annual basis (see appendix A). To use these factors, the appraiser needed only to multiply the dollar amount being considered by the appropriate factor to arrive at present or future value calculations. The tables assumed equal periodic compounding periods, for example, annual or monthly compounding.

With the introduction of calculators and widespread use of computers, the tables have virtually disappeared from use. Financial calculators have the compounding and discounting formulas built in. The table information is therefore at the fingertips of the appraiser and accessible by entering a few simple keystrokes. A discussion follows, covering each of the common six factors typically used. These factors are generally referred to as the "Six Functions of One Dollar." All six factors are mathematically related to each other. This relationship will be demonstrated after a discussion of each of the six factors.

Future Value of One Dollar S^n

The *future value of one dollar* signifies the amount to which an investment of \$1.00 grows with compound interest after a specified number of years at a specified interest rate (column 1 of the compound interest tables in appendix A). The factor for the future value of one dollar is arrived at by adding one to the interest per period (i) and taking this to the exponent that represents the number of years (n): $(1 + i)^n = S^n$.

Formula: $(1 + i)^n = S^n$ (column 1 in the table in appendix A)

where i equals the effective interest rate and n equals the number of time periods (column 1 in the table in appendix A).

Table Relationship.   This factor is the reciprocal of the *present value of one dollar* (column 4 in the table in appendix A).

Example

What will a $10,000 investment made today grow to at the end of 5 years, assuming a 12 percent rate of return?

Year	Beginning Value		Annual Return (12%)		Ending Balance
1	$10,000	+	($10,000 × 0.12) $1,200	=	$11,200
2	11,200	+	(11,200 × 0.12) 1,344	=	12,544
3	12,544	+	(12,544 × 0.12) 1,505	=	14,049
4	14,049	+	(14,049 × 0.12) 1,686	=	15,735
5	15,735	+	(15,735 × 0.12) 1,888	=	17,623

Present Value	*Future Value*	*Future Value Factor*
$10,000	$17,623	$17,623 ÷ $10,000 = 1.7623

Factor Solution.   The 12 percent annual future value of one factor for 5 years may be found in the tables in appendix A. The factor is 1.762342. The factor also can be found using the financial functions of a financial calculator by entering 1.00 as the present value, 5 years as the number of periods (holding period), and 12 percent as the interest, then pressing the future value key. Alternatively, it can be found by solving the following mathematical relationship, using the powers option:

$$(1 + 0.12)^5 = (1.12)^5 = 1.762342$$

Discussion.   The factor represents the basic compound interest concept and is used to convert a single lump-sum payment into a future value estimate. In investment analyses, this factor is used in the first step of calculating an adjusted rate of return (see chapter 8) to estimate the future value numbers for each interim cash flow using a reinvestment rate.

Future Value of One Dollar per Period

The *future value of one dollar per period* is defined as a compound interest factor to which a constant periodic investment of $1.00 per period will grow, assuming compound growth at a specific rate of return for a specific number of compounding periods (column 2 of the compound interest tables in appendix A). In an appraisal (and real estate investment analysis), these payments are generally assumed to be made at the *end* of each period.

NOTE: The annuity factors in the table assume each payment will be received at the end of the year. This type of annuity is referred to as an *ordinary annuity*. Annuities can also be assumed to start at the beginning of the year. This would be referred to as an *annuity in advance*. An example of an annuity in advance is provided later in this chapter.

Formula: $\dfrac{(1 + i)^n - 1}{i} = S_{\overline{n}|}$ (column 2 in the tables in appendix A)

where i equals the effective interest rate and n equals the number of time periods.

Table Relationship.   This factor is the reciprocal of the sinking fund factor (column 3 in the tables in appendix A).

Example

What will a $1,000 investment made at the end of each of the next 5 years grow to at the end of the 5-year period, assuming a 12 percent rate of return?

Annual Investment	Future Value	Future Value Factor
$1,000 (EOY)	$6,352	$6,352 ÷ $1,000 = 6.352

* Proof *

Year	Beginning Balance	Annual Return 12%		Additional Investment		Ending Balance
1	$0	+ $0	+	$1,000	=	$1,000
2	1,000	+ (1,000 × 0.12) $120	+	1,000	=	2,120
3	2,120	+ (2,120 × 0.12) 254	+	1,000	=	3,374
4	3,374	+ (3,374 × 0.12) 405	+	1,000	=	4,779
5	4,779	+ (4,779 × 0.12) 573	+	1,000	=	6,352

Factor Solution.   The 12 percent annual future value of one dollar per period factor for 5 years may be found in the tables in appendix A. The factor is 6.352847. The factor may also be found using the financial functions of a calculator by entering 1.00 for the payment, 5 years as the number of periods (holding period) and 12 percent as the interest rate. When the future value key is pressed, the factor for 12 percent will appear.

The future value of one dollar per period can also be calculated by adding the future value of 1.00 factors for $(n - 1)$ periods and adding 1.00. For example, if we add the future value of 1.00 factors for years 1 through 4 at a 12 percent interest rate and then add 1.00, we obtain the same answer as the future value of an annuity of 1.00 factor for 5 years.[2]

Discussion.   This factor may be used to calculate the future value for a series of equal payments in the first step of calculating an *adjusted rate of return* (to be covered in chapter 8). This factor is probably used the least by an appraiser in typical assignments.

Sinking Fund Factor

The *sinking fund factor* is a compound interest factor that represents the level payment percentage required to be periodically invested and compounded at a specific interest rate to grow to an amount equal to $1.00 over a specific time period (column 3 of the compound interest tables).

Formula: $\dfrac{i}{(1 + i)^n - 1} = 1/S_{\overline{n}|}$ (column 3 in the tables in appendix A)

where *i* equals the effective interest rate and *n* equals the number of time periods.

Table Relationship.   This factor is the reciprocal of the future value of one dollar per period (column 2 in the tables in appendix A).

Example

What level annual payment must be paid at the end of each of 5 years assuming a 12 percent rate of return to grow to $10,000 in 5 years?

Future Value		Sinking Fund Factor		Sinking Fund Payment
$10,000	×	0.1574	=	$1,574

* Proof *

Year	Beginning Balance		Annual Return 12%		Additional Payment		Ending Balance
1	$0	+	$0	+	$1,574	=	$ 1,574
2	1,574	+	(1,574 × 0.12) $189	+	1,574	=	3,337
3	3,337	+	(3,337 × 0.12) 400	+	1,574	=	5,311
4	5,311	+	(5,311 × 0.12) 638	+	1,574	=	7,523
5	7,523	+	(7,523 × 0.12) 903	+	1,574	=	10,000

Factor Solution.   The 12 percent annual sinking fund factor for 5 years may be found in the tables in appendix A. The factor is 0.157410. The factor may also be found using the financial functions of a calculator by entering 1.00 for the future value, 5 years for the holding period and 12 percent as the interest rate. When the payment key is pressed, the factor for 12 percent will appear.

Discussion. This factor can be used to estimate the amount necessary to set aside in a reserve for replacements. The factor is also used in some of the formula approaches to yield capitalization discussed in chapter 9 of this book. It also can be used by appraisers to estimate the periodic annual payment needed to cover a projected loss in value. This concept will be explained in later chapters. A complete understanding of the operation and assumptions made when using a sinking fund factor are required if the appraiser is to understand fully some of the appraisal techniques presented later.

Present Value of One Dollar

The *present value of one dollar* is a compound interest factor typically calculated for an annual interest rate used to discount an expected future cash flow to arrive at its current present value (column 4 of the tables in appendix A).

Formula: $\dfrac{1}{(1 + i)^n}$ = $1/S^n$ (column 4 in the tables in appendix A)

where i equals the effective interest rate and n equals the number of time periods.

Table Relationship. This factor is the reciprocal of the future value of one dollar (column 1 in the tables in appendix A).

Example

What is the present value of $10,000 to be received at the end of 5 years, assuming a 12 percent interest rate?

Future Value		Present Value Factor		Present Value
$10,000	×	0.5674	=	$5,674

* Proof *

Year	Beginning Balance		Additional Return 12%			Ending Balance
1	$5,674	+	($5,674 × 0.12)	$ 681	=	$ 6,355
2	6,355	+	(6,355 × 0.12)	763	=	7,118
3	7,118	+	(7,118 × 0.12)	854	=	7,972
4	7,972	+	(7,972 × 0.12)	957	=	8,929
5	8,929	+	(8,929 × 0.12)	1,071	=	10,000

Factor Solution. The 12 percent annual present value factor for 5 years may be found in the tables in appendix A. The factor is 0.567427. It may also be found using the financial functions of a financial calculator by entering 1.00 as the future value, 5 years as the holding period and 12 percent as the interest rate and pressing the present value key. Alternatively, it can be calculated by solving the following mathematical relationship, using the powers and reciprocal options:

$$\frac{1}{(1 + 0.12)^5} = \frac{1}{1.762342} = 0.567427$$

Discussion. This factor is probably the most important one used by an appraiser. It is the principal factor used to transform either a single-year or a multiple-year cash-flow forecast into a present value estimate. Many of the appraisal techniques used in the income approach mirror this concept. It is, therefore, important that an appraiser completely understand the present value concept and the method used to calculate this present value factor.

Present Value of One Dollar per Period

The *present value of one dollar per period* is a compound interest factor typically calculated for an annual interest rate that is used to discount a series of equal future cash flows in order to arrive at a current present value of the total stream of income (column 5 of the tables in appendix A).

Formula: $\dfrac{1 - \dfrac{1}{(1 + i)^n}}{i} = a_{\overline{n}}$ (column 5 in the tables in appendix A)

where i equals the effective interest rate and n equals the number of time periods.

Table Relationship. This factor is the reciprocal of the payment to amortize one dollar (column 6 in the tables in appendix A).

Example

What is the present worth of receiving 5 annual payments (end of year) of $10,000 over each of 5 years assuming a 12 percent rate of return?

Year	Cash Flow		Present Value Factor 12%		Present Value
1	$10,000	×	0.8929	=	$ 8,929
2	10,000	×	0.7972	=	7,972
3	10,000	×	0.7118	=	7,118
4	10,000	×	0.6355	=	6,355
5	10,000	×	0.5674	=	5,674
Total					$36,048

Present Value	Annual Payment	Present Value Factor
$36,048	$10,000	$36,048 ÷ $10,000 = 3.6048

Factor Solution.   The 12 percent annual present value of one dollar per period for 5 years may be found in the tables in appendix A. The factor is 3.604776. It may also be found using the financial functions of a calculator by entering 1.00 as the payment, 5 years as the holding period and 12 percent as the interest rate. When the present value key is pressed, the factor for 12 percent will appear.

Discussion.   This factor is the sum of the present value factors (column 4 factors, appendix A) for the holding period, as shown below.

Year	Present Value Factors
1	0.892857
2	0.797194
3	0.711780
4	0.635518
5	0.567427
Total	3.604776

This factor is extremely useful to an appraiser who wishes to calculate the present value of a forecast cash-flow schedule containing equal cash flows.[3]

NOTE ON THE PRESENT VALUE OF ANNUITIES IN ADVANCE: The present value of 1 per period factor discussed above assumes that the cash flows are received at the *end* of each year. This is why the first-year cash flow is also discounted. This is referred to as an "ordinary annuity" and is the assumption normally used in financial tables. It is also the assumption used in financial calculators, unless the user changes the mode of the calculator to assume the first cash flow occurs at the *beginning* of the year. When the payments for an annuity are assumed to start at the beginning of the first year the annuity is referred to as an "annuity in advance." The present value of this annuity will be higher than that of an ordinary annuity that uses the same interest rate and number of payments because all cash flows are received one year sooner. In fact, because each cash flow is received one year sooner, the present value of this annuity will be higher by a factor of $(1 + i)$. Using the previous example, if the payments of $10,000 began at the beginning of the first year, the present value of 5 years of payments discounted at a 12 percent interest rate would be

Present Worth of Ordinary Annuity	×	$(1 + i)$	=	Present Worth of Annuity in Advance
$36,048	×	1.12	=	$40,374

Payment To Amortize One Dollar

The *payment to amortize one dollar* is the periodic payment necessary to repay a $1.00 loan with interest paid at a specified rate over a specified time on the outstanding loan balance (column 6 of the tables in appendix A).

Formula: $\dfrac{i}{1 - 1/(1 + i)^n} = 1/a_{\overline{n}}$ (column 6 in the tables in appendix A)

where i equals the effective interest rate and n equals the number of time periods.

Table Relationship.   This factor is the reciprocal of the present value of one dollar per period (column 5 in the tables in appendix A). This factor is also equal to the effective interest rate plus the sinking fund factor for the year selected or, in terms of columns:

$$\text{Column } 6 = \text{Column } 3 + i$$

Example

What level of annual end-of-year payment would be needed to amortize a $10,000 loan payment over 5 years assuming a 12 percent interest rate?

Loan Amount		Installment to Amortize Factor		Annual Payment
$10,000	×	0.2774	=	$2,774

Payment	$2,774
Interest	– 1,200
Sinking Fund Payment	$1,574

NOTE: For proof that five annual payments of $1,574 each, assuming compounding at 12 percent, will grow to $10,000, see the sinking fund factor discussion.

In the above example, the annual payment is $2,774. This is the amount necessary to repay the loan in 5 years (with annual payments) and pay the bank 12 percent interest on the outstanding balance each year. A loan schedule for this example is shown following:

Typical Amortization Schedule

Year	Beginning Balance	Interest	Payment	Principal	Ending Balance
1	$10,000	$1,200	$ 2,774	$ 1,574	$8,426
2	8,426	1,011	2,774	1,763	6,663
3	6,663	800	2,774	1,974	4,689
4	4,689	562	2,774	2,212	2,477
5	2,477	297	2,774	2,477	0
Total		$3,870	$13,870	$10,000	

Factor Solution.   The 12 percent annual payment factor for 5 years may be found in the tables included in appendix A. The factor is 0.277410. The factor may also be found using the financial functions of a calculator by entering 1.00 as the present value, 5 years as the holding period and 12 percent as the interest rate. When the payment key is pressed, the factor for 12 percent will appear.

Another method of obtaining the payment factor is to add the sinking fund factor to the effective interest rate. The sinking fund factor in this instance is 0.157410 (based on a 5-year holding period and a 12 percent interest rate), and the interest rate is 0.120000. The sum is 0.277410. Viewed in this manner, we might say that the installment to amortize 1.00 factor consists of two components:

1. an allowance for interest on the loan (*return on capital*) and
2. repayment of the loan (referred to as *return of capital*).

This can be interpreted as meaning that a borrower could pay interest of 12 percent per year and set aside 15.74 percent of the loan ($1,574.10) in a sinking fund (for example, a bank account) earning 12 percent and accumulate enough money in the sinking fund ($10,000) to repay the loan after 5 years.[4]

Loan Constant.   The payment to amortize one dollar factor can be used to calculate loan payments for level-payment amortizing loans and can be referred to as a *loan constant*. Level-payment amortizing loans are fixed-payment loans over a specific time period (*amortization* period), whose payment includes a combination of interest and principal that would result in total repayment over the amortization period.

In the above example the loan constant would be for a 5-year loan with *annual* payments. Note that the loan constant (27.741 percent) in the above example is greater than the interest rate of 12 percent. It must be higher for the loan to be amortized. In fact, in this example it is quite a bit higher, because the loan is being amortized over only 5 years.

MORTGAGE CAPITALIZATION RATE

In general, a *capitalization rate* is the ratio of some measure of cash flow from an investment to the value of that investment. The measure of cash flow is usually the cash flow during the first year of the investment. In the case of a mortgage loan, the cash flow is the annual payment on the loan and the investment is the initial amount of the loan. In the example considered above, the payment during the first year (which is the same each year) is $2,774. The amount of the loan (which is the lender's investment) is $10,000. Thus the capitalization rate for the mortgage (referred to as a *mortgage capitalization rate*) is $2,774 ÷ $10,000 = 27.74 percent. This is obviously the same as the mortgage constant. The point is that the mortgage constant can be referred to as the "mortgage capitalization rate."

The concept of a capitalization rate is used so frequently in appraisal theory and practice that it is essential for the appraiser to have as much insight into this concept as possible. Therefore, it is important to begin to think about the interpretation of this ratio. Our example and the discussion were related to the relationship between loan payments and the value of that loan (which is the present value of the payments). More generally, a capitalization rate is a relationship between the cash flow on any investment and the present value of those cash flows. If, in the example considered above, the annual payments were for an investment in a property (rather than a loan) that would produce income of $2,774 for the next 5 years (and nothing thereafter), then we could say that the capitalization rate for the property would be 27.74 percent.[5] The relationship between capitalization rates and compound interest theory is discussed extensively in later chapters.

Monthly Payments

As mentioned above, the installment-to-amortize factor is used primarily to calculate loan payments for level-payment, self-amortizing loans. Frequently, loan payments are made monthly. For a 25-year loan at 12 percent interest with monthly payments, the installment-to-amortize factor would be calculated as follows

$$\text{Formula: } \frac{i}{1 - 1/(1 + i)^n} = \frac{1}{a_{\overline{n}|}}$$

$$i = 0.12/12 = 0.01$$
$$n = 25 \times 12 = 300$$

$$\frac{1}{a_{\overline{n}|}} = \frac{0.01}{1 - 1/(1 + 0.01)^{300}} = \frac{0.01}{0.949466} = 0.010532$$

For a $10,000 loan, the monthly payment would therefore be

$$\$10,000 \times 0.010532 = \$105.32$$

We can also determine the loan constant for a loan with monthly payments. In this case it is customary to express the loan constant on an *annual* basis, even though the payments are actually made on a monthly basis. For the above example, the annual constant would be

$$\text{Annual mortgage constant} = [\$105.32 \ / \ \$10,000] \times 12 = 12.64\%$$

Effective Annual Rate

The *effective annual rate* is the rate based on annual compounding that is equivalent to a rate that assumes more frequent compounding. For example, if a loan is made at a 12 percent rate with monthly payments, the effective rate is higher than it would be if payments were made only on an annual basis, because interest compounds each month. The effective annual rate could be calculated as follows:

$$(1 + i)^{12} - 1 \text{ or } (1 + 0.01)^{12} - 1 = 1.1268 - 1 \text{ or } 0.1268 \text{ or } 12.68\%$$

A loan with a nominal annual rate of 12 percent that has monthly payments is equivalent to a loan that has annual payments and an interest rate of 12.68 percent. Thus, we could say that the effective annual rate is 12.68 percent.

INTERRELATIONSHIP AMONG THE FACTORS

It is informative to understand that all of the six factors are mathematically related. Some of the relationships were presented earlier. They are summarized as follows:

- Column 1 is the reciprocal of Column 4
- Column 2 is the reciprocal of Column 3
- Column 5 is the reciprocal of Column 6
- Column 6 = Column 3 + i
- Column 1 × Column 3 = Column 6
- Column 2 × Column 4 = Column 5
- Column 1 × Column 3 × Column 5 = 1
- Column 2 × Column 4 × Column 6 = 1

NOTE: The last two relationships enable the appraiser to calculate what one factor is in terms of the other factors. For example:

$$\text{Column 3} = \frac{1}{\text{Column 1} \times \text{Column 5}} = \frac{\text{Column 4}}{\text{Column 5}}$$

PRESENT VALUE APPLICATIONS

Historically, the tables in appendix A were used by real estate appraisers to estimate the present value of various types of incomes. Today, calculators and computers do the same task, but it is important to understand how the tables can be used to calculate present value.

Present Value of a Level Income Stream

The present value of a given level income stream can be found once a discount (interest) rate is selected, because at that point three of the four essential elements in a compound interest problem would be known (future cash flows, time period and interest rate).

Find the present value of the following end-of-year (EOY) cash flows, assuming a 15 percent annual discount rate:

Year	Cash Flow
1	$2,000
2	2,000
3	2,000
4	2,000
5	2,000

Cash Flow		Present Value of an Annuity Factor @ 15%		Present Value
$2,000	×	3.352155	=	$6,704

Because the five cash flows are equal and equal time periods are assumed in the analysis, the answer can be readily calculated by multiplying the periodic cash flow by the 5-year present value of one dollar per period for 15 percent as shown above. The same answer could have been found by discounting each payment by the appropriate present value of one dollar factor for each year. (This approach is necessary when the cash flows are uneven and tables are used.)

Year	Cash Flow		Present Value @ 15%		Present Value
1	$2,000	×	0.869565	=	$1,739
2	2,000	×	0.756144	=	1,512
3	2,000	×	0.657516	=	1,315
4	2,000	×	0.571753	=	1,144
5	2,000	×	0.497177	=	994
Total					$6,704

Note that the capitalization rate for the above example is $2,000/$6,704, which is 29.83 percent. Based on our earlier discussion about the relationship between factors, it should not be a surprise that the same rate can be found in column 6 (Payment to Amortize $1) of the 15 percent compound interest tables in appendix A.

Present Value of a Level Income Stream Plus a Reversion

Investments are often analyzed for a holding period that is shorter than the time period over which the investment will generate income. In this case the resale price of the property at the end of the holding period must be considered. The term *reversion* is used in real estate appraisal and investment analysis to refer to the proceeds from resale. In the following example it is assumed that income will be $5,000 per year and the property can be sold for $50,000 at the end of a 5-year holding period.

Example

What is the present value of the following 5-year cash flows, assuming a 15 percent annual rate of return?

Year	Cash Flow (EOY)
1	$ 5,000
2	5,000
3	5,000
4	5,000
5	5,000
5	50,000

Cash Flow		*Annuity Factor @ 15%*		*Present Value*
$5,000	×	3.352155	=	$16,761

Cash Flow		*Present Value Factor @ 15%*		
$50,000	×	0.497177	=	+24,859
Total				$41,620

An alternative way of solving the above problem is to determine the present value of each cash flow individually, then add the results of each present value. This is shown as follows:

Year	*Cash Flow*		*Present Value Factor @ 15%*		*Present Value*
1	$ 5,000	×	0.869565	=	$ 4,348
2	5,000	×	0.756144	=	3,781
3	5,000	×	0.657516	=	3,287
4	5,000	×	0.571753	=	2,859
5	55,000	×	0.497177	=	27,345
Total					$41,620

The answer is obviously the same for each approach. The answer also could have been found by using the present value function of a calculator or using a computer.

Present Value of Variable Income

Frequently an appraiser is faced with the task of estimating the present value of a variable cash-flow forecast. Because this type of income stream is not level, the shortcut method using the present value of one dollar per period cannot be used. In this case, the appropriate math is to find the sum of the present values of the income for each year, including any reversion. This is illustrated in the following example, in which income during each year differs and there is a reversion at the end of the holding period.

Example

What is the present value of the following 5-year variable cash flows, assuming a 15 percent annual rate of return?

Year	Cash Flow		Present Value Factor @ 15%		Present Value
1	$ 5,000	×	0.869565	=	$ 4,348
2	5,250	×	0.756144	=	3,970
3	5,600	×	0.657516	=	3,682
4	5,850	×	0.571753	=	3,345
5	65,000	×	0.497177	=	32,317
Total					$47,662

In this case the capitalization rate (ratio of the *first* year cash flow to the present value) is $5,000/$47,662 = 10.49 percent. Because the income is not a level annuity and because there is a reversion, the exact mathematical relationship between the capitalization rate and the discount rate (interest rate) is not obvious. That is, the capitalization rate is *not* the factor in column 6 of the tables in appendix A and it cannot be found by the simple table relationships described earlier. However, there is still a conceptual relationship between the capitalization rate and the discount rate. This relationship will be explored extensively throughout this text.

Typically, most real estate cash-flow forecasts today have a variable cash-flow pattern, unless the payments have been fixed by a long-term absolute net lease. Thus, the approach illustrated in the above example is the most common and most general approach. It can be used to handle any income pattern, as long as the expected future cash flows can be estimated in dollars.[6]

Present Value of Cash Flows Received in Advance

Typically, real estate cash flows are assumed to have been received at the end of a period. Sometimes, however, an appraiser may be faced with estimating the value of income received at the beginning of the period (in advance).

Example

What is the present value of the following 5-year cash flows, assuming the payments are received in advance and assuming a 15 percent rate of return?

Year	Cash Flow		Present Value Factor @ 15%		Present Value
1	$2,000	×	1.000000	=	$ 2,000
2	3,000	×	0.869563	=	2,609
3	3,500	×	0.756144	=	2,646
4	4,000	×	0.657516	=	2,630
5	5,000	×	0.571753	=	2,858
Total					$12,743

Receiving a cash flow at the beginning of year 2 (for example) is the same as receiving it at the end of year 1. The appropriate approach to calculate present value, therefore, is to add the entire beginning payment (because the present value of receiving $2,000 today is $2,000) to the present value of the future cash flows. In this case the present value of the cash flows received at the beginning of year 2 is the same as the present value of the same cash flow assumed to be received at the end of year 1.

Interest Rate Calculation

Whenever a complete set of cash flows is known or assumed, the present value tables may be used to calculate the interest rate. In this case, three of the four elements of compound interest must be known or assumed: the present value, the holding period and the future cash flows. Because of the mathematical complexity of calculating an interest rate, trial and error is the only method of finding an answer. Calculators and computers can be programmed, however, to undertake the trial-and-error process rapidly and find the answer in only a few seconds. The first method illustrated to calculate an interest rate will be trial and error using the table factors.

Example

Find the interest rate, given an initial investment of $10,000 and expected cash flows as follows:

Year	Cash Flow	
0	($10,000)	(Initial Investment)
1	1,200	
2	1,200	
3	12,000	

Solution—Trial and Error

Try 15%:

Year	Cash Flow		Present Value Factor @ 15%		Present Value
0	($10,000)				
1	1,200	×	0.8696	=	$ 1,044
2	1,200	×	0.7561	=	907
3	12,000	×	0.6575	=	7,890
Total					$ 9,841

$9,841 < $10,000, therefore, 15% is too high

Try 14%:

Year	Cash Flow		Present Value Factor @ 14%		Present Value
0	($10,000)				
1	1,200	×	0.8772	=	$ 1,053
2	1,200	×	0.7695	=	923
3	12,000	×	0.6750	=	8,100
Total					$10,076

$10,076 > $10,000, therefore, 14% is too low

IRR	Present Value
14%	$10,076
15%	9,841
Difference	$ 235

IRR	Present Value
14%	$10,076
? %	10,000
Difference	$ 76

Interpolation

14% + (76/235)1% = 14.32%

___

The interest rate can also be found using a hand-held calculator. The answer is found by entering $10,000 as the beginning cash flow, entering *each* future cash flow in the proper register, then pressing the IRR (internal rate of return) key. The calculator will rapidly search for the correct answer and finally print the answer on the display. In this case, the interest rate found was 14.318796, rounded to 14.32 percent.

Year	Cash Flow	
0	($10,000)	
1	1,200	IRR = 14.32%
2	1,200	
3	12,000	

The answer also could have been found using a computer. For example, spreadsheet programs have an internal rate of return calculation option as a built-in function.

To prove that the correct interest rate is 14.32 percent, the analyst need only calculate the present value of the future cash flows using 14.32 percent interest factors to determine if the present value of the future cash flows is equal to the present value of the investment. Following is the proof.

Year	Cash Flow		Present Value Factor @ 14.32%		Present Value
1	$ 1,200	×	0.874738	=	$ 1,050
2	1,200	×	0.765166	=	918
3	12,000	×	0.669319	=	8,032
Total					$10,000

In this instance, the interest rate calculation of 14.32 percent is correct, because the present value of the future cash flows discounted at this rate is equal to the present value of the investment.

The Internal Rate of Return

The *internal rate of return,* or IRR for short, is defined as a rate of return that discounts all expected future cash flows to a present value equal to the original investment. It represents the rate of return on an investment.

The internal rate of return is recognized as a more general term than "interest rate," but the two represent the same concept. In real estate, the term "interest rate" is more commonly used when discussing mortgage financing. In this case, the mortgage interest rate would be the interest rate that discounts all future loan payments to a present value equal to the initial mortgage balance. In other words, the mortgage interest rate calculated would be the internal rate of return to the lender. (If points are charged on the loan, the internal rate of return to the lender would be higher.)

The internal rate of return can also be referred to as a "discount rate" or "yield rate." Typically, when an interest rate is used to discount future cash flow to a present value estimate, it is referred to as a "discount rate." When calculating the interest rate for a set of cash flows, the rate found is usually referred to as a "yield rate" or "internal rate of return." Although the terminology may appear confusing, it is important for an appraiser to understand the terminology and the meaning of each rate. Conceptually, internal rates of return, interest rates, discount rates and yield rates are similar, because each represents the return on an investment and is the rate that discounts all expected future cash flows to a present value. When used in practice, each should have a descriptor attached to it that describes the ownership interest to which the rate applies. For example, a rate used to discount future property cash flows to present value equal to the total property value is referred to as the "property discount rate." Following is a table of the typical internal rates of return used in real estate analyses:

Typical Real Estate Internal Rates of Return

Interest	Discount / Yield Rate	Symbol
Total property	Property discount rate	Y_O
Building value	Building discount rate	Y_B
Land value	Land discount rate	Y_L
Equity	Before-tax equity yield rate	Y_E
Mortgage	Mortgage interest rate	Y_M or i

In using or calculating any of the rates listed above, the only cash flows used are those that are applicable to the property interest appraised, and the present value estimates represent the value of the interest to which the cash flows accrue. For example, when estimating the value of the land, the land discount (Y_L) is used to discount the cash flow attributable to the land.

Internal Rate of Return Issues

There are several issues with regard to use and calculation of an internal rate of return (interest rate in compound interest theory). One issue is the multiple IRR possibilities, and another is whether the calculation assumes reinvestment of interim cash flows. Following are brief discussions of each issue.

Multiple IRR Solutions.   A situation can arise in which two or more rates of return can be used to discount future cash flows to a present value equal to the original investment. Generally, in real estate, the existence of cash-flow patterns that would result in multiple internal rates of return are rare. The multiple rate occurs when the cash-flow schedules vary from positive to negative in future years. For example, the following set of cash flows has only one sign change:

Year	Cash Flow	Sign
0	($100,000)	(−)
1	12,000	(+)
2	12,000	(+)
3	12,000	(+)
4	150,000	(+)

In this case, there can be only one internal rate of return. The following set of cash flows has three sign changes:

Year	Cash Flow	Sign
0	($100,000)	(−)
1	50,000	(+)
2	40,000	(+)
3	30,000	(+)
4	10,000	(+)
5	9,000	(+)
6	8,000	(+)
7	7,000	(+)
8	(50,000)	(−)
9	3,000	(+)
10	2,000	(+)

When there is more than one sign change, there can be more than one IRR. In this case there are two mathematical IRRs. They are −11.42 percent and +10.27 percent, which creates a dilemma! Is this a good or a bad investment? Clearly, it is difficult to make a decision by looking only at the IRR. Fortunately, there is a way to resolve this issue. One way is to calculate the present value of the cash flows for years 1 through 10 at an appropriate discount rate. The difference between this present value and the initial investment is referred to as the *net present value* (NPV). If the NPV is positive, the investment is acceptable. In this case we find that the NPV is positive at a 10 percent discount rate. Thus, the present value of the cash inflows, including the negative $50,000 in year 8 (discounted as a negative), is still greater than the initial investment of $100,000. Thus, it would be a good investment as long as the investor is willing to accept a rate of return of 10 percent or less.[7]

In most cases the appraiser is estimating the present value of the cash flows at a given discount rate, rather than calculating an IRR. Thus, even in situations where a multiple IRR is possible (due to more than one change in the sign of the cash flows), it is not a problem in estimating the appraised value.

Reinvestment Assumptions.   There are two schools of thought concerning implied reinvestment in the calculation of the internal rate of return. One school holds that when calculating an IRR there is no implied *reinvestment assumption* regarding how cash flows received between the beginning and the end of the holding period are reinvested. For example, given the following set of cash flows, the internal rate of return can be calculated as 20 percent without making any assumptions about reinvestment of cash flows.

Year	Cash Flow	
0	($10,000)	
1	3,000	IRR = 20.00%
2	5,000	
3	6,960	

* Proof *

Year	Cash Flow		Present Value Factor @ 20%		Present Value
0	($10,000)				
1	3,000	×	0.833333	=	$ 2,500
2	5,000	×	0.694444	=	3,472
3	6,960	×	0.578704	=	4,028
Total					$10,000

The other school believes that when calculating this return, there is an implicit assumption made that the $3,000 and $5,000 cash flows can be reinvested at a 20 percent rate so that the series of cash flows will actually earn a 20 percent return over the holding period.

Individuals who believe there is an implied reinvestment assumption generally make the following argument: If there is no reinvestment assumption, the total future value of the investment would be:

Year	Cash Flow
1	$ 3,000
2	5,000
3	6,960
Total	$14,960

Using the compound interest tables (see appendix A) or a calculator, the implied annual return, given a $10,000 investment today and a lump-sum payment of $14,960 at the end of 3 years, would be as follows:

$$(\$14,960/\$10,000)^{1/3} -1 = (1.496)^{1/3} -1 = 1.1437 -1, \text{ or } 14.37\%$$

This rate is considerably less than the 20 percent internal rate of return calculated. Now let's assume the interim cash flow may be reinvested at 20 percent.

Year	Cash Flow		Future Value Factor @ 20%		Future Value
1	$ 3,000	×	1.4400	=	$ 4,320
2	5,000	×	1.2000	=	6,000
3	6,960	×	1.0000	=	6,960
Total					$17,280

Again, using the compound interest tables in appendix A or a calculator, the implied annual return, given a $10,000 investment today and a lump-sum payment of $17,280 (after assuming reinvestment of interim cash flow at 20 percent annually) at the end of 3 years, would be as follows:

$$(\$17,280/\$10,000)^{1/3} -1 = (1.728)^{1/3} -1 = 1.20 -1, \text{ or } 20\%$$

In this case, the annual rate found is 20 percent, which is equal to the internal rate of return. Clearly, if the cash flows cannot be reinvested at the 20 percent rate, the investor will not end up with a 20 percent return on funds invested. Whether this means that the internal rate of return implicitly assumes reinvestment at a rate equal to the internal rate of return (20 percent, in this case) is, perhaps, a matter of semantics. The point is that when investors interpret the meaning of the internal rate of return that is calculated for a particular investment, they should be aware that they may not be able to reinvest interim cash flows at the same rate.

Investors who want to consider explicitly how cash flows can be reinvested often calculate what is referred to as an "adjusted rate of return." This is illustrated in the following section.

Adjusted Rate of Return.   To illustrate the calculation of the adjusted rate of return, consider the following set of cash flows:

Year	Cash Flow
0	($10,000)
1	3,000
2	5,000
3	10,400

IRR = 30.00%

The internal rate of return calculated above was 30 percent, which is a significantly high rate of return. When doing investment analysis, because of the reinvestment assumption implied in this IRR calculation, reinvestment at 30 percent probably would be unrealistic when compared to alternative investments available in the market. Several methods have been devised to adjust these interim cash flows, the simplest of which is to compound the interim cash flows forward at a "reinvestment rate," a return typically obtainable in the marketplace. Assuming a real estate investor could readily receive a 12 percent return on periodic cash flows received from the property, the first step in calculating an adjusted rate of return would be to compound the future cash flows forward at 12 percent.

Year	Cash Flow		Future Value Factor @ 12%		Future Value
1	$ 3,000	×	1.2544	=	$ 3,763
2	5,000	×	1.1200	=	5,600
3	10,400	×	1.0000	=	10,400
Total					$19,763

The second step would be to estimate the implied annual rate of return, given the $10,000 investment today and a lump-sum future value in 3 years of $19,763.

$$(\$19,763/\$10,000)^{1/3} - 1 = 1.9763^{1/3} - 1 = 1.2549 - 1, \text{ or } 25.5\%$$

In this instance, the adjusted rate of return is 25.5 percent, or 4.5 percent less than the internal rate of return of 30 percent.

The following is another example of an adjusted rate of return using cash flows similar to those that would be expected from a real estate investment.

Example

Step 1—Future Value Calculation

Given the following set of cash flows, what is the future value, assuming a 10 percent rate of return?

Year	Cash Flow		Future Value Factor @ 10%		Future Value
1	$ 3,000	×	1.4641	=	$ 4,392
2	3,500	×	1.3310	=	4,658
3	4,000	×	1.2100	=	4,840
4	4,500	×	1.1000	=	4,950
5	50,000	×	1.0000	=	50,000
Future Value					$68,840

Step 2—Calculate the Rate of Return

Given a future value of $68,840, what is the annual rate of return assuming an initial investment of $40,000?

$$(\$68,840/\$40,000)^{1/5} - 1 = 1.7210^{1/5} - 1 = 1.1147, \text{ or } 11.47\%$$

The adjusted rate of return is: 11.47%
The IRR is: 11.70%

In this example, the adjusted rates of return and the IRR are virtually equal, because:

- the IRR and the reinvestment rate are reasonably close and
- a significant part of the expected cash flows results from the proceeds from resale.

Because the resale proceeds fall at the end of the holding period, the impact is not affected by the rate adjustment process.

There are several variations of the above theme. For example, other methods of adjusting interim cash flows include:

- discounting negative cash flows by a "safe rate" and adding this number to the original investment[8];
- discounting negative cash flows by a safe rate and netting this number against the first prior positive cash flow; and
- using a two-tier reinvestment assumption, which assumes that interim cash flows are compounded at a safe rate until enough money is accumulated to purchase higher yielding real estate. After that, funds are reinvested at a higher reinvestment rate, representative of what could be earned on other real estate investments.

Other terms used for this type of approach of reinvesting cash flows include "modified internal rates of return" (MIRR) and "financial management rates of return" (FMRR). The adjusted rate of return concept is used primarily in investment analysis and is an attempt by investors to mirror the actual handling of cash flows in a real estate investment.

MORTGAGE LOAN CALCULATIONS

The compound interest concept is the basis for calculating loan payments for level-payment, self-amortizing loans. Each payment includes interest and principal portions that vary over time, as explained earlier in this chapter in discussion of the installment to amortize factor.

The impact of introducing financing into an analysis of real estate is covered in chapter 11. The following discussion covers only the mathematics of calculating mortgage payments, interest rates, remaining loan terms and loan balances, using compound interest tables and calculators.

Calculating Loan Payments—Level Amortizing Mortgages

Calculating a mortgage payment for a self-amortizing loan is a typical compound interest problem. In this case, the analyst is given three of the four variables needed to calculate an answer—the holding period (the amortization term), the interest rate (the mortgage interest rate) and the present value (the beginning loan balance)—and is asked to find the future payments. An example follows:

Example

What is the monthly payment required to amortize a $100,000 loan over 25 years, assuming a 10.5 percent interest rate?

Solution 1 (Compound Interest Table)

Loan Amount		Payment Factor		Monthly Payment
$100,000	×	0.009442*	=	$944.20

* The 0.009442 factor is from the monthly compound interest tables in appendix B.

As in any basic compound interest problem, the time interval between payments must be equal. In many cases, loan payments are required monthly, so the interest rate and number of periods over which the compounding is to take place must be adjusted accordingly.

The answer also could have been found using the financial functions of a calculator by inputting 300 as the number of periods (12 × 25), 0.875 as the monthly interest rate (10.5 ÷ 12) and $100,000 as the present value. Once the payment key is pressed, the monthly payment is displayed.

Example

Solution 2 (Calculator)

n	=	300
i	=	0.875%
PV	=	$100,000
PMT	=	?
Payment	=	$944.18

In this instance, 300 monthly payments of $944.18 (difference due to rounding) would totally pay off the $100,000 loan and provide the lender with an 0.875 percent monthly rate of return, or 10.5 percent on an annual basis. The effective interest rate would not be 10.5 percent but would be $(1.00875)^{12}$, that is, 1.1102 or 11.02 percent. The IRR to the lender would be 0.875 percent per month.

Calculating a Loan Balance—Level Amortizing Mortgages

The compound interest tables or a calculator may be used to calculate the loan balance for a level amortizing loan at any point in time. Conceptually, the easiest way to calculate a loan balance is to realize that the balance at any time is the present value of the remaining series of payments discounted at the effective mortgage interest rate. The example that follows illustrates this point:

Example

What would be the balance of the loan in the previous example after 6 years of payments?

Solution 1 (Compound Interest Tables)

Payment		Monthly Present Value Annuity Factor @ 10.5%, 19 Years		
$944.18	×	98.605822	=	$93,102

In the above example, the present value of one dollar per period for 228 payments (19 × 12) at an 0.875 percent interest rate (10.5% ÷ 12) is 98.605822. Multiplying this factor by the expected monthly payment of $944.18 results in a present value estimate for the income stream of $93,102, which is the loan balance after 72 (6 × 12) months of payments.

The answer also may be found using the financial functions of a calculator by entering the number of remaining time periods (228), the effective interest rate (0.875 percent) and the monthly payment of $944.18, and pressing the present value key. Several additional automatic functions are also built into most calculators that calculate a loan balance.

Example

Solution 2 (Calculator)

n	=	228
i	=	0.875%
PMT	=	$944.18
PV	=	?
Loan Balance	=	$93,102

SUMMARY

Because the value of real estate income property depends on anticipated future benefits, a thorough understanding of time value of money concepts is very important. Although most appraisers use financial calculators or computers to solve the types of problems illustrated in this chapter, a review of the *six functions of one dollar* that form the basis for the traditional financial tables provides insights into the interrelationships between the different compound interest and discounting concepts important in appraisal theory. Whether tables, a financial calculator or a computer is used, appraisers should be able to find the present value of any given series of cash flows, whether the cash flows represent a level annuity, an annuity plus a reversion or an uneven series of cash flows with or without a reversion. All of these situations can be encountered in practice.

Many terms have virtually the same meaning: interest rate, discount rate, yield rate, return on capital and internal rate of return. It is important to understand how to calculate and interpret the meaning of each of these terms because they form the basis for yield capitalization. Because the discount rate used in yield capitalization should reflect the internal rate of return that a typical investor requires if he or she is to invest in the property, it is also important to know how that investor might view the reinvestment assumptions implicit in the interpretation of the internal rate of return, as well as the possibility of there being multiple IRRs for the same investment.

Although the focus of this chapter was on the tools for discounting cash flows that would be used in yield capitalization, a thorough understanding of these concepts is also important to interpret a capitalization rate used in direct capitalization. The relationship between yield rates and capitalization rates was briefly introduced in this chapter. This relationship will be explored in more detail in chapters 8 and 9. However, before we do that we will learn more in chapter 7 about how cash flows can be forecast.

KEY TERMS

adjusted internal rate of return	interest
amortization	interest rate
annuity in advance	internal rate of return
capitalization rate	Inwood annuity factor
compound interest	loan constant
compound interest factor	mortgage capitalization rate
discount rate	net present value
discounting	ordinary annuity
effective annual rate	payment to amortize one dollar
future value of one dollar	present value
future value of one dollar per period	present value annuity of one dollar

present value of one dollar per
   period
principal
reinvestment assumption
reinvestment rate
return of capital

return on capital
reversion
sinking fund factor
six functions of one dollar
time value of money
yield rate

QUESTIONS

1. What is meant by the term "discounting"? How is discounting related to the financial principle of the time value of money?
2. Which financial functions do you think an appraiser would be most likely to use?
3. Which financial function do you think an appraiser could use to determine how much money would have to be set aside in an interest-earning account to replace a roof in 5 years?
4. Why does an appraiser need to distinguish between an ordinary annuity and an annuity in advance?
5. What is the relationship between a loan constant and the interest rate for a fully amortized mortgage?
6. Suppose an investment is estimated to have a cash flow of $100,000 per year for the next 5 years. At the end of the fifth year the property is expected to be sold for $1,000,000. What is the present value of the investment at a 10 percent discount rate?
7. Refer to question 6. Suppose the income is $100,000 for the first year but then increases 5 percent per year over the next 4 years. What is the present value at the same 10 percent discount rate?
8. What causes the possibility of a multiple rate of return?
9. Why is the adjusted rate of return usually less than the internal rate of return?
10. Suppose a loan is made for $5 million. Interest is to be charged at an 8 percent interest rate with payments amortized over 30 years. What is the monthly loan payment? What is the balance of the loan after 5 years?

END NOTES

1. If the future cash flow is the unknown variable and the future cash flow involves more than one period, then it must be assumed to follow a well-defined mathematical pattern (for example, a level annuity) in order to solve for the future cash flow using tables or a financial calculator in a straightforward manner.

2. The reason the future worth of 1.00 factors are for $(n - 1)$ years rather than n years is the assumption that the cash flows are deposited at the end of the year. Thus the deposit during the last year does not earn interest and is only worth 1.00. Only the previous years' cash flows earn interest.

3. Some appraisal textbooks refer to this factor as an "Inwood factor," especially when the resulting present value is contrasted with that found under an alternative way of valuing annuities referred to as the "Hoskold" premise. This is discussed later.

4. Of course, we might question the ability of the borrower to earn 12 percent on the money. However, by making the principal payment to the bank, the net result is the same as if the borrower earned 12 percent on the funds given to the bank.

5. An example of an investment in a property interest that would have this type of income pattern might be a leasehold estate in a property that has a below-market lease that expires in 5 years. The valuation of leasehold estates is discussed in chapter 13.

6. In chapter 9 we will consider situations where the resale price (reversion) is estimated based on a percentage change from the present value of the property. This adds an additional complication when attempting to discount the cash flows.

7. Technically it would have a positive NPV at any discount rate less than 10.27 percent but greater than −11.42 percent. Of course, we would not want a rate less than zero.

8. A "safe rate" is a rate of return that could be earned on a relatively riskless investment such as treasury bills. The idea of discounting at a safe rate is that the resulting present value represents the amount of additional investment that would be necessary to cover the future negative cash flows if these additional funds were invested at the safe rate.

<table>
<tr><td>

CHAPTER 5

</td><td>

Cash-Flow Forecasting

</td></tr>
</table>

REAL ESTATE CASH-FLOW FORECASTS

The income approach theoretically is based on the premise that the value of real estate property is the present value of the anticipated future benefits. These future benefits manifest themselves in the income approach as expected future cash flows, both from the operation of the income-producing property and the expected net proceeds from a forecast resale of the property at the end of a holding period. Preparing a reliable and supportable cash flow can be a difficult task, especially in a highly volatile market, but methods have been developed to test and refine these forecasts. It is important for the appraiser not only to be able to identify and quantify expected cash flows but also to understand the important effect that changes in assumptions have on any final value estimates. Because forecasts reflect expectations for the future and will probably prove to be incorrect, their accuracy should not be judged from a historical perspective but from the perspective of how logical the forecasts appeared at the moment they were made, given the data available to the appraiser.

FORECASTING

Forecasting is accomplished by assimilating information from the past, identifying relationships between influencing factors and drawing conclusions about what will probably happen in the future. The final conclusion will be reached after application of typical forecasting techniques such as modeling, applied judgment, time series analyses and various additional approaches. The sources of forecasting information include historical data and behavior patterns as well as current trends and performances. Key considerations in the forecasting process include:

- Forecasts must be timely, that is, based on the most recent trends.
- Forecasts must be in the units appropriate for the decision (dollars, units, units per period and so forth).
- Forecasts must be as detailed as needed to capture key factors that affect the item being forecast.
- Forecasting assumptions and limitations should be clearly spelled out.

Items usually in a forecast for a real estate appraisal include income, rent, expenses, vacancy, sale prices, interest rates and value. In addition, market demand, supply, absorption, capture rate, market capacity and market potential are key elements in a highest and best use analysis as well as in economic feasibility studies. Note that all forecasts involve estimation of actual cash flows versus cash flows based on accounting or accrual concepts. The purpose of forecasting in real estate appraisal is to identify the dollar amounts actually to be received or paid by typical investors in the property under analysis.

TYPES OF INCOME

Application of the income approach to real estate income property requires one or more measures of the income potential of the property. Commonly used measures include potential gross income, effective gross income, net operating income, before- and after-tax cash flow, and reversion (resale) proceeds.

- Potential gross income (PGI) is the total potential income that could be expected from property at full occupancy before operating expenses are deducted. PGI can be calculated for the first year of ownership of the property and estimated for each year of operation over a typical holding period.
- Effective gross income (EGI) is the anticipated income from operation of the property after vacancy and collection losses. EGI is often based on a percentage of potential gross income that is typical for the area. For a leased fee estate, vacancy losses should include losses due to tenant turnover.
- Net operating income (NOI) is the income remaining after all operating expenses are deducted from effective gross income but before mortgage debt service, tax depreciation, or any state or federal income taxes are deducted. NOI is usually expressed as an annual amount.
- Before-tax cash flow (BTCF) is the portion of net operating income that remains after debt service is deducted but before tax depreciation or income

taxes are deducted. BTCF is also referred to as "equity dividend" or "pretax cash flow."

- After-tax cash flow (ATCF) is the portion of cash flow that remains after state and federal income taxes have been deducted. The amount of ordinary income tax depends on the taxable income that results from owning the property. Taxable income is determined by the amount of interest and tax depreciation that can be deducted from NOI when calculating taxable income. The tax liability depends on the investor's other taxable income.

- Reversion is the cash that an investor receives when the investment is sold. The amount depends on the value of the property at the time of sale, which depends on the income anticipated by the next owner. Thus, the reversion can be viewed as selling the rights to future income to the next investor. The income from reversion may be calculated before or after deduction of the mortgage balance and income taxes and should be consistent with the way cash flow is calculated during the operating years. For example, if the appraiser is analyzing the property before considering financing and taxes, NOI would be estimated during the operating years, and the reversion would be equal to the net resale proceeds (sales price less any selling costs). If, on the other hand, the appraiser wanted to project BTCF, then debt service would be deducted from NOI during each operating year and the mortgage balance would be deducted from the net resale proceeds.

CASH-FLOW FORECASTS FROM OPERATIONS

The cash flow generated annually from the operation of an income-producing property is, basically, the income received less operating expenses. Usually, these estimates are made on an annual basis, assuming that the net cash flows are received at the end of each year. Cash-flow forecasts may be prepared that assume receipt at the beginning of the year, but it is rare to receive all income and pay all expenses at the beginning of the year. There is one instance in which it would be logical to assume that receipt of income would occur at the beginning of the year, namely, when a building is leased on an absolute net basis (tenant pays all operating expenses). Such a lease requires a full annual payment at the beginning of each year. Leases requiring this specific payment structure are rare.

Sources of Annual Income

Income from a real estate property is primarily produced by charging a tenant to occupy the space; in other words, to rent the space through the execution of a lease. It is often said that appraisals are "lease based," because one of the basic assumptions made, whether the space is leased or owner occupied, is that the space could be leased at a certain rental rate. This rental or implied rental typically becomes the primary source of income from the property. The relative level of rent for a specific building is based on the perceived utility and the effective demand for the property as determined by current market conditions for the property type being appraised based on rental ranges for comparable properties. An appraiser may imply a certain level of rent or may actually consider any existing leases for tenant space. If the income forecast includes rent from existing leases, the ownership interest becomes the leased fee interest. If the income forecast is based on market rent levels, the ownership interest appraised is the fee simple interest.

There are a few specialized property types where the income usually analyzed is not actual or implied lease income, for example, hotels, nursing homes and recreational facilities. In each of these cases, the source of the income is the actual charges to tenants to occupy or use the facilities. Conceptually, use charges are similar to rent, but the operating expenses are structured in a different format.

Some properties are able to generate income from sources other than rent. Apartment buildings may contain laundry facilities and/or vending machines that generate additional income from their use. Office buildings may generate income from parking, concessions, antenna rent (on the top of high-rise buildings) and so forth. Shopping centers can generate additional income from such things as selling advertising services and equipment rental. In some instances, it becomes difficult to decide whether the additional funds are income to the real estate or income attributable to nonrealty interests such as business value and personal property rental. When making judgments about whether additional income is attributable to the real estate, the appraiser should weigh all the facts carefully—especially whether additional management expertise is necessary to generate additional income.

Land rent and easement fees are other sources of income prevalent in the market. These incomes would be the result of transferring ownership rights in vacant land.

Operating Expenses

All expenses to operate an income-producing property are deducted from the income in the year the expenses are incurred. Typically, the expenses fall into two categories: fixed expenses or variable expenses.[1] *Fixed expenses* are annual costs that generally do not vary based on the occupancy level of a building. These expenses include property taxes, insurance and some maintenance contracts (an elevator maintenance contract, for example). *Variable expenses* generally do vary with the level of occupancy of the building. Examples include the basic costs of operating the building, including utility costs, janitorial fees, management expenses, maintenance costs (interior, exterior and site) and professional fees.

Each expense must be identified directly as a cost to operate the building. Expenses to manage or operate the ownership entity, such as partnership fees, profit distribution and individual income taxes, are not building operating expenses and should not be included in the calculation of net operating income (NOI). In addition, deductions for depreciation and interest costs for mortgage financing are not included in calculating the NOI for the building. Determination of whether the landlord or tenant pays all or portions of each expense item is typically controlled by a lease contract.

Net Operating Income

The difference between income and operating expenses is referred to as *net operating income* or *NOI*. It is the income an owner would expect to receive prior to making any debt service payments. Forecasts of future NOI are based on expected relative changes in income and expenses over a selected holding period. Practically, a change in income may directly affect the level of an expense. For example, in many cases, management fees are based on income collected. If income were to rise, a corresponding increase in management fees would be expected.

RESALE PROCEEDS FORECAST

In addition to annual income from operations, an owner of an income-producing property could expect to receive *resale proceeds,* that is, the net proceeds generated by resale of the property at the end of a holding period. In most income-producing real estate properties, the property has some value at the end of a typical holding period. In development properties such as subdivision and condominium projects, where lots or units, respectively, are gradually sold, there may be nothing remaining to sell at the end of a typical sellout period. The level of the reversion can have a significant impact on value, so care must be taken when forecasting the reversion.

Holding Period

One of the first inputs to be selected by an appraiser when preparing a cash-flow forecast is the holding period. The period selected should represent the "typical" holding period for the particular class of property. Sometimes it is difficult to determine what a typical holding period is. In the middle 1980s, properties tended to be held from 5 to 10 years. After that, the tax incentives associated with turning over the property to a new owner tended to result in a sale before the fifteenth year of ownership. After the 1986 tax law change, many of the incentives for shorter holding periods disappeared, which currently makes selecting a "typical" holding period difficult. For the purpose of discounted cash-flow analysis the appraiser should attempt to select a holding period for the property being valued that is representative of the typical investor, because the market value of a property should reflect the investment motivations for the typical investor.

Frequently, the terms holding period, marketing period, absorption period and sellout period are confused. *Holding period* is the time period over which an investor holds the property before deciding to sell. *Marketing period* is the time period required to actually sell the property once the decision to sell is made. *Absorption period* is the time required to either rent-up a property or sell out lots in a development. Sellout period and absorption period are basically the same. In appraisal theory, cash flows for an investment property are forecast over a typical holding period and discounted to a present value. There is, however, no adjustment for marketing period, if the value estimate is to represent market value, because the market value definition assumes a typical buyer and seller and a reasonable marketing period. If, on the other hand, an appraisal is made that requires or limits the marketing period to a time period less than what would be considered typical or reasonable by the appraiser, the value estimate would be considered a forced, or liquidation, value.

Because the purpose of most appraisal assignments is to estimate market value, the appraiser generally selects the holding period and simply reports a typical marketing period under current market conditions. As mentioned earlier, selecting and supporting a so-called typical holding period is difficult; in the final analysis, the "correct" period would not necessarily be based on historical evidence. On the contrary, the correct estimate is the "typical" period used in a forecast by "typical" investors when analyzing a real estate investment, rather than how long the investor actually expects to hold the property. In most cases, investors use 5- to 15-year projections, so projections in this range would be reasonable. In theory, an appraiser using a 5-year cash-flow forecast should arrive at exactly the same value as an appraiser using a 15-year forecast. In practice, there may be slight value differences when different holding periods are used, but according to appraisal theory, the appraisers should arrive at identical market values if the values are based on the same premise.

Resale Value

The resale value is the forecast of the price to be received by the property owner at the end of the holding period. It is frequently referred to as the *reversion*. In essence, it represents the probable price that will be paid by the next owner. That price, in theory, depends on the expectations of the next owner at that future time. Again, as in forecasting other values, the quality and reliability of the resale forecast can be judged only against what is logical given today's information, rather than what actually happens to the sales price over time.

There are various methods of estimating resale value. Each is discussed in detail later in this chapter. All methods are designed to mirror typical buying strategies.

Disposition Costs

The actual proceeds from resale used in a discounted cash-flow analysis or yield capitalization (concepts to be explained in detail later) should reflect the actual dollars that will be received by the current owner. Selling costs such as sales commissions and legal fees are usually incurred in a real estate transaction. The magnitude of these *disposition costs* to the seller at reversion depends on the property type, local customs, property size and selling strategy. An appraiser, therefore, must make a judgment of how the estimated disposition costs for the property being appraised would affect its net proceeds from sale (reversion). Sometimes selling costs are not explicitly deducted from the sales price used in a discounted cash-flow forecast. This does not mean that the appraiser does not believe there will be any selling costs. Rather, it is done to simplify the presentation of the cash flows. In this case, the sales price shown in the analysis would be assumed to be already net of selling costs. This approach is used in the examples in this book. In appraisal practice the appraiser should be consistent in either showing or not showing an explicit estimate of selling costs in a discounted cash-flow analysis so that cash-flow estimates will be comparable.

CASH-FLOW FORECASTS

Chapter 5 introduced the key types of income that are relevant in cash-flow forecasts. We will now look in more detail at the estimation of net operating income (NOI), that is, cash flow that is available before deduction of any mortgage financing. Chapter 10 illustrates cash-flow forecasts with mortgage calculations included.

Rental Income Calculations

The rental income forecast is made after comparing the subject with similar properties in its market segment. The rental rate may be calculated on the following basis:

- *Gross lease*—Landlord pays all operating expenses.
- *Net lease*—Tenant pays a portion of the operating expenses (usually everything except taxes, insurance, management and exterior maintenance).
- *Absolute net lease*—Tenant pays all operating expenses (usually with the exception of management fees).[2]

The rental rate is applied to the net usable area, the net leasable area or the gross building area. *Net usable area* is space that can be occupied by tenants. *Net leasable area* may include a pro rata share of the common area. *Gross building area* is the total floor area of the building.[3] Contractual rental payments may or may not be at market rent levels. Methods of analyzing nonmarket contractual rental payments will be discussed in chapter 14. All rental projections made in the remainder of this chapter will be assumed to reflect market rental rates.

Rental rates may vary within a building, based on location, quality of tenant space, condition of the improvements and the use of the space. Any rental rate selected should represent the best estimate of what the space would rent for under current market conditions. The typical *rental units of comparison* for income-producing properties are:

- rent per square foot of gross building area;
- rent per square foot of net leasable area; and
- rent per unit.

In addition, some income-producing properties are rented on a specialized unit basis, such as rent per seat, rent per door and rent per room.

An integral part of any income forecast is the expected pattern of change over the holding period. Historical trends are important considerations in forecasting future rental rate changes, but historical patterns should not be the sole source of support for the rental rates selected for future years. The appraiser must analyze current and expected market conditions in selecting future rental rates. Again, any forecast change must be logical, given current market conditions, and must represent the thought process of a typical investor.

The basic valuation example that will be used frequently in the remainder of the book assumes that NOI is based on a net leasable area of 20,000 square feet and a market rent of $15 per square foot. The *potential gross income (PGI)* for this example is $300,000:

$$20,000 \text{ sq. ft. @ } \$15 \text{ per sq. ft.} = \$300,000$$

Vacancy and Credit Loss Estimate

It would be highly unusual for the subject property and all properties in the market segment in an area to be fully occupied. Low vacancy levels encourage developers to construct new, competing projects. Most cash-flow forecasts, therefore, contain an adjustment for *vacancy and credit loss.* The vacancy and credit loss percentage used when estimating the fee simple interest in a property should be the typical rate for the market. This typical rate may change from year to year, and it could vary from property type to property type and from market to market. In rapidly growing markets, you could expect the typical vacancy rate to be higher than in stable or slow-growing markets. The higher vacancy rate in growing markets is caused by the need to create new space to satisfy the growing need. The higher rate exists because of the lead time needed to receive the proper approvals and construct a new project. Vacancy allowance can also be affected by existing leases on a property. This issue is discussed in chapter 13 of this book.

Vacancy and collection are often expressed as a percentage of potential gross income. Our example will assume a 6 percent stabilized vacancy and credit loss allowance. The vacancy allowance in the first year, therefore, would be

Potential Gross Income		*Vacancy and Credit Loss*		*Vacancy Amount*
$300,000	×	0.06	=	$18,000

Effective Gross Income

The rental income that remains after adjusting for vacancy and credit loss is the *effective gross income (EGI)*. The effective gross income often includes any other income directly attributable to the real estate. Income generated by any nonrealty interest such as personal property or business income would not be included as a part of either potential gross income or effective gross income. For the previous example the effective gross income for the first year is

Potential Gross Income	$300,000
Less Vacancy and Credit Loss	− 18,000
Effective Gross Income	$282,000

OPERATING EXPENSES

As mentioned earlier, *operating expenses* fall into two categories: fixed expenses and variable expenses. The expenses are only those needed to operate the property. Five methods usually used to estimate operating expenses include:

1. direct dollar estimate;
2. expenses per square foot of gross building area;
3. expenses per square foot of net building area;
4. percent of effective gross income; and
5. expenses per unit.

As a rule, the option used to estimate an expense item either is the method used in the market to quote or calculate an expense or reflects a common unit of comparison used in the market. For example, maintenance contracts for elevators are set by contract. The usual method of forecasting the expense for this item is, therefore, a direct dollar estimate. Management fees are usually quoted as a percentage of actual income collected, so the typical estimate is a percent of effective gross income. Utility expenses are usually compared on the basis of a price per square foot of gross building area, so utility expenses are typically forecast on the same basis.

As with income, forecasting future changes in any expense over a holding period requires thorough market analysis. Historical trends are important, but they should not be the sole basis for estimating future trends. Any forecast change must be logical, given market conditions, and represent the expectation of a typical investor. Following is an expense forecast for the property example used in several valuation problems later in this book.

Example

Gross Building Area = 24,000 Square Feet (SF)
Net Building Area   = 20,000 Square Feet (SF)

Fixed Expenses:
Property Tax (Actual)	$11,900
Insurance	4,000
Maintenance Contract	4,000

Variable Expenses:
Management Fee (5% of Effective Gross Income)	14,100
Utilities ($1.25/SF of Gross Building Area)	30,000
Janitorial ($0.90/SF of Net Building Area)	18,000
Total Operating Expenses	**$82,000**

After estimating expenses, the appraiser should test the reasonableness of the estimate by calculating the applicable key ratios:

- expenses per square foot of gross building area;
- expenses per square foot of net building area;
- operating *expense ratio* (total expenses divided by effective gross income); and
- expenses per unit. (Expenses per unit are calculated most often for multifamily income-producing properties.)

In the example above, the key ratios are

- expenses per square foot of gross building area:

$$\$82,000/24,000 \text{ SF} = \$3.42 \text{ per SF}$$

- expenses per square foot of net building area:

$$\$82,000/20,000 \text{ SF} = \$4.10 \text{ per SF}$$

- operating expense ratio:

$$\$82,000/\$282,000 = 0.2908 \text{ or } 29.08\%$$

The ratios should appear reasonable when compared with similar ratios for competitive properties. If not, the expense forecasting process should be reviewed to confirm the reasonableness of each forecast. The operating expense ratio is sometimes calculated using potential gross income rather than effective gross income. The appraiser should be consistent.

REPLACEMENT RESERVES

Frequently, appraisers include a *reserve for replacements* adjustment in an expense forecast. The reserve is a deduction that reflects the fact that components of the building with short economic lives may need to be replaced (requiring a lump-sum payment) before the end of the economic life of the building. For example, assume an air-conditioning compressor with a current replacement cost of $50,000 will need to be replaced in 10 years. An appraiser could adjust for this possibility in six ways.

1. Build a replacement reserve to be deducted in each year that is equal to today's cost of $50,000 divided by the remaining life of the component (10 years): ($50,000 ÷ 10) = $5,000.
2. Estimate the replacement cost in 10 years. Assume this will increase to $70,000 because of inflation. Then calculate the sinking fund payment needed to grow to $70,000 in 10 years and deduct this amount each year from the cash flow. The interest rate chosen for the sinking fund factor is typically a "safe rate" earned on an account in which funds would be deposited each year. Note that it would be incorrect to base a sinking fund payment on $50,000, because $50,000 would not be enough to replace the unit in 10 years.
3. Deduct a lump-sum payment of $70,000 in year 10. In this case, at least a 10-year holding period would need to be used.[4]
4. Reduce the estimated resale price at the end of the holding period by an amount that represents the effect that the physical deterioration of the compressor would have on the price. In our example, this alternative could be used if the holding period were less than 10 years. For example, if the building were to be sold at the end of the ninth year, the purchase price might be reduced by slightly less than $70,000, because the compressor would have to be replaced 1 year later.
5. Include the potential periodic cost as part of the annual maintenance expense for the building. Maintenance expenses usually vary widely from year to year for both the subject property and its competitors, so the maintenance assumption basically reflects a contingency fee.
6. Make no adjustment in the cash flows, which basically means that the risk of possibly having to replace the unit would be reflected in the discount rate used in the analysis.

Any of the above alternatives could be considered a proper way to treat the replacement in appraisal theory. The method of treatment should have no bearing on the final value estimate if that estimate is done logically and consistently. Occasional arguments against using reserves are that reserve items are often not reported in profit-and-loss statements for comparable properties[5] and investors usually do not build reserve replacements into the cash-flow projections used when analyzing investments. The method an appraiser chooses to use is not the important issue. The important issue is that once a method is chosen, to ensure consistency, the appraiser should use the same method when analyzing both comparable data and the subject property. In the valuation examples in the remainder of this book, a reasonable level of maintenance expenses will be assumed and the risk of possible replacement items will be compensated for in the discount rate.

CASH-FLOW EXAMPLE

Following is an example of a typical annual cash flow.

Example

Assumptions:

Income:	Increasing 4 percent per year.
Vacancy:	Level at 6 percent per year.
Management:	5 percent of effective gross income.
Property tax:	$11,900 level for 3 years, increasing to $15,000 in years 4, 5 and 6.
Insurance:	$4,000, increasing by 3 percent per year.
Utilities:	$30,000, increasing by 5 percent per year.
Janitorial:	$18,000, increasing by 4 percent per year.
Maintenance:	$4,000, increasing by 3 percent per year.

	Year 1	Year 2	Year 3	Year 4	Year 5	Year 6
PGI	$300,000	$312,000	$324,480	$337,459	$350,958	$364,996
Vacancy	− 18,000	− 18,720	− 19,469	− 20,248	− 21,057	− 21,900
EGI	$282,000	$293,280	$305,011	$317,211	$329,901	343,096
Management 5%	$ 14,100	$ 14,664	$ 15,251	$ 15,861	$ 16,495	$ 17,155
Property tax	11,900	11,900	11,900	15,000	15,000	15,000
Insurance	4,000	4,120	4,244	4,371	4,502	4,637
Utilities	30,000	31,500	33,075	34,729	36,465	38,288
Janitorial	18,000	18,720	19,469	20,248	21,057	21,899
Maintenance	4,000	4,120	4,244	4,371	4,502	4,637
Total Expenses	$ 82,000	$ 85,024	$ 88,183	$ 94,580	$ 98,021	$ 101,616
NOI	$200,000	$208,256	$216,828	$222,631	$231,880	$241,480

The end result of the income and expense forecast is a series of estimated NOIs.[6] The appraiser should test the reasonableness of the estimates by calculating the implied change in NOI over the holding period. In the above instance, the implied change is ($241,480/$200,000)−1 = 20.74 percent, or approximately 4 percent per year. Typically, the relationship between income and expense is such that each tends to move in relation to the other. An implied NOI trend that is not logical, given the trends assumed for the incomes and expenses, may be a result of faulty forecasts.

ESTIMATING RESALE PROCEEDS

There are three common methods used to estimate a reversionary value.

1. Estimating the resale price as a dollar amount.
2. Estimating a percentage change over the holding period.
3. Applying a terminal (going-out) capitalization rate to estimated income one year after the end of the holding period.

Direct Dollar Forecast

Making a direct dollar forecast of *resale proceeds* without basing it on a calculation method used by typical investors is rare. Using this method, however, may be logical if there is a contractual purchase arrangement that specifies a resale amount, for example, an option to purchase the property at the end of the lease. It is also possible that a dollar estimate was made using some other method, such as another independent discounted cash-flow valuation calculation or a discounted cash-flow approach to the subject after analysis of a holding period following the first assumed investment holding period. For example, a reversion assumed at the end of a 10-year analysis might be logically estimated by first undertaking an analysis of the cash flows to be received in years 10 through 20, then calculating the value of those cash flows in 10 years. This method of analysis may be used in valuing leased fee interests, which will be discussed further in chapter 13.

Estimated Percent Change

A second method is to assume a percent change in value over the holding period. The percent change could either be expressed as an annual or a total change and could reflect either a total increase, a decrease or no change in value over the time period. The relationship of the two should be logical, given the parameters of the appraisal problem. For example, suppose the value of the property with the cash flows illustrated previously is $2 million. What will its value be after 5 years, assuming (1) a 3 percent per year increase in value and (2) a total increase in value of 15 percent? The calculations are as follows:

$$\text{Value} = \$2{,}000{,}000 \qquad \text{Holding Period} = 5 \text{ Years}$$

- Reversion assuming a 3 percent annual change in value:

$$\$2{,}000{,}000 \times (1.03)^5 = \$2{,}318{,}548$$

Note that this is slightly more than a 15 percent total increase, due to compounding.

• Reversion assuming a 15 percent total increase in value:

$$\$2{,}000{,}000 \times 1.15 = \$2{,}300{,}000$$

The Terminal Capitalization Rate

A third method used to forecast the resale proceeds is to use the concept of a capitalization rate to estimate the resale price. Recall that a capitalization rate is the ratio of a single year's cash flow to the value of the total cash flows. Usually the capitalization rate is based on the first-year cash flow, as illustrated in the previous chapter. As discussed in that chapter, although the capitalization rate uses only the first-year cash flow when it is calculated, the resulting capitalization rate is related to the assumptions used to calculate the present value of the cash flows, because the present value is based on anticipation of all future cash flows. Thus, if we knew the appropriate capitalization rate, we could estimate the present value of the future cash flows by dividing the first-year cash flow by the capitalization rate. In fact, this is an approach that will be discussed in chapter 8.

What is important at this time is that there is a relationship between the cash flow at a given time and the present value of all future cash flows that can be captured by selection of an appropriate capitalization rate. We can use this relationship to estimate the resale price of the property at the end of the holding period, because the resale price is theoretically based on the present value of the future cash flows that the new owner will receive. Thus, we can think in terms of a capitalization rate that expresses the relationship between the first-year cash flow to the new owner and the price that the new owner should be willing to pay for the property at that time. Stated slightly differently, we can estimate the resale price of the property by dividing the estimated first-year income to the next buyer by an appropriate capitalization rate. This can be thought of as a shortcut approach to estimating the resale price rather than as attempting to project cash flows over a holding period for the new buyer and discount those cash flows.[7]

When a capitalization rate is used to estimate the resale price, it is referred to as a *terminal capitalization rate*.[8] In theory, the terminal capitalization rate should represent the typical rate that would be expected at the time the property is sold. A slightly higher rate is sometimes used because of the additional uncertainty associated with estimating what the cash flow will be when the property is sold to the new owner, and because the building is older and may not have the same income potential as it had at the beginning of the holding period.

As an example of using the terminal capitalization rate, consider the NOI forecast shown earlier. The NOI in year 6 was estimated to be $241,480. Now assume that an appropriate terminal capitalization rate (R_T) would be 10 percent. Our estimated resale price would then be as follows:

$$\text{Reversionary value} = \frac{\text{NOI (6th year)}}{R_T} = \frac{\$241{,}480}{0.10} = \$2{,}414{,}800$$

Note that the terminal capitalization rate was applied to the year 6 NOI, rather than to the year 5 NOI. The logic here is that the value at the *end* of year 5 is the present value of income that starts in year 6. This is consistent with the way the capitalization rate was calculated in chapter 5. In that case the cash flow was for end of year 1 and the value was for the beginning of year 1 (which is the *end* of year 0).

Once the value is found, the overall capitalization rate should be compared to the terminal capitalization rate to ensure that the implied relationship is logical. In addition, an appraiser should also calculate both the implied change in NOI and the implied change in value to ensure that the implied assumptions are reasonable and supported by current market data.

For example, suppose we discount the cash flows for the above example at a 13 percent discount rate. A summary of the calculation is as follows:

Year	Cash Flow
1	$200,000
2	208,256
3	216,828
4	222,631
5	231,880 + 2,414,800 = 2,646,680

The present value of the above cash flows at a 13 percent discount rate is $2,063,414, or approximately $2,065,000.

Using this present value, note that the capitalization rate based on the first-year NOI would be $200,000/$2,065,000 or approximately 9.70 percent. This is slightly less (30 basis points lower) than the terminal capitalization rate of 10 percent. This difference is logical if we believe that the outlook for future cash flows for the next buyer (starting in year 6) would be about the same as for the first 5 years. The slightly higher terminal capitalization rate could reflect being a little conservative when estimating the resale price, that is, building a slight risk premium into the terminal capitalization rate.

NOTE: Some appraisers prefer to apply the terminal capitalization rate to the income during the last year of the holding period rather than the income 1 year later. For example, in the five-year cash-flow forecast illustrated above, the terminal cap rate would be applied to the income during the fifth ($231,880) rather than the sixth year (holding period plus 1 year). This would give the same answer if the correct terminal capitalization rate is used. In this case the terminal capitalization rate would have to be 9.60 percent to arrive at the same estimated resale price. Dividing $231,880 by 9.60 percent results in approximately the same resale price of $2,414,480. In this case we are using a capitalization rate that is for the same year as the calculated value. To be consistent, this would have to be compared with an initial capitalization rate (going-in capitalization rate) calculated in the same manner. In our example, the year 1 NOI was estimated to be $200,000. This is the NOI at the end of the first year. What would the NOI be at the beginning of year 1 (end of year 0)? Assuming the increase in NOI from year 0 to year 1 would be the same rate of approximately 3 percent per year, NOI would have been about $194,000 at the beginning of year 1. Using this NOI to calculate a capitalization rate (assuming the same present value) we obtain an answer of $194,000/$2,065,000, about 9.39 percent. Note that the difference between the going-in capitalization rate and the terminal capitalization rate is still about 30 basis points, the same as it was before. Thus, the same conclusions will be reached as long as the appraiser is consistent in his or her thinking.

Conceptually, the choice as to which method to use is based on the position an appraiser takes on the definition and method of calculation of the overall capitalization rate. No matter which approach is used, the reversionary value should be the same, because the appraiser is estimating the value on the same date. If the NOI data used to estimate the overall rates for comparable sales reflect last year's or a year 0 forecast, then to be consistent, the appraiser would capitalize year 5's NOI to estimate the resale in the example above. If, on the other hand, the appraiser believes the NOI data used to calculate overall rates for comparable sales represent an end-of-year estimate, year 6's net operating income would be used. An appraiser can only make this decision after a close analysis of comparable data and the methodology used to estimate NOI.

Care should be taken when determining the appropriate relationship between the going-in capitalization rate and the terminal capitalization rate (the "going-out" rate). When estimating ownership interests other than fee simple or when occupancy is not stabilized, there may be little relationship between the two. There are logical circumstances where either one could be higher than the other. In estimating the fee simple interest, however, most appraisers select a terminal rate that is slightly higher than the current rate. As discussed above, one reason given for using a higher rate is that the future forecast is less certain and therefore has greater risk. The riskiness of the property, however, is generally reflected in the discount rate. The appropriate reversionary value to use is the one used by typical investors. The issue, therefore, concerning the relationship between the two is what relationship reflects the current investor thought process. Unless it can be demonstrated either that older buildings sell for higher capitalization rates than newer buildings or that investors always use higher going-out than going-in rates, simply using a higher capitalization because of the risk would not mirror investor expectations.

No matter what relationship is expected, the appraiser should compare the implied current rate with the terminal rate used to see whether the relationship is logical.

SOURCES OF INCOME AND EXPENSE DATA

Income and expense information can be gathered from either primary or secondary sources. Primary sources include building owners and managers, utility companies, accountants, real estate brokers, leasing agents and other appraisers. Secondary sources include professional journal articles, publications by building management associations and lender publications. In all cases the data must be reported in a format suitable for application to the subject property.

Where possible, any income and expense forecast should be compared with the historical performance of the property itself. The subject building may have attributes that would place cost levels for certain expenses outside normally expected levels. For example, a poorly designed or insulated building may have utility costs that exceed normal levels. The expense forecast should reflect what aspects of the property may not fall within a typical range.

SUMMARY

The income approach is based on the premise that the value of real estate property is the present value of anticipated future benefits. For real estate income property, these benefits come from anticipated cash flow that must be forecast by assimilating information from the past, identifying relationships between influencing factors, and drawing conclusions about what will probably happen in the future. Forecasts of cash flows usually begin with an estimate of net operating income. When calculating net operating income, only expenses associated with operating the property are deducted. These expenses are categorized as either fixed expenses or variable expenses, depending on whether they vary with the level of occupancy. A reserve for replacement of short-lived items is sometimes included with operating expenses.

Depending on the interest being appraised, a resale or reversion value of the property may have to be estimated. Two common ways of estimating the resale price are to (1) assume an annual or total change in value from the time the property is purchased until it is sold and (2) use a terminal capitalization rate. Terminal capitalization rates are often estimated by taking the going-in capitalization rate and adding a premium for the uncertainty of estimating income at the time the property is sold. Differences in income potential for the property at the time of resale versus at the time of purchase could also affect the choice of an appropriate capitalization rate.

KEY TERMS

absolute net lease	going-in capitalization rate
absorption period	gross building area
disposition costs	gross lease
effective gross income (EGI)	holding period
fixed expenses	marketing period
forecasting	net leasable area

net lease

reserve for replacement

net operating income (NOI)

reversion

net usable area

terminal capitalization rate

operating expense ratio

units of comparison

operating expenses

vacancy and collection loss

potential gross income (PGI)

variable expense

resale proceeds

QUESTIONS

1. What is meant by forecasting? Why is it necessary for appraisers to forecast income?
2. What is the difference between potential gross income and effective gross income?
3. What are the main categories of operating expenses?
4. How is the holding period determined?
5. What is the difference among a holding period, a marketing period and an absorption period?
6. What is the difference between usable area and leasable area?
7. What is meant by "disposition costs"? How does the appraiser usually consider disposition costs in a discounted cash-flow analysis?
8. What is the difference between a gross lease and a net lease?
9. What are the typical "units of comparison" for rental rates?
10. What are the typical ways that operating expenses are estimated?

END NOTES

1. A third category of expenses that is often included in the calculation of net operating income is called a "reserve for replacements." This category of expenses will be discussed later in this chapter.

2. This is sometimes referred to as a net-net-net lease where the three items that are net are taxes, insurance and exterior maintenance. This terminology is not common today.

3. It is usually measured from the exterior of the walls and includes all enclosed areas, including the basement area.

4. The effect of this alternative on the value of the property would be equivalent to alternative 2 *if* the rate for the sinking fund were assumed to be the discount rate used to calculate the present value rather than a safe rate.

5. Replacements of items that contribute value to the property over a significant number of years would be considered a "capital expenditure" for accounting purposes, not an expense item. Capital expenditures are depreciated for tax purposes and thus would not be deducted as an expense in the year of the replacement.

6. Depending on the appraisal technique being used, there may be a further reduction from NOI to calculate cash flow to a particular interest in the property, for example, deduction of a mortgage payment to estimate cash flow to the equity investor. This will be discussed in the next chapter.

7. In fact, this would not eliminate the need to estimate a resale price for the second investor at the end of the second holding period. To eliminate the need to estimate a resale price, we would have to estimate cash flows for the entire economic life of the property, which is not very practical.

8. Sometimes the terminal capitalization rate is referred to as a residual capitalization rate. The capitalization rate we discussed earlier, which expresses the relationship between the first-year income to the present value of the property (year 0) is sometimes referred to as a going-in capitalization rate to contrast it with the terminal capitalization rate.

CHAPTER 6	# Investment Return Calculations

INTRODUCTION

The purpose of an appraisal is to estimate the market value of a property, assuming its purchase by a knowledgeable, typical investor. Implicit in this approach to estimating market value is that the analytical techniques used by an appraiser to arrive at the market value are duplicates of the methodology used by the typical investor to arrive at a purchase price. For example, when using yield capitalization as an income approach, the appraiser estimates the future benefits (usually in the form of net operating income [NOI] and net proceeds from a forecast resale) and discounts the expected cash flows by a rate of return that reflects the return required by a typical investor, given the ownership interest being appraised. In applying this methodology, it is assumed that:

- the appraiser understands the various investment techniques usually used by investors to analyze an income property and
- the appraiser can select an appropriate discount rate based on rates of return implied by actual sales from the market.

To promote a deeper understanding of appraisal techniques, the various investment analysis measures of return are presented in this chapter. The appraisal techniques that mirror each of the investment analysis techniques are presented in chapter 7.

INVESTOR MOTIVATIONS

An investor usually has two goals when investing funds: preservation of the capital invested and a desire to earn a competitive profit on the capital invested. Numerous investment opportunities are available to an investor in the marketplace. Each has its own specific set of characteristics and its own level of risk. Some investments, such as publicly traded stocks, are highly marketable. Some, including real estate, may require extended periods to sell. There are short-term investments and long-term investments. There are investments with low risks (T-bills backed by the federal government) and investments with high risk (commodities futures). Some provide for gradual payback of the original investment and profit; others have a lump-sum payment at maturity. Investors select the investments that they perceive match their investment goals.

As discussed in chapter 1, real estate has its own set of investment characteristics, including lack of liquidity, differential tax treatment, need for competent management and dependence on location. Because investors do have many alternatives for investing their money, real estate operates in the marketplace and must compete with alternative investments for funds. Expected returns from real estate must be comparable to returns from other investments with similar risk. When an analyst compares the returns from one investment with those from another, the returns must be compared after considering the relative risk of each alternative.

Preservation of Capital

Naturally, the first goal of any investor is the *preservation of capital,* that is, not to lose money. Certainly, in some risky investments, losing the original capital is a distinct possibility. An investor generally expects to have the original investment returned through periodic payment, through the receipt of a lump-sum payment at some time in the future or through a combination of the two. This is sometimes referred to as "return of capital" or "recapture." When a lender advances funds for a loan requiring level amortizing payments over a specific amortization period, the repayment of the loan will occur gradually through periodic payments.[1] Other investments may be expected to hold their value over time, in which case the original capital will be returned at resale. In the early and middle 1900s, when inflation was virtually nonexistent, real estate was expected to lose some value over time because of depreciation of the improvements from age, wear and tear. The investor, therefore, did not expect to recover all the investment at resale, and typical investment approaches required periodic repayment of a portion of the invested capital.

In the 1960s inflation became a fact in the marketplace, driving land prices and construction costs up year by year. The rising land prices and costs resulted in a rise in nominal property value even after adjustment for depreciation. Investors, therefore, could expect return of the invested capital at resale. Investment techniques that assumed the return of capital would occur at resale became popular. In fact, inflation moved at such a rapid pace that an investor could expect to resell the property for more than the original investment, resulting in additional profit. The issue of preservation of capital will be discussed for each of the investment techniques presented in this chapter.

Earning Investment Profit

The second motive of an investor is to earn a profit on invested capital. The amount of expected profit is directly related to the risk inherent in the investment. Low-risk investment would be expected to earn low profits; high-risk investment would be expected to generate high profits. Through the competitive bidding process, the market forces interact and set the return range for each class of investment. Real estate is a major segment of this market, and prices paid for properties, in theory and in practice, reflect the market's perception of the risk in real estate. Unfortunately, because of the lack of a formally organized market and the characteristics of the real estate itself, actual returns are not readily available. In the market for corporate bonds, for example, the returns are published daily for actively traded bonds. In real estate, the returns can only be implied after a detailed analysis of the potential of the property.

When doing an appraisal, several of the techniques used require the input of return measures that are typical for the market. The interesting aspect of real estate is that there are a multitude of interests that could be valued, as well as financing and tax implications to be considered. As a result, there are a number of different returns that can be calculated that use information from the same property but have a different meaning. An appraiser must understand the interrelationship of all possible measures of return for real estate and understand how each can be affected by the structure of a transaction.

REAL ESTATE RETURN MEASURES

Several income investment measures can be extracted from a real estate sale, including payback period, first-year cash-flow ratios, internal rates of return, net present values, profitability indexes and adjusted rates of return.

Payback period is the time that elapses until an initial investment is returned. *Cash-flow ratios* (sometimes called *income rates*) are calculated by dividing the cash flow available to an ownership interest for a single year by the value of the ownership interest itself. Usually, the cash flow is the first year of the investment holding period. In real estate, these first-year cash-flow rates are typically referred to as *capitalization rates* and are preceded by a description identifying the applicable ownership interest. For example, the cash-flow rate that is calculated by dividing the first-year NOI by the total overall property value is referred to as the *overall capitalization rate* (R_O) (or going-in capitalization rate).[2]

Internal rates of return are calculated either by hand or by electronic means using an iterative process to calculate the rate of return that would discount a specific set of forecast periodic cash flows to be received by an ownership interest to a present value equal to the ownership interest itself. In real estate, these internal rates of return are usually called "yield rates" and are preceded by a description identifying the applicable ownership interest. For example, the internal rate of return calculated by comparing the cash flows to be received by the equity investor on a before-tax basis to the equity investment is the *before-tax equity yield rate* or *equity yield rate* for short.

The cash-flow ratios discussed earlier do not specifically address profitability but are only "snapshot" ratios, which can be used for comparison with comparable real estate sales. Yield rates, however, directly address profitability and can be compared with measures of return for alternative investments (real estate as well as other investments) after consideration for relative differences in risk.

Net present value and profitability index calculations are similar to the internal rate of return approach in that profitability is addressed and a complete schedule of future cash flows (income from operations and a forecast resale) are analyzed. However, there are some differences in the calculations. First, a level-of-investment yield rate is selected that represents a target yield rate for the investment. Second, the total present value of future cash flows is calculated, using the target yield rate as a discount rate. Third, the original investment is compared to the total present value to arrive at investment decisions. In the case of the net present value, the original investment is subtracted from the present value. That is,

Net present value = Present value of future cash flows − Original investment

The profitability index is equal to the present value of the cash flows divided by the original investment. That is,

$$\text{Profitability index} = \frac{\text{Present value of future cash flows}}{\text{Original investment}}$$

The calculation of each of these measures is illustrated later.

An *adjusted internal rate of return* (*AIRR*)[3] calculation is similar to the internal rate of return calculation, except that expected future cash flows are compounded forward at a reinvestment rate to arrive at a total expected future value of the future cash flow. Then the future cash flows are compared with the original investment to calculate an implied annual rate of return. Recall that the adjusted internal rate of return was discussed and illustrated in chapter 4.

CALCULATION OF INVESTMENT RETURN MEASURES

In this chapter the various measures of return are calculated on a before-tax basis only, without consideration for financing. The impact of financing on real estate measures of return is discussed in chapter 10. The following set of cash flows will be used to calculate each return measure:

Example

Sample Data

Given:

Value = $1,000,000   Resale Price (10 Years) = $1,200,000
Land Value = $150,000

Year	1	2	3	4	5
GPI	$140,000	$145,000	$150,000	$155,000	$160,000
Vacancy and Credit Loss	− 10,000	− 10,500	− 11,000	− 11,500	− 12,000
EGI	$130,000	$134,500	$139,000	$143,500	$148,000
Operating Expenses	− 30,000	− 32,500	− 35,000	− 37,500	− 40,000
NOI	$100,000	$102,000	$104,000	$106,000	$108,000

Year	6	7	8	9	10
GPI	$165,000	$170,000	$175,000	$180,000	$185,000
Vacancy and Credit Loss	− 12,500	− 13,000	− 13,500	− 14,000	− 14,500
EGI	$152,500	$175,000	$161,500	$166,000	$170,500
Operating Expenses	− 42,500	− 45,000	− 47,500	− 50,000	− 52,500
NOI	$110,000	$112,000	$114,000	$116,000	$118,000

Payback Period

Payback period is the length of time needed to return the initial investment to an investor. Following is a payback calculation for the sample data.

Investment = $1,000,000

Year	NOI	Cumulative Total Cash Flow
1	$100,000	$ 100,000
2	102,000	202,000
3	104,000	306,000
4	106,000	412,000
5	108,000	520,000
6	110,000	630,000
7	112,000	742,000
8	114,000	856,000
9	116,000	972,000
10	118,000	1,090,000

In this instance, payback did not occur until year 10. That is, after 10 years the cumulative NOI totaled more than $1,000,000, which is the amount of the initial investment. The weakness of using payback as an investment measure is that it ignores the time value of money.

Income Multipliers

Ratios calculated by dividing the value of the property by the potential gross income (PGI), effective gross income (EGI), or net operating income (NOI) are called *income multipliers.* If the divisor is the potential gross income, the ratio is referred to as a *potential gross income multiplier (PGIM).* If the divisor is the effective gross income, the ratio is referred to as an *effective gross income multiplier (EGIM).* If the divisor is the net operating income, the ratio is referred to as a *net income multiplier (NIM).*

The gross income multipliers (potential and effective) are expressed as factors rather than as ratios simply because of tradition. In the case of the NIM it is more common to use the reciprocal of this ratio, which is the overall capitalization rate, discussed previously as a cash-flow ratio or income rate. Following are calculations for each income multiplier using the sample data:

$$\text{PGIM} = \$1,000,000/\$140,000 = 7.143$$

$$\text{EGIM} = \$1,000,000/\$130,000 = 7.692$$

$$\text{NIM} = \$1,000,000/\$100,000 = 10.00$$

NOTE: The overall capitalization rate (R_O) is the reciprocal of the NIM, that is, 1/10 or 10 percent.

The income multipliers do not explicitly address profitability and are simple benchmark relationships used to compare real estate sales.

Overall Capitalization Rate

The *overall capitalization rate* is calculated by dividing first-year NOI by the value of the property. It is the reciprocal of the NIM and is more typically calculated in this format. The symbol R_O is used to represent the overall capitalization rate (overall rate). Following is the overall rate calculation using the sample data:

$$R_O = \$100,000/\$1,000,000 = 0.10 \text{ or } 10\%$$

Like the income multipliers, the overall capitalization rate does not explicitly address profitability and is simply a benchmark relationship used to compare real estate sales. If two real estate properties are highly comparable, then an appraiser would expect their income multipliers and overall rates to be similar for each property. There are, however, factors that may logically cause the income multipliers and overall capitalization rates for relatively comparable properties to be substantially different. Following is a list of the key factors:

- differences in financing;
- differences in the ownership interest purchased;
- existence of excess land;
- differences in vacancy and credit loss percentages;
- differences in expense ratios;
- differences in expected future income; and
- differences in expected resale (reversion) proceeds.

Differences in Financing.   Investors will pay a premium for a property that has financing terms more favorable than usual, such as a below-market interest rate. Thus, given two properties, if the price of one of them included an additional premium paid for favorable financing, the amount of the premium must be deducted from that property's price before the income multipliers or overall capitalization rate can be expected to be consistent.

Differences in the Ownership Interest Purchased.   If the price of either property represented a different interest, the income multipliers may not be consistent. For example, suppose the land for one of the properties is leased rather than owned. Then one sale may represent a fee simple interest in the land and building, whereas the other may represent a fee simple interest in the building and a leasehold interest in the land. Thus, the purchase price would not be for comparable property interests. This could make comparison of income multipliers or overall capitalization rates misleading.

Excess Land.   If one sale contained excess land (land in excess of that required by the improvements), the value of the excess land must be deducted before the income multipliers or overall capitalization rates can be expected to be similar because the excess land may not be generating any income. It may be owned to allow for future expansion or as a speculative land investment.

Differences in Vacancy and Credit Loss Percentages.   Depending on the reason for differences in vacancy and credit loss allowance, the gross income multipliers may not be comparable. For example, suppose two properties are purchased by investors at prices that result in EGIMs of 6. If the properties have different amounts of vacancy and credit loss, clearly their PGIMs are not the same. Alternatively, suppose two properties are purchased by investors for about the same PGIMs. If one of the properties has a temporarily higher vacancy rate because some of the space is being renovated, the EGIMs, NIMs and overall capitalization rates would not be comparable.

Differences in Expense Ratios. If the operating expense ratios for the properties are different (and expected to remain different),[4] the PGIMs and the EGIMs are likely to differ because, all else being equal, investors will pay less for the property with greater operating expenses. Because PGI and EGI are calculated before operating expenses, measures that rely on these ratios could be misleading. For example, suppose two properties are purchased by investors at a price that results in a 10 percent overall capitalization rate. However, one of the properties has a 40 percent operating expense ratio and the other has a 50 percent operating expense ratio. Clearly the gross income multipliers could not be the same.

Differences in Expected Future Income. Because income multipliers and capitalization rates are usually calculated using income for the first year of the holding period, differences in expectations for future years can cause the ratios to differ. All else being equal, investors will pay more for a property with greater future income potential. For example, suppose two properties are expected to have the same internal rates of return (property yield rate) over a typical investment holding period. Both properties have the same first-year NOI. Because of differences in lease terms, however, the NOI for one of the properties will be level, whereas the NOI for the other will increase 5 percent each year. Clearly, a higher price will be paid for the second property. Thus, any ratios based on the first-year income are going to differ for the two properties. For example, the overall capitalization rate will be lower for the property with the greater income potential. A more precise relationship between the overall capitalization rate and the property yield rate will be examined in chapter 7.

Differences in Expected Resale (Reversion) Proceeds. The reason differences in expected resale prices will cause any measures based on first-year income to differ is similar to that for future income, discussed above. All else being equal, investors will pay more for a property with a higher expected resale price.

Land and Building Capitalization Rates

Another method of analyzing real estate is by considering its physical components, land and building, separately. In the early and middle 1900s the values of these components were viewed as moving in different patterns. With the absence of significant inflationary trends, land value was viewed as remaining relatively stable, whereas the improvements were viewed as losing value over their economic life as a result of gradual depreciation. The total value was separated into building value and land value and the NOI was divided into income attributable to the land and income attributable to the building. Once both were split, the analyst could then calculate a first-year ratio for the land and a first-year ratio for the building. The first-year ratio for the land, calculated by dividing the income attributable to the land by the land value, became the *land capitalization rate* (R_L); the first-year ratio for the building, calculated by dividing the income attributable to the building by the building value, became the *building capitalization rate* (R_B). Following is the calculation of each, using the sample data and assuming the income attributable to the land is $13,500, based on the amount someone would have to pay to lease the land.

Example

Value	$1,000,000		NOI	$100,000
Less land value	− 150,000		Less land income	− 13,500
Building value	$ 850,000		Building income	$ 86,500

$$R_L = \$13,500/\$150,000 = 0.09 \text{ or } 9\%$$

$$R_B = \$86,500/\$850,000 = 0.1018 \text{ or } 10.18\%$$

The preceding example assumes the land value is known. Historically, the land capitalization rate and the internal rate of return or land discount rate were assumed to be equal because the land value was assumed to remain constant over time. Today we realize that this is not necessarily true. Depending on the expected change in land value, the land capitalization rate could be higher or lower than the internal rate of return on the land. The relationship between the internal rate of return and the capitalization rate will be explored in chapter 7.

Property Yield Rate

The *property yield rate* (Y_O) is the internal rate of return to the total property value and is calculated by finding the interest rate that discounts the expected NOI and net proceeds from resale to a value equal to the total property value. Following is the property yield rate calculation, using the sample data.

Year	Cash Flow
0	($1,000,000)
1	100,000
2	102,000
3	104,000
4	106,000
5	108,000
6	110,000
7	112,000
8	114,000
9	116,000
10*	$1,318,000

$$\text{IRR} = Y_O = 0.1187 \text{ or } 11.87\%$$

*Year 10 includes NOI of $118,000 and resale proceeds of $1,200,000.

The property yield rate in this instance is a measure of profitability for the property. If two real estate properties are highly comparable, the appraiser could expect their property yield rates to be similar. In fact, expected yield rates for different investments should normally be the same unless there are differences in risk. (Differences in tax benefits could also result in differences in before-tax yield rates.) The riskiness of the investment depends on factors such as:

- whether it is an existing project or a development project;
- the lease terms, e.g., whether there are CPI adjustments and expense passthroughs;
- the credit rating of the tenants; and
- the type of ownership interest purchased.

Net Present Value

Net present value (NPV) is a standard measure of return for many investment analysts. It is calculated by selecting a target rate of return, calculating the present value of the future cash flows and comparing this present value estimate to the initial investment. Following is an NPV calculation, assuming an 11 percent target rate and using the sample data:

Year	Cash Flow		Present Value Factor @ 11%		Present Value
1	$ 100,000	×	0.900901	=	$ 90,090
2	102,000	×	0.811622	=	82,785
3	104,000	×	0.731191	=	76,044
4	106,000	×	0.658731	=	69,825
5	108,000	×	0.593451	=	64,093
6	110,000	×	0.534641	=	58,810
7	112,000	×	0.481658	=	53,946
8	114,000	×	0.433926	=	49,468
9	116,000	×	0.390925	=	45,347
10	1,318,000	×	0.352184	=	464,179
Total present value					$1,054,587

Total present value	$1,054,587
Less investment	– 1,000,000
Net present value	$ 54,587

Once the present value is calculated, the NPV is found by subtracting the original investment. If the NPV is greater than 0, the investment promises to provide a return in excess of 11 percent. If the NPV is negative, the expected return would be less than 11 percent and the investment would be rejected. In the above example, an additional $54,587 could be invested and the investor could still expect to earn 11 percent.

The NPVs may not be comparable for two similar properties if the investments required for each are different. A $2 million investment would be expected to have a higher NPV than a $1 million investment, all other things being equal.

Profitability Index

Conceptually, the *profitability index (PI)* and the NPV approaches are basically the same. In each the future cash flows are discounted by a target rate of return and the total present value is compared to the initial investment. In calculating the PI, however, the initial value is divided into the total present value, rather than subtracted from it, as shown below:

$$\frac{\text{Total present value}}{\text{Investment}} = \frac{\$1,054,587}{\$1,000,000} = 1.0546$$

The resulting ratio becomes the PI. An index greater than 1.00 indicates expectations that the investment will earn greater than an 11 percent return. If the index is less than 1.00, the investment is not forecast to earn an 11 percent annual return. Comparing two investments in this manner eliminates the problem found when using the NPV when the investments are of unequal value.

Adjusted Internal Rate of Return

As discussed in chapter 4, the adjusted internal rate of return approach is similar to the internal rate of return approach, except that it assumes future cash flows are compounded forward at a specified reinvestment rate. The reinvestment rate is not necessarily the same as the internal rate of return, which is why the adjusted internal rate of return can differ from the internal rate of return.[5] The reinvestment rate is usually either a *safe rate,* which represents the amount that funds could earn if reinvested in an account in which they would accumulate interest at little risk until the property was sold, or a *speculative rate,* which represents the rate that typically could be earned on comparable real estate investments. In the latter case, the assumption is that funds would be used to purchase other real estate investments, but the other investments might earn an internal rate of return that would be less than the specific project being evaluated.

Following is an adjusted internal rate of return calculation assuming a 10 percent reinvestment rate, using the sample data.

Year	Cash Flow		Future Value Factor @ 10%		Future Value
1	$ 100,000	×	2.357948	=	$ 235,795
2	102,000	×	2.143589	=	218,646
3	104,000	×	1.948717	=	202,667
4	106,000	×	1.771561	=	187,785
5	108,000	×	1.610510	=	173,935
6	110,000	×	1.464100	=	161,051
7	112,000	×	1.331000	=	149,072
8	114,000	×	1.210000	=	137,940
9	116,000	×	1.100000	=	127,600
10	1,318,000	×	1.000000	=	1,318,000
Total future value					$2,912,491

$$AIRR = (\$2,912,491/\$1,000,000)^{1/10} - 1 = 0.1128, \text{ or } 11.28\%$$

In this instance, the adjusted rate of return assuming reinvestment at 10 percent is 11.28 percent, which is less than the property yield or pure IRR of 11.87 percent. The adjusted rate of return is an excellent measure of the potential profitability of an investment if the IRR is higher than one might expect to earn on the interim cash flows.

SUMMARY

It is important to understand investment return calculations because the motivations of the actions of the typical investor ultimately affect the market value of the property. An investor is motivated to purchase income property in anticipation of future benefits in the form of cash flows that recapture the investor's initial investment capital as well as provide a yield rate on the capital.

Cash-flow ratios and income multipliers are often examined by investors to see if they are in line with those of comparable properties. There are, however, many reasons that these ratios could differ for properties that have the same expected yield rate. Thus, appraisers must be careful when these ratios are used as indications of the relationship between income and value.

A number of measures can be used by investors to determine whether the investment meets a target yield rate. These include the internal rate of return, net present value and profitability index. The internal rate of return would be compared with a target yield rate. If the internal rate of return is greater than the target yield rate, then it is a good investment. The target yield rate can also be used as a discount rate to calculate the present value of the expected future cash flows. If the internal rate of return is greater than the target yield rate, the net present value will be positive (greater than zero) and the profitability index will be greater than one.

An adjusted internal rate of return is similar to the internal rate of return but allows the cash flows to be reinvested at a specified reinvestment rate, which might be either the same as the target yield rate or a lower safe rate. When the reinvestment rate is less than the internal rate of return, the adjusted internal rate of return will be less than the internal rate of return.

KEY TERMS

adjusted internal rate of return (AIRR)

before-tax equity yield rate

building capitalization rate (R_B)

capitalization rate

cash-flow ratio

effective gross income multiplier (EGIM)

equity yield rate (Y_E)

income multiplier

income rate

land capitalization rate (R_L)

modified internal rate of return (MIRR)

net income multiplier (NIM)

net present value (NPV)

overall capitalization rate (R_O)

payback period

potential gross income multiplier (PGIM)

preservation of capital

profitability index (PI)

property yield rate (Y_O)

safe rate

speculative rate

QUESTIONS

1. What are the primary motivations for investing in real estate income property?
2. What is meant by the term "payback period"?
3. What is the difference between a cash-flow ratio and an internal rate of return?
4. What is meant by a net present value?
5. Why do you think an adjusted internal rate of return is typically less than an internal rate of return?
6. Suppose a property was just purchased for $1 million that is expected to have net operating income during the first year of $90,000. After the first year, the cash flow is expected to increase by $5,000 per year for 10 years because of the terms of the lease. At the end of the tenth year the property is expected to be sold for $1.4 million to the lessor because of an option in the lease. There will be no loan on the property. Calculate the following:
   a. Overall capitalization rate
   b. Net income multiplier
   c. Internal rate of return (property yield rate)

      d. Net present value by using a 12.5 percent discount rate

      e. Profitability index by using a 12.5 percent discount rate

      f. Adjusted internal rate of return, using a 6 percent reinvestment rate

END NOTES

1. Recall that in chapter 5 we showed how the interest rate on a loan (return *on* capital) plus the sinking fund factor for the same interest rate (return *of* capital) was equal to the loan constant (mortgage capitalization rate).

2. Sometimes the overall capitalization rate is simply referred to as the "cap rate." Another synonymous term is "overall rate."

3. The adjusted rate of return is also referred to as the "adjusted internal rate of return" or "adjusted IRR" for short. Another synonymous term is *modified internal rate of return (MIRR)*.

4. For example, one of the properties may have a much less efficient HVAC system, causing utility expenses to differ.

5. If the reinvestment rate is less than the internal rate of return, the adjusted internal rate of return will also be less than the internal rate of return.

| CHAPTER 7 | # Income Capitalization Approach |

INCOME APPROACH IN THE VALUATION PROCESS

The *income approach* is one of the three approaches to value in appraisal. In the income approach the value of the property is derived using one or more income capitalization procedures to convert the expected income generated from a property into a present value estimate. The term *capitalization* refers to the process of converting income into an estimate of value. The income approach is often called the "income *capitalization* approach."

Application of the income approach involves analyzing the income-producing capabilities of a property, forecasting the periodic income and transforming the income expectations into a value estimate. The income typically forecast includes both the annual income expected from the operation of the property and the net income generated from resale at the end of a selected holding period. The reliability of a value found by this approach depends on an appraiser's ability to forecast and support income forecasts and to apply the appropriate income capitalization technique to arrive at the value estimate. When estimating market value, the income forecast must be considered by the appraiser to be typical and the income capitalization techniques must reflect the way investors usually estimate value. In this approach, the perspective taken must also be that of a typical, knowledgeable investor, whose primary objective is to earn a profit on the money invested. Recall from chapter 1 that the definition of market value assumes the following:

- buyer and seller are typically motivated;
- both parties are well-informed or well-advised, and acting in what they consider their best interests;
- a reasonable time is allowed for exposure in the open market;
- payment is made in terms of cash in United States dollars or in terms of financial arrangements comparable thereto; and
- the price represents the normal consideration for the property sold unaffected by special or creative financing concessions granted by anyone associated with the sale.

The implication of this definition is that the typical buyer is knowledgeable about and uses current techniques to set the price to be paid for the property. In applying the income approach, therefore, it is incumbent on the appraiser to:

- be aware of the modern techniques used by investors to evaluate property;
- constantly monitor the marketplace to keep current as to the actual methods being used to determine price; and
- always use the same techniques that are being used by investors when estimating the value of a property.

The techniques used to capitalize income could be applied to income from the property before consideration of financing, after consideration of financing but before considering income taxes or after consideration of income taxes. The income capitalization methods selected by an appraiser for estimating the value of a property should mirror the techniques actually being used in the marketplace by typical investors.

The theoretical framework of the income approach is based on the economic principles of anticipation, change, substitution, supply and demand, contribution and opportunity cost. (You may want to review the discussion of these principles in chapter 2.) These principles should be kept in mind as the various income capitalization techniques are illustrated.

INCOME CAPITALIZATION METHODS

There are two main income capitalization methods: direct capitalization and yield capitalization. Both methods convert income into an estimate of value, but they differ as to exactly how the income is capitalized.

Direct Capitalization

Direct capitalization is a method used to convert an estimate of a single year's income into an indication of value. It involves either dividing the income estimate by an appropriate capitalization rate (sometimes called an income rate) or multiplying the income estimate by an appropriate factor (sometimes called an income multiplier). The income estimate is usually the expected income for the first year of the investment holding period. The rate is based on an analysis of comparable sales.

For example, a property may sell for $1,000,000 and the buyer expects to receive NOI of $100,000 during the first year of ownership. This implies that the investor paid a price that was 10 times the NOI. Thus, we can say that the NOI multiplier is 10. This is an example of a factor. Alternatively, using the same example, we could say that first-year net operating income is expected to be 10 percent of the value of the property. Thus, the capitalization rate is 10 percent. When the capitalization rate is calculated using NOI, it is referred to as the "overall capitalization rate." Capitalization rates and income multipliers can be developed from any of the measures of income discussed previously, for example, potential gross income, effective gross income, net operating income, before-tax cash flow (equity dividend) and even after-tax cash flow. Capitalization rates also can be developed using just the land or building income. The use of these various capitalization rates in appraisal is discussed in chapter 6.

The advantage of direct capitalization is that the capitalization rates and income multipliers come directly from market indications of the relationship between income and value. However, because they are calculated using a single year's estimate of income, the assumption is that expected changes in income will be similar for the comparable properties and the subject property. In the preceding example the investor also may have expected income to increase 4 percent per year after the first year, with a commensurate increase in the property value each year. As we will see in later chapters, this implies that the investor expects a rate of return that will be greater than the 10 percent capitalization rate, that is, around 14 percent before considering the effect of financing. Thus, the 10 percent capitalization rate should only be used as an indication of the relationship between price and value for properties with similar expectations for increases in income and value. An investor who expected to earn a 14 percent rate of return would not pay $1,000,000 for a property that had the same $100,000 first-year income if that income were not expected to increase.

Yield Capitalization

Yield capitalization is a method used to convert income into an estimate of value by projecting the income or cash flow expected for each year of a typical investment holding period, including any cash flow at reversion. Yield capitalization estimates value by discounting the estimated income or cash flow, using a discount rate that represents the rate of return a typical investor will require if he or she is to invest in the property. Another term for yield capitalization is *discounted cash-flow analysis.*

The advantage of yield capitalization is that the income or cash flow for each year is explicitly identified. The discount rate used in yield capitalization should be the rate of return that investors would expect to earn on comparable properties, that is, properties of similar risk. However, because any change in income and property value is explicit in the discounted cash-flow analysis, the change does not have to be the same for the property being appraised and comparable sales. In fact, yield rates should be similar for any investments that have comparable risk. Thus, appraisers can select an appropriate yield rate without relying directly on comparable sales, assuming they can determine how the market would perceive the risk of the property being appraised relative to other investments.

Appraisers often debate the merits of direct capitalization versus yield capitalization. When adequate data is available, however, both techniques should be used, just as all three approaches to value should be used. They are likely to result in different value estimates because of the imperfections in the market, as discussed in chapter 1. When there is an adequate amount of information on comparable sales with similar income expectations, direct capitalization can be very reliable. When information on comparable sales is lacking, yield capitalization may provide a more reliable estimate of value, because the appraiser may be able to select an appropriate yield rate by determining what investors are requiring as a rate of return on investment of similar risk. Ways of selecting an appropriate yield rate are discussed in chapter 18.

APPLICATION OF THE INCOME APPROACH

Application of the income approach can vary from one property type to another. Typical techniques used vary because of differences in the methods of income collection and expense treatment.

Office Buildings

Office buildings are usually rented to tenants under medium-term and long-term lease agreements. Rents can be collected either on a gross basis with the landlord paying all the operating expenses or on a net basis with the tenant paying some or all of the expenses.[1] Alternatively, leases may include provisions that result in an *expense passthrough,* that is, any increase in certain expenses (over some specified base amount) is "passed through" to the tenant for payment. The base amount is referred to as an "expense stop" and is usually stated on a per-square-foot basis.

Office building leases may also have provisions for increases in the rent tied to increases in, say, the consumer price index (CPI); for example, the base rent might be adjusted upward by 50 percent of any increase in the CPI.[2]

Because office building purchases usually include existing leases, values estimated for office buildings usually represent a leased fee interest. Proper application of the income approach to office buildings requires consideration of how estimated future cash flows and the resale proceeds at the end of the investment holding period are affected by existing leases.

Retail Shopping Centers

Shopping centers are also generally subject to leases. Major tenants usually have long-term leases that have a specified *minimum rent* as well as *percentage rent* provisions that allow the owner to receive a percentage of the tenants' retail sales volumes, if and when they exceed a predetermined level. Any amount received above the minimum rent because of the percentage rent provisions is referred to as *overage rent.* The smaller tenants (sometimes referred to as local tenants) usually have leases for short or medium terms with sales overage clauses. Tenants generally pay their own utilities costs and interior maintenance. Frequently, common area expenses (exterior maintenance, common area utilities, and so on) are shared among tenants on a pro rata basis based on leased area. It is possible that insurance and property taxes may be collected on a pro rata basis. For larger community and regional malls, tenants may also share advertising and management costs. Larger shopping centers require a high degree of marketing and management expertise and as a rule require anchor tenants, such as large national department stores, to sign operating agreements that require the anchor tenant to operate in the shopping center for a specified number of years. A well-managed shopping center that has operating agreements in place and a diversified tenant mix with an established customer base may also include nonrealty interests in the price paid to purchase the shopping center.

Multifamily Residential Properties

Apartments are usually rented to tenants for terms of a year or less. Tenants often pay their own utility expenses, while the project owner pays for taxes, insurance, management, unit maintenance and common area maintenance. With short-term leases, occupancy percentages may vary over time, which may make typical occupancy levels difficult to identify. When the turnover ratio is high, unit maintenance may also be high. The difficult aspect of applying the income approach to a multifamily project is the selection of appropriate expense levels. Differences in project design, construction type and quality, and tenant mix can greatly influence expenses.

Industrial Properties

Major manufacturing and special-use industrial plants are often owner occupied and therefore are not usually rented, so the income approach may not be applicable in appraising these properties. Warehouses and business parks may be rented, however, so the income approach would be a key approach when estimating their value. Warehouses and business parks are usually rented on a medium-term or long-term basis, with the tenant paying most of the operating expenses except for management fees and, possibly, property taxes, insurance and exterior maintenance. When a building is occupied by a single tenant, the tenant usually pays all expenses except for management fees. Because these properties are usually subject to medium-term or long-term leases, the ownership interest valued is usually the leased fee.

Hotels and Motels

As a rule, hotels are not leased; therefore, the income analyzed is the total income generated by the hotel operation. The expenses reflect those required to operate the business. Consequently, the income and expense format is somewhat different from that of offices, apartments, retail and industrial properties. The hotel operation usually includes nonrealty property, including personal property (furniture and fixtures) and business value (that is, the franchise value due to the hotel name, national reservation system and so forth). All of these factors must be considered when estimating the real estate value of a hotel. The difficulty in valuing a hotel is that the incomes and expenses are highly sensitive to changes in average occupancy and daily room rates that, in most cases, are directly related to the quality of management in the hotel. Estimating demand for hotel space is also difficult because there are many sources of clientele—business meetings, tourism, conventions, transient visitors and so forth—which makes forecasting incomes and expenses difficult. Comparable sales are also difficult to analyze because each may include varying degrees of nonrealty interests in their sales prices.

Development Projects

The income approach (sometimes referred to as the *development approach* when valuing development properties) is the primary method used to estimate the value of land development projects. This approach requires a detailed study of market conditions, because the key factors in applying the approach are the absorption rate and market sales prices for the lots. Additional considerations include the timing of the development costs over the development period. Cash-flow forecasting is the difficult aspect of applying the income approach to estimating the value of development projects.

Special-Use Properties

Special-use properties, including health care facilities, recreational facilities and recreational vehicle parks, have unique patterns of income and expense. Frequently, valuation of these properties includes nonrealty interests, as in the case of hotel properties. Care should be taken to support each input of the income and expense forecast as well as the discount rate.

ESTIMATING VALUE USING FIRST-YEAR
CASH-FLOW FACTORS AND RATES OF RETURN

Value estimates for a variety of ownership interests may be calculated by applying an appropriate multiplier or capitalization rate to the property's first-year income or cash-flow forecast. The term *direct capitalization* is sometimes used to refer to the technique of deriving income multipliers or capitalization rates from comparable sales. Capitalization rates and income multipliers derived from comparable sales do not explicitly address profitability; they are simply observed ratios of income to value. However, they can provide a reliable estimate of value if

1. the first-year cash flow is representative and
2. the income multiplier or capitalization rate is derived from comparable sales with the same potential for future income.

The common first-year ratios used by appraisers on an unleveraged basis (without consideration for financing) to estimate the value of an ownership interest include the income multipliers (potential gross income multiplier [PGIM], effective gross income multiplier [EGIM] and net income multiplier [NIM]) and several capitalization rates (overall capitalization rate $[R_O]$, land capitalization rate $[R_L]$ and building capitalization rate $[R_B]$). Use of the income multipliers is presented first. The first step in applying any income multiplier approach is to forecast the appropriate first-year income or cash flow (discussed in chapter 6). The cash-flow forecast in this chapter is used to demonstrate the valuation techniques. In all cases in this chapter, the fee simple (unencumbered) value is estimated. The relevant issues and techniques used to estimate the value of other ownership interests are presented in later chapters.

Example

Cash-Flow Forecast Summary

Building type: office	
Gross building area	24,000 square feet (SF)
Net leasable building area	20,000 SF
Market rent estimate	$15.00/SF
Vacancy and credit allowance	6%
Operating expenses estimate	$4.10/SF
Potential gross income (PGI)	
20,000 SF @ $15.00/SF	$300,000
Less vacancy and credit loss (6%)	– 18,000
Effective gross income (EGI)	$282,000

Less operating expenses	
20,000 SF @ $4.10/SF	− 82,000
Net operating income	$200,000

Direct Capitalization Using PGIM, EGIM and NIM

Potential Gross Income Multiplier.   Using a potential gross income multiplier (PGIM) of 7.0, the value would simply be found by multiplying the potential gross income (PGI) by the PGIM.

PGI		*PGIM*		*Value*
$300,000	×	7.00	=	$2,100,000

The PGIM is found by extracting PGIMs from sales of similar properties, comparing the attributes (physical, locational and financial) of the comparables to the subject property and selecting a multiplier that appears to be the appropriate number to use. When either calculating value or extracting multipliers, it is assumed that the rents are calculated on the same basis with regard to treatment of operating expenses (gross, net and so on).

Although use of the PGIM does not specifically require an appraiser to make cash-flow forecasts beyond the first year, there is an implied assumption that the expected future annual performance (no matter what the cash flows actually turn out to be) will be similar to that of the first year. For example, suppose two properties have the same PGI at the time of the appraisal but the income of property B is projected to increase faster than that of property A. Property B should command a higher price; therefore, its PGIM will be higher because it is measured against first-year income.

Effective Gross Income Multiplier.   Using an effective gross income multiplier (EGIM) of 7.5, the value would simply be found by multiplying the effective gross income (EGI) by the EGIM.

EGI		*EGIM*		*Value*
$282,000	×	7.50	=	$2,115,000

The EGIM is found by extracting EGIMs from sales of similar properties, comparing the attributes (physical, locational, financial) of the comparables to the subject property and selecting a multiplier that appears to be the appropriate number to use.

The primary difference between the EGIM and the PGIM is that the EGIM is applied to income *after* subtracting an estimate of vacancy and collection loss. If a difference in the vacancy rate of the comparable property and that of the subject property exists and is expected to continue, use of the EGIM is likely to be more appropriate because investors are likely to consider the difference in vacancy rate when establishing the value of each property. On the other hand, if the difference in vacancy rate is only temporary, use of the PGIM might be warranted because investors may value the property based on the assumption that the vacancy difference will be eliminated after the property is purchased.

As was the case for the PGIM, use of the EGIM does not specifically require an appraiser to make cash-flow forecasts beyond the first year. Thus, there is an implied assumption that the expected future performance of the properties will be similar.

Net Income Multiplier.   Using a net income multiplier (NIM) of 10.5, the value would simply be found by multiplying the net operating income (NOI) by the NIM.

$$NOI \qquad NIM \qquad Value$$
$$\$200,000 \quad \times \quad 10.5 \quad = \quad \$2,100,000$$

The NIM can be found by extracting NIMs from sales of similar properties, comparing the attributes (physical, locational, financial) of the comparables to the subject property and selecting a multiplier that appears to be appropriate. An advantage of the NIM is that it is applied to income *after* expenses (and vacancy and credit loss) are deducted from the PGI. If there is a difference in the expense ratios of the subject and the comparable properties, the NIM is likely to provide a more reliable value estimate. As for the PGIM and EGIM, extracting a NIM from a comparable property and applying that NIM to the subject property assumes that the future performance of the properties will be similar.

Rather than use an NIM, the tradition in the appraisal field has been to use the reciprocal of the NIM, which is the overall capitalization rate (R_O) introduced in previous chapters. That is, rather than multiplying NOI by the NIM, we would divide the NOI by the overall capitalization rate.

Direct Capitalization Using an Overall Rate

A value estimate may be found by dividing the first-year net operating income (NOI) by an overall capitalization rate (R_O). Using an overall rate of 9.52 percent, the value estimate would be calculated as shown below.

$$NOI \div R_O = \$200,000/0.0952 = \$2,100,000$$

The R_O can be found by extracting overall rates from sales of similar properties, comparing the attributes (physical, locational, financial) of the comparables to the subject property and selecting an overall rate that appears appropriate. As discussed for PGIM, EGIM and NIM, an implied assumption is that the future performances of the comparable sale and the subject will be similar.

Residual Techniques Using Direct Capitalization

Residual techniques are used to estimate the value of a property when one of the components of the total property value is known and the other component is estimated. For example, the known component might be the building value and the unknown component the land value. This is referred to as a *land residual* technique because the land value is the unknown. If, on the other hand, the land value is known and the building value is unknown, this is referred to as a *building residual* technique. In the following sections we give examples of the land and the building residual techniques using direct capitalization. Recall that direct capitalization uses first-year income measures. In this case separate capitalization rates are applied to the land and the building incomes. There are other ways of doing land and building residual techniques, as well as other types of residual techniques. These are discussed later in this text.

Building Residual Example.   As indicated above, with the building residual technique, the land value is known, possibly from a separate analysis of comparable land sales using a sales comparison approach (discussed in chapter 8). The following example assumes that the appraiser has already estimated the land value at $450,000. Furthermore, the appraiser has determined that the appropriate capitalization rates for the land and building are 9.5 percent and 10 percent, respectively. (Later on we will say more about how these rates may be obtained.)

Example

Given:

Land value	$450,000
Land capitalization rate R_L	0.095
Building capitalization rate R_B	0.10

Solution:

NOI	$200,000
Less return to land ($450,000 × 0.095)	− 42,750
Building cash flow	$157,250

Building Cash Flow		Building Cap Rate		Building Value
$157,250	÷	0.1000	=	$1,572,500

Building value	$1,572,500
Plus land value	450,000
Property value	$2,022,500

One possible application of the building residual technique is in estimating the value of special-purpose buildings. In this case there may be comparable land sales, but no sales of comparable buildings.

Land Residual Example. As previously mentioned, the difference between the building residual technique and the land residual technique is that in the land residual technique, the building value is known and the land value is to be estimated. Following is an example of the land residual technique:

Example

Given:

Building value	$1,400,000
Land capitalization rate R_L	0.095
Building capitalization rate R_B	0.10

Solution:

NOI	$200,000
Less return to building ($1,400,000 × 0.10)	− 140,000
Land cash flow	$ 60,000

Land Cash Flow		*Land Capitalization Rate*		*Land Value*
$60,000	÷	0.095	=	$631,579

Building value	$1,400,000
Plus land value	631,579
Total property value	$2,031,579

This particular approach was originally developed to help estimate the highest and best use of the land. The assumption is that if the contemplated use of the land is the highest and best use, the value of the building should equal the cost of constructing it. Thus, the value of the building is assumed to be based on the construction cost. The land residual technique, as outlined above, would be repeated for alternative assumptions about the type of building constructed on the site to determine which use results in the greatest residual value to the land.

This approach to highest and best use analysis requires separate estimates of the land and the building capitalization rates. This can be difficult in practice. An alternative way of doing a highest and best use analysis to estimate residual land value is to first estimate the total property value (land and building), then deduct the building costs to arrive at land value. Using the previous example, suppose the R_O is assumed to be 10 percent and the building value (based on construction cost) is $1.4 million. NOI is still $200,000. The land value could be estimated as follows:

Example

$$\text{NOI} \quad \div \quad R_O \quad = \quad \text{Property Value}$$

$$\$200,000 \quad \div \quad 0.10 \quad = \quad \$2,000,000$$

Property value	$2,000,000
Less building value	1,400,000
Land value	$ 600,000

The reader should note that residual techniques also can use the discounted cash-flow approach. Discounted cash flow is the subject of the next section. [3]

YIELD CAPITALIZATION (DISCOUNTED CASH-FLOW ANALYSIS)

Value estimates for a variety of ownership interests may be calculated by forecasting cash flows over a typical holding period and discounting those cash flows to a present value estimate using a typical discount rate. This valuation approach is called *yield capitalization* or *discounted cash-flow analysis.* The discount rates used in this approach directly address the expected profitability of the investment. This chapter demonstrates discounted cash-flow analysis on an unleveraged basis (without consideration of financing). Discounted cash-flow techniques that consider financing are presented in chapter 14. The cash flows to be forecast with an unleveraged discounted cash-flow approach include NOI and net proceeds from resale. The discount rate is the property discount rate, which is sometimes called the "property yield rate" or *overall yield rate (Y_O).* The first step in applying the discounted cash-flow approach is to forecast the cash flows over a typical holding period, as was discussed in chapter 6. The following cash-flow forecasts will be used to demonstrate the valuation techniques. In the first example, it is assumed that NOI is level. The resale is estimated to be $2.3 million at the end of a 5-year holding period.

Year	1	2	3	4	5
PGI	$300,000	$300,000	$300,000	$300,000	$300,000
Less vacancy and credit loss	− 18,000	− 18,000	− 18,000	− 18,000	− 18,000
EGI	$282,000	$282,000	$282,000	$282.000	$282,000
Less operating expenses	− 82,000	− 82,000	− 82,000	− 82,000	− 82,000
NOI	$200,000	$200,000	$200,000	$200,000	$200,000
Net resale proceeds (5 years)					$2,300,000

The standard discounted cash-flow formula for solving for value on an unleveraged (without financing) basis is

Value = Present value of NOIs + Present value of the net resale proceeds

Using a Y_O of 12 percent to discount the cash flows results in the following present value estimate.

Example

Year	Cash Flow		Present Value Factor @ 12%		Present Value
1	$ 200,000	×	0.892857	=	$ 178,571
2	200,000	×	0.797194	=	159,439
3	200,000	×	0.711780	=	142,356
4	200,000	×	0.635518	=	127,104
5	200,000	×	0.567427	=	113,485
5 (resale)	2,300,000	×	0.567427	=	1,305,082
Total present value					$2,026,037

Shortcut Method

Present Value Annuity @ 12%		Present Value Factor		
$200,000	×	3.604776	=	$ 720,955
$2,300,000	×	0.567427	=	1,305,082
Total present value				$2,026,037

In the analyses, the present value estimate is $2,026,037, which implies an R_O for the property of 9.87 percent ($200,000/$2,026,037). In this instance, the shortcut method could have been used to estimate the present value of the annual incomes because the NOIs were a level ordinary income. The shortcut cannot be used if the NOIs vary over time, as demonstrated below.

Variable Income and a Fixed Resale Price. In the following example, the incomes and expenses are assumed to be increasing over time.

Year	1	2	3	4	5	6
PGI	$300,000	$312,000	$324,480	$337,459	$350,958	$364,996
Less vacancy and credit	− 18,000	− 18,720	− 19,469	− 20,248	− 21,057	− 21,900
EGI	$282,000	$293,280	$305,011	$317,211	$329,901	$343,096
Less operating expenses	− 82,000	− 85,024	− 88,183	− 94,580	− 98,021	−101,616
NOI	$200,000	$208,256	$216,828	$222,631	$231,880	$241,480
Resale proceeds (5 years)						$2,300,000

Using a property discount rate (Y_O) of 12 percent results in the following present value estimate:

Year	Cash Flow		Present Value Factor @ 12%		Present Value
1	$ 200,000	×	0.892857	=	$ 178,571
2	208,256	×	0.797194	=	166,020
3	216,828	×	0.711780	=	154,334
4	222,631	×	0.635518	=	141,486
5	231,880	×	0.567427	=	131,575
5 (resale)	2,300,000	×	0.567427	=	1,305,082
Total present value					$2,077,068

In this analysis, the present value estimate is $2,077,068, which implies an R_O for the property of 9.63 percent ($200,000/$2,077,068). The value is slightly higher than the value found assuming level income, obviously because of the additional income to be received.

NOTE: This also results in a lower implied R_O, even though the discount rate is the same, because the value is based on future income, whereas the capitalization rate uses the first-year income in the numerator. Thus, the more a property is expected to increase in value, the higher its present value and the lower its first-year capitalization rate.

It is important to understand how expected future income affects observed capitalization rates. That is why we stress that comparable sales should have the same expected future income when capitalization rates are derived from comparable sales. It would be incorrect to use a capitalization rate obtained from a comparable sale with little expectation of increase in future income to appraise a property with a much greater expectation of increase in income. Although the appraiser may feel that both properties have about the same risk, and thus would require the same Y_O, the R_O would have to be quite different. The relationship of these two rates (yield rate and capitalization rate) is stressed frequently in this text because although they are very different, they are often confused.

In the previous examples, the mathematics of applying the discounted cash-flow technique is relatively simple because all future cash flows are known before solving for present value. This situation can occur when the reversion is forecast by capitalizing the last-year or last-year-plus-one-year NOI by a terminal capitalization rate (see chapter 6).

Variable Income and Resales Based on a Terminal Capitalization Rate.   Recall that in chapter 6 we discussed the concept of a terminal capitalization rate. The terminal capitalization rate can be applied to an estimate of income for the next owner to estimate the resale price. This income depends on how market rates are expected to change over the first owner's holding period and whether any of the original leases are still in effect. (Ideally, all the leases will have been renewed at an estimated market rental rate before the end of the holding period, so the estimated resale price is not affected by any below-market or above-market rent.)

Following is a discounted cash-flow analysis that assumes the resale price is estimated using a 10 percent terminal capitalization rate (based on year 6 NOI) and a 12 percent property discount rate.

Example

$$\text{Estimated year 6 NOI} = \$241,480$$

$$\text{Resale} = \text{NOI (6th year)} \div \text{Terminal } R_O$$

$$\text{Resale} = \$241,480 \div 0.10$$

$$\text{Resale} = \$2,414,800$$

Year	Cash Flow		Present Value Factor @ 12%		Present Value
1	$ 200,000	×	0.892857	=	$ 178,571
2	208,256	×	0.797194	=	166,020
3	216,828	×	0.711780	=	154,334
4	222,631	×	0.635518	=	141,486
5	231,880	×	0.567427	=	131,575
5 (resale)	2,414,800	×	0.567427	=	1,370,223
Total present value					$2,142,209

In the analysis, the present value of the total property value is $2,142,209, which implies an R_O of 9.34 percent ($200,000/$2,142,209). When using a terminal capitalization rate to estimate the reversion, an appraiser should compare the implied overall capitalization rate (in this case, 9.34 percent) with the terminal capitalization rate (10 percent), to see whether the proper relationship is implied. In this instance, would it be logical that today's overall capitalization rate would be 0.66 percent lower than the terminal capitalization rate (perhaps due to the higher risk associated with estimating the resale price)? We are much less sure of the NOI in year 6 than we are of the NOI today. Therefore, because we are estimating the resale price based on the uncertain NOI in year 6, it may be appropriate to add a risk premium to the terminal capitalization rate. This strategy is conceptually the same as using a higher discount rate to discount cash flows beyond year 5 to estimate the resale price in year 5. Another possible reason for using a higher terminal capitalization rate is that the NOI growth will be less after year 5 than it was during the first 5 years. (Recall how the expected growth in NOI affects capitalization rates: The less the expected growth, the higher the capitalization rate.)

On the contrary, there may be a circumstance where it would be logical for the terminal rate to be lower than the going-in capitalization rate. For example, the potential for income growth might be expected to be greater after the property is sold because of changing economic conditions or, perhaps, a planned renovation of the property during the holding period.

The appraiser also should calculate the implied change in value over the holding period and compare it with the change implied in the NOI. In this instance, the NOI increased from $200,000 to $241,480, a total of about 21 percent over the 5 years from year 1 to year 6. Over the same 5 years value would increase from $2,142,209 to $2,414,800, a total of about 13 percent. Would a 21 percent increase in income and a 13 percent increase in property value reflect the expectations of a typical investor? If not, the appraiser may need to alter the input assumptions.

NOTE: In this case the increase in income is greater than the increase in property value. This could reflect a situation in which there are below-market leases that will expire during the holding period. Income will rise more than the property value in this situation because the fact that income is expected to increase is already reflected in the initial present value estimate when it is found by discounting estimated future cash flows (including the reversion).

Percentage Change in Value.   Frequently, an appraiser may wish to solve for value, assuming the resale will change by a certain percentage (annual or total) over the holding period. In this instance, the resale price will not be known until the value is found because the resale price depends on the present value being calculated. At the same time, the present value depends on the resale price. Although this may be a valid appraisal assumption, it presents a mathematical problem when we attempt to solve for present value. There are many ways of solving this type of problem:

• using algebra;
• using a *yield capitalization formula;* and
• using a computer.

We will demonstrate the use of algebra and the yield capitalization formula to show that yield capitalization formulas were developed, in effect, to presolve the algebra by solving for an R_O that gives the same answer as the algebra. The same answer also can be found using a computer. In this case, the computer can be programmed to solve for the present value while allowing the resale price to depend on the present value. A discussion of the procedure that computers use to solve the problem is beyond the scope of this book. However, the reader should be aware that there are a number of commercially available software programs as well as electronic spreadsheets, that can solve this type of problem.[4,5]

Level Income and an Unknown Resale Price.   Following is an example of using algebra to solve for present value, assuming level income over 5 years, a resale value that increases by 15 percent over the 5 years and a 12 percent property discount rate, which results in the present value estimate. (V represents property value.)

Example

Year	Cash Flow		*Present Value Factor @ 12%*		*Present Value*
1	$ 200,000	×	0.892857	=	$ 178,571
2	200,000	×	0.797194	=	159,439.
3	200,000	×	0.711780	=	142,356
4	200,000	×	0.635518	=	127,104
5	200,000	×	0.567427	=	113,485
5 (resale)	$(V + 0.15V)$	×	0.567427	=	$0.652541 V$
Total present value					$720,955 + 0.652541 V$

$$V = \$720,955 + 0.652541V$$
$$0.347459V = \$720,955$$
$$V = \$2,074,936$$

The resale value is

$$\text{Resale price} = \$2,074,936 \times 1.15 = \$2,386,176$$

* *Proof* *

Year	Cash-flow
0	($2,074,936)
1	200,000
2	200,000
3	200,000
4	200,000
5	2,586,176

$$\text{IRR} = 12.0\%$$

In the analysis, the present value is $2,074,936, which implies an R_O for the property of 9.64 percent ($200,000/$2,074,936). Proof that the answer is correct is that the internal rate of return for the implied cash flows is equal to the property discount rate (Y_O) used in the analysis.

Finding the answer to a problem that requires algebra is not only tedious, it is usually time-consuming. Fortunately, computer programs have been developed that facilitate rapid solutions of even the most complex circular reference problems. In the 1990s many, if not most, appraisers are using personal computers to help forecast future cash flows and solve for value in discounted cash-flow analysis.

Estimating Value Using Yield Capitalization Formulas

In the 1960s and 1970s, before the introduction of personal computers, a series of formulas were developed to shortcut the calculation of discounted cash-flow problems with circular logic. One of the early pioneers was L. W. Ellwood. Ellwood not only developed a series of mortgage and equity formulas but he also was responsible for publishing tables of precalculated constants that could be used to solve valuation problems. (Ellwood's contribution will be presented in detail in chapter 14.) Although the formulas Ellwood developed were based on financing, they can be used to solve problems on an unleveraged basis, simply by making the loan-to-value ratio equal to zero.

The use of a formula approach to solving discounted cash-flow problems is sometimes referred to as *yield capitalization* because it involves developing a capitalization rate based on an assumed yield rate. That is, rather than obtaining the capitalization rate from comparable sales, it is mathematically derived from an assumption about the yield rate that the typical investor would require to invest in the property. As we shall see, this capitalization rate gives an estimate of value consistent with discounting the implied cash flows.

Although this approach produces a capitalization rate, the logic used to arrive at that rate is quite different from that used in direct capitalization. The formula is used instead of discounting the cash flows because the resale price is assumed to depend on the unknown property value. This results in an algebraic problem with an unknown value on both sides of the equation. The yield capitalization formulas presented in the remainder of this chapter were developed as an alternative to solving the problem algebraically. In effect, these formulas result from solving the problem in terms of an overall rate that can be used in more general cases.

The basic unleveraged yield capitalization formula was derived by beginning with the basic discounted cash-flow relationship and algebraically solving for the R_O, as demonstrated below.

Derivation of a Yield Capitalization Formula (Optional). The following example shows how a yield capitalization formula can be derived for the case of level NOI and a resale price based on a percentage change in value. The idea is to solve for the property value based on the premise that

Property value = Present value of NOI + Present value of net resale

The first step in developing the yield capitalization formula is to state the discounted cash-flow relationship in terms of relevant symbols, as shown below.

$$V = \text{Property Value}$$

- Present value of NOI (assuming level income) =

$$V \times R_O \times \text{col. 5 @ } Y_O$$

- Present value of net resale =

$$V (1 + \Delta) \times \text{col. 4 @ } Y_O$$

Col. 5, col. 4 and so forth refer to columns in the compound interest tables in appendixes A and B.

- Estimating the present value of NOI, because a level pattern is assumed, is accomplished by multiplying the first-year NOI by the present value of an annuity factor (column 5 in the tables in the appendixes) at the yield rate (Y_O).
- The resale is the original value plus the percentage change (Δ) expected over the holding period. The present value is then calculated by multiplying the resale by the present value factor at the end of the holding period (column 4 in the tables in the appendixes) at the discount rate (Y_O).

The resulting relationship follows.

Basic Yield Capitalization Formula Derivation

V	$= V\,(R_O)\text{col. }5 + V\,(1 + \Delta)\text{col. }4$	(Divide by V)
1	$= R_O\,(\text{col. }5) + \text{col. }4 + \Delta\text{col. }4$	(Rearrange)
$R_O\,(\text{col. }5)$	$= 1 - \text{col. }4 - \Delta\text{col. }4$	(Divide by col. 5)
R_O	$= 1/\text{col. }5 - \text{col. }4/\text{col. }5 - \Delta\text{col. }4/\text{col. }5$	(col. 4/col. 5 = col. 3, and 1/col. 5 = col. 6)
R_O	$= \text{col. }6 - \text{col. }3 - \Delta\text{col. }3$	(col. 6 – col. 3 = Y_O)
R_O	$= Y_O - \Delta\text{col. }3$	(The symbol for col. 3 is $1/S_{\overline{n}}$)

The basic yield capitalization formula is $R_O = Y_O - \Delta 1/S_{\overline{n}}$

Column numbers refer to the compound interest tables in appendixes A and B.

COMMENTS: A view of the formula reveals that if property value is expected to remain constant over the holding period, R_O equals the discount rate (Y_O).

Value Solution Assuming Level Income and No Change in Resale Price. Following is a value solution assuming level NOI at \$200,000 per year, no change in value over a 5-year holding period and a 12 percent property discount rate (Y_O). The sinking fund factor $(1/S_{\overline{n}})$ for 5 years at 12 percent is 0.157410.

Example

$$R_O = Y_O - \Delta 1/S_{\overline{n}}$$
$$R_O = 0.12 - (0)(0.157410)$$
$$R_O = 0.12$$

$$\text{Value} = \text{NOI}/R_O = \$200,000/0.12 = \$1,666,667$$

* Proof *

Year	Cash Flow
0	($1,666,667)
1	200,000
2	200,000
3	200,000
4	200,000
5	$1,866,667

IRR = 12.0%

NOTE: In this case R_O is the same as Y_O. A situation in which income is level and value does not change over time is called a *perpetuity*. A perpetuity can be expressed as:

$$R_O = Y_O$$

Value Estimate Assuming Level Income and a Changing Resale Price. Following is a value solution assuming level NOI at $200,000, a 15 percent increase in value over a 5-year period and a 12 percent property discount rate (Y_O). The sinking fund factor for 5 years at 12 percent is 0.157410.

Example

$$R_O = Y_O - \Delta 1/S_{\overline{n}}$$
$$R_O = 0.12 - (0.15)(0.157410)$$
$$R_O = 0.096388$$

Value = NOI/R_O = $200,000/0.096388 = $2,074,947

* Proof *

Year	Cash Flow
0	($2,074,947)
1	200,000
2	200,000
3	200,000
4	200,000
5	$2,586,189

IRR = 12.0%

The value found using the formula is the same as that using the algebraic approach in the discounted cash-flow discussion. In this instance, the R_O

is less than the Y_O because additional profit (return *on*) will come from the increase in property value at resale.

Level Income with No Reversion (Inwood Premise).   In some valuation situations the income may be level for a specified holding period but there may be no reversion at the end of the holding period. For example, suppose a special-purpose building is leased to the user with a level lease that has a term equal to the economic life of the building. In this situation the income is simply a level annuity. One way to value this annuity is simply to use the present value of an annuity factor (column 5) from the compound interest tables in appendixes A and B.

For example, suppose you are valuing the personal property in a hotel. The personal property (that is, furniture and fixtures) is estimated to have a 5-year economic life. The appraiser estimates that $10,000 of the NOI from the hotel can be attributed to the personal property and the NOI is assumed to be level for the 5-year economic life. What is the value of this property, using a 10 percent discount rate?

One approach is to use the present value of $1 per period from the compound interest tables in appendix A, which is 3.790787. Thus, we have:

$$\$10,000 \quad \times \quad 3.790787 \quad = \quad \$37,908$$

Alternatively, we can use the yield capitalization formula introduced above to solve for an overall capitalization rate as follows:

$$R_O \quad = \quad Y_O \quad - \quad \Delta_O \; 1/S_{\overline{n}}$$

Because there is no reversion, we can say that the property will lose 100 percent of its value, which means that Δ_O is -1.0. Thus, the yield capitalization formula becomes:

$$
\begin{aligned}
R_O \quad &= \quad Y_O \quad + \quad 1/S_{\overline{n}} \\
&= \quad 0.10 \quad + \quad 0.163797 \\
&= \quad 0.263797
\end{aligned}
$$

Using this overall rate, the value is estimated as follows:

$$\$10,000/0.263797 \quad = \quad \$37,908$$

Note that the sinking fund factor $1/S_{\overline{n}}$ is based on a 10 percent discount rate. This implies that a portion of the NOI could be reinvested at 10 percent to replace the investment. We could say that Y_O represents return on capital and $1/S_{\overline{n}}$ represents return of capital. Historically, appraisers have referred to this as the *Inwood premise*. This differs from an alternative assumption about the return of capital known as the *Hoskold premise,* which is discussed below.

The Hoskold Premise.   In contrast to Inwood, Hoskold assumes that the portion of the NOI necessary to replace the equipment (capital recovery or return of capital) is reinvested at a *safe rate* that is lower than the discount rate used to value the rest of the NOI. Like the Inwood premise, the Hoskold technique was designed for situations where the property value would decrease to zero over a holding period. However, Hoskold also assumed that funds would be set aside to replace the asset at the end of the holding period. This might make sense for personal property.[6]

Using the previous example, suppose we now assume that a portion of the NOI has to be set aside at a 5 percent rate to replace the personal property every 5 years. All other assumptions remain the same. We solve this problem by calculating an overall rate, as follows:

$$
\begin{aligned}
R_O &= Y_O + 1/S_{\overline{n}} \\
&= 0.10 + 0.180975 \\
&= 0.280975
\end{aligned}
$$

In this case the sinking fund factor ($1/S_{\overline{n}}$) is calculated at a 5 percent rate rather than the 10 percent used in the Inwood premise. This has the effect of increasing the capitalization rate and lowering the value. The value is now

$$
\$10,000/0.280975 = \$35,590
$$

The value is lower because a portion of NOI had to be set aside at 5 percent to have $35,590 after 5 years to replace the property. This can be seen as follows:

NOI	$10,000
Sinking fund	− 6,441
Balance	$ 3,559

The future value of $6,441 at 5 percent for 5 years is $35,590 (rounded), which replaces the investment. The balance of the NOI of $3,559 is like a perpetuity and at 10 percent is worth $35,590.

Value Solution Assuming Income and Value Are Changing at the Same Rate.
A yield capitalization formula can be used in another special situation, when NOI and property value are expected to change by the same annual compounded rate. In this case the formula is

$$
R_O = Y_O - CR
$$

where CR is the annual rate of change.

The interesting fact about using this formula is that the overall rate is the same for all holding periods. Following is the solution for value assuming a property discount rate of 12 percent (Y_O) and a 3 percent annual change in NOI and resale:

Example

$$R_O = Y_O - CR$$
$$R = 0.12 - 0.03$$
$$R_O = 0.09$$

$$\text{Value} = \text{NOI}/R_O = \$200,000/0.09 = \$2,222,222$$

* Proof *

Year	Cash Flow
0	($2,222,222)
1	200,000
2	206,000
3	212,180
4	218,545
5*	$2,801,266

$$\text{IRR} = 12.0\%$$

$$* [\$225,102 + (\$2,222,222)(1.03)^5] = \$2,801,266$$

NOTE: If the NOI continues to increase 3 percent per year it will be $231,855 in year 6. Using this sixth-year NOI, we can calculate the terminal capitalization rate as follows:

$$R_T = \$231,855/\$2,576,164$$
$$= 9\%$$

where R_T equals the terminal capitalization rate.

This is exactly the same as the going-in capitalization rate that was calculated above. This is not a coincidence. This yield capitalization formula implicitly assumes that the capitalization rate will be constant through time and, therefore, the terminal capitalization rate will always equal the going-in capitalization rate.

We can certainly envision situations where it is reasonable to assume that income and value will increase at the same compound rate. In fact, for fee simple estates or leased fee estates, where leases have clauses to keep rent at the market rate, this is probably a reasonable approximation. However, recall our earlier discussion of the relationship between the going-in capitalization rate and the terminal capitalization rate. An assumption that they are going to be the same implies that expectations for increases in income will be the same at resale as they are at the time the property is being appraised. This assumption does not allow for economic deterioration in the value of the property. Thus, it should be made only when it is warranted based on a careful analysis of the property's potential. Furthermore, recall that the terminal capitalization rate often includes a risk premium, even if the antici-pated future growth in NOI is expected to be the same at resale as it is at the time of the appraisal.

Straight-Line (Constant Amount) Change in Income per Period. A yield capitalization formula that was historically frequently used by appraisers is referred to as the *straight-line capitalization* formula. As we will see, it really is a special case in that very precise assumptions are made about both the income pattern and the implied change in property value.

This means NOI increases by the same dollar amount each year. The formula is as follows:

$$R_O = Y_O - \Delta_O 1/n$$

where *n* is the holding period.

Δ_O is the total change in value over the holding period, and $\Delta_O 1/n$ gives the percentage drop in value the first year.

Example

Assume that the first-year NOI is $16,000. The property value is estimated to decrease a total of 20 percent over a 5-year holding period. What is the value, using a 12 percent discount rate?

$$\Delta_O 1/n = -0.20/5 = -0.04$$
$$R_O = 0.12 - (-0.04) = 0.16$$
$$V = \$16,000/0.16 = \$100,000$$

The straight-line capitalization formula is deceptively simple to use. It does not require the use of compound interest tables to calculate the overall rate and estimate the value, which accounts for its popularity before the advent of hand-held electronic calculators and personal com-puters. But what do we have to assume about the pattern of NOI to prove our answer using discounted cash-flow analysis?

In this case the implied change in NOI must be found by the follow-ing formula:

$$\Delta_I = V \times \Delta_O 1/n \times Y_O$$

where Δ_I is the *first-year* change in income.

Thus, we have:

$$\Delta_I = \$100,000 \times (-0.04) \times 0.12 = -\$480$$

Therefore, NOI is assumed to decrease by $480 per year.[7] So NOI for the 5 years is as follows:

Year	1	2	3	4	5
NOI	$16,000	$15,520	$15,040	$14,560	$14,080

Because it was assumed that value would decrease by 20 percent, the implied resale price after 5 years is $100,000 \times (1 - 0.2) = \$80,000$. Thus the total cash flow in year 5 is $80,000 + $14,080 = $94,080. Note that this could not be determined until *after* we found the value of $100,000. Using the above NOI and estimated resale, the cash flows for 5 years are as follows:

Year	1	2	3	4	5
Cash-flow	$16,000	$15,520	$15,040	$14,560	$94,080

The present value of these cash flows at 12 percent is $100,000, which proves the answer using discounted cash-flow analysis.

The question that the appraiser should always ask is whether the assumptions about changes in income and value are logical. In the example, income and value both decrease. We know that value decreases 20 percent, because that was assumed to begin with. If income decreases by the same $480 after year 5, the NOI will be $13,600 in year 6. This would be a 15 percent change in income over a 5-year period. Note that this is less than the decrease in value. Because of the way the straight-line capitalization formula works, the change in income will not equal the change in value. Also note that the annual change in income depends on the yield rate Y_O, as shown in the above formula for Δ_I.

The point is that the appraiser should be aware of the implications about the pattern of change in income and value whenever a yield capitalization formula is used. These formulas are, by nature, shortcut techniques that can be used to solve discounted cash-flow problems quickly, *if* we are comfortable with the implied income pattern and the relationship between the change in income and the change in property value.

Residual Techniques Using Yield Capitalization Formula.   Before the 1970s, when annual inflation became an accepted fact in the marketplace and mortgage loans became important in the financing of real estate transactions, a segment of investors separated real estate into its physical components (land and building) and analyzed each separately when arriving at a purchase price.

The basic assumption then was that the land value would basically remain stable over time and that the building would lose value over its economic life because of depreciation. Ultimately, at the end of the life of the building, the property value would equal the original land value. Appraisal techniques developed to mirror this purchasing strategy were called residual techniques (land residual and building residual). When solving for value in the building residual technique the value of the land was calculated first, by direct market comparison, and the building value became the unknown (the residual). In the land residual technique, the value of the building was assumed and the land value became the unknown to be found (the residual). Once the unknown component was estimated, it was then added to the known component to arrive at a value estimate for the total property.

As mentioned earlier in this text, the two basic motives of an investor are

1. to recover the initial investment and
2. to earn a profit.

In appraisal terminology the act of recovering an investment is referred to as *return OF capital* and any additional profit earned is referred to as *return ON capital*. Because land value was assumed to be level over the life of the building, total return *of* the land investment was expected at resale. All annual income, therefore, attributable to the land represented return *on,* or profit, owing to the land. On the other hand, the building was expected to lose its total value over its life. Therefore, the income attributable to the building must provide for both total return *of* the original investment as well as a reasonable return *on* capital.

The problems that arose when applying the residual techniques in estimating value were, first, in estimating the NOI over the entire life of the building and, second, dividing the income into the portion attributable to the land and the portion attributable to the building. In addition, the land and building capitalization rates, unlike overall capitalization rates, were not readily extractable from comparable sales. If they were known, solving for value would have been a simple matter, as shown in the example demonstrating the building residual technique.

Because building and land capitalization rates were not readily observable in the market, yield capitalization techniques were used to estimate the building and land capitalization rates. In essence, the land capitalization rate was assumed to be equal to the return *on* profit rate (often referred to as the land yield rate or the discount rate) and the building capitalization rate was a combination of the return *on* or profit rate (yield or discount rate) plus an adjustment added to ensure full return *of* the building investment over its life. The return *of* rate was referred to as the "recapture rate."

The following example shows how we can use the yield capitalization formula for level income and a change in property value discussed earlier to develop a land and building capitalization rate.

Example

Building Residual

Given:

Land value	$450,000
Discount rate estimate (Y_O)	0.095
Land capitalization rate R_L	0.095*
Building life	25 Years

* Same as discount rate because the change in land value (Δ_L) is assumed to be zero (a perpetuity).

Sinking fund factor   0.01096†

† Sinking fund factor for 25 years at a 9.5 percent internal rate. Referred to as the recapture rate (return of capital) for the building.

Because the holding period is the entire economic life of the property and value is zero at the end of the holding period, the change in building value, Δ_B, would be −1. Therefore, $R_B = Y_O + 1/S_{\overline{n}}$.

Building capitalization rate (R_B)	=	*Discount rate*	+	*Recapture rate*
		0.095	+	0.01096
	=	0.10596		

Solution:

Net operating income	$200,000
Less return to the land ($450,000 × 0.095)	− 42,750
Building cash flow	$157,250

Building Cash Flow		*Building Cap Rate*		*Building Value*
$157,250	÷	0.10596	=	$1,484,051

Building value	$1,484,051
Plus land value	450,000
Total property value	$1,934,051

The above example assumes that NOI is level. The reader should note that other assumptions about the income pattern could also be used to develop land and building capitalization rates. For example, it could be assumed that the building income is falling with the building value, even though the land income and land values are constant. This assumption about income might be captured by using the straight-line capitalization formula to develop a building capitalization rate. In this case we would have

$$
\begin{aligned}
R_B &= Y_B & + & \quad 1/n \\
&= 0.095 & + & \quad 1/25 \\
&= 0.095 & + & \quad 0.04 \\
&= 0.135
\end{aligned}
$$

The value of the building would now be $157,250/0.135 = $1,164,815. Note that the building value is now lower than when we assumed that the building income was level because we are now assuming that the building income is declining. The implied decline in building income would be found as follows:

$$
\begin{aligned}
\Delta_I &= V_B & \times & \Delta_B\, 1/n & \times & Y_O \\
&= \$1,164,815 & \times & -1/25 & \times & 0.095 \\
&= -\$4,426 \text{ per year}
\end{aligned}
$$

As previously stressed, these techniques should be used only when they represent a reasonable approximation of the expected pattern of NOI. If we do not feel that the building NOI will decrease $4,426 per year, the straight-line capitalization formula should not be used in this case.

STABILIZING INCOME

We have discussed several yield capitalization formulas that can be used to estimate value. These formulas required very specific assumptions about the expected change in income and property value. A more general way of dealing with a variable income pattern is to stabilize the income pattern, (i.e., convert the variable income pattern into an equivalent level income pattern). We can then estimate the value of the stabilized income pattern using the level income yield capitalization formula discussed earlier in this chapter.

To stabilize a variable income pattern, we need to calculate an equivalent level income with the same present value. This can be done with the following two steps:

1. Find present value of nonlevel income stream using appropriate yield rate (Y_O or Y_E); and
2. Multiply the present value from step 1 by the installment-to-amortize-$1 factor (using the same yield rate and holding period) to obtain an equivalent level income stream.*

Example

Assume the following:

NOI in Year 1	$100,000
Increase in NOI after Year 1	4%
Increase in value over 5 years	15%
Y_O	12%
Holding period	5 years

Stabilize the income and estimate the property value using a yield capitalization formula.

Calculation of equivalent level income

Present Value of NOI

Year	NOI	×	PV factor	=	Present Value
1	$100,000	×	0.892857	=	$ 89,286
2	104,000	×	0.797194	=	82,908
3	108,160	×	0.711780	=	76,986

---

*Alternatively we could divide the result from step 1 by the present value of $1 factor. This step can be thought of as finding payments for a loan.

4	$112,486	×	0.635518	=	$ 71,487
5	116,986	×	0.567427	=	66,381
					$387,048

Total present value of NOI × Installment-to-amortize-$1 factor = Equivalent level income

$$\$387,048 \times 0.277410 = \$107,371$$

Calculation of capitalization rate

Application of level income yield capitalization formula:

$$R_O = Y_O - \Delta_O\ 1/S_{\overline{n}}$$
$$= 0.12 - 0.15\ (0.157410)$$
$$= 0.096389$$

Calculation of value

$$\text{Value} = \$107,371\ /\ 0.096389$$
$$= \$1,113,934$$

* Proof *

Year	Income
0	($1,113,934)
1	100,000
2	104,000
3	108,160
4	112,486
5*	$1,398,010

$$IRR = 12\%$$

$$*\$116,986 + (1.15 \times \$1,113,934)$$

Income Stabilization Factor

An alternative way of stabilizing income is to calculate a factor that when multiplied by the first year's income, results in the equivalent level income. This is illustrated below using the information from the previous example.

Example

Refer to the previous example. Calculate the equivalent level income based on a factor.

Calculation of factor

Year	Δ in NOI*		PV Factor @ 12%		Present Value
1	1.000000	×	0.892857	=	0.892857
2	1.040000	×	0.797194	=	0.829081

3	1.081600	×	0.711780	=	0.769861
4	1.124864	×	0.635518	=	0.714871
5	1.169859	×	0.567427	=	0.663809
Total					3.870480

*The change in NOI from Year 1. In this case the change is $(1.04)^{(n-1)}$ where n is the year.

Calculation of Income Stabilization Factor.   The income stabilization factor (X) is found by multiplying the present value calculated above by the installment-to-amortize-$1 factor.

Income stabilization factor = 3.870480 × 0.277410 = 1.073709

Calculation of Level Income.   1.073709 × $100,000 = $107,371. The answer is the same as calculated previously.

Adjusting the Capitalization Rate

The previous example estimated the value of the property with the following two steps:

1. Stabilize the income by multiplying the first year income by an income stabilization factor.
2. Divide the income from step 1 by a capitalization rate that assumes the income is level.

A slight variation of this approach is as follows:

1. Divide the capitalization rate (for level income) by the same income stabilization factor as calculated above.
2. Divide the first-year income (unadjusted) by the adjusted capitalization rate calculated in step 1.

The difference in the latter approach is that the capitalization rate is adjusted rather than the income. The result of each approach is mathematically the same. An advantage of adjusting the overall capitalization rate rather than income is that capitalization rates can be compared with capitalization rates from other properties.

Example

Using the same information as the previous example, estimate the value of the property by adjusting the capitalization rate.

Using the symbol X for the income stabilization factor, we have

$$R_O = (Y_O - \Delta_O \, 1/S_{\overline{n}}) \div X$$

$$= [0.12 - 0.15 \, (0.157410)] \div 1.073709$$
$$= 0.089772$$
$$V_O = \$100,000 \div 0.089772$$
$$= \$1,113,933$$

This is the same answer as found previously ($1 difference due to rounding).

K Factor (a special case)

When income is changing at a the *same compound rate* (C) each year, the income stabilization factor (X) is referred to as a *K factor* and can also be calculated by the following equation:

$$K = \frac{1 - [(1 + C)^n / (1 + Y)^n]}{(Y - C)a_n}$$

where

C is the annual compound rate of change in income;
Y is the discount rate used to estimate the property value; and
a_n is the present value of an ordinary annuity of $1 factor.

In the previous example the income is increasing by 4 percent per year over a 5-year holding period and the discount rate is 12 percent. Thus, the K factor is as follows:

$$K = \frac{1 - [(1.04)^5 / (1.12)^5]}{(.12 - 0.04)3.604776}$$

K = 1.073709

This is the same answer as calculated for the X factor in the previous example. Tables have historically been published for appraisers to use to obtain precalculated K factors. The reader should keep in mind, however, that the K factor can only be used to stabilize income that is changing (increasing or decreasing) at the same compound rate each year. The more general process of stabilizing income, however, can be used to estimate the value for any variable income pattern.

Example

Assume an NOI beginning at $200,000 and assume the pattern of change found in the income and expense forecast on page 155 earlier in this chapter. Further assume a 15 percent increase in value over a 5-year period and a 12 percent property discount rate (Y_O). Following is the derivation of the income stabilization factor (X):

Year	NOI/Beginning NOI		% Change		Present Value Factor @ 12%		Present Value
1	(200,000 ÷ 200,000)	=	1.000000	×	0.892857	=	0.892857
2	(208,256 ÷ 200,000)	=	1.041280	×	0.797194	=	0.830102
3	(216,828 ÷ 200,000)	=	1.084140	×	0.711780	=	0.771669
4	(222,631 ÷ 200,000)	=	1.113155	×	0.635518	=	0.707430
5	(231,880 ÷ 200,000)	=	1.159400	×	0.567427	=	0.657875

Total present value   3.859933

Total Present Value		Installment to Amortize Factor @ 12%		X Factor
3.859933	×	0.277410	=	1.070784

The sinking fund factor for 5 years at 12 percent is 0.157410.

$$R_O = \frac{Y_O - \Delta_O \frac{1}{S_n}}{X}$$

We can now use this factor to adjust the overall capitalization rate:

$$R_O = \frac{.12 - 0.15(0.157410)}{1.070783}$$

$$R_O = \frac{.096389}{1.070783}$$

$$R_O = 0.090017$$

$$Value = NOI/R_O = \$200,000/0.090017 = \$2,221,803$$

* Proof *

Year	Cash Flow
0	($2,221,803)
1	$ 200,000
2	$ 208,256
3	$ 216,818
4	$ 222,631
5	$2,786,944*

*$231,880 + ($2,221,803) 1.15 = $2,786,944

The IRR for the above cash flows is 12.0 percent as assumed.

J Factor

As noted in the previous section, an income stabilization factor (X) can be calculated for any income pattern. However, appraisers have historically used income stabilization factors for income patterns that had certain mathematical properties. One that we have already mentioned is the K factor for income that is changing at a compound rate.

Another income stabilization factor that was historically used by appraisers is referred to as the *J factor*. The J factor is used for a curvilinear income pattern that is based on compound interest tables. Appraisers typically obtained the J factor from special tables where the factors were precalculated, using the following formula:

$$J = \left(\left[\frac{n}{1 - \dfrac{1}{(1 + Y_E)^n}} - \frac{1}{Y_E} \right] \right) \frac{1}{S_n}$$

Example

Assume that NOI will be $25,000 at the *beginning* of the first year. The NOI is expected to increase by a total of 20 percent over a 10-year holding period. Property value is also expected to increase by 20 percent over the 10-year holding period. The appropriate discount rate (Y_O) is 15 percent. Calculate the stabilized income and estimate the value of the property.

The J factor is calculated as follows:

$$J = \left(\left[\frac{10}{1 - \dfrac{1}{(1 + 0.15)^{10}}} - \frac{1}{0.15} \right] \right) 0.049252$$

$$J = 0.325891$$

When the J factor is used, the income stabilization factor (X) is calculated as follows:

$$X = (1 + \Delta_I \, J)$$

where Δ_I is the total change in income.

$$X = 1 + (0.20 \times 0.325891)$$
$$X = 1.065178$$

We can now calculate the overall capitalization rate and estimate the value of the property as follows:

$$R_O = (Y_O - \Delta_O \, 1/S_n) / X$$
$$R_O = .15 - (.20 \times .049252) / 1.065178$$
$$R_O = .131574$$

$$V = \frac{\$25,000}{.131574} = \$190,007$$

J Factor Income Pattern. Although we have estimated the value of the property, we have not yet seen what the income pattern actually looks like when we use the J factor to stabilize the income. We have only described the income pattern as curvilinear. The net operating incomes for the projection period that are implied by the J-factor premise are calculated below.

Step 1: Calculate the change in income for the first year.

$$\text{First year income adjustment} = \Delta_I \times 1/S_n$$

where Δ_I is the total change in income over the holding period and $1/S_n$ is the sinking fund factor using the 15 percent yield rate for the 10-year holding period.

Therefore,

First year-income adjustment = $5,000 × 0.049252
First-year income adjustment = $246.26

Step 2: Calculate the change in income for each year of the holding period.

Year	First Year Adjustment		Future Value of an Annuity Factor		Cumulative Adjustment to Base Year NOI*
1	$246.26	×	1.000000	=	$ 246
2	246.26	×	2.150000	=	529
3	246.26	×	3.472500	=	855
4	246.26	×	4.993375	=	1,230
5	246.26	×	6.742381	=	1,660
6	246.26	×	8.753738	=	2,156
7	246.26	×	11.066799	=	2,725
8	246.26	×	13.726819	=	3,380
9	246.26	×	16.785842	=	4,134
10	246.26	×	20.303718	=	5,000

*The base *NOI* is the income at the *beginning* of the first year.

The cumulative NOI adjustment calculated above is added to the base year NOI ($25,000) to obtain the NOI for each year of the holding period. For example, the NOI during year 1 is $25,000 plus $246, or $25,246. The NOI for the second year is $25,000 plus $529, or $25,529. Note that the NOI for year 10 will be $25,000 plus $5,000, or $30,000. This is a 20 percent increase ($5,000 / $25,000) from the base year. An idiosyncrasy of this income pattern is that the base year NOI is one year *prior* to the first year of NOI received by the investor. Use of the J factor to stabilize income assumes that the capitalization rate will be divided into this base year NOI, as was done previously. The logic is that this is the NOI at the date the value is being estimated. Another peculiarity of the J factor income pattern is that it uses the discount rate, 15 percent in this example, as part of the process of spreading the change in income over the holding period. That is, the shape of the curve (not the total change in income) depends on the discount rate. Thus, the periodic adjustment would be slightly different for a different discount rate!

Using the income adjustments calculated above, the curvilinear income pattern implied by use of the J factor to stabilize income is shown below.

Year	NOI
1	$25,246
2	25,529
3	25,855
4	26,230
5	26,660
6	27,156
7	27,725
8	28,380
9	29,134
10	30,000

Although the process of generating the income implied by the J factor is cumbersome, the income pattern that results may be a reasonable approximation for the income expected for a property. A closer examination of the income pattern reveals that the compound rate of change is not the same each year. The rate of change is low during the early years and increases over time. For example, the income increases by about 1 percent (from $25,246 to $25,529) from year 1 to year 2 but it increases by almost 3 percent from year 9 to year 10. Thus, if the income were plotted over time, the curve would be very flat (almost linear) during the first couple of years, but the curvature would increase over time; hence the name *curvilinear income pattern.*

Prior to widespread use of personal computers to estimate value, using precomputed J factors from tables was a relatively easy way to stabilize income. Recall that the value could be calculated without actually projecting the income each year. Also note that the J factor itself does not depend on the amount that the income is projected to change. The J factor is multiplied by the change in income. Thus, it is easy to prepare J factor tables, because the J factor is independent of the actual change in income. This advantage of the J factor is reduced significantly with the ability to easily stabilize any income pattern with a spreadsheet program or computer software specifically developed for this purpose.

Now that we have calculated the curvilinear income pattern implied by the J factor, we can verify that the present value of the NOI plus the present value of the implied resale price is, in fact, equal to the estimated value of $190,007. This is shown below.

Valuation of Equity

Year	Cash Flow		PVF at 15%		Present Value
1	$25,246	×	0.869565	=	$21,953
2	25,529	×	0.756144	=	19,303
3	25,855	×	0.657516	=	17,000
4	26,230	×	0.571753	=	14,997
5	26,660	×	0.497177	=	13,255
6	27,156	×	0.432328	=	11,740
7	27,725	×	0.375937	=	10,423
8	28,380	×	0.326902	=	9,277
9	29,134	×	0.284262	=	8,282
10	258,008*	×	0.247185	=	63,776

The sum of the above present values is equal to $190,006, which is the value previously estimated ($1 difference due to rounding).

*$30,000 from NOI plus $228,008 from resale. The resale price ($228,008) is based on the assumed 20 percent increase in value, i.e., $190,007 × 1.20 = $228,008.

SUMMARY

This chapter presented a variety of techniques used to value real estate income property. In general, these techniques could be categorized as either direct capitalization or yield capitalization. Direct capitalization uses first-year measures of income or cash flow to estimate value. This includes the use of income multipliers such as the potential gross income multiplier, effective gross income multiplier and net income multiplier, as well as the use of capitalization rates such as the overall capitalization rate, land capitalization rate and building capitalization rate.

Yield capitalization requires an assumption about the estimated future income of the property. Value is estimated by discounting this income, including any proceeds from reversion, at an appropriate yield rate. Another term for yield capitalization is discounted cash-flow analysis. When estimating value using yield capitalization, the first-year NOI must always be explicitly estimated. Income after the first year must be either explicitly estimated for each year of the investment holding period or assumed to change according to a particular mathematical process. Several common alternative income patterns were discussed, such as level income, compound change and straight-line change.

Similarly, either the proceeds from reversion must be estimated as a dollar amount or the property value must be assumed to change by some specified percentage amount over the holding period. A common way of estimating the reversion proceeds as a dollar amount is to apply a terminal capitalization rate to the NOI during the first year following the end of the assumed investment holding period. When value is assumed to change by a specified percentage amount per year or a total percentage change over the holding period, the value must be estimated either by solving an algebraic equation or by using an appropriate yield capitalization formula. Yield capitalization formulas have traditionally been used for specific assumptions about the manner in which income and value will change over the investment holding period. These formulas require simplifying assumptions about the pattern of income, but were useful to appraisers before the advent of personal computers allowed appraisers to solve more complex discounted cash-flow problems. Whether the value is estimated by hand using a formula or with the aid of a computer, it is important to recognize that the value simply represents the present value of the future cash flows that the investor expects to receive over the investment holding period. The appraiser can always "prove" this by discounting the implied cash flows.

The yield capitalization process automatically ensures that the investor will receive a return *on* capital in addition to return *of* capital invested. Normally the appraiser does not have to be concerned with what the property owner does with the return of capital each year. However, in the case of short-lived assets such as personal property, appraisers sometimes feel that it is appropriate to make an explicit assumption that a portion of the return of capital will be used to establish a sinking fund to periodically replace the asset. The Hoskold premise assumes that this sinking fund earns interest at a rate lower than the yield rate assumed to represent the rate of return on capital that must be earned on the investment.

Residual techniques allow the appraiser to apply an income approach to estimate the value when one of the components of value is assumed to be known. In this chapter the land and building residual techniques were introduced. In the case of the land residual technique, the building value must already be specified. This technique is sometimes used in a highest and best use analysis because the building value is assumed to equal the cost of constructing the building when the building represents the highest and best use of the site. Similarly, in the case of the building residual technique, the land value must already be specified. This approach is sometimes used to estimate the value of special-purpose buildings where land value is assumed to be known, for example, from a separate analysis of comparable land sales.

In this chapter, value was estimated without explicitly considering the effect of debt financing. Chapter 10 discusses how financing affects yield rates and other investment measures. This sets the stage for chapter 11, which illustrates how financing can be incorporated into the valuation process, using either direct capitalization or yield capitalization.

KEY TERMS

building capitalization rate
building residual technique
capitalization
direct capitalization
discounted cash-flow analysis

discount rate
effective gross income multiplier
 (EGIM)
expense passthrough
holding period

Hoskold premise

income stabilization factor

Inwood premise

J Factor

K Factor

land capitalization rate

land residual technique

minimum rent

net income multiplier (NIM)

overage rent

overall yield rate (Y_O)

perpetuity

potential gross income multiplier
   (PGIM)

residual techniques

return of capital

return on capital

safe rate

straight-line capitalization

yield capitalization

yield capitalization formulas

QUESTIONS

1. What is the difference between a potential gross income multiplier (PGIM) and an effective gross income multiplier (EGIM)? Under what circumstances might use of a PGIM be more appropriate than use of an EGIM?
2. What is the relationship between a net income multiplier (NIM) and an overall capitalization rate (R_O)?
3. What is the difference between a land residual technique and a building residual technique?
4. What is the primary difference between direct capitalization and yield capitalization?
5. Is there a difference between yield capitalization and discounted cash-flow analysis?
6. What is the difference between the Inwood and the Hoskold premises?
7. A property is expected to have NOI of $100,000 during the first year. Using a 10 percent yield rate (Y_O) and a 5-year holding period, estimate the value under the following assumptions:
   a. NOI will be level but the property value will increase by a *total* of 15 percent over the 5 years.
   b. Both the NOI and property value will increase by 3 percent *per year* over the 5-year holding period.
   c. The property value will increase by a total of 15 percent over the 5-year holding period and income will increase according to the straight-line (constant amount) assumption.
8. Refer to problem 7. Contrast the answers for each part of the problem. What is the reason for the differences in the estimated value?
9. An appraiser is estimating the value of the furniture, fixtures and equipment (FF&E) in a hotel. She estimates that income attributable to FF&E amounts to $500,000 per year. Assume that the FF&E has to be replaced every 10 years and that the typical owner of a hotel will set up a sinking fund account to replace the equipment every 10 years. Although the

appraiser believes that investors would require a 12 percent return on capital invested in FF&E, she knows that funds set aside in a sinking fund account can earn only 8 percent per year. What is the value of the equipment under the above assumptions?

10. An appraiser is estimating the highest and best use of a vacant site. One of the alternatives being considered as a use for the site is a building that would cost $1 million to construct the improvements. Under this use, NOI is estimated to be $120,000 per year. Assume that an appropriate building capitalization rate (R_B) is 10 percent and an appropriate land capitalization rate is 8 percent. What is the estimated residual value of the land under this use? What is the total property value?

11. The NOI for a property is expected to be $100,000 in year 1 and increase 3 percent per year over a five year holding period. The property value is expected to increase by a total of 15 percent over the same period. Investors require a 12 percent overall yield rate.
    a. Calculate the stabilized income.
    b. Estimate the value of the property.

END NOTES

1. The term "net net net" or triple net lease is sometimes used when property taxes, insurance and maintenance are paid by the tenant.

2. A 100 percent increase in the base rent is not necessary when the lease also has provisions for expense passthroughs, because increases in expenses due to inflation will result in additional income to the owner because of the passthrough provision in the lease.

3. Several of the examples in the section, "Yield Capitalization (Discounted Cash-Flow Analysis)," first appeared in *Income Property Appraisal* by Jeffrey D. Fisher and Robert S. Martin, Dearborn Financial Publishing, Inc. (1991) and were subsequently used with the permission of Dearborn Financial Publishing, Inc. in Course 510, Advanced Income Capitalization, developed by Jeffrey D. Fisher and published by the Appraisal Institute, Chicago, IL (1993).

4. The authors of this text have developed software that can solve all of the discounted cash-flow valuation examples illustrated in this text. For more information write to ValuSoft, Inc., 119 Brookstown Ave., Winston-Salem, NC 27101, or call (919) 721-0233.

5. Readers are referred to an article titled "Using Circular Reference in Spreadsheets to Estimate Value," Jeff Fisher, *The Quarterly Byte* 5 (fourth quarter 1989), which illustrates how a spreadsheet can be used to solve this type of problem.

6. Hoskold applied his technique to "wasting assets," for example, mines where the value decreased to zero as the minerals were removed and funds had to be set aside to invest in a new mine after the minerals were depleted (zero reversion).

7. Note that because income does not increase until *after* the first year, the total change in income over the holding period would be $\Delta_I (n - 1)$. In this case the total change in income is $-\$480 \times 4 = -\$1,920$. That is, income starts at $16,000 and decreases by a total of $-\$1,920$, to $14,080, as illustrated. It is insightful to note that at the same rate of change, income would change by $-\$2,400$ over a 5-year period, that is, from year 0 to year 5. Over the same 5-year period the total dollar change in value is $-0.20 \times \$100,000$, or $20,000. These two dollar amounts of change are related by the yield rate (Y_O), which is 12 percent in this example. That is, $-\$20,000 \times 0.12 = -\$2,400$.

CHAPTER 8

Sales Comparison Approach

INTRODUCTION

The *sales comparison* approach is one of the three methods of estimating the value of an income-producing property. A value is estimated by comparing the subject property to recent sales of similar properties on a physical unit or income ratio basis. The basis of the approach relies on the proposition that an informed purchaser will pay no more for a property than the cost of acquiring a similar property having the same utility. The approach is based primarily on the economic principles of substitution and supply and demand, in that the price paid for comparable properties is affected by the supply and demand conditions at the date of sale as well as by the price being asked for properties with the same utility.

This approach is applicable when there is an active market for the property type in the market area plus an adequate number of sales that can be compared to the subject. It is essential that adequate information for each sale be available from an authoritative and reliable source. Comparisons cannot be made without accurate and complete data, and the direct sales comparison approach cannot be used if there is a lack of recent sales. In addition, it is difficult to apply if the comparable sales are not highly similar to the subject property, if the data cannot be reliably verified, if local market conditions are changing rapidly or if regional or national economic factors are changing. For example, in 1986 a major income tax change occurred that had a significant impact on the market for many property types, which made sales that occurred prior to the tax change difficult to use to estimate value after 1986.

SOURCES OF COMPARABLE DATA

Information on *comparable sales* may be available from several sources. Primary sources include the buyer and seller, brokers, public records, professional data companies, multiple listing services and other appraisers. When gathering data, the appraiser should be aware of the applicable information needed and must seek to confirm all data reported. It is important that the data be reported using the same units of comparison. For example, operating expenses reported for one building as dollars per square foot of gross building area and for another building as dollars per square foot of net rentable area would obviously not be directly comparable. It also is important that the appraiser gather data in units of comparison that are considered important by the typical investor in the marketplace. As with the income approach, the direct comparison approach should mirror the considerations, concerns and actions of typical investors. For example, reports on sales of office buildings are typically based on a price per square foot of either gross building area or net building area. Reporting a sale on a price per square foot of land area would be inappropriate.

When gathering comparable information, the appraiser must consider not only the physical improvements but also the market area characteristics. For larger properties, such as hotels or regional malls, there may be few or no sales of similar properties in the general market area, simply because there are no or only a few similar properties in the area itself. In this instance, it would be logical to use sales outside the general market as long as the comparable areas are similar. Under these circumstances, it is also important to consider whether the typical investors for each property type would be similar. In other words, two markets could be considered comparable, even if they are located in different market areas, if the buildings are similar and the investors for both properties could be considered similar.

IDENTIFICATION OF UNITS OF COMPARISON

As mentioned earlier, estimating value by the direct sales comparison approach is accomplished by comparing sales of similar properties with the subject by using either a price per physical unit basis or income ratios. Typical *units of comparison* on a physical unit basis include:

- price per square foot of gross building area;
- price per square foot of net building area;

- price per unit (apartments, miniwarehouses, hotels, health care);
- price per seat (restaurants and theaters);
- price per door (truck terminals and distribution centers);
- price per boat slip (marinas);
- price per parking space (parking decks);
- price per hole (golf courses);
- price per lane (bowling alleys); and
- price per lot or pad (subdivisions, mobile home parks, RV parks).

The important consideration for an appraiser is to properly identify the units of comparison used for the different property types in the marketplace and to calculate the unit value correctly for the comparable property. Without accurate information, the direct sales comparison approach is difficult to use.

The common units of comparison on an income unit basis include:

- potential gross income multiplier (PGIM) (value divided by potential gross income);
- effective gross income multiplier (EGIM) (value divided by effective gross income);
- gross rent multiplier (GRM)[1] (value divided by gross rent); and
- net income multiplier (NIM)[2] (value divided by net operating income).

The proper use of the income multiplier was presented in chapter 9. As a short review, the multipliers represent relationships between various levels of income and the sales price of a comparable property. Once the factors are properly extracted from each sale, they are compared with the subject and an appropriate multiplier is selected to estimate the value of the subject property. Differences in factors for comparable properties may be caused by one or more of the following:

- differences in ownership interests;
- noncash equivalent sales prices;
- excess land;
- possible differences in lease terms, market condition and expense treatment in leases; and
- differences in occupancy levels.

ELEMENTS OF COMPARISON

On identification and calculation of the appropriate unit of comparison, each is compared to the subject property and adjusted for differences. Potentially the typical adjustment could be for one or more of the following *elements of comparison*:

- ownership interest:
  a. fee simple or
  b. leased fee;

- nonmarket financing (cash equivalency);
- conditions of sale (buyer and seller motivations);
- change in market conditions (sometimes referred to as time);
- locational characteristics:
  a. access to transportation patterns,
  b. neighborhood land use pattern,
  c. existence of public utilities and facilities, and
  d. existence or lack of support facilities;
- physical characteristics:
  a. appearance and design,
  b. effective age,
  c. construction type and quality,
  d. condition,
  e. size and finished area,
  f. floor height/ceiling height,
  g. equipment,
  h. amenities, and
  i. site improvements;
- economic characteristics:
  a. operating expenses,
  b. management,
  c. lease terms and concessions, and
  d. tenant mix;
- use:
  a. existing versus highest and best use or
  b. intended use;
- nonrealty components of value:
  a. business value and
  b. personalty.

Ownership Interest

The subject and/or comparable sales may represent differences in *ownership interests.* One sale may represent a leased fee interest, whereas another sale may include nonrealty interest items such as personal property. In each case, if the assignment is to estimate the fee simple interest value for the subject, no comparable would give a reliable indication of value without adjusting the sales to make each sale represent a value indication of a fee simple ownership interest. In addition, sometimes the subject and a comparable may represent the same ownership interest but still not be comparable. A leased fee interest in the subject may not be directly comparable to the sale of a leased fee interest (all other elements being equal), simply because the existing leases for each may affect the properties by differing percentages (the market rent equivalency adjustment may represent different relative percentages). For example, a multitenant office building with one below-market-rate lease representing only about 5 percent of the rentable area would be expected to be influenced to a lesser degree than a multitenant office building having many leases at rates substantially below the market. (Approaches to estimating the impact of leases are presented in chapter 12.)

Cash Equivalency

It is possible for the reported sales price for an income-producing property to include a premium paid for the assumption of a below-market-rate loan. If this is the case for a selected comparable, the amount of the premium paid must be deducted from the transaction price before comparing the comparable with the subject. This adjustment is referred to as a *cash equivalency* adjustment, and the adjusted sales price would then become a cash equivalent price. (Methods of calculating this adjustment are presented in chapter 14 of this book.) The amount of the adjustment should reflect the additional value placed on the loan assumption by the buyer. In other words, the amount of the adjustment should be calculated from the buyer's point of view rather than from the lender's.

Conditions of Sale

Changes in the market are not the only conditions that need to be researched. Motivations behind a sale (the *conditions of sale*) must also be investigated to ensure that neither party in the transaction was under any undue pressure and that the transaction was at arm's length and not between related parties. Forced sales where the seller is under unusual pressure to sell the property are generally not good indications of the value of a property.

Market Conditions

After adjusting the sales to reflect cash equivalent indications of the same ownership interest, each must be modified to reflect changes in market conditions between the date of the sale and the effective date of the appraisal. This adjustment is frequently referred to as the "time adjustment." The market changes may be positive or negative and could represent minor or major adjustments, depending on the magnitude of the changes in market conditions.

Locational Attributes

Since real estate is immobile, location is a key element affecting an income-producing property. Probably the most important *locational attribute* is current neighborhood land use and potential patterns of change. Compatibility of land use as well as absence of and protection from adverse influences is a highly desirable trait and, therefore, is a major contributor to value. Differences in additional location features such as neighborhood and property accessibility, transportation patterns, existence of neighborhood support facilities such as shopping and schools, and access to adequate utilities can result in differences in property values.

Physical Characteristics

The most obvious adjustment made in the direct sales comparison approach is for differences in the *physical characteristics* of two properties. Differences in condition, quality, design, age and equipment are generally readily discernible. Adjustment for differences in physical characteristics should reflect the contributing value of the attribute itself, not just the cost to reproduce or replace the items.

THE ADJUSTMENT PROCESS

In adjusting sales of income-producing properties the key test of the relative worth of an attribute is its ability to generate income (specifically in the form of net operating income).

There are several methods of reporting or basing adjustments, including:

- percentage adjustment;
- dollar adjustment;
- qualitative analysis; and
- statistical analysis.

Percentage adjustments and *dollar adjustments* are quantitative in nature and should reflect the relative differences between the comparable and the subject. Most of the ownership interests, cash equivalency, and functional and economic obsolescence adjustments are made on a lump-sum dollar basis, whereas the locational and physical characteristics adjustments are typically based on percentage differences. Qualitative adjustments are usually confined to those instances where the adjustments are large or where any adjustment would be so small that, basically, only a reconciliation of an estimate for the subject is needed. The method used by an appraiser should be dictated by the concerns and activities of a typical investor in the property's market segment.

Making adjustments is somewhat subjective, so the best approach to developing a reliable estimate of value by the sales comparison approach is to find sales of improved properties that are obviously highly similar to the subject property. If highly similar properties are not available, little weight should be placed on any value estimate made by this approach because of the variety of factors that could contribute to differences in unit value indications for apparently similar properties.

Once adjustments are made to the comparables, the various adjusted prices can be reconciled to estimate a value for the subject property. Typically, a range of values will result because of imprecision in the market. However, this range should not be too varied. When reconciling the value, greater weight may be placed on the values of comparables that are most similar to the subject property. However, it is common to report a range of values in the appraisal report rather than a single specific value.

SALES COMPARISON APPROACH EXAMPLE

Following is the information from three office building sales similar to the subject property. The effective date of the appraisal is 1/1/91. The subject building has the following characteristics.

Example

Gross building area	24,000 square feet (SF)
Net building area	20,000 SF
Market rent/SF net	$15.00
Market expenses/SF	$4.10
Market vacancy	6%
Age of building	New

Comparable Office Building Sales

Property Number	1	2	3
Date of Sale	5/90	10/89	12/90
Age	1 Year	4 Years	3 Years
Sales Price	$2,675,000	$4,200,000	$1,750,000
Property Rights Purchased	Fee Simple	Fee Simple	Leased Fee
Site Area	74,300 SF*	84,000 SF	35,000 SF
Gross Building Area	26,500 SF	46,200 SF	22,300 SF
Net Building Area	22,200 SF	40,150 SF	18,300 SF
Potential Gross Income	$ 344,000	$ 592,000	$ 227,000
Vacancy/Credit Loss	5%	6%	0%
Effective Gross Income	326,800	556,500	227,000
Operating Expenses	99,000	172,500	72,000
Net Operating Income	227,800	384,000	155,000
Loan Amount	$2,000,000	$2,750,000	$1,400,000
Interest Rate	9.75%	8.75%**	9.5%

*Contains 28,000 square feet or $200,000 of excess land.
**Market interest rate was 9 75% at date of sale.

All three sales have locations similar to that of the subject. Comparable 1 is built of better quality materials than the subject and both of the other comparables. Following are the key ratios calculated for each sale before making any adjustments.

Example

Ratio Extraction—No Adjustments

Property Number	1	2	3
Price/SF Gross Area	$100.94	$ 90.91	$73.99
Price/SF Net Area	$120.50	$104.61	$ 9.16
Building Efficiency Ratio	83.8%	86.9%	82.1%
PGIM	7.78	7.09	7.27
EGIM	8.19	7.55	7.27
Expense Ratio	30.3%	31.0%	31.7%
Expense/SF Gross Area	$ 3.75	$ 3.73	$ 3.23
Overall Rate	0.085	0.091	0.094
Rent/SF Gross Area	$ 12.98	$ 12.81	$10.18
Rent/SF Net Area	$ 15.50	$ 14.75	$12.40
Floor Area Ratio	41.2%	55.0%	63.7%

Note the differences in several of the rates and ratios, even though the sales are highly similar. The first step is to adjust the sales for differences in ownership interest, financing and excess land.

Example

Sale Price Adjustment Chart

Property Number	1	2	3
Sales Price	$2,675,000	$4,200,000	$1,650,000
Property Rights Appraised	0	0	+200,000*
Excess Land Adjusted	200,000	0	0
Financing Adjustment	0	215,000	0
ADJ Price (Fee Simple)	$2,475,000	$3,985,000	$1,850,000
Potential Gross Income	$ 344,000	$ 592,000	$ 265,350**
Vacancy	5%	6%	6%
Effective Gross Income	$ 326,800	$ 556,500	$ 249,429
Operating Expenses	$ 99,000	$ 172,500	$ 78,000
Net Operating Income	$ 227,800	$ 384,000	$ 171,429

*Market equivalency adjustment.
**Potential gross income and expense based on market.

After adjustments, the key ratios are again calculated for each sale.

Example

Ratio Extraction—After Adjustment

Property Number	1	2	3
Price/SF Gross Area	$ 93.40	$86.26	$ 82.96
Price/SF Net Area	$111.49	$99.25	$101.09
Building Efficiency Ratio	83.8%	86.9%	82.1%
PGIM	7.19	6.73	6.97
EGIM	7.57	7.16	⁌.42
Expense Ratio	30.3%	31.0%	31.3%
Expense/SF Gross Area	$ 3.75	$ 3.73	$ 3.50
Overall Rate	0.092	0.096	0.093
Rent/SF Gross Area	$ 12.98	$12.81	$ 11.08
Rent/SF Net Area	$ 15.50	$14.75	$ 13.50
Floor Area Ratio	57.2%	55.0%	63.7%

Following is an adjustment grid based on the price per square foot of gross building area.

Example

Property Number	1	2	3
Price/SF Gross Area	$93.40	$86.26	$82.96
Market Indications	1.87	3.45	0
Adjusted Price/SF	$95.27	$89.71	$82.96
Location	0	0	0
Age	+1%	+4%	+3%
Size	0	+2%	0
Quality	−5%	−5%	+5%
Condition	0	0	0
Total Adjustment	−4%	+1%	+8%
Price/SF	$89.55	$90.61	$89.60

Before making the adjustment the range of indications for the subject would have been as follows:

Example

	Unadjusted Indications			% Difference
Potential gross income multipliers (PGIM)	7.09	to	7.78	9.7%
Effective gross income multipliers (EGIM)	7.27	to	8.19	12.6%
Overall rate	8.5%	to	9.4%	10.5%
Price/SF of gross building area	$73.99	to	$100.94	36.4%

After Adjustments

	Adjusted Indications			% Difference
PGIM	6.73	to	7.19	6.8%
EGIM	7.16	to	7.57	5.7%
Overall rate	9.20%	to	9.6%	4.3%
Price/SF of gross building area	$89.55	to	$90.61	1.2%

The reduction in the range highlights the importance of a logical and supportable adjustment process.

Following is a discussion of the strengths and weaknesses of each technique used to estimate value.

Example

Appraisal of the Subject Property

Potential gross income (24,000 SF × $15.00/SF)	$300,000
Vacancy and credit loss (6%)	− 18,000
Effective gross income	$282,000
Operating expenses (24,000 SF × $4.10/SF)	− 82,000
Net operating income	$200,000

Potential Gross Income Multiplier

$$\$300,000 \times 7.0 = \$2,100,000$$

COMMENTS: This technique is reliable when the interests appraised are identical and the building efficiency ratios for the subject and the comparable fall within a narrow range (as is the case in the example). If any comparable or the subject is rented under different terms (say, gross lease versus net or absolute net basis), the *potential gross income multipliers* (PGIM) will not logically fall within a narrow range. It is also extremely difficult to use this method if either the comparable or the subject represents a leased-fee interest. In the example, after adjustment the indications appear to give a good indication of value after adjusting each comparable for the ownership interest and adjusting Comparable 3 income to represent market income.

Effective Gross Income Multiplier

$282,000 × 7.5 = $2,115,000

COMMENTS: The *effective gross income multiplier* (EGIM) gives a good indication of value when the subject and the comparable represent the price of the same interest and the leases are based on the same terms (say, gross versus net or absolute net). Unlike the PGIM, it gives a good indication even if the efficiency ratios are not in a reasonable range. After adjusting each sale for ownership interests, the three appear to give good indications of value. It should be noted that the range of indicators is not affected by minor age, quality, or size differentials between the comparables and the subject. This factor only analyzes the comparable sales and the subject based on their relative income-producing potential.

NOTE: In residential property, the gross rent multiplier (GRM) is classified as an income approach. On income-producing properties, the PGIM, EGIM and net income multiplier (NIM) are classified as direct sales comparison approach indicators. When single family homes are rented, the tenant typically pays all operating expenses, except, possibly, for taxes (maybe insurance) and major maintenance, so the GRM is the only income test ratio available.

Net Income Multiplier or Overall Rate

$200,000/0.094 = $2,127,660

or

$200,000 × 10.6 = $2,120,000

COMMENTS: The overall rate gives a good indication of value if the properties represent the same interest and are similar in other respects. Some appraisers classify the overall rate analysis as an income approach; others place it in the direct sales comparison approach. This book does not take a position as to where it should be classified; however, it has characteristics highly similar to the PGIM and EGIM. Any value indication and the implied overall rate produced using a discounted cash-flow or yield capitalization approach should be comparable to the overall rates indicated by sales. Typically, if the sales have a wide range in their overall rates, the differences primarily are due to differences in ownership interests or level of occupancy assumed.

Price per Square Foot of Gross Building Area

24,000 SF × $90.00/SF = $2,160,000

COMMENTS: The *price per square foot* of gross building area will give a good indication of the value of a subject property only after ensuring that each sale represents the same ownership interests and that adjustments have been made for differences in the locational and physical characteristics of the subject and the comparable. If the building efficiency ratios are not similar, the price per square foot of net rentable area would probably be a better indicator of value.

Summary of Value Indicators

Method Used	Value Indication
PGIM	$2,100,000
EGIM	2,115,000
NIM (overall rate)	2,127,660
Price per square foot of gross building area	2,160,000

COMMENTS: The four approaches resulted in a reasonably small range of value indications. This is obviously because each sale is highly similar to the subject. The indications were arrived at without having to make a significant number of adjustments. The value of the 24,000 SF office building falls in the range of $2,100,000 to $2,160,000, or around $2,125,000.

SUMMARY

The sales comparison approach estimates value by comparing the subject property with other comparable properties that recently have sold. This approach is best used when an adequate number of sales of similar properties exist and data can be retrieved from accurate sources.

Price can be compared through units of comparison, such as price per square foot. The units used to compare prices differ for different property types. Income units such as the potential gross income multiplier can also be used to compare properties. The sales price of comparables must also be adjusted for elements of comparison such as ownership interest, nonmarket financing, market conditions, location, physical characteristics, economic characteristics, use and nonrealty components of value.

To estimate the value of the property, a sales adjustment grid is created, in which elements of comparable properties are adjusted to reflect differences from the subject property. These adjustments can be made through dollar, percentage, qualitative or statistical adjustments. The adjusted sales prices of the comparables will indicate a value for the subject.

This approach can give a very strong indication of value when the comparable sales are similar and represent the same ownership interest. Care should be taken when analyzing leased fee interests because each may be affected to different degrees by the lease terms and tenant creditworthiness. Just because two sales represent a leased fee interest does not mean they are similar.

KEY TERMS

adjusted sales price
adjustments
cash equivalency adjustment
comparable sales
conditions of sale
direct sales comparison approach
dollar adjustment
effective gross income multiplier

elements of comparison
locational attributes
ownership interest
percentage adjustment
physical characteristics
potential gross income multiplier
price per square foot
units of comparison

QUESTIONS

1. What are the limitations of using the sales comparison approach?
2. On which appraisal principles is the sales comparison approach primarily based?
3. What is an appropriate unit of comparison for apartments? for theaters?
4. What income units can be used to compare properties in the sales comparison approach?
5. Why might income units vary among comparable properties?
6. What are the nine elements of comparison used to compare properties?
7. Under what conditions is the potential gross income multiplier most reliable?
8. For what type of property is the gross rent multiplier typically used?
9. A comparable property sold for $800,000 and had potential gross income of $105,000. What is the indicated value for a subject property that has a potential gross income of $120,000?
10. If the subject property in question 9 had vacancy and collection losses of $14,000 and the appropriate effective gross income multiplier is 8.6,

what is the indicated value for the property based on the effective gross income multiplier?

END NOTES

1. The gross rent multiplier is typically used for residential rental properties and usually represents a monthly multiplier.

2. The net income multiplier is the reciprocal of the overall rate.

CHAPTER 9

Site and Improvements Description and Analysis

SITE DESCRIPTION

A parcel of land is an integral part of any income-producing property. Land that has been graded and prepared for a specific purpose is commonly referred to as a *site*. A site has features that can generally be classified as physical, locational, legal and economic. Land itself is immobile and therefore significantly influenced by its surroundings. Its value is a function of its ability to satisfy a market need. In the case of income-producing properties, the value of the land is a function of its ability to serve as a site for either existing or proposed income-producing improvements. In addition, its value is determined by its highest and best use under current market conditions.

Physical Features

Size and Shape. Each parcel of land has a specific size and shape. Its size depends on both its frontage and its depth. The size and shape can sometimes be changed through subdividing or assemblage with adjacent land. In the absence of these acts, however, each parcel has its own characteristic physical layout. The size of a site affects the number of alternatives for which it may be used: A tract containing one acre is certainly too small to accommodate the demands of a regional mall. The shape of a parcel may affect its utility by affecting the percentage of usable land area. Usable area is the minimum land needed to construct specific improvements, including all site improvements typically needed to support the use: parking lots, buffer areas and landscaping, all required to meet both development specifications and market demands. An unusual shape can limit buildable area and result in an inefficient layout.

Topography.   *Topography* refers to the lay of the land. Topography is an important attribute because income-producing improvements are usually constructed on relatively level sites. Topography is usually classified as level, gently sloping, rolling, moderately sloping, severely sloping, or any combination thereof. A site with irregular topography may require significant development costs before it becomes suitable for construction of improvements. The increased development costs could include additional clearing, grading, soil testing, erosion control, storm drainage, rock removal, plus above-average utility installation costs. In addition, the developer may need to truck in fill material or, possibly, to remove material from the site, both of which are costly activities. The cost of the development activities involved in preparing a site may be difficult to determine before construction is begun; therefore, construction on a site with poor topography is riskier than on a level site.

Frontage.   A site having direct or other access to a street is said to "front" on the thoroughfare, or have *frontage*. The desirability of having frontage varies from one property type to another. Frontage serves two functions: First, it provides a point or points of access; second, it possibly enhances visibility of the site. (The importance of visibility will be discussed in a later section.) Businesses that need high traffic volumes (shopping centers, fast-food restaurants, and service stations) are greatly benefited by ample frontage. Industrial sites that can be served by one access point and do not require visibility are functional with only minimum frontage. Frontage is both a quantitative and a qualitative attribute of a site. A site with poor topography along its frontage may be less desirable than the same-sized site with less frontage but with level topography because of additional development costs needed to provide access.

Drainage and Water Runoff.   Site drainage is vitally important and greatly affects the use of a site. Frequently, portions of a site may be located in a floodway or flood plain. A *floodway* is a ground area usually covered annually by water. As a rule, any type of construction or filling is not allowed in a floodway without specific permission. Construction in a floodway would require significant costs to control or move the natural path of water flow. A *floodplain* is the area outside the floodway that is subject to periodic flooding. Typically, the high-water mark is the highest point that flood waters are expected to reach at least once every 100 years. Generally, flood plains may be filled to a level above the 100-year flood level and developed, unless the flood-plain area is determined to be wetlands. If classified as wetlands, there may be restrictions on filling the area. Parking areas and recreation facilities usually may be constructed in flood-plain areas without being filled.

An appraiser should be cautious when investigating flood-plain areas. Site development restrictions generally include requirements for handling water control and runoff from the site. Such control frequently involves the construction of storm drainage facilities and erosion control ponds. A site with poor drainage may require significant costs to rectify drainage or flood problems.

Soil Conditions.   The physical attributes of the soil can have a significant impact on the usability of a site. Soil attributes include permeability, stability, load-bearing capability and the ability to physically support structural improvements. *Permeability* addresses a soil's ability to absorb water. In areas where public sewers are unavailable, soil with little ability to absorb water probably will not support septic tank usage. Unstable soils that are subject to landslides, earthquakes, and shifts because of subsurface water movement are generally unstable for construction without the addition of costly subsurface support. The existence of subsurface rock can greatly increase development costs. Constructing improvements on unstable soils is risky.

Environmental Conditions.   Increasing emphasis on *environmental conditions* has made them important to any site analysis. Unfortunately, many sites have been polluted by prior users or by infiltration of pollutants from adjacent sites. Many environmental problems are not readily observable and require specialized testing to be found. The existence of subsurface toxic waste may render a site unsuitable for development. Therefore, an appraiser should be thorough in the visual inspection of the site and should seek information from knowledgeable individuals when investigating the history of a site. Potential environmental hazards may exist within a site and some, such as air and noise pollution, may originate from neighboring properties.

Locational Attributes

Site Access and Transportation Patterns.   Physical *access* is a requirement of virtually all income-producing real estate. The issue when analyzing a site, therefore, is the quality of the access. The quality of the accessibility to a site is generally a function of convenience. The importance of the quality of access varies significantly from one property type to another. For example, convenience may not be important to an industrial site as long as the access is good enough to accommodate the vehicles visiting the plant, but the quality of access is extremely important to a fast-food restaurant site. Convenience is judged by the effort it takes to enter the site. A site that requires a significant number of turns or that can be reached only by indirect routing would rank low in access quality. A site with multiple access points and no traffic controls that prohibit direct entrance into the site from any direction on a thoroughfare would be rated as having excellent accessibility.

Visibility. *Visibility* is associated with the ability of a site and/or improvements to be seen, usually from a transportation thoroughfare. As with frontage, the importance of having visibility depends on the property type. A business catering to travelers on a thoroughfare would desire visibility. On the other hand, visibility would be of little concern in the decision of where to locate an industrial plant.

Neighboring Property Uses. Compatibility of neighboring land uses is a key factor that affects the utility and, therefore, the value of a site. As mentioned earlier, existing or expected pollution from a neighboring source is a key issue. A neighboring property, however, may also indirectly adversely affect a neighboring property simply by its existence. The neighboring property uses determine and establish the reputation for the area through visual impressions. The proper neighborhood mix of land uses can create an environment that enhances profit potential, but neighborhoods with properties in poor physical condition or with incompatible land uses can create negative visual impressions and destroy this potential. Neighborhood compatibility is a major issue in selecting appropriately supported land use.

GOVERNMENT AND LEGAL RESTRICTIONS

Zoning

As described in chapter 3, virtually all communities now have *zoning* ordinances that control land use in their jurisdictions. Zoning ordinances may vary widely from one community to another both in land-use classifications and in methods of implementation. The pattern of zoning in a community is theoretically based on an overall land-use plan established after a thorough analysis of the area needs. In practice, however, it is sometimes difficult to predict future patterns of growth, so petitions asking for changes in land use are common. An appraiser may be faced with a situation in which a property is not zoned to allow what appears to be its highest and best use. Because it is an appraiser's job to estimate market value based on a property's highest and best use, a value may be reported that requires a change in zoning. An appraiser who makes a zoning change assumption in an appraisal must be able to support the conclusion by presenting evidence of land-use changes in the area, by citing comparable successful zoning petitions and by quoting support for a zoning change from appropriate public officials.

Building Permits and Inspections

Proposed site and building plans usually must be reviewed and approved by the appropriate government officials. The *building permit* process, therefore, serves as an additional form of land-use control. The site plan is reviewed to ensure adherence to zoning restrictions (setback, side yard, parking, signage, density and building coverage ratios), and the building plans are inspected to ensure compliance with building codes. Traffic control and utility engineers are consulted to ascertain that existing public facilities can adequately serve the new facility. In some areas, environmental impact studies are required to show that construction of the facility will not have an adverse impact on the community's environment, including air and water quality, traffic patterns, and quality of public service such as education, police and fire protection and medical facilities.

Legal Restrictions

Frequently developers place legal restrictions on lots that are rented or sold. This is usually true of residential subdivisions, but it can also be true of commercial and industrial developments. Specific limitations could include restrictions on building size, lot size, property uses, architectural appearance, construction type and operating hours. In addition, leases may contain clauses that affect neighboring properties by creating exclusive territories. For example, a food store lease for a shopping center may contain a provision that no additional space in the center will be leased to another food store.

Easements are legal restrictions that affect the use (but not the ownership) of property. Typical easements are those providing for access, pathways for utilities (both public and private), drainage and maintaining existing views. The impact of easements may influence property values significantly, sometimes positively and sometimes negatively. Analysis of the impact of easements is a highly specialized field within the appraisal profession.

Taxation

One of the powers granted to government is the right to tax. In many communities, taxation of real and/or personal property is the prime source of revenue for funding education and other public services. Real estate taxation is a three-step process.

1. An appropriate *assessed value* for a property is established.
2. An appropriate tax rate is set.
3. The assessment is multiplied by the rate to arrive at the amount of taxes due.

The value placed on an income-producing property may bear little relationship to the actual market value of the property.

Reassessment of property values is undertaken periodically. The length of time between reassessments can vary widely from one jurisdiction to another. The important issue, however, is not what the relationship between the absolute level of assessment for a given property and its market value is but how the property's assessment compares with that of other properties in the community. A property may have an assessment that is relatively too high or too low compared with similar properties. If the assessment is relatively higher, it can have an adverse impact on the desirability of the property. In the appraisal of real estate, analysis of property taxes is a vital factor that cannot be omitted.

ECONOMIC ISSUES

Plottage

Plottage is the additional value that results when two or more sites are combined under one ownership so that the value of the two as a whole is greater than the sum of the values of each individual site. This process of combining sites is referred to as "assemblage." Plottage value can arise when the tract created by the assemblage has a higher unit value because the new site represents an optimum mix of attributes. For example, two small tracts of downtown office land might be combined into a larger tract that will allow the construction of a high-rise office building with optimum bay depth to provide for an economic rentable area ratio, thus creating value from assemblage.

Excess Land

It is possible for a site to have more land than is needed for a specific improvement. For example, a 35,000-square-foot site on a major commercial street would be considered to have *excess land* if it were to be used as a fast-food restaurant site (typical size of 25,000 square feet). Once the existence of excess land is confirmed, the next issue to be addressed is, What is the most logical use of the excess? Typically, four options are available:

1. Selling the site and developing it separately;
2. Selling the site for assemblage purposes to an adjacent owner;
3. Retaining the property as a buffer area; and
4. Retaining the property for potential expansion of existing improvements.

For an appraiser to select the best use and therefore the appropriate way to estimate the value of the excess land, the utility of the excess land must be analyzed. If the excess land can physically be separated from the original site and developed itself, adding the value of the developed site would appear appropriate. If the land cannot be developed, the choice to keep the property or sell it depends on the status of the adjoining properties and their potential for expansion. If little expansion potential exists, the approach then must be to retain the land and consider its suitability for expansion. If expansion appears out of the question, often because of physical problems with the excess land, the last option is to retain it as a buffer zone.

Under the last scenario, the land would have little utility and, therefore, little value.

SITE ANALYSIS

The site attributes all contribute to the functional utility and, therefore, to the value of the site. The key points to be considered in analyzing a site for an income-producing property are:

- Will the site be able to physically support the existing or proposed improvements?
- Is the use legally permissible?
- Does the site have the attributes desired by the market to make its development financially feasible?

For example, a retail site containing five acres on a heavily traveled street is large enough to support the construction and provide parking for up to 50,000 square feet of retail space. If, however, the frontage is small and requires constructing improvements facing a side street rather than facing the commercial street, the site will be able to physically support the construction of the improvements but will lack the attributes required by the market. Noncoincidentally, the aforementioned three factors are the first three tests considered when determining the highest and best use for the site; the fourth test is the selection of the specific use that will result in the highest value. When deciding whether a site will physically support the construction of improvements, major factors to be considered are the size and shape of the site. Can the improvements be built on the site and provide adequate parking, landscaped areas and buffer zones? Additional factors include topography, drainage, soil and access. Will site costs be reasonable or, possibly, high and unpredictable? Once the site has been determined to be physically capable of accommodating the improvements, the next question is whether the use is legally permissible. If the zoning appears favorable and the improvements are designed to meet the proper codes, the use would appear to pass the legality test. If current zoning will not allow the improvements in question, a judgment must be made about whether the zoning is likely to be changed. A conclusion that the zoning may be changed requires detailed analysis and support. Once the legality test has been passed, the last question becomes, "Does the site have the characteristics demanded by the market for the use?" Factors to be considered along with the site's physical characteristics include accessibility, visibility, environmental conditions and relationship to neighborhood property uses. Once all attributes of a property have been considered, the final judgment made for the site is the selection of its highest and best use, which, in turn, determines the valuation methodology and comparables to be used when finally estimating the value of the vacant land.

IMPROVEMENTS DESCRIPTION

The physical improvements are the second component of an income-producing property. These improvements include any structures on the site as well as any improvements added to the site, such as parking lots, utility lines, storm drainage and landscaping. Each improvement has its own specific characteristics that must be thoroughly investigated and analyzed by the appraiser. The structural improvements are generally classified as residential, commercial, industrial, agricultural or special use. (Because this book specifically deals with income-producing real estate, only apartments will be considered among the residential uses.) Structural improvements consist of a combination of physical components designed to serve a specific purpose. In the case of income-producing properties, the structural improvements are constructed with the express purpose of generating rental and business income. For the improvements to reach their full potential (generate the most income), the components must be combined in the optimum mix. A building can be described either by listing its general characteristics or by detailing its actual physical components.

General Characteristics

Use.   Buildings are usually designed and built with a specific use in mind. Some building types provide for more flexibility than others. For example, a generic neighborhood shopping center could accommodate a wider range of tenants than a garden apartment building. Each use generally requires specific design features, both in land and building improvements, that satisfy the specific needs of tenants. These design features frequently contribute little or no value if the use is changed. For example, the drive-in windows required by branch banks are of little use if the bank building is converted to general office use.

Size.   Each structure has a gross building area that most often is calculated using exterior measurements. Some building designs contain *common areas* that serve all tenants. Deducting the common area from the gross area results in the calculation of net *usable area,* typically the area actually occupied by tenants. In some lease contracts, a tenant pays rent for a pro rata share of common areas, in addition to that paid for the space actually occupied. An area reported that includes a share of the common area is referred to as *net leasable area.* Some buildings are designed to accommodate multiple uses. For example, warehouses may contain varying percentages of office space and research and development space.

Architectural Style.   Architectural style is the manner in which building components are combined to create a visual impression while providing for a specific level of utility. It comprises the various building characteristics, including appearance, space handling, functionality and the structure itself. Architectural style is influenced by current market tastes and trends, as well as by technological advancement in structural components and design. Architectural trends change over time as a result of interplay between the desire to maintain tradition and the market's desire for efficiency, variety and change. As a result, contemporary structures frequently contain elements that combine traditional standards with modern methods. Architectural trends are subject to cyclical swings over time as certain styles become popular, gradually lose favor and then reemerge in a slightly different format. An excellent example of this cyclical movement can be seen in the current trend in the construction of high-rise office buildings. In the early part of the twentieth century new buildings were highly ornate. In the 1960s and 1970s, most new buildings were constructed with mirrored glass with little ornamentation. Today, new buildings combine mirrored glass with unique, ornate facades.

Construction Type.   Buildings are generally built using one of five methods of construction. The methods are categorized based primarily on the load-bearing characteristics of the building. The five methods are

1. heavy steel frame;
2. reinforced concrete frame;
3. masonry load-bearing walls;
4. frame exterior walls; and
5. prefabricated metal.

Heavy steel frame and reinforced concrete frame construction are usually reserved for multistory office buildings, apartment buildings and regional malls. Heavy steel frame is almost exclusively used in high-rise buildings. Masonry load-bearing walls are used for low-rise office, retail, manufacturing and distribution warehouse buildings. Wood frame exterior walls are used primarily for low-cost, low-rise office buildings and apartment buildings. Prefabricated metal is often used for warehousing and distribution facilities and some light manufacturing. It is possible for a structure to contain more than one type of construction; usually, however, construction type is uniform throughout a building. An architect selects the construction type based on the projected size and use of the building. The construction type also can be influenced by cost constraints. Typically, cost new is directly related to the construction type, with heavy steel frame construction being the most expensive and prefabricated metal being the least expensive on a per-square-foot basis.

Construction Components

Site Preparation and Foundation.   *Site preparation* includes the excavation and grading of the site as well as compaction of the soil. For small, single-story buildings the site preparation costs are minimal. For high rise office buildings, the site preparation costs can be significant. After the site is prepared, the *foundation* is installed. The foundation for a single-story building usually consists of concrete footings under the load-bearing walls and the supporting frame members. The foundation cost is a direct function of the construction type, the height of the building, and the weight of the load it supports.

Frame.   The *frame* includes the posts, columns, beams, girders, sills, underpinning and bracing in a structure. The frame can be totally independent of the other components of the building, including the exterior walls, or can actually be the exterior walls and roof supports themselves. Independent frames may be constructed of either steel or reinforced concrete. This method of framing is used for high-rise buildings. In this use, the exterior walls bear no weight and are therefore referred to as curtain walls. The frame for single-story and some low-rise buildings can be built directly into the exterior walls. The points of support may be reinforced, if necessary, with pilasters. The cost of the framing members is directly related to the load supported. In areas that may be unstable, such as earthquake zones or beach areas subject to hurricanes, the framing requirements may be subject to special standards. Prefabricated metal buildings are a special case for single-story buildings where a steel frame is used to support the structure and the metal walls are curtain walls.

Floor Structure.   Typically, the *floor structure* in a commercial or industrial building is a reinforced concrete slab on the ground floor and metal joists covered by metal decking and a concrete slab for above-ground floors. Apartments, however, may have wooden joists covered by wood subflooring. Some industrial buildings have raised floors to facilitate the loading and unloading of trucks.

Floor Cover.   The covering over the subflooring may be made of various types of material, including carpeting, terrazzo, wood, brick or various types of tile. The quality of the *floor cover* material is generally directly related to the quality of the building.

Ceiling.   The *ceiling* covering may be made of various materials including fiber, wood, plaster and metal. The covering may be attached directly to the floor above or may be hung from a suspension system. Ceilings vary from relatively plain and inexpensive to highly ornate and high priced.

Interior Construction.   *Interior construction* covers the basic cost of such items as partitions, doors, hardware, stairs, closets and cabinet work. In occupancies such as apartments and offices, the cost is typically uniformly related to the building area. Other occupancies such as stores and industrial buildings, which have large total area with very little partitioning, may have varying percentages of partitioned area. The cost of the interior construction items may vary widely from one building to another, even though the uses are the same. The cost of the interior partitioning is dependent on the quality of the materials, the room size and layout, the number of doors, the quality of the hardware and the number of built-in features such as cabinets and shelves.

Plumbing.   *Plumbing system* costs include the complete plumbing installation, rough and finished, and any associated structural allowances. The amount of plumbing is directly related to the property use. For example, a warehouse would be likely to have very little plumbing, whereas a bottling plant would require a significant amount of plumbing in the form of added drains and piping. Generally, the plumbing costs depend directly on the property use and the quality of the building.

Sprinkler System.   Not every building has a *sprinkler system,* but the current trend is toward a higher percentage of new construction having sprinkler systems. The sprinkler system can be wet or dry, depending on whether water circulates continuously in the lines.

Heating, Ventilation and Air-Conditioning.   *Heating, ventilation and air-conditioning (HVAC) systems* include the basic heating units: boilers, pumps and/or gas burners, cooling towers, piping and ducts, registers, operating motors and fans needed to control the temperature and airflow in a building. This component's cost may vary widely and is based on the type of system used in the structure. In addition, the costs are related to the climate of the area as well as the quality and efficiency of the building insulation. Basic system types include heat pumps, hot and chilled water, space heaters, and gas forced warm air units. Many systems currently in use have sophisticated electronic controls for controlling heating, cooling and air flow in an attempt to maintain proper temperature control and reduce energy costs.

Electrical System.   *Electrical system* costs allow for the service distribution, light fixtures, receptacles and convenience outlets, as well as any special industrial use requirements. The cost of electrical components is directly related to the overall quality of the structure itself. Industrial plants, however, may house operations with significant electrical requirements, so an appraiser must consider the electrical capacity of an industrial plant with care.

Exterior Walls.   Exterior wall costs include the complete outer wall covering, including the windows, doors, and any special ornamentation. The *exterior walls* are generally classified as wood, masonry, ornamental glass, composite preengineered metal and ornamental stone. The relative exterior wall cost depends on the quality of materials, the percentage of fenestration and the wall height.

Roof.   The *roof* includes the structure and the roof cover. The roof structure includes the joists, trusses, rafters, purlins and sheathing or decking, together with the bracing and ties. The roof cover includes the roofing as well as the flashing, gravel stops, gutters and skylights. There are a multitude of roof covers in use, including tar and gravel, rubber, shingles, wood, tile, slate, copper and galvanized steel. The cost is based on the quality of the material as well as on the roof style.

Insulation.   As a rule, the walls, ceilings and floor are insulated. The relative cost of *insulation* depends on the materials used, the climate, and the thickness of the material. Energy-efficient buildings are usually more attractive to the market because of the degree of control that can be exercised over utility costs.

Special Building Features and Additions.   Specialized building additions include balconies, canopies, loading docks, elevators, escalators and ornamental fountains; all of which may increase the utility and attractiveness of a building.

Site Improvements.   *Site improvements* include improved parking areas, sidewalks, landscaping, exterior lighting, signs, entrances, utility lines and fencing. Parking facilities can vary from paved areas to high-rise parking decks. The site improvements should complement the improvements and generally be of the same quality.

Functional Utility

The ability of a property to satisfy a need is referred to as its *functional utility*. In the case of an income-producing property, this ability is generally reflected by the level of rental and/or business income the improvements are capable of generating. In appraisal theory, it is assumed that land is valued based on its highest and best use. For an improved site, this implies that of the income generated by a property, the land is allocated its full share of the income first, with the remainder being applicable to the improvements. If the capitalized value of the income applicable to the improvements is not equal to their cost new, the functional utility of the improvements is not at its maximum potential, which indicates the improvements have lost value over time. The amount of value loss is referred to as depreciation. This loss in value can be caused by physical or functional problems with the improvements themselves or possibly by external problems in the market. The delineation of whether the loss in improvement value is due to physical, functional, or external problems or a combination of factors is accomplished only through a thorough analysis of the market and property itself.

Physical Depreciation

Physical depreciation is generally due to normal aging as well as to wear and tear on the improvements. Physical depreciation is sometimes referred to as physical deterioration. Older properties, even if they are located in healthy markets and are of efficient design, generally do not generate incomes equal to those of new buildings. Physical depreciation can also result from damage to the property. Physical depreciation of an item can usually be eliminated by repair or by replacing the damaged or worn item.

Functional Depreciation

Functional depreciation is traditionally referred to as *functional obsolescence.* It represents any loss in value due to structural attributes that do not meet the efficiency standards of the current market. Potential functional problems include an inefficient design or floor plan, *superadequate* construction components and/or inadequate construction features. An office building that has an *efficiency ratio* (net rentable building area divided by gross building area) of 75 percent in a market where the typical efficiency ratio is 85 percent cannot generate an optimum level of income and therefore would suffer a loss in value due to poor design. A warehouse built with heavy masonry walls and a precast concrete roof structure that has the same utility as a prefabricated metal building of the same size cannot generate the additional rental needed to support the cost of its existing building components. In this instance, masonry construction would be considered superadequate for the market if competitive buildings were prefabricated metal construction. A two-bedroom apartment containing only one bathroom cannot generate the same income as a two-bedroom unit containing the current market-standard two bathrooms. The loss in value may be greater than the original cost of adding another bath, so the project suffers a loss in value because of inadequate construction. Methods of calculating the loss in value caused by functional problems will be demonstrated in later chapters of this book.

External Depreciation

External depreciation is often referred to as *external obsolescence,* either locational or economic. It is the loss in value due to adverse market conditions. The adverse conditions could exist in a general market area or just in the neighborhood. External obsolescence can be permanent or temporary, depending on the source of the problem. If the source is an excess of supply over demand in the subject's market segment (*economic obsolescence*), the appraiser may conclude that the adverse market condition is temporary. If the imbalance is forecast to remain, such as the existence of excess warehouse space in a market with an expected static or decreasing population (*locational obsolescence*), the external obsolescence may be long term. Another factor that may result in external obsolescence is the existence of adverse influences in the immediate area: pollution, poor property compatibility, poor physical condition of the neighborhood properties. All could result in below-optimum rent levels for the subject property.

Economic Life

Each improvement has a physical life and an actual chronological age. In appraisal, however, the key factors are effective age, total economic life and remaining economic life. The *effective age* is the actual age, adjusted upward or downward for the physical condition of the improvements and current market conditions. The *remaining economic life* is the appraiser's estimate of the time period over which the improvements are expected to add value above and beyond the value of the land. Remaining economic life and remaining physical life may bear little relationship to each other when the highest and best use of the land and the highest and best use of the improvements do not coincide. In addition, the economic life of a poorly designed building may be significantly different from that of an efficiently designed building, even if they are built of the same quality materials and are the same age. The concept of economic life is a market-driven concept that was founded on the economic principles of contribution and supply and demand. It is essential that an appraiser carefully consider all market elements when estimating the economic age and remaining useful life for a subject property. The total of the effective age and remaining economic life is the estimate of the *total economic life* of the improvements.

SUMMARY

Physical real estate comprises a parcel or tract of land and any improvements on that land. A site is land that has been graded and readied to be improved with buildings. Because land is immobile, its value can be affected greatly by its surroundings, including physical, locational, legal and economic factors.

When analyzing a site, the following factors must be considered in determining its highest and best use.

1. Is the proposed project physically possible?
2. Is it legally permissible?
3. Is it financially feasible?
4. Is it maximally productive?

Highest and best use is further discussed in chapter 19.

Improvements include any structures on the land, as well as parking lots, utility lines, landscaping and other such items. Structural improvements are generally classified as residential, commercial, industrial, agricultural, or special use. This book considers only those types of properties that produce income. General characteristics such as use, size, architectural style and construction components should be considered when valuing improvements.

Loss in property value can result from physical deterioration, functional obsolescence or external depreciation. The cause and measurement of these factors are discussed in detail in chapter 11.

KEY TERMS

access
assessed value
building permits
ceiling
common area
easements
economic obsolescence
effective age
efficiency ratio
electrical system
environmental conditions
excess land
exterior walls
external depreciation
external obsolescence
flood plain
floodway
floor cover
floor structure
foundation
frame
frontage
functional obsolescence

functional utility
heating, ventilation and air-
    conditioning (HVAC) systems
insulation
locational obsolescence
net leasable area
permeability
physical depreciation
plottage
plumbing system
remaining economic life
roof
site
site improvements
site preparation
sprinkler system
superadequacy
topography
total economic life
usable area
visibility
zoning

QUESTIONS

1. What is meant by the term "site"?
2. What physical features of a site should be considered when estimating the value and how can they affect the use of the site?
3. What four general classifications of features affect the value of a site?
4. What type of property would require good access? For what type of property would access be less important? Why?
5. How can legal restrictions affect property value?
6. What four factors determine the highest and best use of a site?
7. Besides buildings, what other features can be considered improvements?
8. What is meant by the term "plottage"?
9. What factors cause physical depreciation?
10. What causes functional depreciation?
11. An excess of supply over demand in a property's marketplace would be considered what type of depreciation?

| CHAPTER 10 | # Site Valuation |

INTRODUCTION

This chapter applies the sales comparison approach and the income approach discussed in previous chapters to valuation of a site. The purpose of site valuation is to estimate the value of the site separate from the value of any building improvements that may exist on the site. This is important because an appraisal should normally show the contributing value of the site and improvements to the total property value. You may recall that the value of the site depends on its highest and best use as if the site were vacant. Furthermore, the cost approach to appraisal (discussed in the following chapter) requires a separate estimate of the site value using one of the other two approaches to value.

APPROACHES TO SITE VALUATION

The first phase of estimating value by the cost approach is to estimate the value of the *site,* defined as a plot of land improved for a specific purpose. Typical approaches used to estimate site value include

- direct sales comparison approach;
- extraction method;
- development approach;

- capitalization of ground rent; and
- allocation; or
- land residual.

Sales Comparison Approach

The sales comparison approach is the most common method used to estimate the value of a site. Application of this approach involves gathering information from recent sales of similar properties and comparing each to the subject. Each comparable sale is adjusted for dissimilarities to arrive at an indication of value for the subject property. Attributes compared include method of financing the transaction, changes in market conditions since date of sale and differences in locational characteristics and physical features. (A discussion of the relative importance of locational and physical attributes was presented in chapter 9.) Any adjustments needed to arrive at an indication of value of the subject land are usually summarized in an adjustment grid, followed by narrative commentary explaining the reasoning behind making the adjustments. Typical adjustments made to comparable land sales include:

- financing differences;
- changes in market conditions (sometimes referred to as the time adjustment);
- locational features:
  —access and transportation patterns,
  —zoning and other land-use restrictions,
  —neighborhood development pattern and
  —visibility; and
- physical attributes:
  —size and shape,
  —topography and drainage,
  —frontage and accessibility,
  —soil conditions,
  —access to public utilities and
  —easements and encroachments.

The purpose of the adjustment process is ultimately to arrive at an adjusted indication of value for each comparable sale that mirrors the attributes of the subject property. For example, if the subject property has rolling topography and market information indicates the market will pay 10 percent more for a level site, the sales price of a level site (all other attributes being equal) is adjusted downward by 10 percent so the adjusted price will be an indication of value for a rolling site. Following is a sample adjustment grid. The site is a 38,000 square feet lot that is the site of the 24,000 square feet office building used as an example in the income approach section of this report.

Example

Sale	Subject	Comp 1	Comp 2	Comp 3
Sales price	N/A	$285,000	$250,000	$300,000
Date of sale	1/1/91	6/90	10/90	1/90
Size, square feet (SF)	38,000	40,312	35,400	44,840

Adjustment Grid

Sale	Comp 1	Comp 2	Comp 3
Price per SF	$7.07	$7.06	$6.69
Financing adjustment	0	0	0
Cash equivalent price	$7.07	$7.06	$6.69
Market conditions	+2%	+1%	+4%
Adjusted price per SF	$7.21	$7.13	$6.96
Location	+10%	0	+10%
Size	0	−5%	+5%
Utilities	0	0	0
Topography	−5%	+10%	−5%
Total adjustments	+5%	+5%	+10%
Adjusted price per SF	$7.57	$7.48	$7.65

The top portion of the grid contains a brief description of the subject and of each comparable sale. The lower section is the adjustment grid itself. The adjustments reflect differences between the subject and the comparables. For example, comparable sale 3 is larger than the subject (44,840 square feet versus 38,000 square feet). After an analysis of comparable sales, the appraiser has made the judgment that smaller lots sell for slightly higher unit prices than larger lots. If this is the case, the unit price paid for comparable 3 would be expected to be slightly lower than the subject, simply because of the difference in size. To adjust for this factor, the appraiser made a 5 percent upward adjustment to the comparable for size.

Adjustments may be made and reported either on a quantitative or a qualitative basis. The usual quantitative methods employed are adjustments based on either percentage differences or actual dollar estimates. The adjustments illustrated in the previous grid are reported and calculated using percentages. When using dollar adjustments, the appraiser strives to identify the actual marginal contribution of a specific attribute on a dollar basis. The best method of arriving at and supporting a level of adjustment is through the analysis of comparable properties, referred to as "paired sales analysis." Following is an example:

Example

Paired Sales Analysis

Comparable	1	2
Sales price	$74,250	$60,000
Date of sale	3/90	4/90
Size (acres)	2.25	2.0
Location	Good	Good
Topography	Level	Rolling
Utilities	All city	All city
Price per acre	$33,000	$30,000

COMMENTS: The two comparable sales are highly similar to each other in size, date of sale, location and access to utilities. The only major difference appears to be that comparable 1 has level topography, whereas comparable 2 has rolling topography. In this situation, the appraiser is able to estimate and support an adjustment for topography by comparing the two sales.

$$\frac{\text{Price per acre comparable 1}}{\text{Price per acre comparable 2}} = \frac{\$33,000}{\$30,000} - 1 = 0.10, \text{ or } 10\%$$

NOTE: It may be difficult to find properties that have only one dissimilar attribute. The adjustment process requires a significant amount of judgment on the part of the appraiser. Paired sales analysis, however, can help an appraiser refine the judgment process.

The second approach to making adjustments involves use of qualitative statements such as "superior" and "inferior" to describe differences between the subject property and the comparable. This approach usually is used when the range of sales is so diverse that quantitative adjustments would be difficult to select and support or when comparable properties and the subject are so similar that the unadjusted indications fall in a very narrow range. In this latter case, the adjustment process, in essence, becomes a reconciliation of the unadjusted indications. No matter what method of adjustment is selected, the appraiser must fully and logically explain the justification for the adjustment process. It is important that the reader of an appraisal report be able to follow and fully understand the steps taken in the adjustment process.

Using the sales comparison approach, the range of value indication after adjusted, falls in the range from $7.48 per sq. ft. to $7.65 per sq. ft., averaging $7.56. The three sales appear to be very similar and require little adjustment. Based on the analysis, the appraiser selected $7.50 per square foot as the best estimate of value for the subject land. The appraiser should not automatically select the averaged indication; he or she should rely heavily on the most similar, and least adjusted indication to arrive at a final value conclusion.

Land Value Estimate: 38,000 SF × $7.50 per SF = $285,000

Extraction Method

In the *extraction method,* the appraiser estimates the value of the total property and subtracts the contributing value of any improvements to estimate site value. This method is often used when there is an absence of recent comparable land sales in the market area. When applied to new improvements that represent the highest and best use of the site, this process mirrors the methodology used to determine the highest and best use of the land as if vacant. Following is an example of the extraction approach.

Total property value	$1,200,000
Less contributing value of improvements	− 900,000
Land value estimate	$ 300,000

The extraction method should be used only in unusual circumstances, because the land value found using this approach may not accurately reflect the value of the site as if it were vacant and ready for its highest and best use. In addition, the extraction method is highly speculative when the improvements are old and/or do not represent the highest and best use of the site. In either case the estimate of the contributing value of the improvements would be highly subjective.

Development Approach

The *development approach* often is used to estimate the value of a large tract of land that has the potential of being subdivided and sold separately as smaller lots. It makes no difference whether the land could be used for residential, commercial or industrial development, the valuation approach is the same. Conceptually, estimating land value by the development approach is similar to the income approach: The value of the site is the present value of the future cash flows (attributable to the land ownership) discounted at a rate of return considered typical for investors purchasing development land.

The first step in estimating land value by the development approach is to prepare a cash-flow forecast covering the expected sellout period of the project. Typical sources of income or cash include lot sales proceeds and, possibly, income from the operation of recreational amenities and/or assessment fees to cover common area expenses. The primary source usually is income from lot sales. The expenses or uses of cash include site development costs, amenity costs (possibly), sales and marketing expense, administration and overhead expenses, and developer fees (sometimes referred to as "developer profit"). The cash-flow forecast should match incomes and expenses in the periods when they are expected to be received or paid.

Unit Sales Income.   Forecasting *unit sales income* involves undertaking a detailed study of the market area, neighborhood and market segment of each type of property to be constructed on the site. The purpose of the market studies is, to estimate the lot sale prices and the lot absorption rate. The lot sales prices are found using the direct sales comparison approach by comparing sales prices of lots in the area that are similar to the proposed subject lots. The absorption rate is forecast by estimating future demand for the sites, based on an analysis of historical and expected population, employment, household and/or business growth trends and patterns, and comparing this demand with the current and proposed supply of competitive lots. Once the lot prices and absorption rate have been selected, the potential periodic income is found by multiplying the forecast sales prices by the expected unit sales in the period. Unit prices may increase, remain constant or decrease during this sellout period. The appraiser must address this issue and take a supportable stand, given current conditions and expectations of price changes over the absorption period.

Other Income.   Some developments contain amenities such as recreational facilities that generate income over the sellout period. If the proposed development is to have income-producing amenities, the appraiser must include and be able to support logically a forecast of income from this source because these amenities frequently do not generate a positive cash flow by themselves. In addition, some developments have all or a portion of the operating expenses paid by lot owners through periodic assessment fees. The fees may cover expenses such as landscaping, security and amenities operation. In this instance, these fees would be a source of income; however, this income would be offset by operating expenses for the development and thus would not be a net source of profit to a developer.

Site Development Costs.   *Site development costs* include expenses for clearing and grading the land as well as for installation of roads, utilities and amenities. These costs could be relatively minor for a simple single-road subdivision and enormous for a major resort development that incorporates significant recreational facilities. Direct-site costs include clearing, grading, soil testing, engineering, surveying, erosion control and soil stabilization. Road costs may include pavement, curb and gutters, streetlights, sidewalks, and storm drainage. Utilities can include the cost of providing sewer, water, gas, telephone and electrical service to each site. Additional site costs might include signage, bridges, lakes, on-site sewage disposal systems and so on. Determining the appropriate timing of incurrence of each development cost, as well as the magnitude of the cost, is essential in the preparation of a development cash-flow forecast. Many developments have failed because too great a percentage of the site was developed in early years. The initial site costs should be no more than needed to produce a 2- or 3-year inventory of lots. In other words, a large development (absent any unusual circumstances) should be phased properly, and the cash-flow forecast should accurately reflect the phasing strategy.

Sales and Marketing Expenses.   Developers will incur costs to market lots. These costs typically include sales commissions and advertising and promotional material. Many developers are geared to handle the marketing effort in house. This should not preclude the appraiser's making a deduction in the cash-flow forecast for *sales and marketing expenses.* As with all appraisals, the value sought is the price to be paid by the next buyer of the property, who probably will incur marketing expenses.

Administrative, Overhead and Operating Expenses.   *Administrative expenses* and *overhead* are incurred by the developer of a property to run the business operation while the development activity and sellout of the lots occur. These expenses include property taxes (not paid by the lot owners), insurance, office rent, telephone, secretarial fees and so forth. The amount of typical overhead expense may vary significantly from one property type to another. Operating expenses are the cost to operate the project itself. For smaller subdivisions the operating and overhead expenses frequently are combined. When a specific ownership association, however, has been established and lot buyers are paying part of the expenses to operate the property in the form of assessment dues, operating expenses are generally listed as a separate category. When an owners' association is involved, the expense incurred by the developer is usually the difference between the total expense and the owners' association contribution.

Entrepreneurial Profit.   Developing a subdivision is a management-intensive and time-consuming job. Typically a developer seeks to earn profit above all costs needed to complete the project as a reward for successfully completing the venture. The profit is earned for the effort expended to locate a subdivision site, plan the project, secure all government approvals, coordinate the construction work and sales effort, and handle other administrative details.

   Entrepreneurial profit is the compensation a developer receives for these activities. Because an entrepreneur's efforts are independent of other roles he or she may play, the source of entrepreneurial profit is unrelated to these other roles. Therefore, entrepreneurial profit should not be viewed as compensation for such activities as those of a general contractor, capital supplier or real estate broker.

   Several methods are used to compensate for entrepreneurial profit in a cash-flow forecast, including:

- deducting a line item expense based on a percentage of sales income (for example, 12 percent of total sales income);
- making no line item deduction and assuming a higher discount rate (In this instance, the rate of return would reflect both profit in the invested capital and entrepreneurial profit.); and

- deducting expenses periodically from cash flows that are calculated by means other than a percentage of sales income.

The common method is to deduct a line item expense based on sales income. This method will be used in the example shown later in this chapter.

Discount Rate Selection. The discount rate selected should reflect the typical rate required by investors in land suitable for development. The analysis can be done either on an unleveraged or leveraged (with consideration for financing) basis. The discount rate used on an unleveraged basis is the land discount rate (Y_L). If land financing is considered, the discount rate becomes the before-tax equity yield rate (Y_E). The example below represents a cash-flow forecast on an unleveraged basis.

Example

Land Valuation—Development Approach Example

The following is an example of estimating land value using a development approach.

Assumptions:

Analysis period length	Semiannual
Total periods	5
Construction period	6 Months
Sellout period	2 Years
Number of lots	86
Typical lot price	$45,000, increasing by 2% per semiannual period

Development Costs:

Engineering	Period 1 = $25,000
	Period 2 = $10,000
	Period 3 = $20,000
Clearing/grading	Period 1 = $50,000
	Period 3 = $10,000
Roads	Period 1 = $300,000
	Period 3 = $175,000
Utilities	$4,000 per unit built, increasing by 2% per period
Sales costs	8% of sales income
Overhead	2% of sales income
Real estate taxes	$250 per remaining lot
Developer profit	12% of sales income
Land discount rate	15%

Sales and Construction Schedule

Semiannual Period	1	2	3	4	5
Beginning Balance Construction	0	46	16	36	16
Total Construction	46	0	40	0	0
Sales	0	30	20	20	16
Ending Balance	46	16	36	16	0
Cumulative Sales	0	30	50	70	86
Unsold developable sites at year's end	86	56	36	16	0
Average unsold during year	86	71	46	26	8

Example

Lot Sales Prices

Period	1	2	3	4	5
Sales price per lot	$45,000	$45,900	$46,818	$47,754	$48,709

Net Cash Flows

Semiannual period	1	2	3	4	5	Totals
Source of Cash						
Sales income						
Typical lot	$ 0	$1,377,000	$936,360	$955,087	$779,351	$4,047,798
Total cash	$ 0	1,377,000	936,360	955,087	779,351	4,047,798
Use of Cash						
Development cost						
Engineering	25,000	10,000	15,000	0	0	50,000
Clearing/grading	50,000	0	10,000	0	0	60,000
Roads	300,000	0	175,000	0	0	475,000
Utilities	184,000	0	166,480	0	0	350,480
Total	559,000	10,000	366,480	0	0	935,480
Selling Costs	0	110,160	74,909	76,407	62,348	323,824
Total	0	110,160	74,909	76,407	62,348	323,824
Administration and Overhead						
Overhead	0	27,540	18,727	19,102	15,587	80,956
Real estate tax	21,500	17,750	11,500	6,500	2,000	59,250
Total	21,500	45,290	30,227	25,602	17,587	140,206
Developer's profit (12%)	0	165,240	112,363	114,610	93,522	485,735
Total uses	580,500	330,690	583,979	216,619	173,457	1,885,245
Net cash flow	−580,500	1,046,310	352,381	738,468	605,894	2,162,553
Present value cash flow*	−540,000	905,406	283,653	552,965	422,040	1,624,064
Value						$1,624,064

*At a 15% discount rate.

COMMENTS: The subdivision was assumed to be constructed in two phases, with the first phase (46 units) completed in the first period and the second phase (40 units) completed in the third period. The total present value of the income to be received by the land owner, when discounted at 15 percent, is $1,624,064, which is the land value estimate.

Capitalization of Ground Rent

In markets where land is usually leased rather than sold (some portions of Hawaii, for example), the *capitalization of ground rent* can be a useful tool. This approach mirrors income approach techniques in which the typical rent (lease payment) for a tract of land is estimated as well as the typical lease terms. This future cash-flow forecast is translated into a present value, using either a land capitalization rate (R_L) or a land discount rate (Y_L). Capitalization of the first year's land rent by an estimated capitalization rate would generally be reliable if land lease terms are consistent in the marketplace and if tracts of land subject to leases are being sold in the market unimproved. If this is not the case, the best method is to forecast a set of land lease payments and discount the payments plus any reversionary value to a present value estimate. An example follows:

Example

Estimate Market Rent Land Lease Payments

Years	1–10	11–20	21–30	31–40
	$45,000	$60,000	$95,000	$140,000

Projected Resale in 40 Years = $1,500,000

Year	Cash Flow		Present Value Factor @ 12%		Present Value
1–10	$ 45,000	×	5.650223	=	$254,260
11–20	60,000	×	1.819219	=	109,153
21–30	95,000	×	0.585742	=	55,645
31–40	140,000	×	0.188593	=	26,403
Resale	1,500,000	×	0.010747	=	16,120
Total					$461,581

Land value estimate = $461,581

Allocation

One additional method of estimating site value is called *allocation*. It is applied by estimating the value of the property and multiplying that value by a typical land ratio observed in the market. This is a seldom-used method because it does not specifically address the highest and best use of the site. It is used, however, when land sales are not directly available, for example, in the analysis of patio homes, where the land is not sold separately, so no vacant land sales representing the same type of land are available in the market.

Land Residual

The land residual technique is an income approach to site valuation. This technique is discussed in chapter 7.

EXCESS LAND

Frequently an income-producing property may include excess land. *Excess land* may include either land that could be split from the improved portion and sold separately or land suitable only for the expansion of the existing improvements. The additional benefit of being able to market a tract separately without affecting the utility of the existing improvements should be considered in estimating the value of any excess land.

The value of excess land is not, as a rule, considered directly in the income approach unless a level of land rent has been added to the income from the improvements to reflect its existence. Excess land is usually added as a separate item in both the income and direct sales comparison approaches so that each value indication reflects numbers for the same real estate interest.

SUMMARY

The cost approach bases value on the contribution of any improvements (after deduction for accrued depreciation) to the value of the land as if vacant, based on its highest and best use. Therefore, the first phase of estimating value by the cost approach is to estimate the value of the site. Typical approaches used to estimate site value include the direct sales comparison approach, extraction method, development approach, capitalization of ground rent, and the allocation method.

The direct sales comparison approach is the most common method of valuing a site. In this approach, comparable sales are adjusted for dissimilarities in a sales comparison grid to arrive at an indication of value for the subject property. A paired sales analysis can be used to determine the amount of an adjustment.

In the extraction method, the appraiser estimates the value of the total property and subtracts the contributing value of any improvements to estimate site value. This method is used on a restricted basis because of the subjectivity of the technique and is primarily used when recent comparable land sales cannot be found.

The development approach estimates site value by the present value of future cash flows. It is most often used for larger lots that will be divided and sold in smaller parcels.

Capitalization of ground rent is used in markets where land is usually leased rather than sold. A future cash-flow forecast of the probable rent for a tract of land is made and discounted to a present value through a land capitalization or a land discount rate.

The allocation method estimates site value by estimating the value of a property and multiplying it by a typical land ratio observed in the market. This method is seldom used because it does not specifically address the highest and best use of the site.

KEY TERMS

administrative expenses	land residual
allocation	overhead
capitalization of ground rent	paired sales analysis
development approach	sales and marketing expenses
entrepreneurial profit	site
excess land	site development costs
extraction method	unit sales income

QUESTIONS

1. How is value estimated in the cost approach?
2. Upon what appraisal principle is the cost approach based?
3. Name five methods used to estimate site value.
4. What is the most common method used to estimate site value?
5. What method is primarily used to estimate site value if recent comparable sales of land can not be found?
6. What method is primarily used to estimate site value if land is usually leased rather than owned?
7. What method is primarily used to estimate the value of large tracts of land that are expected to be subdivided and sold as smaller tracts?
8. How does the allocation method estimate site value? What is the weakness of this approach?
9. What income and expense items should be considered when estimating the value of a site by the development approach?
10. What factors should be compared when valuing a site through the direct sales comparison approach?
11. Based on the information below, what dollar adjustment would be made for the location of a property with poor access in a sales adjustment grid?

	Comp 1	*Comp 2*
Sales price	$84,000	$125,000
Date of sale	8/91	9/91
Size (acres)	1.00	1.00
Location	Poor access	Good
Topography	Level	Level
Utilities	City	City

12. Would land being developed as a parking lot for an office building be considered excess land? Why or why not?

13. Refer to the development approach example in the chapter. Assume that lot sales will be as follows:

Year	*1*	*2*	*3*	*4*	*5*
Sales	0	16	20	20	30

Estimate the land value using the above sales schedule with all other assumptions the same as before. Note that sales costs, overhead and developer profit will be different because they are a percentage of sales income. Real estate taxes also will change because only unsold lots are taxed.

CHAPTER 11

The Cost Approach

INTRODUCTION

The cost approach in the appraisal analysis is based on the proposition that the informed purchaser would pay no more than the cost of producing a substitute property with the same utility as the subject property. (Recall the principle of substitution.) It is particularly applicable when the property being appraised involves relatively new improvements that represent the highest and best use of the land or when relatively unique or specialized improvements, for which there exist no comparable properties in the market, are placed on the site.

The cost approach is defined as one of the three traditional appraisal approaches to estimating value. In this approach, value is based on adding the contributing value of any improvements (after deduction for accrued depreciation) to the value of the land as if it were vacant, based on its highest and best use. If the interest appraised is other than fee simple, additional adjustments may be necessary for nonrealty interest and/or the impact of existing leases or contracts.

Traditionally, appraisal texts have presented the cost approach prior to the income approach. However, many of the adjustments made in the cost approach for beneficial financing, ownership interests plus functional and external obsolescence are calculated using techniques presented in the income approach. For this reason, we have elected to cover the income approach first in presenting the appraisal techniques used to estimate the value of income producing properties.

The cost approach is useful in estimating the value of an income-producing property when the property is unique and/or when the property is reasonably new and the improvements represent the highest and best use of the site. Chapter 10 was devoted to estimating the value of the site. This chapter is devoted to estimating the contributing value of the improvements (both building and site) on the site. The contributing value of the improvements is equal to the reproduction cost new of the improvements less loss in value because of depreciation caused by age, wear and tear, and functional and external problems. Ultimately the contributing value of the improvements, as well as compensation for entrepreneurial profit, is added to the estimated site value to estimate the value of the fee simple interest in the property. When estimating the value of an ownership interest other than fee simple, the value indication by the cost approach at this point must be further adjusted for the market rent equivalency adjustment and/or the value of any nonrealty interests such as personal property, financing and lease premiums and business interests.

COST NEW

The first step in estimating the contributing value of improvements is to estimate the cost new of the improvements. There are two criteria by which the cost new is estimated: reproduction cost new and replacement cost new. *Reproduction cost* is the cost of construction at current prices of an exact duplicate or replica using the same materials, construction standards, design, layout and quality of workmanship, embodying all the deficiencies, super-adequacies and obsolescence of the subject building.

Reproduction cost new can usually be readily calculated for new or nearly new improvements that represent contemporary construction methods. If the building is older, is unusually ornate and/or contains materials either no longer available or too expensive to use in modern building, calculating reproduction cost new can be difficult. It also can be difficult when building standards have changed, because of lack of availability of cost information on a method that is no longer used. For example, most warehouses prior to the 1960s were masonry construction with bowstring roofs, whereas today, most are prefabricated metal.

A second method of estimating cost new is to estimate the replacement cost rather than the reproduction cost new. *Replacement cost* is the cost of construction at current prices of a building having utility equivalent to the building being appraised but built with modern materials and according to current standards, design and layout. The use of the replacement cost concept presumably eliminates most forms of functional obsolescence; therefore, the only depreciation to be measured is physical deterioration and external obsolescence.

For a new or nearly new building, reproduction cost and replacement cost are generally identical. For older buildings built of outdated materials, there could be a significant difference between reproduction and replacement cost. Functional problems usually eliminated when estimating replacement costs include superadequate construction and overcapacity. Inadequate construction or design, conditions that occur infrequently, must be adjusted for separately.

Type of Costs

The typical improvement costs include costs for direct and indirect costs. *Direct* expenses include materials and labor incurred when constructing the building. In addition, the building contractor's fee is generally included. *Indirect* costs include all other expenses, including administrative costs, financing fees, taxes and insurance during construction, professional fees, leaseup fees, plus architectural and survey costs.

To properly estimate costs, appraisers must be familiar with and understand architectural plans, building techniques, construction types and component specifications. Appraisers must undertake detailed inspections of improvements and construction plans. In addition to knowing indirect and direct costs, appraisers also must modify the total of these costs to reflect an adjustment for entrepreneurial profit levels that are typical of the market. *Entrepreneurial profit* is the additional return expected by the developer for the risk and effort associated with the completion of a successful project. The date when entrepreneurial profit can be properly recognized is a subject of debate, but certainly when the project has been completed and rented to stabilized levels and is not having any functional or external problems, all of the entrepreneurial profit will have been realized. If the developer and the contractor are the same entity, one could expect both full contractor's profit and full entrepreneurial profit to have been realized; however, each would be reported at a separate level. Debate has also arisen about whether entrepreneurial profit should be added to the site value portion of the investment. Because levels of entrepreneurial profit are set in market transactions, the dollar amount is, therefore, theoretically fixed. Consequently, whether entrepreneurial profit is viewed as accruing to the land plus improvements or to improvements only would not affect the total dollar amount; but it *would* affect the percentage selected to arrive at the profit amount. This is demonstrated below.

Land costs	$ 2,000,000
Building costs	10,000,000
Entrepreneurial profit (market derived)	1,200,000
Total	$13,200,000

NOTE: The total amount of $13.2 million and $1.2 million are fixed in the market. An appraiser who believes entrepreneurial profit is attributable only to the building would report a 12 percent ($1,200,000/$10,000,000) profit on the building. An appraiser who believes entrepreneurial profit is attributable to both land and building would report a 10 percent ($1,200,000/$12,000,000) profit on both land and building.

Methods of Estimating Costs

Four methods are used to estimate the cost new of improvements, when calculating either reproduction or replacement cost new:

1. comparative unit method;
2. segregated cost method;
3. unit in place method; and
4. quantity survey method.

To apply one of these methods, the appraiser must have inspected and analyzed the improvements and gathered information in the proper format for analysis. The complexity of the calculation increases dramatically from the comparative unit method to the quantity survey method. The appropriate method to use depends on the size, shape and design of the improvements and which cost is being estimated, as well as on the scope of the assignment. For standard buildings, the comparative unit method usually will result in a reasonable cost estimate, especially when the cost is to represent replacement cost rather than reproduction cost.

Comparative-Unit Method.   The *comparative-unit method* is used to derive a cost estimate from a lump-sum unit cost based on either the square footage or the cubic footage measurement for a structure. The unit costs are found by extracting unit costs from completed buildings within various categories. The categories are clearly defined, and each may contain many classifications for a property type. For example, there are five basic types of construction, classified according to frame and exterior wall type. The five types include:

1. heavy steel frame with exterior curtain walls;
2. reinforced concrete frame with exterior curtain walls;
3. reinforced concrete or masonry exterior load-bearing walls;
4. frame construction exterior load-bearing walls; and
5. prefabricated metal frame.

An office building, for example, could be constructed using any of these methods. Heavy steel frame construction is generally limited to multistory buildings. Reinforced concrete frame is generally used for low-rise and high-rise office buildings, but it is not suitable for buildings taller than 10 to 20 stories. Masonry and frame load-bearing exterior walls are used for one-story or two-story buildings, and prefabricated metal is used for inexpensive office buildings. In some instances, a building may contain two types of construction or combinations of methods, which may affect the way the cost estimate is developed. An appraiser must be able to distinguish between types of construction to be able to develop reliable cost estimates.

The categories also may be segregated by the quality of materials used. The quality of materials used depends on the intended purpose of the structure and the quality and condition of competing buildings. Obviously, the cost increases as the quality of the materials used increases. An appraiser must be able to identify the quality of construction materials accurately to arrive at a reliable cost estimate.

Once the building has been classified in regard to construction type and quality, the next step in using the comparative-unit cost method is to search for a unit cost measure for similar structures. Once a suitable estimate is found, it may need to be further refined for possible differences in mechanical systems (heating, air-conditioning and ventilation systems, plumbing, electrical and elevators), size, ceiling height, shape, sprinkler systems, loading docks and so forth. Sources of cost information are presented later in this chapter. After the appropriate adjustments have been made, the final estimate is found by multiplying modified unit cost by the actual size of the subject structure. A comparative unit example for estimating the reproduction cost new for a proposed office building follows.

Example

Comparative Unit Cost Example

Gross building area	24,000 square feet (sq. ft.)
Construction type	Masonry load
Bearing walls quality	Good
Number of stories	2
Number of elevators	1
Base building cost/SF	$ 64.00
Plus HVAC adjustment	+ 1.04
Plus sprinkler adjustment	+ 2.06
Adjusted unit cost	$ 67.10
Story height multiplier	× 1.030
Perimeter multiplier	× 0.947
Adjusted unit cost	$ 65.45
Building cost ($65.45 × 24,000 sq. ft.)	1,570,800
Elevator	55,000
Reproduction cost new	$1,625,800

Segregated Cost Method.   The *segregated cost method* employs cost estimates for the various components in the structure. The cost of each component (for example, roof cover) is estimated separately, and the sum of all the component costs becomes the cost estimate for the building. Various units of measure are used to estimate the cost of each component, including cost per square foot, cost per lineal foot and unit cost. In appraisal, the segregated cost often is used when the comparative unit method is difficult to apply because of an unusual design or mix of components or lack of unit cost data. This method is also useful when all components in the building do not represent the same level of quality. Following is an example showing the development of reproduction cost new for the same office building as in the preceding example.

Example

Item	Size, sq. ft.		Unit Cost, per sq. ft.		Cost
Site preparation	12,000	×	$ 0.67	=	$ 8,040
Foundation	24,000	×	2.57	=	61,680
Frame	24,000	×	5.47	=	131,280
Floor structure—1st fl.	12,000	×	3.31	=	39,720
Floor structure—2nd fl.	12,000	×	9.88	=	118,560
Floor cover—carpet	24,000	×	3.70	=	88,800
Ceiling	24,000	×	6.20	=	148,800
Interior partitions	24,000	×	15.78	=	378,720
Sprinkler	24,000	×	2.06	=	49,440
Plumbing	24,000	×	3.40	=	81,600
HVAC	24,000	×	4.45	=	106,800
Electrical/lighting	24,000	×	4.51	=	108,240
Exterior wall	12,480	×	12.77	=	159,370
Roof structure	12,000	×	6.07	=	72,840
Roof cover	12,000	×	1.85	=	22,200
Elevator	24,000	×	2.30	=	55,200
Total					$1,631,290

Unit-in-Place Method.   The *unit-in-place method* uses costs for the various components in a structure based on the makeup of the different sections of the building. Components within the structure are identified specifically (for example, interior framing) and costs are estimated based on a square foot, lineal foot or cubic foot basis. This method differs from the segregated method in that cost estimates for the various components of a building element (for example, roof structure, including joists, roof deck and sheathing) are performed separately with the unit in place method, whereas they are considered as a total unit with the segregated cost method. This method differs from the quantity survey method (discussed next) in that in the quantity survey method the roof structure would be appraised by counting the number of roof joists, decking plates and sheets of sheathing needed; applying specific costs for each; and later adding a contractor's profit and overhead to the total. When using the unit-in-place method an allowance for contractor's profit and overhead would have been built into the unit costs used.

Quantity Survey Method.   The most accurate method of estimating cost is the *quantity survey method,* in which each item is identified and the cost estimated separately. This method mirrors the method used by contractors to arrive at an original bid estimate. Not only is the cost of each individual item, such as a light fixture, identified but also the number of hours of labor that would be expected to install that item. Once each unit cost is estimated and totaled, the contractor then applies the appropriate adjustments for overhead and profit. Accurately estimating value after the fact by this method is a time-consuming task, especially if some of the construction materials are not readily visible. For this reason, an appraiser seldom is required to estimate cost using the quantity survey method. The method, however, may be used to estimate the value of unusual components if they exist in a structure.

Sources of Cost Information

There are four basic sources of cost new information: professional cost estimating companies, actual costs of newly completed buildings, contractor's estimates and an appraiser's files. A cost estimate arrived at by one of these services should be tested for reasonableness using another method. Appraisers frequently estimate costs using cost source data and test the reliability of the estimate against costs of similar new buildings that have been constructed. Several prominent cost-estimating services publish data for estimating costs. A few of these are Marshall and Swift Publication Company, Boeckh Publications and F. W. Dodge Corporation. These companies publish updated information frequently. A few offer on-line computer estimating services. Each service structures its data somewhat differently, so the appraiser should be fully aware of the assumptions and methods of the service being used.

Some services include an adjustment for indirect costs, and others do not. They also may differ in the handling of architectural fees. Information is updated periodically using a series of cost indexes that modify published changes in market conditions and relative differences between locations in the areas served. Each service's unit costs are calculated and periodically updated by comparing the original unit costs with actual costs of new buildings.

Example

In order to estimate the total value for the 24,000 square feet new office building used as an example in the income section of this book, the value of the site improvements and an adjustment for entrepreneurial profit is made.[1] The site contains 38,000 square feet and is improved with a 25,000 square feet parking lot, accommodating 65 automobiles. The landscaping contributing value is $5,000 and entrepeneurial profit is based on 12% of the total improvement cost. Entrepreneurial profit is the return expected by the developer and is compensation for efforts in planning and completing the development and renting the project at a stabilized occupancy level. In this example, it is assumed that the building is new and would not be subject to physical depreciation or deduction for functional or economic obsolescence.

Reproduction cost new (comparative cost method)	$1,625,800
Plus:	
Parking lot: 25,000 SF × $1.25 sq. ft.	31,250
Landscaping:	5,000
Total reproduction cost new	1,662,050
Plus:	
Entrepreneurial profit (12%)	199,446
Land value	285,000
Total indicated value by the cost approach	$2,146,496

DEPRECIATION

Depreciation is the difference between the cost new (either reproduction or replacement) and the contributing value of the improvements representing the fee simple interest. Differences between the values of the fee simple interest and other ownership interests are not depreciation but are a result of contractual or business arrangements affecting the property. Methods for adjusting the cost approach for nondepreciable items (such as the market rent equivalency adjustment, financing premiums and personal property) will be presented in later chapters in this book. Several of the methods used to estimate the impact of these contractual arrangements (for example, leases), however, mirror some of the methods used to estimate adjustments for depreciation.

If the contributory value of the improvements is less than the cost new, the difference is a result of depreciation arising from physical, functional and/or external problems affecting the property. In income-producing property, the loss in value (or utility) manifests itself in the failure of the improvements to be able to generate the rents that are needed to support the cost new. Physical problems include loss in value due to age and wear and tear. Functional obsolescence results from design features that do not represent current building standards, including superadequacies, inadequacies and absence of desired features. External problems are a result of adverse locational or economic factors. Three of the methods used to estimate depreciation are:

1. the age-life method;
2. the breakdown method; and
3. the market extraction method.

The Age-Life Approach

In applying the *age-life approach,* the appraiser estimates the effective age, the total economic life and the remaining economic life of the building. The effective age is defined as the age of an improvement determined by its current condition and utility based on its design, location and current competitive market conditions. The effective age may be greater than, less than or equal to the actual age of the improvements, depending on the current condition and history of periodic maintenance of the structure. The total economic life is the estimated time period during which an improvement yields a return over the economic rent that is attributable to the land itself, that is, the estimated time period over which an improved property has value in excess of its salvage value. The remaining economic life equals the time period over which an improvement is expected to add value above the value of the land as if vacant and valued at its highest and best use. The remaining economic life may or may not be equal to the remaining physical life, depending on current and foreseeable market conditions.

A ratio then can be calculated by dividing the effective age by the economic life (economic life = effective age + remaining economic life). This ratio is multiplied by the cost new to arrive at the depreciation estimate. The following example shows how the age-life approach is used.

Example

Reproduction cost new (30,000 sq. ft. @ $19/sq. ft.)		$570,000
Total economic life	40 years	
Remaining economic life	30 years	
Effective age	10 years	
Depreciation %: 10/40 (25%)		− 142,500
Depreciation value of improvements		$427,500
Contributing value of site improvements		+ 15,000
Land value		+ 65,000
Total value		$507,500

NOTE: *Deferred maintenance* (items that need to be repaired or replaced immediately) frequently is deducted first from the cost new, and the effective age is modified to reflect the effective age assuming the deferred maintenance items are repaired. Under this circumstance, the depreciation method is referred to as the "modified" age-life approach.

The Breakdown Method

In the *breakdown method,* the physical, functional and external factors contributing to the loss in value of the improvements are isolated and estimated separately. The physical and functional factors are further divided into curable and incurable items. *Curable physical depreciation* items represent costs to repair components. Items are classified as curable if the cost to repair them does not exceed the value they will contribute to the property after repair. *Incurable physical depreciation* encompasses items that would not be repaired immediately (for example, a roof cover that is 5 years old and has a 20-year life) and if the cost to repair would not add value greater than that cost.

Curable functional obsolescence refers to items that are superadequacies or deficiencies when the cost to cure them is less than the value added to the structure. When the cost to cure a functional problem is greater than the value added, the item is classified as incurable. Such a situation is called *incurable functional obsolescence. Superadequacies* are caused by a structural component that is too large or of a higher quality than that needed for the highest and best use of the property. The cost of superadequate features exceeds their value. Superadequacies are also referred to as "over-improvements." Deficiencies are inadequate features in a structure or one of its components.

Problems resulting from external forces such as adverse neighborhood or economic conditions are incurable and are classified as *external obsolescence.* The depreciation deduction could be permanent or temporary, depending on the nature of the problem. *Economic external obsolescence* (adverse market or economic conditions) can change over time, whereas *locational external obsolescence* (neighborhood incompatibility of land uses and/or other adverse influences) typically requires a significant period of time to change, if ever.

The first step in applying the breakdown method is to identify each component cost. Typically, replacement cost new is estimated for income-producing properties to eliminate possible functional problems with the structure. To illustrate methods of adjusting for superadequate construction, however, the cost of superadequate exterior wall construction (brick veneer) has been included in the following example.

Example

All the costs below include allocation for indirect costs and entrepreneurial profit attributable to the building.

30,000-sq.-ft. Warehouse—Reproduction Cost New

Excavation and site preparation	$ 9,600
Frame	97,500
Floor structure	67,200
Floor cover, office	3,850
Ceiling, office	13,500
Partitions, office	36,000
Sprinkler	40,500
HVAC, warehouse	21,950

HVAC, office	11,700
Plumbing	47,200
Electrical	53,000
Exterior wall	93,000
Roof cover	25,000
Roof structure	40,000
Total	$560,000

The first depreciation deduction calculated is deferred maintenance, which consists of costs to cure physical problems that need immediate attention. In the sample building the two items that need immediate attention are the repair of roof damage caused by a storm and the replacement of all the space heaters in the building that were found to be defective. The cost to replace the space heaters would be greater than the cost new because of the added cost of new wiring.

Example

Deferred Maintenance

	Replacement Cost New	Cost To Cure	Remainder
Roof leak	$25,000	$ 3,500*	$21,500
Space heaters	21,950	$23,500†	0
		$27,000	

*It will require $3,500 to repair a leak caused by storm damage.
†Three space heaters need to be replaced.

The second depreciation deduction is for incurable physical depreciation for short-lived items (components that have shorter economic lives than the basic structure itself). Once the components are identified, the appraiser estimates an effective age and useful economic life for each. The actual age and effective age of any component may be different, because of the maintenance history of the component. Once the effective age and economic life for each have been selected, the depreciation deduction for each is calculated by multiplying the depreciation percentage by the replacement (or reproduction) cost new. The cost base for any components affected by deferred maintenance must be reduced by the cost to cure before applying the depreciation percentage to avoid double counting.

Example

Physical Incurable Depreciation—Short-Lived Items

	Replacement Cost	Effective Age	Economic Life	% Depreciation	Depreciation
Roof cover*	$21,500	10	15	67	$14,405
Floor cover	3,850	2	8	25	962
Ceiling	13,500	10	20	50	6,750
HVAC, office	11,700	10	15	67	7,839
Plumbing fixtures†	6,500	10	20	50	3,250
Electrical fixtures‡	14,300	8	15	53	9,699
	$75,350				$42,905

*The roof cover replacement cost is net of the cost of repairs.
†The portion of the plumbing costs attributable to the plumbing fixtures only.
‡The portion of the electrical costs attributable to the light fixtures only.

The final physical depreciation deduction is attributable to loss in value of long-lived items. To arrive at the appropriate deduction for this depreciation item, the cost new is first reduced by the deferred maintenance estimate and the total replacement cost of all short-lived items (not just the depreciation amount), again, to avoid double counting. In addition, estimates are made of the effective age of the long-lived components as well as of their remaining economic life alone. The effective age and remaining economic life of the long-lived components would probably differ from the effective age and remaining economic life used in the age-life method, because the effective age and remaining economic life in the age-life method reflect a composite rating for all components. The amount of depreciation for the long-lived components is calculated by multiplying their cost new by the ratio found by dividing their effective age by their total economic life.

Example

Physical Incurable Depreciation—Long-Lived Items

Replacement cost new		$560,000
Less		
Deferred maintenance	$27,000	
Incurable short-lived items	$75,350	
Total short-lived items		− 102,350
		$457,650
Effective age	8 years	
Remaining useful life	42 years	
Depreciation percentage	16%	$ 73,224

Functional problems are caused by either a deficiency or by super-adequate construction. The building used to illustrate the depreciation deductions has a brick veneer exterior wall that would be considered to be superadequate, based on current standards. In addition, the building does not have a truck-height loading dock, which is a disadvantage, so it also has a deficiency. To estimate the impact of a deficiency, the cost to add the item today is contrasted to the cost to add the component originally. The depreciation deduction is the difference between the two. The deduction, however, must be less than the value added by adding or modifying the existing structure. If the deficiency would result in the replacement of an existing item, any remaining value attributed to the item at this point must also be deducted.

Curable Functional Obsolescence

Deficiency:

Installation of truck-height loading dock	$4,500
Original cost of installation	− 2,500
Loss in value	$2,000

Frequently, functional items may be incurable. The depreciation deduction for this type of item can be calculated in two ways.

1. The extra cost of construction (remaining after deducting physical depreciation already taken) is deducted.
2. The income difference (net operating income [NOI]) between the level needed to support the superadequacy and current functional income levels is capitalized by the overall capitalization rate.

The first method illustrates the cost difference approach.

Example

Method 1: Excess Cost Adjustment

Incurable Functional Obsolescence: Superadequacy

Exterior wall (added cost)	$40,000
Less depreciation taken	− 6,400
Depreciation	$33,600

NOTE: The physical depreciation taken amounts to 16 percent of $40,000, or $6,400.

The second method is to compare rent levels needed to support the super-adequate construction with rent levels currently available and estimate the difference in NOI after considering any impact on operating expenses and then to calculate the loss in value by capitalizing the NOI by the appropriate overall capitalization rate.

Example

Method 2: Rent Loss

Incurable Functional Obsolescence: Superadequacy

Rent needed to support masonry construction	$2.10 per sq. ft.
Market rent	− 1.95 per sq. ft.
Rent difference	$0.15 per sq. ft.

NOTE: In this example, the operating expenses are assumed to be identical for either rent, except that management fee is 3 percent of the difference, so the net loss in NOI per square foot is $0.1455 per square foot [0.15(1 − 0.97)] or $4,365 per year, which results in a loss of value, assuming an overall capitalization rate of 10.5 percent, of $41,571 ($4,365/0.105). This estimate represents the loss in value caused by the superadequate construction. This estimate must be reduced further by the depreciation deduction taken with the long-lived item depreciation to arrive at the functional obsolescence adjustment.

Value loss	$41,571
Less depreciation taken	− 6,400
Depreciation	$35,171

NOTE: The depreciation numbers found by each method are similar, and they should be.

The final type of depreciation estimated is incurable external obsolescence, which is a result of adverse locational and/or economic conditions. The primary method used to estimate this type of depreciation is the capitalization method, which is basically the same approach previously used to estimate incurable functional obsolescence for a superadequacy. The amount of depreciation is the present value of the NOI lost, which is calculated either by dividing the first-year NOI difference by the appropriate overall capitalization rate (R_O) or by estimating the lost NOI over a specific holding period and then estimating the present value using an appropriate property discount rate (Y_O). When the external obsolescence is a result of temporary economic conditions (high interest rates, excess of supply over demand, employment problems and so forth, the latter method is the best way of estimating the depreciation. In the following example, the rent levels expected for the subject property are $0.20 per square foot less than rates for similar properties in other similar areas because of poor property use compatibility in the subject property's neighborhood.

Example

External Obsolescence: Locational

Market rent	$1.95 per sq. ft.
Current rent	− 1.75 per sq. ft.
Rent difference	$0.20 per sq. ft.

NOTE: In this example the operating expenses are assumed to be identical for either rent, except that management fee is 3 percent of the difference, so the net loss in NOI is $0.194 per square foot [$0.2(1 − 0.97)], or $5,820 per year, which results in a loss of value, assuming an overall rate of 10.5 percent, of $55,429 ($5,820/0.105). The value represents the loss in total property value attributable to the entire property. Assuming the land represents 80 percent of value and because the loss in land value attributable to the locational problem would have been considered when estimating the value of the site itself, only 80 percent of the lost value is attributable to the improvements ($55,429 × 0.80 = $44,343).

In some instances, the amount of external obsolescence can be estimated using a paired sales analysis by comparing sales of similar buildings, some of which are affected by neighborhood problems and others that are outside the influence. The percentage difference would be an estimate of external obsolescence. This method, however, generally would not result in a precise answer.

Example

Depreciation Summary

Physical Deterioration

Curable, deferred maintenance	$ 27,000
Incurable, short-lived items	42,905
Incurable, long-lived items	73,224
Total	$143,129

		$143,129
Functional Obsolescence		
Curable	$ 2,000	
Incurable	33,600	
Total	$ 35,600	35,600
External obsolescence		44,343
Total accrued depreciation		$223,072

Example

Summary of Final Value Estimate

Reproduction cost new	$560,000
Less accrued depreciation	− 223,072
Depreciated value of improvements	$336,928
Plus contributing value of site improvements	15,000
Plus land value	65,000
Fee simple value indication	$416,928

NOTE: The estimate may be adjusted further to reflect the value of an ownership interest other than fee simple.

The Market Extraction Method

Probably the best method used to estimate depreciation is the *market extraction method,* in which the percentage loss is extracted from market sales of similar properties. Obviously, one key element in applying this method is the availability of similar sales. Implied depreciation percentage may be extracted by deducting the value of the land and any contributing value of site improvements from the sales price, then dividing this number by the cost new for the improvements. The complement of the answer would be the implied depreciation percentage from all sources. Following is an example.

Example

Sales price	$1,400,000
Less land value	− 300,000
Less contributing value of site improvements	− 50,000
Depreciated value of the improvements	$1,050,000

$$\text{Depreciated \%} = 1 - \frac{\text{Depreciation value of improvements}}{\text{Cost new of improvements}}$$

$$= 1 - \frac{\$1,050,000}{\$1,625,000}$$

$$= 1 - 0.65$$

$$= 0.35, \text{ or } 35\%$$

If the effective age of the building is 15 years, the annual depreciation percentage would be 0.35/15 = 0.023, or 2.3% per year.

NOTE: This method is difficult to apply if the building and the subject differ somewhat in age, quality and/or condition. Using this method assumes each has been affected by the same market forces.

SUMMARY

The cost approach estimates value as the value of the land as if vacant based on its highest and best use plus the contributing value of any improvements minus depreciation. This approach primarily is useful for calculating the value of properties that are unique or that are reasonably new and represent the highest and best use of the site.

Valuation of the land was discussed in chapter 15. This chapter focused on the second step of the cost approach, valuing the cost of improvements. The cost new of the improvements can be calculated as either a reproduction cost or a replacement cost. The reproduction cost represents the cost to construct an exact duplicate of the subject property. The replacement cost represents the cost to construct a replica of the subject property with current construction standards, layout, materials and design.

Costs can include direct and indirect expenses. Costs can be estimated by four methods: comparative unit method, segregated method, unit in place method or quantity survey method.

Depreciation is the difference between the cost new and the contributing value of the improvements representing the fee simple interest. Depreciation can be calculated through several methods, including the age-life method, the breakdown method, and the market extraction method. The breakdown method further classifies depreciation as curable physical, incurable physical, curable functional, incurable functional and external obsolescence.

KEY TERMS

age-life approach
breakdown method
comparative-unit method

curable functional obsolescence
curable physical depreciation
deferred maintenance

depreciation
direct cost
economic obsolescence
entrepreneurial profit
external obsolescence
incurable functional obsolescence
incurable physical depreciation
indirect cost

locational obsolescence
market extraction method
quantity survey method
replacement cost
reproduction cost
segregated cost method
superadequacy
unit-in-place method

QUESTIONS

1. What are the limitations of using the cost approach to estimate value? For what types of properties is it best used?
2. What is the difference between reproduction cost and replacement cost?
3. What factors can cause the reproduction cost to be hard to estimate?
4. Why are most forms of functional obsolescence eliminated by the replacement cost but not the reproduction cost?
5. The building contractor's fee is generally classified as what type of cost?
6. How is entrepreneurial profit handled when estimating costs?
7. What four methods are typically used to estimate costs?
8. How is a cost estimate derived through the comparative unit method?
9. What is the most accurate method of estimating cost of construction? Why is this method seldom used in appraisal?
10. What three methods are used to estimate depreciation?
11. What is the relationship between the effective age and the actual age of an improvement?
12. Assume a building has a total economic life of 50 years, a remaining economic life of 30 years and a reproduction cost new of $340,000. What is the depreciated value of the building using the age-life method?
13. What is meant by the term "superadequacy"?
14. Describe two methods to estimate incurable functional obsolescence.
15. A retail property is located in an area in which the neighborhood is becoming increasingly run down. Net income of the property has fallen by $0.15 per square foot. If the property encompasses 1,500 square feet and the overall capitalization rate is 9 percent, what is the value of the external obsolescence?
16. What are the limitations in using the market extraction method to estimate depreciation?

END NOTE

1. This example was introduced in chapter 5. The cash flows are projected on page 106 and the resale price was estimated on page 120. The value is estimated in chapter 7 on page 157.

<table>
<tr><td>

CHAPTER 12

</td><td>

Leased Fee and Leasehold Valuation

</td></tr>
</table>

INTRODUCTION

Up to this chapter, the income, expenses and discount rates used assumed typical market levels. Frequently, however, income-producing properties are subject to one or more existing leases that may or may not be at market levels. Existing leases can affect the typical investment returns by their impact on one or more of the following four factors:

1. net operating income;
2. reversionary value estimate;
3. financing options; and
4. investment risk.

Ownership interests subject to existing leases in which the right to occupy and use a property is conveyed to an outside party are referred to as *leased fee interests* or "leased fee estates." An appraisal that requires estimating the market value of a property subject to one or more existing leases therefore is an assignment requiring estimation of the market value of the leased fee estate. The ownership interest held by a tenant who has an existing lease is referred to as the *leasehold interest* or "leasehold estate." An appraisal that requires estimating the market value of a tenant's interest created by a lease is an assignment requiring estimation of the market value of the leasehold estate. According to the Uniform Standards of Professional Appraisal

Practice (USPAP), any property subject to an existing lease to a nonrelated party must be considered in an appraisal.

The value of a leased fee interest could be greater than, less than, or equal to the market value of the fee simple (unencumbered) interest, depending on the circumstances. The market value of the leased fee interest is the most probable price that a property would bring in an open market after consideration of the impact of existing leases. The typical purchaser of a leased fee interest is a real estate investor. (Fee simple interests might be held by businesses that use the space. Leasehold estates usually would be held by tenants.) The market value, therefore, is the most probable price a "typical" purchaser of a leased fee interest would pay for the property assuming the effect of the leases.

The value of the leased fee interest equals the sum of the present value of the net operating income (NOI) generated by a property with consideration of any existing leases plus the present value of the reversionary proceeds from the resale of the property at the end of the holding period. It represents the value to a typical investor in leased real estate. The discount rate used is the rate desired by that investor, considering the riskiness of the interest.

The value of the leasehold interest is the present value of the rent differentials created by a lease under which the contract rent is not equal to the current market rent. The contract rent may be higher or lower than the market rent. The leasehold value is the present value of the incremental rent differentials discounted at a rate of return desired by purchasers of leasehold interests, usually other tenants.

The value of the leased fee interest(s) plus the value of the leasehold interest(s) may or may not equal the value of the fee simple interest(s). Real estate investors who buy leased fee estates and tenants who buy leasehold estates operate in different markets and may have different investment criteria. Furthermore, the investment horizons of these two classes of owners may be different. For example, the typical real estate investor may be considering a 10-year holding period for an investment in a leased fee estate, whereas a typical tenant for a food store may be considering acquiring a leasehold estate in a below-market lease that has a remaining term of 20 years.

There may be more than one below-market lease in a property, a circumstance that would result in the creation of multiple leasehold estates, all with different lease terms and, therefore, different potential buyers. Some textbooks present methods of valuing leased fee and leasehold interests that assume the sum of the leased fee interest and the leasehold interest equals the fee simple interest. However, one must be careful when making this assumption.

CASH-FLOW FORECASTING WITH EXISTING LEASES

The first step in estimating the market value of a leased fee interest is to prepare a cash-flow forecast that considers the impact of any leases. The existing leases may affect the income, operating expenses, holding period selected and resale forecast. As when forecasting cash flows representing the fee simple interest, appraisers must consider all factors affected by a lease agreement, including occupancy, tenant turnover at the expiration of the lease, renewal options and expense treatment, and must consider all relevant market factors when estimating leased fee cash flows.

Even when estimating the value of a leased fee estate, the appraiser begins by considering market conditions and market rental rates that would apply for evaluation of a fee simple estate. This provides the appraiser with a benchmark with which to compare the contractual lease terms. The appraiser must then read and consider the contractual arrangements in each lease. The degree of difference between the existing contractual agreement and other typical market lease arrangements may have a significant impact on the most logical approach to forecasting the lease income. For example, a renewal option with payments that appear to be significantly below projected market rates is much more likely to be exercised than one with an option requiring payments higher than current market rates.

THE LEASE AGREEMENT

The basic lease instrument contains the following elements and provisions:

- date of agreement and parties to the lease;
- description of the leased premises;
- uses allowed for the property;
- commencement date and length of time of the lease;
- payment amount or method of calculation of rent;
- responsibility for expenses:
    —property taxes,
    —insurance,
    —utilities,
    —janitorial and maintenance and
    —management;
- method of handling of delinquent payments;
- records and books of account;
- alteration or improvement restrictions;
- restrictions on the operation of the tenant's business;
- restrictions on assignment or subletting;
- use of common areas and facilities;
- responsibility for maintenance of tenant space;
- conditions for surrender of premises;
- rules and regulations;
- liability insurance;
- indemnification of landlord;
- government regulations;

- remedies in the event of total or partial destruction;
- rights in the event of condemnation;
- right of entry;
- responsibility for legal expense;
- statement that the lease represents the entire agreement;
- requirements for any notices;
- future options in the lease; and
- subordination and partial invalidity of the lease.

The appraiser must read each lease agreement in detail and be aware of the common provisions. The following sections consist of brief discussions of some of the key provisions.

Date of Agreement and Parties to the Lease

The *date of agreement* is a key consideration in estimating the income to be collected under a lease. The key dates are the date of execution of the lease, the date the rental payments begin, the date the lease expires, the date of any renewal options and the date of notice. Additionally, an appraiser should identify the *parties to the lease* in order to ascertain whether the transaction is arm's length. A non-arm's length lease is not usually considered in estimating the value of a leased fee interest because the owner could conceivably cancel the lease before selling the property.

Description of the Leased Premises and Uses Allowed for the Property

The leased premises must be legally described and the use identified for the lease to be enforceable. Care should be taken to ensure that the description of the leased premises matches the space being occupied. Failure to describe accurately the property being leased may result in cancellation of the lease.

Commencement Date and Length of Time of the Lease

When making projections of rental income, the starting and ending dates of each lease must be considered. When leases expire, the appraiser must make an assumption about how that space will be leased in the future. The income expected from lease renewals can be quite different from that expected during the current lease term.

Payment Amount or Method of Calculation of Rent

Either the rental amount or the method of calculating the rental payment under the current terms and option periods must be clearly defined. As indicated in earlier chapters, market rent is the typical rent for a tenant space under current market conditions. There are other terms used to identify rent paid under a lease agreement.

- *Contract rent* is the actual rental payment specified in a lease. Contract rent may be greater than, less than or equal to economic rent and/or market rent.
- *Percentage rent* is a type of rent that is based on a percent of sales from the property, usually associated with a guaranteed base rent.
- *Overage rent* is rent paid in addition to a fixed base rent; it is usually based on a variable figure, such as a percent of sales or an index.
- *Excess rent* is the amount by which contract rent exceeds market rent because of unfavorable lease terms. The additional rent could be a result of market changes, sales overage clauses, and/or poor negotiating skills on the part of the tenant.

Contract rent can include fixed payments (either level or with gradual changes) or payments that vary based on changes in a specific *price index* such as the Consumer Price Index. The perceived investment risk associated with a leased fee cash-flow forecast may be affected by the contract rent provisions. A lease with a fixed rental payment would typically be a riskier arrangement for a property owner than rental payments that provided for rental increases based on changes in an index.

Responsibility for Expenses

All leases specifically identify the party responsible for paying for building operating expenses. If all operating expenses are paid by the landlord, the lease is referred to as a *gross lease.* If all the operating expenses (except, possibly, for management fees) are paid by the tenant, the lease is referred to as an *absolute net lease.* If responsibility for expenses is shared by the tenant and the landlord, the lease is referred to as a *net lease.* The degree of "netness" of a lease depends on the proportion of operating expenses paid by the tenant. Historically, a net lease meant that the tenant paid for property taxes, insurance and exterior maintenance. The term "net net net lease" or "triple net lease" was sometimes used to refer to each of these expense items that were net. In today's market, however, there is no obvious set pattern of expense treatment for specific property types. It is vital, therefore, that an appraiser actually identify the method of expense treatment in every lease affecting a property. It is likely that the method of expense treatment may vary for different tenants in the same building. In some instances, a portion or all of an operating expense is "passed through" to a tenant. The amount of the *expense passthrough* could be based on a pro rata share of space leased or be based on an increase in an expense over a base level. Following is an example of an expense passthrough.

Example

Tenant name	ABC Bank
% Net rental area occupied	20%
Property tax base amount (1985 expense)	$22,500
Current property tax amount (1990 expense)	$28,600

Expense stop: Pro rata share of property taxes above 1985 levels.

Passthrough Calculation

1990 Expense		*1985 Base*		*Excess*
$28,600	−	$22,500	=	$6,100

Excess		*% Occupied*		*Passthrough*
$6,100	×	0.20	=	$1,220

Remaining Lease Provisions

The remaining provisions listed address specific issues such as the ability to alter or sublet the space; remedies in case of condemnation, bankruptcy or destruction of the premises; and rules pertaining to the use of the property. These provisions do not usually have a direct impact on the cash-flow forecast but are vitally important should a controversy arise between tenant and landlord. It is important for an appraiser to know whether any of the provisions of a lease are being disputed or litigated. Many of these issues are legal in nature, and an appraiser should never attempt to practice law. If an issue arises that an appraiser cannot answer, outside professional advice should be sought.

NET OPERATING INCOME FORECASTS

Forecasting net operating income (NOI) for a leased fee interest may be simple or may be one of the most complicated and time-consuming tasks an appraiser can undertake. The net income from a single tenant building subject to a long-term, absolute net fixed payment lease would be the contract income less a minor adjustment for management fees. Conversely, an NOI forecast for a multitenant office building with a variety of indexed leases with varying expiration dates, expense passthroughs and multiple renewal options requires making judgments and performing mathematical calculations for numerous variables. Ultimately, the forecast should represent the appraiser's best judgment, given current market conditions and the existing leases.

The starting point of any forecast begins with determination of the contractual rent for each leased space. If unleased space exists, the appraiser must consider whether that space will eventually be leased. This involves making an assumption about what rate the space will lease for and how long it will take for the space to be absorbed by the market.

The vacancy and credit loss allowances should be forecast after consideration of the impact of the leases. If a property is subject to long-term leases covering 100 percent of the tenant space, it would appear logical to assume no or below-market vacancy during the term of the lease. Again, it is important to remember that the leased fee cash-flow forecast should theoretically reflect the expectations of the typical investor for the property type being appraised.

Income from sources other than space rentals may be considered in the NOI forecast. This forecast could be affected by a contractual arrangement (radio tower rent on the top of a high-rise building, for example) that may not equal market rent for the income source. In estimating other income in this instance, the actual contractual income rather than market income should be included in the income forecast for the leased fee interest.

Finally, the operating expenses are deducted from the income each year to arrive at each year's NOI. The operating expenses must be adjusted for the impact of expense-stop (passthrough) provisions in the leases. Expense passthrough income may be reported directly as income or as an offset to expenses. In either case, the net effect should be the same. Total annual fixed expenses such as property tax and insurance are typically affected little by existing leases. Total annual charges for some variable expenses such as management fees, however, can vary significantly from property to property if they are a function of collected income. The appraiser must recognize this and consider the relationship between incomes and expenses in a leased fee analysis.

RESALE PROCEEDS FORECAST

The value of a leased fee estate includes the rights to cash flow from sale of the property at the end of the investment holding period. The estimated value of the reversion may or may not be the same as would be expected for a fee simple estate, depending on whether all existing leases have expired by the end of the investment holding period. Recall that the following three methods were discussed to estimate the sales price of a fee simple estate:

1. actual dollar forecast;
2. change in value over the holding period; and
3. using a terminal capitalization rate.

Estimating the resale price (reversion) for a leased fee estate can be a more difficult task because the NOI is affected by existing leases. This could mean that the percentage change in the NOI over time for the leased fee estate may be significantly different than what the expected change in NOI would be for a fee simple estate. For example, consider the following projections:

Percentage Change in NOI

Year	1	2	3	4	5	% Change
Market NOI	$100,000	$105,000	$110,000	$115,000	$120,000	+20%
Leased fee NOI*	75,000	75,000	90,000	105,000	120,000	+60%

*In this instance, the first-year leased fee NOI is well below the $100,000 market estimate because of a series of below-market leases. By year 5, however, all of the leases have expired and the NOI is equal to market levels.

In this case, the leased fee NOI increased by 60 percent, whereas the market NOI increased by only 20 percent. The leased fee NOI increased at a greater percentage rate because of the assumption that leases were renewed at the higher market rate.[1]

It is important for the appraiser to recognize that in cases where there is a significant change in NOI because of lease renewals, the change in the value of the leased fee estate over the same time period may not be nearly as great. To understand why this is the case, we must consider two factors:

1. The value of the leased fee estate depends on both the NOI from the existing leases and the proceeds from resale of the property at the end of the holding period.
2. The resale price of the property at the end of the holding period depends on the expected NOI in the years after the property is sold.

If most or all of the leases have been renewed at the market rental rate by the time the property is sold, then the estimated value of the reversion may be virtually the same as the estimated value for a fee simple estate would have been. Thus, although the NOI for the leased fee estate may be significantly lower than that of a fee simple estate over the investment holding period, the value of the leased fee estate may not be affected nearly as much because of the contribution of the resale proceeds to the total value of the leased fee estate.

In the above example, suppose we want to estimate the value of the property at the end of a 4-year holding period by applying a terminal capitalization rate to the NOI for year 5.[2] Using a 10 percent terminal capitalization rate, we have:

Year	NOI	Terminal Cap Rate	Estimated Resale
5	$120,000	0.10	$1,200,000

The estimated reversion is $1.2 million. Because all existing leases have been renewed at the market rate by year 5, this value is the same as it would have been for a fee simple estate. Now consider the value of the leased fee estate for the 4-year holding period by discounting the leased fee NOI and reversion estimate calculated above. If the appropriate discount rate is 15 percent, the value of the leased fee estate is as follows:

Estimated Value of Leased Fee Estate

Year	1	2	3	4
Cash flow	$75,000	$75,000	$90,000	$1,305,000*
Discount rate (15%)	0.86957	0.75614	0.65752	0.57175
Present value†	$65,218	$56,711	$59,177	$746,134
Total present value	$927,240			

*Includes the reversion.
†At a 15% discount rate.

Now consider the value of the fee simple estate, using the same 15 percent discount rate:[3]

Estimated Value of Fee Simple Estate

Year	1	2	3	4
Cash flow	$100,000	$105,000	$110,000	$1,315,000*
Discount rate (15%)	0.86957	0.75614	0.65752	0.57175
Present value†	$86,957	$79,395	$72,327	$751,851
Total present value	$990,530			

*Includes the reversion.
†At a 15% discount rate. Assumed to be the same as for the fee simple estate.

Note that the impact of the below-market leases on the value of the leased fee estate is not as great as the impact on the NOI. Whereas the NOI for the leased fee estate increased by 60 percent from the end of year 1 to the end of year 5, the value of the leased fee estate increased by slightly less than 30 percent from the beginning of year 1 to the beginning of year 5 (end of year 4 when sold). In contrast, NOI and value for the fee simple estate both increased by about 20 percent over the same period.[4]

In the above example, the terminal capitalization rate for the leased fee estate was assumed to be the same as that of a fee simple estate. This was based on the assumption that all leases had expired. If some of the leases had not expired by the end of the holding period, the terminal capitalization rate would have to be adjusted accordingly. For example, suppose that in the previous example one of the leases would not expire until after year 5, making the leased fee NOI lower than the fee simple NOI in year 5 by $5,000. If the same terminal capitalization rate of 10 percent were used, the estimated reversion would be lower by $50,000.[5] This would not be correct: It would be analogous to assuming that the $5,000 loss in income would have a permanent impact on value, rather than an impact for only 1 year. Clearly, the effect of $5,000 less income for 1 year cannot exceed $5,000! A slightly lower terminal capitalization rate could be used to reflect the $5,000 increase in the leased fee NOI after year 5 because of the lease renewal.[6] Because the increase in NOI due to the lease renewal is for 1 year only, the impact on the terminal capitalization rate would not be great, but it clearly must be considered.

It is obviously easier to project the reversion if we can select a holding period that extends beyond the expiration of the last lease. If it is not possible to select such a holding period, extreme care should be taken when estimating the reversion. The reversion at that time should reflect the present value of the future benefits to be received by the next buyer after consideration of the remaining lease(s) at that point.

Whichever method is used to forecast the reversion, the appraiser should test the reasonableness of the estimate by comparing the implied change in NOI, value and capitalization rates to ensure that the relationships are logical, given current and expected market conditions.

LEASED FEE DISCOUNT (YIELD) RATE

The leased fee discount rate is the interest rate that discounts all expected future leased fee cash flows to a present value equal to the present value of the leased fee interest. The leased fee discount rate can be higher, lower, or equal to the fee simple property discount rate, depending on the circumstances. The relative position of the leased fee discount rate compared with the fee simple property discount rate depends on the relationship of risk in the two interests. It is possible that because of the excellent credit of a building tenant, a strong below-market lease and/or a lease with built-in risk protection such as a CPI adjustment and expense stops, the leased fee discount rate logically could be below the property discount rate. When preparing the leased fee cash-flow forecasts, the appraiser should consider the risk implications involved in the assumptions selected and should translate these judgments into relative changes in the ultimate leased fee discount rate selected to estimate leased fee value.

LEASED FEE CASH-FLOW FORECAST—A CASE STUDY

Following are assumptions for a leased fee cash-flow forecast for an office building. The building and expense assumptions are the same as those used in examples in chapters 7 and 9, except that it is now assumed that three tenants have existing leases in the building.

Example

Given:

Gross building area	24,000 square feet (sq. ft.)
Net building area	20,000 sq. ft.

Tenant	Leased Area	Current Annual Rent	Contract Rent per sq. ft.	Remaining Term	Market Rent per sq. ft.	Comments
C&B Bank	10,000 sq. ft.	$100,000	$10.00	4 yrs.	$15.00	Tax stop above $0.20 per sq. ft.
Valley Mortage	6,000 sq. ft.	69,000	11.50	1 yr.	15.00	2-year option @ $13.00 per sq. ft.
Apex Insurance	4,000 sq. ft.	48,000	12.00	3 yrs.	15.00	2% annual increase

Assumptions:

Market rent	Increasing by 4% per year.
Vacancy	6% of released space; 0 during term of existing leases.
Management	5% of effective gross income.
Property tax	$11,900; level for 3 years, increasing to $15,000 in years 4 and 5.
Insurance	$0.20 per sq. ft. net rentable area, increasing by 3% per year.
Utilities	$1.25 per sq. ft. of gross area, increasing by 5% per year.
Janitorial	$0.90 per sq. ft. of net rentable area, increasing by 4% per year.
Maintenance	$4,000, increasing by 3% per year.

The projected cash flows based on the above assumptions are as follows:

Example

Income and Expense Forecast

Year	1	2	3	4	5
Income:					
C&B Bank	$100,000	$100,000	$100,000	$100,000	$175,479
Valley Mortgage	69,000	78,000	78,000	101,238	105,287
Apex Insurance	48,000	48,960	49,939	67,492	70,192
Total	$217,000	$226,960	$227,939	$268,730	$350,958
Vacancy @ 6%	– 0	– 0	– 0	– 10,124	– 21,057
Effective gross income	$217,000	$226,960	$227,939	$258,606	$329,901
Expenses:					
Management	$ 10,850	$ 11,348	$ 11,397	$ 12,930	$ 16,495
Property tax	11,900	11,900	11,900	15,000	15,000
Insurance	4,000	4,120	4,244	4,371	4,502
Utilities	30,000	31,500	33,075	34,729	36,465
Janitorial	18,000	18,720	19,469	20,248	21,057
Maintenance	4,000	4,120	4,244	4,371	4,502
Total expenses	$ 78,750	$ 81,708	$ 84,329	$ 91,649	$ 98,021
Passthroughs	3,950*	3,950*	3,950*	5,500	0
NOI	$142,200	$149,202	$147,560	$172,457	$231,880

*$11,900/20,000 sq. ft. = $0.595 − $0.20 = $0.395 × 10,000 sq. ft. = $3,950

The NOI calculated above begins at $142,200 in year 1 and increases to $231,880 in year 5. By year 5, all existing leases have expired. Once a lease expired, rental rates were increased to the implied market rent at that time, and the vacancy allowance was based on 6 percent of this market income. Before estimating the leased fee value we analyze the cash flows for the fee simple value estimate (based on market rents) in the following section. Before estimating the leased fee value we analyze the cash flows for the fee simple value estimate (based on market rents) in the following section.

FEE SIMPLE VALUE ESTIMATE

Following is a review of the fee simple cash-flow assumptions and the property value estimates found in chapter 7. The value of the fee simple interest is as follows:

Example

Assumptions:

Market rent	$15.00 per sq. ft.
Income	Increasing 4% per year for 5 years.
Vacancy	Level at 6% per year.
Management	5% of effective gross income.
Property tax	$11,900 level for 3 years, increasing to $15,000 in years 4, 5 and 6.
Insurance	$0.20 per sq. ft. of net rentable area, increasing by 3% per year.
Utilities	$1.25 per sq. ft. of gross area, increasing by 5% per year.
Janitorial	$0.90 per sq. ft. of net rentable area, increasing by 4% per year.
Maintenance	$4,000 per year increasing by 3% per year.

Year	1	2	3	4	5	6
Potential gross income	$300,000	$312,000	$324,480	$337,459	$350,958	$364,996
Vacancy @ 6%	− 18,000	− 18,720	− 19,469	− 20,248	− 21,057	− 21,900
EGI	$282,000	$293,280	$305,011	$317,211	$329,901	$343,096
Management	$ 14,100	$ 14,664	$ 15,251	$ 15,861	$ 16,495	$ 17,155
Property tax	11,900	11,900	11,900	15,000	15,000	15,000
Insurance	4,000	4,120	4,244	4,371	4,502	4,657
Utilities	30,000	31,500	33,075	34,729	36,465	38,288
Janitorial	18,000	18,720	19,469	20,248	21,057	21,899
Maintenance	4,000	4,120	4,244	4,371	4,502	4,637
Total expenses	$ 82,000	$ 85,024	$ 88,183	$ 94,580	$ 98,021	$101,616
NOI	$200,000	$208,256	$216,828	$222,631	$231,880	$241,480

The fee simple value using a 12 percent property discount rate and an estimated resale price of $2,414,800 was shown in chapter 7 to be as follows:[7]

Example

Estimated year-6 NOI = $241,480

Resale = NOI (sixth year)$/R_T$

= $241,480/0.10

= $2,414,800

Year	Cash Flow		Present Value Factor @ 12%		Present Value
1	$ 200,000	×	0.892857	=	$ 178,571
2	208,256	×	0.797194	=	166,020
3	216,828	×	0.711780	=	154,334
4	222,631	×	0.635518	=	141,486
5	231,880	×	0.567427	=	131,575
5 (resale)	2,414,800	×	0.567427	=	1,370,223
Total present value					$2,142,209

LEASED FEE VALUE ESTIMATE

The leased fee value estimate can now be found by discounting the leased fee NOI, and resale can be forecast by the leased fee discount rate. Assuming that all leases have expired after the 5-year holding period, the same resale price can be used that was used when estimating the fee simple value, as shown above.

The value found by assuming the leased fee discount rate is 12 percent.

Year	Cash Flow		Present Value Factor @ 12%		Present Value
1	$ 142,200	×	0.892857	=	$ 126,964
2	149,202	×	0.797194	=	118,943
3	147,560	×	0.711780	=	105,030
4	172,456	×	0.635518	=	109,599
5	231,880	×	0.567427	=	131,575
5 (resale)	2,414,800	×	0.567427	=	1,370,223
Total present value					$1,962,334

Under the above assumptions, the leased fee value estimate is $1,962,334. The implied overall capitalization rate (in this case, the leased fee capitalization rate) is 7.25 percent ($142,200/$1,962,334), and the implied change in value over the holding period is 23.06 percent ($2,414,800/$1,962,334 − 1).

If the appraiser believes the leased fee investment would be less risky because of the tenant mix and/or the level of market rents and, therefore, selected a leased fee discount rate lower than the property discount rate of 12 percent, say 11 percent, the leased fee value estimate would be as follows:

Year	Cash Flow		Present Value Factor @ 11%		Present Value
1	$ 142,200	×	0.900901	=	$ 128,108
2	149,202	×	0.811622	=	121,096
3	147,560	×	0.731191	=	107,895
4	172,457	×	0.658731	=	113,602
5	231,880	×	0.593451	=	137,609
5 (resale)	2,414,800	×	0.593451	=	1,433,065
Total present value					$2,041,375

Assuming a leased fee discount rate of 11 percent, the leased fee value estimate is $2,041,375. The reduction in the discount rate has resulted in a value estimate of $79,041, or about 4 percent higher. The best method of testing which leased fee discount rate to use is to analyze sales of comparable leased fee interests and examine the discount rate and income pattern change relationships implied by the price paid for properties, as demonstrated in the previous rate analysis example.

MARKET RENT EQUIVALENCY ADJUSTMENT

In the preceding tables the value of the fee simple interest is $2,142,209 and the value of the leased fee interest, assuming a 12 percent leased fee discount rate, is $1,962,334; assuming an 11 percent leased fee discount rate, the value is $2,041,375. The difference in value between each of these numbers is:

	Leased Fee Discount Rate	
	11%	*12%*
Fee simple interest	$2,142,209	$2,142,209
Leased fee interest	− 2,041,375	− 1,962,334
Difference	$ 100,834	$ 179,875

The bottom line represents the differences between the value of the fee simple ownership interest and the leased fee ownership interest for both rates. The conclusion about which of the amounts is the best estimate of the difference depends on the appraiser's assessment of current market conditions and the tenant profile. The chosen amount represents the difference between the property interests appraised and is referred to as the *market rent equivalency adjustment*. It is the value loss attributable to the existing leases. It represents the value of the property without consideration of the leases less the value of the property to a typical investor after consideration of the leases.

Some textbooks advocate estimating the impact of the leases by discounting the NOI difference by a rate of return and deducting this amount from the fee simple interests. In this case, the NOI difference is as follows:

Year	1	2	3	4
Fee simple NOI	$200,000	$208,256	$216,828	$222,631
Leased fee NOI	− 142,200	− 149,202	− 147,560	− 172,457
Rent difference	$ 57,800	$ 59,054	$ 69,268	$ 50,174

The leases expire in 4 years, so only 4 years were used in the above analysis. Discounting the above cash flows at 12 percent results in a present value of $179,875. This is the same as the difference in the value of the fee simple estate and leased fee estate shown above, if the leased fee estate and fee simple estate are both valued at a 12 percent discount rate. However, if the leased fee estate and fee simple estate are not valued using the same discount rate, discounting the difference in rents, as illustrated above, will not give the correct difference in value. For example, when the leased fee estate was valued at an 11 percent discount rate, the difference in value between the leased fee estate and the fee simple estate was $100,834. To obtain the same answer by discounting, the NOI difference would require a discount rate in excess of 100 percent! The best approach to estimating the market rent equivalency adjustment, therefore, is to estimate the value of each interest by either the discount cash flow approach or yield capitalization and find the difference between the two.

As a final comment, it should be noted that the market rent equivalency adjustment discussed above represents a difference between the value of the leased fee estate and fee simple estate. This adjustment is necessary when using the cost approach to estimate the value of a leased fee estate because without this adjustment, the value arrived at with the cost approach represents the value of a fee simple estate. However, this difference in value does not necessarily represent the value of the leasehold estate. As discussed earlier, the value of the leased fee estate plus the value of the leasehold estate do not necessarily have to add to the value of the fee simple estate. To value the leasehold estate, we take the perspective of a typical tenant who is concerned with the rent savings as discussed next.

LEASEHOLD VALUE ESTIMATE

The leasehold interest is the ownership interest of a lessee or tenant. The value of any leasehold interest is the leasehold estate and is the present value of any net benefits to another tenant. From a cash-flow standpoint, the benefits arise when the effective contract rental payments are less than current market rental rates for the space. It is possible for a property to be attractive to another tenant for reasons other than potential rental savings, but consideration of these factors is beyond the scope of this book.

As mentioned earlier, the cash flows arise from effective rental savings throughout the term of a lease. To translate these future benefits into a present value, each must be discounted by an interest rate. The interest rate used represents the "typical" return requirement for a "typical" purchaser of the interest and is referred to as the "leasehold discount rate."

Following is an example showing the calculation of a leasehold value, assuming a 5-year lease.

Example

Market Rent Estimate for Term of Lease

Market rent for 20,000 square feet is $15 per square foot, increasing by 4 percent per year. The contract rent equals $225,000 per year for 5 years. The value of the leasehold estate, assuming a 12 percent leasehold discount rate, is as follows:

Year	Market Rent		Contract Rent		Difference		Present Value @ 12%		Present Value
1	$300,000	–	$225,000	=	$ 75,000	×	0.8929	=	$ 66,967
2	312,000	–	225,000	=	87,000	×	0.7972	=	69,356
3	324,480	–	225,000	=	99,480	×	0.7118	=	70,810
4	337,459	–	225,000	=	112,459	×	0.6355	=	71,468
5	350,958	–	225,000	=	125,958	×	0.5674	=	71,469
Value of leasehold									$350,070

In this case, the present value of the rent savings is $350,070, which represents the value of the leasehold estate.

SUPPORTING LEASEHOLD DISCOUNT RATES

The best source of discount rates is sales of leasehold interests. The rate is found by finding the internal rate of return that discounts the rental benefits over the term of the lease to a present value equal to the price paid for the leasehold. For example, suppose a lease is purchased by Tenant B from

Tenant A for $225,000. The lease is for 10 more years and the contract rent is $175,000 for each of those 10 years. The current market rent for the space is $200,000, and it is anticipated that market rent will increase by 2 percent each year. We see that the implied leasehold discount rate is slightly above 12 percent, as shown below.

Year	Market Rent		Contract Rent		Rental Savings
0					($225,000)
1	$200,000	–	$175,000	=	25,000
2	204,000	–	175,000	=	29,000
3	208,080	–	175,000	=	33,080
4	212,242	–	175,000	=	37,242
5	216,486	–	175,000	=	41,486
6	220,816	–	175,000	=	45,816
7	225,232	–	175,000	=	50,232
8	229,737	–	175,000	=	54,737
9	234,332	–	175,000	=	59,332
10	239,019	–	175,000	=	64,019

Leasehold discount rate = 0.1211, or 12.11%

SUMMARY

Many types of income property are purchased subject to existing leases. Thus, the investor is purchasing a leased fee estate, not a fee simple estate. To estimate the value of the leased fee interest, the appraiser must consider how the terms of the existing leases will affect the projected net operating income (NOI) and resale price of the property.

This chapter discussed typical lease provisions that can affect the projected NOI and discussed how the NOI and resale price can be estimated for a leased fee estate. The relationship between the discount rate for leased fee estates versus fee simple estates was shown to depend on the relative riskiness of each estate.

The relationship between the value of the leased fee estate and fee simple estate is referred to as a "market rent equivalency adjustment." It was emphasized that this difference in the value between the two estates does not necessarily represent the value of the leasehold estate, because the typical tenant who would purchase an interest in a leasehold estate may have a different investment perspective. The value of a leasehold estate depends on the rent savings associated with that estate. The value of these rent savings may or may not be equivalent to the difference in value between the leased fee estate and fee simple estate.

KEY TERMS

absolute net lease

contract rent

date of agreement

excess rent

expense passthrough

fee simple interest

gross lease

leased fee interest

leasehold interest

market rent equivalency
  adjustment

net lease

overage rent

parties to the lease

percentage rent

price index

QUESTIONS

1. How do existing leases affect the estimated NOI for a property?
2. Should the value of a fee simple estate be equal to the sum of the values of the leased fee estate and the leasehold estate?
3. Do you think the same discount rate should be used to estimate the value of the fee simple estate and that of the leased fee estate?
4. What is meant by a market rent equivalency adjustment?
5. What lease provisions do you think would have the greatest impact on the estimated NOI?
6. What is the difference between overage rent and excess rent? How do you think each of these kinds of rent affects the riskiness of a leased fee estate?
7. What is meant by a "net" lease? What expenses are typically net?
8. What is an expense passthrough? How do you think the existence of expense passthroughs affects the riskiness of the leased fee estate?
9. Why is it desirable to use an investment projection period that extends beyond the term of existing leases?
10. Due to existing leases, a property is projected to have NOI of $90,000 per year for each of the next 5 years. All of the leases will have expired at the end of the 5 years. If the property were not encumbered by existing leases, the appraiser estimates that the NOI would be $100,000 for the first year and increase by 3 percent each year over a projected holding period of 5 years.
    a. Estimate the value of the fee simple estate by discounting the cash flows at a 12 percent discount rate. Assume that the resale price at the end of the fifth year can be estimated by applying a 9 percent terminal capitalization rate to the sixth-year NOI.
    b. Estimate the value of the leased fee estate by discounting the appropriate cash flows at an 11 percent discount rate.
    c. What does the difference in the answers for parts A and B represent?

END NOTES

1. If market rents are falling and existing leases are above market rental rates, the NOI could decrease at a much greater rate than the market rate.

2. Recall that we apply the terminal capitalization rate to the NOI 1 year after the end of the holding period because this is the NOI to the next owner.

3. For simplicity the discount rate for the leased fee estate and fee simple estate is assumed to be the same. They would differ if there were a difference in the riskiness associated with investing in each estate.

4. For fee simple estates, it is logical that NOI and value change at approximately the same rate over time.

5. $5,000/0.10 = $50,000.

6. Recall that the capitalization rate depends on the expected change in NOI. Thus an additional increase in NOI due to lease renewals implies a lower terminal capitalization rate.

7. Refer to chapter 9 to review the assumptions. The resale price was estimated by applying a terminal capitalization rate to an estimate of the year-6 NOI.

CHAPTER 13

Investment Measures with Mortgage Financing

IMPACT OF FINANCING ON REAL ESTATE CASH-FLOW FORECASTS

In the 1960s, mortgage financing became an important factor in many real estate transactions. Currently, a multitude of financing options are available to an investor. When an investor secures a mortgage loan for an income-producing property, the investor becomes the owner of the *equity interest* and the lender has a *mortgage interest.* In essence, the two have become partners in the real estate. Under the terms of a mortgage loan agreement, for advancing a portion of the funds to finance the purchase, the lender receives periodic payments over a specified time period known as the *amortization period.* The periodic loan payments include provisions for a complete return of the principal balance (return *of* capital), as well as a competitive profit (return *on* capital) to the lender. Generally, the lender has first right to receive the payments required by the loan contract and is in what is typically referred to as first position. Should the equity investor fail to meet the required payment schedule, the investor will ultimately lose the property and, therefore, the equity investment. Since the lender is in first position, the mortgage position usually involves less risk. This suggests that the expected profit level rate (mortgage interest rate) for the lender would be less than the equity investor's profit rate (*equity yield rate*).

An owner has, basically, two motives when financing a real estate purchase with a mortgage. The first is to secure the level of funds needed to purchase the property, and the second is to increase the equity profits through the use of financial leverage. The concept of financial leverage will be discussed later in this chapter.

Real estate cash flows are affected because the periodic debt payments are deducted from each year's forecast net operating income (NOI) and any remaining loan balance is deducted from the resale proceeds. Once the mortgage payments have been deducted, the resulting annual cash flows are referred to as the *before-tax cash flows (BTCF)* from operations. In appraisal literature, these cash flows have also been referred to as the *equity dividend* or *cash throwoff (CTO)*. The net reversion after deducting any remaining loan balance is referred to as the "before-tax cash flow from reversion."

CALCULATION OF INVESTMENT RETURNS, ASSUMING FINANCING

The typical investment measures calculated in chapter 6, including payback, capitalization rates, internal rates of return, net present value, profitability index and adjusted rates of return, can also be calculated for the equity investor. The same set of cash flows used in chapter 6 to calculate investment measures on an unleveraged basis will be used to calculate the leveraged return, except that a $750,000 loan at a 10 percent interest rate for 25 years will be assumed.

Example

Given:

Value	$1,000,000
Loan amount	$750,000
Mortgage interest rate	10%
Amortization period	25 Years (Monthly)
Equity value	$250,000
Resale price	$1,200,000 (10 Years)

Year	1	2	3	4	5
NOI	$100,000	$102,000	$104,000	$106,000	$108,000
Annual debt service	− 81,783	− 81,783	− 81,783	− 81,783	− 81,783
BTCF	$ 18,217	$ 20,217	$ 22,217	$ 24,217	$ 26,217

Year	6	7	8	9	10
NOI	$110,000	$112,000	$114,000	$116,000	$118,000
Annual debt service	− 81,783	− 81,783	− 81,783	− 81,783	− 81,783
BTCF	$ 28,217	$ 30,217	$ 32,217	$ 34,217	$ 36,217

Resale price	
(reversion)	$1,200,000
Loan balance	− 634,210
BTCF from reversion	$ 565,790

NOTE: In this instance, the mortgage capitalization rate (R_M), sometimes referred to as the mortgage constant, is 0.1090 ($81,783/$750,000).

Payback Period

Payback period is the length of time it takes an equity investor to regain the initial equity investment. The following demonstrates how payback is calculated for the sample data.

Equity Investment = $250,000

Year	Before-Tax Cash Flow	Cumulative Total Cash Flow
1	$18,217	$ 18,217
2	20,217	38,434
3	22,217	60,651
4	24,217	84,868
5	26,217	111,085
6	28,217	139,302
7	30,217	169,519
8	32,217	201,736
9	34,217	235,953
10	36,217	272,170

In this instance, payback did not occur until year 10. That is, it took 10 years of BTCF from operations to receive sufficient cash flow to return the original equity investment.[1] The weakness of using payback as an investment measure is that it ignores the time value of money.

Equity Capitalization Rate

The *equity capitalization rate* (R_E), frequently referred to as the *equity dividend rate*, is calculated by dividing the first-year BTCF by the equity value. Following is the R_E calculation using the sample data.

$$R_E = \text{BTCF}/V_E = \$18,217/\$250,000 = 0.0729, \text{ or } 7.29\%$$

where V_E represents equity value.

The equity capitalization rate does not explicitly address profitability and is simply a benchmark relationship used to compare real estate sales. If two real estate properties are highly comparable, the appraiser could expect their equity dividend rates to be similar. One must be very careful, however, if financing of the properties differs. For example, equity dividend rates can and should in theory differ for different loan-to-value ratios. As we will see later, the higher the loan-to-value ratio, the greater the risk.

Before-Tax Equity Yield Rate

The *before-tax equity yield rate* or "equity discount rate" is the internal rate of return to the equity value calculated by finding the interest rate that discounts the expected BTCF and the equity proceeds from resale to a value equal to the original equity investment. The symbol used to represent the before-tax equity yield rate is Y_E. Following is the before-tax Y_E calculation using the sample data.

Year	BTCF
0	($250,000)
1	18,217
2	20,217
3	22,217
4	24,217
5	26,217
6	28,217
7	30,217
8	32,217
9	34,217
10*	602,007

$$\text{IRR} = Y_E = 0.1590, \text{ or } 15.9\%$$

*Year 10 BTCF and resale proceeds.

The yield rate in this instance is a measure of profitability for the equity investor. The before-tax Y_E of 15.90 percent is significantly higher than the property yield rate of 11.87 percent (from chapter 6). The increase in the yield rate is a result of positive leverage, which will be discussed in a later section of this chapter.

If two real estate properties are highly comparable, the appraiser could expect the before-tax equity yields to be similar. As with the equity capitalization rate, however, the before-tax yields may not be comparable if the financing structures are not similar. If, for example, the property was financed with a loan for $650,000 instead of $750,000 but at the same interest rate (10 percent) for the same time period (25 years) with monthly payments, the before-tax Y_E would be

---

Example

Given:

Value	$1,000,000
Loan amount	$650,000
Mortgage interest rate	10%
Amortization period	25 Years (Monthly)
Equity value	$350,000
Resale price	$1,200,000

Year	1	2	3	4	5
NOI	$100,000	$102,000	$104,000	$106,000	$108,000
Annual debt service	− 70,879	− 70,879	− 70,879	− 70,879	− 70,879
BTCF	$ 29,121	$ 31,121	$ 33,121	$ 35,121	$ 37,121

Year	6	7	8	9	10
NOI	$110,000	$112,000	$114,000	$116,000	$118,000
Annual debt service	− 70,879	− 70,879	− 70,879	− 70,879	− 70,879
BTCF	$ 39,121	$ 41,121	$ 43,121	$ 45,121	$ 47,121

Resale price	$1,200,000
Loan balance	− 549,649
Before-tax proceeds	$ 650,351

The before-tax Y_E, assuming a $650,000 loan, is calculated as follows:

Year	BTCF
0	($350,000)
1	29,121
2	31,121
3	33,121
4	35,121
5	37,121
6	39,121
7	41,121
8	43,121
9	45,121
10	697,472

$$\text{IRR} = Y_E = 0.1458, \text{ or } 14.6\%$$

By dropping the loan-to-value ratio from 75 percent to 65 percent, the before-tax Y_E for the same set of cash flows, interest rate and amortization structure dropped from 15.9 percent to 14.6 percent. It should be noted, however, that there is also less risk for the equity investor when less debt is used. This is discussed in chapter 16.

Net Present Value

The net present value (NPV) may be calculated using the equity cash flows. The NPV under these circumstances becomes the NPV for the equity investment. It is calculated by selecting a target rate of return, calculating the present values of the forecast before-tax cash flows and comparing the present value estimate with the initial equity investment. Following is an NPV calculation assuming a 15 percent target rate and using the sample data.

Year	BTCF		Present Value Factor @ 15%		Present Value
1	$ 18,217	×	0.869565	=	$ 15,841
2	20,217	×	0.756144	=	15,287
3	22,217	×	0.657516	=	14,608
4	24,217	×	0.571753	=	13,846
5	26,217	×	0.497177	=	13,034
6	28,217	×	0.432328	=	12,199
7	30,217	×	0.375937	=	11,360
8	32,217	×	0.326902	=	10,532
9	34,217	×	0.284262	=	9,727
10	602,007	×	0.247185	=	148,807
					$265,241

Total present value	$265,241
Less equity investment	− 250,000
NPV	$ 15,241

Once the present value is calculated, the NPV is found by subtracting the original value. If the NPV is greater than zero, the investment promises to provide a return in excess of 15 percent. If the net present value were negative, the expected return would be less than 15 percent and would be rejected. In the above example, the investor could invest an additional $15,241 of equity capital and still earn 15 percent. This assumes the amount of the loan would remain the same.

Differences in NPV could occur for the same reasons that differences in the yield rate could occur. In addition, the NPVs are not comparable for two similar properties if the equity investment required for each one is different.

Profitability Index

Conceptually, the *profitability index* approach and the NPV approach are basically the same. In each, future cash flows are discounted by a target rate of return and the total present value is compared to the initial investment. In calculating the profitability index, however, the initial equity value is divided into the total present value rather than subtracted from it, as shown below.

Total present value/Equity investment = $265,241/$250,000 = 1.061

The resulting ratio becomes the profitability index. An index greater than 1.00 indicates that the investment is expected to earn greater than a 15 percent return. If the index is less than 1.00, the investment is not forecast to earn a 15 percent annual return.

Adjusted Internal Rate of Return

As we have discussed, the *adjusted internal rate of return (AIRR)* approach is similar to the internal rate of return approach, except that it is assumed that future cash flows will be compounded forward at a typical investment rate. In chapter 8 we illustrated calculating the AIRR before considering financing. Following is an AIRR calculation, using a 12 percent reinvestment rate and the sample data we have been analyzing in this chapter.

Year	BTCF		Future Value Factor @ 12%		Future Value
1	$ 18,217	×	2.773079	=	$ 50,517
2	20,217	×	2.475963	=	50,057
3	22,217	×	2.210681	=	49,115
4	24,217	×	1.973823	=	47,800
5	26,217	×	1.762342	=	46,203
6	28,217	×	1.573519	=	44,400
7	30,217	×	1.404928	=	42,453
8	32,217	×	1.254400	=	40,413
9	34,217	×	1.120000	=	38,323
10	602,007	×	1.000000	=	602,007
Total future value					$1,011,288

$$\text{AIRR} = (\$1,011,288/\$250,000)^{1/10} - 1 = 0.1500, \text{ or } 15\%$$

In this instance, the AIRR, assuming reinvestment at 12 percent, is 15 percent, which is less than the before-tax equity yield or unadjusted internal rate of return (IRR) of 15.90 percent. The AIRR is an excellent measure of the potential profitability of an investment if the IRR is higher than an investor might expect to earn on the interim cash flows.

FINANCIAL LEVERAGE

Financial leverage is defined as the use of borrowed funds in the purchase of an investment. If the addition of the mortgage increases the return to the equity, the addition of the mortgage has resulted in *positive leverage.* If the addition of the mortgage decreases the return to the equity, the addition of the mortgage has resulted in *negative leverage.*

As shown earlier in this chapter, borrowing funds at an interest rate or mortgage yield rate (Y_M) that is below the property yield rate (Y_O) results in a positive impact on the before-tax equity yield rate (Y_E). In addition, generally the higher the loan-to-value ratio the higher the before-tax Y_E. This circumstance is referred to as "positive (or favorable) leverage" because the equity investor is able to increase the rate of return through borrowing funds. Should the mortgage interest rate, however, be higher than the property yield rate (Y_O), the before-tax Y_E will be lower than the Y_O, which would result in "negative (or unfavorable) leverage." The phenomenon of negative leverage is presented in the next example by using the sample data, except, in this case, the $750,000 mortgage is assumed to have a 12.5 percent interest rate for 25 years (monthly payments). The before-tax Y_E is calculated as follows:

Example

Given:

Value	=	$1,000,000
Loan amount	=	$750,000
Mortgage interest rate	=	12.5%
Amortization period	=	25 years (Monthly)
Equity value	=	$250,000
Resale price (10 Years)	=	$1,200,000

Year	1	2	3	4	5
NOI	$100,000	$102,000	$104,000	$106,000	$108,000
Annual debt service	− 98,132	− 98,132	− 98,132	− 98,132	− 98,132
BTCF	$ 1,868	$ 3,868	$ 5,868	$ 7,868	$ 9,868

Year	6	7	8	9	10
NOI	$110,000	$112,000	$114,000	$116,000	$118,000
Annual debt service	− 98,132	− 98,132	− 98,132	− 98,132	− 98,132
BTCF	$ 11,868	$ 13,868	$ 15,868	$ 17,868	$ 19,868

Resale price	$1,200,000
Loan balance	− 663,490
Before-tax proceeds	$ 536,510

Year	BTCF
0	($250,000)
1	1,868
2	3,868
3	5,868
4	7,868
5	9,868
6	11,868
7	13,868
8	15,868
9	17,868
10	$556,378

IRR = Y_E = 0.1066, or 10.66%

With the interest rate at 12.5 percent instead of 10 percent, the before-tax Y_E is only 10.7 percent, which is less than the 11.87 percent Y_O. By borrowing the money at an interest rate higher than the Y_O, the before-tax Y_E was negatively affected, an example of negative leverage. Normally we would expect positive leverage based on anticipated cash flows at the time the property is purchased. We expect the Y_E to be greater than the mortgage yield rate (Y_M) because of the additional risk incurred by the equity investor compared with the mortgage lender. Of course, it may turn out after the property is purchased that the equity investor does not earn the originally expected return.

Cash-Flow Leverage

The concept of positive and negative leverage can also be viewed on a first-year cash-flow basis alone. In essence, if the mortgage capitalization rate (R_M) is less than the overall rate (R_O), then positive leverage will result, and the equity dividend rate (R_E) will be greater than R_O. In periods of no inflation or deflation this would be the case. Caution should be exercised, however, when analyzing leverage on a first-year cash-flow basis only. Unfavorable leverage can occur on a cash-flow basis even though it is favorable over the holding period.

This was true for the first example using the sample data in this chapter. The overall yield rate (Y_O) of 11.87 percent exceeded the interest rate on the mortgage (Y_M) of 10 percent, which magnified the equity yield rate (Y_E) to 15.9 percent with a 75 percent loan-to-value ratio. Thus, there was favorable financial leverage based on yield rates. For this same example, the overall capitalization rate (R_O) is 10 percent, which is less than the mortgage constant (R_M) of 10.90 percent.* Recall that the equity dividend rate (R_E) calculated earlier for this sample data is 7.29 percent. Thus, there is negative leverage when viewed in terms of the effect of leverage on the equity dividend rate whereas there is positive leverage when viewed in terms of the effect of leverage on the equity yield rate.

Effect of Leverage on Equity Dividend Rate

The effect of leverage on the equity dividend rate can be shown as follows:

$$R_E = R_O + (R_O - R_M) \, M \, / \, (1-M)$$

where M is the loan-to-value ratio. Using the above example, we have

$$
\begin{aligned}
R_E \ &= \ 10 + (10 - 10.90) \times .75 \, / \, .25 \\
&= \ 10 - (.90 \times 3) \\
&= \ 10 - 2.70 \\
&= \ 7.30
\end{aligned}
$$

---

*Note that the mortgage constant is higher than the interest rate of 10 percent because the loan is amortized.

This is the same equity dividend rate as calculated earlier. (The difference from 7.29 percent is due to rounding.) The formula shown above makes it clear that R_O must exceed R_M for leverage to be positive and increase R_E. Furthermore, the effect of leverage increases as the loan-to-value ratio (M) increases.

Effect of Leverage on Equity Yield Rate

The effect of leverage on the equity yield rate Y_E can be *estimated* using a similar formula as follows:

$$Y_E = Y_O + (Y_O - Y_M) \, M \, / \, (1-M).$$

Note that in this case we use the mortgage interest rate Y_M, which is a yield rate rather than the loan constant that is a cash flow rate. Using the same example, we have

$$
\begin{aligned}
Y_E &= 11.87 + (11.87 - 10) \times .75 \, / \, .25 \\
&= 11.87 + (1.87 \times 3) \\
&= 17.48
\end{aligned}
$$

This is higher than the equity yield rate calculated earlier which was 15.9 percent. This is because the above formula uses the initial loan-to-value ratio (M) and assumes that the loan-to-value ratio (M) is constant over the investment holding period. This is not true when the loan is amortized and/or the property value changes. In the example above the loan balance decreases over a period of time and the property value increases over a period of time. Both of these factors result in a buildup of equity over the holding period that reduces the loan-to-value ratio each year. This is why the equity yield rate is overestimated when the above formula is used. The formula gives an exact answer if the loan is not amortized, i.e., interest only, and the property value does not change over the holding period. Even when this is not true, however, the formula is still useful in understanding the relationships between Y_O, Y_M and Y_E.

Figure 13-1 uses the sample data from the beginning of this chapter (loan at a 10 percent interest rate) where there is positive leverage to illustrate how the investor's return on equity (Y_E) increases with increasing amounts of leverage, i.e., higher loan to value ratios. In that example, the property value was assumed to increase from $1 million to $2 million over the ten-year holding period. But what if the property value does not actually increase? Suppose instead that the property value decreases to $800,000. Figure 13-2 shows what would happen to the investor's return on equity (Y_E) at different amounts of leverage if the property value decreases to $800,000. In this case there is negative financial leverage. The more the investor had borrowed, the lower his or her expected rate of return on equity. This illustrates the risk associated with the use of financial leverage. We don't know what will actually happen to the property value over a period of time. The investor may have expected the property value to increase to $1,200,000 and borrowed money based on the expectation of positive financial leverage. That is, if

FIGURE 13-1   Positive Leverage

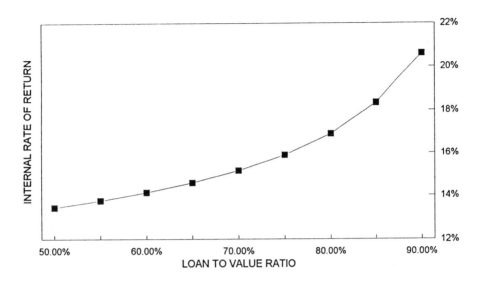

no money had been borrowed, the investor's expected return on equity would have been 11.87 percent whereas with a 75 percent loan, the expected return on equity would be 15.9 percent. If the property value actually declines to $800,000, however, the investor's actual rate of return would have been 9.47 percent if no debt had been used but it would be 8.06 percent with a 75 percent loan. Leverage works against the investor in the latter case. This is why the investor must expect a higher rate of return if he or she is going to use leverage to begin with when purchasing an investment. The expected return must consider the risk that the actual return may be higher or lower depending on what actually happens to market rental rates, vacancy rates, property values, etc. over the investment holding period. Chapter 14 illustrates how the use of financial leverage increases the variance of the investor's rate of return (risk analysis).

Summary of Leverage Relationships

We can summarize the leverage relationships discussed above as follows:

If $R_O > R_M$ then $R_E > R_O$ positive leverage of equity dividend rate
If $R_O = R_M$ then $R_E = R_O$ neutral leverage of equity dividend rate

FIGURE 13-2 Negative Leverage

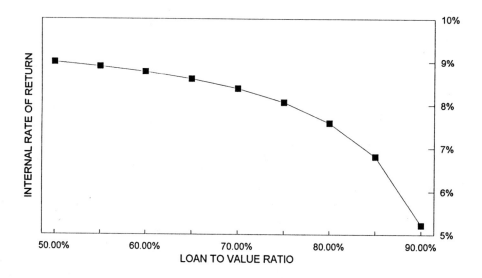

If $R_O < R_M$ then $R_E < R_O$ negative leverage of equity dividend rate
If $Y_O > Y_M$ then $Y_E > Y_O$ positive leverage of equity yield rate
If $Y_O = Y_M$ then $Y_E = Y_O$ neutral leverage of equity yield rate
If $Y_O < Y_M$ then $Y_E < Y_O$ negative leverage of equity yield rate

Leverage and Market Value

Note that when we discussed leverage in the examples above we did not suggest that leverage affects the market value of the property. Positive leverage increases the investor's *expected* return but at the same time it increases the riskiness of the investment. With greater amounts of leverage, however, the investor's *actual* rate of return also is more uncertain. This is because any factor that affects Y_O such as an increase in vacancy will have a greater affect on Y_E with higher amounts of leverage. Because risk also increases with financial leverage, the equity investor requires a higher expected rate of return on the investment. Thus, the value of the investment does not necessarily increase. Appraisers must be careful when discounting cash flows to value the equity position to select a discount rate that reflects the risk associated with the level of financial leverage. Otherwise they may over- or underestimate the market value of the property.

Loan Amount Determination

Typically, lenders have two methods of selecting the level of funds to be advanced to a property owner. These two so-called *loan constraints* are the *loan-to-value ratio* (M) and the first-year debt service coverage ratio (DCR). The M for the sample data is calculated as follows:

$$M = \frac{\text{Loan Amount}}{\text{Property Value}} = \frac{\$750,000}{\$1,000,000} = 0.75, \text{ or } 75\%$$

The *debt service coverage ratio* (debt coverage ratio, or DCR for short) is calculated by dividing the first year's NOI by the annual mortgage payment, as shown below.

$$DCR = \frac{\text{NOI}}{\text{Annual Debt Payment}} = \frac{\$100,000}{\$81,783} = 1.22$$

A ratio greater than 1.00 means that a lender would require that the first-year NOI be greater than the annual debt service payment. In some instances, the maximum a lender can loan on a property is set by law. In other cases, the maximum loan amount is a policy decision of the lending institution. It is possible for the lending constraint to vary by property type, age, location, tenant mix and borrower, especially if any of these result in differences in risk. The formula for finding a loan balance using a DCR is as follows:

$$\text{Mortgage value } (V_M) = \frac{\text{NOI}}{\text{DCR} \times R_M}$$

The NOI equals the first-year NOI, the R_M is the mortgage capitalization rate (see chapter 6) and the DCR is the first-year ratio required by a lender. Following is an example of the use of the DCR to find the loan amount.

Example

DCR	1.2
First-year NOI	$200,000
Loan term	9.75% interest; 30 years, monthly payment

Therefore, $R_M =$ 0.103099

$$V_M = \frac{\$200,000}{1.2 \times 0.103099} = \$1,616,569$$

The annual payment for a $1,616,569 loan is $166,666, which indicates a 1.2 ($200,000/$166,666) DCR.

Frequently, lenders look at both the loan-to-value ratio (*M*) and the DCR. It is highly unlikely that a loan amount would exactly satisfy both a specific *M* and a specific DCR. A lender, therefore, picks a controlling restraint and tests to see whether the sister constraint falls within a reasonable range. An example appears below.

Example

Lender Constraints   DCR = 1.20 − 1.30

Given: Value $2,000,000
          Loan amount $1,600,000 @ 10.5% interest
                                   20 years (monthly payments)
          First year NOI $225,000

$$M = \frac{\$1,600,000}{\$2,000,000} = 0.80 \text{ or } 80\%$$

$$DCR = \frac{\$225,000}{\$191,689} = 1.174$$

In this instance, *M* is exactly 80 percent, but the DCR is only 1.174, which is less than the required rate. The loan as structured, therefore, would not meet the lender's constraints.

Loan Types

The loan used in the examples in this chapter is a level-payment, fully amortized loan. Loans of this type are prevalent in the marketplace. Other loan types, however, exist and are currently available from lenders active in the marketplace. The predominant loan types are

- Interest only mortgage;
- Adjustable rate mortgage;
- Negative amortization mortgage; and
- Loan participation.

Interest Only Mortgages. *Interest only mortgages* are structured so that the entire annual payment just covers the interest; this results in no amortization (repayment) of the mortgage (principal), which remains constant. The lender receives the entire principal at the expiration of the loan. Payment of this balance is referred to as a *balloon payment.* Interest only mortgages typically have shorter amortizing periods than level-payment, self-amortizing loans. Following is an example of an interest only loan for $750,000 at 10 percent interest for 10 years, using the sample data.

Example

Interest Only Mortgage

Given:

Value	$1,000,000
Loan amount	$750,000 interest only @ 10%
Equity value	$250,000
Resale (tenth year)	$1,200,000

Year	1	2	3	4	5
NOI	$100,000	$102,000	$104,000	$106,000	$108,000
Annual debt payment	− 75,000	− 75,000	− 75,000	− 75,000	− 75,000
BTCF	$ 25,000	$ 27,000	$ 29,000	$ 31,000	$ 33,000

Year	6	7	8	9	10
NOI	$110,000	$112,000	$114,000	$116,000	$118,000
Annual debt payment	− 75,000	− 75,000	− 75,000	− 75,000	− 75,000
BTCF	$ 35,000	$ 37,000	$ 39,000	$ 41,000	$ 43,000

Resale price	$1,200,000
Loan balance	− 750,000
Before-tax reversion	$ 450,000

Year	BTCF
0	($250,000)
1	25,000
2	27,000
3	29,000
4	31,000
5	33,000
6	35,000
7	37,000
8	39,000
9	41,000
10	493,000

$$\text{IRR} = Y_E = 0.1633, \text{ or } 16.33\%$$

The before-tax yield rate is slightly higher with the interest only loan, which suggests that the equity investor would prefer an interest only loan to a level amortizing loan at the same rate. The interest only loan, however, is due in 10 years, which would probably increase the risk to the equity, thus offsetting any benefits from the interest only structuring of the payment.

Adjustable Rate Mortgages. *Adjustable rate mortgages* are structured so that payments vary over time, either contractually or as a result of general interest rate changes. These loans can be structured on an interest only basis or can have gradual amortization built in. The following example shows a variable rate loan structured on an interest only basis for 10 years. In this case the interest rate for each year is given. In practice, however, the interest rate for each year would be calculated after comparison with some index specified in the loan contract. Under these circumstances, an appraiser would not know the future interest rate and would therefore need to forecast rates to analyze the impact of the loan.

Example

Adjustable Rate Mortgage

Given:

Value	$1,000,000
Loan amount	$750,000 interest only with variable interest rate
Equity value	$250,000
Resale (tenth year)	$1,200,000

Year:	1	2	3	4	5	6	7	8	9	10
Interest, %	9%	9%	9.5%	10%	10%	11%	11%	10%	10%	10%

Year	1	2	3	4	5
NOI	$100,000	$102,000	$104,000	$106,000	$108,000
Annual debt payment	− 67,500	− 67,500	− 71,250	− 75,000	− 75,000
BTCF	$ 32,500	$ 34,500	$ 32,750	$ 31,000	$ 33,000

Year	6	7	8	9	10
NOI	$110,000	$112,000	$114,000	$116,000	$118,000
Annual debt payment	− 82,500	− 82,500	− 75,000	− 75,000	− 75,000
BTCF	$ 27,500	$ 29,500	$ 39,000	$ 41,000	$ 43,000

Resale price	$1,200,000
Loan balance	− 750,000
Before-tax reversion	$ 450,000

Year	BTCF
0	($250,000)
1	32,500
2	34,500
3	32,750
4	31,000
5	33,000
6	27,500
7	29,500
8	39,000
9	41,000
10	493,000

$$\text{IRR} = Y_E = 0.1694, \text{ or } 16.94\%$$

The before-tax Y_E for a variable rate loan is higher than that for an interest only loan, assuming payments at a 10 percent rate. The variable nature of the loan payments, if not specifically set by contract, results in a riskier situation for the equity investor. This type of loan, however, would probably represent a lower risk to the lender if payments depend on future market conditions, because of the opportunity to increase payments if interest rates increase.

Negative Amortization Mortgages.   *Negative amortization mortgages* are structured so that early payments are below the level needed to meet the interest payments fully. Therefore, the loan balance increases in early years. Loans structured in this manner help investors during periods of temporary high interest rates or during early rent-up of a new project. The mathematics of calculating the interest and principal payment in any year may be complicated, and for this reason, an example of a negative amortization loan is not given in this book.

Loan Participation.   *Loan participation* mortgages are structured to include both a constant payment over time and additional payments based on a property's performance over time. The additional income can come from resale proceeds, as well as from annual operating income. A multitude of methods are used to calculate additional payments, including percentages of

- gross income;
- gross income above a threshold amount;
- NOI;
- NOI above a threshold amount;
- BTCF (after regular debt service but before the participation);

- BTCF above a threshold amount;
- resale proceeds;
- gain at resale (over the original purchase price); and
- cash flow at resale (sales price less mortgage balance).

Typically, these loans initially are structured with lower interest rates because of the potential for increased returns to the lender. Following is an example of a loan participation, assuming a $750,000 loan at 9.5 percent interest for 25 years (monthly payments) with an additional income participation based on 25 percent of any NOI above $100,000.

Example

Loan Participation Mortgage

Given:

Value	$1,000,000
Loan amount	$750,000 (@ 9.5% interest for 25 years; monthly payments)
Equity value	$250,000
Resale (tenth year)	$1,200,000
Participation	25% of NOI increase

Year	*1*	*2*	*3*	*4*	*5*
NOI	$100,000	$102,000	$104,000	$106,000	$108,000
Annual debt payment	− 78,633	− 78,633	− 78,633	− 78,633	− 78,633
Participation payment	− 0	− 500	− 1,000	− 1,500	− 2,000
BTCF	$ 21,367	$ 22,867	$ 24,367	$ 25,867	$ 27,367

Year	*6*	*7*	*8*	*9*	*10*
NOI	$110,000	$112,000	$114,000	$116,000	$118,000
Annual debt payment	− 78,633	− 78,633	− 78,633	− 78,633	− 78,633
Participation payment	− 2,500	− 3,000	− 3,500	− 4,000	− 4,500
BTCF	$ 28,867	$ 30,367	$ 31,867	$ 33,367	$ 34,867

Resale price	$1,200,000
Loan balance	− 627,521
Before-tax reversion	$ 572,479

Year	BTCF
0	($250,000)
1	21,367
2	22,867
3	24,367
4	25,867
5	27,367
6	28,867
7	30,367
8	31,867
9	33,367
10	607,346

$$\text{IRR} = Y_E = 0.1644, \text{ or } 16.44\%$$

Other Types of Financing

A multitude of other mortgage types exist, including fixed principal repayment loans, convertible mortgages, mortgages that are of one type for a certain period and change to another type later, and various types of joint venture arrangements. Each financing alternative should be judged based on the potential risks to the lender and to the equity holder.

SUMMARY

The use of debt to finance real estate creates both a mortgage and an equity interest in the property. Each of these interests can be analyzed separately, and a market value is associated with each interest. The total value of the property equals the total values of these interests.

The investment return calculations discussed in chapter 8 for evaluating the entire property (before considering financing) can also be applied to analysis of the equity interest. Typical measures include the payback period, the equity capitalization rate, the equity yield rate, the net present value of the cash flows to the equity investor, and the adjusted rate of return. These measures usually differ from those for the entire property because of the impact that debt has on cash flows to the equity position.

The concept of financial leverage deals specifically with the impact of debt on the equity investor's cash flow and rate of return. Leverage can either be favorable or unfavorable, depending on the cost of the debt. Conditions for either favorable or unfavorable leverage to be favorable were discussed in terms of the effects on both equity yield rates and equity dividend rates.

The amount of debt that can be obtained for real estate income property is often limited by either a maximum loan-to-value ratio or a minimum debt coverage ratio. A maximum loan-to-value ratio ensures a minimum initial equity investment, whereas a minimum debt coverage ratio ensures that net operating income is sufficient to cover the mortgage payment during the first year of the investment.

A variety of different types of mortgages, in addition to fully amortized fixed rate mortages, are available to finance real estate income property. These include interest only mortgages, adjustable rate mortgages, negative amortization mortgages and mortgages with participation.

KEY TERMS

adjustable rate mortgage
adjusted internal rate of return
  (AIRR)
amortization term
balloon payment
before-tax cash flow (BTCF)
before-tax equity yield rate
cash throwoff (CTO)
debt coverage ratio (DCR)
equity capitalization rate (R_E)
equity dividend
equity dividend rate
equity interest

equity yield rate (Y_E)
financial leverage
interest only mortgage
loan constraints
loan participation
loan-to-value ratio
mortgage interest
negative amortization
negative leverage
net present value
payback period
positive leverage
profitability index

QUESTIONS

1. What is the difference between an equity capitalization rate and an overall capitalization rate?
2. What is the difference between an equity yield rate and an equity capitalization rate?
3. What factors would tend to cause expected equity yield rates to differ for different properties?
4. What is meant by financial leverage? What causes leverage to be positive?
5. Can leverage be evaluated by considering the effect on first-year cash flows?
6. Suppose a property is projected to have a first-year net operating income of $250,000. The lender requires a 1.25 debt coverage ratio. The loan would have a 10 percent interest rate and be amortized over 25 years with monthly payments. How large a loan can be obtained?

7. What is meant by a negative amortization mortgage?
8. What is meant by a loan participation? What is the participation based on?
9. What is meant by a balloon payment?
10. An investor is considering purchasing a property for $2.5 million by obtaining a loan for 80 percent of the purchase price at a 9 percent interest rate with monthly payments over 30 years. The net operating income is expected to be $200,000 the first year and then increase by 4 percent per year until the property is sold. The investor expects to sell the property for $3 million at the end of the fifth year.
   a. What is the debt coverage ratio?
   b. What is the equity capitalization rate?
   c. What is the equity yield rate?
   d. What is the net present value of the cash flows to the equity investor using a 12 percent equity discount rate?

END NOTE

1. In this case the payback of capital was received by the tenth year without considering any cash flow from resale (reversion). If the property was sold before year 10, the payback period would be the same as the holding period, assuming sufficient funds were received from its sale to return any capital not yet received through cash flow from operations.

CHAPTER 14	# Valuation of Mortgage and Equity Interests

INTRODUCTION

Chapter 7 presented the various techniques used to estimate property value on an unleveraged basis. This chapter is devoted to presenting and explaining the various techniques that include provisions for financing. The appraisal strategy for estimating value assuming financing is the same as that of the unleveraged approach: The appraiser uses methods that mirror current market expectations and investor motivations. If properties are frequently financed in the market and typical investors consider the impact of financing in their buying decisions, it is necessary for an appraiser to use an analytic technique that considers financing when estimating value.

The two basic approaches to estimating value on a leveraged basis include

1. use of first-year cash-flow ratios (capitalization rates) and
2. use of internal rates of return (before tax equity yield [discount] rates).

The first-year cash-flow ratios using capitalization rates are presented first, followed by yield capitalization using yield capitalization formulas as well as more general discounted cash-flow analysis. Appraisal techniques that consider financing are called mortgage/equity techniques.

ESTIMATING VALUE USING FIRST-YEAR CAPITALIZATION RATES

Value estimates for equity interests may be calculated by dividing a first-year before-tax cash-flow (BTCF) forecast by the appropriate capitalization rate. Capitalization rates based on equity interests do not explicitly address profitability; they are simply observed ratios that can be extracted from comparable sales. The ultimate actual profitability to an equity owner can be determined only after analyzing the complete pattern of cash flows over a holding period. The first-year capitalization rate used is called the *equity capitalization rate* (R_E), also referred to as the *equity dividend rate*. Three common methods are used to estimate property value using equity capitalization rates. Each is based on the loan constraint assumed in the analysis. The three possible loan determinants are

1. loan-to-value ratio,
2. debt coverage ratio and
3. fixed loan amount.

In all cases in this chapter, the fee simple (unencumbered) value is estimated. The relevant issues and techniques used to estimate the value of other ownership interests are presented in later chapters.

R_E and a Loan-to-Value Ratio (Band of Investment)

An overall capitalization rate can be calculated by taking a weighted average of the mortgage constant (R_M) and the equity dividend rate (R_E). These two rates are weighted by the proportion of mortgage funds[1] (M) and the proportion of equity (E) to be invested in the property. The sum of M and E must be 1 or 100 percent (or $E = 1 - M$). The *band-of-investment* equation is written as follows:

$$R_O = (M \times R_M) + (E \times R_E)$$

This can be proved mathematically by substituting the definition of each of the terms in the equation, as follows:

$$R_O = \frac{\cancel{\text{Loan}}}{\text{Value}} \times \frac{\text{Payment}}{\cancel{\text{Loan}}} + \frac{\cancel{\text{Equity}}}{\text{Value}} \times \frac{\text{Equity dividend}}{\cancel{\text{Equity}}}$$

$$= \frac{\text{Payment}}{\text{Value}} + \frac{\text{Equity dividend}}{\text{Value}}$$

$$= \frac{\text{Payment} + \text{Equity dividend}}{\text{Value}}$$

$$= \frac{\text{NOI}}{\text{Value}}$$

Some authors have suggested that the band-of-investment formula might be calculated with the loan interest rate substituted for the mortgage loan constant in the above equation, but this is not mathematically correct. If the interest rate rather than the loan constant were used in the band-of-investment formula, it could not be proved as shown above. Appraisers must take care to use equations that are technically correct.

Example

Using a $200,000 first-year net operating income (NOI) and assuming a first mortgage at 10.25 percent interest for 30 years (monthly payments) with a loan-to-value ratio of 75 percent and an R_E of 7 percent, the value estimate would be calculated as shown below:

Mortgage (M)	0.75	×	0.1075 (R_M)*	=	0.0806
Equity (E)	0.25	×	0.0700 (R_E)	=	0.0175
Overall rate (R_O)					0.0981

NOI		R_O		Value
$200,000	÷	0.0981	=	$2,038,736

*R_M for a loan with an interest rate of 10.25 percent and monthly payments for a term of 30 years.

The R_E is found by extracting R_Es from sales of similar properties, comparing the attributes (physical, locational and financial) of the comparables, and selecting the R_E that appears to be the best rate to use. The following formula can be used to calculate an R_E from an overall rate derived from a comparable sale and information about financing.

$$R_E = \frac{R_O - M(R_M)}{E}$$

When selecting the R_E, the appraiser must consider factors that could cause the rates to differ for comparable sales. In the case of the R_E, it is especially important to consider whether the loan-to-value ratio, interest rate and amortization terms are similar. For example, an R_E from a sale financed with an 80 percent loan with level amortizing payments over 25 years would not be expected to be in the same range as an R_E extracted from a sale financed with a 60 percent loan with a variable interest rate and a 5-year balloon payment.

Although use of the R_E does not specifically require an appraiser to make cash-flow forecasts beyond the first year, there is an implied assumption made that future performance (no matter what the cash flows turn out to be) will be similar for the subject and the comparables.

R_E and a Fixed Loan Amount (Equity Residual Technique)

The R_E can be used if the loan balance is known. This might be the case if the loan were assumable or if the loan already had been determined by applying the *debt coverage ratio* (DCR) to the first-year NOI, as discussed previously. Using a $200,000 first-year NOI and assuming a first mortgage at 10.25 percent interest for 30 years (monthly payments) with a current loan balance of $1,450,000 and an R_E of 7 percent, the value estimate would be calculated as shown below.

NOI	$200,000
Less mortgage payment	− 155,922
BTCF	$ 44,078

BTCF		R_E		Equity Value
$44,078	÷	0.07	=	$629,686

Equity value	$ 629,686
Plus mortgage balance	1,450,000
Total property value	$2,079,686

This method is commonly referred to as the *equity residual technique* because the income to the equity position is the residual. Note that the format for finding the solution is similar to that for the land residual and building residual techniques. When using the equity residual technique, the appraiser must be careful if the financing is not typical. For example, if the loan has a below-market interest rate, the resulting equity value will include a premium for the financing, which is a nonrealty interest.

Underwriter's Method

A third method used to estimate value assuming financing is the *underwriter's method,* which is used to calculate the overall rate, using the following formula:

$$R_O = M \times R_M \times DCR$$

where R_M is the mortgage capitalization rate.

This formula is used to find the value that would satisfy the dual requirements of a lender, that is, the loan-to-value ratio and the DCR. None of these inputs explicitly considers the requirements of an equity investor, so the approach is not likely to be appropriate for estimating market value. The calculation above implies a specific R_E. Only if the implied R_E is reasonable will an estimate found by using this formula be an estimate of market value.

ESTIMATING VALUE USING DISCOUNTED CASH-FLOW ANALYSIS [2]

Value estimates for a variety of ownership interests may be calculated by forecasting cash flows over a typical holding period and discounting each to a present value using a typical discount rate. This valuation approach is referred to as *discounted cash-flow analysis* (DCF). The DFC techniques discussed in chapter 7 were applied without consideration for financing. These techniques can also be used assuming financing. When using financing, the cash flows analyzed become those to be received by an equity investor. The discount rate used is the before-tax equity yield rate (Y_E). This discount rate addresses the expected profitability of the equity investor. The first step in applying the discounted cash-flow approach is to forecast the BTCFs over a typical holding period. (Cash-flow forecasting was discussed in chapter 5.)

The following cash-flow forecasts will be used to demonstrate the valuation techniques. The example assumes that NOI is level. The resale was estimated to be $2.3 million at the end of a 5-year holding period, and the first mortgage was assumed to be for $1.5 million at a 10.25 percent interest rate for 30 years with monthly payments.

Year	1	2	3	4	5
NOI	$200,000	$200,000	$200,000	$200,000	$200,000
Debt service	− 161,298	− 161,298	− 161,298	− 161,298	− 161,298
BTCF	$ 38,702	$ 38,702	$ 38,702	$ 38,702	$ 38,702
Resale					$2,300,000
Loan balance					− 1,450,967
BTCF from resale					$ 849,033

The standard discounted cash-flow formula for solving for the value of the equity is

Equity value = Present value of BTCF + Present value of BTCF
from operations   from reversion

Using a before-tax equity discount rate (Y_E) of 15 percent results in the following present value estimate:

Example

Year	BTCF		Present Value Factor @ 15%		Present Value
1	$ 38,702	×	0.869565	=	$ 33,654
2	38,702	×	0.756144	=	29,264

Year	BTCF		Present Value Factor @ 15%		Present Value
3	$ 38,702	×	0.657516	=	25,447
4	38,702	×	0.571753	=	22,128
5	38,702	×	0.497177	=	19,242
5 (resale)	849,033	×	0.497177	=	422,120

Present value of equity	$ 551,855
Plus loan amount	1,500,000
Property value	$2,051,855

Shortcut Method

		Present Value Annuity @ 15%		Present Value
$ 38,702	×	3.352155	=	$ 129,735

		Present Value Factor @ 15%		
$849,033	×	0.497177	=	$ 422,120

Total equity value	$ 551,855
Plus loan amount	1,500,000
Total property value	$2,051,855

COMMENTS: In the analysis, the present value of the equity is $551,855 and the total property value estimate is $2,051,855, which implies an R_E of 7.01 percent ($38,702/$551,855) and an R_O of 9.75 percent ($200,000/$2,051,855). In this instance, the shortcut method can be used to estimate the present value of the BTCFs because they were level. The shortcut method could not be used if the NOIs vary over time, as demonstrated below.

Year	1	2	3	4	5
NOI	$200,000	$208,256	$216,256	$222,631	$231,880
Debt service	− 161,298	− 161,298	− 161,298	−161,298	−161,298
BTCF	$ 38,702	$ 46,958	$ 54,958	$ 61,333	$ 70,582

Resale price (5 years)	$2,300,000
Loan balance	− 1,450,967
Before-tax proceeds	$ 849,033

Variable BTCF and Fixed Resale Price

Using a before-tax Y_E of 15 percent results in the following present value estimate for the equity.

Year	BTCF		Present Value Factor @ 15%		Present Value
1	$ 38,702	×	0.869565	=	$ 33,654
2	46,958	×	0.756144	=	35,507
3	54,958	×	0.657516	=	36,136
4	61,333	×	0.571753	=	35,067
5	70,582	×	0.497177	=	35,092
5 (resale)	849,033	×	0.497177	=	422,120

Present value of equity	$ 597,576
Plus loan amount	1,500,000
Total property value	$2,097,576

In the above analysis, the present value estimate for the equity is $597,576 and the total property value is $2,097,576, which implies an R_E of 6.48 percent ($38,702/$597,576) and an R_O of 9.53 percent ($200,000/$2,097,576). Note that both R_E and R_O are now lower.

In the previous examples, the NOIs, the resale price and the loan amount were given. The resale could have been found using a terminal capitalization rate (see chapter 7). Using a terminal capitalization rate results in a dollar forecast for the resale price.

Level BTCF and Resale Using Terminal Capitalization Rate

Assume a property will have level NOI of $200,000 per year for a 5-year holding period. Furthermore, no change in NOI is expected after the property is sold. Suppose the property can be financed with a loan for $1.5 million at a 10.25 percent interest rate for 30 years with monthly payments. The reversion is to be estimated by applying a 10 percent terminal capitalization rate to the sixth-year NOI. Using a before-tax Y_E of 15 percent, the value estimate is found as follows:

Example

$$\text{Resale} = \frac{\text{NOI (6th year)}}{\text{Terminal } R_O} = \frac{\$200,000}{0.10} = \$2,000,000$$

Before-Tax Resale Proceeds:

Resale price	$2,000,000
Less loan balance	− 1,450,967
BTCF from resale	$ 549,033

Year	BTCF		Present Value Factor @ 15%		Present Value
1	$ 38,702	×	0.869565	=	$ 33,654
2	38,702	×	0.756144	=	29,264

Year	BTCF		Present Value Factor @ 15%		Present Value
3	$ 38,702	×	0.657516	=	$ 25,447
4	38,702	×	0.571753	=	22,128
5	38,702	×	0.497177	=	19,242
5 (resale)	549,033	×	0.497177	=	272,967
Present value of equity					$ 402,702
Plus loan value					1,500,000
Total property value					$1,902,702

In the preceding analysis, the present value of the equity is $402,702 and the total property value is $1,902,702, which implies an R_E of 9.6 percent ($38,702/$402,702) and an R_O of 10.51 percent ($200,000/$1,902,702).

As we have stressed several times, when using a terminal capitalization rate to estimate the reversion, the appraiser should compare the implied R_O (in this case 10.51 percent) with the terminal R_T (10 percent) to see whether the proper relationship is implied. In this instance, would it be logical that today's R_O would be 0.5 percent higher than the terminal R_T? Under certain special circumstances, it may be logical for the terminal R_T to be lower than the going-in capitalization rate. However, as we discussed earlier, in a typical circumstance the terminal rate would be equal to or slightly higher than the going-in capitalization rate.

The appraiser also should calculate the implied change in value over the holding period and compare it with the change implied in the NOI. In this instance, the NOI was not assumed to change over the 5 years. Comparing the total property value with the estimated resale price reveals that the implied decrease in value over the 5 years would be 5.1 percent [($2,000,000/$1,902,702) − 1]. Would level income and a 5 percent change in the resale price be logical and reflect the expectations of a typical investor? If not, the appraiser may need to alter the input assumptions.

The loan amount was given in the first two DCF examples. The loan amount could also have been determined by assuming a debt coverage ratio (DCR). Using a debt coverage ratio results in a dollar forecast for the loan amount.

Level Income, Fixed Resale and Debt Coverage Ratio

Using level NOI of $200,000 over a 5-year holding period, assuming a resale of $2.3 million in 5 years, and using a DCR of 1.2 for a mortgage at a 10.25 percent interest rate for 30 years with monthly payments and a before-tax Y_E of 15 percent, the value estimate would be as follows:

Example

$$\text{Loan amount} = \frac{\text{NOI}}{\text{DCR} \times R_M} = \frac{\$200,000}{1.20 \times 0.1075} = \$1,550,387$$

Year	1	2	3	4	5
NOI	$200,000	$200,000	$200,000	$200,000	$200,000
Annual debt service	− 166,716	− 166,716	− 166,716	− 166,716	− 166,716
BTCF	$ 33,284	$ 33,284	$ 33,284	$ 33,284	$ 33,284
Resale price					$2,300,000
Less loan balance					− 1,499,707
BTCF from resale					$ 800,293

Year	BTCF		Present Value Factor @ 15%		Present Value
1	$ 33,284	×	0.869565	=	$ 28,943
2	33,284	×	0.756144	=	25,167
3	33,284	×	0.657516	=	21,885
4	33,284	×	0.571753	=	19,030
5	33,284	×	0.497177	=	16,548
5	800,293	×	0.497177	=	397,887
					$509,460

Present value of equity	$ 509,460
Plus loan amount	1,550,387
Total property value	$2,059,847

The implied loan-to-value ratio is 75.27 percent ($1,550,387/$2,059,847). If the implied loan-to-value ratio is above the requirements of a typical lender, a higher DCR will be required. In addition, the appraiser must compare the before-tax Y_E used to ensure that its level will be consistent with the implied loan-to-value ratio. As demonstrated earlier, the expected BTCF is directly related to the percentage of equity in the property.

Level Income, Unknown Sales Price and Loan-to-Value Ratio

In the previous examples, the mathematics of applying the discounted cash-flow is relatively simple because all future cash flows are known or can be readily calculated after the NOI forecast has been made. Frequently, however, the appraiser may wish to assume that one or more inputs in the analysis are functions of the value estimate to be found. In chapter 9, the issue of calculating a resale by assuming a specific change over time was discussed. Recall that this required us to either solve an algebraic equation or use a special yield capitalization formula. The same issue arises here. To illustrate, the algebraic approach will first be used to solve for value, assuming level income over 5 years, a resale price based on the assumption that value will increase by 15 percent over 5 years and a loan balance for a first mortgage at a 10.25 percent interest rate for 30 years with monthly payments with a beginning loan balance equal to 75 percent of the value calculated.

Using a before-tax Y_E of 15 percent results in the following present value estimate.

Example

Year	NOI		Annual Debt Service		BTCF
1	$200,000	–	$V(0.75)(0.107532)$	=	$200,000 – 0.080649V$
2	200,000	–	$V(0.75)(0.107532)$	=	$200,000 – 0.080649V$
3	200,000	–	$V(0.75)(0.107532)$	=	$200,000 – 0.080649V$
4	200,000	–	$V(0.75)(0.107532)$	=	$200,000 – 0.080649V$
5	200,000	–	$V(0.75)(0.107532)$	=	$200,000 – 0.080649V$
5	$1.15V$	–	$V(0.75)(1 – 0.032688)$	=	$0.424516V$

Year	BTCF		Present Value Factor @ 15%		Present Value
1	$200,000 – 0.080649V$	×	0.869565	=	$173,913 – 0.070130V$
2	200,000 – 0.080649V	×	0.756144	=	151,229 – 0.060982V
3	200,000 – 0.080649V	×	0.657516	=	131,503 – 0.053028V
4	200,000 – 0.080649V	×	0.571753	=	114,360 – 0.046111V
5	200,000 – 0.080649V	×	0.497177	=	99,435 – 0.040097V
5	0.424516V	×	0.497177	=	0.211060V

Present value of equity $670,440 – 0.059288V$

$$\begin{aligned}
\text{Value} &= \text{Loan value} + \text{Equity Value} \\
V &= 0.75V + (\$670,440 - 0.059288V) \\
0.309288V &= \$670,440 \\
V &= \$2,167,688
\end{aligned}$$

Implied resale	=	$2,492,842
Implied loan amount	=	$1,625,766
Implied equity value	=	$ 541,922

Example

* Proof *

Year	1	2	3	4	5
NOI	$200,000	$200,000	$200,000	$200,000	$200,000
Annual debt service	− 174,822	− 174,822	− 174,822	− 174,822	− 174,822
BTCF	$ 25,178	$ 25,178	$ 25,178	$ 25,178	$ 25,178
Resale price					$2,492,842
Loan amount					− 1,572,622
Before-tax proceeds					$ 920,220

Year	BTCF
0	($541,922)
1	25,178
2	25,178
3	25,178
4	25,178
5	$945,398

$$IRR = Y_E = 0.1500, \text{ or } 15.0\%$$

The implied equity value is $541,922, and the implied loan amount is $1,625,766. The R_E is 4.65 percent ($25,178/$541,922), and the R_O is 9.23 percent ($200,000/$2,167,688). Proof that the answer found is correct is that the internal rate of return to the equity is 15.0 percent, which equals the before-tax Y_E used.

This algebraic approach can be used to estimate value in a discounted cash-flow format for any pattern of NOI, resale price and loan term. However, the mathematics can become tedious. As of the 1990s, most appraisers are using personal computers and either spreadsheet programs or specially designed menu-driven programs to solve for value. These types of problems may be solved using the "circular reference" mode incorporated into most spreadsheet programs, which employs an iterative process to find the answer. Other computer programs use either a trial-and-error process or a series of yield capitalization formulas to solve for value directly. Using yield capitalization formulas is the most efficient and therefore the fastest method of solving for value.

ESTIMATING VALUE USING YIELD CAPITALIZATION

In the 1960s and 1970s, L. W. Ellwood introduced a series of yield capitalization formulas that provided the appraiser with the option of solving for value using a mortgage/equity approach. The formulas provided a direct method of solving for value, even though both the resale and the loan amounts were a function of (dependent on) value (circular logic). In addition, a series of tables containing solutions for many of the variables needed to solve the formulas was published. The tables became widely used, because handheld electronic calculators had not yet achieved market acceptance. Currently, however, technological advances have made the tables virtually obsolete. Handheld calculators and personal computers can be programmed to provide the appropriate numbers rapidly. It is important, however, for an appraiser to be aware of these basic yield capitalization formulas to understand how they relate to the discounted cash-flow approach.

Basic Mortgage/Equity Discounted Cash-Flow Relationship

Present value (PV) of equity = PV of BTCF + PV of equity reversion

Ellwood Formula

$$R_O = Y_E - M[Y_E + P(1/S_{\overline{n}}) - R_M] - [\Delta_O(1/S_{\overline{n}})]$$

where R_O = Overall capitalization rate
M = Loan-to-value ratio
Y_E = Before-tax equity discount (yield) rate
P = Percentage of mortgage paid off
$1/S_{\overline{n}}$ = Sinking fund factor at the before-tax equity discount rate (Y_E)
R_M = Mortgage constant
Δ_O = Percent change in property value over the holding period

The Ellwood equation is sometimes expressed as follows:

$$r = Y_E - M[Y_E + P(1/S_{\overline{n}}) - R_M]$$

and

$$R_O = r - [\Delta_O(1/S_{\overline{n}})]$$

where r indicates a "basic rate." The basic rate is an intermediate step in the calculation of an overall rate that considers everything except any change in property value. The basic rate (r) is then adjusted upward or downward to reflect the effect of any change in property value (Δ_O) on the overall rate (R_O).

Value Solution Assuming Level Income, Percent Change in Value and Loan-to-Value Ratio

The *Ellwood formula* may be used to find the value of a property, assuming level income of $200,000 per year for 5 years, and a resale price that assumes value will increase by 15 percent over 5 years, a loan at a 10.25 percent interest rate for 30 years with a beginning loan balance of 75 percent of value, and a 15 percent before-tax equity discount rate.

Example

Ellwood Formula

$$R_O = Y_E - M[Y_E + P(1/S_{\overline{n}}) - R_M] - [\Delta_O(1/S_{\overline{n}})]$$

where Y_E = 0.15
P = 0.032688
Δ_O = 0.15
M = 0.75
R_M = 0.107532
$1/S_{\overline{n}}$ = 0.148316 (from tables)

R_O = 0.15 − 0.75 {0.15 + [(0.032688)(0.148316)] − 0.107532} − [0.15(0.148316)]
= 0.15 − 0.035487 − 0.022247
= 0.092266

$$\text{Value} = \frac{\text{NOI}}{R_O} = \frac{\$200,000}{0.092266} = \$2,167,646$$

Implied resale = $2,167,646 × 1.15 = $2,492,793
Loan amount = 0.75 × $2,167,646 = $1,625,735
Equity = 0.25 × $2,167,646 = $541,911

The answer is nearly identical to the one found using the discounted cash-flow approach with the algebraic solution. The slight difference is due to rounding of some of the input variables. Following is the implied cash-flow assumption when using the Ellwood formula.

Example

Year	1	2	3	4	5
NOI	$200,000	$200,000	$200,000	$200,000	$200,000
Annual debt service	− 174,819	− 174,819	− 174,819	− 174,819	− 174,819
BTCF	$ 25,181	$ 25,181	$ 25,181	$ 25,181	$ 25,181
Resale					$2,492,793
Less loan balance					− 1,572,592
Before-tax proceeds					$ 920,201

* Proof *

Year	BTCF
0	($541,911)
1	25,181
2	25,181
3	25,181
4	25,181
5	$945,382

IRR = Y_E = 0.1500, or 15%

It is important that an appraiser understand the pattern of cash flows assumed when using yield capitalization formulas. If the implied cash flows are not supportable by current market information, alternative solution approaches should be used. One of the problems that arose when using the Ellwood equation in the 1970s and 1980s was how to adjust the formula to mirror changing income patterns. L. W. Ellwood himself introduced the "J Factor," which was introduced in chapter 7.

AUTHOR'S NOTE: In the early 1970s an approach was introduced called "Ellwood without algebra," which is now commonly referred to as the *Akerson method.* The calculator format of this method appeared as follows:

Step 1	$M \times R_M$
Step 2	$+ (1-M) \times Y_E$
Step 3	$- M \times P \times 1/S_{\overline{n}}$
Basic rate	$= r$
Step 4	$- \Delta_O\, 1/S_{\overline{n}}$
Overall rate	$= R_O$

The first two steps look like the "band-of-investment" approach. However, note that the proportion of equity $(1-M)$ is multiplied by the equity yield rate (Y_E), not the equity dividend rate (R_E). Conceptually, this is because we are now basing value on an equity yield rate, not an equity dividend rate. Mathematically, steps 3 and 4 are necessary because the equity yield rate is affected by equity buildup through amortization of the loan (step 3) and any change in the property value over the holding period (step 4).

The Akerson format is really simply a restatement of the Ellwood equation that has been rearranged in the above four steps to make its calculation more tractable for people who are not comfortable with dealing with all the terms in the Ellwood equation at one time. When written on one line, the Akerson format appears as follows:

$$(M \times R_M) + [(1 - M)Y_E] - M[P(1/S_{\overline{n}})] - \Delta_O(1/S_{\overline{n}}) = R_O$$

This can be expanded to obtain:

$$(M \times R_M) + [(Y_E - M)Y_E] - M[P(1/S_{\overline{n}})] - \Delta_O(1/S_{\overline{n}}) = R_O$$

Collection of terms results in the following relationship:

$$Y_E - M[Y_E + P(1/S_{\overline{n}}) - R_M] - \Delta_O(1/S_{\overline{n}}) = R_O$$

which is the Ellwood equation.

The reader should verify that for the example considered earlier, substituting the input assumptions into the four steps in the Akerson equation above results in the same overall rate that was obtained from the Ellwood equation.

STABILIZING INCOME WITH THE ELLWOOD FORMULA

The Ellwood formula introduced in the previous section can be used to estimate the value of only a *level* income stream. Only the property value can change over the holding period. If the income is not level, we have to stabilize the income using one of the techniques introduced in chapter 7. Recall that we can develop an adjusted overall capitalization rate by dividing the rate that would apply to a level income stream by the income stabilization factor X. The same technique works when the capitalization rate is developed using the Ellwood formula. The revised Ellwood formula is as follows:

$$R_O = \frac{Y_E - M[Y_E + P(\frac{1}{S_n}) - R_M] - [\Delta_O \frac{1}{S_n}]}{X}$$

The income stabilization factor (X) can be calculated using any of the techniques illustrated in chapter 7, including the K factor for compound growth or the J factor for curvilinear income.

Example

Assume the NOI is expected to be $10,000 during the first year and increase by 4 percent per year over a 5-year holding period. The property value is expected to increase by a total of 20 percent over the 5 years. A mortgage can be obtained for 75 percent of the property at a 12 percent interest rate to be amortized with monthly payments over a 15-year loan term. Equity investors require a 15 percent discount rate.

The first step is to calculate the income stabilization factor.

Total Growth in NOI	*PV Factor @ 15%*	*Present Value*
1	0.869565	0.869565
1.04	0.756144	0.786390

Total Growth in NOI	*PV Factor @ 15%*	*Present Value*
1.0816	0.657516	0.711169
1.124864	0.571753	0.643144
1.169859	0.497177	0.581627
Total		3.591895

Present worth of $1 per period ($a_{\overline{n}}$) = 3.352155

$X = 3.591895 \div 3.352155$
$X = 1.071518$

We can now calculate the overall rate as follows:

$$R_O = \frac{Y_E - M[Y_E + P(\frac{1}{S_n}) - R_M] - [\Delta_O \frac{1}{S_n}]}{X}$$

$$R_O = \frac{0.15 - 0.75[0.15 + (0.163477) \times (0.148316) - 0.14402] - 0.2(0.148316)}{1.071518}$$

$R_O = 0.09767 \div 1.071518$
$R_O = 0.91151$, or 9.115%
$V = NOI / R_O$
$V = \$10,000 \div 0.09115$
$\quad = \$109,709$

The Ellwood formula can also be used with a curvilinear income stream as discussed in chapter 7 if the income is stabilized with the J factor.

Example

Assume NOI at the beginning of the first year will be $200,000.[3] Both income and property value are expected to increase by a total of 20 percent over a 5-year holding period. Investors require a 15 percent return on equity.

$$J = [\frac{n}{1 - \frac{1}{(1 + Y_E)^n}} - \frac{1}{Y_E}] \frac{1}{S_n}$$

$$J = [\frac{5}{1 - \frac{1}{(1 + 0.15)^5}} - \frac{1}{0.15}][0.148316]$$

$J = 0.486059$

$$R_O = \frac{0.15 - 0.75[0.15 + (0.032688)(0.148316) - 0.107532] - [0.15(0.148316)]}{1 + (0.15)(0.486059)}$$

$$R_O = \frac{0.15 - 0.035487 - 0.022247}{1.072909}$$

$$R_O = 0.0859961$$

$$V = \frac{NOI}{R_O} = \frac{200,000}{0.0859961}$$

$$V = \$2,325,687$$

* Proof *

Now that we know the value we can prove the answer.

Resale price	$= \$2,325,687 \times 1.15 =$	$2,674,540
Loan amount	$= \$2,325,687 \times 0.75 =$	1,744,265
Equity investment	$= \$2,325,687 \times 0.25 =$	581,422

Following is the implied cash-flow assumption when using this Ellwood formula.

Example

Year	1	2	3	4	5
NOI*	$204,449	$209,566	$215,451	$222,218	$230,000
Annual debt service	− 187,565	− 187,565	− 187,565	− 187,565	− 187,565
BTCF	$ 16,884	$ 22,001	$ 27,886	$ 34,653	$ 42,435
Reversion					$2,674,540
Less: loan balance					− 1,687,248
Before-tax proceeds					$ 987,292

*Calculated using the technique illustrated in chapter 7 for the curvilinear (J factor) income pattern.

Year	BTCF
0	($ 581,422)
1	16,884
2	22,001
3	27,886
4	34,653
5	1,029,727

The IRR (Y_E) of the above cash flows is 15 percent, which is what was assumed in the problem. Thus the value estimate is verified.

Ellwood Equation with a Debt Service Coverage Ratio

The Ellwood formula was originally designed to use a loan-to-value ratio (M) to specify the amount of debt financing available from the lender. This assumes that this loan can be obtained regardless of the implied debt coverage ratio. Such an assumption can be unrealistic when the NOI is low during the initial years of the holding period, because lenders typically require that the debt coverage ratio exceed a specified minimum amount, e.g., 1.20 based on the *first-year* NOI. Thus, if a significant portion of the property value comes from expected future NOI and/or price appreciation, a loan based on a percentage of that value may result in an unsatisfactory debt coverage ratio from the lender's perspective. This is particularly true during an inflationary environment, when much of the value is based on expected increases in income and property value due to inflation. A low first-year NOI (and consequently a low DCR) also can result from existing leases that have a below-market rental rate. The value of the property may be expected to increase because the leases will expire sometime after the first year. Developed projects also may have a low DCR during the initial years because the space takes a couple of years to be leased up to a stabilized occupancy level.

The Ellwood formula can be modified to find the value of a property, assuming financing is based on a minimum debt coverage ratio rather than a maximum loan-to-value ratio. The modified formula is as follows:

$$R_O = \frac{(Y_E - \Delta_O \, 1/S_n) \, (\text{DCR}) \, (R_M)}{Y_E + P[1/S_n] - R_M + (\text{DCR})(R_M)}$$

Example

Assume that a property will have level income at $200,000 per year for 5 years due to an existing lease. Because the lease will expire after 5 years, the resale price is expected to increase by 15 percent over the 5-year holding period. A loan can be obtained at a 10.25 percent interest rate, amortized over 30 years. The lender requires a minimum first-year debt service coverage ratio of 1.20. Investors require a 15 percent before-tax equity yield rate.

Y_E = 0.15
P = 0.032688
R_M = 0.107532
DCR = 1.20
Δ_O = 0.15
$1/S_n$ = 0.148316

$$R_O = \frac{[0.15 - (0.15)(0.148316)][(1.2)(0.107532)]}{0.15 + (0.032688)(0.148316) - 0.107532 + (1.2)(0.107532)}$$

$$R_O = \frac{0.016485}{0.176355}$$

$$R_O = 0.093476$$

$$V = \frac{\$200,000}{0.093476} = \$2,139,577$$

This is the value that meets the 1.2 debt coverage constraint and provides the investor with an expected IRR of 15 percent. To prove that this is the correct answer, we can use the value to calculate the following implied cash flows:

Resale price = $V \times 1.15 = \$2,139,577 \times 1.15 = \$2,460,514$
Debt service = NOI / DCR = \$200,000 / 1.2 = \$166,667
Loan amount = Debt service / R_M = \$166,667 / 1.2 = \$1,549,992
Equity = Value − Loan amount = \$2,139,577 − \$1,549,992 = \$ 589,585

Cash flows:

Year	1	2	3	4	5
NOI	\$200,000	\$200,000	\$200,000	\$200,000	\$200,000
Annual debt service	− 166,667	− 166,667	− 166,667	− 166,667	− 166,667
BTCF	\$ 33,333	\$ 33,333	\$ 33,333	\$ 33,333	\$ 33,333
Resale					\$2,460,514
Less: Loan balance					− 1,499,372
Before-tax proceeds					\$ 961,142

Year	BTCF
0	(\$589,585)
1	33,333
2	33,333
3	33,333
4	33,333
5	994,475

IRR = Y_E = 0.1500, or 15%

This modified Ellwood formula also can be used with the income stabilization factor X, including the special case factors K and J that we discussed earlier. The Ellwood formula can also be modified to handle other assumptions about financing. With the availability of personal computers, however, use of these specialized formulas is seldom necessary.

SUMMARY

Appraisal techniques that explicitly consider the effect of financing on cash flows are referred to as mortgage/equity techniques. This chapter discussed several ways to apply mortgage equity techniques to the valuation of real estate income property. Some techniques, such as the band-of-investment technique and equity residual technique, rely solely on first-year cash-flow measures such as the equity capitalization rate and mortgage constant. The underwriter's method also uses first-year cash-flow measures but only considers lender's criteria such as the loan-to-value ratio, the mortgage constant and the debt coverage ratio.

Discounted cash-flow analysis also can be used to value the equity position by discounting the estimated cash flows to the equity investor. The value of the equity interest is equal to the present value of the before-tax cash flow from operations and the before-tax cash flow from reversion. The total property value is then equal to the sum of the value of the equity interest plus the value of the mortgage interest.

There are a variety of ways of projecting cash flows from operations and resale. In some cases, all cash flows can be projected in dollar amounts. This makes the discounting procedure very straightforward. In other cases, cash flows may depend in some way on the unknown appraised value being estimated. For example, the loan may be assumed to be a percentage of the appraised value or the resale price may be assumed to be based on a projected change from the initial appraised value. In these cases, the valuation procedure becomes more complex and must be solved by using algebra, special formulas (such as the Ellwood formula) or a computer. However, it is important to realize that the resulting value conclusion still represents the price that is the present value of the mortgage and equity interests in the property. Furthermore, the price simply represents the amount that the investor would have to pay to expect to earn the specified equity yield rate.

KEY TERMS

Akerson method
band-of-investment
debt coverage ratio
discounted cash-flow analysis
Ellwood formula

equity capitalization rate
equity discount rate
equity dividend rate
equity residual technique
underwriter's method

QUESTIONS

1. A property is expected to have first-year NOI of $250,000. A loan for 75 percent of the property value can be obtained with a 12 percent mortgage constant. An analysis of comparable sales indicates that equity investors require an 8 percent equity capitalization rate for comparable properties with similar financing. Estimate the value of the property using the band-of-investment formula.

2. Refer to problem 1. Suppose that financing has already been determined to be for $2 million with the same 12 percent mortgage constant. Assuming the appropriate equity capitalization rate is still 8 percent, what is the estimated value of the property?

3. Refer to question 1. A mortgage lender indicates that it is willing to make a loan with a 75 percent loan-to-value ratio, a 12 percent mortgage constant and a 1.25 debt coverage ratio. What does this imply about the value that the lender would place on the property for underwriting purposes? Is this likely to be the market value of the property?

4. A property is projected to have NOI of $250,000 during the first year and increase by 2 percent per year thereafter. The appraiser estimates that it can be sold after 5 years based on applying a 10 percent terminal capitalization rate to the year 6 NOI. A loan can be obtained at an 11 percent interest rate with monthly payments amortized over a 30-year term. The lender requires a 1.2 debt coverage ratio applied to the first-year NOI. What is the value of the property based on a 12 percent equity yield rate? What overall capitalization rate is implied by the answer?

5. A property is projected to have level NOI of $500,000 per year for the next 5 years because of existing leases. However, because market rents are increasing, the value of the property is expected to increase by 15 percent over the 5-year holding period. A loan can be obtained for 70 percent of the estimated value of the property. The loan will have an 11 percent interest rate and be amortized over 30 years with monthly payments. What is the value of the property, based on a 12 percent equity yield rate?

6. How does using the Ellwood equation to estimate value differ from doing mortgage equity analysis with discounted cash-flow analysis?

7. What type of valuation problem is the Akerson method designed to solve? How does it differ from the band-of-investment technique?

END NOTES

1. This is the loan-to-value ratio.

2. Several of the examples in the section, "Estimating Value Using Discounted Cash-Flow Analysis," first appeared in *Income Property Appraisal* by Jeffrey D. Fisher and Robert S. Martin, Dearborn Financial Publishing, Inc. (1991) and were subsequently used with the permission of Dearborn Financial Publishing, Inc. in Course 510, Advanced Income Capitalization, developed by Jeffrey D. Fisher and published by the Appraisal Institute, Chicago, IL (1993)."

3. Recall that the overall rate found by using the J factor to stabilize the income is divided into the income at the beginning of the first year.

CHAPTER 15

Valuation of Nontypical Mortgage Financing

INTRODUCTION

Many real estate sales are financed with mortgage loans. The purpose of including mortgage financing is, first, to ensure adequate funding for completing the transaction and, second, to enhance the return to the equity investor through the use of leverage. The concept of leverage is discussed in chapter 13. During periods of high interest rates or shortages of mortgage financing, financing incentives frequently are offered to investors in the form of beneficial interest rates and/or loan terms. In some instances, financing arrangements (either loan assumptions or owner financing) represent terms significantly better than those available in the market, including below-market interest rates, higher than typical loan-to-value ratios, and/or unusual repayment terms. Below-market financing terms can benefit the investor by improving the before-tax cash flows and enhancing the impact of leverage. When the loan terms are better than the terms usually available in the market, a buyer may be justified in paying an additional premium just for the financing, which would result in a purchase price above what would be expected for the real estate alone. Payments made in excess of the real estate value represent nonrealty interests. In this case, the additional payment would be referred to as a financing premium.

The appraiser may be asked to estimate the value of a financing premium, either in conjunction with estimating the value of the subject property or when analyzing comparable sales. In some instances, a comparable sales price may include additional money paid specifically for beneficial financing terms in the transaction. In this instance, to arrive at the portion of the sales price attributable to the real estate ownership interest only, the appraiser would be asked to adjust the sales price by deducting the amount paid for this non-realty interest (the financing premium). A sales price that has had the value of any financing premiums deducted is referred to as a "cash equivalent" price and the process used to make this modification is referred to as a *cash equivalency adjustment*. When considering financing premiums in an analysis of a subject property, the purpose would be to estimate the contributing value of any favorable assumable financing available for that property. The value of any such benefit would be listed as a nonrealty interest in the subject property.

Estimating the contributing value of beneficial financing is accomplished by first estimating the value of the real estate alone, then estimating the most probable price an investor would pay for the property after considering the impact of the beneficial financing. The difference between the two is the contributing value of the below-market financing—the *financing premium*. When adjusting comparable sales, the procedure is to identify the amount of any financing premium and deduct it from the actual sales price. There are several methods of estimating the cash equivalency adjustment, including application of paired sales analysis and discounted cash-flow techniques. Each approach is demonstrated in this chapter.

MORTGAGE LOAN REVIEW

The amount of money a lender will advance on an income-producing property is generally determined using one of two constraints: a loan-to-value ratio or a debt coverage ratio (DCR). In most instances, lenders have specific goals to meet with regard to each of the two constraints, but usually only one of the two will be the limiting factor. It would be unlikely that both constraints (for example, a loan-to-value ratio of 75 percent and a DCR of 1.15) would be met exactly in a transaction. The controlling factor may vary as market conditions vary. During periods of low interest rates, the controlling factor is generally the loan-to-value ratio, and during periods of high interest rates, the DCR. The following equations show application of the two loan constraints, assuming a level-payment, self-amortizing loan:

Loan Amount—75% Loan-to-Value Ratio

Property Value		Loan-to-Value Ratio		Loan Amount
$1,000,000	×	0.75	=	$750,000

Loan Amount—1.2 DCR

$$VM = \frac{NOI}{DCR \times R_M} = \frac{\$100,000}{1.2 \times 0.113302} = \$735,497$$

In this instance, the DCR results in the lowest loan amount and would probably be the controlling constraint.

Mortgages may be of varying types, including

- level-payment, self-amortizing;
- interest only;
- fixed principal payment;
- variable interest rate;
- negative amortization; and
- lender participation.

These are the major types of loans, but there are many combinations of these terms available in the market today. The remainder of this chapter focuses on level-payment, self-amortizing loans, although the same techniques also apply to the other loan types.

PAYMENT AND ENDING BALANCE REVERSION

Find the annual payment and loan balance at the end of a 10-year period for the following level-payment, self-amortizing loan.

Example

Loan amount	$750,000
Interest rate	10.5%
Loan term (years)	25 (monthly payments)

Loan Balance		*Monthly Payment Factor*		*Monthly Payment*
$750,000	×	0.0094418	=	$7,081.35

Monthly Payment			*Annual Payment*
$7,081.35	× 12 =		$84,976.20

Present Value

Monthly Payment		*Annuity @ 10.5% (180 mo.)*		*Loan Balance*
$7,081.35	×	90.465078	=	$640,615

IMPACT OF BELOW-MARKET FINANCING

The first step in identifying the impact of below-market financing is to actually determine what would be the typical financing terms in the current market for the subject property and what they are for a comparable property at the date of its sale. In this chapter, only self-amortizing mortgages are analyzed.

Beneficial loans frequently are not based on a self-amortizing payment structure; therefore, calculation of a financing premium for both the subject and the comparables is more difficult. When faced with this situation, the appraiser should attempt to identify a loan based on a payment structure similar to that of the assumable loan. For example, if the assumable loan is structured on an interest-only basis for 10 years, the appraiser should attempt to identify the usual loan terms of a 10-year, interest only loan in the current market. By operating in this manner, the appraiser eliminates the problem of possible differences in the risk associated with two contrasting loan types.

Once the typical terms are identified, the assumable (or assumed) loan is compared with these terms to identify whether it offers (or offered) better terms. The benefits could arise from one or more of the following four factors:

1. below-market interest rates;
2. longer amortization terms;
3. assumability of loan at resale; and
4. higher loan-to-value ratio.

Below-Market Interest Rates

Obviously, if a mortgage has a *below-market interest rate* of 8.5 percent and the typical rate today (assuming the same amortization terms) is 10 percent, the loan offers a benefit. In the example in this chapter, this is the case. Problems arise, however, as mentioned earlier, if the typical and the actual loan terms are not basically the same.

Longer Amortization Terms

Amortization terms are the restrictions placed on repayment of a loan. Amortization terms are broken down into two elements:

1. The time period at which the loan will ultimately come due and
2. The periodic principal payment required in interim years

An interest only loan, for example, contains no provisions for principal payment in interim years, whereas a self-amortizing loan requires principal payments that fully repay the loan by the end of the amortization period. In general, an investor prefers paying back as little principal as possible during the holding period.

Assumability of Loan at Resale

The *assumability* of a mortgage is vitally important when estimating a financing premium for the subject and may be an issue in adjusting comparable sales. If a beneficial loan on the subject property is not assumable by the next buyer, it has no benefit in the next transaction, so no financing premium exists. When analyzing the impact of financing premiums on comparable sales, the assumability question is "If the loan created a benefit at the last sale, can it also be expected to generate a benefit the next time the property is sold?" The answer to this question lies in the assumability of the loan by the next buyer plus the projected loan-to-value ratio and the remaining amortization term at the projected point of disposition. Certainly if the loan is not assumable by the next buyer, no benefit can be expected at resale. In addition, even if the loan is assumable, if the loan balance is low relative to the property value or if it matures shortly after the purchase, its existence would be of little benefit to the next buyer. In the analysis in this chapter, this issue is eliminated by assuming the loan becomes due at resale. The appraiser should be careful to ensure logical handling of the reversion for either the subject or the comparables.

Higher Loan-to-Value Ratio

The act of borrowing additional money, in itself, does not create additional value. As pointed out in chapter 13, in cases where the mortgage interest rate is less than the property yield rate (Y_O), borrowing additional money increases leverage, which increases risk, which in turn increases the before-tax equity yield rate (Y_E). Borrowing additional money without a corresponding increase in the mortgage interest rate, however, can create a situation where the loan-to-value ratio is above the norm. In other words, the loan-to-value ratio and the mortgage interest rate are interrelated. When the appraiser selects the loan terms, the loan-to-value ratio of the assumable loan should be considered. For example, if the assumable loan for $1 million has an interest rate of 10 percent and the average loan is for $800,000 at a 10 percent rate, the assumable loan would probably be beneficial and may command a financing premium. This is not necessarily because of the higher loan-to-value ratio; it may be because the interest rate (although equal for the two different loan amounts) for the assumable loan is below the usual rate for a $1 million loan on the property as opposed to an $800,000 loan.

NOTE: Lenders often increase the interest rates as the loan-to-value ratios rise because the risk of default rises as the loan amount increases.

ESTIMATING THE IMPACT OF BENEFICIAL FINANCING

To illustrate the impact of beneficial financing, we begin with a simple example. More realistic assumptions are made in later examples.

Example

A property that sold for $1,000,000 was financed with a $700,000 loan by the seller at an interest rate of 8 percent, amortized monthly over 15 years. Typical market terms for a fixed interest rate loan at that time were 10 percent interest and a 15-year term. Assume that the buyer will benefit from the below-market interest rate for the full 15 years. What is the cash equivalent value of the property?

The total (overall) value of the property V_O is equal to the sum of the value of the mortgage (V_M) plus the value of the equity V_E invested in the property. That is,

$$V_O = V_M + V_E$$

The monthly payment for a $700,000 loan at 8 percent interest, amortized over 15 years, is $6,689.56. The value of the mortgage (V_M) is equal to the present value of the payments (debt service) discounted at the *market* interest rate of 10 percent per year or .8333 percent per month.* Thus we have

$$V_M = \text{PV of \$6,689.56 monthly for 15 years (180 months)}$$
$$\text{at a 10 percent annual discount rate}$$
$$V_M = \$622,514$$

The value of the equity (V_E) is the amount of cash that has been invested in the property, $300,000 in this example. Therefore, the total value of the property is as follows:

$$V_E = \$300,000$$
$$V_M = \$622,514$$
$$V_O = V_M + V_E$$
$$= \$622,514 + \$300,000$$
$$= \$922,514$$

This implies that the *premium* paid for the favorable financing was $1,000,000 − $922,514 − $77,486, which represents the present value of the payment savings to the buyer (payment subsidy by the seller). We can obtain the same financing premium ($77,486) by discounting the payment savings over the 15 years at a 10 percent rate. The savings is the difference between the payments for a loan at the market rate of 10 percent versus the payments for a loan at the actual rate of 8 percent. This can be illustrated as follows:

---

*Because we are finding the present value of mortgage payments, we use *monthly* discounting. Thus, the discount rate is 10/12 = .8333 percent per month.

Monthly Payment

Market debt service, 10%	$7,522.24
Less actual service, 8%	6,689.56
Savings	$ 832.68

The present value of $832.68 per month for 15 years discounted monthly at a 10% annual rate is $77,487, the same answer as above. ($1 difference due to rounding.)

Interpretation of Cash Equivalency

In the above example, the value of the property can be summarized as follows:

Value of Mortgage (V_M)	$622,514	(Cash equivalent value of mortgage)
Value of Equity (V_E)	300,000	(Cash equity)
Total (Overall) Value (V_O)	$922,514	(Total cash equivalent value)

The value is based on market interest rates of 10 percent with a below-market interest rate loan at 8 percent. If the loan had *not* been at a below-market interest rate, i.e., if market interest rates were actually 8 percent, then the value of the mortgage (V_M) would be $700,000, the present value of the payments at an 8 percent discount rate. The market interest rate is 10 percent, so the value of the loan (to the lender) decreases from $700,000 to $622,514. Because the equity investor benefits from the lower mortgage payments, she is willing to invest an additional $77,486 in the property. Thus, the value of the equity increases by $77,486. The additional funds that the equity investor is willing to invest in the property (with a below-market interest rate loan) are exactly offset by the decrease in the value of the mortgage loan to the lender. For this reason, the total value of the property does not change with below-market financing. Although the financing may be *favorable* from the investor's perspective, it is *unfavorable* from the lender's perspective.

More Realistic Assumptions

In practice, the actual premium that is typically paid for favorable financing tends to be less than suggested by the previous illustration. The above example assumed that the buyer would benefit from the below-market interest rate loan for the full 15 years. This may not be realistic for a number of reasons.

First, market interest rates may drop in the future. As the current interest rate drops, the below-market financing is less favorable, because the borrower can usually refinance the loan if market interest rates fall.

Second, the buyer may not plan to hold the property for the full 15 years. Thus, the first buyer may benefit from the below-market interest rate only until the property is sold to a second buyer. Whether the second buyer also will pay a premium (to the first buyer) for the financing depends on whether the loan is assumable and whether the market rate is still greater than the contract rate on the loan. Furthermore, because the loan has been amortized over the time it was held by the first buyer, it is less valuable because there is less loan balance to assume.[1] Thus, the first buyer may be willing to pay a premium only for savings the first buyer expects to receive during the period he or she will hold the property.

Third, the assumable loan may include a provision that requires payment in full (balloon payment) before the loan is fully amortized. Again, this would mean that the borrower definitely can benefit only until the loan must be repaid.

Example

To illustrate, we now modify the previous example by assuming that the loan will be repaid at the end of year 5. It is still assumed that the buyer will benefit by the difference between the market rate and the contract rate for the full 5 years.

The loan balance (balloon payment) after 5 years is $551,364. The value of the mortgage is now equal to the present value of the mortgage payments (discounted for 60 months) plus the present value of the mortgage balance after 60 months. This is calculated as follows:

$$V_M = \text{PV of \$6,689.56 for 60 months} + \text{PV of the balloon payment of \$551,364 at the end of 60 months.}$$
$$V_M = \$649,959$$

The total value of the property is again found by adding the value of the mortgage and the value of the equity. We have

$$V_O = \$649,959 + \$300,000$$
$$V_O = \$949,959$$

This implies a financing premium of $1,000,000 - $949,959 = $50,041. Note that this is less than the premium of $77,486 calculated, assuming the loan is held for the full term. The premium is smaller because the benefit of a lower payment is received over a shorter time period.

An alternative way of obtaining the same financing premium ($77,486) is to discount the payment savings over the 5 years at a 10 percent rate. In this case we also must consider the loan balance after 5 years. This is illustrated as follows:

	Monthly Payment	*Loan Balance, Year 5*
Market debt service 10%	$7,522.24	$569,216
Less actual debt service 8%	6,689.56	551,364
Savings	$ 832.68	$ 17,852

Financing premium = PV of $832.68 per months for 60 months +
                    PV of $17,852 after 60 months
                  = $39,190 + $10,850
Financing premium = $50,040

This is the same answer as before ($1 difference due to rounding).

Cash Equivalency Based on Investor's Expectations

As we have seen, finding the financing premium as we did above assumes, in effect, that the value of the favorable financing to the equity investor is equal to the present value of the savings at the market interest rate for *mortgages*. This implies that the risk associated with the payment savings is the same as that of a regular mortgage loan. It could be argued, however, that because the equity investor is investing additional equity funds in the property to obtain the favorable loan, the expected savings should be discounted at the investor's required equity yield rate.

To illustrate, we now assume that the payment savings for the previous example (5-year holding period) are discounted at a 19 percent rate. In this case, we use *annual* discounting to be consistent with the way equity investors calculate rates of return. The calculations are shown below.

Market debt service	10%	$7,522.24 × 12 =	$90,267
Less actual debt service	8%	6,689.56 × 12 =	80,275
Difference		$1,711.62	$ 9,992
Loan balance	10%	$ 569,216	
Less loan, balance	8%	551,364	
Difference		$ 17,852	

The present value of the *difference* in payments plus the *difference* in loan balances after 5 years, using a 19 percent discount rate, is $38,033. Therefore, the equity investor would be willing to pay only $38,033 more for the property to assume the favorable loan. This is lower than the amount calculated in the previous example ($50,040), because the previous example implicitly assumed that the investor only required a 10 percent rate of return (rather than 19 percent) on any additional equity capital invested in the property.

Alternative Solution

An alternative way to obtain the same answer as the previous example is to analyze the cash flows that the equity investor expects to receive with the favorable loan versus a market rate loan.

Example

To illustrate, assume the property we have been analyzing produces an NOI of $96,350 per year and is expected to be sold in year 5 for

$1,150,000. The equity investor expects a return of 19 percent (annual discounting) on all equity funds invested in the property, including any premium paid for financing.

With *below-market* financing the annual cash flows are as follows:

NOI	$ 96,350
Less debt service	80,275
BTCF	$ 16,075
Resale price	$1,150,000
Less loan balance	551,364
BTCF (reversion)	$ 598,636

To calculate the equity value with the below-market financing, we discount the above cash flows at a 19 percent rate over the 5-year holding period. The present value of $16,075 per year for 5 years plus the present value of $598,636 received in year 5 equals a present value of $300,000 (rounded). This suggests that the investor would be willing to invest about $300,000 in the property with favorable financing. Adding this to the loan amount of $700,000 results in the *purchase price* (including the financing premium) of $1,000,000. Note that this is the same purchase price as before.

We now repeat the calculations based on *market* financing.

NOI	$ 96,350.00
Less debt service	90,267.00
BTCF	$ 6,083.00
Resale price	$1,150,000.00
Less loan balance	569,216.00
BTCF (reversion)	$ 580,784.00

The equity value is again found by discounting the cash flows over the 5 years at a 19 percent discount rate. The value is $261,977. Adding this to the loan amount of $700,000 results in a cash equivalent value of the property of $961,977. Comparing the cash equivalent value with the purchase price of $1,000,000, the implied financing premium is $1,000,000 − $961,977 = $38,023.

This is the same answer as that obtained by simply discounting the payment savings at a 19 percent rate, because the present value of the NOI and resale price is the same under both alternatives (slight difference due to rounding). Looking at it this way emphasizes, however, that we have now calculated the value of the financing premium so that the equity investor earns the same rate of return (19 percent) on all funds invested in the property.

Conclusions About Cash Equivalency

We have calculated the financing premium under a variety of assumptions. Which is the correct answer? This can be discovered only by knowing how investors are analyzing properties with favorable loans. The answer may depend on market conditions and the sophistication of the typical investor who would purchase the property.

Paired Sales Analysis

One of the best methods of estimating the value of a financing premium is to compare sales affected by below-market financing with others not so affected. Using this method to approach the problem can give the appraiser an indication of the true value buyers place on financing. The difficulty in applying paired sales analysis is that it is difficult to compare beneficial financing terms that involve different relative interest rates, loan terms and balances. An appraiser, however, should be able to quantify the relative importance that buyers place on beneficial financing.

MORTGAGE VALUATION

The previous section dealt with estimating the effect of nontypical mortgage financing on the price paid for a property. One way this was done was to calculate the market value of the mortgage based on the actual terms of the loan. That is, we calculated the price that an investor would pay for the right to receive the cash flow from the mortgage. We can apply the same valuation concepts to the valuation of other types of mortgages. In this section we illustrate the valuation of a participating mortgage.

Valuation of Mortgages with Participations

Recall that a participating mortgage allows the lender to participate in the performance of the property in addition to receiving contract interest payments. To estimate the value of a participating mortgage, we need to calculate the present value of the interest income as well as the present value of the expected income from the participation provisions. Because the expected cash flow from the participation is riskier than the contract interest rate, this income is often discounted at a higher rate. This is illustrated in the following example.

Example

A loan was issued two years ago for $3,000,000 at a contract rate of 9 percent with *annual* payments over a 15-year amortization period and a balloon payment due in the 7th year. In addition, the lender will receive 10 percent of the NOI each year, plus 10 percent of either property reversion or property value at the end of 7 years, whichever occurs first.

Given the following projected income for the next 6 years, estimate the value of the lender's interest today, assuming the debt service is discounted at 10 percent, the participations are discounted at 12 percent and the terminal capitalization rate, applied to the NOI 6 years from now, is 8 percent.

	Year 1	*Year 2*	*Year 3*	*Year 4*	*Year 5*	*Year 6*
NOI	$500,000	$510,000	$520,000	$530,000	$540,000	$550,000
Participation						
10%	50,000	51,000	52,000	53,000	54,000	—

$$\text{Property reversion} = \$550,000 \div 0.08$$
$$= \$6,875,000$$

Loan payment on $3,000,000 loan, 9%, 15 years = $ 372,177
Loan balance end of year 7 (5 years from now) = $2,059,930

Property reversion	$6,875,000
Less mortgage balance	2,059,930
Cash flow	$4,815,070
Participation (10%)	$ 481,507

$$V_M = \text{PV of debt service and balloon} + \text{PV of participations}$$

PV of debt service and balloon = PV of annual payment of
$372,177 for 5 years at 10% +
PV of $2,059,930 end of year 7
at 10%
= $2,689,898

	Year 1	*Year 2*	*Year 3*	*Year 4*	*Year 5*
10% of NOI	$50,000	$51,000	$52,000	$53,000	$ 54,000
10% of reversion					481,507
					$535,507

PV at 12% = $459,856

$$V_M = \text{PV of debt service} + \text{PV of participation}$$
$$= \$2,689,898 + \$459,856$$
$$= \$3,149,754$$

NOTE: The value of the mortgage is higher than the original loan amount of $3,000,000. This could occur if the participation is higher than originally projected or marketed interest rates have changed.

SUMMARY

The market value of a real estate investment is based on the assumption that the property is or can be financed with a loan that represents the norm for that type of property. That is, the amount of financing, the interest rate, the amortization period and other relevant loan terms are at current market rates. For a variety of reasons, a particular property may have financing available that is not at current market rates. When available or existing financing on a property is more favorable than what is typically available in the market, a potential benefit accrues to the equity interest in the property. Thus, a buyer of the equity position may pay a premium for the property for the right to receive the benefits of the favorable financing. In theory, any premium paid for the equity interest is offset by a corresponding loss in the value of the mortgage interest. Because the value of the property is equal to the sum of the mortgage and equity interests, the total property value is not affected by the favorable financing.

For several reasons, appraisers must understand the effect that favorable financing can have on the price paid by an equity investor. First, the appraiser may be asked to value a property subject to existing financing. In this case the appraiser must determine if and how the existing financing will affect what an equity investor will pay relative to what would be paid if the financing were at current market rates. Any difference in this price must be attributed to the effect of the nonmarket financing, not the value of the real property.

Second, when selecting comparable sales, the appraiser must be aware of any unusual financing that may have affected the price paid for the comparable. If the financing for the comparable property was not at market rates at the time it was purchased, the appraiser must make a cash equivalency adjustment. Such an adjustment involves determining how the financing affected the price paid for the comparable so that the price can be adjusted to reflect what would have been paid if financing had been at market rates.

Several techniques of making cash equivalency adjustments were discussed in this chapter. Considerable judgment must be used in making cash equivalency adjustments because of insufficient market data to allow the appraiser to determine the effect favorable financing has on the price paid by equity investors.

KEY TERMS

amortization term
assumability
balloon payment
below-market interest rate

beneficial loan
cash equivalency adjustment
financing premium
market value of a loan

QUESTIONS

1. What is meant by an adjustment for cash equivalency? When is this adjustment necessary?
2. How might an assumable loan have benefits that differ from those that are typical in the market?
3. What is meant by the market value of a loan? How is this used to make a traditional cash equivalency adjustment?
4. How might a balloon payment on an assumable loan affect the financing premium paid to assume the loan?
5. Why might a different cash equivalency adjustment result when considering the return required by equity investors?
6. A property sold for $1 million with an assumable loan for $700,000. The loan has an 8 percent interest rate with a remaining term of 15 years and payments of $6,689.56 per month. Local lenders indicate that market rates for a loan for about 70 percent to 75 percent of the property value would be 10 percent interest with a 15-year loan term. What is the cash equivalent value of the property, assuming the buyer will hold the loan for the full loan term?
7. Refer to problem 6. How would your answer change if you found out that the assumable loan had a balloon payment due after 5 years?
8. A property is projected to have NOI of $100,000 per year for the next 5 years. At the end of the fifth year the investor expects to sell the property for $1.2 million. The seller of the property is willing to provide a loan for $750,000 at an 8 percent interest rate. The loan would be amortized over 25 years, but a balloon payment would be due after 5 years. Local lenders indicate that the rate for a $750,000 loan on the same property would have an interest rate of 10 percent if amortized over 25 years with a 5-year balloon payment. The investor normally requires a 12 percent equity yield rate (Y_E).
   a. How large a financing premium should the investor pay for the property, assuming the same 12 percent equity yield rate is required whether the investor gets the seller financing or a loan at the market interest rate?
   b. How does the answer obtained in part a differ from the answer that would be obtained by discounting the loan savings at the mortgage rate of 10 percent? What is the reason for the difference in answers?
9. A loan was issued two years ago for $4,000,000 at a contract rate of 8 percent with annual payments over a 25-year term. The lender also receives 50 percent of the cash flow (after the contract mortgage payment) each year plus 50 percent of cash flow from sale (after payment of the mortgage balance). NOI is projected to be $400,000 per year for the next 3 years and the property is expected to sell for $5,000,000 after 3 years.

What is the value of the participation loan today, assuming all cash flows are discounted at a 10 percent rate?

END NOTE

1. This also means that the second buyer has to either invest more equity in the property or obtain a second mortgage to make up the difference.

CHAPTER 16	# Risk Analysis

INTRODUCTION

Risk can be defined as the probability that events will not occur as expected. For example, vacancy rates may be higher than anticipated, market rental rates at the time of lease renewals may be lower than predicted, terminal capitalization rates at the time of resale may be higher than expected. Because actual events in the market can differ from what the investor contemplated at the time the property was purchased, the investor's actual rate of return can differ from the return hoped for when the property was purchased. Thus, we can view risk as the probability that the actual rate of return earned by the investor will differ from the return that was expected when the investment was made.

Risk is important for several reasons. First, the investor's desired rate of return depends on the degree of risk. Second, comparable sales should have the same degree of risk for extraction of capitalization rates or rates must be adjusted for differences in risk. Third, discount rates used to calculate the present value of cash flows must be commensurate with the level of risk.

TYPES OF RISK

There are a number of different types of risk that can affect real estate investors. Knowing the sources of risk that can affect a particular real estate investment is the first step in risk analysis. Following is a discussion of the main types of risk.[1]

Space Market Risk

Space market risk is the risk that changes in the market for real estate space will affect market rents, vacancy rates and net operating income (NOI). This can result from either changes in the demand for space by users or changes in the supply of space from new construction. Space market risk is affected by the type of property (office, retail, residential, etc.) and the location of the property. Space market risk deals with uncertainty in the market for the space provided by real estate to potential tenants.

Capital Market Risk

Capital market risk is the risk that changes in the market for capital will affect the value of the real estate. Note that this differs from changes in the market for space (discussed above). Changes in the capital market can be caused by changes in mortgage interest rates (Y_M) or changes in equity yield rates (Y_E). A change in either of these rates will also result in a change in overall yield rates (Y_O). Overall capitalization rates (R_O) may also be affected because they are related to overall yield rates as discussed in chapter 7. Capital market risk is affected by changes in the level of interest rates, changes in the availability of mortgage and equity capital and changes in the rate of return for alternative investment opportunities. Capital market risk affects investors regardless of whether they use debt to finance the investment.

Financial Risk

Financial risk results from use of debt to finance an investment. We saw in chapter 13 that the use of leverage can increase an investor's return on equity if the leverage is positive, but it will decrease the return on equity if the leverage is negative. Investors normally expect leverage to be positive when they purchase and finance property. Due to unexpected changes in market conditions, however, the leverage may turn out to be negative. The impact of space market risk (discussed above) on the investor's overall return on the property (Y_O) is magnified by the use of financial leverage. This is illustrated later in the chapter after we discuss ways of measuring risk. The use of debt also increases the risk of default on mortgage from use of debt. The degree of financial risk increases with the amount of debt. This is illustrated later in this chapter.

Liquidity Risk

Liquidity risk refers to the difficulty of converting an investment into cash at a price close to market value in a reasonable time. Real estate has a relatively high degree of liquidity risk because there are few potential buyers for a particular type of property at any given point in time. Also, real estate is not publicly traded like stocks and bonds.

Inflation Risk

Inflation risk is the risk that unexpected inflation will cause future income from operations and reversion to lose purchasing power, owing due to the probability that actual inflation will differ from the amount of inflation that was expected when the investment was made. Historically, there has been a relatively low level of inflation risk for real estate investments because inflation tends to increase the replacement cost of properties. For example, construction costs tend to increase with inflation. This puts upward pressure on market values. Because real estate is not a fixed income investment (like a bond), market rents can often increase if inflation is greater than expected. Furthermore, lease provisions like CPI adjustments and expense passthrough provisions in office building leases allow the rental income to increase with inflation. In a weak market, however, building owners may not be able to raise rents to match inflation, and property values may not keep up with replacement costs. This is especially true when vacancy rates are high and new construction is not feasible.

Environmental Risk

Environmental risk is the risk that the value of a property will be affected by environmental factors that affect the owner's ability to develop or lease the space. Examples include properties that contain asbestos or that are exposed to toxic waste. Environmental risk is often difficult to measure and the costs associated with curing the problem can exceed the value of the property.

Legislative Risk

Legislative risk is the risk that changes in laws and regulations and will affect the market value of the property. Examples of legislative risk include

- Federal income tax law changes,
- Environmental regulations,
- Changes in zoning,
- Change in land-use regulations and
- Building codes.

Legislative risk increases when changes in legislation are unexpected, especially when they have an unfavorable effect on real estate investments.

Management Risk

Income producing real estate investments require property management. *Management risk* exists because management can affect the performance of the property. Some properties require more specialized management than others, e.g., convention hotels and regional malls. These properties have greater management risk.

SENSITIVITY ANALYSIS

Sensitivity analysis measures how a change in one of the assumptions affects the performance of the property. Examples of assumptions to vary in sensitivity analysis include projected market rental rates, vacancy rates at lease renewals, expense ratios and price appreciation (or depreciation).

Scenarios are alternative assumptions about how the property might perform. It is an extension of sensitivity analysis that recognizes if a change occurs in one variable, other variables are also likely to be affected, e.g., if the market softens, rents may decline and vacancy rates may increase. Three alternative scenarios are usually considered, e.g., a pessimistic scenario, a most likely scenario, and an optimistic scenario. This captures the range of alternatives.

EXPECTED RETURN

A range of possible outcomes such as the equity dividend rate or equity yield rate can be identified from the analysis of scenarios. Each scenario can then be assigned a probability of occurrence based on the appraiser's judgment. The expected rate of return is found by weighing each possible return according to its probability. For example, suppose that the probabilities of occurrence of each scenario are estimated as follows:

Scenario	Overall Yield (Y_O)	Probability
Pessimistic	5	.30
Most likely	10	.40
Optimistic	20	.30

What is the expected return (overall yield rate)?

Solution:

$$\text{Expected return} = 0.05(0.30) + 0.10(0.40) + 0.20(0.30)$$
$$= 0.1150, \text{ or } 11.5\%$$

Note that the expected return is not necessarily the same as the most likely return.

VARIANCE AND STANDARD DEVIATION

Variance is a measure of the uncertainty or risk associated with an investment. It measures the tendency of individual returns to vary from the expected return. The variance is calculated as the mean of the squares of the deviations from the mean of the frequency distribution. The *standard deviation* (SD) is the square root of the variance. The larger the SD or variance, the greater the risk. For a normal distribution, there is about a 68 percent chance that the outcome will fall within plus or minus one SD from what was expected. There is about a 95 percent chance that the outcome will fall within two SDs and there is a greater than 99 percent chance that the outcome will fall within three SDs. (The relationships are discussed in statistics books.)

Using the previous example, the variance is calculated as follows:

$$\text{Variance} = 0.30(0.05 - 0.1150)^2 + 0.40(0.10 - 0.1150)^2 +$$
$$0.30(0.20 - 0.1150)^2$$
$$= 0.003525$$

The standard deviation is found by taking the square root of the variance, e.g., $\sqrt{0.003525} = 0.05937$ or 5.937%.

The expected (mean) return is 11.50 percent, and the calculated SD is about 6 percent. Thus, assuming the returns are normally distributed, there is about a 68% probability that the overall yield will fall within the range of 11.50 percent ± 6 percent, or between 5.5 percent and 17.5 percent.

The mean and variance also can be calculated for equity yield rates (Y_E) and other measures of investment performance.

Ranking Investments

The expected return and standard deviation (of returns) can be used to compare investment alternatives. This is illustrated in an example.

Example

How would you rank the following properties in terms of risk and return?

	Expected Return	*Standard Deviation*
Property A	9%	4.0%
Property B	9	2.0
Property C	10	4.0

Solution: A and B have the same expected return, but A has a higher standard deviation. Thus, B is better than A.

C has the same standard deviation as A but has a higher expected return. Thus, C also is better than A.

Because C has a higher return but more risk than B, it is not possible to say whether B or C is more desirable. This decision depends on the amount of risk the investor is willing to incur for the increase in the expected return. Given the standard deviations, property C could do worse than B.

EXPECTED PRESENT VALUE

We can also identify scenarios for the cash flows for a property and calculate the expected value of the property. This is illustrated in the following example.

Example

A property is projected to have an NOI of $100,000 in year 1.

	Pessimistic	Most Likely	Optimistic
Increase in NOI	0	2%	4%
Resale in year 5	$1,000,000	$1,200,000	$1,400,000
Probability	20%	50%	30%

Do the following exercises, using the assumptions in pessimistic, most likely and optimistic scenarios.

1. Using an overall yield rate (Y_O) of 10 percent to discount the cash flows, calculate the present value of the property for each scenario.

Scenario	Year 1 Cash Flows	Year 2	Year 3	Year 4	Year 5
Pessimistic	$100,000	$100,000	$100,000	$100,000	$100,000 + $1,000,000
Most likely	100,000	102,000	104,040	106,120	108,243 + 1,200,000
Optimistic	100,000	104,000	108,160	112,486	116,986 + 1,400,000

PV @ 10%

Pessimistic	$1,000,000
Most likely	1,138,171
Optimistic	1,276,880

2. Considering the likelihood that each scenario will occur, wh-- is the expected present value?

Expected PV = 0.20($1,000,000) + 0.50($1,138,171) + 0.30($1,276,880)
= $1,152,150

3. Calculate the variance and standard deviation for the present values calculated in exercise 2.

Variance = $0.20(1,000,000 - 1,152,150)^2 + 0.50(1,138,171 - 1,152,150)^2 + 0.30(1,276,880 - 1,152,150)^2 =$
$9,394,902,591

Standard deviation = $\sqrt{9,394,902,591}$ = $96,927

4. Within what range of values could you predict the true value to fall with 95 percent accuracy?

$1,152,150 $\pm$ 2 × $96,927 or $958,296 to $1,346,004

The above analysis indicates the degree of precision of the estimated value. Most appraisers report a single value estimate, e.g., $1,152,150. Based on this analysis, however, we see that this is the midpoint of a range of values that may be correct.

PARTITIONING THE IRR

The expected cash flow from a real estate investment comes from different sources that do not necessarily have the same degree of risk.

Partitioning the IRR is a method of calculating the relative contribution of different components of cash flow to the expected IRR. For example, IRR for a real estate investment can be broken down into the following components:

1. Net operating income
   a. Income from existing leases
   b. Income from expected lease renewals
2. Reversion
   a. Cash flow from recapture of original investment (i.e., purchase price)
   b. Cash flow from expected price appreciation

Partitioning also can be used to break down the cash flows that contribute to the equity yield rate (Y_E). For example, how much of the value comes from the pretax cash flow (NOI – debt service) versus the reversion to the equity investor? Partitioning uses the IRR as a discount rate to calculate the present value of each component of cash flow that is partitioned. By definition, the total present value of all partitioned cash flows must equal the original amount of the investment (e.g., equity investment or purchase price). The relative contribution of each component provides insight into the riskiness of the investment.

Example

An investor considers purchasing one of the following properties. Each can be purchased for $500,000 and would have NOI and an expected sale price after 5 years as follows:

Property	Purchase Price	NOI	Sale Price
A	$500,000	$50,000	$500,000
B	500,000	10,000	744,204

Calculate the IRR, *and partition the IRR for each property.*

Solution:

Property	Year 0	Year 1–5	Year 5	IRR
A	($500,000)	$50,000	$500,000	10%
B	(500,000)	10,000	$744,204	10

Partitioning the IRR using a 10% discount rate

Property	PV of NOI	%	PV of Sale Price	%	Total PV	%
A	$189,539	38	$310,461	62	$500,000	100
B	37,908	8	462,092	92	500,000	100

Property *B* could be considered riskier than property A. A greater proportion of its value depends on the cash flow from the sale in year 5 that relies on price appreciation.

It is insightful to note that the adjusted IRR for property B is higher than that of property A, which is consistent with the differences in risk. Using a 5 percent reinvestment rate, for example, the adjusted IRRs are 9.2 percent and 9.8 percent for properties A and B, respectively.

DISCOUNTING NOI AND REVERSION AT DIFFERENT RATES

Rather than use a single discount rate, it is appropriate to discount sources of cash flow with different degrees of risk at a different discount rate. The NOI is often considered less risky than cash flow from reversion. NOI is

NOI is more dependent on income from existing leases than the reversion that depends on future lease renewals. Therefore the NOI could be discounted at a lower rate than the reversion.

Example:

A property is leased for 5 years with a net lease at $90,000 per year. It is expected to sell for $1,200,000 in 5 years, when the lease expires. The discount rate for the leased portion of the cash flow is 9 percent and the discount rate for the reversion is 12 percent. What is the indicated value?

PV of $90,000 for 5 years at 9% = $350,069
PV of $1,200,000 at the end of 5 years at 12 percent = $680,912
$350,069 + $680,912 = $1,030,981

The value of the property is $1,030,981. Assuming the property is purchased for this amount, what is the IRR?

Year 0	Year 1–5	Year 5
($1,030,981)	$90,000	$1,200,000

IRR = 11.34%

NOTE: In the above example the IRR falls between the discount rate of 9 percent used for the NOI and the discount rate of 12 percent used for the reversion. Conceptually the IRR of 11.34 percent is a weighted average of the 9 percent discount rate for the NOI and the 12 percent discount rate for the reversion. To arrive at the same present value either the NOI and reversion must be discounted at 9 percent and 12 percent respectively, or all the cash flow (income and reversion) must be discounted at 11.34 percent.

EFFECT OF LEVERAGE ON FINANCIAL RISK

This use of debt can result in positive financial leverage as illustrated in chapter 13. The use of leverage also increases financial risk, however, as illustrated in the following example.

Example

Consider the following assumptions about a proposed investment:

Purchase price = $100,000
Debt financing: 10% interest; 30 year amortization

Scenario	NOI	Resale	Probability
Pessimistic	$10,000 per year	$ 90,000	.30
Most likely	12,000 per year	100,000	.60
Optimistic	14,000 per year	110,000	.10

Calculate Y_E at loan-to-value ratios of 0 percent, 30 percent, 60 percent, and 90 percent. How does risk change with different levels of financing?

Loan/value (%)	Pessimistic Return (%)	Most Likely Return (%)	Optimistic Return (%)	Expected Return (%)	Standard Deviation (%)
0	8.31	12.00	15.47	11.24	2.17
30	7.57	12.86	17.70	11.76	3.09
60	5.66	14.97	23.02	12.98	5.34
90	−12.54	28.72	54.38	18.91	21.92

As the loan/value ratio increases, so does the expected return. Thus, there is positive financial leverage. The SD also increases, however, due to an increase in financial risk. An investor choosing no debt can expect no more than an 11.24 percent return, but that investor's pessimistic return is 8.31 percent. An investor who used 90 percent debt would have an expected return of 18.91 percent but could have a negative return of −12.54 percent under the pessimistic scenario.

Financial leverage clearly magnifies the risk in this example. The SD increases from 2.17 percent with no debt to 21.92 percent with 90 percent debt.

SUMMARY

Although difficult to quantify, risk must be considered when doing investment analysis or appraisal. Investors cannot interpret expected returns without considering risk. Appraisers should not select discount rates (Y_O or Y_E) or capitalization rates (R_O or R_E) without considering the riskiness of the interest being valued. In highest-and-best-use analysis of a site, the riskiness of each possible use must be considered when selecting a discount rate or a capitalization rate.

This chapter discussed the different sources of risk that may affect a real estate investment. These risks are interrelated. For example, higher than expected inflation (inflation risk) can also cause interest rates and equity yield rates to increase (capital market risk). Changes in federal income tax laws (legislative risk) can lead to changes in the required before-tax equity yield rate (capital market risk). A decrease in the availability of capital for real estate (capital market risk) can make it more difficult to sell the property (liquidity risk). Environmental problem (environmental risk) can lead to new environmental laws (legislative risk). Alternative ways of measuring the risk include sensitivity analysis, calculating the mean and variance, and partitioning the IRR.

KEY TERMS

capital market risk
environmental risk
expected return
financial risk
inflation risk
legislative risk
liquidity risk
management risk

partitioning the IRR
risk
scenarios
sensitivity analysis
space market risk
standard deviation
variance

QUESTIONS

1. In the context of real estate investment, what do we mean by risk?
2. What is the difference between space market risk and capital market risk?
3. a. What is the purpose of sensitivity analysis
   b. How does the use of scenarios improve on sensitivity analysis?
4. A property is projected to have NOI as shown below. Partition the IRR based on NOI and reversion.

	Year 1	Year 2	Year 3	Year 4	Year 5
NOI	$75,000	$80,000	$85,000	$88,000	$90,000

Reversion (after Year 5) $1,000,000

Assume that the property can be purchased for $800,000.

5. The distribution of expected cash flow from a subject property produces an expected value of $100,000, with a standard deviation of $2,000. What does this suggest about the precision of the value estimate?

6. Would capital market risk affect an investor who does not have a mortgage on the property?

7. A single-use property is leased absolute net for $200,000 per year for the next 10 years to a tenant with an excellent credit rating. The appraiser has applied a terminal capitalization rate to the estimated NOI in year 11 and arrived at an estimated resale price of $2,500,000 when the lease expires at the end of year 10. Based on the yield currently quoted for the tenant's corporate bonds, the appraiser believes that if the income stream were discounted separately from the reversion, it would be discounted at a 9 perent rate. Due to uncertainty about the NOI after the lease expires, the appraiser believes the reversion should be discounted at a 12 percent rate.

   a. What is the value of the property?
   b. What single discount rate would result in the same value?

8. An investor has projected three possible scenarios for a project:

   Pessimistic: NOI will be $500,000 the first year and decrease 3 percent per year over a 5-year holding period. The property will sell for $4,500,000 after 5 years.

   Most likely: NOI will be level at $500,000 per year for the next 5 years. The property will sell for $5,000,000.

   Optimistic: NOI will be $500,000 the first year and increase 3 percent per year over a 5-year holding period. The property then will sell for $5,500,000.

   The asking price is $5,000,000.
   The investor thinks there is about a 20 percent probability for the pessimistic scenario, a 40 percent probability for the most likely scenario, and a 40 percent probability for the optimistic scenario.

   a. Compute the IRR *for each scenario.*
   b. Compute the expected IRR.
   c. Compute the variance and standard deviation of the IRRs.
   d. Would this project be better than one with a 13% expected return and a standard deviation of 4%?

9. Refer to Problem 8. Assume a loan for $4,000,000 is obtained at a 10 percent interest rate and a 20-year term.

   a. Calculate the expected IRR on equity and the standard deviation of the return on equity.
   b. Contrast the results of problem 9 with those of problem 8. Has the loan increased the risk?

END NOTE

1. The types of risk discussed in this section are fairly standard in the finance literature. There are some differences, however, to capture that unique nature of real estate, e.g., the term "space market risk." The discussion of sources of risk in this chapter was influenced by the discussion found in Course 510, Advanced Income Capitalization, published by the Appraisal Institute, 1993.

CHAPTER 17

Tax Considerations in Income Property Valuation

INTRODUCTION

Income from the operation and sale of real estate income property is subject to federal income taxes. Federal income taxes affect the after-tax cash flow and after-tax rate of return available to investors. Thus, investors are concerned about how taxes affect real estate as well as other investment alternatives. This affects the investment value of real estate because the price that investors are willing to pay for a property depends in part on how that property is taxed. All else being equal, investors will pay a higher price for investments that receive a more favorable tax treatment and vice versa. Historically real estate investors received favorable tax treatment, although this has diminished substantially since the Tax Reform Act of 1986.

It is often argued that taxes affect only the investment value of a property because the amount of taxes depends on the particular investor's tax status. Market value does reflect the price that a typical investor is willing to pay. Thus, if the typical investor is concerned about the after-tax IRR, the taxes ultimately affect market value.

This chapter provides an overview of tax considerations that are important to real estate investors. Investment analysis calculations from previous chapters are then extended to show how taxes affect the investor's rate of return and other investment performance measures. The implications for valuation of real estate income property are then discussed.

TAXABLE INCOME FROM OPERATION OF REAL ESTATE

Recall that the calculation of net operating income (NOI) involved deducting expenses associated with operating a property, such as property taxes, insurance, maintenance, management and utilities. After subtracting the mortgage payment from the NOI, before-tax cash flow from operating the property results. Taxable income from operating real estate income property differs from before-tax cash flow derived from operations for two main reasons:

1. Only the interest portion of a loan payment, not the total payment, is deductible from NOI for tax purposes.
2. The tax code allows owners to deduct an allowance for depreciation from NOI.

Thus, taxable income from operating a real estate income property can be stated as follows:

$$\begin{array}{l} \text{NOI} \\ -\ \text{Interest} \\ \underline{-\ \text{Depreciation allowance}} \\ =\ \text{Taxable income} \end{array}$$

The amount of interest deductible in a given taxable year is equal to the total interest paid to the lender during that year.

Depreciation Allowances

Physical assets such as buildings suffer from physical depreciation over time, which reduces their economic value. Because buildings must eventually be replaced and because investment in improvements is allowed to be recovered before income produced from the improvement is taxed, a deduction for depreciation is allowed prior to the determination of taxable income. Otherwise, taxable income would be overstated. Tax laws have historically allowed investors to write off buildings for tax purposes at a rate that exceeds the actual loss in value. Even under the current tax law, buildings can be depreciated on a straight-line basis over a period of either 27½ years for residential properties or 39 years for nonresidential properties.

Depreciation of Personal Property

When investors acquire real estate income property, they also often purchase furniture and fixtures in addition to the land and building. For example, apartments may include stoves and refrigerators, and hotels and motels usually include beds, tables, lobby furniture, kitchen equipment and so on. Furniture and fixtures are categorized as personal property, not real property and may be depreciated over 7 years, using the double-declining balance method. The following table shows the percent of the depreciable basis that would apply for personal property.

Year	Depreciation %
1	14.286
2	24.490
3	17.493
4	12.495
5	8.925
6	8.925
7	8.925
8	4.461
Total	100.000

The first-year depreciation allowance is lower than the second year because the tables assume that the property is purchased in the middle of the tax year. This is also why the property is not fully depreciated until the eighth year.

Loan Points

Points paid in connection with obtaining a loan to purchase, refinance or operate a real estate income property investment must be deducted ratably over the term of the loan. For example, suppose a loan for $1,000,000 is made to purchase an office building. The loan is to be amortized over a 25-year term. Suppose two points, or $20,000, are paid on the loan. For tax purposes, the $20,000 would have to be amortized over 25 years, or $800 per year. If the property is sold before the points are completely amortized, the balance can be expensed in the year of sale. Thus, in the above example, if the property is sold and the loan is repaid after 5 years, $16,000 could be expensed.

The deductibility of points is based on the **term** of the loan, not the amortization period. If the loan in our example had a balloon payment due in the tenth year, then the points could be deducted over 10 years, even though the loan payments are based on a 25-year amortization.

TAXABLE INCOME FROM SALE
OF DEPRECIABLE REAL PROPERTY

To determine whether a taxable gain or loss has occurred when a property is sold, the gross sales price must first be established. The gross sales price is equal to any cash or other property received in payment for the property sold, plus any liabilities against the property assumed by the buyer. Any selling expenses, e.g., legal fees, recording fees and brokerage fees, may then be deducted to establish net sales proceeds. To determine gain or loss, the adjusted basis of the property is subtracted from net sales proceeds. The adjusted basis of a property is its original basis (cost of land and improvements) plus the cost of any capital improvements, made during the period of ownership, less accumulated depreciation taken to date. Any excess of net sales proceeds over the adjusted basis results in a taxable gain, and any deficit results in a taxable loss.

Calculations of taxable income from the operation and disposition of real estate are illustrated in the following section.

AFTER-TAX INVESTMENT ANALYSIS

Let us consider the effect of federal income taxes on the investment analysis example from the beginning of chapter 13, Investment Measures with Mortgage Financing. Our example applies to a depreciable property held by an individual to produce income in a trade or business. We assume that the property is an apartment building. As a starting point for our discussion, Table 17-1 shows the summary calculation of before-tax cash flow from that example.

Table 17-1
Estimates of Cash Flow from Operations

	Year				
	1	*2*	*3*	*4*	*5*
A. Before-tax cash flow					
NOI	$100,000	$102,000	$104,000	$106,000	$108,000
Less: debt service	81,783	81,783	81,783	81,783	81,783
Before-tax cash flow	$ 18,217	$ 20,217	$ 22,217	$ 24,217	$ 26,217

	Year				
	6	*7*	*8*	*9*	*10*
NOI	$110,000	$112,000	$114,000	$116,000	$118,000
Less: debt service	81,783	81,783	81,783	81,783	81,783
Before-tax cash flow	$ 28,217	$ 30,217	$ 32,217	$ 34,217	$ 36,217

After-Tax Cash Flow from Operation

We have estimated before-tax cash flows from the investment. Now we must determine the increase or decrease in the investor's taxable income as a result of undertaking this investment. The investor's federal income tax will either increase or decrease as a result of the investment. We must consider how much taxable income is produced each year from operations and then consider taxes in the year that the property is sold. Table 17-2 shows the calculation of taxable income and after-tax cash flow from operating the property.

Table 17-2
Taxable Income and After-Tax Cash Flow from Operations

	Year				
	1	*2*	*3*	*4*	*5*
B. Taxable income or loss					
NOI	$100,000	$102,000	$104,000	$106,000	$108,000
Less: Interest	74,680	73,937	73,115	72,207	71,205
Depreciation	30,909	30,909	30,909	30,909	30,909
Taxable income (loss)	(5,589)	(2,846)	(24)	2,884	5,886
Tax or (savings)	(1,565)	(797)	(7)	807	1,648
C. After-tax cash flow					
Before-tax cash flow	$ 18,217	$ 20,217	$ 22,217	$ 24,217	$ 26,217
Less tax or add (savings)	(1,565)	(797)	(7)	807	1,648
After-tax cash flow	$ 19,782	$ 21,014	$ 22,224	$ 23,410	$ 24,569

	Year				
	6	*7*	*8*	*9*	*10*
B. Taxable income or loss					
NOI	$110,000	$112,000	$114,000	$116,000	$118,000
Less: Interest	70,097	68,873	67,521	66,028	64,378
Depreciation	30,909	30,909	30,909	30,909	30,909
Taxable income (loss)	8,994	12,218	15,570	19,063	22,713
Tax or (savings)	2,518	3,421	4,359	5,338	6,360
C. After-tax cash flow					
Before-tax cash flow	$ 28,217	$ 30,217	$ 32,217	$ 34,217	$ 36,217
Less tax or add (savings)	2,518	3,421	4,359	5,338	6,360
After-tax cash flow	$ 25,699	$ 26,796	$ 27,857	$ 28,879	$ 29,857

In Table 17-2, we see that taxable income is found by subtracting interest and depreciation from the NOI. Note that only the interest, not the total loan payment, is tax deductible. In our example, interest was based on having a $750,000 loan amortized over a 25-year term with monthly payments based on a 10 percent interest rate. Table 17-3 shows a summary loan schedule for the property.

Table 17-3
Summary Loan Information

End of year	1	2	3	4	5
Payment	$ 81,783	$ 81,783	$ 81,783	$ 81,783	$ 81,783
Mortgage balance	742,897	735,051	726,383	716,807	706,228
Interest	74,680	73,937	73,115	72,207	71,205
Principal	7,103	7,847	8,668	9,576	10,579

End of year	6	7	8	9	10
Payment	$ 81,783	$ 81,783	$ 81,783	$ 81,783	$ 81,783
Mortgage balance	694,542	681,632	667,370	651,615	634,210
Interest	70,097	68,873	67,521	66,028	64,378
Principal	11,686	12,910	14,262	15,755	17,405

Depreciation

Taxable income is also affected by an allowance for depreciation. As discussed earlier in the chapter, residential properties may be depreciated over 27½ years and nonresidential real property must be depreciated over 39 years. Both must be depreciated in a straight-line basis. Also recall that only the improvements, not the land, can be depreciated. Thus, we need to know what portion of the $1,000,000 purchase price of the office building represents building improvements. For our case example, we assume that expenditures for land are 15 percent of the purchase price, or $150,000, leaving improvements of $850,000. Dividing improvement cost by 27½ results in an annual depreciation deduction of 30,909.09.[1]

Depreciation allowances do not represent an actual cash outflow for the investor. The deduction only affects taxable income and after-tax cash flows. In our example, taxable income is −$5,589 in year 1. Assuming the investor is in a 28 percent tax bracket and can use this loss to offset other income,[2] the decrease in tax liability as a result of owning the property will be .28 × $5,589 = $1,565. Adding this to before-tax cash flow results in after-tax cash flow of $19,782 in year 1.

After the third year the taxable income is positive, and additional taxes must be paid as a result of this investment. Note, however, that the taxable income is still much less than the before-tax cash flow.

After-Tax Cash Flow from Sale

Table 17-4 illustrates how sale of the property affects the investor's taxable income.

Table 17-4
After-Tax Cash Flow from Sale

Estimates of Cash Flows from Sale in Year 10

Sales price		$1,200,000
Mortgage balance		634,210
Before-tax cash flow (BTCF)		$565,790

Sales price		$1,200,000	
Original cost basis	$1,000,000		
Accumulated depreciation	309,091		
Adjusted basis		$ 690,909	
Capital gain		$ 509,091	
Tax from sale ($509,091 × 0.28)*			142,545
After-tax cash flow from sale			$ 423,244

*Assumes investor is in the 28 percent tax bracket.

In our example, depreciation was $30,909.09 per year for 10 years, resulting in accumulated depreciation of $309,091. Subtracting the accumulated depreciation from the original cost basis of the property (cost of the land and improvements) results in an adjusted basis of $690,909. The difference between the adjusted basis ($690,909) and the sale price ($1,200,000) is the capital gain, which is $509,091. As discussed earlier, under current tax law the entire taxable gain is taxed at the same rate as ordinary income. Thus, assuming the investor is still in the 28 percent tax bracket upon sale of the property (and assuming tax laws haven't changed again), taxes resulting from sale of the property would be $142,545. Subtracting the tax from the before-tax cash flow results in after-tax cash flow of $423,244.

After-Tax IRR

Using the information from Tables 17-2 and 17-4 we may now calculate the after-tax internal rate of return (IRR). The cash flows are summarized in Table 17-5, along with the before-tax cash flows for comparison.

Table 17-5
Cash-Flow Summary

Cash-flow (CF) summary:

End of year	0	1	2	3	4	5
Before-tax CF	($250,000)	$18,217	$20,217	$22,217	$ 24,217	$26,217
After-tax CF	(250,000)	19,782	21,014	22,224	23,410	24,569

Table 17-5 (continued)

End of year	6	7	8	9	10
Before-tax CF	$28,217	$30,217	$32,217	$34,217	$602,007
After-tax CF	25,699	26,796	27,857	28,879	453,101

Before-tax IRR	15.90%
After-tax IRR	13.27
Effective tax rate	16.57

The after-tax IRR is lower than the before-tax IRR. However, although the investor's tax rate was 28 percent, the after-tax IRR is about 16.5 percent lower than the before-tax IRR. That is,

$$1 - (13.27/15.90) = 16.54\%$$

Thus, the *effective tax rate* for this investment is 16.54 percent.

CLASSIFICATION OF INCOME

The current tax law requires that income and loss from all sources, including real estate, be divided into three categories.[3]

1. Passive income (loss): Income or loss from a trade or business where the investor does not materially participate in the management or operation of the property. Material participation is defined as "involvement in the operations of the activity on a regular, continuous and substantial basis." Real estate investment is considered to be a passive activity. Hence, unless an investor materially participates in the operation of the property, income and losses earned from such activity are categorized as passive income or loss. Income (or loss) received by a limited partner in a partnership is considered passive by definition.
2. Active income (loss): Salaries, wages, fees for services and income from a trade or business in which the investor materially participates. Even if a taxpayer materially participates, however, income or loss from "rental activity" is not considered active income. Thus, income from rental housing, office buildings, shopping centers and other real estate activities in which a taxpayer is a landlord are not classified as active income (or loss). They are classified as passive income. The operation of a hotel, other transient lodging or a nursing home, however, is not a rental activity; therefore, its owners will have active income if they materially participate.
3. Portfolio income (loss): Interest and dividend income from stocks, bonds and some categories of real estate that are classified as capital assets. Examples of portfolio income from real estate activity are (1) dividends

received on shares in a Real Estate Investment Trust (REIT) or (2) income received on long-term land leases or net leases on real estate where the owner does not materially participate in its operation.

In general, passive losses cannot be used to offset income from another category. This is referred to as the "passive activity loss limitation." Passive losses produced from real estate investments and other passive activities must be used to offset passive income earned during the tax year. Any remaining, or unused, passive losses must be "suspended" and carried forward to offset any passive income earned in future years.

When an investment producing passive income is sold and a capital gain occurs, any unused or "suspended" losses from that activity may be

- used to offset any capital gain from the sale of that activity;
- then used to offset any other passive income produced from other passive activities during that year; and
- then used to offset any income, including active and portfolio income, earned during that year.

To the extent that unused losses remain, they may be carried forward into succeeding years as capital losses, not subject to passive loss rules.

Special Exceptions: Loss Allowances for Rental Real Estate

One special exception to the passive activity loss limitation applies to individual rental property owners (other than limited partners). These investors are allowed to offset active income with up to $25,000 of passive activity losses (to the extent they exceed income from passive activities) from rental real estate activities in which the individual "actively" participates. Active participation is less restrictive than the material participation standard referred to earlier and requires less personal involvement. In general, the individual must own a 10 percent or greater interest in the activity and must either be involved in management decisions, selection of tenants and determination of rents or arrange for others to provide services (e.g., a property manager to manage the property on a day-to-day basis).

This special rule is phased out for individuals with adjusted gross incomes between $100,000 and $150,000. When an individual's adjusted gross income for the taxable year exceeds $100,000, the $25,000 loss allowance is reduced by 50 percent of the amount of the excess. Thus, individuals with an adjusted gross income of $120,000 would only be allowed to use up to $15,000 of any passive losses to reduce active income.* An individual with adjusted gross income in excess of $150,000 receives no loss allowance.[4]

---

*The $25,000 loss allowance would be reduced by $10,000 which is 50 percent of the $20,000 when the adjusted gross income exceeds $100,000.

VALUATION USING AN AFTER-TAX APPROACH (OPTIONAL)

It should be clear that federal income taxes affect the investor's after-tax rate of return. Because real estate has some tax benefits (even under the current tax law), investors can afford to accept a lower before-tax IRR on real estate than they would require for a fully taxable investment with similar risk. Thus, taxes affect the investment value of a real estate investment. Although we can still estimate the value on a before-tax basis by selecting the proper before-tax discount rate, doing an after-tax analysis provides a good test of the reasonableness of the value estimate. That is, even though the price is estimated on a before-tax basis, an investor who purchases the property at the appraised value should expect a favorable after-tax IRR. This can be tested in one of two ways:

1. Calculate the after-tax IRR based on the purchase price implied by a before-tax valuation;
2. Estimate the value using an after-tax discount rate.

The valuation techniques discussed in previous chapters were all based on a before-tax analysis. That is, we used a before-tax overall yield rate (Y_O) and a before-tax equity yield rate (Y_E) to estimate value by discounting before-tax cash flows. Property value also may be estimated using an after-tax approach. Conceptually the idea is to find the price that results in a specified after-tax rate of return. In addition to the information required for a before-tax discounted cash-flow analysis, we need to select an after-tax discount rate, a building depreciation method, a building ratio or land value and a tax rate.

Solving for value using an after-tax approach is difficult mathematically because the capital gain will always depend on the price paid for the property, i.e., the unknown value being estimated. This is analogous to the problem discussed in chapters 7 and 14 that occurred when the resale price was expressed as a change from the appraised value. Recall that this requires the use of algebra, yield capitalization formulas or a computer to solve for value. Although this type of problem is best solved with a computer, we will show how the Ellwood yield capitalization formula can be modified to arrive at the same answer. The equation in the following example assumes that NOI is level. However, it can be stabilized using the same techniques discussed in chapter 7.

Example

Assume that a property will have level income of $200,000 per year. The property value will increase by 15 percent over five years. A loan for 75 percent of the appraised value can be obtained at a 10.25 percent interest rate for 30 years (monthly amortization). The building value will be 85 percent of the appraised value, and it will be depreciated on a straight-line basis over 27½ years. The investor will be in a 28 percent tax bracket and require an after-tax equity discount rate of 12 percent.

The modified Ellwood equation that can be used is

$$R_O = \frac{Y_t - M\,[Y_t + P(1/S_n) - R_m + Ft] - Bdt - [\Delta_O(1-t) - nBdt]\,(1/S_n)}{1 - t}$$

Where Y_t = after-tax discount rate
P = percentage of loan paid off over the holding period
Δ_O = change in property value
M = loan-to-value ratio
R_M = mortgage constant
$1/S_n$ = sinking fund factor
B = building-to-value ratio
d = annual tax depreciation rate
t = tax rate
F = interest factor

Using the information from the example we have

Y_t = 0.12
P = 0.032688
Δ_O = 0.15
M = 0.75
R_m = 0.107532
$1/S_n$ = 0.15741
B = 0.85
d = 1/27.5 = 0.036364
t = 0.28
F = 0.101143 (mortgage interest factor calculated below)
n = 5

The F factor transforms the mortgage interest payments into their level equivalent annual annuity. The method used is the same as the method used to calculate the X factor for transforming variable NOIs into their level equivalent annuity. The factor is needed because only the interest payments on a mortgage are deductible for tax purposes. Following is the derivation of the F factor:

Example

Year	Interest* Payment		Present Value Factor @ 12%		Present Value
1	0.102256	×	0.892857	=	0.091300
2	0.101691	×	0.797194	=	0.081067
3	0.101061	×	0.711780	=	0.071933
4	0.100369	×	0.635518	=	0.063786
5	0.099596	×	0.567427	=	0.056513

Present Value   0.364599

	Present Value		Factor @ 12%†		
F =	0.364599	×	0.277410	=	0.101143

*The amounts in this column are the amount of interest each year (sum of the interest for each month) expressed as a percentage of the original loan amount. For example, interest during the first year is 10.2256 percent of the original loan amount. These amounts can be obtained from a loan schedule for a loan of $1.00.
†Installment to amortize $1 factor @ 12 percent.

We can now substitute the above information into the modified Ellwood equation.

$$R_O = \frac{0.12 - 0.75\,[0.12 + (0.032688)(0.157410) - 0.107532 + (0.101143)(0.28)] -}{1 - 0.28}$$

$$\frac{[0.85\,(0.036364)(0.28)] - [0.15(1 - 0.28) -}{1 - 0.28}$$

$$\frac{5\,(0.85)\,(0.036364)(0.28)]\,(0.15741)}{1 - 0.28}$$

$$R_O = \frac{0.12 - 0.034450 - 0.008655 - 0.010189}{.72}$$

$$R_O = 0.092648$$

Value
$$= \frac{NOI}{R_O} = \frac{\$200,000}{0.092648} = \$2,158,715$$

The investor should be willing to pay $2,158,715 for the property. This is the price that will result in an expected after-tax IRR of 12 percent. To show that this is true, we can now calculate the following:

Implied resale	1.15	×	$2,158,715	=	$2,482,522
Loan amount	0.75	×	$2,158,715	=	$1,619,036
Equity	0.25	×	$2,158,715	=	$539,679
Building value	0.85	×	$2,158,715	=	$1,834,908

Using this information we can develop the following five-year cash-flow forecast.

Value Solution Summary
After-Tax Cash Flow (ATCF)

	Year 1	Year 2	Year 3	Year 4	Year 5
NOI	$200,000	$200,000	$200,000	$200,000	$200,000
Debt service 1	− 174,098	− 174,098	− 174,098	− 174,098	− 174,098
Cash flow (BT)	$ 25,902	$ 25,902	$ 25,902	$ 25,902	$ 25,902
NOI	$200,000	$200,000	$200,000	$200,000	$200,000
Interest	165,557	164,640	163,623	162,498	161,251
Depreciation	− 66,724	− 66,724	− 66,724	− 66,724	− 66,724
Taxable income	− 32,281	− 31,363	− 30,347	− 29,221	− 27,975
Taxes	− 9,039	− 8,782	− 8,497	− 8,182	− 7,833
Cash flow (AT)	$ 34,940	$ 34,683	$ 34,399	$ 34,084	$ 33,735

After-Tax Cash Flow from Reversion

Resale price	$2,482,522	Resale price	$2,482,522
Adjusted basis	− 1,825,095	Loan balance 1	− 1,566,113
Taxable gain	657,427	Before-tax proceeds	916,410
Taxes at resale	184,080	Taxes	− 184,080
		After-tax proceeds	732,330

Year	ATCF
0	($539,679)
1	34,940
2	34,683
3	34,399
4	34,084
5	766,065

$$Y_t = \text{IRR} = 0.12, \text{ or } 12\%$$

The IRR for the above after-tax cash flows is 12 percent, which is what we used as a basis for estimating the value using the modified Ellwood equation. This proves that the equation gave us the correct value.

Conclusion

The above analysis is rather cumbersome. We could have arrived at the same answer, however, with a computer program. For example, we could have used a trial-and-error process to estimate the price that would result in the same 12 percent after-tax IRR with the same assumptions about financing, depreciation, taxes, etc. The computer can be programmed to do this very quickly, eliminating the need to use any special equations. The approach above was used to illustrate the technique of after-tax valuation.

SUMMARY

Federal income tax laws affect the after-tax cash flows that are available from a real estate income property investment. The taxation of real estate differs from many other investments such as stocks and bonds. Therefore, many investors believe that they must compare the after-tax cash flows and after-tax IRRs when evaluating different investment alternatives.

Because taxes can affect investment decisions, it is useful for appraisers to be able to calculate the after-tax IRR for a real estate investment. If the typical investor for a property being appraised is a taxable investor, then the expected after-tax IRR must be sufficient to attract investment capital.

This chapter discussed the key tax considerations that affect real estate income property and illustrated the calculation of the after-tax IRR. An optional technique for estimating the value of a property on an after-tax basis was also demonstrated. In practice, the same answer can be obtained by using a discounted cash-flow computer program to determine the purchase price that results in a specified after-tax IRR.

The purpose of this chapter was to provide a general overview of how federal income taxes might affect the price a typical investor might pay for a real estate income property. The purpose was not to provide sufficient information to allow tax planning for a particular individual. This is not within the purview of a real estate appraiser. Investors should consult their tax accountant for advice as to the tax consequences of their specific investments.

KEY TERMS

accumulated depreciation
active income
adjusted basis
after-tax cash flow
after-tax IRR
capital gain
depreciation allowance

effective tax rate
gross sale price
net sale proceeds
passive income
portfolio income
taxable income

QUESTIONS

1. Why should appraisers be concerned about the effect of federal income taxes on real estate returns?
2. What is meant by "passive income"? Why is this important to real estate investors?
3. How is the gain from the sale of real estate taxed?

4. What is meant by an "effective tax rate"? What does it measure?
5. Do you think taxes affect the value of real estate versus that of other investments?
6. A property is projected to have NOI of $100,000 per year for the next five years. It can be purchased for $1,000,000 and financed with a $750,000 loan at a 10 percent interest rate with monthly payments over a 25-year term. For tax purposes, 15 percent of the purchase price would be considered land and the rest would be considered improvements that would be depreciated over 27½ years using straight-line depreciation. The property is expected to be sold for $1,200,000 at the end of a five-year holding period. The investor is in a 30 percent tax bracket and can use any tax losses from this investment to offset other income.
   a. Calculate the after-tax cash flow from operations and reversion.
   b. What is the after-tax IRR?
   c. What is the effective tax rate?
   d. Suppose an appraiser is asked to value this property and believes that the investor described above is typical except that the appraiser thinks the after-tax discount rate should be 12 percent. Does this imply that the property value would be higher or lower than $1,000,000? Explain but do not calculate.

END NOTES

1. The IRS publishes tables that taxpayers must use to calculate depreciation deductions. The tables assume that the investor purchases the property in the middle of the month and prorate the first-year depreciation according to the actual month of the year the property is purchased. We are simply dividing by 27½ years.

2. As discussed later in this chapter, there are severe limits on the ability of real estate investors to use tax losses to offset income from other investments.

3. The following tax rules are based on the Tax Reform Act of 1986. See Chapter 11, *Real Estate Finance and Investments* by William B. Brueggeman and Jeffrey D. Fisher, published by Richard D. Irwin, Inc., 9th edition, 1993 for a further discussion and numerical examples of the effect of tax rules on real estate investors.

4. For further discussion see P. Fass, R. Haft, L. Loffman and S. Presant, *Tax Reform Act of 1986* (New York: Clark Boardman Co., Ltd., 1986).

CHAPTER 18

Selecting and Supporting the Discount Rate

INTRODUCTION

The keys to the reliability of a value estimate found by using either discounted cash flow or yield capitalization lie both in the quality of the cash-flow forecast and in the proper selection of the discount rate. As indicated earlier, the term "discount rate" is another name used to identify a yield rate. The term discount rate is usually used when the purpose of the analysis is to find the present value of a series of cash flows using a specified yield rate. That is, the discount rate represents the yield rate that the investor requires to make the investment. Because a number of values could represent various ownership interests (property, equity, mortgage, leased fee and so on) and, therefore, a number of discount rates, a descriptor must be included with the discount rate to identify the interest being appraised. For example, if a property value is being estimated using an unleveraged analysis on a before-tax basis, the discount rate used would be referred to as the "overall discount rate." Because this is conceptually the same as the overall yield rate, the same symbol (Y_O) is used for both. Conversely, if the equity interest is being appraised using a mortgage/equity approach, the discount rate used to arrive at the present value of the equity cash flows is referred to as the "equity discount rate" (Y_E). Discount rates address profitability directly and are comparable to yield rates for alternative investments available in the market. In theory, expected yield rates for alternative investments should differ only if there is a difference in the riskiness of the investment alternatives.[1]

DISCOUNT RATE EXAMPLES

For review, the property overall yield rate (Y_O) and before-tax equity yield rate (Y_E) will be extracted from the following example.

Example

Cash-Flow Summary

Given:

Value	$1,000,000
Loan amount	$700,000
Loan term	25 years
Interest rate	10%
Payments	Monthly
Equity	$300,000
Holding period	5 years
NOI (level)	$100,000
Resale	$1,100,000

Year	1	2	3	4	5
NOI	$100,000	$100,000	$100,000	$100,000	$100,000
Debt service	− 76,331	− 76,331	− 76,331	− 76,331	− 76,331
BTCF	$ 23,669	$ 23,669	$ 23,669	$ 23,669	$ 23,669

Resale price	$1,100,000
Less loan balance	− 659,146
Before-tax proceeds	$ 440,854

Summary of Yield Rates

Year	Y_O	Y_E
0	($1,000,000)	($300,000)
1	100,000	23,669
2	100,000	23,669
3	100,000	23,669
4	100,000	23,669
5	100,000	23,669
5 (resale)	1,100,000	440,854

Overall Yield Rate	Equity Yield Rate
$Y_O = 11.59\%$	$Y_E = 14.87\%$

The rates are referred to as yield rates because they represent internal rates of return that are calculated from the cash flows for each of the two interests.

Property Yield (Discount) Rate: Y_O

In the previous example the property yield rate (Y_O) is the interest rate that discounts all cash flows to be received by the property owner on an unleveraged basis to a present value equal to the property value. This rate of return is relatively comparable to that on alternative investments, including

- commercial mortgage rate,
- corporate bond rate and
- corporate junk bond rate.

Each of these rates is quoted on a before-tax unleveraged basis. In most cases, the real estate investment is generally riskier than most of the above investments, except, possibly, for certain classes of junk bonds.

Before-Tax Equity Yield (Discount) Rate: Y_E

The before-tax equity yield rate (Y_E) is the interest rate that discounts all future cash flows to be received by the equity investor to a present value equal to the equity. These rates are comparable to returns on the kinds of investments listed above, except that real estate returns reflect the impact of financing. Because many other investments cannot be financed on a similar basis, before-tax Y_E should be significantly higher than the unleveraged rates.

SELECTION OF RATES

There are three basic approaches to selecting discount rates, including the buildup approach, the alternative investment comparison method and the implied rate extraction approach.

Buildup Method

The traditional *buildup method* of selecting discount rates attempts to build up a rate by first identifying the return on a risk-free investment, then adding a premium for the risk associated with real estate. Real estate is riskier than relatively riskless investments like short-term Treasury bills.

In theory a yield rate consists of a safe real rate plus expected inflation plus a risk premium:

$$Y_O = \text{risk-free real rate} + \text{expected inflation} + \text{risk premium}$$

The risk-free real rate is compensation for the time value of money, i.e., for waiting to receive the cash flow from an investment. This rate tends to fall in the 2 percent to 3 percent range over extended periods of time. An adjustment for expected inflation is added to the risk-free real rate as an adjustment for the loss in purchasing power due to inflation over the investment holding period. This is not a risk premium. This adjustment would be necessary even if we were certain about the future rate of inflation. Any risk resulting from the rate of inflation differing from expectations should be reflected in the risk premium.

The risk premium is compensation for the different types of risk that may affect the investment, as discussed in chapter 16, Risk Analysis. For example, a premium would be added for market risk, management risk, liquidity risk and so on. An additional risk premium would have to be added to overall discount rate (Y_O) to obtain an equity discount rate (Y_E) because of the additional financial risk due to financial leverage as discussed in chapter 13.

In practice it is difficult to build up a discount rate for real estate by using these theoretical components. The safe real rate is difficult to measure at any given point in time, and it is very difficult to quantify each type of risk that must be included in the risk premium.

In theory, this method should provide an excellent way of estimating a discount rate. In practice, it is difficult to translate risk factor segments into supportable number estimates. The method, however, provides a foundation for the next approach, alternative investment rate comparison.

Alternative Investment Comparison

A second approach to selecting discount rates is the alternative investment comparison method, which compares real estate investments with alternative investments in the market and makes adjustments for dissimilarities. The primary comparisons include commercial mortgage interest rates and corporate bond rates (typically, Baa and junk bonds). Concerning commercial mortgages, a commercial lender occupies the "first position" in a property, a position that is said to be less risky than the owner's position on an unleveraged basis. Therefore, the property yield would be expected to be higher than that at regular mortgage interest rates. Mortgage interest rates and corporate Baa rates have been observed to move in the same relative direction over time and to be at comparable levels over time. Property yields, though, are expected to be slightly higher than Baa bond rates. The risk associated with junk bonds led to theories that junk bond rates and unleveraged real estate yields were reasonably comparable.

In the early and middle 1980s, after the high inflation of 1980 and 1981 and the tax law changes of 1981, the real estate market became oriented to tax-shelter benefits. These tax benefits became so substantial that in some cases, before-tax yields fell below mortgage interest rates, a situation that could be justified only after consideration of the considerable tax benefits available. The tax laws were changed in 1986, and many of the tax benefits were removed. In 1987, real estate analysis became less tax-oriented and more oriented toward the economics of the property itself. This condition remained as we entered the 1990s.

Discount Rate Extraction from Comparables

Property Discount Rate. Another potential source of discount rate information is comparable sales data. The discount rate itself, however, is not directly extractable because it is a function of the property's expected performance over time. In other words, it cannot be calculated without identifying the future cash-flow expectations of the buyer.

Obviously, the best method of obtaining an investor's discount rate is simply to ask the investor what rate of return was the target rate used to determine the purchase price. If an investor is willing to report the target rate, the appraiser should also inquire as to what the investor's cash-flow expectations were. On receiving the information, the appraiser should test the consistency of the data by calculating the internal rate of return (on either a leveraged or unleveraged basis), given the price paid and the investor's cash-flow expectations, as demonstrated below.

Example

Sample Rate (Y_O) Extraction: Sale No. 1

Sales Price	$2,650,000

Investor's Expectations:

Target property yield rate (Y_O)	13%
Net operating income (NOI) (first year)	$275,000
Assumed change in NOI	3% per year
Assumed resale price	15% increase over 5 years
Disposition costs	2% of sales

Year	Implied Cash Flows
0	($2,650,000)
1	275,000
2	283,250
3	291,747
4	300,500
5*	$3,296,065

*{$309,515 + [($2,650,000)(1.15)] (1 − 0.02)} = $3,296,065

$$IRR = Y_O = 12.90\%$$

In this instance, the rate of return found, given the investor assumptions, was 12.90 percent, which supports the 13 percent rate reported.

Frequently, however, buyers will not divulge their investment criteria, or they may be difficult to contact. In this instance, an appraiser can analyze the sales price using sensitivity analysis by calculating a yield rate for an assumed cash-flow pattern based on the appraiser's understanding of the market. This technique is presented below.

Example

Sample Rate (Y_O) Extraction: Sale No. 2

Sales price	$1,200,000
NOI	$ 115,000
Overall rate	0.0958

Estimate the property yield rate (Y_O) assuming a 3 percent annual change in value and income over a 5-year holding period.

Year	Forecast Cash Flow
0	($1,200,000)
1	115,000
2	118,450
3	122,004
4	125,664
5*	$1,520,563

*{$129,434 + [($1,200,000)(1.03)^5]} = $1,520,563

$$\text{IRR} = Y_O = 0.1258, \text{ or } 12.58\%$$

In this instance the implied property rate (Y_O) is 12.58 percent, assuming a 3 percent annual change in income and resale. The rate can also be calculated assuming various other levels and income and value changes.

Income and Resale Percent Change

% Change	1%	2%	3%	4%
Year	Cash Flow	Cash Flow	Cash Flow	Cash Flow
0	($1,200,000)	($1,200,000)	($1,200,000)	($1,200,000)
1	115,000	115,000	115,000	115,000
2	116,150	117,300	118,450	119,600
3	117,311	119,646	122,004	124,384
4	118,485	122,039	125,664	129,359
5	1,380,882	1,449,377	1,520,563	1,594,517
Y_O	10.58%	11.58%	12.58%	13.58%

NOTE: A shortcut method of calculating Y_O by adding the percent change to the overall rate of 9.58 percent can be used in the preceding example because the income and resale are assumed to be changing annually at the same compounded rate. This shortcut approach does *not* work if NOI and resales are not moving at the same annual rate (maybe because of an existing lease structure) or if you are extracting before-tax Y_Es after consideration for financing.

As demonstrated above, there is a different property Y_O for each change pattern. Which pattern represents the expectations of a typical investor? Assuming the information from data sample 1 regarding the expected change in income and value (about 3 percent per year) is typical, the information from data sample 2 suggests a property yield rate of about 12.5 percent (rounded). We have therefore narrowed the range for a discount rate from 12.5 percent to 13 percent. We would use a rate in this range to value similar properties.

It should be noted that the yield rate is directly affected by the level of change assumed in future cash flows. The importance of understanding this relationship is that when selecting a discount rate, the appraiser should be aware of the implied change in the cash-flow forecast. In other words, the appraiser should not select the cash-flow pattern and discount rate independently of each other. The pattern and rate should be selected simultaneously, with consideration for this interrelationship.

Graphical Analysis

It is useful to use the information in the above table to graph the relationship between the yield rate (Y_O) and the change in income and property value. This is done in Figure 18.1. Calculations of (Y_O) for some additional growth rates were added to extend the range of the graph.

The figure shows the yield rate that would be consistent with an assumption about the growth rates (for income and property value). Any of the points

FIGURE 18.1   Yield Versus Growth Rate

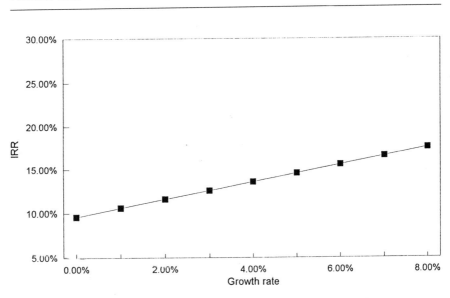

on the line in the graph would justify the price actually paid for property number 2. That is, if the investor expected income and property value to increase 3 percent per year, then he or she could have expected a yield rate of about 12.5 percent. Or if the investor expected income and property value to increase 6 percent per year, he or she could have expected a yield rate of about 15.5 percent. Any of the combinations of yield rate and growth rate that are on the line in the graph would explain the price actually paid for the property. Therefore, if an appraiser used one of these combinations as assumptions in a discounted cash-flow analysis, she or he would have estimated a value for property 2 that is the same as the price the investor actually paid. On the other hand, combinations of yield rate and growth rate that are **not** on the graph would not result in a value estimate equal to the price paid for the comparable sale. For example, if the appraiser assumed a 2 percent change in income and property value and a 15 percent yield rate, she or he would obtain a higher value than actually paid for the property.

Although the appraiser may not know what assumptions the investor really had in mind, the above graphic analysis helps narrow the range of possibilities. Furthermore, the appraiser may have other information that helps narrow the range even further. For example, we saw that the investor in property number 1 indicated that he expected income and property value to increase 3 percent per year and expected a yield of 13 percent, which is close to the points on the graph for property number 2. Because the market is not perfect and the two properties are not exactly the same, we should not expect the relationship between the growth rate and yield rate to be exactly the same for both properties. The appraiser also may have done her own analysis of recent trends in rental rates and market values and may believe that a 3 percent growth rate is reasonable. Thus, the appraiser would feel comfortable assuming a 3 percent growth rate and selecting a 12.5 percent yield rate to appraise a property similar to the two comparable sales we just analyzed.

Before-Tax Equity Discount Rate.   Like property yield rates, before-tax Y_Es also can be selected by direct investor contact or through sensitivity analysis of a comparable sale. When gathering rates or applying sensitivity analysis, it is essential not only to identify any future patterns of change in the cash flows but also to investigate the method of financing, because the before-tax equity yield rate is influenced by the financing structure, as will be demonstrated below. The data below include financing data gathered from the buyer of each property.

Example

Sample Rate (Y_E) Extraction: Sale No. 1

Sales Price	$2,650,000
Investor's Expectations:	
Target equity yield rate (Y_E)	18%
NOI (first year)	$275,000

Assumed change in NOI	3% per year
Assumed resale price change	15% increase over 5 years
Disposition costs	2% of sales
Loan amount	$2,000,000
Loan term (monthly payments)	25 years
Interest rate	11%

The implied cash flows would be as follows:

Year	1	2	3	4	5
NOI	$275,000	$283,250	$291,748	$300,500	$309,515
Debt service No. 1	− 235,227	− 235,227	− 235,227	− 235,227	− 235,227
Cash flow (BTCF)	$ 39,773	$ 48,023	$ 56,521	$ 65,273	$ 74,288

Reversion Cash Flow

Resale price	$3,047,500
Selling cost	− 60,950
Loan balance No. 1	− 1,899,098
Before-tax proceeds	1,087,452

Year	Implied BTCF
0	($ 650,000)
1	39,773
2	48,023
3	56,521
4	65,273
5	1,161,740

$$\text{IRR} = Y_E = 0.1776, \text{ or } 17.76\%$$

In this instance the before-tax Y_E is 17.76 percent, approximately equal to the investor's expectations. The implied loan-to-value ratio is 75.47 percent ($2,000,000/$2,650,000). The use of the mortgage to finance the property resulted in positive leverage and raised the equity investor's return by 4.86 percent (from 12.90 percent to 17.76 percent).

Sensitivity analysis also may be used to extract data from data sample 2. In this instance the property was financed with a $780,000 loan at a 10.5 percent interest rate for 25 years. The before-tax Y_E, assuming a 3 percent annual change in NOI and resale, is calculated as follows:

Example

Sample Rate (Y_E) Extraction: Sale No. 2
Annual Cash-Flow Summary

Year	1	2	3	4	5
NOI	$115,000	$118,450	$122,004	$125,664	$129,434
Debt service No. 1	− 88,375	− 88,375	− 88,375	− 88,375	− 88,375
BTCF	$ 26,625	$ 30,075	$ 33,629	$ 37,289	$ 41,059

Reversion Cash Flow

Resale price	$1,391,129
Loan balance	− 737,657
Before-tax proceeds	$ 653,472

Year	BTCF
0	($420,000)
1	26,625
2	30,075
3	33,629
4	37,289
5	694,531

$$\text{IRR} = Y_E = 0.1588, \text{ or } 15.88\%$$

In this instance, assuming a 3 percent annual change in income and resale results in an implied before-tax Y_E of 15.88 percent. This is significantly below the 17.76 percent found using data sample 1. These yields are not comparable, however, because the loan-to-value ratios are not the same. This property has a loan-to-value ratio that is lower than the property in data sample 1 (65 percent versus 75 percent). Thus, we would expect the equity yield rate to be lower because there is less leverage. (Leverage is favorable for both properties.) If a 75 percent loan were used for this property, the equity yield rate would be 17.60% as shown below.

Loan-to-Value Ratio	65%*	75%†
Year	BTCF	BTCF
0	($420,000)	($300,000)
1	26,625	13,028
2	30,075	16,478
3	33,629	20,032
4	37,289	23,692
5	694,531	567,449
$Y_E =$	15.88%	17.60%

*Actual loan.
†Recalculated with same loan-to-value ratio as property 1.

Using a loan representing a 75 percent loan-to-value ratio would have resulted in a before-tax Y_E of 17.6 percent for property 2, which is almost equal to the implied rate in property 1.[2] Thus, if an equity yield rate was being selected to value a property with a 75 percent loan, a range of Y_E from about 17.5 percent to 18 percent appears to be supported by these two comparable sales.

This analysis highlights the fact that an appraiser must select a discount rate that is consistent with the other assumptions about the property, such as the expected change in income and value and the loan-to-value ratio.

Graphic Analysis.   Graphic analysis can be used to analyze the relationship between the equity yield rate (Y_E) and growth rate (for income and property value), as was done earlier to analyze the overall yield rate (Y_O). This is shown in Figure 18.2.

The interpretation of this graph would be similar to that of Figure 18.1, except that we now are analyzing combinations of growth rate and equity yield rate that are consistent with the price actually paid for property number 2 as well as the way it was financed. The appraiser would estimate a value that was the same as the price actually paid for property 2 if one of the points on the graph were used for assumptions about the growth rate and discount rate and the same assumption were made about the way the property was financed.

These graphs are simply a way of graphically representing the results of a sensitivity analysis of the assumptions for a discounted cash-flow analysis. An approach to this type of graphic analysis that was used before the advent of personal computers was to use the Ellwood equation (discussed in chapter 14) to solve for the points on the graph. To use this approach, simplifying assumptions had to be made about the change in income, e.g., that the income was level (and only the value changed) or that the income changed according to the J factor premise introduced in chapter 7. This is illustrated in the appendix to this chapter.

Estimating a Discount Rate Based on Surveys.   A survey of market participants as to their yield expectations is another way to select an appropriate

FIGURE 18.2   Equity Yield Versus Growth Rate

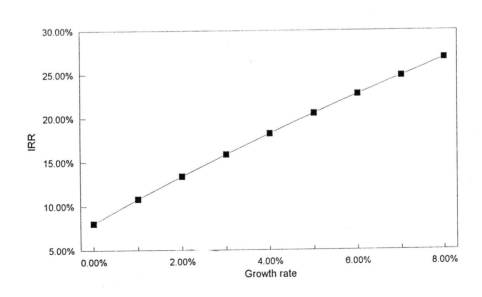

capitalization rate or discount rate. Surveys are regularly taken by professional associations and appraisal companies, and the results are published in newsletters.[3] They typically include information on current overall capitalization rates, terminal capitalization rates, equity capitalization rates and expected yield rates. The information is usually reported for different geographic areas and property types.

Example

Following is an example of a typical survey:

Real Estate Investment Criteria

Property Type	Industrial	Retail		Office		Apartment
		Regional Centers	Community/ Neighborhood/	CBD	Suburban	
Overall yield (IRR) range, %	11–14	10–14	11.0–14.0	11–15	12–16	11–14
Average, %	11.9	11.6	12.1	12.9	13.0	11.4
Going-in cap rate, %	9.6	7.7	9.9	9.7	10.0	9.1
Terminal cap rate, %	9.7	8.3	10.1	9.6	9.9	9.3
Year capped	11	11	11	11	11	11
Change in Income, %	1.0–2.0	3–5	2–4	3.0–4.0	2.0–2.5	3.0–4.0
Anticipated holding period (years)	10	10	10	10	10	10

The results of surveys can be used as further support for the assumptions derived from the analysis of comparable sales, as discussed earlier in this chapter. For example, suppose we are appraising a CBD office building, and we feel that the above survey is representative. The survey indicates that investors are looking for an overall yield rate in the range of 11 percent to 15 percent. (Note that this is within the range we obtained from the graphic analysis discussed earlier in the chapter, although we did not specify the property type in those examples.) The survey also indicates a going-in capitalization (cap) rate of 9.7 percent and a change in income of 3 percent to 4 percent. This is the capitalization rate that would be used to estimate the value of the property at the date of the survey, i.e., applied to the income expected the year following the survey. Note that if the change in income is added to the going-in cap rate, we obtain an estimate of the overall yield rate (assuming income and property value change at the same rate) of 12.7 percent to 13.7 percent, which is consistent with the survey results for the yield rate.

The survey indicates that investors are estimating the resale price by applying an 9.6 percent terminal capitalization rate to the income in year 11 (which would suggest a 10-year holding period). The terminal cap rate is slightly lower than the going-in cap rate. The slightly lower terminal cap rate suggests investors expect office market to improve over the next ten years.

Surveys must be used with caution because they may not be representative of the property being appraised. However, they do provide a good test of the reasonableness of the discount rate and other assumptions used in a discounted cash-flow analysis.

YIELD FOR ALTERNATIVE INVESTMENTS

An estimate of the yield of real estate can be obtained by examining trends in the yield for alternative investments. These trends can then be compared with those for real estate yields obtained from surveys as discussed in the previous section.

Example

The following table illustrates yields for mortgages, 10-year Treasuries and real estate.

	1989	1990	1991	1992
Average real estate yield (%)*	11.3	11.4	11.9	12.2
Long-term mortgages	10.2	10.0	8.5	9.3
10-Year Treasuries (%)	8.7	8.4	7.9	6.9

*From surveys as discussed earlier.

Note that the spread between real estate and 10-year Treasuries widened over the period shown in the table. This suggests investors believe the risk for real estate was increasing from 1989 through 1992.

REAL VERSUS NOMINAL DISCOUNT RATES

A *real* discount rate is the return that would be required if there was no inflation. The term *nominal discount rate* refers to the rate that can be observed in the market. It includes inflation expectations. It is the rate that is typically used by appraisers because it is what we observe on alternative investments. Similarly, lenders quote a nominal mortgage interest rate. Their perceived risk and their expectation for inflation over the term of the loan are built into this rate.

It is necessary, therefore, that forecasts of income and reversion also reflect inflation expectations of the typical investor. That is, to be consistent with the use of a nominal discount rate, we must project nominal income. Note that the growth rate for income and property value discussed in the earlier examples also included inflationary expectations. It is difficult to separate changes in income and property value that are due to expected inflation from changes that are due to changes in market conditions.

Some appraisers attempt to get around this problem by projecting cash flows in real terms and discounting the cash flows with a real discount rate. The *real cash flow* is the cash flow that would occur in the absence of inflation. Similarly, the *real discount rate* is the rate that would occur if there were no inflation.

As already discussed, it is difficult to use a real discount rate because most rates are quoted on a nominal basis. We do not know what rate of return investors would require for real estate if there were no inflation because the risk relative to alternative investments also would change if there were no inflation. Real estate historically has been a better hedge against inflation than other investments. Thus, real estate is more desirable during periods of high and uncertain inflation. For example, if inflation is expected to be 3 percent per year but is actually 5 percent, real estate rents and values may rise by an additional 2 percent to compensate investors for the higher rate of inflation. In contrast, the interest income and face value of fixed-income investments like corporate bonds cannot increase to compensate the investor for the loss in purchasing power due to the higher inflation rate. Thus real estate may be perceived as less risky in an inflationary environment, and a greater risk premium may be required for real estate investments than for corporate bonds.

Relationship Between Real and Nominal Rates

Although it is difficult to know the real discount rate, in theory the relationship between the nominal and real discount rates can be expressed as follows:

$$(1 + \text{nominal rate}) = (1 + \text{real rate}) \times (1 + \text{expected rate of inflation})$$

For example, suppose the real rate of return that investors want for a risk-free investment like a Treasury bill is 3 percent and the expected rate of inflation is 2 percent. The nominal rate of return is

$$(1 + \text{nominal rate}) = (1 + 0.03) \times (1 + .02)$$
$$\text{nominal rate} \quad = 1.0506 - 1$$
$$= .0506, \text{ or } 5.06\%$$

As an approximation, the real rate and expected inflation rate simply are added. Using the above example, we obtain a nominal rate of

$$3\% + 2\% = 5\%$$

We also can solve for the implied real rate, given a nominal rate and inflation expectations. The formula is

$$(1 + \text{real rate}) = (1 + \text{nominal rate}) \div (1 + \text{expected inflation})$$

For example, if the nominal rate for a Treasury bill is 10 percent and inflation is expected to be 3 percent, then the real rate is found as follows:

$$(1 + \text{real rate}) = (1 + 0.10) \div (1 + 0.03)$$
$$= 1.068$$
$$\text{real rate} \quad = 1.068 - 1$$
$$= .068, \text{ or } 6.8\%$$

If the projected cash flows and the discount rate are both properly adjusted for inflation, the resulting estimate of value will be exactly the same, whether we discount nominal cash flows using a nominal discount rate or use discount real cash flows that use a real discount rate. This can be illustrated with the two examples that follow.

Example

Assume that vacant land values are expected to increase at the inflation rate. A particular investment in land is expected to have a nominal value of $100,000 one year from now. This estimate was based on an increase in land area values due to inflation, which is expected to be 4 percent. What is the present value using a **nominal** discount rate of 10.24 percent?

Using a nominal discount rate of 10.24 percent, the estimate of present value is $100,000 ÷ 1.1024 = $90,711.

Example

Refer to the previous example. What is the estimate of present value using a **real** discount rate?

$$\text{Real discount rate} \quad = (1.1024 \div 1.04) - 1$$
$$= 6\%$$

$$\text{Real value of land reversion} = \$100,000 \div 1.04$$
$$= \$96,153.80$$

By discounting the real reversion at a real discount rate, the estimate of present value is $\$96,153.80 \div 1.06 = \$90,711$.

Note that the answers for the above two examples are the same. In theory it should not make a difference whether we discount real or nominal cash flows as long as we select the appropriate discount rate. This also is true if there are annual cash flows from operations in addition to a reversion. (The above example had only a reversion to simplify the calculations.) The questions are what investors expect the cash flow to be and what discount rate is appropriate. On balance, it is probably easier to do the analysis in nominal terms for the reasons discussed earlier.

REVIEW OF RELATIONSHIPS AMONG RATES[4]

The focus of this chapter has been on selection of a proper discount rate. We have discussed a number of ways to do this. Also, throughout the text we have discussed a number of relationships between various yield rates. In this section we summarize the key relationships.

Expected Relationship Between Y_O (Fee Simple) and Y_{LF} (Leased Fee)

Recall that a leased fee estate is subject to existing leases. This means there are tenants who have signed leases. Assuming those tenants have a good credit rating, Y_{LF} (leased fee) is probably less than Y_O (fee simple). If the leases are at below market rents there is *less* risk involved because tenants are less likely to default on leases. On the other hand, if rents are above market and the tenants are more likely to default, Y_{LF} (leased fee) is probably greater than Y_O (fee simple).

Expected Relationship Between Y_O and R_O

Recall that R_O and Y_O are only equal for perpetuity. If income and property value is expected to increase, the overall rates should be less than the overall yield rate. Similarly, if income and property value is expected to fall, the overall rate should be greater than the overall yield rate.

If income and property values are changing in opposite directions, the relationship is uncertain and depends on the magnitude of change of each. This is unlikely, however, because changes in property value are related to changes in income.

Expected Relationship Between Y_E and R_E

Recall that the equity capitalization rate (R_E) considers the cash flow during the *first* year of the holding period; however, the equity yield rate (Y_E) considers the cash flow over the entire holding period, including resale. If the equity value is expected to increase over time owing to price appreciation and/or amortization of the loan, then the equity yield rate should be greater than the equity capitalization rate. However, if the equity is expected to decrease over time owing to price depreciation and/or negative amortization of the loan, then the equity yield rate should be less than the equity capitalization rate.

Expected Relationship Between R_O and R_E

Both the overall capitalization rate (R_O) and the equity capitalization rate (R_E) are based on the first year of the holding period. Recall from our discussion of the band of investment technique in chapter 14 that the overall capitalization rate (R_O) is a weighted average of the mortgage constant (R_M) and the equity dividend rate (R_E). However, an investor may purchase a property with $R_O < R_M$ and still expect $Y_E > Y_M$ because the equity investor benefits from loan amortization and any expected increase in property value. Thus, the relationship between R_O and R_E is ambiguous.

Expected Relationship Between R_O (Going-In Cap Rate) and R_T (Terminal Cap Rate)

We know that the overall capitalization rate depends on the expected yield rate and expected change in income and property value **at the time the property is purchased.** Similarly, the terminal capitalization depends on the expected yield rate and expected change in income and property value **at the time the property is to be sold.**

Whether the terminal cap rate is higher or lower than the going-in capitalization rate depends on how yield rates and rates of growth for income and property values are likely to change over the investment holding period. If yield rates and market conditions are expected to remain the same over time, these two rates should be about the same, with the exception that a risk premium is typically added to the going-in capitalization rate to obtain the terminal capitalization rate, as discussed earlier. The terminal capitalization rate could be lower than the going-in capitalization rate, however, if yield rates are expected to fall significantly and/or the market is expected to improve rates are expected to fall significantly and/or the market is expected to improve significantly and if higher growth rates for income and property value are expected in the future.

Expected Relationships Between Y_O, Y_E and Y_M

The overall yield rate (Y_O) is a weighted average of the mortgage yield rate (Y_M) and the equity yield rate (Y_E). In theory, we have

$$Y_O = \overline{M} \times (Y_M) + (1-\overline{M}) \times Y_E$$

Where $\overline{M}$ is the average loan-to-value ratio over the investment holding period. The loan-to-value ratio (M) *usually is not the same each year* because the loan is amortized and the property value usually changes over time. Thus, the above formula only provides an approximation of Y_O if we use the *initial* loan-to-value ratio (M) in the formula.

The expected equity yield rate (Y_E) should be higher than the mortgage rate, (Y_M) because the equity investor incurs more risk than the mortgage lender. Of course, the equity investor's *actual* Y_E could be lower than the Y_M depending on what actually happens after the property is purchased.

As discussed above Y_O is a weighted average of Y_M and Y_E. Because Y_E is expected to exceed Y_M, it follows that we should expect Y_E to exceed Y_O.

The above relationship is what should be *expected* at the time that the investment is purchased. The point is that the appraiser should select an equity yield rate that is higher than an overall yield rate that would be selected for the same property.

Expected Relationship Between Y_E (Pretax) and Y_E (After Tax)

The current tax law still provides some tax benefits to real estate investors. Taxable income is usually less than before-tax cash flow.

Because interest is fully tax deductible, we have

$$Y_M \text{ (after-tax)} = Y_M \text{ (pretax)} \times (1 - \text{actual tax rate})$$

Because the use of debt (assuming positive leverage) magnifies tax benefits, we have

$$Y_E \text{ (after-tax)} = Y_E \text{ (pretax)} \times (1 - \text{effective tax rate})$$

Recall from chapter 17 that the effective tax rate is usually less than the investor's actual tax rate.

SUMMARY

Proper application of discounted cash-flow analysis requires selection of an appropriate discount rate that can be supported by market evidence. The discount rate should reflect the expected rate of return required by typical investors for the ownership interest being valued. There are different discount rates for each ownership interest. This chapter emphasized selection of the property yield rate (Y_O) and the equity yield rate (Y_E).

This chapter illustrated various ways of selecting and supporting the discount rate chosen for a discounted cash-flow analysis. One approach is to use information from surveys of investors. This can provide valuable insights into their yield expectations as well as going-in and terminal capitalization rates for different property types. A second approach is to examine the historical relationship between real estate and other investments such as mortgages and 10-year Treasuries. In theory, expected rates of return for different investments and different ownership interests should differ only because of differences in perceived risk. Thus, yield rates for real estate should be comparable to rates of return expected on alternative investments with similar risk. We should normally expect the yield for real estate equity investments to be higher than mortgages or Treasuries because of their higher risk. The risk premium can change over time, however, as illustrated in the chapter. Information from sales of comparable real estate investments can be used to provide an indication of the rate of return the purchaser might have expected. Graphical analysis can be used to examine how this rate of return is related to the projected change in the property's value over the investment holding period. Finally, discount rates and capitalization rates should be selected to be consistent with the theoretical relationships among these rates.

KEY TERMS

buildup method
graphical analysis
nominal discount rate

rate extraction
real discount rate

QUESTIONS

1. What is meant by the "buildup method" of developing a discount rate? What factors are considered in using this method to develop a rate?
2. What alternative investments do you think would have expected rates of return that are comparable to real estate? Explain.
3. How can a discount rate be extracted from comparable sales? What assumptions must be made to do this?
4. How would selection of the equity yield rate differ from selection of the overall yield rate to use when discounting cash flows to estimate value?
5. How would the overall yield rate be expected to differ from the mortgage yield rate for the same property?

6. How would the loan-to-value ratio for a property affect selection of a discount rate to estimate the value of the equity position?
7. What is the difference between a real discount rate and a nominal discount rate?

END NOTES

1. Differences in the taxation of alternative investments can also cause *before-tax* yield rates to differ. Investors may be willing to accept a lower before-tax yield rate on an investment that has favorable tax treatment because after-tax yield rates will be comparable. Prior to the Tax Reform Act of 1986, which eliminated much of the favorable tax treatment of real estate, real estate had relatively low before-tax rates of return because investors could also shelter other taxable income by owning real estate.

2. It should also be noted that property 2 had a slightly lower mortgage interest rate (10.5 percent versus 11 percent), which is consistent with the fact that the lender's risk is slightly less with a lower loan-to-value ratio. Thus, it could be argued that we should have used an 11 percent interest rate when calculating the equity yield for property 2 at a higher loan-to-value ratio.

3. Examples include the *Korpacz Real Estate Investor Survey* published quarterly by Peter F. Korpacz & Associates, Inc. and the *Real Estate Outlook* published quarterly by Cushman & Wakefield, Inc.

4. A similar "Review of Relationships Among Rates" discussion appears in Course 510, Advanced Income Capitalization, published by the Appraisal Institute, Chicago, Illinois (1993).

APPENDIX: Graphic Analysis with Ellwood Equation

In chapter 18 we saw how graphic analysis could be used to analyze yield rates. The approach used in the chapter was to solve for the yield rate based on different assumptions about the change in income and property value. This relationship was then plotted on a graph. Another way to calculate the points for this type of graph is to solve for the change in income and property value necessary to obtain a specified yield rate. The difference is that we specify the range of yield rates, then solve for the rate of change rather than starting with a rate of change and solving for the yield rate. This does not change the appearance of the graph. It is simply a different way of selecting the points to plot on the graph.

In this appendix we will show how to solve for the change in property value for a specified range of yield rates by using a modification of the Ellwood formula, described in chapter 14. This approach was used before the advent of personal computers when the Ellwood formula provided a convenient way to solve this type of problem.

Example

The following information is given for a comparable sale:

Sale price	$1,200,000
NOI in year 1	$ 115,000
Overall rate	0.0958

Change in NOI	Related to change in value (J factor pattern)
Loan terms	75% loan-to-value ratio; 10.5% interest rate, 25 years (monthly payments)

Income is assumed to follow the J factor pattern described in chapter 7. Although this pattern of change over time is hard to describe, it is a convenient way to have the income and property value change by the same total amount over the holding period. Its mathematical properties are such that it also can be conveniently used with the Ellwood equation to solve discounted cash-flow problems. The Ellwood formula is normally used to solve for an overall rate that is then used to calculate the property value. In this case we will start with the overall rate implied by the comparable sale in the above example. The unknown that we will solve for is the total change in income and value (represented by Δ) necessary to achieve a range of specified equity yield rates. To do this, we can rearrange the Ellwood formula as follows:

$$\Delta = \frac{Y_E - M[Y_E + P(1/S_n) - R_M] - R_O}{R_O J + 1/S_n}$$

where Δ is the change in income and property value. From chapter 14, recall that M is the loan to value ratio, Y_E is the equity yield rate, P is the percentage of the loan repaid during the holding period, R_M is the mortgage loan constant, R_O is the overall capitalization rate, $1/S_n$ is a sinking fund factor (based on the equity yield rate and the holding period) and J is the factor that allows income to change in the Ellwood equation. (An alternative assumption that we could have made is that income is level and only the value changes, as specified by Δ. In this case J would be zero in the above equation.)

Using the above equation, we can solve for Δ. This is done for both 5-year and 10-year holding periods in the following table:

5-Year Holding Period				10-Year Holding Period			
Y_E	$1/S_n$	J	Δ	Y_E	$1/S_n$	J	Δ
14%	0.1513	0.4932	9.08%*	14%	0.0517	0.3387	21.96%
16	0.1454	0.4789	12.16%	16	0.0469	0.3133	31.21%
18	0.1398	0.4650	15.43%	18	0.0425	0.2893	41.98%
20	0.1344	0.4514	18.95%	20	0.0385	0.2668	54.50%

*[0.14 − 0.75 (0.14 + (0.054286)(0.151283) − 0.113302) − 0.0958] / [(0.0958)(0.4932) + 0.1513] = 0.0908 or 9.08%.

As was done in this chapter, the relationship between the yield rate and the change in income and value can be plotted as shown in Figure 18A.1.

Based on this graphical analysis, the investor would earn a 16 percent before-tax equity yield rate if NOI and value increase by a total of about 12 percent over a 5-year holding period or about 31 percent over a 10-year holding period. This is a change of about 3 percent per year. The interpretation of the graph would be the same as discussed in this chapter. The only

FIGURE 18A.1   Equity Yield Rate Versus Change in Income and Value

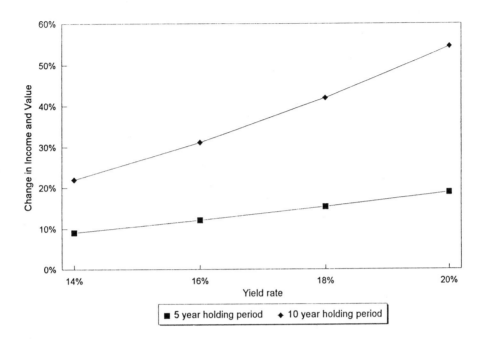

difference here is that the Ellwood formula is used to calculate the points plotted in the graph.

The relationship between the equity yield rate and the change in income and value depends on the amount of financing. To illustrate this, suppose we use the same example as before but assume that the loan-to-value ratio is 85 percent. The results are shown in the following table.

Y_E	$1/S_n$	J	Δ	Y_E	$1/S_n$	J	Δ
14%	0.1513	0.4932	7.32%*	14%	0.0517	0.3387	17.89%
16	0.1454	0.4789	9.29	16	0.0469	0.3133	24.25
18	0.1398	0.4650	11.40	18	0.0425	0.2893	31.61
20	0.1344	0.4515	13.66	20	0.0385	0.2668	40.09

*[0.14 − 0.85 (0.14 + (0.054286)(0.1513) − 0.113302 − 0.0958] / [(0.0958)(0.4930) + 0.151283] = 0.0732 or 7.3%.

A graph of the results is shown in Figure 18A.2.

Note that the required change in income and value (Δ) is now less than before for the same yield rate. Conversely, the same change in income and value will result in higher equity yield rates owing to the effect of financial leverage. This is illustrated in Figure 18A.3. Because the change in NOI and

---

FIGURE 18A.2   Equity Yield Rate Versus Change in Income and Value (85% loan)

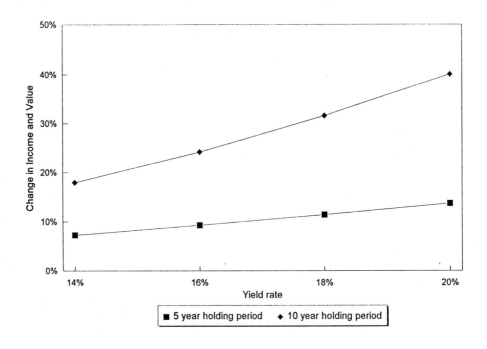

value should be independent of the amount of financing, this analysis again highlights the impact of the loan-to-value ratio on the before tax equity yield rate. As emphasized in this chapter, the yield rate selected in a discounted cash-flow analysis must consider the amount of financial leverage. The lesson to be learned is that the appraiser must be careful when comparing the yield rate graphs for comparables that were financed with different loan-to-value ratios, because the graphs could not be expected to depict the same pattern regarding equity yield rate and change in NOI and value.

FIGURE 18A.3 Equity Yield Rate Versus Change in Income and Value: 75% and 85% loan

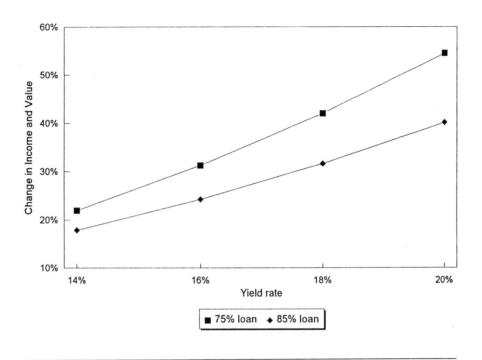

CHAPTER 19

Highest and Best Use Analysis: Applications

INTRODUCTION

This chapter is devoted to presenting analytical approaches to estimating the *highest and best use* of a site as if vacant and "as improved." The techniques are presented last for this reason: An appraiser must have a prior understanding of the three approaches to estimating value because the analytical approaches used to estimate value are the same techniques used to analyze highest and best use. Actually, a highest and best use analysis starts with a series of value estimates (assuming different uses), and the scenario that results in the highest value (either land or as improved) for the property is the highest and best use.

Highest and best use of land as if vacant is defined as that use, from among reasonably probable and legal alternative uses, found to be physically possible, appropriately supported, financially feasible and that results in the highest land value.

The highest and best use of the site as improved is defined similarly, except it is the use that results in the highest property value.

Highest and best use for the property as improved may be the same as or different from the highest and best use of the land as if vacant. If the highest and best use of the improvements is not the same as the land as if vacant, the highest and best use as improved is referred to as the highest and best "interim" use of the property.

If the value estimate for the land as if vacant and assuming its highest and best use alone is higher than the value estimate of the improved property assuming its highest and best use, then the value of the property is equal to the value of the land alone less costs to demolish the existing improvements.

IMPORTANCE OF HIGHEST AND BEST USE

Making judgments of the highest and best use of the land and property as improved are key elements in an appraisal report. The highest and best use judgment directly determines which comparable sales are applicable and which valuation methods are the most appropriate. If the highest and best use of the vacant land were judged to be commercial but the property was improved with apartment units, it would be inappropriate to use multifamily land sales to estimate the value of the land. Highest and best use is essentially a selection standard for the "best course of action" for a typical investor to follow from among those alternatives that meet the basic standards of acceptability. It is the "best" among those alternative uses that are physically possible, legally permissible, appropriately supported and financially feasible. Traditionally, in the valuation of real estate, uses that are strictly for the "public good" without a judgment as to their economic viability are not considered.

Selecting the potential uses for the vacant land and improvements requires a detailed analysis of both current market conditions and the property itself. Market, marketability, investment analyses and feasibility studies all play important roles in selecting the highest and best use and form the backbone of the analytical framework of the real estate appraisal.

A highest and best use study involves testing many alternative uses to select the one that appears to be the optimum under current market conditions. The key words in the previous sentence are "current market conditions" because, although a use may appear to be obvious at first, an oversupply condition in that particular market may mean that another use is dictated at that moment.

THE FOUR TESTS OF HIGHEST AND BEST USE

The four tests used to select the highest and best use of a site as if vacant and as currently improved are:

1. Is the use physically possible?
2. Is the use legally permitted?
3. Would the use be financially feasible?
4. Would the use be maximally productive (result in the highest value)?

Typically, these tests are applied in the order listed above, but the sequencing of the tests should have no impact on the final highest and best use selected for either the land or the improvements. A sequencing that began with legally permitted use may reduce the number of choices, but it would not change the conclusion as to the ultimate highest and best use for a property.

When estimating the highest and best use of the site, the appraiser should not only identify the use in general but also identify the general characteristics of improvements that, if constructed, would represent the optimum improvement for the site.

Physically Possible

The first consideration generally tested in making a highest and best use judgment is whether the use is *physically possible.* Factors that include topography, soil conditions, subsurface or surface water, land size and/or shape, and possibly even weather patterns can make the construction of a particular improvement impossible. This first test is generally the easiest hurdle to overcome, because there are generally a great number of physically possible uses for a site. Because the appraiser is asked not only to identify the use for the site but also to identify the characteristics of optimum improvements, care should be taken to ensure that the apparent optimum improvement could be physically built on the site.

Legally Permitted

The second test involves making a judgment of which of the physically possible uses selected are *legally permitted.* Legal restrictions could include zoning, subdivision restrictions, setback, side yard, parking and building coverage restrictions, easements, leases, operational restrictions such as rent controls and/or building height limits. Making judgments concerning these factors may be difficult because some are subject to change. In some instances, logical changes may not take place because of political reasons. For example, most appraisers have been exposed to spot zoning where a zoning change occurred because of political influence rather than as a result of logical thought processes.

Probably the most difficult assignment an appraiser or analyst has is to analyze or estimate the value of a parcel of land that does not appear to be zoned correctly, given current market conditions or trends in the marketplace. It is possible and logical for an appraiser to select a highest and best use not allowed under current zoning if market conditions, trends, activities or opinions of knowledgeable people (the zoning director, for instance) indicate a change of zoning is likely. An appraiser should not assume a zoning change is likely, however, without substantial evidence to support such a conclusion.

A similar problem arises when an existing improvement does not conform to existing zoning restrictions because it was constructed before the implementation of the zoning ordinance. In this instance, the use is "grand-fathered" in, but severe limitations are likely to be placed on the operation itself and changes that can be made. In most instances, a change in use is not allowed, and restrictions are placed on expanding and/or replacing the improvements if they are damaged.

Financially Feasible

The third test involves a detailed market analysis of each use that passes the physical and legal tests to ensure that a use is *financially feasible.* For those uses that appear to be market supported (conform with the current and fore-seeable land use patterns), data needed to undertake financial feasibility tests should be gathered, including information on rents, expenses, absorption rates, construction costs, discount rates and desired profit levels. Analytical models should be created for each use, to estimate the residual value of the land after consideration of the costs involved to construct the theoretically ideal improvements for the use being considered. For example, if one of the possible uses of a site is as a shopping center, an appraiser must create a valuation model that mirrors the key factors involved in building a center on the site, for example, construction type and quality, building design, tenant mix, rental rate range, absorption period, operating expenses and reasonable rates of return. Obviously, these valuation models would mirror those presented in the "valuation" chapters of this book. Once the models are created, the next task is to eliminate the uses that do not appear to be feasible, that is, uses that do not appear to have potential values in excess of costs.

Maximally Productive

After eliminating the uses that are not physically possible, legally permitted, market supported or economically feasible, the remaining potential uses would probably be limited. The final step is to select the use that is *maximally productive,* that results in the highest value for the land and highest and best use of the improvements (if applicable). A highest and best use determination in essence cannot be made before application of the valuation approaches to the subject property. In many cases the highest and best use of the land and improvements may be obvious, but an appraiser must analyze each option thoroughly to ensure that the judgments made are supported.

Some textbooks suggest that the test of highest and best use is the use that provides the highest return to the land. An assumption made when using this test is that the land value is known before the analytical tests are applied. This assumption appears to be in conflict with the purpose of highest and best use, which is to determine the use that maximizes the value of the land. In addition, a test that emphasizes the level of the rate of return without recognition of the fact that one type of use may be riskier than another (a regional shopping center versus a recreational theme park) may result in an illogical conclusion about the highest and best use of the site.

HIGHEST AND BEST USE OF THE LAND

The first use selection made by an appraiser is the highest and best use of the site as if it were vacant and ready for development. With properties that are already improved, this premise is somewhat theoretical in nature. However, although theoretical, this approach is required to appropriately address the valuation issues that are the foundation of appraisal theory, including the concepts of anticipation and contribution. Each potential use is subjected to the four tests until a single use emerges as the highest and best use. The best method to test each choice is to "build" the "optimum" improvement for each use, estimate the value of each property after construction of the improvement, subtract the cost to improve the property and test to see whether the use selected results in the highest land value.

Sometimes the highest and best use selected represents a general use such as commercial or industrial. Because numerous commercial (retail, hotel, office, restaurant and so on) uses exist for a tract of land, it seems desirable, where appropriate, to select the narrowest choice possible. For example, density is a key issue in multifamily property, so it would appear that a highest and best use judgment should also include a density quantifier or at least a range of densities.

Key data in estimating the highest and best use of land include vacant land sales, zoning, demographic data for the neighborhood, market trends with regard to land use, recent income and expense data for improvements for various uses, physical information for the site and demand and supply data for the market.

HIGHEST AND BEST USE OF IMPROVED PROPERTY

If the property has an existing, income-generating improvement, after determining the highest and best use of the site as if the improvements were not in existence, the appraiser is asked to select the highest and best use of the property as currently improved.

The first step an appraiser takes when making this judgment is to select a list of possible uses for the property. Generally, this list is relatively small and includes the current use plus several closely related alternatives.

In some instances, however, there may be conversion or rehabilitation potential that can complicate the analysis. For example, a building may be used for low-quality offices, but its location on a major thoroughfare may suggest that rehabilitation into retail space would generate higher net operating income. In this case, an additional consideration in the highest and best use judgment would be the cost to rehabilitate the space plus any costs needed to attract the appropriate tenants. Another possibility might be to rehabilitate the current building while maintaining the same general use. In this case, the rehabilitation costs must be considered as well as rentup of the rehabilitated space.

Even when highest and best use of the land corresponds with the highest and best use of the improvements, the highest and best use issue may not be totally resolved because the improvements may not meet the test of providing optimum efficiency. For example, the improvements may be too small, resulting in the existence of excess land; or the improvements may be functionally inefficient, which would result in obsolescence adjustments in the valuation approaches.

The financial analysis of highest and best use of the improvements may become very complex and require numerous calculations. Financial scenarios for each possible legal and appropriately supported use must be developed, including estimates of value assuming typical absorption rates, costs of conversion or rehabilitation and rates of return typical of the use.

The highest and best use of the property as improved is the use that results in the highest present property value. The present value is the present worth of all forecast future net cash flows discounted at a typical market rate of return. Should the value of the improvements, based on their highest and best use, be less than the value of the land, based on its highest and best use, minus the cost of demolition of the improvements, the improvements would contribute no value. The highest and best use would be to remove the improvements.

If the highest and best use for the site and improvements are different, the highest and best use of the improvements becomes the highest and best *interim use.* Typically, in this case, if land values based on the highest and best use of the site are increasing at a faster rate than the value as improved, the economic life of the building is reduced. This suggests that the improvements will be removed some time in the future before the end of their remaining physical life.

HIGHEST AND BEST USE EXAMPLES

Following are examples of typical approaches to estimating the highest and best use of a site and of existing improvements.

Highest and Best Use of Vacant Land

Description of the Land.   The subject land is a rectangular tract containing 4.6 acres with frontage on Maple Avenue, a major commercial street. The tract is gently rolling and has 400 feet of frontage. It is readily visible from Maple Avenue as well as Interstate 100, just to the west. There is a major interchange at the intersection of Maple and Interstate 100.

Neighborhood Description.   Both employment and population have increased at a steady pace in recent years. The neighborhood has an above-average income level and has a high percentage of midpriced to high-priced residential housing. Currently the office vacancy rate is 6 percent, the retail vacancy is 10 percent and the typical hotel occupancy is 70 percent.

Preliminary Findings.   The site appears suitable for a high-rise office building, a small specialty shopping center or a hotel. Following is an analysis of each option. Each analysis assumes the construction of what would be considered an optimum structure for the site for each use.

Example

Office Building Option:

Proposed building size	90,000 square feet (SF)
Efficiency ratio	85%
Net rentable area	76,500 SF
Market rent/SF rentable area	$14.00
Market operating expenses/SF gross building area (GBA)	$4.50
Market vacancy rate	6% (in the 3rd year)
Building cost/SF GBA	$55.00
Cost of site improvements	$200,000
Rentup period	1 year

The typical property discount rate (Y_O) for office buildings appears to be 12 percent, assuming a 3 percent annual change in incomes and expenses. Following is a 5-year discounted cash-flow analysis for the project, which assumes a 1-year construction period, a 1-year rentup and a reversion calculated by capitalizing the fifth-year income by 10 percent.

Example, *continued*

Five-Year Discounted Cash Flow

Year	1	2	3	4	5
Income	$ 0	$1,103,130	$1,136,224	$1,170,311	$1,205,420
Vacancy %	N/A	50%	6%	6%	6%
Vacancy	0	− 551,565	− 68,173	− 70,219	− 72,325
Effective gross income	$ 0	$ 551,565	$1,068,051	$1,100,092	$1,133,095
Operating expenses	− 0	− 417,150	− 429,665	− 442,554	− 455,831
NOI	$ 0	$ 134,415	$ 638,386	$ 657,538	$ 677,264
Improvements cost	− 5,150,000	0	0	0	0
Net cash flow	−$5,150,000	$ 134,415	$ 638,386	$ 657,538	$ 677,264

$$\text{Resale} = \frac{\$677,264}{0.10} = \$6,772,640$$

Year	Cash Flow		Present Value Factor @ 12%		Present Value
1	−$5,150,000	×	0.892857	=	−$4,598,214
2	134,415	×	0.797194	=	107,155
3	638,386	×	0.711780	=	454,390
4	657,538	×	0.635518	=	417,877
5	677,264	×	0.567427	=	384,298
5	6,772,640	×	0.567427	=	3,842,977
Present value					$ 608,483

Comments: The present value of the land under this scenario is $608,483, or $3.04 per square foot.

Example

Shopping Center Option:

Proposed building size	65,000 SF
Market rent/SF GBA	$10.00
Market operating expenses/SF GBA	$2.00
Market vacancy rate	10% (in year 4)
Building cost/SF GBA	$50.00
Cost of site improvements	$300,000
Rentup period	2 years

The typical property discount rate (Y_O) for shopping centers appears to be 12 percent, assuming a 3 percent annual change in income and expenses. Following is a 5-year discounted cash-flow analysis for the project, which assumes a 1-year construction period, a 2-year rentup period and a reversion calculated by capitalizing the fifth-year income by 10 percent.

Example, continued

Five-Year Discounted Cash Flow

Year	1	2	3	4	5
Income	$ 0	$669,500	$689,585	$710,273	$731,581
Vacancy %	N/A	67%	33%	10%	10%
Vacancy	− 0	− 448,565	− 227,563	− 71,027	− 73,158
Effective gross income	$ 0	$220,935	$462,022	$639,246	$658,423
Operating expenses	− 0	− 133,900	− 137,917	− 142,055	− 146,316
NOI	$ 0	$ 87,035	$324,105	$497,191	$512,107
Improvements cost	− 3,550,000	0	0	0	0
Net cash flow	−$3,550,000	$ 87,035	$ 324,105	$ 497,191	$ 512,107

$$\text{Resale} = \frac{\$512,107}{0.10} = \$5,121,070$$

Year	Cash Flow		Present Value Factor @ 12%		Present Value
1	−$3,550,000	×	0.892857	=	−$3,169,642
2	87,035	×	0.797194	=	69,384
3	324,105	×	0.711780	=	230,691
4	497,191	×	0.635518	=	315,974
5	512,107	×	0.567427	=	290,583
5	$5,121,070	×	0.567427	=	2,905,833
Present value					$ 642,823

The present value of the land under this scenario is $642,823, or $3.21 per square foot.

Example

Hotel Option:

Proposed building size	130,000 SF (225 rooms)
Average room rent/night	$55.00
Occupancy, %	70%
% income attributable to room rent	65%
Typical profit percentage	20%
Building cost/room	$30,000
Cost of site improvements	$200,000
Cost of personal property/room	$5,000

The typical property discount rate (Y_O) for hotels appears to be 14 percent, assuming a 3 percent increase in room rental rates and a constant occupancy of 70 percent. Following is a 5-year discounted cash-flow analysis for the project, which assumes a 1-year construction period, an immediate achievement of 70 percent occupancy and a reversion calculation based on capitalizing the fifth-year NOI using an 11 percent overall rate.

Example, continued

Five-Year Discounted Cash Flow

Year	1	2	3	4	5
Room rate	$ 55.00	$ 56.65	$ 58.35	$ 60.10	$ 61.90
Room nights	82,125	82,125	82,125	82,125	82,125
Potential room income	4,516,875	4,652,381	4,791,994	4,935,712	5,083,537
Occupancy	0%	70%	70%	70%	70%
Room income	0	3,256,667	3,354,396	3,454,998	3,558,476

Year		1	2	3	4	5
Total income		0	5,010,256	5,160,609	5,315,382	5,474,578
Profit, %		20%	20%	20%	20%	20%
Cash flow	$	0	$1,002,051	$1,032,122	$1,063,076	$1,094,916
Improvements*	− 8,075,000 −		0 −	0 −	0 −	0
Net cash flow	−$8,075,000		$1,002,051	$1,032,122	$1,063,076	$1,094,916

*Hotel, Site Improvements, Personal Property

$$\text{Resale} = \frac{\$1,094,916}{0.11} = \$9,953,782$$

Year	Cash Flow		Present Value Factor @ 14%		Present Value
1	−$8,075,000	×	0.877193	=	−$7,083,333
2	1,002,051	×	0.769468	=	771,046
3	1,032,122	×	0.674972	=	696,653
4	1,063,076	×	0.592080	=	629,426
5	1,094,916	×	0.519369	=	568,665
5	$9,953,782	×	0.519369	=	5,169,686
Present value					$ 752,143

The present value of the land under this scenario is $752,143, or $3.75 per square foot.

Summary

Office building	$608,483
Shopping center	$642,823
Hotel	$752,143

Conclusion. In this instance, the highest and best use of the site is for a hotel. The 2-year rentup caused by low shopping center occupancy has adversely affected the value for the shopping center and the office rent levels, the office value. Note that the size of the building and the income-generation potential were not overriding factors in this analysis.

Land Density Issue

Description of the Land. The subject land is an 8.2-acre tract that has a highest and best use as a site for multifamily dwellings. The issue, however, is what type of project would represent the highest and best use: a 125-unit apartment project or a low-density, 68-unit condominium project.

Neighborhood Description. The neighborhood appears suitable to support either a high-end apartment project or a condominium project.

Apartment Project Option:

Proposed number of units	125
Average unit size	840 SF
Average monthly rent	$420
Stabilized vacancy %	8%
Operating expense ratio	35%
Building costs/SF GBA	$34.00
Cost of site improvements	$200,000
Rentup period	6 months

COMMENTS: The typical property discount rate (Y_O) for apartment projects is 12 percent, assuming a 4 percent change in income and expense. Following is a 5-year discounted cash-flow analysis for the project, which assumes a 6-month construction period, a 6-month rentup period and a reversion calculated by capitalizing the fifth-year NOI by 10 percent.

Example

Five-Year Discounted Cash Flow

Year	1 (6 months)	2	3	4	5
Income	$ 315,000	$655,200	$681,408	$708,664	$737,011
Vacancy %	50%	8%	8%	8%	8%
Vacancy	− 157,500	− 52,416	− 54,513	− 56,693	− 58,961
Effective gross income	$ 157,500	$602,784	$626,895	$651,971	$678,050
Operating expenses	− 55,125	− 210,974	− 219,413	− 228,190	− 237,317
NOI	$ 102,375	$391,810	$407,482	$423,781	$440,733
Improvements cost	− 3,720,000	− 0	− 0	− 0	− 0
Net cash flow	−$3,667,625	$391,810	$407,482	$423,781	$440,733

$$\text{Resale} = \frac{\$440,733}{0.10} = \$4,407,330$$

Year	Cash Flow		Present Value Factor @ 12%		Present Value
1	−$3,667,625	×	0.892857	=	−$3,274,665
2	391,810	×	0.797194	=	312,349
3	407,482	×	0.711780	=	290,038
4	423,781	×	0.635518	=	269,320
5	440,733	×	0.567427	=	250,084
5	$4,407,330	×	0.567427	=	2,500,838
Present value					$ 347,964

Condominium Project Option:

Proposed number of units (2 phases)	68
Average unit size	1,100 SF
Average unit price/SF	$70.00
Average unit cost/SF	$40.00

Development costs
　　Amenities $80,000
　　Site cost—phase I $220,000
　　Site cost—phase II $140,000

Sales expense (% of sales income)   8%
Overhead
　　Year 1: $75,000
　　Year 2: $75,000
　　Year 3: $50,000

COMMENTS: The typical *land discount rate* (Y_L) for condominium projects is 15 percent. It is assumed that unit sales prices and unit construction
costs will increase by 3 percent per year. The sellout is expected to occur
over 3 years, and developer profit is assumed to be 10 percent of sales income
in each year. Units will be sold as follows: 24 in the first year, 24 in the
second year and the remaining 20 in the third year. The project will be built
in two phases, with half of the units built the first year and the remaining
half built the second year.

Years	1	2	3	Totals
Source of Cash				
Sales income	$1,848,000	$1,903,440	$1,633,786	$5,385,226
Total cash	1,848,000	1,903,440	1,633,786	5,385,226
Use of Cash				
Development cost	300,000	140,000	0	0
Unit construction	1,496,000	1,540,880	0	3,036,880
Selling cost	147,840	152,275	130,703	430,818
Administration & Overhead	75,000	75,000	50,000	200,000
Developer's profit	184,800	190,344	163,379	538,523
Total uses	2,203,640	2,098,499	344,082	4,646,221
Net cash flow	−355,640	−195,059	1,289,705	739,005
PV cash flow	−309,252	−147,493	848,002	391,257

Value............$391,257
Annual IRR 0.150000

Summary

	Price	Price/Acre
Apartment site	$347,964	$42,435
Condominium site	$391,257	$47,714

Conclusion.   It appears from the above analysis that the highest and best
use of the site is for condominium development. The difference in the two
analyses appears to be the price being paid for condominiums in the neighborhood versus apartment rental ranges, plus the projected rapid absorption
of the condominium units. The conclusion would probably be different if

only 10 to 12 condominium units could be absorbed annually. It is interesting to note that differences in market conditions could cause the highest and best use of a site to shift back and forth from year to year.

Underimprovement

The property you are appraising is currently improved with an old distribution warehouse that was constructed in the early 1960s on a 1.1-acre tract of land. Since its construction, however, a new office park was opened on an adjacent tract, and now the park is improved with numerous office buildings, all built in the 1980s. Currently there are 12 office buildings in the park with only one remaining vacant site. Thus, the appraiser believes that the old distribution warehouse may be an underimprovement. In addition, two sites adjacent to the subject that were originally improved with single-family residences built in 1929 were cleared and a new office building is now being constructed. When the office park was built, the road fronting on the north side of the subject was connected with the other streets in the park, so the subject site is readily accessible and visible from the park. After a thorough analysis of the property, you conclude that the highest and best use of the vacant land is as an office building site, based on analyzing office building inventory and space demand. Based on an analysis of comparable data, you decide $6 per square foot is the best estimate of value for the vacant site, which results in a vacant land value of $287,496 (say, $287,500). You estimate it will cost $8,000 to remove the existing building.

You then analyze the building to make a judgment about its highest and best use. The building contains 18,000 square feet, is in fair condition and is currently renting for $1.50 per square foot on an absolute net basis. An analysis of recent comparables indicates that the $1.50 per square foot is equal to the current market rent. It appears that the existing building has neither conversion potential nor excess land. Analysis of recent sales of older warehouses indicates that the best estimate of the applicable overall capitalization rate for this property type is in the neighborhood of 11.5 percent. Your estimate of the value of the property "as improved" with the warehouse is, therefore, as follows:

Net operating income = 18,000 SF @ $1.50/SF = $27,000

Value = $27,000/0.115 = $234,782, say, $235,000

Value of land as if vacant	$287,500
Less demolition costs	− 8,000
Value of land as is	$279,500
Value of property as a warehouse	$235,000

Conclusion.   Since the value of the land net of demolition costs is higher than the value of the property as improved, the highest and best use of the site is as a vacant office site.

Highest and Best Interim Use

You have been asked to appraise an older apartment project that is located on a 1.3-acre tract in the fringe area of the central business district. The site has frontage on a major street and is sandwiched between a restaurant and an office building. The apartments were built in 1958 with good-quality materials. The apartment building is three stories high and contains 30 two-bedroom units that are all 800 square feet. There are 48 parking spaces on the northern side of the lot. The units currently rent for $375 per month and all but one of the units are rented. Operating expenses have averaged 42 percent of EGI over the past 2 years and vacancy has averaged 6 percent. It is your opinion that market rent for the building is $385 per month.

In a separate analysis on the land as if vacant similar to that demonstrated earlier in this chapter, it was determined that the highest and best use of the site as if vacant would be for a hotel site. Your estimate of the land value is $12 per square foot or $679,536 (say, $680,000). In analyzing the improvements, you do not believe the site contains excess land. You undertake a financial analysis to ascertain what appropriate value the property has as an apartment project. Following are the results:

Income ($385 × 12 × 30)	$138,600
Less vacancy @ 6%	− 8,316
	$130,284
Less operating expenses	− 54,719
NOI	$ 75,565

Analysis of recent sales of older apartment buildings reveals that the best estimate of the overall capitalization rate for this type of property would be on the order of 10 percent. The value estimate, therefore, would be:

Value = $75,565/0.10 = $755,650, rounded to $755,000

Conclusion.   The highest and best use of the land alone is for a hotel site, but the value of the property as improved with the apartments is $755,000 or $75,000 higher. The use as apartments, therefore, is the highest and best use of the property as improved and is called the "highest and best *interim use.*" The highest and best use of the property will remain apartments until the land value less demolition costs exceeds the value of the property as improved.

NOTE: When an existing building is an interim use, its remaining economic life will be shorter than if it represented the highest and best use as if vacant. This results in functional obsolescence, which must be considered when making adjustments in the cost approach. The appraiser first subtracts physical depreciation due to age, wear and tear, and so on. Then to reflect the functional obsolescence due to the improvements' failure to generate enough income to satisfy the required return to the land plus the value of the improvements, an adjustment is made for functional obsolescence. (Some people argue the loss in value should be called *external obsolescence.*) The amount of the deduction for this factor is calculated by estimating the remaining economic life of the building, which is the number of years remaining before the value as if vacant exceeds the value of the property as improved. Following is an example of how the depreciation deduction could have been handled in the cost approach.

To estimate the remaining economic life of the building, you have projected value changes over time, assuming land value is increasing by 5 percent per year and apartment value is increasing by 3 percent per year. Assuming that in 7 years it will cost about $25,000 to demolish the improvements, the land value less demolition costs would exceed the value as used as apartments by year 7. The remaining useful life would, therefore, be reduced from 25 to 7 years because the improvements are an underimprovement.

Year	Vacant Land Value	Apartment Value
0	$680,000	$755,000
1	714,000	777,650
2	749,700	800,980
3	787,185	825,009
4	826,544	849,759
5	867,871	875,252
6	911,265	901,510
7	956,828	928,555

Cost Approach:

Reproduction cost new (24,000 SF @ $25/SF)	$600,000
Less physical depreciation (25/40 yrs)	− 375,000
Depreciated value	$225,000
Less functional depreciation (8/15 yrs)*	− 120,000
Depreciated value of the building	$105,000
Plus land value	680,000
Value estimate by the cost approach	$785,000

*Based on economic age-life method.

NOTE: A highest and best interim use may occur not only because the property use will change sometime in the near future but also because the existing buildings may be an underimprovement. For example, a site suitable for a 10-story office building may have an old two-story office building on it. The highest and best use would be a more intensive use.

Conversion

A client requests that you appraise an old two-story building located on a small lot (10,000 SF) in the central business district. It was used as a retail store originally, but 10 years ago the original tenant moved the business to a suburban mall. The property is currently rented to a pawnshop that uses the second floor as warehouse space. The pawnshop pays $4 per square foot, based on the first floor area. The building was built in 1930 and has solid brick walls that are 1.5 feet thick. The interior has a heavy wooden frame typical of construction of the era. A decade ago, most of the high-quality retailers left the neighborhood and low-quality retail businesses and offices moved into the space. Five years ago, however, renovation began on several of the buildings and now more than half of the older buildings in the block have been purchased and converted into high-quality office space. The neighborhood is very near to the state and federal courthouses two blocks away, so a majority of the new tenants are law firms.

Based on your analysis of the market, it is your opinion that the highest and best use of the lot is for downtown commercial development. The lot itself, however, is too small to support a large building, but it could be improved with either a small office building or a retail store. After analyzing recent comparable sales, you believe the value of the land as if vacant is $20 per square foot, or $200,000.

Next you analyze the building and estimate its value based on its current use. After analyzing comparable sales in the area, you believe the current market rent for the subject based on its current use is only $4 per square foot (first floor only). After subtracting vacancy of 5 percent, management fees of 3 percent, taxes of $1,800, insurance of $1,600, and capitalizing the net operating income by 11 percent, you arrive at the following value of the property based on its current use:

Gross income	$40,000
Less vacancy @ 5%	− 2,000
	$38,000
Less management	− 1,140
Less taxes and insurance	− 3,400
NOI	$33,460

Value = $33,460/0.11 = $304,182, rounded to $305,000

After completion of your analysis, it appears the improvements add value to the property. You have noticed, however, that many properties have been converted in the immediate area; therefore, you decide to test the *conversion* possibilities for the subject.

Having appraised several of the buildings that have been converted in the area, you estimate that once converted, the building would have about 16,500 square feet of rentable area, and you believe that conversion costs would be about $50 per square foot based on gross area, including the installation of an elevator. Once completed, you believe the space could command rates of $12.50 per square foot with operating expenses based on $4 per square foot of net rentable area. You believe vacancy will be 6 percent at stabilized occupancy. Following is a 5-year discounted cash-flow analysis, assuming a 14 percent property discount rate, a 6-month construction period, a 6-month lease-up period, assuming rents and expenses increase by 3 percent per year, and assuming the reversion is based on capitalizing the fifth-year NOI by a 10.5 percent capitalization rate.

Example

Five-Year Discounted Cash Flow

Year	1	2	3	4	5
Gross income	$103,125	$212,437	$218,811	$225,375	$232,136
Vacancy %	50%	6%	6%	6%	6%
Vacancy	− 51,562	− 12,746	− 13,129	− 13,522	− 13,928
Effective gross income	$ 51,563	$199,691	$205,682	$211,853	$218,208
Operating expenses	− 33,000	− 67,980	− 70,019	− 72,120	− 74,284
NOI	$ 18,563	$131,711	$135,663	$139,733	$143,924
Improvements cost	− 825,000	− 0	− 0	− 0	− 0
Net cash flow	−$806,437	$131,711	$135,663	$139,733	$143,924

$$\text{Resale} = \frac{\$143,924}{0.105} = \$1,370,705$$

Year	Cash Flow		Present Value Factor @ 14%		Present Value
1	− $806,437	×	0.877193	=	−$707,401
2	131,711	×	0.769468	=	101,347
3	135,663	×	0.674972	=	91,569
4	139,733	×	0.592080	=	82,733
5	143,924	×	0.519369	=	74,750
5	$1,370,705	×	0.519369	=	711,902
Total					$354,900

Conclusion.   The value as a conversion is higher than the value of the land alone and the value "as is." It is, therefore, your opinion that the highest and best use of the property is for conversion to offices. The higher discount rate was used to reflect the added risk associated with a conversion.

SUMMARY

Highest and best use analysis provides the foundation for real estate appraisal. The topic was first discussed in chapter 2. However, a complete understanding of how to apply highest and best use analysis to real estate income property requires an understanding of all three approaches to value, especially the income approach. Thus, this chapter presented several examples of applications of highest and best use analysis using income capitalization techniques presented in previous chapters.

Highest and best use analysis applies to both the land as if it were vacant and the property as currently improved. The land is always valued under its highest and best use as if it were vacant. The existing improvements may or may not be the same as those that represent the highest and best use of a vacant site. However, the existing improvements will remain if they contribute value to the site. In this case the existing use is referred to as an "interim use." The existing improvements are likely to be removed when the value of the entire property under its existing use is less than the value of the land alone (less demolition costs) under its highest and best use.

In some cases the value of an existing building may reflect its ability to be converted to a better use through renovation. This is the case when the value under its converted use less the costs of conversion is greater than the value under either its existing use or the value of the land alone under its highest and best use as if vacant.

It should be clear that although the appraiser may have a preliminary idea what the highest and best use of a property is before applying one or more of the three approaches to value, the ultimate determination of highest and best use requires application of all relevant approaches to value to be sure he or she knows what use maximizes the value of both the land as if vacant and the value of the property as improved.

KEY TERMS

conversion	interim use
financially feasible	land density
highest and best use	legally permissible
highest and best use of improved site	maximally productive
	physically possible
highest and best use of vacant land	underimprovement

QUESTIONS

1. What are the four tests of highest and best use? Does the order of the tests matter?
2. Why does the appraiser determine the highest and best use of the site as if vacant when improvements are already on the property?
3. What might cause the highest and best use of an improved site to differ from the highest and best use of the site as if vacant?
4. What is meant by an underimprovement? Do you think a site can be overimproved?
5. What is meant by an interim use? How could you estimate the remaining economic life of an interim use?

6. What adjustments are necessary when applying the cost approach to a building that is an interim use?

7. Under what conditions is an existing building likely to be demolished? Why do demolition costs have to be considered?

8. A property with an existing building generates NOI of $9,500 per year. The appraiser believes that a 10 percent overall capitalization rate is appropriate to estimate the value of the existing property as improved. The value of the site as if vacant is determined to be $100,000 before considering demolition costs.

   a. Do you think the existing building should be demolished if there are no demolition costs?

   b. Do you think the existing building should be demolished if demolition costs are $10,000?

9. Refer to problem 8. Suppose the existing building could be converted at a cost of $40,000 to a use that would increase the NOI by $4,000 during the first year after conversion. The appraiser believes that an overall capitalization rate of 9.50 percent would be appropriate for the converted use because of lower risk and greater potential for increase in NOI in the future. Should the existing building be converted or demolished if there are no demolition costs?

10. Two potential uses of a vacant site have been identified. Office space could be constructed at a cost of $5 million, which would produce NOI of $300,000 the first year and $600,000 per year for the next four years. It is expected to be sold for $5.2 million at the end of year 5. Alternatively, retail space could be constructed at a cost of $4 million that would produce NOI of $300,000 the first year and $500,000 per year for the next four years. It is expected to sell for $4.5 million at the end of year 5. Suppose that the appropriate discount rates were 10 percent for office and 11 percent for retail. What is the highest and best use of the site?

CHAPTER 20

Valuation of Proposed Projects

INTRODUCTION

Up to this chapter, the properties used in the examples were complete and occupied. Methods of estimating the value of a proposed project will be presented in this chapter. When estimating the value of a proposed project, the appraiser is asked not only to estimate the value of a property *"as is"* but also to estimate two values in the future that will be referred to as *prospective value estimates*. The purpose of estimating prospective values for the project is to assist lenders in the underwriting process. Following are definitions of the three values to be estimated for proposed projects.

Value "As Is"

This is the value of the project as of the date of its last physical inspection. Typically in an appraisal assignment for a proposed project, this value represents the value of the land only, except where construction of the improvements has begun. When construction has commenced, the "as is" value is the value of the vacant land plus any contributing value of improvements that exist as of the effective date of the appraisal report.

Prospective Value on Completion but Prior to Rentup

This is the expected value of the property on completion of the improvements but before occupancy by any tenants. The effective date of this estimate is the future date when construction of the improvements is expected to be complete. In addition, this prospective value is estimated assuming the property is yet to be occupied, which means this estimate must be adjusted downward for the impact of the cost to rent the space. Methods of estimating the rentup adjustment will be presented later in this chapter.

Prospective Value on Reaching Stabilized Occupancy

This is the expected value of the property at the time when the building is forecast to be occupied to a stabilized level. The effective date of this value estimate falls at the end of the typical construction period plus the estimated time needed to rent the property. The time to rentup the property is estimated after the appraiser has undertaken a thorough supply and demand analysis of the market to forecast the expected absorption period.

Where possible, the appraiser should support the two prospective value estimates using all three approaches to value: the income approach, the cost approach and the sales comparison approach.

Another key issue to be addressed is at what point the earning of entrepreneurial profit is recognized. Because recognition of full entrepreneurial profit occurs only after the completion and successful rentup of the project is achieved, only a part of entrepreneurial profit will be recognized when estimating the prospective value of the project on completion but prior to rentup.

This issue will be discussed in greater detail in this chapter.

VALUE "AS IS"

When estimating the value of a proposed project "as is," the value generally represents the value of the land only. Estimating the value is generally accomplished using the sales comparison approach by comparing the subject land with comparable recent land sales. In some instances construction may have begun on the project as of the effective date of the appraisal. In this case, the contributing value of any improvement must be added to the land value to arrive at a value estimate "as is." The contributing value of the site improvement may be greater than, equal to or less than the cost of the improvements at that time. The appraiser must be careful to report the contributing value of the improvements only.

Example

Office Building

Gross building area	24,000 sq. ft.
Net building area	20,000 sq. ft.
Land area	38,000 sq. ft.

The information given for the 24,000-square-foot office building used in chapter 8 will be used to demonstrate the valuation techniques in this chapter. The only difference in the assumptions is the construction time needed to build the building. The effective date of the "as is" value is January 1, 1991. The building should require six months to complete.

The value of the land was estimated in chapter 10. Following is a restatement of the adjustment grid and an estimate of the market value of the vacant land, which in this example is the "as is" value because it is assumed that construction had not begun as of January 1, 1991.

Sale	*Subject*	*Comp 1*	*Comp 2*	*Comp 3*
Sales price	N/A	$285,000	$250,000	$300,000
Date of sale	1/1/91	6/90	10/90	1/90
Size (sq. ft.)	38,000	40,312	35,400	44,840

Adjustment Grid

Sale	*Comp 1*	*Comp 2*	*Comp 3*
Price per sq. ft.	$7.07	$7.06	$6.69
Financing adjustment	-0-	-0-	-0-
Cash equivalent price	$7.07	$7.06	$6.69
Market conditions	+2%	+1%	+4%
Adjusted price per sq. ft.	$7.21	$7.13	$6.96
Location	+10%	-0-	+10%
Size	-0-	-5%	+5%
Utilities	-0-	-0-	-0-
Topography	−5%	+10%	−5%
Total adjustments	+5%	+5%	+10%
Adjusted price per sq. ft.	$7.57	$7.48	$7.65

After adjustment, the "as is" value of the land was estimated to be $7.50 per square foot, or $285,000 ($7.50 × 38,000 sq. ft.).

PROSPECTIVE VALUE ON COMPLETION BUT PRIOR TO RENTUP

The effective date of the prospective value on completion but prior to rentup is the date at which the improvements are expected to be complete but before occupancy by any tenant. Typically, the construction period is provided to the appraiser by either the developer or the construction contractor. The appraiser, however, should test the reasonableness of a projected construction period against actual construction periods for similar projects. Once the period length is selected, the effective date of this prospective value estimate becomes the future date at which the building should be complete. In the example being used to demonstrate the valuation technique, a 6-month projected construction period would mean the effective date of the prospective value estimate would be July 1, 1991.

Where possible, all three valuation approaches (cost, income and sales comparison) should be used to estimate this prospective value for the subject property. All three approaches should be adjusted for market condition changes that may be expected to occur as of the future date. For example, if land values, rents, construction costs, operating expenses, etc., are expected to increase owing to inflation during the construction period, each factor must be appropriately adjusted. The prospective value estimates by each approach must reflect the appraiser's best judgment as to what is likely to occur as of this future date.

Income Approach

The prospective value on completion but prior to rentup estimated using the income approach is the present value of all expected cash flows beginning as of the future effective date. The factors to be considered when estimating the net operating income (NOI) include an estimate of the market rent in future years as well as the forecast absorption period and pattern of rentup of the space. The annual allowance for vacancy and credit loss is considered during the rentup period and in future years in which the project would most likely be operating at stabilized occupancy levels. The estimate of the rentup pattern and time is made after a detailed analysis of the market and consideration of current and future expected supply and demand for competitive space. The operating expenses are those expected to occur during rentup of the property and during later periods of stabilized occupancy. Fixed operating expenses such as taxes, insurance and maintenance contracts may vary little during the rentup period, whereas variable expenses such as management, utilities, janitorial and maintenance expenses may be small in the beginning and then may increase rapidly during the rentup of a project. The expected NOI for each year is the potential rental income adjusted for vacancy and credit loss and typical operating expenses.

Other possible deductions from NOI include leasing commissions and costs of tenant improvements if the building is not expected to be totally complete prior to rentup. Leasing commissions are deducted if the typical leaseup activity in the market area includes payment of leasing commissions to leasing agents. In this example we are assuming that leasing is part of the management operation and would therefore be reflected as part of typical management fees; therefore, no separate deduction for leasing commissions will be made. If, however, leasing commissions are typically paid separate from management fees in property's market, then a separate deduction should be made.

The final income to be forecast is the reversionary value to be received at the end of the typical holding period. There are two methods of selecting when the reversion will be received. One method is to assume that the end of the holding period in the analysis is the date at which the property is to reach stabilized occupancy. In this case, the reversionary value will be equal to the prospective value of the property on reaching stabilized occupancy. The derivation and meaning of this value estimate will be discussed later in this chapter.

The second method is to assume the reversion will be received at the end of a typical holding period, which includes both the rentup period and a number of years during which the property will be operating at stabilized occupancy. Methods of estimating the reversion were presented in earlier chapters of this book.

The final factor considered in estimating the prospective value on completion but prior to rentup is the selection of the appropriate discount rate for calculating the present value of the expected future cash flows. Typically, the rate would be the same rate used to estimate the value of a project at stabilized occupancy. Some appraisers argue that the discount rate should be increased to compensate for the additional risk associated with rentup of the project. But if a proper market analysis is undertaken when estimating the absorption period for a proposed project, there may not be any greater risk in a proposed project than in a project operating at stabilized occupancy levels.

In addition to estimating the prospective value of the project, the income approach also can be used to estimate the rentup adjustment to be used in the cost and sales comparison approaches. The technique used is to estimate a "theoretical" stabilized value as of the date the project is to be completed. The difference between this theoretical stabilized value and the prospective value on completion becomes an estimate of the rentup adjustment. Conceptually calculating the rentup adjustment in this manner is similar to the approach used to estimate the market rent equivalency adjustment in the earlier leased fee valuation chapter. In essence, the rentup adjustment is the difference between the value of the property without consideration of the rentup impact and the value of the property after consideration of the lost income expected during rentup. An alternative approach is to estimate the lost income during the rentup phase and estimate the present value of this lost income using the appropriate discount rate. If the same property discount rate is used to estimate the theoretical stabilized value, the prospective value on completion and the rent loss, then either approach used to estimate the rentup adjustment will result in the same adjustment.

The following example of estimating the prospective value on completion used the office building example introduced in chapter 7. Again, it is assumed that construction will require 6 months. In addition, after undertaking a thorough analysis of the market, it is our conclusion that rentup to a 94 percent occupancy should occur on a straight-line basis over 2 years after completion of the project. In addition, the income and expense rates are assumed to be applicable as of July 1, 1991.

Example

Estimating the Theoretical Stabilized Value as of July 1, 1991:

Gross building area	24,000 sq. ft.
Net building area	20,000 sq. ft.
Market rent	$15/sq. ft. as of 7/1/91
Stabilized vacancy rate	6%

continued

Fixed expenses:

Property tax	$ 11,900
Insurance ($0.20/sq. ft. net area, then increasing at 3% per year)	4,000

Variable expenses:

Management fee (5% of effective gross income)	14,100
Utilities ($1.25/sq. ft. of gross building area, then increasing at 5% per year)	30,000
Janitorial ($0.90/sq. ft. of net building area, then increasing at 4% per year)	18,000
Maintenance	4,000

Reversion in 5 years (NOI year $6/R_T$)	$241,480/0.10	2,414,800

Following is the cash-flow forecast over a 5-year holding period, assuming the property is at stabilized occupancy as of July 1, 1991. This annual cash-flow forecast is used to estimate the theoretical stabilized value of the property as of July 1, 1991.

Year	1	2	3	4	5	6
Potential gross income	$300,000	$312,000	$324,480	$337,459	$350,958	$364,996
Vacancy @ 6%	− 18,000	− 18,720	− 19,469	− 20,248	− 21,057	− 21,900
EGI	$282,000	$293,280	$305,011	$317,211	$329,901	$343,096
Management	14,100	14,664	15,251	15,861	16,495	17,155
Property tax	11,900	11,900	11,900	15,000	15,000	15,000
Insurance	4,000	4,120	4,244	4,371	4,502	4,637
Utilities	30,000	31,500	33,075	34,729	36,465	38,288
Janitorial	18,000	18,720	19,469	20,248	21,057	21,899
Maintenance	4,000	4,120	4,244	4,371	4,502	4,637
Total expenses	$ 82,000	$ 85,024	$ 88,183	$ 94,580	$ 98,021	$101,616
NOI	$200,000	$208,256	$216,828	$222,631	$231,880	$241,480

The theoretical value of the property, assuming a 12 percent property discount rate as of July 1, 1991, is as follows:

Year	Cash Flow		Present Value Factor @ 12%		Present Value
1	$ 200,000	×	0.892857	=	$ 178,571
2	208,256	×	0.797194	=	166,020
3	216,828	×	0.711780	=	154,334
4	222,631	×	0.635518	=	141,486
5	231,880	×	0.567427	=	131,575
5	2,414,800	×	0.567427	=	1,370,223
Total present value					$2,142,209

Implied R_O = $200,000/$2,142,209 = 0.093362

The $2,142,209 value estimate is the theoretical stabilized value, assuming the property is at stabilized occupancy as of the date of completion of the building. The term is preceded by the word *theoretical* because this value is not expected to be an accomplished fact. This estimate is used to calculate only the rentup adjustment.

continued

The next step is to prepare a cash-flow forecast beginning as of July 1, 1991, that incorporates the impact of the 2-year expected rentup period.

Space Absorption and Cash-Flow Schedule

Year	1	2	3
Beginning occupied space, sq. ft.	-0-	9,400	18,800
Absorption of space, sq. ft.	9,400	9,400	-0-
Ending occupied space	9,400	18,800	18,800
Average space occupied, sq. ft.	4,700	14,100	18,800
Rent/sq. ft.	$ 15.00	$ 15.60	$ 16.22
Rental income	$70,500	$219,960	$305,011
Management*	$ 3,525	$ 10,998	$ 15,251
Property Tax	11,900	11,900	11,900
Insurance	4,000	4,120	4,244
Utilities†	16,465	26,665	33,075
Janitorial‡	7,525	15,158	19,469
Maintenance	4,000	4,120	4,244
Total expenses	$47,415	$ 72,961	$ 88,183
NOI	$23,085	$146,999	$216,828

*Management is below stabilized estimates because management fees are a function of calculated rental income.

†The utility forecast during rentup assumes that $0.50/sq. ft. of gross is fixed and $0.95/sq. ft. is variable, based on occupancy.

‡The janitorial forecast during rentup assumes that $0.20/sq. ft. of the rentable area is fixed and $0.75/sq. ft. is variable, based on occupancy.

In the previous cash-flow forecast, the third-year NOI is equal to the third-year NOI forecast assuming stabilized occupancy. The NOI for years 4 and 5 as well as the reversion in year 5 also will be the same.

The prospective value of the property on completion but prior to rentup, is the present value of the NOI with year 1 and year 2 changed to reflect the impact of the gradual absorption of the office space.

Year	Cash Flow		Present Value Factor @ 12%		Present Value
1	$ 23,085	×	0.892857	=	$ 20,612
2	146,999	×	0.797194	=	117,187
3	216,828	×	0.711780	=	154,334
4	222,631	×	0.635518	=	141,486
5	231,880	×	0.567427	=	131,575
5	2,414,800	×	0.567427	=	1,370,223
Total present value					$1,935,417

The prospective value on completion but prior to rentup is equal to $1,935,417.

continued

Theoretical stabilized value, July 1, 1991	$2,142,209
Prospective value on completion, July 1, 1991	$1,935,417
Rentup adjustment	$ 206,792

The difference between the theoretical stabilized value and the prospective value on completion is the rentup adjustment that will be used to adjust the value indications by the cost and sales comparison approaches.

Cost Approach

The prospective value on completion but prior to rentup is estimated by the cost approach by estimating the prospective value of the land and improvements as of the expected date of completion, then adjusting this indication for rentup. The purpose of the rentup adjustment is to adjust for the fact that the property is expected to be vacant as of the effective date of valuation. Because the property will be new at this date, it would not be adjusted for physical depreciation. Care should be taken to ensure, however, that the project is feasible. If the prospective value estimate completion is significantly below the cost estimate, the project may not be feasible.

In addition, the actual cost to build the improvements may be lower than the reproduction cost estimate as of the prospective date. In times of rapidly increasing construction costs, the actual costs will most certainly be below the reproduction cost new at this time because actual costs may have been based on negotiated costs that were in effect during the construction and may not be applicable today.

Example

The cost approach estimate for the subject building presented in chapter 11 (see pages 233 and 234) will be used. The assumption is that this is the value as of January 1, 1991.

Building cost	$1,625,800
Parking lot	31,250
Landscaping	5,000
Total cost	$1,662,050
Plus: Entrepreneurial profit	199,446
Total value of improvements	$1,861,496
Plus: Land value	285,000
Total value	$2,146,496

Assuming land values are increasing by 4 percent per year and building costs are increasing by 3 percent per year, the reproduction cost new and land value as of July 1, 1991, would be as follows:

Total costs of improvements ($1,662,050 × 1.015)	$1,686,981
Plus: Entrepreneurial profit (12%)	202,438
Total value of improvements	$1,889,419
Plus: Land value (285,000 × 1.02)	290,700
Total value	$2,180,119

The value at this point reflects that of a project at stabilized occupancy and is an indication of the theoretical stabilized value. The final adjustment is for rentup, which must be made so that the value estimate reflects the value of the property prior to occupancy.

Total value	$2,180,119
Less: Rentup adjustment	− 206,792
Value indication by the cost approach	$1,973,327

The value at this point is the indication of the prospective value of the property on completion but prior to rentup.

Sales Comparison Approach

The prospective value on completion but prior to rentup is estimated by the sales comparison approach by estimating the value of the project expected as of the date of completion, then adjusting this indication for rentup. The purpose of the rentup adjustment is to adjust for the fact that the property is expected to be vacant as of the effective date of valuation. The property will be new at this point, so the comparable sales must be adjusted for this fact. In addition, if the market value is expected to change during the construction period owing to changes in market conditions, these factors must be considered.

Example

The sales comparison approach estimate for the subject building presented in chapter 8 was $2,125,000 (see page 194). The assumption is that this is the value as of January 1, 1991. Assuming market values of office buildings are increasing by 3 percent per year, the value estimate as of July 1, 1991, must be increased by 1.5 percent reflect the value as of this prospective date.

Value 1/1/91		*Market Condition Adjustment*		*Value Indication*
$2,125,000	×	1.015	=	$2,156,875

The value at this point reflects the stabilized value as of July 1, 1991, and is an indication of the theoretical stabilized value. The appraiser, however, must be certain that the comparable sales price and therefore the adjusted value indication reflect the value of the comparable property at stabilized occupancy. For example, if a comparable building used to estimate the value of the subject sold and was only at a 50 percent occupancy level, its price would most probably have been reduced because of the occupancy problem. This situation can be handled in one of two ways. The first method is to adjust the value upward to represent occupancy, then take a full deduction for rentup. A second method is to adjust the sales price for the relative difference between the impact of the 50 percent occupancy in the comparable and the 0 percent occupancy level in the subject on completion but prior to rentup.

In our example, the theoretical stabilized occupancy indication must be adjusted now for the impact of rentup.

Total value	$2,156,875
Less: Rentup adjustment	− 206,792
Value indication by the sales comparison approach	$1,950,083

Summary of Value Conclusions, July 1, 1991

Theoretical Stabilized Values

Income approach	$2,142,209
Cost approach	2,180,119
Sales comparison approach	2,156,875

Prospective Value on Completion Prior to Rentup

Income approach	$1,935,417
Cost approach	1,973,327
Sales comparison approach	1,950,083

The value indications at this point indicate a relatively narrow range of value. The theoretical stabilized value is used to estimate the rentup adjustment only and is not an estimate that is expected to be achieved. The prospective value on completion but prior to rentup is a value that is expected to be achieved and is generally used by lenders as a benchmark in the underwriting process. In this instance, a value estimate of about $1,950,000 appears supportable by all three approaches to value.

PROSPECTIVE VALUE ON REACHING STABILIZED OCCUPANCY

The effective date of the prospective value on reaching stabilized occupancy is the date at which the project is expected to reach stabilized occupancy. The effective date is selected by the appraiser after a detailed analysis of the market and a forecast of the absorption rate are made. Once the absorption period is estimated, the effective date is estimated as the date when the building is completed plus the absorption period. In the example used to demonstrate the valuation technique, a 6-month construction period plus a 2-year rentup period means the effective date of this prospective value estimate is July 1, 1993.

Where possible, all three valuation approaches (cost, income and sales comparison) should be used to estimate this prospective value for the subject property. All three approaches should be adjusted for all market condition changes that may be expected to occur as of this future date. For example, if land values, rents, construction costs, operating expenses, etc., are expected to increase owing to inflation during the construction and rentup periods, each factor must be appropriately adjusted. The prospective value estimates by each approach must reflect the appraiser's best judgment as to what is likely to occur as of this future date.

Income Approach

The prospective value on reaching stabilized occupancy is the present value of all expected cash flows, beginning as of the future effective date. The factors to be considered when estimating the NOI include an estimate of the market rent in future years. The annual allowance for vacancy and credit loss should reflect stabilized occupancy levels. The operating expenses are those that are expected to occur once the property is at stabilized occupancy.

Additional deductions from NOI could include leasing commissions and costs of tenant improvement for re-upfitting the space as it is released. Leasing commissions are deducted if the typical leaseup activity in the market area includes payment of leasing commission to leasing agents. In the example we are using in this chapter, we assume that leasing is part of the management operations and would therefore be reflected as part of typical management fees, so no separate deduction for leasing commissions is made. If, however, leasing commissions are typically paid separate from management fees in your property's market, than a separate deduction should be made in your analysis.

The final income to be forecast in using the income approach is the reversionary value to be received at the end of the typical holding period. Methods of estimating the reversion were presented in earlier chapters of this book.

The final factor considered in estimating the prospective value on reaching stabilized occupancy is the selection of the appropriate discount rate for calculating the present value of the expected future cash flows. Typically, the rate would be the same rate used to estimate the value of a project at stabilized occupancy today.

The following example estimates the prospective value on reaching stabilized occupancy by using the office building example discussed earlier in this chapter. Again, it is assumed construction will require six months and rentup will require two years.

Example

Estimating Prospective Stabilized Value as of July 1, 1993:

Gross building area	24,000 sq. ft.
Net building area	20,000 sq. ft.
Market rent	$15/sq. ft. as of 7/1/91, increasing 4% per year
Stabilized vacancy rate	6%

Fixed expenses:		
Property tax		$ 11,900
Insurance ($0.20/sq. ft. net area)		4,000
Variable expenses:		
Management fee (5% of effective gross income)		14,100
Utilities ($1.25/sq. ft. of gross building area)		30,000
Janitorial ($0.90/sq. ft. of net building area)		18,000
Maintenance		4,000
Reversion in 5 years as of 7/1/98	$257,893/.10	$2,578,930

Following is the cash-flow forecast over a 5-year holding period, assuming the property is at stabilized occupancy as of July 1, 1993. This annual cash flow forecast will be used to estimate the theoretical stabilized value of the property as of July 1, 1993.

Income and Expense Forecast Beginning July 1, 1993

Year	1	2	3	4	5	6
Potential gross income	$324,480	$337,459	$350,958	$364,996	$379,596	$394,780
Vacancy @ 6%	− 19,469	− 20,248	− 21,057	− 21,900	− 22,776	− 23,687
EGI	$305,011	$317,211	$329,901	$343,096	$356,820	$371,093
Management	15,251	15,861	16,495	17,155	17,841	18,555
Property tax	11,900	15,000	15,000	15,000	18,908	18,908
Insurance	4,244	4,371	4,502	4,637	4,776	4,919
Utilities	33,075	34,729	36,465	38,288	40,202	42,213
Janitorial	19,469	20,248	21,057	21,899	22,775	23,686
Maintenance	4,244	4,371	4,502	4,637	4,776	4,919
Total expenses	$ 88,183	$ 94,580	$ 98,021	$101,616	$109,278	$113,200
NOI	$216,828	$222,631	$231,880	$241,480	$247,542	$257,893

The property value of the property at stabilized occupancy, assuming a 12 percent property discount rate, is as follows:

Year	Cash Flow		Present Value Factor @ 12%		Present Value
1	$ 216,828	×	0.892857	=	$ 193,596
2	222,631	×	0.797194	=	177,480
3	231,880	×	0.711780	=	165,048
4	241,480	×	0.635518	=	153,465

| 5 | 247,542 | × | 0.567427 | = | 140,462 |
| 5* | 2,578,930 | × | 0.567427 | = | $1,463,355 |

Total present value $2,293,406

Resale $257,893/0.10 = $2,578,930

The $2,293,406 value is the estimate for the prospective value on reaching stabilized occupancy as of July 1, 1993. An alternative method of estimating this stabilized value is to divide the first year NOI (in this case $216,828) by the implied overall rate calculated earlier when estimating the theoretical stabilized value as of July 1, 1991. The implied overall rate at that point is approximately 0.094. Assuming the same rate would apply in 1993, the resulting value estimate would be as follows:

| *NOI* | | R_O | | *Value Estimate* |
| $216,828 | ÷ | 0.094 | = | $2,306,681 |

This value is nearly equal to the value found using discounted cash flow.

The prospective value on reaching stabilized occupancy as of July 1, 1993, using the income approach is approximately $2,300,000. In essence, this is the expected value of the property when it becomes occupied to a stabilized occupancy level of 94 percent.

Cost Approach

The prospective value on reaching stabilized occupancy is estimated by the cost approach by estimating the prospective value of the land and improvements as of the expected date of reaching stabilized occupancy. Because the property will not be new as of this date, the value will need to be adjusted for physical depreciation.

In addition, the actual cost to build the improvements may be lower than the reproduction estimate as of the prospective date. In times of rapidly increasing construction costs, the actual costs will most certainly be below the reproduction cost new at this time because actual costs may have been based on negotiated costs that were in effect during the construction and may not be applicable today.

Example

The cost approach estimate for the subject building presented earlier will be used again. The assumption is that this is the value as of January 1, 1991.

Building	$1,625,800
Parking lot	31,250
Landscaping	5,000
Total cost	$1,662,050
Plus: Entrepreneurial profit	199,446
Total value of improvements	$1,861,496
Plus: Land value	285,000
Total value	$2,146,496

Assuming land values are increasing by 4 percent per year and building costs are increasing by 3 percent per year, the reproduction cost new and land value as of July 1, 1993, would be as follows:

Total costs of improvements ($1,662,050 × 1.076814)*	$1,789,719
Plus: Entrepreneurial profit (12%)	214,771
Total value of improvements	$2,004,490
Less: Physical depreciation 2/50† = 4%	− 80,181
Plus: Land value (285,000 × 1.103232)	314,421
Total value	$2,238,730

*(1.03 × 1.03 × 1.015 = 1.076814)
†Assumes a 50-year economic life and an effective age of two years.

The value at this point reflects that of a project at stabilized occupancy, as estimated by the cost approach.

Sales Comparison Approach

The prospective value upon reaching stabilized occupancy is estimated by the sales comparison approach by estimating the value of the project expected as of the date the project is occupied at a stabilized level. The property will be two years old at this point so the comparable sales must be adjusted for the fact. In addition, if the market value is expected to change during the construction and rentup periods, due to changing market conditions, this factor must be considered.

Example

The sales comparison approach estimate for the subject building presented earlier in this chapter as of January 1, 1991, was $2,125,000. The assumption is that this is the value as of January 1, 1991. Assuming market values of office buildings are increasing by 3 percent per year, the value estimate as of July 1, 1993, must be increased by 7.6814 percent to reflect the value as of this prospective date:

			Prospective Value
Value 1/1/91	*Market Condition Adjustment*		*Indication 7/1/93*
$2,125,000	× 1.076814	=	$2,288,230

The value at this point reflects the stabilized value as of July 1, 1993, and is an indication of the prospective stabilized value.

Prospective Stabilized Value on Reaching Stabilized Occupancy

Income approach	$2,300,000
Cost approach	2,238,730
Sales comparison approach	2,288,230

The value indications at this point indicated a relatively narrow range of value. In this instance, a prospective stabilized value estimated at $2,250,000 appears supportable by all the approaches to value.

SUMMARY

For proposed projects, the appraiser may be required to estimate three different values. The value of the property "as is" is the value of the land and any existing improvements. In addition to this value, there are two prospective values that are estimates of what the property should be worth at some future point in time. The first prospective value is an estimate of the value of the property at the date construction of the improvements is expected to be complete but prior to rentup of the space in the building. The second prospective value is the value after the property has been rented up such that occupancy is at a stabilized level.

Understanding the difference between each of these values is especially important for the purpose of loan underwriting. Lenders should be certain that they do not agree to advance funds in excess of the value of property at any given point in time. For example, a construction lender may commit to a maximum loan amount that is a percentage of the prospective value that the property is expected to have after it reaches stabilized occupancy. However, the lender does not want to advance funds in excess of the as is value until construction begins. Construction funds will then be advanced during construction as the value increases to the value on completion but prior to rentup. Depending on the loan agreement, the lender may be willing to advance additional funds during the rentup period.

All three approaches can be used to estimate the above values. Additional adjustments must be made in the process, however, to be sure that the value is being estimated at the proper point in time. For example, the cost approach must consider what it will cost to construct the property at the date of the prospective value. Similarly, the sales comparison approach must consider what the comparable would sell for at the date of the prospective value.

KEY TERMS

prospective value

value as is

value on completion but prior to
rentup

value on reaching stabilized
occupancy

QUESTIONS

1. What is meant by the "as is" value?
2. What are the two prospective values that are estimated for proposed projects?
3. How do the projected cash flows differ when estimating the two prospective values versus the value as is?
4. What adjustments have to be made in the sales comparison approach to estimate the prospective values?
5. What adjustments have to be made in the cost approach to estimate the prospective values?
6. In the first example in chapter 19 the value of vacant land was estimated under the assumption that an office building would be constructed on the site. The answer of $608,483 would be the "value as is" under the assumption that an office building is the highest and best use of the site. Use the same cash flow projections and discount rate that was used in that example.
   a. Estimate the prospective value on completion but prior to rentup to stabilized occupancy.
   b. Estimate the prospective value on reaching stabilized occupancy.

CHAPTER 21

Valuation of Distressed Properties

INTRODUCTION

Frequently, appraisers are asked to appraise distressed properties, which certainly can be a difficult task. The problems, which cause the property to be distressed, may result from an oversupplied market, poor design or improper location of the improvements, inadequate maintenance and possibly poor decisions made by the owner of the property. The problems generally result in low occupancy, higher operating cost and/or low rent levels. In some instances, the problems may be incurable; in others the property condition or design may be altered or market conditions may change over time and the problems disappear.

When problems occur, the appraiser is asked to identify the cause and potential cure and estimate the impact caused by the troubled situation. Generally the adjustments required in the appraisal are for deferred maintenance, functional obsolescence, economic obsolescence and/or the impact of rentup of the property (occupancy obsolescence). The remainder of this chapter is devoted to presenting methods to estimate the various adjustments needed. The adjustments then will be made in three valuation approaches to estimate the value of a troubled property.

EXTERNAL OBSOLESCENCE

External obsolescence is defined as a loss in property value resulting from negative influence outside the property itself; an element of accrued depreciation.

External obsolescence is generally incurable and can be further defined as either economic obsolescence or locational obsolescence. Economic obsolescence is caused by a negative economic force that affects an entire area, whereas locational obsolescence is caused by environmental or social forces that negatively affect a specific property owing to its location. In the cost approach, the total loss in value from external obsolescence is distributed between the land and the improvements. External obsolescence can be measured either by capitalizing the income loss due to the negative influence or by comparing sales of similar properties that are subject to the negative influence with sales of similar properties that are not subject to the negative influence.

Economic Obsolescence

Economic obsolescence is defined as a type of external obsolescence in which value loss is caused by an occurrence or situation that adversely affects the employment, quality of life or economics of an area, e.g., loss of a major employer, a high tax base or changes in zoning. Frequently, economic obsolescence may disappear over time.

Locational Obsolescence

Locational obsolescence is defined as a type of external obsolescence in which value loss is caused by a negative influence outside the property because of its location, e.g., a corner location in a residential area, a health hazard close to the property or a change of property use close to the property. Locational obsolescence is generally considered to be incurable and will more or less permanently impair property value.

OCCUPANCY OBSOLESCENCE

Occupancy obsolescence is defined as a loss in the value of real estate improvements due to an occupancy that is less than the stabilized occupancy that the property should achieve in the current market. It is generally the present value of income loss during the rentup of a property. This form of obsolescence is generally curable. If it is not curable, the obsolescence becomes locational obsolescence.

FUNCTIONAL OBSOLESCENCE

Functional obsolescence is defined as a loss in the value of real estate improvements due to functional inadequacies or superadequacies due to poor design and/or change in market standards or requirements for building components. Functional obsolescence may be curable or incurable.

PROPERTY INSPECTION AND ANALYSIS

The first step in estimating the value of a distressed property is to inspect the property and review its financial history. In some instances a financial history may be difficult to obtain, but the appraiser must use his or her best judgment to try to identify the cause of the problem. Frequently low occupancy and low rent are a result of an oversupplied market. If an oversupplied market exists, as evidenced by above-average vacancy rates, the appraiser must undertake a thorough analysis of the market for competitive projects and determine whether the oversupply condition is temporary or permanent. If expected market growth trends appear positive and the oversupply market appears to be a temporary condition, the appraisers must consider this in estimating the market value of the property and make an adjustment for external economic obsolescence. If the adverse market conditions appear to be incurable in the foreseeable future, an adjustment for locational obsolescence must be made in the valuation process.

If the problem with the property is not a result of poor market conditions, the appraiser must make a judgment of whether the cause is incurable or curable. In the case of a poorly designed or maintained property, redesign, conversion or rehabilitation may restore the property to a competitive position. In this instance, the cost to cure must be considered in the valuation of the property. If the problem is incurable, a deduction for functional obsolescence must be made when estimating the value of the property.

The three approaches to estimating value (the income approach, the cost approach and the sales comparison approach) are applicable to problem properties.

Income Approach

When estimating the value of a distressed property by the income approach, emphasis is placed on the development of a cash-flow forecast that considers all the elements discussed in chapter 20 when estimating the value of the property "as is." In addition, it may be desirable (as when estimating the values for a proposed project) to estimate one or more theoretical values as of various key effective dates to estimate adjustments for deferred maintenance, external obsolescence, functional obsolescence and/or the impact of gradual rentup of the property. In addition, the appraiser must estimate the prospective stabilized value for the property. Examples of methods used to estimate the various adjustments that may need to be made when estimating the value of a distressed property will be presented later in this chapter.

To estimate theoretical values for distressed properties, several rent levels must be considered. The first is feasibility rent. *Feasibility rent* is the rent level needed to support the depreciated value of the property after consideration of deductions for normal physical depreciation in the improvements but before the consideration of any adverse conditions such as external obsolescence, functional obsolescence, occupancy obsolescence, rehabilitation costs or conversion costs. For example, if feasibility rents are greater than market rents that have been adversely affected by an oversupplied market, the difference between the value estimated assuming feasibility rent levels and the value found using market rents is an estimate of the external obsolescence of a property.

The proper allowance for vacancy and credit loss is a key element in estimating the value of a distressed property. The actual vacancy rate is certainly considered when estimating the value of a property "as is." In addition, a judgment must be made of the most appropriate stabilized occupancy level when estimating the prospective stabilized value for a property. Several factors are considered when estimating the date on which the estimated prospective stabilized value will occur. In an oversupplied market, the prospective stabilized value will occur when the supply and demand for competitive space reaches balanced levels, and the subject would then be expected to generate feasibility rent levels and reach a stabilized occupancy level. If the market, however, is not expected to be in balance in the foreseeable future and the property is more or less permanently affected by external conditions or suffers functional obsolescence, the effective date of the estimated prospective stabilized value is when the property is expected to reach stabilized occupancy at the highest rent for the property once the market is in balance. If the property needs rehabilitation or conversion, the effective date of the prospective stabilized value is after the rehabilitation or conversion has taken place and when the property is expected to reach a stabilized occupancy level at feasibility rent levels.

Operating expense forecasts may vary depending on the value that is estimated. When estimating the value of the property "as is," the expense levels are those that the appraiser believes actually will occur. When estimating theoretical values for identifying adjustments to be made to the cost or sales comparison approaches, however, the expenses are based on the rent and occupancy levels assumed in the analyses. For example, management fees may increase significantly in a cash flow forecast that assumes large occupancy increases over time when estimating the "as is" value of property that is at low occupancy levels as of the effective date of the appraisal. On the other hand, when estimating a theoretical stabilized value for the current date, the management fee would be that expected if the property were generating feasibility rents at stabilized occupancy levels.

Once the various value estimates are calculated for the property, the difference between the value estimates will be used as adjustments that must be made to the cost approach and, in some cases, to the sales comparison approach. The methodology used is similar to the approach used to estimate the market rent equivalency adjustment in chapter 12, except the impact of poor market or property characteristics is addressed rather than the effect of lease contracts on value.

Cost Approach

When estimating the value of a distressed property by the cost approach, the improvements value may need to be adjusted for more than physical depreciation. If the subject suffers from external obsolescence (either location or economic obsolescence), the appraiser must make a judgment of whether the land value estimate also reflected the impact of the external obsolescence. If the land value estimate included the external obsolescence adjustment, the adjustment may need to be allocated between land and building. If the feasibility rent selected to estimate the theoretical stabilized value was based on a land value estimate after consideration of any external obsolescence, then the adjustment for this obsolescence should reflect the loss in value to the improvements alone and should not be allocated between land and building. An example exploring this issue will be presented later in this chapter.

If the subject's vacancy is greater than what would be expected at stabilized levels, the cost approach estimate must be adjusted for any occupancy obsolescence. The adjustment is found by estimating the present value of the lost income during the projected absorption period. An adjustment also must be made if the subject suffers from functional obsolescence. If the functional obsolescence is curable, the adjustment should reflect the cost to cure plus the present value of the lost income during rehabilitation. If the functional obsolescence is incurable, the adjustment should reflect the lost income attributable to the functional problem over the life of the improvements.

Two methods may be used to estimate the adjustment for economic, functional and occupancy obsolescence. The income approach may be used where values are estimated both before and after making adjustment for the impact of the obsolescence, with the differences between the two values being the adjustment. In addition, paired sales analysis may be used where comparable property sales both with and without the obsolescence are compared to estimate the adjustment. Care must be taken when using either approach to ensure that the impact of only one type of obsolescence is considered at a time.

Sales Comparison Approach

When estimating the value of a distressed property, the important factor considered is to make the appropriate adjustment to comparable sales so their adjusted value indications reflect the true circumstances of the subject property "as is." Frequently, in distressed markets, comparable property sales are scarce, which makes application of the sales comparison approach difficult.

When adjusting comparables to reflect the "as is" condition of the property, not only relative differences in age, condition, quality, property rights appraised and market trends but also differences in occupancy, economic conditions and functionality of the properties must be considered.

When both the comparable sales and the subject suffer from the same form of obsolescence, the comparable must be adjusted for relative differences in the obsolescence category as well. For example, if a comparable sold property was 70 percent occupied at closing and the subject is 50 percent occupied currently, a downward adjustment must be made to the comparable for the relative difference in occupancy obsolescence between the two.

Following are several examples of estimating the "as is" value of a property that suffers from various forms of obsolescence. The same example used to estimate property value in the income, cost and sales comparison approaches in earlier chapters of this book is used. Following is a summary of the property information and value estimates for the property, assuming it is complete and at stabilized occupancy levels.

Value Estimates with No Problem

Summary of Value Indication

Value Estimate

Income approach	$2,142,209
Cost approach	2,146,996
Sales comparison approach	2,160,000

Building Type—Office

Gross building area	24,000 sq. ft.
Net leasable area	20,000 sq. ft.
Land area	38,000 sq. ft.
Market rent estimate	$15.00/sq. ft.
Vacancy and credit allowance	6%
Operating expense estimate	$4.10/sq. ft.

The value estimate at this point is in the range of $2,150,000, as indicated by the three approaches.

Example

Functional Obsolescence

Suppose the 24,000-square-foot office building was designed so that only 18,000 square feet (rather than 20,000 square feet) were rentable and that this design flaw is incurable. The resulting efficiency ratio would be only 75 percent, rather than the market expected ratio of 83 percent to 85 percent. The design flaw would result in incurable functional obsolescence. Following is an estimate of the value of the property using the three approaches.

Income Approach

Following is a 6-year cash-flow forecast that assumes the rent for the leasable area is $15 per square foot. The reversionary value was calculated by capitalizing the sixth year's NOI by a 10 percent terminal cap rate.

continued

Year	1	2	3	4	5	6
Potential gross income	$270,000	$280,800	$292,032	$303,713	$315,862	$328,496
Vacancy, 6%	− 16,200	− 16,848	− 17,522	− 18,223	− 18,952	− 19,710
EGI	$253,800	$263,952	$274,510	$285,490	$296,910	$308,786
Management	$ 12,690	$ 13,198	$ 13,726	$ 14,275	$ 14,845	$ 15,439
Property tax	11,900	11,900	11,900	15,000	15,000	15,000
Insurance	4,000	4,120	4,244	4,371	4,502	4,637
Utilities	30,000	31,500	33,075	34,729	36,465	38,288
Janitorial	18,000	18,720	19,469	20,248	21,057	21,899
Maintenance	4,000	4,120	4,244	4,371	4,502	4,637
Total expenses	$ 80,590	$ 83,558	$ 86,658	$ 92,994	$ 96,371	$ 99,900
NOI	$173,210	$180,394	$187,852	$192,496	$200,539	$208,886

Year	Cash Flow		Present Value Factor @ 12%		Present Value
1	$ 173,210	×	0.892857	=	$ 154,652
2	180,394	×	0.797194	=	143,809
3	187,852	×	0.711780	=	133,709
4	192,496	×	0.635518	=	122,335
5	200,539	×	0.567427	=	113,791
5	2,088,860	×	0.567427	=	1,185,276
Total present value					$1,853,572

The value estimated, assuming a 12 percent property discount rate, is $1,853,572. The difference in value between the value estimated assuming a typical efficiency ratio ($2,142,209) and the value estimated using the actual efficiency ratio of the building ($1,853,572) is an estimate of the functional obsolescence.

Value—Optimum ratio	$2,142,209
Value—Actual ratio	− 1,853,572
Functional obsolescence	$ 288,637

Cost Approach

To arrive at a value estimate for the property by the cost approach, the improvements value must be adjusted for functional obsolescence.

Unadjusted improvements value	$1,861,993
Less: Functional obsolescence	− 288,637
Value of the improvements	$1,573,356
Plus: Land value	285,000
Total property value	$1,858,356

Sales Comparison Approach

To arrive at a value estimate for the property by the sales comparison approach, the indicated property value must be adjusted for functional obsolescence. Take care to ensure that the comparable sales have been properly adjusted for any functional problem before making a full deduction for the functional obsolescence of the subject property.

continued

Value indication—No obsolescence	$2,160,000
Less: Functional obsolescence	− 288,637
Value of the improvements	$1,871,363

Value Estimates with Functional Obsolescence

Summary of Value Indication

Value Estimate

Income approach	$1,853,239
Cost approach	1,858,356
Sales comparison approach	1,871,363

The value estimate at this point, after consideration of the functional incurable obsolescence, is $1,850,000, as indicated by the three approaches.

Example

External Obsolescence, Locational

Suppose the property is adversely influenced because it is located in a neighborhood adversely affected by the poor condition of other neighborhood properties. The adverse location results in rent levels lower than would be expected for an identical property in a different neighborhood. Based on an analysis of the market, it appears that the best estimate of the market rent is $13 rather than $15 per square foot. It is the appraiser's opinion that the locational problem is incurable in the foreseeable future, so an adjustment for location obsolescence is required. In addition, based on an analysis of land sales, it appears that land value also has been affected by the locational problem and that the value of the land is $200,000. Following is an estimate of the value of the property using the three approaches.

Income Approach

Following is a 6-year cash-flow forecast using the expected rent for the building. The reversionary value was calculated by capitalizing the sixth year's NOI by 10 percent.

Year	1	2	3	4	5	6
Potential gross income	$260,000	$270,400	$281,216	$292,465	$304,163	$316,330
Vacancy, 6%	− 15,600	− 16,224	− 16,873	− 17,548	− 18,250	− 18,980
EGI	$244,400	$254,176	$264,343	$274,917	$285,913	$297,350
Management	$ 12,220	$ 12,709	$ 13,217	$ 13,746	$ 14,296	$ 14,867
Property tax	11,900	11,900	11,900	15,000	15,000	15,000
Insurance	4,000	4,120	4,244	4,371	4,502	4,637
Utilities	30,000	31,500	33,075	34,729	36,465	38,288

continued

Janitorial	18,000	18,720	19,469	20,248	21,057	21,899
Maintenance	4,000	4,120	4,244	4,371	4,502	4,637
Total expenses	$ 80,120	$ 83,069	$ 86,149	$ 92,465	$ 95,822	$ 99,328
NOI	$164,280	$171,107	$178,194	$182,452	$190,091	$198,022

Year	Cash Flow		Present Value Factor @ 12%		Present Value
1	$ 164,280	×	0.892857	=	$ 146,679
2	171,107	×	0.797194	=	136,405
3	178,194	×	0.711780	=	126,835
4	182,452	×	0.635518	=	115,952
5	190,091	×	0.567427	=	107,863
5	1,980,200	×	0.567427	=	1,123,630
Total present value					$1,757,364

The value estimated, assuming a 12 percent property discount rate, is $1,757,398. The difference in value between the value estimate assuming no locational obsolescence ($2,142,209) and the value estimate using the rental estimate for the subject, after consideration of the effect of the location problem ($1,757,398), is an estimate of the locational obsolescence.

Value—No obsolescence	$2,142,209
Value—With locational obsolescence	– 1,757,364
Locational obsolescence	$ 384,845

Cost Approach

To arrive at a value estimate for the property by the cost approach, the improvements value must be adjusted for locational obsolescence. Because the land value was impacted adversely by the locational problem, the locational obsolescence must be allocated between the land and the building value.

Land value—No obsolescence	$285,000
Land value—With obsolescence	– 200,000
Land value obsolescence	$ 85,000
Unadjusted improvements value	$1,861,991
Less: Allocated obsolescence ($384,845 – $85,000)	299,845
Value of improvements	$1,562,146
Plus: Land value	200,000
Total property value	$1,762,146

Sales Comparison Approach

To arrive at a value estimate for the property by the sales comparison approach, the indicated property value must be adjusted for locational obsolescence. Take care to ensure that the comparable sales have been properly adjusted for any locational problem before making a full deduction for the locational obsolescence of the subject property.

continued

Value indication—No obsolescence	$2,160,000
Less: Locational obsolescence	− 384,845
Value indication	$1,775,155

Value Estimates with Locational Obsolescence

Summary of Value Indication

Value Estimate

Income approach	$1,757,364
Cost approach	1,762,146
Sales comparison approach	1,775,155

The value estimate at this point, after consideration of the locational obsolescence, is $1,750,000, as indicated by the three approaches.

Example

External Obsolescence, Economic

Suppose the property were adversely affected by an oversupply of office space. The adverse conditions results in rent levels lower than would be expected and a need to offer rent concessions to attract tenants. Based on an analysis of the market, it appears that the best estimate of the market rent is $13 rather than $15 per square foot and the typical tenant requires 2 months' free rent. Based on this analysis, the appraiser concludes that the market will restabilize in 5 years, with rent concessions disappearing in 3 years. In addition, based on an analysis of land sales, it appears that land values have been affected by the oversupply problem and that the value of the land is $200,000. Following is an estimate of the value of the property using the three approaches.

Income Approach

Following is a 6-year cash-flow forecast using the expected rent for the building. The reversionary value was calculated by capitalizing the sixth year's NOI by 10 percent.

Year	1	2	3	4	5	6
Market rent	$13.00	$13.25	$14.50	$16.25	$17.55	$18.25
Potential gross income	$260,000	$265,000	$290,000	$325,000	$350,958	$364,996
Vacancy, 6%	− 15,600	− 15,900	− 17,400	− 19,500	− 21,057	− 21,900
Concessions	− 40,733	− 41,517	− 45,433	-0-	-0-	-0-
EGI	$203,667	$207,583	$227,167	$305,500	$329,901	$343,096
Management	$ 10,183	$ 10,379	$ 11,358	$ 15,275	$ 16,495	$ 17,155
Property tax	11,900	11,900	11,900	15,000	15,000	15,000
Insurance	4,000	4,120	4,244	4,371	4,502	4,637
Utilities	30,000	31,500	33,075	34,729	36,465	38,288

continued

Janitorial	$ 18,000	$ 18,720	$ 19,469	$ 20,248	$ 21,057	$ 21,899
Maintenance	4,000	4,120	4,244	4,371	4,502	4,637
Total expenses	$ 78,083	$ 80,739	$ 84,290	$ 93,994	$ 98,021	$101,616
NOI	$125,584	$126,844	$142,877	$211,506	$231,880	$241,480

Year	Cash Flow		Present Value Factor @ 12%		Present Value
1	$ 125,584	×	0.892857	=	$ 112,129
2	126,844	×	0.797194	=	101,119
3	141,877	×	0.711780	=	101,697
4	211,506	×	0.635518	=	134,416
5	231,880	×	0.567427	=	131,575
5	2,414,800	×	0.567427	=	1,370,222
Total present value					$1,951,159

The value estimated, assuming a 12 percent property discount rate, is $1,915,159. The difference in value between the value estimate assuming no locational obsolescence ($2,142,209) and the value estimate using the rental estimate for the subject, after consideration of the effect of the economic problem ($1,951,159), is an estimate of the obsolescence.

Value—No obsolescence	$2,142,209
Value—With economic obsolescence	− 1,951,159
Economic obsolescence	$ 191,050

Cost Approach

To arrive at a value estimate for the property by the cost approach, the improvements value must be adjusted for economic obsolescence. Because the land value was adversely affected by the economic problem, the economic obsolescence must be allocated between the land and the building value.

Land value—No obsolescence	$ 285,000
Land value—With obsolescence	− 200,000
Land value obsolescence	$ 85,000
Unadjusted improvements value	$1,861,991
Less: Allocated obsolescence ($191,050 − $85,000)	− 106,050
Value of improvements	$1,755,941
Plus: Land value	200,000
Total property value	$1,955,941

Sales Comparison Approach

To arrive at a value estimate for the property by the sales comparison approach, the indicated property value must be adjusted for economic obsolescence. Take care to ensure that the comparable sales have been properly adjusted for any economic problem before making a full deduction for the economic obsolescence of the subject property.

continued

Value indication—No obsolescence	$2,160,000
Less: Economic obsolescence	− 191,050
Value indication	$1,968,950

Value Estimates with Economic Obsolescence

Summary of Value Indication

Value Estimate

Income approach	$1,951,159
Cost approach	1,955,941
Sales comparison approach	1,968,950

The value estimate at this point, after consideration of the economic obsolescence, is $1,950,000, as indicated by the three approaches.

Example

External Obsolescence, Economic and Occupancy Obsolescence

Suppose the property used in the previous example suffered from an occupancy problem as well as being affected by an oversupply condition. The property value then must be adjusted for both economic and occupancy obsolescence. In this example we assume the same circumstance for the property as in the previous example, except that occupancy as of the date of valuation is 40 percent rather than 94 percent and the property will require 3 years to rentup. In addition, we also assume that the land value has been adversely affected by the oversupplied market and the land value is $200,000. Following is an estimate of the value of the property using the three approaches.

Income Approach

Following is a 6-year cash-flow forecast using the expected rent for the building. The reversionary value was calculated by capitalizing the sixth year's NOI by 10 percent.

Year	1	2	3	4	5	6
Market rent	$ 13.00	$ 13.25	$ 14.50	$ 16.25	$ 17.55	$ 18.25
Potential gross income	260,000	265,000	290,000	325,000	350,958	364,996
Vacancy	− 130,000 −	79,500 −	34,800 −	19,500 −	21,057 −	21,900
	(50%)	(30%)	(12%)			
Concessions	− 21,667 −	44,167 −	42,533	-0-	-0-	-0-
EGI	$108,333	$141,333	$212,667	$305,500	$329,901	$343,096
Management	$ 5,417	$ 7,067	$ 10,633	$ 15,275	$ 16,495	$ 17,155
Property tax	11,900	11,900	11,900	15,000	15,000	15,000
Insurance	4,000	4,120	4,244	4,371	4,502	4,637
Utilities	30,000	31,500	33,075	34,729	36,465	38,288

continued

Janitorial	$ 9,000	$ 13,104	$ 17,135	$ 20,248	$ 21,057	$ 21,899
Maintenance	4,000	4,120	4,244	4,371	4,502	4,637
Total expenses	$ 64,317	$ 71,811	$ 81,231	$ 93,994	$ 98,021	$101,616
NOI	$ 44,016	$ 69,522	$131,436	$211,506	$231,880	$241,480

Year	Cash Flow		Present Value Factor @ 12%		Present Value
1	$ 44,016	×	0.892857	=	$ 39,300
2	69,522	×	0.797194	=	55,423
3	131,436	×	0.711780	=	93,554
4	211,506	×	0.635518	=	134,416
5	231,880	×	0.567427	=	131,575
5	2,414,800	×	0.567427	=	1,370,223
Total present value					$1,824,491

The value estimated, assuming a 12 percent property discount rate, is $1,824,491. The difference in value between the value estimate assuming no economic obsolescence ($2,142,209) and the value estimate using the rental estimate for the subject, after consideration of the effect of the economic and occupancy problems ($1,824,491), is an estimate of both the economic and the occupancy obsolescence.

Value—No obsolescence	$2,142,209
Value—With economic and occupancy obsolescence	− 1,824,491
Economic and occupancy obsolescence	$ 317,718

Note: As calculated earlier, the economic obsolescence is $191,050, so the occupancy obsolescence must be $126,668.

Cost Approach

To arrive at a value estimate for the property by the cost approach, the improvements value must be adjusted for economic and occupancy obsolescence. Because the land value was adversely affected by the economic and occupancy problems, the obsolescence must be allocated between the land and the building values.

Land value—No obsolescence	$ 285,000
Land value—With obsolescence	− 200,000
Land value obsolescence	$ 85,000
Unadjusted improvements value	$1,861,991
Less: Allocated obsolescence ($191,050 − $85,000)	− 106,050
Less: Occupancy obsolescence	− 126,668
Value of improvements	$1,629,273
Plus: Land value	200,000
Total property value	$1,829,273

continued

Sales Comparison Approach

To arrive at a value estimate for the property by the sales comparison approach, the indicated property value must be adjusted for economic and occupancy obsolescence. Take care to ensure that the comparable sales have been properly adjusted for any economic problem before making a full deduction for the economic and occupancy obsolescence of the subject property:

Value indication—No obsolescence	$2,160,000
Less: Economic obsolescence	− 191,050
Less: Occupancy obsolescence	− 126,668
Value indication	$1,842,282

Value Estimates with Occupancy and Economic Obsolescence

Summary of Value Indication

Value Estimate	
Income approach	$1,824,491
Cost approach	1,829,273
Sales comparison approach	1,842,282

The value estimate at this point, after consideration of the economic and occupancy obsolescence, is $1,825,000, as indicated by the three approaches.

SUMMARY

Appraisers are often required to estimate the value of a property that has problems due to factors such as an oversupplied market, poor design or improper location of the improvements, inadequate maintenance and poor management decisions. This chapter illustrated how the value of a property can be adjusted to capture these problems.

The starting point for estimating the value of a troubled property is usually the value that would exist if the property did not have any problems. All three approaches can usually be used to estimate this value. For example, the cost approach would be used to estimate the value of constructing the property as if it did not have the problem. Similarly, income can be projected as if the property did not have any problems and comparable sales would most likely not have the same problems as the subject property.

The value adjustment necessary to capture the property's problems are often based on using the income approach because the loss in value is directly related to the loss in income due to the problem affecting the property. Once this adjustment is calculated from the income approach it also can be used to adjust the value estimates for the cost and sales comparison approaches.

KEY TERMS

distressed property
economic obsolescence
external obsolescence
feasibility rent

functional obsolescence
locational obsolescence
occupancy obsolescence

QUESTIONS

1. What factors can result in a "distressed property"?
2. In general, how is the loss in value due to the problems associated with a distressed property usually estimated?
3. What are the two types of external obsolescence that can affect distressed properties?
4. What is meant by the term occupancy obsolescence?
5. Can the sales comparison approach be used to estimate the value of a distressed property?
6. Can you think of any specific examples of problems that are not mentioned in the chapter that would result in a distressed property?

CHAPTER 22

Case Study: Appraisal of Bay Hill Apartments

INTRODUCTION

This chapter includes a complete narrative appraisal of an apartment building. All three approaches to value are included. This sample appraisal illustrates the format typically used in an appraisal report, including the letter of transmittal, summary of conclusions, description of the property and neighborhood, highest and best use analysis, cost approach, income approach, sales comparison approach, and reconciliation and final value estimate. A listing of the typical addenda is also included in the report's table of contents.

The sample appraisal is based on an actual property. The case should be viewed as an example of one of many ways of approaching this type of appraisal problem. Other appraisers may approach the same problem in a slightly different manner and arrive at a slightly different value. What is important is that the report makes it clear how the appraiser arrived at the estimate of value. The reader can decide whether this was accomplished in this appraisal.

APPRAISAL REPORT
BAY HILL APARTMENTS
528 MAIN STREET
NORTHWOODS, NORTH CAROLINA

PREPARED FOR:

MR. JOHN LENDER
ABC NATIONAL BANK
POST OFFICE BOX 15008
NORTHWOODS, NORTH CAROLINA

PREPARED BY:

SMITH & ASSOCIATES
119 FIRST AVENUE
NORTHWOODS, NORTH CAROLINA

AS OF:

JANUARY 1, 1993

January 1, 1993

Mr. John Lender
ABC National Bank
Post Office Box 15008
Northwoods, North Carolina

Re: Appraisal Report
     Bay Hill Apartments
     528 Main Street
     Northwoods, North Carolina

Dear Mr. Lender:

As you requested, I have inspected the above-referenced property for the purpose of estimating the market value of the fee simple interest in the property. The last date of inspection of the property was January 1, 1993, which will be considered the effective date of the value estimate. I have analyzed information pertinent to the formulation of the value estimate and am reporting the conclusions in this report. Market value is defined in the report. We believe the following report meets the requirements of ABC National Bank and the Uniform Standards of Professional Appraisal Practice.

Based on my analysis of the property, it is my opinion that the best estimate of the market value of the fee simple interest in the property as of January 1, 1993, was in the order of:

One million four hundred fifty thousand dollars
($1,450,000)

If any additional information or further clarification is needed, please do not hesitate to contact me.

Respectfully submitted,

SMITH & ASSOCIATES

John Smith, State Certification #1

JS:cb

SUMMARY OF CONCLUSIONS

SUBJECT PROPERTY:

Bay Hill Apartments
528 Main Street
Northwoods, North Carolina

The subject property contains the Bay Hill apartment complex containing eight buildings with a total of 44,712 square feet. The project was built in 1983. The buildings are two story, wood frame with brick veneer and contain 64 apartment units. The site has 3.76 acres and is known as Lot 100, Tax Block 6043, Northwoods, Forsyth County, North Carolina.

OWNER:

Bay Hill Partnership

CLIENT:

Mr. John Lender
ABC National Bank of North Carolina
Post Office Box 15008
Northwoods, North Carolina

EFFECTIVE DATE:

January 1, 1993

ZONING:

R-MF (Multifamily)

HIGHEST AND BEST USE:

As improved with an apartment project.

INTEREST APPRAISED:

Fee Simple Interest

VALUE ESTIMATE:

$1,450,000

TABLE OF CONTENTS

Part I: Preface

Title Page
Letter of Transmittal
Summary of Conclusions
Table of Contents

Part II: Description, Analysis and Conclusions

Identification of the Property
Scope of the Appraisal
Purpose of the Appraisal
Ownership of the Property
Area Description
Neighborhood Description
Site Description
Zoning
Assessment and Taxes
Improvements Description
Highest and Best Use
Valuation Methodology
Cost Approach
Income Approach
Sales Comparison Approach
Reconciliation and Final Value Estimate

Part III: Addenda

Photographs of the Subject/Comparables
Area Map
Neighborhood Map
Deeds
Tax Map
Subject Site Map
Land Sales Location Map
Comparable Rental Location Map
Improved Sales Map
Profit/Loss Statement
Rent Roll
Letter of Engagement
Certification of the Appraiser
Assumptions and Limiting Conditions of the Appraisal
Qualifications of the Appraiser

APPRAISAL REPORT
BAY HILL APARTMENTS
528 MAIN STREET
NORTHWOODS, NORTH CAROLINA

IDENTIFICATION OF THE PROPERTY

The property to be appraised consists of approximately 3.76 acres of land containing eight apartment buildings with 64 units located on the south side of Main Street between Maple Street and Elm Street in the southern section of Northwoods, North Carolina. The property is locally referred to as Bay Hill Apartments, 528 Main Street, Northwoods, North Carolina.

The property is further identified as Lot 100, Tax Block 6043, Northwoods Township in the Forsyth County Tax Assessors Office.

SCOPE OF THE APPRAISAL

The scope of this appraisal report included the research and collection of data pertaining to recent economic trends and multifamily real estate sales and leasing activity in Forsyth County. Information was collected from courthouse records, the files of reliable real estate professionals, members of the local planning staff and utilities staff, contiguous land owners and developers who are presently offering vacant land and/or improved real estate for sale or lease in the subject's market area.

All sales and leasing information used in the report has been confirmed by the appraiser or was obtained from reliable sources who confirmed the data. Sales data include the location of the comparable, date of sale, sale price, financing (if available), grantor and grantee, land size, size and condition of improvements (if any), current or proposed use, topography and availability of utilities. Further, I have analyzed the sales using the appropriate units of measure recognized in the market. Comments have been added where necessary to explain any significant items not considered in the above factual presentation.

PURPOSE AND FUNCTION OF THE APPRAISAL

The purpose of the appraisal is to estimate the market value of the fee simple interest in the property. The last date of inspection of the property was January 1, 1993, which will be considered the effective date of this report. Market value is defined by the Uniform Standards of Professional Appraisal Practice:

    (i) The most probable price that a property should bring in a competitive and open market under all conditions requisite to a fair sale, the buyer and seller each acting prudently and knowledgeably, and assuming the price is not affected by undue stimulus. Implicit in this definition is the consummation of a sale as of a specified date and the passing of title from seller to buyer under conditions whereby: (A) buyer and seller are typically motivated; (B) both parties are well informed or well advised, each acting in what he or she considers his or her own best interest; (C) a reasonable time is allowed for exposure in the open market; (D) payment is made in terms of cash in U.S. dollars or in terms of financial arrangements comparable thereto; and (E) the price represents the normal consideration for the property sold, unaffected by special or creative financing or sales concessions granted by anyone associated with the sale.

   (ii) Adjustments to the comparables must be made for special or creative financing or sales concessions. No adjustments are necessary for those costs that are normally paid by sellers as a result of tradition or law in a market area; these costs are readily identifiable because the seller pays these costs in virtually all sales transactions. Special or creative financing adjustments can be made to the comparable property by comparisons with financing terms offered by a third-party institutional lender that is not already involved in the property or transaction. Any adjustment should not be calculated on a mechanical dollar-for-dollar cost of the financing or concession, but the dollar amount of any adjustment should approximate the market's reaction to the financing or concessions based on the appraiser's judgment.

Fee simple interest is the unencumbered rights to property except for the government powers of escheat, eminent domain, police power and taxation.

The appraisers have received specific guidelines from the client and have relied on standards required by ABC National Bank and the USPAP to obtain appraisals that clearly report the realty interest, timing, support and assumptions made in the appraisal of the subject property.

The function of this appraisal is to serve as a guideline of market value for the subject property for financing purposes.

OWNERSHIP OF THE PROPERTY

The subject property is currently owned by Bay Hill Partnership, which purchased the property from AYZ Building Company. The transaction is summarized in the chart below.

Block 6043/100

Grantor	Grantee	Date	Price	Deed Book/Page
AYZ Building Company	Bay Hill Partnership	8/4/83	$1,300,000	643/892

AREA DESCRIPTION

The subject property is located in Northwoods, Forsyth County, North Carolina. The town of Northwoods is centrally located within the Piedmont region of the state, being 10 miles east of Winston-Salem, 17 miles west of Greensboro, and 8 miles north of High Point. Interstate 40 provides direct access to both Winston-Salem and Greensboro. U.S. Highway 66 provides access to High Point. Other major highways serving Northwoods include U.S. Highway 421 and N.C. Highways 66 and 150. Interstate 85 is approximately 25 miles east at Greensboro and Interstate 77 is about 50 miles to the west at Statesville.

Northwoods is part of the Greensboro/Winston-Salem/High Point Standard Metropolitan Statistical Area (SMSA), which is the largest SMSA in North Carolina.

Northwood's growth has substantially exceeded that of the SMSA, including Winston-Salem and Forsyth County. For example, the U.S. Census shows the town's population grew by 59.75 percent, from 6,802 in 1980 to 10,863 in 1990. Forsyth County, on the other hand, grew by only 9.1 percent, from 243,683 to 265,878. Northwoods should continue to grow in the future due to its central location among the Piedmont's three principal cities.

Northwoods has historically been a bedroom community of Winston-Salem, Greensboro, and High Point. The town officials, however, feel that Northwoods has become more than just a residential community. For example, there are nearly 400 businesses with Northwoods addresses.

Major employers include Thomas-Hall Corporation (textile) with 650 persons, Highway Express (freight transportation) with 550 persons, America Buildings (metal building fabrication) with 250 persons and Knitwear Industries (textile) with 100 persons. The N.C. Employment Security Commission does not record unemployment figures for the town of Northwoods.

Unemployment is not a significant problem in Northwoods, however, owing to the close proximity of major employment centers in Winston-Salem, Greensboro and High Point. Further, the increase in the township's assessed values from $233.4 million in 1982 to $417.1 million in 1990, a 78.7 percent increase, is due in part to commercial and industrial growth and not wholly due to residential growth. Northwood's financial resources have also grown from one local bank in 1965 to five banks and four savings and loan association branches in 1992. Town officials and local REALTORS® estimate the vacancy at 5 percent for commercial buildings, rental homes and apartments. The new Interstate 40 Bypass will be located only two miles south of Northwoods and should provide renewed interest in all types of development.

Although located in the center of the state's largest metropolitan area, Northwood still retains a small-town image. It has one weekly newspaper, two city parks, its own Chamber of Commerce and one branch library. The town is governed by a mayor–board of aldermen form of government with day-to-day duties carried on by a town manager. The town also has its own police department and the schools are consolidated with the Winston-Salem/Forsyth County School System. There are various nursing homes in the town, and major hospitals (Baptist and Forsyth) are located within a twenty-minute drive to the west in Winston-Salem. The town also has its own water and sewer system. Electricity is provided by Duke Power Company and Piedmont Natural Gas provides gas service.

In conclusion, Northwoods is a very pleasant community. While historically it has been a bedroom community of Winston-Salem, Greensboro and High Point, growth in the economic base has resulted in the town's having its own viable economy, which is augmented by major employment centers in the aforementioned three Piedmont cities. Indications are that growth in the Northwoods area will continue to be very good owing to its central location, transportation system and abundance of available land. Northwoods represents a viable area for well-conceived real estate investments, including apartment projects.

NEIGHBORHOOD DESCRIPTION

A neighborhood is best defined as a portion of a larger community or an entire community in which there is a homogeneous grouping of inhabitants, buildings or business enterprises. Inhabitants of a neighborhood typically have a more than casual community of interest and similarity of economic level or cultural background. Neighborhood boundaries may consist of well-defined natural or man-made barriers or they may be more or less well defined by a distinct change in land use or in the character of the inhabitants.

The subject neighborhood is located south of Interstate 40, east of Oak Street, west of N.C. Highway 66 and north of the city limits in the southern portion of Northwoods, Forsyth County, North Carolina. Broad Street is the major east-west artery through this neighborhood, and both N.C. Highway 66 and Oak Street run north-south along the boundaries of the subject neighborhood, as defined above. The subject property, Bay Hill Apartments, is located along the southern side of Main Street, which runs east-west connecting Maple Street and Elm Street. The commercial/industrial development along Interstate 40 and N.C. Highway 66 and the rural character of the area south of the city limits is the reason I have defined the subject neighborhood as above.

The northern side of Main Street contains a small mobile home park and several older single family residences located directly across from the subject property. The subject neighborhood primarily contains a mixture of older single family residential and multifamily properties, except for the Northwoods Public Works facility located at the northwest corner of the Broad Street and Maple Street intersection and the commercial properties located along the north side of Spring Street. Although the majority of this neighborhood is developed, there is some vacant land available in this area for additional development in the future.

Access into the area is good via N.C. Highway 66, Elm Street, Spring Street and Broad Street. These roadways provide direct access to surrounding neighborhoods, the northern section of Northwoods and Interstate 40 and N.C. Highway 150, as well as the Interstate 40 Bypass scheduled for completion in late 1993. Main, Broad, Elm and surrounding streets are paved, two-lane streets with curbs and gutters. All city utilities are available to the area, including public water and sewer, telephone, electricity, police, fire and garbage service.

Other apartment complexes in this neighborhood include Oakwood Manor (Phases I and II), Forest Lake, Robin Townhouses and 418 Thomas Street. Oakwood Manor contains 222 units, and the other complexes are smaller developments.

Topographically, the neighborhood is moderately rolling and partially wooded. Silver Creek runs north-south across a portion of the neighborhood, which hinders development to a degree in the immediate vicinity of the creek.

In summary, it appears that the subject neighborhood should continue to be a viable location for multifamily housing. This neighborhood offers good access to major transportation routes, shopping and employment centers, availability of public utilities, usable topography and compatibility with other multifamily properties in the surrounding area.

A map of the neighborhood is included in the Addenda to this report.

SITE DESCRIPTION

The subject property lies on the south side of Main Street between Maple Street and Lee Street in the southern portion of Northwoods, Forsyth County, North Carolina. The site is located approximately two blocks south of Interstate 40, which separates the central business district of Northwoods from the southern portion of the township. Main Street, Elm Street and Maple Street are paved, two-lane public streets with curbs, gutters and lighting.

The subject property contains a total of 3.76 acres of land, which is irregularly shaped and contains 420 feet of road frontage along Main Street, 262 feet of frontage along Maple Street and 300 feet of frontage along Broad Street. It is improved with eight two-story multifamily buildings containing 64 units.

The topography of the subject site is generally level. A sanitary sewer easement also runs north-south across a portion of the subject site, but this does not appear to adversely affect the subject property. The total density for the improved portion of the subject site is 17.02 units per acre, which is typical for the Northwoods market.

The site is located within the city limits of Northwoods and is served by all city utilities such as public water and sewer, telephone, electricity, trash collection, police and fire protection. The site is zoned R-MF, allowing multifamily housing. Access to the improved portion of the site is via four curb cuts along Main Street leading into the four separate parking areas providing parking along the front of each building.

In conclusion, the site exhibits all the attributes of a good multifamily site: adequate size, usable topography, good access, visibility and all city utilities. The site should be well received as a multifamily location.

Copies of the site survey and tax map are included in the Addenda to this report.

ZONING

The subject property is located within the city limits of Northwoods and is under the zoning jurisdiction of the Town of Northwoods Planning Board. The property is zoned R-MF Residential Multifamily. R-MF zoning permits up to 17.63 units per acre, not limited by size or number of bedrooms, and 1.5 parking spaces per apartment unit. The subject property has 64 units and 100 parking spaces on 3.76 acres of land for a density of 17.02 units per acre and a parking ratio of 1.56 spaces per unit. It appears the development meets all current zoning requirements.

TAXES AND ASSESSMENTS

The property is currently assessed as follows for 1992 tax purposes. The assessment was performed in 1988. The following chart provides the tax assessment for the improved portion of the site and the undeveloped, excess land as follows:

Block 6043/Lot 100

Land	$ 245,600	$ 1.50/sq. ft. of land area
Improvements	1,137,200	25.40/sq. ft. of building area
Total	$1,382,800	$30.88/sq. ft. of building area

The subject property is located within the city limits of Northwoods, so it is responsible for city/county taxes. The 1992 city/county tax rate is $1.2425 per $100 of assessed value and we estimate the rate will increase 3 percent for 1993, for a tax rate of $1.28 per $100 of assessed value. Based on this estimate, the tax burden can be calculated as follows:

Block 6043/Lot 100

Assessed value	$1,382,800
Tax rate	× 1.28/100
Property tax	$ 17,700

To check the reasonableness of the subject's tax assessment, we will use the assessment of some of the surrounding apartment developments as follows:

Oakwood Manor Apartments

Land	$ 542,354	$ 1.13/sq. ft. of land area
Improvements	2,728,919	27.15/sq. ft. of building area
Total	$3,271,273	$32.54/sq. ft. of building area

Lake View Apartments

Land	$ 887,200	$ 1.46/sq. ft.
Improvements	5,373,600	26.92/sq. ft.
Total	$6,260,800	$31.37/sq. ft.

Briar Creek Apartments

Land	$1,506,200	$ 1.14/sq. ft.
Improvements	6,628,300	26.45/sq. ft.
Total	$8,134,500	$32.46/sq. ft.

The tax assessment for the improvement is very close to the range of these nearby apartment developments and appears reasonable because these properties are all similar.

IMPROVEMENTS DESCRIPTION

The subject site is improved with eight two-story apartment buildings built in 1983, which contain a total of 64 units. The workmanship and quality of materials are of average quality for the Northwoods market.

Improvement details are as follows:

Paving: Asphalt covering over gravel in parking areas and driveways; concrete dumpster pads.

Foundations: Poured concrete footings and concrete slabs on grade on first floors.

Framing: Wood wall framing, roof trusses and floor trusses.

Exterior Walls: Brick veneer surfaces on all sides.

Roofing: Asphalt roof shingles, aluminum gutters and downspouts.

Doors and Windows: Exterior wooden doors, aluminum double-hung windows with one-half screens.

Interior Finish: Painted sheetrock walls, textured ceilings, painted (or stained) doors and trim, wallpaper in kitchens and bathrooms.

Kitchen Appliances: Range/oven, hood fan, frost-free refrigerator, double sink, eat-on bar and dishwasher (two bedroom units only).

Finish Floors: Carpet over particle board on upper floor and concrete slab on ground level floors. Bath and kitchen flooring are vinyl.

HVAC: One-bedroom units have electric baseboard heating and through-wall air conditioning. Two-bedroom units have central heating and cooling. All electric.

Washer/Dryer Connections: All units have washer and dryer connections.

Front Walks/Balconies: Concrete on grade walks for ground level units and wood balconies for upper level units.

The unit breakdown for the subject improvements is as follows:

No. of Units	Unit Type	Size (sq. ft.)
32	1BR/1BA	550
32	2BR/1BA	750

All units have either entrance porches or covered walkways. Parking is in the front of each building with approximately 1.5 parking spaces per unit on a per-building basis. Landscaping is modest and consists of ornamental bushes, trees and native grasses.

The units appear to have a functional design and suffer no obsolescence. The buildings were built in 1983 and appear to have received adequate maintenance. The improvements are in average to good condition with an estimated effective age of nine years. Buildings of this type and quality typically have useful lives of 40 to 45 years.

Photographs of the improvements and floor-plan sketches for each of the unit types are included in the Addenda to this report.

HIGHEST AND BEST USE

Highest and best use is defined in *The Language of Real Estate Appraisal** as:

> The reasonable and probable use that results in the highest present value of the land after considering all legally permissible, physically possible and economically feasible uses. Capitalization rates or discount rates for each feasible use should reflect typical returns expected in the market. Highest and best use is usually determined under two different premises: as if the site was vacant and could be improved in the optimal manner or as the site is currently improved.
>
> In the latter premise, the highest and best use of the site will either be to keep the existing building or to demolish the building and develop a building that is the highest and best use. In general, it is not feasible to demolish an existing building as long as it contributes to the value of the site.

In developing a highest and best use analysis, it is necessary to consider the highest and best use of the site, as though it were vacant, and the highest and best use of the site as improved.

Site as though Vacant

In developing a highest and best use analysis, four questions must be answered.

1. Is the proposed use legally permissible or reasonably possible?
2. Is the proposed use physically possible on the site?
3. Is the proposed use economically and financially feasible under existing and projected market conditions?
4. Is the proposed use estimated to be the most profitable among the alternatives that are legally permitted, physically possible and economically feasible?

Physically Possible. As can be seen from a review of the previous Neighborhood Description section of the report, the site is located in the southern section of Northwoods, which enjoys a variety of land uses. Due to the proximity of the subject to Oak Street, N.C. Highway 66, Interstate 40 and N.C. Highway 150, the subject has good access to surrounding neighborhoods and employment centers. In my judgment, the site has good potential for multifamily use, and such a use conforms to surrounding uses and provides a transition from the single-family uses to the east and south and commercial and industrial uses to the north along Springs Drive and Interstate 40. The physical features of the site, such as its size, shape, frontage, depth, topography, ingress/egress and presence of utilities, also permit such a use.

The Language of Real Estate Appraisal by Jeffrey D. Fisher, PhD; Robert S. Martin, MAI, SREA, CRE; and Paige Mosbaugh (Chicago: Dearborn Financial Publishing, Inc., 1991).

As discussed in the Site Description section of the report, soil and subsoil conditions also appear to be adequate to support low-rise multifamily structures. There are no adverse easements or encroachments noted that would prohibit multifamily use or impair the marketability of the site. Given the physical features of the site, a multifamily use of the site is physically possible.

Legally Permissible. The present R-MF, Residential Multifamily zoning permits multifamily development and other uses such as churches, parks and several public utility uses. Given compliance with various height, density, setback and minimum lot area requirements, any of these uses would be legally permissible.

Economically Feasible. Given the location of the site in close proximity to major transportation routes, shopping and employment centers, I believe the subject site, if vacant and ready for development, could be leased or sold as a multifamily site in a reasonably short marketing time at a rate and/or price sufficient to recover the cost of acquisition and development. Vacant multifamily land in the Northwoods area is relatively scarce and is selling in the $30,000 to $40,000 per acre range, depending on the size and location of each tract. Apartments of similar quality in the general market area are leasing in the $0.42 to $0.57 per square foot per month range. As will be seen in the income approach, this rent level will provide the necessary net operating income to cover debt service and provide a reasonable return to equity to the owner, assuming proper design and siting of the improvements. Based on the vacancy survey I have presented in the income approach, multifamily projects in the area are experiencing occupancy rates between 90 percent and 100 percent. Based on the successful operation of other apartment complexes in the immediate area and the location of the subject with good access to major traffic thoroughfares, employment and shopping centers, the subject should be more competitive in the market than other projects of similar quality in inferior locations. Thus, I have concluded that a multifamily use of the site is economically feasible, given the rent and price available for such units and the relative costs of construction.

Most Economically Productive. The general use R-MF zoning permits a variety of uses such as multifamily residential, single family residential, church, medical/dental offices and hotel/motels. The site could physically support any of these uses. Single-family development typically results in a lesser land value than multifamily use, and most hotels/motels and office properties are found in a location with significantly higher visibility and traffic flow than the subject site. Based on these observations, I have concluded that a low-rise multifamily use of the site conforms with the surrounding properties and represents the most profitable among alternative uses that are legally permitted, physically possible and economically feasible.

In my judgment, the subject, as if vacant, has good potential for a multifamily residential site. The site is located in an area of Northwoods that is predominantly multifamily and single-family residential in nature and has excellent access to major traffic arteries and employment centers. Additionally, the site has adequate public utilities, has a size and shape that lends itself to multifamily development and is adequately zoned for multifamily use.

Site as Improved

As described in the Improvements Description section of the report, the subject site is currently improved with eight two-story brick veneer apartment buildings containing 64 units. Given the fact that the subject site is improved with a use that is basically compatible with the determination of the highest and best use of the site as if vacant and whose value exceeds the value of the site as if vacant, it is appropriate to consider the highest and best use of the site as improved. Again, four questions must be asked.

1. Is the use legally permissible or reasonably possible?
2. Is the use physically possible on the site?
3. Is the use economically and financially feasible under existing and projected market conditions?
4. Is the use estimated to be the most profitable among the alternatives that are legally permitted, physically possible and economically feasible?

First, the physical siting of the existing improvements on the site, with acceptable ingress and egress, indicates that the existing improvements are physically possible on the site. The availability of utilities and access to major traffic arteries is further evidence of the conformity with the requirement of physical possibility. As discussed in the Site Description section of the report, no unusual soil or subsoil conditions were noted that would prohibit the use of the site as currently improved.

When considering whether the existing improvements comply with the requirements of legal permissibility, I examined the permitted uses, density and the various physical restraints imposed by any public or private restrictions, including the zoning regulations. As I noted earlier in the report, no private restrictions exist; therefore, I will discuss only public restrictions, including zoning requirements.

Current zoning limits density to 17.63 units per acre and 1.5 parking spaces per apartment unit. The subject property consists of 3.76 acres of land, for a legal maximum limit of 66 units. The subject property contains 64 units and approximately 100 parking spaces for a parking space per unit ratio of 1.56. Therefore, the improvements meet these requirements. The siting of the subject improvements also appear to conform to the zoning requirements, such as setback, height, etc. Thus, the subject is in compliance with the legal requirements and is, therefore, a legally permissible use.

Next I must consider the economic feasibility of continued use of the subject properties as multifamily apartment buildings. The subject properties and competing facilities are all enjoying occupancy rates in excess of 90 percent and, as demonstrated in the income approach section of this report, the present improvements can provide an adequate net income to cover debt service and provide the owner with an adequate rate of return on his equity investment. Therefore, based on an analysis of the net operating income that can be derived from the operation of the subject property, I have concluded that the existing improvements are financially feasible.

Finally, the question arises whether the existing use of each site is estimated to be the most profitable among the alternatives that are physically possible, legally permitted and economically feasible. As noted in my discussion of the highest and best use as if vacant, it appears reasonable that only use as a multifamily property appears to be maximally productive. The successful operation of the subject property, as demonstrated in the income approach section of this report, is further evidence of this highest and best use. Based on these observations, an apartment use appears most profitable. The only question that remains, then, is whether the existing improvements should be modified or expanded to increase efficiency. As noted in the discussion of physically possible uses, it does not appear that the property can be further improved owing to the topography and siting of the current improvements on the subject site. Based on these considerations, it would appear that the present use of the site is representative of the most profitable of alternative uses that are legal, possible and economically feasible.

VALUATION METHODOLOGY

There are three commonly accepted approaches used in valuing real estate. These are the Cost Approach, the Income Approach and the Sales Comparison Approach, they are defined as follows:

Cost Approach—One of the three traditional appraisal approaches to estimating value. In this approach, value is based on adding the contributing value of any improvements (after deduction for accrued depreciation) to the value of the land as if it were vacant, based on its highest and best use. If the interest appraised is other than fee simple, additional adjustments may be necessary for nonrealty interest and/or the impact of existing leases or contracts.

Income Approach—One of the three traditional appraisal approaches to estimating value. In this approach, value is based on the present value of future benefits of property ownership. In direct capitalization, a single year's income is converted to a value indication using a capitalization rate. In yield capitalization, future cash flows are estimated and discounted to a present value using a capitalization rate.

Sales Comparison Approach—One of the three traditional appraisal approaches to estimating value. Value is estimated by comparing similar properties that have sold recently to the subject property. Formerly referred to as the "market approach."

Each of these approaches and their relationship to the appraisal process are discussed in greater detail under the appropriate sections of the report.

COST APPROACH

Estimating the market value of a property by the cost approach is accomplished by first determining the current market value of the site as if vacant and put to its highest and best use and then adding the depreciated value of the improvements (total reproduction cost new minus loss in utility due to age, wear and tear, design and/or location). The land value will be estimated by comparing the subject property with sales of similar parcels of vacant land in the area. The reproduction cost new will be developed from the Marshall-Swift Valuation Service as well as a consideration of the actual costs of constructing two nearby apartment projects. The Marshall-Swift Valuation Service is a nationally recognized cost estimating guide that is easily adapted to local markets through the application of local and current multipliers and has proven to result in reliable estimates of what buildings can be built for across the country.

Land Value Estimate

In this approach, the subject site is valued as though it were vacant and ready for development into its highest and best use. Several sales similar to the subject in terms of location, utility and type of use have been analyzed to estimate the subject's site value.

The valuation method used is sales comparison. This is the method used by those active in the market to purchase or sell sites similar to the subject site. Direct sales comparison is based on the principle of substitution. This is the premise that an informed, prudent and rational purchaser/investor would pay no more for a site than the cost of acquiring a similar, competitive site with the same utility as the subject site. Direct sales comparison is based on the requirements that there be an active market for sites such as the subject site and that reliable, comparable data be available in sufficient quantity and quality to allow for a proper application of this analysis.

After investigating the local market for sites such as the subject, it is my opinion that these requirements are satisfied and that direct sales comparison is a valid method for estimating the value of the subject site.

Land transactions throughout the market have been researched. The search has centered on three recent sales near the subject. The unit of comparison used is the price per unit. Based on discussions with buyers and sellers in the marketplace, I have noted that the price per unit is a common reference in decisions to buy or sell land similar to the subject site. Because land is commonly purchased and sold on this basis, and owing to features such as size, shape and topography, it is my judgment that the price per unit is a better indicator of value than the price per square foot or price per acre for a site similar to the subject.

Land Sale Number One:

Location:	North side of Main Street and Quail Lane Northwoods, North Carolina
Tax block/lot:	5093/5 and 6
Grantor:	Thomas Johnson, Jr., and wife, Kathryn
Grantee:	James Jones
Date:	December 17, 1992
Deed book/page:	888/420
Price:	$85,000
Size:	2.20 acres
Price per acre:	$40,909
Price per unit:	$2,237
Zoning:	Multifamily residential
Topography:	Level, wooded
Utilities:	No public water or sewer

Comments:

Located adjacent to northwestern portion of the subject site. Quail Lane is a gravel roadway, and although public water and sewer are not available directly to the property, these could be extended to the property. The property can be developed with 38 units.

Land Sale Number Two:

Location:	128 West Road Northwoods, North Carolina
Tax block/lot:	5341/108
Grantor:	T & M Partnership
Grantee:	Northwoods Limited Partnership
Date:	October 11, 1992
Deed book/page:	882/321
Price:	$180,000
Size:	6.00 acres
Price per acre:	$30,000
Price per unit:	$2,143
Zoning:	Multifamily residential—approved for 84 units
Topography:	Relatively level
Utilities:	Public water

Comments:
This property is located on West Road near its intersection with Old Church Road in Northwoods. The site was purchased subject to rezoning to multifamily use.

Land Sale Number Three:

Location:	West side of Second Street Northwoods, North Carolina
Tax block/lot:	6106/202
Grantor:	Sara Thomas Hicks, Executrix
Grantee:	William Edward, et al.
Date:	November 9, 1992
Deed book/page:	884/106
Price:	$150,000
Size:	4.38 acres
Price per acre:	$34,262
Price per unit:	$2,027
Zoning:	Multifamily residential—approved for 74 units
Topography:	Sloping
Utilities:	All public

Comments:
The subject property is to be the site of a new 74-unit apartment project known as Oak Tree Village.

Land Sales Summary and Adjustment Grid

Sale	1	2	3
Sale date	12/17/92	10/11/92	11/9/92
Price	$85,000	$180,000	$150,000
Size (acres)	2.20	6.00	4.38
Units app	38	84	74
Price/unit	$2,237	$2,143	$2,027
Time	-0-	-0-	-0-
Net	$2,237	$2,143	$2,027
Location	+5%	+5%	-0-
Size	-0-	-0-	-0-
Topography	−5%	−5%	-0-
Utilities	+5%	+5%	-0-
Density	-0-	−5%	-0-
Net adj.	+5%	-0-	-0-
Price/unit	$2,349	$2,143	$2,027

Comments on the Adjustments

Following is information for three recent multifamily land sales in Northwoods. Each of the adjustments and the reasoning behind them are more fully explained in this section.

Time Adjustment.   All three sales were recent sales, so no adjustment for time was made.

Location Adjustment.   Sale one was judged inferior owing to its location along a gravel roadway with more limited visibility and access relative to the subject site. This adjustment would have been larger except for this site being located adjacent to other multifamily projects near the central business district of Northwoods and Interstate 40. Sale two was also adjusted upward to reflect its inferior location in a more sparsely developed area with more indirect access to Interstate 40 relative to the subject. Sale three is located in an area of multifamily development near the central business district of Northwoods that is judged similar to the location of subject and no adjustment was deemed necessary.

Size Adjustment.   All three sales are similar in size, so no adjustment was made.

Topography Adjustment.   This adjustment is intended to reflect the power line easement that burdens the eastern portion of the subject site. This easement runs across only a small portion of the subject site, but it is my opinion that some negative adjustment is reasonable to reflect the decreased utility. Therefore, all of the comparables, except sale three, are adjusted downward. Sale three required additional site work relative to the subject, and I feel this offsets the diminished utility and no adjustment was required.

Utilities Adjustment. Sales one and two were adjusted upward to reflect the additional costs associated with running water and/or sewer lines to these sites.

Density Adjustment. Sale two was adjusted downward to reflect the typically higher price per unit commanded by sites with lower permitted density levels.

The sales represent recent transactions of multifamily land sales in the Northwoods market. I feel the adjustments are logical and the indicated values provide a good indication of value for the subject site. The range of indicated values is from $2,027 to $2,349 per unit with an average indicated value of $2,173 per unit for the subject. I have given the greatest weight to sales two and three because of their similar location and, based on this analysis, I have chosen $2,100 per unit as the best indication of value for the subject site. Using this value estimate and the 64 units on the subject site, the land value can be calculated as follows:

64 units @ $2,100 per unit	$134,400
Rounded to	135,000

Improvements Value Estimate

Marshall Swift Valuation Service served as a guide in estimating the reproduction cost new of the improvements. The service is a nationally recognized cost manual that is readily adapted to local markets through the application of current and local multipliers. It is our opinion that the subject property would qualify as Average Quality, Multiple Residence, Cost Class D, as described in Section 12, Page 10, of the current Marshall Valuation Service Manual. Site improvement costs were taken from Section 66, Pages 1 and 2.

The cost estimate follows:

Calculation of Building Size

No. of Buildings		Size	Total Area
4	×	4,725 sq. ft.	18,900 sq. ft.
4	×	6,475 sq. ft.	25,900 sq. ft.
Total			44,800 sq. ft.

Calculation of Base Costs

Size (sq. ft.)	4,725	6,475
Base cost	$30.24	$34.48
Area multiplier	× 1.09	× 1.01
Cost multiplier	× 1.04	× 1.04
Local multiplier	× 0.84	× 0.84
Adjusted base cost	$28.80	$30.42

Improvements Cost New

18,900 sq. ft. @ $28.80/sq. ft.	$ 544,320
25,900 sq. ft. @ $30.42/sq. ft.	787,878
Cost new—Buildings	1,332,198
Porches/balconies 6,500 sq. ft. @ $10.00/sq. ft.	65,000
Appliances (units) 32 @ $1,125 each	36,000
32 @ $1,500 each	48,000
Total cost new—Buildings	$1,481,198
Price per square foot	$ 33.06

Following is the actual cost information for two apartment projects in the Northwood area:

Construction Costs for Two Similar Projects

Project Name	Date of Completion	No. of Units	Bldg/sq. ft.	Cost	Cost/sq. ft.
Mill Creek Apts.	10/5/92	36	28,980 sq. ft.	$ 975,000	$33.64
College Village Apts.	3/1/92	96	71,400 sq. ft.	$2,200,000	$30.81

The implied building cost for the subject falls in the range of costs for these two similar projects.

Site Improvements Cost

Item	Size	Cost/Unit	Total Cost
Asphalt paving	36,000 sq. ft.	$1.00	$36,000
Landscaping		Lump sum	5,000
Miscellaneous		Lump sum	5,000
Subtotal			$46,000
Cost multiplier			× 1.04
Local multiplier			× 0.84
Cost new—Site improvements			$40,186

Cost Approach Summary

Building improvements	$1,481,198
Site improvements	40,186
Total cost—Improvements	$1,521,384
Plus: Entrepreneurial profit (10%)	152,138
Subtotal	$1,673,522
Less: Depreciation on building (9 yrs. ÷ 45 yrs. = 20%)	− 325,863
Depreciation on site improvements (9 yrs. ÷ 15 yrs. = 60%)	− 26,523
Total depreciated value	$1,321,136
Plus: Land value	135,000
Total value by the cost approach	$1,456,136
Rounded to	$1,450,000

Cost Approach Value Estimate
One million four hundred fifty thousand dollars
($1,450,000)

INCOME APPROACH

The value by the income approach is estimated by first determining the economic rent (rent indicated by charges for similar space in the market) for the subject; second, subtracting expenses typically incurred in the operation of similar properties; and finally, by capitalizing the resulting net operating income (NOI) before debt service by the appropriate rate as indicated by current market conditions.

This method of valuation is generally the most important method in the estimation of the value of a commercial (income-generating) property because it duplicates the behavior of a typical, knowledgeable investor who desires a financial return on his invested capital.

I was provided a rent roll for the property dated December 23, 1992. This rent roll indicated that the property had only two vacant two-bedroom units at that time. All of the one-bedroom units were leased at $285 per month and all of the two-bedroom units occupied were leased at $345 per month. A copy of the rent roll is included in the addenda to this report.

To estimate the market rental for the subject, rentals for similar types of units were analyzed. The following pages give information about units available in the immediate area.

Comparable Rent Number One:

Name/Location: Parkwood
Maple Street
Northwoods, North Carolina

		Unit Mix		
No. of Units	*Type*	*Mo. Rent*	*Size*	*Rent/sq. ft.*
7	1BR/1BA	$299–$305	615 sq. ft.	$0.49–$0.50
138	2BR/1BA	$335–$340*	780 sq. ft.	$0.43–$0.44

*Lower rents are for 12-month lease terms and higher rental rates are for 6-month lease terms.

Occupancy: 93%
Age: 1973
Construction: Two-story buildings, wood frame with brick veneer and/or wood shingles

Comments:
This complex consists of ten buildings and has an office/clubhouse, swimming pool, two laundry rooms and tennis court. All units include carpet, range, no-frost refrigerator, dishwasher, disposal, central heat and air conditioning, and either a patio or a balcony.

Comparable Rent Number Two:

Name/Location: Pinewood Apartments
Pinewood Drive
Northwoods, North Carolina

		Unit Mix		
No. of Units	*Type*	*Mo. Rent*	*Size*	*Rent/sq. ft.*
36	2BR/2BA	$400	950 sq. ft.	$0.42

Occupancy: 100% (average 97%)
Age: 1985
Construction: Two-story buildings, wood frame with brick veneer and
wood shingles
Comments:
Units are energy-efficient and contain range, refrigerator, dishwasher, washer/dryer connections, carpet and walk-in closets. No amenities.

Comparable Rent Number Three:

Name/Location: Springhouse Apartments
515 Main Street
Northwoods, North Carolina

		Unit Mix		
No. of Units	*Type*	*Mo. Rent*	*Size*	*Rent/sq. ft.*
154	1BR/1.0BA	$285–$290*	600 sq. ft.	$0.48
148	2BR/1.0BA	$325–$345†	780 sq. ft.	$0.42–$0.44
44	3BR/1.5BA	$445†	1,078 sq. ft.	$0.41–$0.42
		$455*		

*Washer/dryer connections; balcony
†Washer/dryer connections

Occupancy: 94.5% (average 94% to 96%)
Age: 1985
Construction: Two-story buildings, wood frame with brick veneer
Comments:
Units include range, frost-free refrigerator and carpet. Two- and three-bedroom units have dishwasher and central air-conditioning. Amenities include two swimming pools, laundry room and playground area.

Comparable Rent Number Four:

Name/Location: Forrestgate Apartments
                  2718 Mountain Street
                  Northwoods, North Carolina

Unit Mix

No. of Units	Type	Mo. Rent	Size	Rent/sq. ft.
46	1BR/1BA	$285	575 sq. ft.	$0.50

Occupancy: 93.5% (average 93% to 95%)
Age: 1983
Construction: Two-story buildings, wood frame with brick veneer
Comments:
Units include range, refrigerator, washer/dryer connections and carpet.

Comparable Rent Number Five:

Name/Location: Oakwood Manor Apartments (Phase I & II)
                  480 Broad Street
                  Northwoods, North Carolina

Unit Mix

No. of Units	Type	Mo. Rent	Size	Rent/sq. ft.
64	1BR/1BA	$315–$340	578–594 sq. ft.	$0.54–$0.57
60	2BR/1.5BA	400	810 sq. ft.	0.49
23	2BR/1.5BA	375	854 sq. ft.	0.44
47	2BR/2BA	440	955 sq. ft.	0.46
12	3BR/1.5BA	515	1,005 sq. ft.	0.51
16	3BR/2BA	535	1,005 sq. ft.	0.53

Occupancy: 99% (average 95% to 97%)
Age: 1985–1989
Construction: Three-story buildings, wood frame with brick veneer
Comments:
Development built in two phases with the majority of the two-bedroom units of newer construction in Phase II. Units include range, refrigerator, dishwasher, washer/dryer connections, wallpaper, chair rails and carpet. Fifteen of the two-bedroom units in Phase II also have vaulted ceilings and ceiling fans and rent from $420 to $460 per month, dependent on the number of bathrooms. Amenities include laundry room, tennis court and a swimming pool. Water is not included in these units and the resident manager indicated that the rental rate and the sizes are the same as the Phase I units. The manager indicated she feels the additional water expense offsets any rental rate increase due to the newer age of these buildings.

Comparable Rent Number Six:

Name/Location:	Lake View Apartments
	549 Elm Street
	Northwoods, North Carolina

Unit Mix

No. of Units	Type	Mo. Rent	Size	Rent/sq. ft.
210	2BR/2BA	$420–$455	900 sq. ft.	$0.47–$0.51

Occupancy:	100% (average 95% to 98%)
Age:	1986
Construction:	Three-story buildings, wood frame with wood siding
Comments:	

Units include range, refrigerator, disposal, dishwasher and washer/dryer connections. The units that rent for $455 per month have lakefront locations within this development. Amenities include swimming pool and two tennis courts.

Summary of Market Rents

Name	Units	Type	Size (sq. ft.)	Rent (sq. ft.)
Parkwood	145	1BR/1BA	615	$0.49–$0.50
		2BR/1BA	780	$0.43–$0.44
Pinewood Apartments	36	2BR/2BA	950	$0.42
Springhouse Apartments	346	1BR/1BA	600	$0.48
		2BR/1BA	780	$0.42–$0.44
		3BR/1.5BA	1,078	$0.41–$0.42
Forrestgate Apartments	46	1BR/1BA	575	$0.50
Oakwood Manor Apartments	222	1BR/1BA	578–594	$0.54–$0.57
		2BR/1BA	810	$0.49
		2BR/1.5BA	854	$0.44
		2BR/2BA	955	$0.46
		3BR/1.5BA	1,005	$0.51
		3BR/2BA	1,005	$0.53
Lake View Apartments	210	2BR/2BA	900	$0.47–$0.51

Comparable Rentals Summary and Adjustment Grid—1 Bedroom

Comp	1	2	3	4	5	6
Mo. rent	$299	N/A	$290	$285	$315–340	N/A
Size, sq. ft.	615	N/A	600	575	578–594	N/A
Rent/sq. ft.	$0.50	N/A	$0.48	$0.50	$0.54–0.57	N/A
Time	-0-	N/A	-0-	-0-	-0-	N/A
Net	$0.50	N/A	$0.48	$0.50	$0.54–0.57	N/A
Location	-0-	N/A	-0-	+5%	-0-	N/A
Size	+5%	N/A	+5%	-0-	-0-	N/A
Age	+10%	N/A	-0-	-0-	−5%	N/A
Condition	-0-	N/A	-0-	-0-	-0-	N/A
Quality	−3%	N/A	-0-	-0-	−3%	N/A
Amenities	−5%	N/A	−5%	-0-	−5%	N/A
Net adj.	+7%	N/A	-0-	+5%	−13%	N/A
Value/sq. ft.	$0.54	N/A	$0.48	$0.53	$0.47–0.50	N/A

Comments on the Adjustments

Location Adjustment.   All of the rent comparables are located within Northwoods in close proximity to the subject and, except for comparable four, no location adjustment is deemed necessary. Comparable four is located just west of Northwoods in a more sparsely developed area judged inferior to that of the subject.

Size Adjustment.   Comparables one and three were adjusted upward for their larger size due to typically lower rents per square foot for larger apartments with the same bedroom count.

Age Adjustment.   Comparable one was adjusted upward owing to the older construction of this development and the greater degree of physical deterioration suffered relative to the subject property. Comparable five was adjusted downward by 5 percent because it is slightly newer.

Quality Adjustment.   Comparables one and five were judged superior in quality owing to having central heating/cooling systems compared with the subject property's through-wall air-conditioning. Cost figures from the Marshall Valuation Service manual are used to determine the amount of this adjustment as follows:

Heatpump cost/sq. ft.		$3.40
Electric BB cost/sq. ft.	$1.80	
A/C window unit cost/sq. ft.	0.65	
		− 2.45
		$0.95

Cost difference/sq. ft. ($0.95/$31.30 = $3.03%)

Therefore, a 3% downward adjustment is deemed reasonable for this factor.

Amenities Adjustment.   Comparables one, three and five were judged superior because these complexes contained a swimming pool and/or tennis court and were adjusted downward to reflect the higher rents per square foot that these amenities typically command.

No other adjustments were deemed necessary. The range of indicated rents per square foot for the one-bedroom units in the subject property is $0.48 to $0.54 per month. The current rental rates for the subject's one-bedroom units are $0.52 per square foot. Because the subject's one-bedroom unit rent rates per square foot fall within the above-indicated range, it appears that its current rental rates for the one-bedroom units are at or near market rental rates. Therefore, the current monthly rent of $285 for the one-bedroom units in the subject property will be used in the income analysis.

Following is the adjustment grid for the two-bedroom/one-bathroom units in the subject:

Comparable Rentals Summary and Adjustment Grid—2 Bedroom

Comp	1	2	3	4	5	6
Mo. rent	$340	$400	$335	N/A	$400	$420
Size, sq. ft.	780	950	780	N/A	810	900
Rent/sq. ft.	$0.44	$0.42	$0.44	N/A	$0.49	$0.47
Time	-0-	-0-	-0-	N/A	-0-	-0-
Term	-0-	-0-	-0-	N/A	-0-	-0-
Net	$0.44	$0.42	$0.44	N/A	$0.49	$0.47
Location	-0-	-0-	-0-	N/A	-0-	-0-
Size	-0-	+10%	-0-	N/A	-0-	+5%
Age	+10%	-0-	-0-	N/A	−5%	-0-
Condition	-0-	-0-	-0-	N/A	-0-	-0-
Quality	+5%	−5%	-0-	N/A	-0-	−5%
Amenities	−5%	-0-	−5%	N/A	−5%	-0-
Net adj.	+10%	+5%	−5%	N/A	−10%	-0-
Value/sq. ft.	$0.48	$0.44	$0.42	N/A	$0.44	$0.47

Comments on the Adjustments

Location Adjustment.   No adjustments were deemed necessary owing to the comparables' similar location near Interstate 40 and other major transportation routes within Northwoods.

Size Adjustment.   Comparables two and six were adjusted upward to reflect the typically lower rents per square foot for larger apartments with the same bedroom count.

Age Adjustment.   Comparable one is of older construction and was adjusted upward to reflect the greater physical deterioration suffered by this development relative to the subject property. Comparable five was adjusted down slightly because it is newer.

Quality Adjustment.   Comparable one was judged inferior because of not having washer/dryer connections and was adjusted upward. Comparables two and six were adjusted downward to reflect their extra bathrooms and the typically higher rent per square foot charged for units with an extra bathroom and the same bedroom count.

Amenities Adjustment.   Comparables one, three and five were adjusted downward to reflect that these complexes have swimming pools and/or tennis courts and the typically higher rent per square foot that these amenities command, all other things being equal.

No other adjustments were deemed necessary. The range of indicated monthly rents for the subject's two-bedroom/one-bathroom units is from

$0.42 to $0.48 per square foot. Because the subject rent for these unit types is $0.46 per square foot, it appears that the subject property's current rental rates for the two-bedroom/one-bathroom units are at or near market rates.

Using the estimated market rental rates for each of the units in the subject property as discussed above, the gross potential income for the subject can be calculated as follows:

32	1BR/1BA units @ $285 per mo.	$ 9,120
32	2BR/1BA units @ $345 per mo.	11,040
Subtotal		$ 20,160
Multiplied by 12 mos.		× 12
Total gross potential income		$241,920

Vacancy and Collection Loss

A survey of the local market provided the vacancy rates for the rent comparables listed above and additional complexes in Northwood with which we are familiar. The data indicate that most developments are enjoying vacancy rates between 0 percent and 10 percent with the majority of similar type projects enjoying vacancy rates between 0 percent and 5 percent. The subject property had two vacant units, or a 3.4 percent vacancy rate, according to the December 23, 1992, rent roll. Based on these observations and the successful operating history of the subject, we will use a 5 percent stabilized vacancy and collection loss estimate. The resulting effective gross income for the subject is as follows:

Gross potential rental income	$241,920
Less: Vacancy/collection loss (5%)	− 12,096
Effective gross income	$229,824

The operating statement for the first nine months of 1992 provides for $229,931 in annual effective gross rental income for 1992. Our estimate for the coming year appears reasonable because it is very close to the annualized 1992 figures.

Other income includes forfeited security deposits, which have averaged approximately $2,500 per year over the project's recent history. I will include $2,500 as other income in my income and expense forecast for the subject property.

Expense Estimate

Normally, the most relevant evidence of the likely expense level to be incurred in the operation of the subject comes from a review of the recent operating results from the subject itself. In reviewing the operating history of the subject, we were provided with financial statements for the first nine months of 1992 and financial statements dating back through 1987. The actual subject operating data provided for 1992 year-to-date and through 1989 are reproduced below.

Bay Hill Apartments—Historical Operating Information

	1992 Jan.–Sept.	1991	1990	1989
Rental income	$172,448	$232,263	$221,851	$209,791
Other income	1,300	2,304	2,104	2,539
Total income	$173,748	$234,567	$223,955	$212,330
Expenses:				
Management fee	$ 12,048	$ 15,888	$ 14,974	$ 13,464
Utilities	12,244	16,306	15,089	14,874
Insurance	2,711	3,154	3,321	3,484
Repairs/maintenance	16,407	31,581	37,213*	26,241
Taxes	-0-	19,059	17,479	16,071
Other	1,452	3,721	3,279	4,485
Total expenses	$ 44,862	$ 89,709	$ 91,355	$ 78,619
NOI	$128,886	$144,859	$132,600	$133,711

*The 1990 maintenance expense included $9,700 for new roof installation.

Total operating expenses before reserves for Bay Hill Apartments, all as a function of effective gross income and cost per unit, are set forth in the following table:

Year	Total Expense	% of EGI	Cost/Unit
1992	$44,862*	25.8	$ 701
1991*	89,709	38.2	1,402
1990	91,355	40.8	1,427
1989	78,619	37.0	1,228

*Taxes are not included in the 1992 expenses, which results in the lower expense levels.

The actual expenses from other apartment projects in the local market, some of which are used as sales in the sales comparison approach, are as follows:

Expense Comparables for Winston-Salem/Greensboro MSA

Project	No. of Units	Expenses	% EGI	Per Unit
Chatham Wood*	208	$446,800	43.7	$2,148
Old Town	60	67,492	33.0	1,125
Grosvenor Square	145	225,560	44.3	1,556
Quail Oaks	152	342,000	43.9	2,250
WIllow Creek	144	248,103	39.0	1,723
St. Croix	216	539,179	39.5	1,496

*This project has a pool and tennis courts.

The survey of complexes in the Winston-Salem/Greensboro area, performed by IREM, revealed that expenses before reserves and replacements ranged from 35.4 percent to 39.7 percent of gross potential income and 41.6 percent to 43.1 percent of effective gross income.

The above expense data typically do not include a reserves and replacements charge. We considered all of this data and also examined each item of expense, as discussed below, in arriving at our expense estimate.

Discussion of Individual Expenses

Real Estate Taxes.   Taxes were estimated earlier in this report to be $17,700 per year.

Insurance.   The annualized cost for the subject property in 1992 equals $3,615, or $0.08 per square foot. The median expense for this item noted in the IREM survey is $0.11 per square foot, which would equate to a charge of $4,928 for the 44,800 square feet of building area. The figures in the 1989 to 1991 financial statements show the insurance expense for the subject to be decreasing over this period. Based on this data, we chose $3,600 as a reasonable estimate of the insurance cost for expense.

Utilities.   This item covers charges for telephone, water and sewer, and common-area electric. The annualized cost for the subject property in 1992 is $16,325, which represents an increase of only $19 over the 1991 utilities expense. This expense category has been increasing at approximately 4 percent per year since 1988, and based on these actual costs, we have chosen $16,950, rounded, for next year's utility costs.

Repairs/Maintenance.   This is the largest single category of expense associated with the operation of the subject. The 1992 annualized cost for the subject is $21,867, which would result in the lowest expenditure in this category since 1987. Excluding the expenditure for the new roof in 1990, this expense category has been fairly consistent between 1988 and 1991, when it ranged from $26,241 to $31,581, with an average expense level of $28,350, rounded. This equates to a cost of $0.63 per square foot. The IREM survey indicates a total maintenance cost of $0.48 per square foot, including amenity maintenance. Based on the age of the subject and the relatively constant indication of the cost of this item, we project a cost of $30,000 for these items for the first year of our analysis.

Administrative/Management Costs.   In addition to management fees, there is currently one full-time on-site employee who oversees the entire Bay Hill complex. The total of this expense has been consistent at approximately 8.25 percent of total income since 1988 for the subject property. Based on this expense level at similar type apartment projects with which we are familiar, it is our opinion that a 8.25 percent charge for this expense appears reasonable. Therefore, a management fee of $18,960 appears reasonable to cover the management fee, on-site manager's salary and payroll costs, and utilities for the office space.

The only other cost that does not appear in the owner operating statement is a reserve for the eventual replacement of long-lived items. Although it is not possible to predict precisely when short-lived items such as appliances, HVAC and roof cover will have to be replaced, some deduction from net income is appropriate to recognize that these expenses will be incurred over time. Several investors we are familiar with who invest in multifamily properties included a provision of approximately 2 percent of effective gross income in their projections to reflect the cost of these eventual replacements. We have adopted their estimate of the appropriate deductions for reserves for replacements in our analysis.

Based on the discussions above, first-year expenses total $91,806, which equates to 39.5 percent of effective gross income, $2.05 per square foot of gross building area and $1,434 per unit, including reserves. We find this line-by-line analysis of the expenses likely to be incurred in the operating of the subject to give the most reliable estimate of net income of all of the analysis presented. The expenses appear reasonable; they are supported by the historical operation of the subject and fall within the ranges indicated by the comparable sales analyzed in the sales comparison approach.

All of the above items of income and expense are combined in the following income and expense forecast:

Bay Hill Apartments
Income and Expense Forecast

Gross potential income	$241,920
Less: Vacancy and credit loss	− 12,096
Plus: Other income	+ 2,500
Effective gross income	$232,324
Less: Expenses	
Management/A&G	$ 18,960
Utilities	16,950
Maintenance	30,000
Taxes (est. earlier in report)	17,700
Insurance	3,600
Total operating expenses (37.5% of EGI and $1,363 per unit)	$ 87,210
Reserves	4,596
Total expenses (39.5% of EGI and $1,434 per unit)	$ 91,806
Net operating income	$140,518
Rounded to	$140,500

Capitalization of Income

Three methods of transforming the income forecast into an estimate of value will be used; direct capitalization, band of investment and yield capitalization.

The yield capitalization approach will be employed using discounted cash flow on both a leveraged and an unleveraged basis. The leverage analysis will assume typical financing of the project at market interest rates.

Direct Capitalization.   Direct capitalization is accomplished by dividing a market overall rate into the first-year NOI forecast for the property. This approach results in a reliable estimate of value when the comparable property sales are similar to the subject because the sales reflect the same interest as the subject and when occupancy levels are highly similar. Following is a list of the three overall rates extracted from the comparable sales listed in the sales comparison approach.

Sale	Overall Rate
1	9.5%
2	10.1
3	9.9

All the sales represent the same interest and each transaction was financed with a loan at market rates, so no adjustment for cash equivalency was required. Sale two is of an older property, which may have had a negative impact on the overall rate. The overall rates for sales one and three reflect a somewhat narrow range. It is therefore my opinion that the best estimate of the overall rate for the subject would be 9.75 percent. Following is the value calculation.

$$\frac{\text{NOI}}{R_M} = \frac{\$140,500}{0.0975} = \$1,441,026$$

Band of Investment.   The band-of-investment method (using mortgage and equity components) calculates an overall rate by analyzing the relationship between the debt and the equity capital that is used to purchase properties. This method is useful when the mortgage constant (annual debt service/mortgage amount) and the required equity dividend rate (return on investment/equity capital) can be derived from the marketplace. The formula for deriving the overall rate using the band-of-investment method is as follows:

$$R_O = M \times R_M + (1-M) \times R_E$$

where:

R_O = overall rate
M = loan-to-value ratio
R_M = mortgage constant
R_E = equity dividend rate

Analysis of the sales in the sales comparison approach provided the following information concerning mortgage rates and equity dividend rates.

(See the overall rate analysis section of the sales comparison approach for details on the mortgage financing and calculation of the equity dividend rates.)

Sale	Equity Dividend Rate	Loan-to-Value Ratio	Mortgage Interest Rate	Mortgage Constant
1	0.059	78.1%	9.50%	0.1048
2	0.087	70.4	9.75	0.1069
3	0.080	71.9	9.50	0.1048

The data indicate that the typical loan-to-value ratio ranges from 70 percent to 80 percent. Mortgage constants range from 0.1048 to 0.1069, with the typical amortization period being 25 years. Balloons are common in the 5-year to 10-year period with interest rate calls as early as 3 years into the holding period. Interviews with investors indicate anticipated typical holding periods range from 5 to 10 years. Equity dividend rates range from 5.9 percent to 8.7 percent.

A search of available financing from local lending institutions indicates a variety of financing alternatives would be available for the subject. The typical financing for many recent loans, including the sales comparables, indicated a mortgage interest rate in the range of 9.5 percent to 9.75 percent amortized over 25 years with a 75 percent loan-to-value ratio. Many of these loans included a balloon payment at 5-year to 10-year intervals. Some loans have been written to fluctuate with the prime rate.

The equity dividend range indicated by the comparables is from 5.9 percent to 8.7 percent. The equity dividend rate is affected by the loan terms and the loan-to-value ratio. Assuming the typical loan-to-value ratio is 75 percent, it appears the best estimate of the equity dividend rate would be higher than 5.9 percent but lower than 8.0 percent or 8.7 percent. It is my opinion that the best estimate of the equity dividend rate for the subject would be 7 percent.

Given these data, the following inputs were selected for the derivation of the overall rate using the band-of-investment method.

Summary of Inputs

Loan-to-value ratio [M]	0.7500
Mortgage constant [R_M]	0.1048
Equity dividend rate [R_E]	0.0700

Overall Rate Solution

0.7500×0.1048	0.0786
0.2500×0.0700	0.0175
R_O	0.0961

$$\text{Value} = \frac{\text{NOI}}{R_O} = \frac{\$140,500}{0.961} = \$1,462,019$$

Yield Capitalization. Yield capitalization is a capitalization method that converts future benefits to present value by applying an appropriate yield discount rate. The yield discount rate is derived by analyzing market evidence concerning the yield anticipated by typical investors. The method requires the following four steps:

1. Selection of a typical holding period.
2. The generation of future cash flows that anticipate the behavior of the NOI over the holding period that was calculated above.
3. Selection of the appropriate yield (discount) rate.
4. Conversion of future benefits of the periodic cash flows to value by discounting each annual cash flow to present value.

Capitalization of the Income.   With the aid of a computer specially programmed to solve for the value using selected inputs, a discounted cash-flow technique will be used to calculate the value estimate. The computer program uses the mortgage-equity technique with the Ellwood formula. This technique considers the potential investor's required rate of return on equity, the current mortgage terms available in the marketplace and the potential changes in the value of the property in the form of equity reversion at the end of the holding period, as well as changes in the income stream.

Following is a summary of the forecast inputs selected and the value solution, plus a schedule of the cash flows implied in the computer analysis, which uses a discounted cash-flow approach to calculate the value indication. In addition, the implied overall rate, the mortgage value and the equity value will be presented to illustrate the discounting process for the annual cash flows and to show the implied debt coverage ratio (DCR) and the equity dividend rate for each year during the holding period. The discounted cash-flow analysis has become a widely accepted method of analyzing income-producing properties by buyers and sellers in the local market.

Leveraged Analysis

Required Inputs:

- A first mortgage with a 9.5 percent rate with level payments over 25 years with a loan-to-value ratio of 25 percent was selected and is based on information provided by several local lenders regarding reasonable financing rates for the subject property.
- NOI was previously estimated in this section of the report and is $140,500. I have assumed that NOI will increase 2.5 percent per year.
- I assumed 5 percent selling costs would be incurred.
- A 16 percent before-tax required equity yield rate was selected as sufficient to compensate the typical investor for the risks inherent in an apartment investment such as the subject. The following before-tax yield rates are currently available in the financial markets as of October 16, 1992:

1–10 Year Corporate Bonds—Medium Quality	6.95%
1–10 Year Corporate Bonds—High Quality	6.49
Long Term Treasuries (10+ Years)	7.48
High Yield Corporate Bonds (Junk Bonds)	11.31

Source: *The Wall Street Journal.*

A 16 percent equity yield rate is nearly twice the rate of return available on risk-free investments of a maturity equal to the projected holding period. The premium over the risk-free rate is intended to compensate an investor for the risks inherent in real estate investments such as the subject where the tenancies are transient and local and national economic events, including sporadic increases in the supply of competing multifamily projects, cause temporary increases in vacancy rates. The Laventhol & Horwath investor survey indicates that a typical property yield rate for investments in multifamily projects ranges from 11.5 percent to 12.3 percent for unleveraged investments, with three of the five investor classifications indicating a required yield rate of between 11.8 percent and 12.0 percent for unleveraged multifamily investment.

Based on alternative yields available in the financial markets and based on the required equity yield rates for unleveraged investments, I chose 16 percent as the required before-tax equity yield rate in the analysis where I assumed typical financing. I chose a higher discount rate for the leveraged analysis to compensate for the additional risk associated with the use of financing. To check the reasonableness of this value solution, I also performed a discounted cash-flow analysis with a 12 percent required discount rate, assuming the investment was unleveraged. The inputs used in the discounted cash-flow analysis assuming a leveraged investment are summarized below.

Summary of Input Assumptions

Basic Inputs

Equity Yield rate	0.16000	Net operating income	$140,500
Holding period	10	Change in NOI	0.24886
Resale value	$1,798,519	Income adjustment factor	G1
Selling cost	0.05000	Annual change	0.02500

Loan Inputs

Loan Number	1
Interest rate	0.09500
Loan term	25.00000
Payments per year	12
Loan constraints	0.75000

Annual Inputs

	Year 1	Year 2	Year 3	Year 4	Year 5
NOI	$140,500	$144,013	$147,613	$151,303	$155,086

	Year 6	Year 7	Year 8	Year 9	Year 10
NOI	$158,963	$162,937	$167,010	$171,186	$175,465

The computer program uses an Ellwood formula to determine the proper dollar relationship between the specified market investor's equity return and the mortgage terms, given the NOI of the subject property. The cash-flow forecast that follows presents a summary of the market investor's equity payment, the annual before-tax cash flows and the reversion (after payment of selling cost and loan balances), which is discounted at the specified rate of 16 percent so that the value of the equity position equals the present value of the anticipated cash flows from the property if purchased at the value indicated. The value solution summary, which sets forth the implied value solution, mortgage and equity values and the implied overall rate, follows.

Value Solution Summary

Value	$1,458,058
Before-tax discount rate	0.16000
Overall rate	0.09636
Mortgage constant	0.10484
Mortgage value	$1,093,543
Equity value	$ 364,515

Annual Cash Flow Summary

	Year 1	Year 2	Year 3	Year 4	Year 5
NOI	$140,500	$144,013	$147,613	$151,303	$155,086
Debt service #1	− 114,651	− 114,651	− 114,651	−114,651	− 114,651
Cash flow (BT)	$ 25,849	$ 29,362	$ 32,962	$ 36,652	$ 40,435

	Year 6	Year 7	Year 8	Year 9	Year 10
NOI	$158,963	$162,937	$167,010	$171,186	$175,465
Debt service #1	− 114,651	− 114,651	− 114,651	− 114,651	− 114,651
Cash flow (BT)	$ 44,312	$ 48,286	$ 52,359	$ 56,535	$ 60,814

Reversion Cash Flow

Resale price	$1,798,519
Selling cost	− 89,926
Loan balance #1	− 914,962
Before-tax proceeds	$ 793,631

Equity Cash-Flow Summary

Year	Cash Flow	P.V. Factor	Present Value	Debt Coverage Ratio	Equity Dividend
0	−$364,515				
1	25,849	0.86207	$ 22,284	1.22546	0.07091
2	29,362	0.74316	21,821	1.25610	0.08055
3	32,962	0.64066	21,117	1.28750	0.09043
4	36,652	0.55229	20,243	1.31969	0.10055
5	40,435	0.47611	19,252	1.35268	0.11093
6	44,312	0.41044	18,188	1.38650	0.12156
7	48,286	0.35383	17,085	1.42116	0.13247
8	52,359	0.30503	15,971	1.45669	0.14364
9	56,535	0.26295	14,866	1.49310	0.15510
10	$854,445	0.22668	193,689	1.53043	0.16684
Total			$364,516		

The preceding analysis indicates an investor could purchase the property for up to $1,458,058, retire the debt on a $1,093,543 mortgage and earn a 16 percent before-tax yield rate on $364,516 in equity. The equity cash-flow summary indicates a modest but increasing equity dividend and a debt coverage ratio within generally acceptable levels and within the range specifically required by lenders I spoke with. When the equity dividend rates and debt coverage ratios implied in the analysis are within the range typical investors and lenders find acceptable, the value indication from the discounted cash-flow analysis appears reasonable, and these ratios lend additional support and credibility to the value indicated.

To confirm the reasonableness of the value estimate resulting from this analysis, I will next perform a second discounted cash-flow analysis assuming an unleveraged investment in the project.

Unleveraged Analysis. The following analysis incorporates all of the same assumptions included in the initial discounted cash-flow analysis with the exception that the mortgage financing was deleted and the required yield rate was changed to 12 percent from 16 percent to account for the lesser risk associated with an unleveraged investment. The summary of input assumptions below is followed by the value solution summary and the cash flows implied in the analysis.

Listed below are the input assumptions used in analyzing an unleveraged investment in the subject.

Summary of Input Assumptions

Basic Inputs

Property yield rate	0.12000	Net operating income	$140,500
Holding period	10	Change in NOI	0.24886
Resale value	$1,798,519	Income adjustment factor	G1
Selling cost	0.05000	Annual change	0.02500

Annual Inputs

	Year 1	Year 2	Year 3	Year 4	Year 5
NOI	$140,500	$144,013	$147,613	$151,303	$155,086

	Year 6	Year 7	Year 8	Year 9	Year 10
NOI	$158,963	$162,937	$167,010	$171,186	$175,465

Value Solution Summary

Value	$1,419,516
Property yield rate	0.12000
Overall capitalization rate	0.09898

Annual Cash-Flow Summary

	Year 1	Year 2	Year 3	Year 4	Year 5
NOI	$140,500	$144,013	$147,613	$151,303	$155,086
Cash flow (BT)	$140,500	$144,013	$147,613	$151,303	$155,086

	Year 6	Year 7	Year 8	Year 9	Year 10
NOI	$158,963	$162,937	$167,010	$171,186	$175,465
Cash flow (BT)	$158,963	$162,937	$167,010	$171,186	$175,465

Reversion Cash Flow

Resale price	$1,798,519
Selling cost	− 89,926
Before-tax proceeds	$1,708,593

Equity Cash-Flow Summary

Year	Cash Flow	P.V. Factor	Present Value
0	−$1,419,516		
1	140,500	0.89286	$ 125,446
2	144,013	0.79719	114,806
3	147,613	0.71178	105,068
4	151,303	0.63552	96,156
5	155,086	0.56743	88,000
6	158,963	0.50663	80,536
7	162,937	0.45235	73,704
8	167,010	0.40388	67,453
9	171,186	0.36061	61,731
10	1,884,058	0.32197	606,616
Total			$1,419,516

Yield Capitalization Approach Summary and Conclusions

On the preceding pages, the cash-flow summaries indicate the before-tax cash flow from operations, with and without debt service requirements, for each of the 10 years in the projected holding period. Proceeds from resale after payment of debt service in the leveraged analysis are also illustrated.

The equity cash-flow summaries, which follow the pro forma operating statements showing the before-tax cash flows, show the yearly cash flows to the equity position, including the equity necessary to acquire the property at the indicated value (in year 0) and the combination of operating income and reversion at the end of year 10.

The value indicated by direct capitalization is $1,411,026, and using the band-of-investment approach it is $1,462,019.

The leveraged and unleveraged before-tax yield capitalization analyses indicated a value from $1,458,058 to $1,419,516 for the value estimate as of January 1, 1992. Based on this analysis, I have chosen $1,450,000 as the best estimate of value for the subject property.

Income Approach Summary and Conclusions

The implied overall rate in the DCF analysis is consistent with the overall rates found in the sales in the sales comparison approach. The debt coverage ratio and equity dividend rates implied in the leveraged before-tax yield capitalization method are within limits generally acceptable to lenders and investors in multifamily investments, according to recent investor surveys and lenders and investors with whom I am familiar. When debt coverage ratios and equity dividend rates fall within typical ranges, the value solution implied in the leveraged discounted cash-flow analysis appears reasonable and enjoys additional credibility. Because most investors in the marketplace use discounted cash-flow analysis in their evaluation of investments in income-producing real estate and typical investors would employ some level of leverage in making their investment, I consider the value indication from the leveraged before-tax yield capitalization analysis to represent the most likely price that would be paid for the property.

Value Indication by the Income Approach
One million four hundred fifty thousand dollars
($1,450,000)

SALES COMPARISON APPROACH

The value by the sales comparison approach is estimated by comparing the subject property with sales of similar properties in the market area. The sales comparison approach is based on the principle that informed, prudent and rational buyers (investors) will pay no more for a property than the cost to them for acquiring a substitute property with the same utility.

In analyzing the property in the sales comparison approach, three approaches are usually used to develop a pattern of indicated value.

1. *Gross Income Multiplier*—This term is preferred to "Gross Rent Multiplier" because other income in addition to rentals may be generated by the property. Gross rentals are, of course, included as part of gross income. This is often a meaningful unit of comparison and is frequently used in conjunction with one or more other units of comparison to generate property value estimates for the subject property. Sales price divided by gross annual income equals gross income multiplier (GIM). A similar unit of comparison is the effective gross income multiplier (EGIM). Effective gross income (EGI) is the income received by the property after vacancy and collection loss. Sales price divided by EGI equals EGIM.

2. *Overall Rate*—Overall Rates (OARs) can be derived directly from evidence of recent sales transactions of similar, competitive properties sold under market conditions similar to those applicable to the property being appraised. All that is necessary is to obtain the verified sales price and NOI for each such comparable sale property. If the properties are truly similar and competitive, both with one another and the subject property, then the OAR for each can be derived simply by dividing NOI by sales price. Truly similar and competitive properties will produce a pattern of OARs that fall into a narrow range. The appropriate OAR for the subject property can then be selected form the range indicated by the sales. Provided good, reliable market data are available, this direct method of OAR estimating is both defensible and valid.

3. *Economic Unit of Comparison*—Economic Units of Comparison have also been called "Operating Units" or "Income Production Units." Income property is valued in terms of its capacity to generate income. The unit in terms of which income is generated is held to be more meaningful in some instances than mere physical units. Of course, in some cases, the physical unit (e.g., square feet of building area) is the more meaningful and appropriate unit of income production.

Different units may be used for different types of properties. Analysis in terms of economic units recognizes the fact that properties and structures of different sizes may be producing the same level of income and that the number of units of income production is the more meaningful consideration.

A requirement for the proper application of the sales comparison approach is that there must be an active market for properties that are similar to the property being appraised. Our search revealed several sales in Northwoods. The value by the sales comparison approach is estimated by comparing the subject property with sales of similar properties in the market area. Discussions with several buyers and sellers indicate that these are all common references in their decision-making process when purchasing or selling properties of this type. Several recent sales in the subject's market area have been selected as indicative of the subject property's value. The sales descriptions will be followed by an adjustment grid that compares the existing sales to the subject. The unit of comparison used is the price per square foot.

Improved Sale Number One:

Project/location:	Village Square Apartments
	407 Quail Lane
	Northwood, North Carolina
Grantor:	William M. Thomas, Jr., and wife, Jane
Grantee:	Tracy Real Estate Company
Deed book/page:	874/216
Date:	April 24, 1992
Price:	$384,000
Financing:	Conventional ($300,000 @ 9.5% for 25 years)
Number of units:	20
Year built:	1987
Net rentable area:	11,520 sq. ft.
Average unit size:	576 sq. ft.
Potential gross income:	$66,000
Vacancy:	− 3,760 (6%)
EGI:	$62,040
Expenses:	$25,600 ($1,280/Unit; $2.22/sq. ft.; 41.3% EGI)
NOI:	$36,440
Price per unit:	$19,200
Price per square foot:	$33.33
EGIM:	6.19
OAR:	0.095
R_E:	0.059

Description: All units are one bedroom with one bath. Laundry facilities are available, but no other amenities.

Unit Breakdown

Unit Type	No. of Units	Size	Mo. Rent	Rent/sq. ft.
1BR/1BA	20	576 sq. ft.	$275	$0.48

Improved Apartment Sale Two:

Project/location:	Pinetree Apartments
	Maple Avenue
	Northwoods, North Carolina
Grantor:	Steven D. Smith & Company
Grantee:	Thomas Hill
Date:	January 12, 1992
Deed book/page:	866/932
Price:	$1,350,000
Financing:	Conventional ($950,000 @ 9.75% for 25 Years)
Number of units:	60
Year built:	1976
Net rentable area:	50,360 sq. ft.
Average unit size:	839 sq. ft.
Potential gross income:	$242,160
Vacancy:	− 7,440 (3%)
EGI:	$234,720
Expenses:	$67,492 ($1,125/Unit; $1.38/ sq. ft.; 33% EGI)
NOI:	$136,508
Price per unit:	$22,500
Price per square foot:	$26.81
EGIM:	6.62
OAR:	0.1011
R_E:	0.087

Comments: Complex developed and built by grantee, sold to grantor and repurchased by grantee. Complex has a pool but no clubhouse.

Unit Breakdown

Unit Type	No. of Units	Size, sq. ft.	Mo. Rent	Rent/sq. ft.
1BR/1BA	4	615	$275	$0.45
1BR/1BA/DELUXE	20	615	310	$0.50
2BR/1BA	4	900	340	$0.38
2BR/1BA/DELUXE	32	1,000	360	$0.36

Improved Apartment Sale Three:

Project/location:	Quail Lakes 126 Main Street Northwoods, North Carolina
Grantor:	American Federal Savings & Loan Assoc.
Grantee:	The Swiss American Realty Group/Quail Lake Apts. Limited Partnership
Date:	June 30, 1992
Deed book/page:	875/321
Price:	$3,200,000
Financing:	See comments
Number of units:	114
Year built:	1985
Net rentable area:	82,650 sq. ft.
Average unit size:	725 sq. ft.
Potential gross income:	$581,400
Vacancy:	− 30,779 (5.3%)
EGI:	$550,621
Expenses:	$233,900 ($2,051/Unit; $2.83/ sq. ft.; 42.5% EGI)
NOI:	$316,721
Price per unit:	$28,070
Price per square foot:	$38.71
EGIM:	5.81
OAR:	0.099
R_E:	0.080

Comments: $900,000 cash; $2,300,000 adjustable rate mortgage to New West Federal Savings & Loan originated at 9.5% with a 25-year amortization period with a 10-year balloon. Two-story wood frame complex situated on a sloping site. On-site amenities include a clubhouse with exercise room, laundry facilities, swimming pool, hot tub and tennis courts.

Unit Breakdown

Unit Type	No. of Units	Size, sq. ft.	Mo. Rent	Rent/sq. ft.
1BR/1BA/GARDEN	38	547	$350	$0.68–$0.71
1BR/1BA/GARDEN	38	767	425	0.57–0.59
2BR/2BA/GARDEN	38	861	500	0.59–0.60

Improved Sales Summary and Adjustment Grid (Price/sq. ft.)

Sale	1	2	3
Date	4/24/92	1/12/92	6/30/92
Price/unit	$19,200	$22,500	$28,070
Price/sq. ft.	$33.33	$26.81	$38.71
Time adj.	-0-	-0-	-0-
Net price/sq. ft.	$33.33	$26.81	$38.71
Location	-0-	+10%	-0-

Sale	1	2	3
Quality	+5%	-0-	-0-
Age/cond.	-0-	+15%	-0-
Amenities	-0-	-5%	−10%
Design/appeal	-0-	-0-	-0-
Net adjustment	+5%	+20%	−10%
Ind. price/sq. ft.	$35.00	$32.17	$34.84

Comments on the Adjustments

The improved sales adjustment grid on the previous pages presented the adjustments required to make the comparables more similar to the subject property. Because the comparable sales consisted of different types of units, we chose the value per square foot as the best indicator of value for the subject property. The reasoning behind the required adjustments is set forth below.

Time Adjustment.   All three sales are recent sales so no adjustment for time was necessary.

Location Adjustment.   Sale one is located in close proximity to the subject property and no adjustment is deemed necessary. Sale two is located within Northwoods but is judged inferior, owing to being situated on the outskirts of the city with a greater distance to the major traffic routes. Sale three is located in the westernmost section of Northwood with inferior access to U.S. Highway 421 relative to the subject. However, because this location is in close proximity to high-quality residential areas, no overall adjustment was required.

Quality Adjustment.   Sale one was judged inferior in quality to the subject owing to the lack of a central HVAC system and adjusted downward. Sales one, two and three were judged similar overall in construction quality to the subject property, and no adjustment was required.

Age/Condition Adjustment.   Sale two is of significantly older construction and inferior in condition relative to the subject property. While sales one and three are newer than the subject, our visual inspection of the properties did not appear to warrant any adjustment for this age differential.

Amenities Adjustment.   All of the comparables except sale one enjoyed a swimming pool, tennis court and/or laundry facility, which required a downward adjustment.

Conclusion.   After adjustments, the indicated range of value per square foot is between $32.17 and $35.00, with an average indicated sales price of $34 per square foot. I find sale one to give the best indication of the comparable sales given because of its similarity in location and the few required adjustments, which are reasonable. Based on these data, a value estimate of $35 per square foot appears to represent a supportable estimate of the value of the subject property. Thus, the value estimate of the subject property can be calculated as follows:

$$41,600 \text{ sq. ft. @ } \$35.00/\text{sq. ft.} = \$1,456,000$$
$$\text{Rounded to} \quad \$1,450,000$$

To support the value estimate, the overall capitalization and GIM rates are examined. We have selected a rate from within the ranges indicated by the comparables based on the expense ratios and overall similarity of each comparable to the subject property. Sale three has a higher expense level than the subject property, whereas sale two has a lower expense level. The chart below summarizes the OAR and GIM for the sale comparables, and this analysis indicates that an OAR on the order of 9.75 percent and an EGIM of 6.25 appear reasonable for the subject.

Sale	OAR	EGIM
1	9.5%	6.19
2	10.1	6.62
3	9.9	5.81

NOI	OAR	Value
$140,500	9.75%	$1,441,026

EGI	EGIM	Value
$232,324	6.25	$1,452,025

The value indication by the square-foot method falls very close to this range, and these value estimates provide further support for each other. Based on this analysis, I will give the greatest weight to the square-foot method, and the value indication for the sales comparison approach is therefore $1,450,000, rounded.

Value Indication by the Sales Comparison Approach
One million four hundred fifty thousand dollars
($1,450,000)

RECONCILIATION AND FINAL VALUE ESTIMATE

Summary of Values

Land value	$ 135,000
Cost approach	1,450,000
Income approach	1,450,000
Sales comparison approach	1,450,000

Before arriving at a final value conclusion, I reviewed the data and conclusions set forth in each of the three approaches. In reviewing the report, I have considered both the quantity and quality of the data available to apply each approach to determine the relative strength and defensibility of the conclusions derived therefrom. In arriving at my final value estimate, I have considered the probable accuracy of these conclusions and the inherent strengths and weaknesses of the various approaches themselves, particularly with respect to their application to the subject property. In the following reconciliation and final value estimate, I will explain why I have chosen the value indication from the income approach as the most reliable estimate of value from the value indications from the three approaches.

In reviewing the cost approach, I find that the land value estimate is well supported by multifamily land sales located within this community. Even before adjustments, the land sales gave a relatively narrow indication of the per-unit value of the subject, and I therefore developed substantial confidence in the land value estimate.

The estimate of the reproduction cost new for the improvements was taken from a national cost service that allows for adjustments for local and current costs and has proven to result in reliable estimates of what buildings can be constructed for across the country. The weaknesses of the cost approach are that apartment buildings are not normally purchased based solely on their cost. The depreciation estimate was supported by actual case studies, published by the Marshall Swift Valuation Service, and the extent of the required adjustment was substantial. The cost approach did, however, serve as a useful benchmark in confirming the reasonableness of the value indications from the other approaches.

In reviewing the income approach, I find that the estimate of market rents is well supported by comparable rentals in the immediate market area of the subject. Estimates of the likely vacancy and collection loss are similarly well supported not only by the experience data from the comparable rentals but also by a recent survey of the multifamily housing market. Expense data were also available from the historical operation of the subject and of the comparables as well. A reconstruction of the operating statement for the subject resulted in a ratio of expenses to EGI that was comparable to the range indicated by the comparables. Based on all of this information, the estimate of NOI that would be derived from an investment in the subject appears well supported.

I found support for financing assumptions and equity return requirements by referring to recent investor surveys and interviewing investors and lenders to determine their current requirements for investment in multifamily projects such as the subject. Based on these market-supported inputs, a computer-assisted discounted cash-flow analysis resulted in debt coverage ratios and equity dividends that appear reasonable and are within the ranges indicated by discussions with lenders and investors. The availability of NOI information on comparable sales in the sales comparison approach made comparison of the OAR and EGIMs implied in the discounted cash-flow analysis with market implied rates possible. I find the value indication by the income approach is reasonable and supported by the value indications from the OAR analysis in the sales comparison approach.

In the sales comparison approach I analyzed sales involving multifamily projects in the market area. Of these transactions, all of the sales were similar in many aspects. All of these sales gave reasonably good indications of the value of the subject, and after relatively minor adjustments for location, condition and amenities, the sales did give a very consistent indication of the per-unit value of the subject. A further analysis indicates a similarly narrow range of OARs, which were implied by the sales.

Based on my judgment that the most likely purchaser of the subject would be an investor requiring a financial return on his or her investment, and based on both the sufficiency and consistency of the data available to arrive at the value indication from the income approach, I have placed the greatest weight on the income approach when arriving at my final value estimate. The value estimate by this approach is well supported by the other approaches. In light of all of these considerations, it is my opinion that the best estimate of the value of the fee simple interest in the subject is

Final Value Indication
One million four hundred fifty thousand dollars
($1,450,000)

ADDENDA* (not included)

---

*For illustration of typical addenda. Purposely omitted from this case study.

QUESTIONS FOR CASE STUDY:
APPRAISAL OF BAY HILL APARTMENTS

1. How was the value of the land estimated in the cost approach?
2. What adjustments were made to the base cost to derive an adjusted base cost per square foot when estimating the improvements value in the cost approach?
3. In addition to land and building costs, what other factors were considered when estimating the total value by the cost approach?
4. What type of rent was used to estimate value in the income approach and how was it derived?
5. What expense did not appear on the owner's operating statement but was used in the appraisal when estimating value through the income approach and how was it estimated?
6. How was the overall capitalization rate chosen in the income approach?
7. How did the appraiser adjust for differences in financing when choosing and using a yield rate in the income approach?
8. What units of comparison were used to analyze comparable sales in the sales comparison approach?
9. What weaknesses in the cost approach were identified by the appraiser?

Annual Compound Interest Tables

ANNUAL COMPOUND INTEREST TABLES

6.00% ANNUAL INTEREST RATE

YEARS	1 FUTURE VALUE OF $1	2 FUTURE VALUE ANNUITY OF $1 PER YEAR	3 SINKING FUND FACTOR	4 PRESENT VALUE OF $1 (REVERSION)	5 PRESENT VALUE ANNUITY OF $1 PER YEAR	6 PAYMENT TO AMORTIZE $1	YEARS
1	1.060000	1.000000	1.000000	0.943396	0.943396	1.060000	1
2	1.123600	2.060000	0.485437	0.889996	1.833393	0.545437	2
3	1.191016	3.183600	0.314110	0.839619	2.673012	0.374110	3
4	1.262477	4.374616	0.228591	0.792094	3.465106	0.288591	4
5	1.338226	5.637093	0.177396	0.747258	4.212364	0.237396	5
6	1.418519	6.975319	0.143363	0.704961	4.917324	0.203363	6
7	1.503630	8.393838	0.119135	0.665057	5.582381	0.179135	7
8	1.593848	9.897468	0.101036	0.627412	6.209794	0.161036	8
9	1.689479	11.491316	0.087022	0.591898	6.801692	0.147022	9
10	1.790848	13.180795	0.075868	0.558395	7.360087	0.135868	10
11	1.898299	14.971643	0.066793	0.526788	7.886875	0.126793	11
12	2.012196	16.869941	0.059277	0.496969	8.383844	0.119277	12
13	2.132928	18.882138	0.052960	0.468839	8.852683	0.112960	13
14	2.260904	21.015066	0.047585	0.442301	9.294984	0.107585	14
15	2.396558	23.275970	0.042963	0.417265	9.712249	0.102963	15
16	2.540352	25.672528	0.038952	0.393646	10.105895	0.098952	16
17	2.692773	28.212880	0.035445	0.371364	10.477260	0.095445	17
18	2.854339	30.905653	0.032357	0.350344	10.827603	0.092357	18
19	3.025600	33.759992	0.029621	0.330513	11.158116	0.089621	19
20	3.207135	36.785591	0.027185	0.311805	11.469921	0.087185	20

n							n
21	0.085005	11.764077	0.294155	0.025005	39.992727	3.399564	21
22	0.083046	12.041582	0.277505	0.023046	43.392290	3.603537	22
23	0.081278	12.303379	0.261797	0.021278	46.995828	3.819750	23
24	0.079679	12.550358	0.246979	0.019679	50.815577	4.048935	24
25	0.078227	12.783356	0.232999	0.018227	54.864512	4.291871	25
26	0.076904	13.003166	0.219810	0.016904	59.156383	4.549383	26
27	0.075697	13.210534	0.207368	0.015697	63.705766	4.822346	27
28	0.074593	13.406164	0.195630	0.014593	68.528112	5.111687	28
29	0.073580	13.590721	0.184557	0.013580	73.639798	5.418388	29
30	0.072649	13.764831	0.174110	0.012649	79.058186	5.743491	30
31	0.071792	13.929086	0.164255	0.011792	84.801677	6.088101	31
32	0.071002	14.084043	0.154957	0.011002	90.889778	6.453387	32
33	0.070273	14.230230	0.146186	0.010273	97.343165	6.840590	33
34	0.069598	14.368141	0.137912	0.009598	104.183755	7.251025	34
35	0.068974	14.498246	0.130105	0.008974	111.434780	7.686087	35
36	0.068395	14.620987	0.122741	0.008395	119.120867	8.147252	36
37	0.067857	14.736780	0.115793	0.007857	127.268119	8.636087	37
38	0.067358	14.846019	0.109239	0.007358	135.904206	9.154252	38
39	0.066894	14.949075	0.103056	0.006894	145.058458	9.703507	39
40	0.066462	15.046297	0.097222	0.006462	154.761966	10.285718	40
41	0.066059	15.138016	0.091719	0.006059	165.047684	10.902861	41
42	0.065683	15.224543	0.086527	0.005683	175.950545	11.557033	42
43	0.065333	15.306173	0.081630	0.005333	187.507577	12.250455	43
44	0.065006	15.383182	0.077009	0.005006	199.758032	12.985482	44
45	0.064700	15.455832	0.072650	0.004700	212.743514	13.764611	45
46	0.064415	15.524370	0.068538	0.004415	226.508125	14.590487	46
47	0.064148	15.589028	0.064658	0.004148	241.098612	15.465917	47
48	0.063898	15.650027	0.060998	0.003898	256.564529	16.393872	48
49	0.063664	15.707572	0.057546	0.003664	272.958401	17.377504	49
50	0.063444	15.761861	0.054288	0.003444	290.335905	18.420154	50

ANNUAL COMPOUND INTEREST TABLES

8.00% ANNUAL INTEREST RATE

YEARS	1 FUTURE VALUE OF $1	2 FUTURE VALUE ANNUITY OF $1 PER YEAR	3 SINKING FUND FACTOR	4 PRESENT VALUE OF $1 (REVERSION)	5 PRESENT VALUE ANNUITY OF $1 PER YEAR	6 PAYMENT TO AMORTIZE $1	YEARS
1	1.080000	1.000000	1.000000	0.925926	0.925926	1.080000	1
2	1.166400	2.080000	0.480769	0.857339	1.783265	0.560769	2
3	1.259712	3.246400	0.308034	0.793832	2.577097	0.388034	3
4	1.360489	4.506112	0.221921	0.735030	3.312127	0.301921	4
5	1.469328	5.866601	0.170456	0.680583	3.992710	0.250456	5
6	1.586874	7.335929	0.136315	0.630170	4.622880	0.216315	6
7	1.713824	8.922803	0.112072	0.583490	5.206370	0.192072	7
8	1.850930	10.636628	0.094015	0.540269	5.746639	0.174015	8
9	1.999005	12.487558	0.080080	0.500249	6.246888	0.160080	9
10	2.158925	14.486562	0.069029	0.463193	6.710081	0.149029	10
11	2.331639	16.645487	0.060076	0.428883	7.138964	0.140076	11
12	2.518170	18.977126	0.052695	0.397114	7.536078	0.132695	12
13	2.719624	21.495297	0.046522	0.367698	7.903776	0.126522	13
14	2.937194	24.214920	0.041297	0.340461	8.244237	0.121297	14
15	3.172169	27.152114	0.036830	0.315242	8.559479	0.116830	15
16	3.425943	30.324283	0.032977	0.291890	8.851369	0.112977	16
17	3.700018	33.750226	0.029629	0.270269	9.121638	0.109629	17
18	3.996019	37.450244	0.026702	0.250249	9.371887	0.106702	18
19	4.315701	41.446263	0.024128	0.231712	9.603599	0.104128	19
20	4.660957	45.761964	0.021852	0.214548	9.818147	0.101852	20

n							n
21	0.099832	10.016803	0.198656	0.019832	50.422921	5.033834	21
22	0.098032	10.200744	0.183941	0.018032	55.456755	5.436540	22
23	0.096422	10.371059	0.170315	0.016422	60.893296	5.871464	23
24	0.094978	10.528758	0.157699	0.014978	66.764759	6.341181	24
25	0.093679	10.674776	0.146018	0.013679	73.105940	6.848475	25
26	0.092507	10.809978	0.135202	0.012507	79.954415	7.396353	26
27	0.091448	10.935165	0.125187	0.011448	87.350768	7.988061	27
28	0.090489	11.051078	0.115914	0.010489	95.338830	8.627106	28
29	0.089619	11.158406	0.107328	0.009619	103.965936	9.317275	29
30	0.088827	11.257783	0.099377	0.008827	113.283211	10.062657	30
31	0.088107	11.349799	0.092016	0.008107	123.345868	10.867669	31
32	0.087451	11.434999	0.085200	0.007451	134.213537	11.737083	32
33	0.086852	11.513888	0.078889	0.006852	145.950620	12.676050	33
34	0.086304	11.586934	0.073045	0.006304	158.626670	13.690134	34
35	0.085803	11.654568	0.067635	0.005803	172.316804	14.785344	35
36	0.085345	11.717193	0.062625	0.005345	187.102148	15.968172	36
37	0.084924	11.775179	0.057986	0.004924	203.070320	17.245626	37
38	0.084539	11.828869	0.053690	0.004539	220.315945	18.625276	38
39	0.084185	11.878582	0.049713	0.004185	238.941221	20.115298	39
40	0.083860	11.924613	0.046031	0.003860	259.056519	21.724521	40
41	0.083561	11.967235	0.042621	0.003561	280.781040	23.462483	41
42	0.083287	12.006699	0.039464	0.003287	304.243523	25.339482	42
43	0.083034	12.043240	0.036541	0.003034	329.583005	27.366640	43
44	0.082802	12.077074	0.033834	0.002802	356.949646	29.555972	44
45	0.082587	12.108402	0.031328	0.002587	386.505617	31.920449	45
46	0.082390	12.137409	0.029007	0.002390	418.426067	34.474085	46
47	0.082208	12.164267	0.026859	0.002208	452.900152	37.232012	47
48	0.082040	12.189136	0.024869	0.002040	490.132164	40.210573	48
49	0.081886	12.212163	0.023027	0.001886	530.342737	43.427419	49
50	0.081743	12.233485	0.021321	0.001743	573.770156	46.901613	50

ANNUAL COMPOUND INTEREST TABLES

9.00% ANNUAL INTEREST RATE

YEARS	1 FUTURE VALUE OF $1	2 FUTURE VALUE ANNUITY OF $1 PER YEAR	3 SINKING FUND FACTOR	4 PRESENT VALUE OF $1 (REVERSION)	5 PRESENT VALUE ANNUITY OF $1 PER YEAR	6 PAYMENT TO AMORTIZE $1	YEARS
1	1.090000	1.000000	1.000000	0.917431	0.917431	1.090000	1
2	1.188100	2.090000	0.478469	0.841680	1.759111	0.568469	2
3	1.295029	3.278100	0.305055	0.772183	2.531295	0.395055	3
4	1.411582	4.573129	0.218669	0.708425	3.239720	0.308669	4
5	1.538624	5.984711	0.167092	0.649931	3.889651	0.257092	5
6	1.677100	7.523335	0.132920	0.596267	4.485919	0.222920	6
7	1.828039	9.200435	0.108691	0.547034	5.032953	0.198691	7
8	1.992563	11.028474	0.090674	0.501866	5.534819	0.180674	8
9	2.171893	13.021036	0.076799	0.460428	5.995247	0.166799	9
10	2.367364	15.192930	0.065820	0.422411	6.417658	0.155820	10
11	2.580426	17.560293	0.056947	0.387533	6.805191	0.146947	11
12	2.812665	20.140720	0.049651	0.355535	7.160725	0.139651	12
13	3.065805	22.953385	0.043567	0.326179	7.486904	0.133567	13
14	3.341727	26.019189	0.038433	0.299246	7.786150	0.128433	14
15	3.642482	29.360916	0.034059	0.274538	8.060688	0.124059	15
16	3.970306	33.003399	0.030300	0.251870	8.312558	0.120300	16
17	4.327633	36.973705	0.027046	0.231073	8.543631	0.117046	17
18	4.717120	41.301338	0.024212	0.211994	8.755625	0.114212	18
19	5.141661	46.018458	0.021730	0.194490	8.950115	0.111730	19
20	5.604411	51.160120	0.019546	0.178431	9.128546	0.109546	20

n							n
21	0.107617	9.292244	0.163698	0.017617	56.764530	6.108808	21
22	0.105905	9.442425	0.150182	0.015905	62.873338	6.658600	22
23	0.104382	9.580207	0.137781	0.014382	69.531939	7.257874	23
24	0.103023	9.706612	0.126405	0.013023	76.789813	7.911083	24
25	0.101806	9.822580	0.115968	0.011806	84.700896	8.623081	25
26	0.100715	9.928972	0.106393	0.010715	93.323977	9.399158	26
27	0.099735	10.026580	0.097608	0.009735	102.723135	10.245082	27
28	0.098852	10.116128	0.089548	0.008852	112.968217	11.167140	28
29	0.098056	10.198283	0.082155	0.008056	124.135356	12.172182	29
30	0.097336	10.273654	0.075371	0.007336	136.307539	13.267678	30
31	0.096686	10.342802	0.069148	0.006686	149.575217	14.461770	31
32	0.096096	10.406240	0.063438	0.006096	164.036987	15.763329	32
33	0.095562	10.464441	0.058200	0.005562	179.800315	17.182028	33
34	0.095077	10.517835	0.053395	0.005077	196.982344	18.728411	34
35	0.094636	10.566821	0.048986	0.004636	215.710755	20.413968	35
36	0.094235	10.611763	0.044941	0.004235	236.124723	22.251225	36
37	0.093870	10.652993	0.041231	0.003870	258.375948	24.253835	37
38	0.093538	10.690820	0.037826	0.003538	282.629783	26.436680	38
39	0.093236	10.725523	0.034703	0.003236	309.066463	28.815982	39
40	0.092960	10.757360	0.031838	0.002960	337.882445	31.409420	40
41	0.092708	10.786569	0.029209	0.002708	369.291865	34.236268	41
42	0.092478	10.813366	0.026797	0.002478	403.528133	37.317532	42
43	0.092268	10.837950	0.024584	0.002268	440.845665	40.676110	43
44	0.092077	10.860505	0.022555	0.002077	481.521775	44.336960	44
45	0.091902	10.881197	0.020692	0.001902	525.858734	48.327286	45
46	0.091742	10.900181	0.018984	0.001742	574.186021	52.676742	46
47	0.091595	10.917597	0.017416	0.001595	626.862762	57.417649	47
48	0.091461	10.933575	0.015978	0.001461	684.280411	62.585237	48
49	0.091339	10.948234	0.014659	0.001339	746.865648	68.217908	49
50	0.091227	10.961683	0.013449	0.001227	815.083556	74.357520	50

ANNUAL COMPOUND INTEREST TABLES

10.00% ANNUAL INTEREST RATE

YEARS	1 FUTURE VALUE OF $1	2 FUTURE VALUE ANNUITY OF $1 PER YEAR	3 SINKING FUND FACTOR	4 PRESENT VALUE OF $1 (REVERSION)	5 PRESENT VALUE ANNUITY OF $1 PER YEAR	6 PAYMENT TO AMORTIZE $1	YEARS
1	1.100000	1.000000	1.000000	0.909091	0.909091	1.100000	1
2	1.210000	2.100000	0.476190	0.826446	1.735537	0.576190	2
3	1.331000	3.310000	0.302115	0.751315	2.486852	0.402115	3
4	1.464100	4.641000	0.215471	0.683013	3.169865	0.315471	4
5	1.610510	6.105100	0.163797	0.620921	3.790787	0.263797	5
6	1.771561	7.715610	0.129607	0.564474	4.355261	0.229607	6
7	1.948717	9.487171	0.105405	0.513158	4.868419	0.205405	7
8	2.143589	11.435888	0.087444	0.466507	5.334926	0.187444	8
9	2.357948	13.579477	0.073641	0.424098	5.759024	0.173641	9
10	2.593742	15.937425	0.062745	0.385543	6.144567	0.162745	10
11	2.853117	18.531167	0.053963	0.350494	6.495061	0.153963	11
12	3.138428	21.384284	0.046763	0.318631	6.813692	0.146763	12
13	3.452271	24.522712	0.040779	0.289664	7.103356	0.140779	13
14	3.797498	27.974983	0.035746	0.263331	7.366687	0.135746	14
15	4.177248	31.772482	0.031474	0.239392	7.606080	0.131474	15
16	4.594973	35.949730	0.027817	0.217629	7.823709	0.127817	16
17	5.054470	40.544703	0.024664	0.197845	8.021553	0.124664	17
18	5.559917	45.599173	0.021930	0.179859	8.201412	0.121930	18
19	6.115909	51.159090	0.019547	0.163508	8.364920	0.119547	19
20	6.727500	57.274999	0.017460	0.148644	8.513564	0.117460	20

21	0.115624	8.648694	0.135131	0.015624	64.002499	7.400250
22	0.114005	8.771540	0.122846	0.014005	71.402749	8.140275
23	0.112572	8.883218	0.111678	0.012572	79.543024	8.954302
24	0.111300	8.984744	0.101526	0.011300	88.497327	9.849733
25	0.110168	9.077040	0.092296	0.010168	98.347059	10.834706
26	0.109159	9.160945	0.083905	0.009159	109.181765	11.918177
27	0.108258	9.237223	0.076278	0.008258	121.099942	13.109994
28	0.107451	9.306567	0.069343	0.007451	134.209936	14.420994
29	0.106728	9.369606	0.063039	0.006728	148.630930	15.863093
30	0.106079	9.426914	0.057309	0.006079	164.494023	17.449402
31	0.105496	9.479013	0.052099	0.005496	181.943425	19.194342
32	0.104972	9.526376	0.047362	0.004972	201.137767	21.113777
33	0.104499	9.569432	0.043057	0.004499	222.251544	23.225154
34	0.104074	9.608575	0.039143	0.004074	245.476699	25.547670
35	0.103690	9.644159	0.035584	0.003690	271.024368	28.102437
36	0.103343	9.676508	0.032349	0.003343	299.126805	30.912681
37	0.103030	9.705917	0.029408	0.003030	330.039486	34.003949
38	0.102747	9.732651	0.026735	0.002747	364.043434	37.404343
39	0.102491	9.756956	0.024304	0.002491	401.447778	41.144778
40	0.102259	9.779051	0.022095	0.002259	442.592556	45.259256
41	0.102050	9.799137	0.020086	0.002050	487.851811	49.785181
42	0.101860	9.817397	0.018260	0.001860	537.636992	54.763699
43	0.101688	9.833998	0.016600	0.001688	592.400692	60.240069
44	0.101532	9.849089	0.015091	0.001532	652.640761	66.264076
45	0.101391	9.862808	0.013719	0.001391	718.904837	72.890484
46	0.101263	9.875280	0.012472	0.001263	791.795321	80.179532
47	0.101147	9.886618	0.011338	0.001147	871.974853	88.197485
48	0.101041	9.896926	0.010307	0.001041	960.172338	97.017234
49	0.100946	9.906296	0.009370	0.000946	1057.189572	106.718957
50	0.100859	9.914814	0.008519	0.000859	1163.908529	117.390853

ANNUAL COMPOUND INTEREST TABLES

11.00% ANNUAL INTEREST RATE

YEARS	1 FUTURE VALUE OF $1	2 FUTURE VALUE ANNUITY OF $1 PER YEAR	3 SINKING FUND FACTOR	4 PRESENT VALUE OF $1 (REVERSION)	5 PRESENT VALUE ANNUITY OF $1 PER YEAR	6 PAYMENT TO AMORTIZE $1	YEARS
1	1.110000	1.000000	1.000000	0.900901	0.900901	1.110000	1
2	1.232100	2.110000	0.473934	0.811622	1.712523	0.583934	2
3	1.367631	3.342100	0.299213	0.731191	2.443715	0.409213	3
4	1.518070	4.709731	0.212326	0.658731	3.102446	0.322326	4
5	1.685058	6.227801	0.160570	0.593451	3.695897	0.270570	5
6	1.870415	7.912860	0.126377	0.534641	4.230538	0.236377	6
7	2.076160	9.783274	0.102215	0.481658	4.712196	0.212215	7
8	2.304538	11.859434	0.084321	0.433926	5.146123	0.194321	8
9	2.558037	14.163972	0.070602	0.390925	5.537048	0.180602	9
10	2.839421	16.722009	0.059801	0.352184	5.889232	0.169801	10
11	3.151757	19.561430	0.051121	0.317283	6.206515	0.161121	11
12	3.498451	22.713187	0.044027	0.285841	6.492356	0.154027	12
13	3.883280	26.211638	0.038151	0.257514	6.749870	0.148151	13
14	4.310441	30.094918	0.033228	0.231995	6.981865	0.143228	14
15	4.784589	34.405359	0.029065	0.209004	7.190870	0.139065	15
16	5.310894	39.189948	0.025517	0.188292	7.379162	0.135517	16
17	5.895093	44.500843	0.022471	0.169633	7.548794	0.132471	17
18	6.543553	50.395936	0.019843	0.152822	7.701617	0.129843	18
19	7.263344	56.939488	0.017563	0.137678	7.839294	0.127563	19
20	8.062312	64.202832	0.015576	0.124034	7.963328	0.125576	20

n							n
21	0.123838	8.075070	0.111742	0.013838	72.265144	8.949166	21
22	0.122313	8.175739	0.100669	0.012313	81.214309	9.933574	22
23	0.120971	8.266432	0.090693	0.010971	91.147884	11.026267	23
24	0.119787	8.348137	0.081705	0.009787	102.174151	12.239157	24
25	0.118740	8.421745	0.073608	0.008740	114.413307	13.585464	25
26	0.117813	8.488058	0.066314	0.007813	127.998771	15.079865	26
27	0.116989	8.547800	0.059742	0.006989	143.078636	16.738650	27
28	0.116257	8.601622	0.053822	0.006257	159.817286	18.579901	28
29	0.115605	8.650110	0.048488	0.005605	178.397187	20.623691	29
30	0.115025	8.693793	0.043683	0.005025	199.020878	22.892297	30
31	0.114506	8.733146	0.039354	0.004506	221.913174	25.410449	31
32	0.114043	8.768600	0.035454	0.004043	247.323624	28.205599	32
33	0.113629	8.800541	0.031940	0.003629	275.529222	31.308214	33
34	0.113259	8.829316	0.028775	0.003259	306.837437	34.752118	34
35	0.112927	8.855240	0.025924	0.002927	341.589555	38.574851	35
36	0.112630	8.878594	0.023355	0.002630	380.164406	42.818085	36
37	0.112364	8.899635	0.021040	0.002364	422.982490	47.528074	37
38	0.112125	8.918590	0.018955	0.002125	470.510564	52.756162	38
39	0.111911	8.935666	0.017077	0.001911	523.266726	58.559340	39
40	0.111719	8.951051	0.015384	0.001719	581.826066	65.000867	40
41	0.111546	8.964911	0.013860	0.001546	646.826934	72.150963	41
42	0.111391	8.977397	0.012486	0.001391	718.977896	80.087569	42
43	0.111251	8.988646	0.011249	0.001251	799.065465	88.897201	43
44	0.111126	8.998780	0.010134	0.001126	887.962666	98.675893	44
45	0.111014	9.007910	0.009130	0.001014	986.638559	109.530242	45
46	0.110912	9.016135	0.008225	0.000912	1096.168801	121.578568	46
47	0.110821	9.023545	0.007410	0.000821	1217.747369	134.952211	47
48	0.110739	9.030221	0.006676	0.000739	1352.699580	149.796954	48
49	0.110666	9.036235	0.006014	0.000666	1502.496533	166.274619	49
50	0.110599	9.041653	0.005418	0.000599	1668.771152	184.564827	50

ANNUAL COMPOUND INTEREST TABLES

12.00% ANNUAL INTEREST RATE

YEARS	1 FUTURE VALUE OF $1	2 FUTURE VALUE ANNUITY OF $1 PER YEAR	3 SINKING FUND FACTOR	4 PRESENT VALUE OF $1 (REVERSION)	5 PRESENT VALUE ANNUITY OF $1 PER YEAR	6 PAYMENT TO AMORTIZE $1	YEARS
1	1.120000	1.000000	1.000000	0.892857	0.892857	1.120000	1
2	1.254400	2.120000	0.471698	0.797194	1.690051	0.591698	2
3	1.404928	3.374400	0.296349	0.711780	2.401831	0.416349	3
4	1.573519	4.779328	0.209234	0.635518	3.037349	0.329234	4
5	1.762342	6.352847	0.157410	0.567427	3.604776	0.277410	5
6	1.973823	8.115189	0.123226	0.506631	4.111407	0.243226	6
7	2.210681	10.089012	0.099118	0.452349	4.563757	0.219118	7
8	2.475963	12.299693	0.081303	0.403883	4.967640	0.201303	8
9	2.773079	14.775656	0.067679	0.360610	5.328250	0.187679	9
10	3.105848	17.548735	0.056984	0.321973	5.650223	0.176984	10
11	3.478550	20.654583	0.048415	0.287476	5.937699	0.168415	11
12	3.895976	24.133133	0.041437	0.256675	6.194374	0.161437	12
13	4.363493	28.029109	0.035677	0.229174	6.423548	0.155677	13
14	4.887112	32.392602	0.030871	0.204620	6.628168	0.150871	14
15	5.473566	37.279715	0.026824	0.182696	6.810864	0.146824	15
16	6.130394	42.753280	0.023390	0.163122	6.973986	0.143390	16
17	6.866041	48.883674	0.020457	0.145644	7.119630	0.140457	17
18	7.689966	55.749715	0.017937	0.130040	7.249670	0.137937	18
19	8.612762	63.439681	0.015763	0.116107	7.365777	0.135763	19
20	9.646293	72.052442	0.013879	0.103667	7.469444	0.133879	20

n							n
21	10.803848	81.698736	0.012240	0.092560	7.562003	0.132240	21
22	12.100310	92.502584	0.010811	0.082643	7.644646	0.130811	22
23	13.552347	104.602894	0.009560	0.073788	7.718434	0.129560	23
24	15.178629	118.155241	0.008463	0.065882	7.784316	0.128463	24
25	17.000064	133.333870	0.007500	0.058823	7.843139	0.127500	25
26	19.040072	150.333934	0.006652	0.052521	7.895660	0.126652	26
27	21.324881	169.374007	0.005904	0.046894	7.942554	0.125904	27
28	23.883866	190.698887	0.005244	0.041869	7.984423	0.125244	28
29	26.749930	214.582754	0.004660	0.037383	8.021806	0.124660	29
30	29.959922	241.332684	0.004144	0.033378	8.055184	0.124144	30
31	33.555113	271.292606	0.003686	0.029802	8.084986	0.123686	31
32	37.581726	304.847719	0.003280	0.026609	8.111594	0.123280	32
33	42.091533	342.429446	0.002920	0.023758	8.135352	0.122920	33
34	47.142517	384.520979	0.002601	0.021212	8.156564	0.122601	34
35	52.799620	431.663496	0.002317	0.018940	8.175504	0.122317	35
36	59.135574	484.463116	0.002064	0.016910	8.192414	0.122064	36
37	66.231843	543.598690	0.001840	0.015098	8.207513	0.121840	37
38	74.179664	609.830533	0.001640	0.013481	8.220993	0.121640	38
39	83.081224	684.010197	0.001462	0.012036	8.233030	0.121462	39
40	93.050970	767.091420	0.001304	0.010747	8.243777	0.121304	40
41	104.217087	860.142391	0.001163	0.009595	8.253372	0.121163	41
42	116.723137	964.359478	0.001037	0.008567	8.261939	0.121037	42
43	130.729914	1081.082615	0.000925	0.007649	8.269589	0.120925	43
44	146.417503	1211.812529	0.000825	0.006830	8.276418	0.120825	44
45	163.987604	1358.230032	0.000736	0.006098	8.282516	0.120736	45
46	183.666116	1522.217636	0.000657	0.005445	8.287961	0.120657	46
47	205.706050	1705.883752	0.000586	0.004861	8.292822	0.120586	47
48	230.390776	1911.589803	0.000523	0.004340	8.297163	0.120523	48
49	258.377669	2141.980579	0.000467	0.003875	8.301038	0.120467	49
50	289.002190	2400.018249	0.000417	0.003460	8.304498	0.120417	50

ANNUAL COMPOUND INTEREST TABLES

13.00% ANNUAL INTEREST RATE

YEARS	1 FUTURE VALUE OF $1	2 FUTURE VALUE ANNUITY OF $1 PER YEAR	3 SINKING FUND FACTOR	4 PRESENT VALUE OF $1 (REVERSION)	5 PRESENT VALUE ANNUITY OF $1 PER YEAR	6 PAYMENT TO AMORTIZE $1	YEARS
1	1.130000	1.000000	1.000000	0.884956	0.884956	1.130000	1
2	1.276900	2.130000	0.469484	0.783147	1.668102	0.599484	2
3	1.442897	3.406900	0.293522	0.693050	2.361153	0.423522	3
4	1.630474	4.849797	0.206194	0.613319	2.974471	0.336194	4
5	1.842435	6.480271	0.154315	0.542760	3.517231	0.284315	5
6	2.081952	8.322706	0.120153	0.480319	3.997550	0.250153	6
7	2.352605	10.404658	0.096111	0.425061	4.422610	0.226111	7
8	2.658444	12.757263	0.078387	0.376160	4.798770	0.208387	8
9	3.004042	15.415707	0.064869	0.332885	5.131655	0.194869	9
10	3.394567	18.419749	0.054290	0.294588	5.426243	0.184290	10
11	3.835861	21.814317	0.045841	0.260698	5.686941	0.175841	11
12	4.334523	25.650178	0.038986	0.230706	5.917647	0.168986	12
13	4.898011	29.984701	0.033350	0.204165	6.121812	0.163350	13
14	5.534753	34.882712	0.028667	0.180677	6.302488	0.158667	14
15	6.254270	40.417464	0.024742	0.159891	6.462379	0.154742	15
16	7.067326	46.671735	0.021426	0.141496	6.603875	0.151426	16
17	7.986078	53.739060	0.018608	0.125218	6.729093	0.148608	17
18	9.024268	61.725138	0.016201	0.110812	6.839905	0.146201	18
19	10.197423	70.749406	0.014134	0.098064	6.937969	0.144134	19
20	11.523088	80.946829	0.012354	0.086782	7.024752	0.142354	20

n							n
21	13.021089	0.010814	92.469917	0.076798	7.101550	0.140814	21
22	14.713831	0.009479	105.491006	0.067963	7.169513	0.139479	22
23	16.626629	0.008319	120.204837	0.060144	7.229658	0.138319	23
24	18.788091	0.007308	136.831465	0.053225	7.282883	0.137308	24
25	21.230542	0.006426	155.619556	0.047102	7.329985	0.136426	25
26	23.990513	0.005655	176.850098	0.041683	7.371668	0.135655	26
27	27.109279	0.004979	200.840611	0.036888	7.408556	0.134979	27
28	30.633486	0.004387	227.949890	0.032644	7.441200	0.134387	28
29	34.615839	0.003867	258.583376	0.028889	7.470088	0.133867	29
30	39.115898	0.003411	293.199215	0.025565	7.495653	0.133411	30
31	44.200965	0.003009	332.315113	0.022624	7.518277	0.133009	31
32	49.947090	0.002656	376.516078	0.020021	7.538299	0.132656	32
33	56.440212	0.002345	426.463168	0.017718	7.556016	0.132345	33
34	63.777439	0.002071	482.903380	0.015680	7.571696	0.132071	34
35	72.068506	0.001829	546.680819	0.013876	7.585572	0.131829	35
36	81.437412	0.001616	618.749325	0.012279	7.597851	0.131616	36
37	92.024276	0.001428	700.186738	0.010867	7.608718	0.131428	37
38	103.987432	0.001262	792.211014	0.009617	7.618334	0.131262	38
39	117.505798	0.001116	896.198445	0.008510	7.626844	0.131116	39
40	132.781552	0.000986	1013.704243	0.007531	7.634376	0.130986	40
41	150.043153	0.000872	1146.485795	0.006665	7.641040	0.130872	41
42	169.548763	0.000771	1296.528948	0.005898	7.646938	0.130771	42
43	191.590103	0.000682	1466.077712	0.005219	7.652158	0.130682	43
44	216.496816	0.000603	1657.667814	0.004619	7.656777	0.130603	44
45	244.641402	0.000534	1874.164630	0.004088	7.660864	0.130534	45
46	276.444784	0.000472	2118.806032	0.003617	7.664482	0.130472	46
47	312.382606	0.000417	2395.250816	0.003201	7.667683	0.130417	47
48	352.992345	0.000369	2707.633422	0.002833	7.670516	0.130369	48
49	398.881350	0.000327	3060.625767	0.002507	7.673023	0.130327	49
50	450.735925	0.000289	3459.507117	0.002219	7.675242	0.130289	50

ANNUAL COMPOUND INTEREST TABLES

14.00% ANNUAL INTEREST RATE

YEARS	1 FUTURE VALUE OF $1	2 FUTURE VALUE ANNUITY OF $1 PER YEAR	3 SINKING FUND FACTOR	4 PRESENT VALUE OF $1 (REVERSION)	5 PRESENT VALUE ANNUITY OF $1 PER YEAR	6 PAYMENT TO AMORTIZE $1	YEARS
1	1.140000	1.000000	1.000000	0.877193	0.877193	1.140000	1
2	1.299600	2.140000	0.467290	0.769468	1.646661	0.607290	2
3	1.481544	3.439600	0.290731	0.674972	2.321632	0.430731	3
4	1.688960	4.921144	0.203205	0.592080	2.913712	0.343205	4
5	1.925415	6.610104	0.151284	0.519369	3.433081	0.291284	5
6	2.194973	8.535519	0.117157	0.455587	3.888668	0.257157	6
7	2.502269	10.730491	0.093192	0.399637	4.288305	0.233192	7
8	2.852586	13.232760	0.075570	0.350559	4.638864	0.215570	8
9	3.251949	16.085347	0.062168	0.307508	4.946372	0.202168	9
10	3.707221	19.337295	0.051714	0.269744	5.216116	0.191714	10
11	4.226232	23.044516	0.043394	0.236617	5.452733	0.183394	11
12	4.817905	27.270749	0.036669	0.207559	5.660292	0.176669	12
13	5.492411	32.088654	0.031164	0.182069	5.842362	0.171164	13
14	6.261349	37.581065	0.026609	0.159710	6.002072	0.166609	14
15	7.137938	43.842414	0.022809	0.140096	6.142168	0.162809	15
16	8.137249	50.980352	0.019615	0.122892	6.265060	0.159615	16
17	9.276464	59.117601	0.016915	0.107800	6.372859	0.156915	17
18	10.575169	68.394066	0.014621	0.094561	6.467420	0.154621	18
19	12.055693	78.969235	0.012663	0.082948	6.550369	0.152663	19
20	13.743490	91.024928	0.010986	0.072762	6.623131	0.150986	20

n							n
21	0.149545	6.686957	0.063826	0.009545	104.768418	15.667578	21
22	0.148303	6.742944	0.055988	0.008303	120.435996	17.861039	22
23	0.147231	6.792056	0.049112	0.007231	138.297035	20.361585	23
24	0.146303	6.835137	0.043081	0.006303	158.658620	23.212207	24
25	0.145498	6.872927	0.037790	0.005498	181.870827	26.461916	25
26	0.144800	6.906077	0.033149	0.004800	208.332743	30.166584	26
27	0.144193	6.935155	0.029078	0.004193	238.499327	34.389906	27
28	0.143664	6.960662	0.025507	0.003664	272.889233	39.204493	28
29	0.143204	6.983037	0.022375	0.003204	312.093725	44.693122	29
30	0.142803	7.002664	0.019627	0.002803	356.786847	50.950159	30
31	0.142453	7.019881	0.017217	0.002453	407.737006	58.083181	31
32	0.142147	7.034983	0.015102	0.002147	465.820186	66.214826	32
33	0.141880	7.048231	0.013248	0.001880	532.035012	75.484902	33
34	0.141646	7.059852	0.011621	0.001646	607.519914	86.052788	34
35	0.141442	7.070045	0.010194	0.001442	693.572702	98.100178	35
36	0.141263	7.078987	0.008942	0.001263	791.672881	111.834203	36
37	0.141107	7.086831	0.007844	0.001107	903.507084	127.490992	37
38	0.140970	7.093711	0.006880	0.000970	1030.998076	145.339731	38
39	0.140850	7.099747	0.006035	0.000850	1176.337806	165.687293	39
40	0.140745	7.105041	0.005294	0.000745	1342.025099	188.883514	40
41	0.140653	7.109685	0.004644	0.000653	1530.908613	215.327206	41
42	0.140573	7.113759	0.004074	0.000573	1746.235819	245.473015	42
43	0.140502	7.117332	0.003573	0.000502	1991.708833	279.859237	43
44	0.140440	7.120467	0.003135	0.000440	2271.548070	319.016730	44
45	0.140386	7.123217	0.002750	0.000386	2590.564800	363.679072	45
46	0.140338	7.125629	0.002412	0.000338	2954.243872	414.594142	46
47	0.140297	7.127744	0.002116	0.000297	3368.838014	472.637322	47
48	0.140260	7.129600	0.001856	0.000260	3841.475336	538.806547	48
49	0.140228	7.131228	0.001628	0.000228	4380.281883	614.239464	49
50	0.140200	7.132656	0.001428	0.000200	4994.521346	700.232988	50

ANNUAL COMPOUND INTEREST TABLES

15.00% ANNUAL INTEREST RATE

YEARS	1 FUTURE VALUE OF $1	2 FUTURE VALUE ANNUITY OF $1 PER YEAR	3 SINKING FUND FACTOR	4 PRESENT VALUE OF $1 (REVERSION)	5 PRESENT VALUE ANNUITY OF $1 PER YEAR	6 PAYMENT TO AMORTIZE $1	YEARS
1	1.150000	1.000000	1.000000	0.869565	0.869565	1.150000	1
2	1.322500	2.150000	0.465116	0.756144	1.625709	0.615116	2
3	1.520875	3.472500	0.287977	0.657516	2.283225	0.437977	3
4	1.749006	4.993375	0.200265	0.571753	2.854978	0.350265	4
5	2.011357	6.742381	0.148316	0.497177	3.352155	0.298316	5
6	2.313061	8.753738	0.114237	0.432328	3.784483	0.264237	6
7	2.660020	11.066799	0.090360	0.375937	4.160420	0.240360	7
8	3.059023	13.726819	0.072850	0.326902	4.487322	0.222850	8
9	3.517876	16.785842	0.059574	0.284262	4.771584	0.209574	9
10	4.045558	20.303718	0.049252	0.247185	5.018769	0.199252	10
11	4.652391	24.349276	0.041069	0.214943	5.233712	0.191069	11
12	5.350250	29.001667	0.034481	0.186907	5.420619	0.184481	12
13	6.152788	34.351917	0.029110	0.162528	5.583147	0.179110	13
14	7.075706	40.504705	0.024688	0.141329	5.724476	0.174688	14
15	8.137062	47.580411	0.021017	0.122894	5.847370	0.171017	15
16	9.357621	55.717472	0.017948	0.106865	5.954235	0.167948	16
17	10.761264	65.075093	0.015367	0.092926	6.047161	0.165367	17
18	12.375454	75.836357	0.013186	0.080805	6.127966	0.163186	18
19	14.231772	88.211811	0.011336	0.070265	6.198231	0.161336	19
20	16.366537	102.443583	0.009761	0.061100	6.259331	0.159761	20

n							n
21	18.821518	118.810120	0.008417	0.053131	6.312462	0.158417	21
22	21.644746	137.631638	0.007266	0.046201	6.358663	0.157266	22
23	24.891458	159.276384	0.006278	0.040174	6.398837	0.156278	23
24	28.625176	184.167841	0.005430	0.034934	6.433771	0.155430	24
25	32.918953	212.793017	0.004699	0.030378	6.464149	0.154699	25
26	37.856796	245.711970	0.004070	0.026415	6.490564	0.154070	26
27	43.535315	283.568766	0.003526	0.022970	6.513534	0.153526	27
28	50.065612	327.104080	0.003057	0.019974	6.533508	0.153057	28
29	57.575454	377.169693	0.002651	0.017369	6.550877	0.152651	29
30	66.211772	434.745146	0.002300	0.015103	6.565980	0.152300	30
31	76.143538	500.956918	0.001996	0.013133	6.579113	0.151996	31
32	87.565068	577.100456	0.001733	0.011420	6.590533	0.151733	32
33	100.699829	664.665524	0.001505	0.009931	6.600463	0.151505	33
34	115.804803	765.365353	0.001307	0.008635	6.609099	0.151307	34
35	133.175523	881.170156	0.001135	0.007509	6.616607	0.151135	35
36	153.151852	1014.345680	0.000986	0.006529	6.623137	0.150986	36
37	176.124540	1167.497532	0.000857	0.005678	6.628815	0.150857	37
38	202.543324	1343.622161	0.000744	0.004937	6.633752	0.150744	38
39	232.924823	1546.165485	0.000647	0.004293	6.638045	0.150647	39
40	267.863546	1779.090308	0.000562	0.003733	6.641778	0.150562	40
41	308.043078	2046.953854	0.000489	0.003246	6.645025	0.150489	41
42	354.249540	2354.996933	0.000425	0.002823	6.647848	0.150425	42
43	407.386971	2709.246473	0.000369	0.002455	6.650302	0.150369	43
44	468.495017	3116.633443	0.000321	0.002134	6.652437	0.150321	44
45	538.769269	3585.128460	0.000279	0.001856	6.654293	0.150279	45
46	619.584659	4123.897729	0.000242	0.001614	6.655907	0.150242	46
47	712.522358	4743.482388	0.000211	0.001403	6.657310	0.150211	47
48	819.400712	5456.004746	0.000183	0.001220	6.658531	0.150183	48
49	942.310819	6275.405458	0.000159	0.001061	6.659592	0.150159	49
50	1083.657442	7217.716277	0.000139	0.000923	6.660515	0.150139	50

ANNUAL COMPOUND INTEREST TABLES

16.00% ANNUAL INTEREST RATE

YEARS	1 FUTURE VALUE OF $1	2 FUTURE VALUE ANNUITY OF $1 PER YEAR	3 SINKING FUND FACTOR	4 PRESENT VALUE OF $1 (REVERSION)	5 PRESENT VALUE ANNUITY OF $1 PER YEAR	6 PAYMENT TO AMORTIZE $1	YEARS
1	1.160000	1.000000	1.000000	0.862069	0.862069	1.160000	1
2	1.345600	2.160000	0.462963	0.743163	1.605232	0.622963	2
3	1.560896	3.505600	0.285258	0.640658	2.245890	0.445258	3
4	1.810639	5.066496	0.197375	0.552291	2.798181	0.357375	4
5	2.100342	6.877135	0.145409	0.476113	3.274294	0.305409	5
6	2.436396	8.977477	0.111390	0.410442	3.684736	0.271390	6
7	2.826220	11.413873	0.087613	0.353830	4.038565	0.247613	7
8	3.278415	14.240093	0.070224	0.305025	4.343591	0.230224	8
9	3.802961	17.518508	0.057082	0.262953	4.606544	0.217082	9
10	4.411435	21.321469	0.046901	0.226684	4.833227	0.206901	10
11	5.117265	25.732904	0.038861	0.195417	5.028644	0.198861	11
12	5.936027	30.850169	0.032415	0.168463	5.197107	0.192415	12
13	6.885791	36.786196	0.027184	0.145227	5.342334	0.187184	13
14	7.987518	43.671987	0.022898	0.125195	5.467529	0.182898	14
15	9.265521	51.659505	0.019358	0.107927	5.575456	0.179358	15
16	10.748004	60.925026	0.016414	0.093041	5.668497	0.176414	16
17	12.467685	71.673030	0.013952	0.080207	5.748704	0.173952	17
18	14.462514	84.140715	0.011885	0.069144	5.817848	0.171885	18
19	16.776517	98.603230	0.010142	0.059607	5.877455	0.170142	19
20	19.460759	115.379747	0.008667	0.051385	5.928841	0.168667	20

Year							Year
21	0.167416	5.973139	0.044298	0.007416	134.840506	22.574481	21
22	0.166353	6.011326	0.038188	0.006353	157.414987	26.186398	22
23	0.165447	6.044247	0.032920	0.005447	183.601385	30.376222	23
24	0.164673	6.072627	0.028380	0.004673	213.977607	35.236417	24
25	0.164013	6.097092	0.024465	0.004013	249.214024	40.874244	25
26	0.163447	6.118183	0.021091	0.003447	290.088267	47.414123	26
27	0.162963	6.136364	0.018182	0.002963	337.502390	55.000382	27
28	0.162548	6.152038	0.015674	0.002548	392.502773	63.800444	28
29	0.162192	6.165550	0.013512	0.002192	456.303216	74.008515	29
30	0.161886	6.177198	0.011648	0.001886	530.311731	85.849877	30
31	0.161623	6.187240	0.010042	0.001623	616.161608	99.585857	31
32	0.161397	6.195897	0.008657	0.001397	715.747465	115.519594	32
33	0.161203	6.203359	0.007463	0.001203	831.267059	134.002729	33
34	0.161036	6.209792	0.006433	0.001036	965.269789	155.443166	34
35	0.160892	6.215338	0.005546	0.000892	1120.712955	180.314073	35
36	0.160769	6.220119	0.004781	0.000769	1301.027028	209.164324	36
37	0.160662	6.224241	0.004121	0.000662	1510.191352	242.630616	37
38	0.160571	6.227794	0.003553	0.000571	1752.821968	281.451515	38
39	0.160492	6.230857	0.003063	0.000492	2034.273483	326.483757	39
40	0.160424	6.233497	0.002640	0.000424	2360.757241	378.721158	40
41	0.160365	6.235773	0.002276	0.000365	2739.478399	439.316544	41
42	0.160315	6.237736	0.001962	0.000315	3178.794943	509.607191	42
43	0.160271	6.239427	0.001692	0.000271	3688.402134	591.144341	43
44	0.160234	6.240886	0.001458	0.000234	4279.546475	685.727436	44
45	0.160201	6.242143	0.001257	0.000201	4965.273911	795.443826	45
46	0.160174	6.243227	0.001084	0.000174	5760.717737	922.714838	46
47	0.160150	6.244161	0.000934	0.000150	6683.432575	1070.349212	47
48	0.160129	6.244966	0.000805	0.000129	7753.781787	1241.605086	48
49	0.160111	6.245661	0.000694	0.000111	8995.386873	1440.261900	49
50	0.160096	6.246259	0.000599	0.000096	10435.648773	1670.703804	50

ANNUAL COMPOUND INTEREST TABLES

17.00% ANNUAL INTEREST RATE

YEARS	1 FUTURE VALUE OF $1	2 FUTURE VALUE ANNUITY OF $1 PER YEAR	3 SINKING FUND FACTOR	4 PRESENT VALUE OF $1 (REVERSION)	5 PRESENT VALUE ANNUITY OF $1 PER YEAR	6 PAYMENT TO AMORTIZE $1	YEARS
1	1.170000	1.000000	1.000000	0.854701	0.854701	1.170000	1
2	1.368900	2.170000	0.460829	0.730514	1.585214	0.630829	2
3	1.601613	3.538900	0.282574	0.624371	2.209585	0.452574	3
4	1.873887	5.140513	0.194533	0.533650	2.743235	0.364533	4
5	2.192448	7.014400	0.142564	0.456111	3.199346	0.312564	5
6	2.565164	9.206848	0.108615	0.389839	3.589185	0.278615	6
7	3.001242	11.772012	0.084947	0.333195	3.922380	0.254947	7
8	3.511453	14.773255	0.067690	0.284782	4.207163	0.237690	8
9	4.108400	18.284708	0.054691	0.243404	4.450566	0.224691	9
10	4.806828	22.393108	0.044657	0.208037	4.658604	0.214657	10
11	5.623989	27.199937	0.036765	0.177810	4.836413	0.206765	11
12	6.580067	32.823926	0.030466	0.151974	4.988387	0.200466	12
13	7.698679	39.403993	0.025378	0.129892	5.118280	0.195378	13
14	9.007454	47.102672	0.021230	0.111019	5.229299	0.191230	14
15	10.538721	56.110126	0.017822	0.094888	5.324187	0.187822	15
16	12.330304	66.648848	0.015004	0.081101	5.405288	0.185004	16
17	14.426456	78.979152	0.012662	0.069317	5.474605	0.182662	17
18	16.878953	93.405608	0.010706	0.059245	5.533851	0.180706	18
19	19.748375	110.284561	0.009067	0.050637	5.584488	0.179067	19
20	23.105599	130.032936	0.007690	0.043280	5.627767	0.177690	20

n							n
21	0.176530	5.664758	0.036991	0.006530	153.138535	27.033551	21
22	0.175550	5.696375	0.031616	0.005550	180.172086	31.629255	22
23	0.174721	5.723397	0.027022	0.004721	211.801341	37.006228	23
24	0.174019	5.746493	0.023096	0.004019	248.807569	43.297287	24
25	0.173423	5.766234	0.019740	0.003423	292.104856	50.657826	25
26	0.172917	5.783106	0.016872	0.002917	342.762681	59.269656	26
27	0.172487	5.797526	0.014421	0.002487	402.032337	69.345497	27
28	0.172121	5.809851	0.012325	0.002121	471.377835	81.134232	28
29	0.171810	5.820386	0.010534	0.001810	552.512066	94.927051	29
30	0.171545	5.829390	0.009004	0.001545	647.439118	111.064650	30
31	0.171318	5.837085	0.007696	0.001318	758.503768	129.945641	31
32	0.171126	5.843663	0.006577	0.001126	888.449408	152.036399	32
33	0.170961	5.849284	0.005622	0.000961	1040.485808	177.882587	33
34	0.170821	5.854089	0.004805	0.000821	1218.368395	208.122627	34
35	0.170701	5.858196	0.004107	0.000701	1426.491022	243.503474	35
36	0.170599	5.861706	0.003510	0.000599	1669.994496	284.899064	36
37	0.170512	5.864706	0.003000	0.000512	1954.893560	333.331905	37
38	0.170437	5.867270	0.002564	0.000437	2288.225465	389.998329	38
39	0.170373	5.869461	0.002192	0.000373	2678.223794	456.298045	39
40	0.170319	5.871335	0.001873	0.000319	3134.521839	533.868713	40
41	0.170273	5.872936	0.001601	0.000273	3668.390552	624.626394	41
42	0.170233	5.874304	0.001368	0.000233	4293.016946	730.812881	42
43	0.170199	5.875473	0.001170	0.000199	5023.829827	855.051071	43
44	0.170170	5.876473	0.001000	0.000170	5878.880897	1000.409753	44
45	0.170145	5.877327	0.000854	0.000145	6879.290650	1170.479411	45
46	0.170124	5.878058	0.000730	0.000124	8049.770061	1369.460910	46
47	0.170106	5.878682	0.000624	0.000106	9419.230971	1602.269265	47
48	0.170091	5.879215	0.000533	0.000091	11021.500236	1874.655040	48
49	0.170078	5.879671	0.000456	0.000078	12896.155276	2193.346397	49
50	0.170066	5.880061	0.000390	0.000066	15089.501673	2566.215284	50

ANNUAL COMPOUND INTEREST TABLES

18.00% ANNUAL INTEREST RATE

YEARS	1 FUTURE VALUE OF $1	2 FUTURE VALUE ANNUITY OF $1 PER YEAR	3 SINKING FUND FACTOR	4 PRESENT VALUE OF $1 (REVERSION)	5 PRESENT VALUE ANNUITY OF $1 PER YEAR	6 PAYMENT TO AMORTIZE $1	YEARS
1	1.180000	1.000000	1.000000	0.847458	0.847458	1.180000	1
2	1.392400	2.180000	0.458716	0.718184	1.565642	0.638716	2
3	1.643032	3.572400	0.279924	0.608631	2.174273	0.459924	3
4	1.938778	5.215432	0.191739	0.515789	2.690062	0.371739	4
5	2.287758	7.154210	0.139778	0.437109	3.127171	0.319778	5
6	2.699554	9.441968	0.105910	0.370432	3.497603	0.285910	6
7	3.185474	12.141522	0.082362	0.313925	3.811528	0.262362	7
8	3.758859	15.326996	0.065244	0.266038	4.077566	0.245244	8
9	4.435454	19.085855	0.052395	0.225456	4.303022	0.232395	9
10	5.233836	23.521309	0.042515	0.191064	4.494086	0.222515	10
11	6.175926	28.755144	0.034776	0.161919	4.656005	0.214776	11
12	7.287593	34.931070	0.028628	0.137220	4.793225	0.208628	12
13	8.599359	42.218663	0.023686	0.116288	4.909513	0.203686	13
14	10.147244	50.818022	0.019678	0.098549	5.008062	0.199678	14
15	11.973748	60.965266	0.016403	0.083516	5.091578	0.196403	15
16	14.129023	72.939014	0.013710	0.070776	5.162354	0.193710	16
17	16.672247	87.068036	0.011485	0.059980	5.222334	0.191485	17
18	19.673251	103.740283	0.009639	0.050830	5.273164	0.189639	18
19	23.214436	123.413534	0.008103	0.043077	5.316241	0.188103	19
20	27.393035	146.627970	0.006820	0.036506	5.352746	0.186820	20

n							n
21	0.185746	5.383683	0.030937	0.005746	174.021005	32.323781	21
22	0.184846	5.409901	0.026218	0.004846	206.344785	38.142061	22
23	0.184090	5.432120	0.022218	0.004090	244.486847	45.007632	23
24	0.183454	5.450949	0.018829	0.003454	289.494479	53.109006	24
25	0.182919	5.466906	0.015957	0.002919	342.603486	62.668627	25
26	0.182467	5.480429	0.013523	0.002467	405.272113	73.948980	26
27	0.182087	5.491889	0.011460	0.002087	479.221093	87.259797	27
28	0.181765	5.501601	0.009712	0.001765	566.480890	102.966560	28
29	0.181494	5.509831	0.008230	0.001494	669.447450	121.500541	29
30	0.181264	5.516806	0.006975	0.001264	790.947991	143.370638	30
31	0.181070	5.522717	0.005911	0.001070	934.318630	169.177353	31
32	0.180906	5.527726	0.005009	0.000906	1103.495983	199.629277	32
33	0.180767	5.531971	0.004245	0.000767	1303.125260	235.562547	33
34	0.180650	5.535569	0.003598	0.000650	1538.687807	277.963805	34
35	0.180550	5.538618	0.003049	0.000550	1816.651612	327.997290	35
36	0.180466	5.541201	0.002584	0.000466	2144.648902	387.036802	36
37	0.180395	5.543391	0.002190	0.000395	2531.685705	456.703427	37
38	0.180335	5.545247	0.001856	0.000335	2988.389132	538.910044	38
39	0.180284	5.546819	0.001573	0.000284	3527.299175	635.913852	39
40	0.180240	5.548152	0.001333	0.000240	4163.213027	750.378345	40
41	0.180204	5.549281	0.001129	0.000204	4913.591372	885.446447	41
42	0.180172	5.550238	0.000957	0.000172	5799.037819	1044.826807	42
43	0.180146	5.551049	0.000811	0.000146	6843.864626	1232.895633	43
44	0.180124	5.551737	0.000687	0.000124	8076.760259	1454.816847	44
45	0.180105	5.552319	0.000583	0.000105	9531.577105	1716.683879	45
46	0.180089	5.552813	0.000494	0.000089	11248.260984	2025.686977	46
47	0.180075	5.553231	0.000418	0.000075	13273.947961	2390.310633	47
48	0.180064	5.553586	0.000355	0.000064	15664.258594	2820.566547	48
49	0.180054	5.553886	0.000300	0.000054	18484.825141	3328.268525	49
50	0.180046	5.554141	0.000255	0.000046	21813.093666	3927.356860	50

ANNUAL COMPOUND INTEREST TABLES

19.00% ANNUAL INTEREST RATE

YEARS	1 FUTURE VALUE OF $1	2 FUTURE VALUE ANNUITY OF $1 PER YEAR	3 SINKING FUND FACTOR	4 PRESENT VALUE OF $1 (REVERSION)	5 PRESENT VALUE ANNUITY OF $1 PER YEAR	6 PAYMENT TO AMORTIZE $1	YEARS
1	1.190000	1.000000	1.000000	0.840336	0.840336	1.190000	1
2	1.416100	2.190000	0.456621	0.706165	1.546501	0.646621	2
3	1.685159	3.606100	0.277308	0.593416	2.139917	0.467308	3
4	2.005339	5.291259	0.188991	0.498669	2.638586	0.378991	4
5	2.386354	7.296598	0.137050	0.419049	3.057635	0.327050	5
6	2.839761	9.682952	0.103274	0.352142	3.409777	0.293274	6
7	3.379315	12.522713	0.079855	0.295918	3.705695	0.269855	7
8	4.021385	15.902028	0.062885	0.248671	3.954366	0.252885	8
9	4.785449	19.923413	0.050192	0.208967	4.163332	0.240192	9
10	5.694684	24.708862	0.040471	0.175602	4.338935	0.230471	10
11	6.776674	30.403546	0.032891	0.147565	4.486500	0.222891	11
12	8.064242	37.180220	0.026896	0.124004	4.610504	0.216896	12
13	9.596448	45.244461	0.022102	0.104205	4.714709	0.212102	13
14	11.419773	54.840909	0.018235	0.087567	4.802277	0.208235	14
15	13.589530	66.260682	0.015092	0.073586	4.875863	0.205092	15
16	16.171540	79.850211	0.012523	0.061837	4.937700	0.202523	16
17	19.244133	96.021751	0.010414	0.051964	4.989664	0.200414	17
18	22.900518	115.265884	0.008676	0.043667	5.033331	0.198676	18
19	27.251616	138.166402	0.007238	0.036695	5.070026	0.197238	19
20	32.429423	165.418018	0.006045	0.030836	5.100862	0.196045	20

21	0.195054	5.126775	0.025913	0.005054	197.847442	38.591014	21
22	0.194229	5.148550	0.021775	0.004229	236.438456	45.923307	22
23	0.193542	5.166849	0.018299	0.003542	282.361762	54.648735	23
24	0.192967	5.182226	0.015377	0.002967	337.010497	65.031994	24
25	0.192487	5.195148	0.012922	0.002487	402.042491	77.388073	25
26	0.192086	5.206007	0.010859	0.002086	479.430565	92.091807	26
27	0.191750	5.215132	0.009125	0.001750	571.522372	109.589251	27
28	0.191468	5.222800	0.007668	0.001468	681.111623	130.411208	28
29	0.191232	5.229243	0.006444	0.001232	811.522831	155.189338	29
30	0.191034	5.234658	0.005415	0.001034	966.712169	184.675312	30
31	0.190869	5.239209	0.004550	0.000869	1151.387481	219.763621	31
32	0.190729	5.243033	0.003824	0.000729	1371.151103	261.518710	32
33	0.190612	5.246246	0.003213	0.000612	1632.669812	311.207264	33
34	0.190514	5.248946	0.002700	0.000514	1943.877077	370.336645	34
35	0.190432	5.251215	0.002269	0.000432	2314.213721	440.700607	35
36	0.190363	5.253122	0.001907	0.000363	2754.914328	524.433722	36
37	0.190305	5.254724	0.001602	0.000305	3279.348051	624.076130	37
38	0.190256	5.256071	0.001347	0.000256	3903.424180	742.650594	38
39	0.190215	5.257202	0.001132	0.000215	4646.074775	883.754207	39
40	0.190181	5.258153	0.000951	0.000181	5529.828982	1051.667507	40
41	0.190152	5.258952	0.000799	0.000152	6581.496488	1251.484333	41
42	0.190128	5.259624	0.000671	0.000128	7832.980821	1489.266356	42
43	0.190107	5.260188	0.000564	0.000107	9322.247177	1772.226964	43
44	0.190090	5.260662	0.000474	0.000090	11094.474141	2108.950087	44
45	0.190076	5.261061	0.000398	0.000076	13203.424228	2509.650603	45
46	0.190064	5.261396	0.000335	0.000064	15713.074831	2986.484218	46
47	0.190053	5.261677	0.000281	0.000053	18699.559049	3553.916219	47
48	0.190045	5.261913	0.000236	0.000045	22253.475268	4229.160301	48
49	0.190038	5.262112	0.000199	0.000038	26482.635569	5032.700758	49
50	0.190032	5.262279	0.000167	0.000032	31515.336327	5988.913902	50

| APPENDIX B |

Monthly Compound
Interest Tables

MONTHLY COMPOUND INTEREST TABLES

6.00% ANNUAL INTEREST RATE

0.5000% MONTHLY EFFECTIVE INTEREST RATE

	1 FUTURE VALUE OF $1	2 FUTURE VALUE ANNUITY OF $1 MONTH	3 SINKING FUND FACTOR	4 PRESENT VALUE OF $1 (REVERSION)	5 PRESENT VALUE ANNUITY OF $1 MONTH	6 PAYMENT TO AMORTIZE $1	
MONTHS							MONTHS
1	1.005000	1.000000	1.000000	0.995025	0.995025	1.005000	1
2	1.010025	2.005000	0.498753	0.990075	1.985099	0.503753	2
3	1.015075	3.015025	0.331672	0.985149	2.970248	0.336672	3
4	1.020151	4.030100	0.248133	0.980248	3.950496	0.253133	4
5	1.025251	5.050251	0.198010	0.975371	4.925866	0.203010	5
6	1.030378	6.075502	0.164595	0.970518	5.896384	0.169595	6
7	1.035529	7.105879	0.140729	0.965690	6.862074	0.145729	7
8	1.040707	8.141409	0.122829	0.960885	7.822959	0.127829	8
9	1.045911	9.182116	0.108907	0.956105	8.779064	0.113907	9
10	1.051140	10.228026	0.097771	0.951348	9.730412	0.102771	10
11	1.056396	11.279167	0.088659	0.946615	10.677027	0.093659	11
12	1.061678	12.335562	0.081066	0.941905	11.618932	0.086066	12
YEARS							MONTHS
1	1.061678	12.335562	0.081066	0.941905	11.618932	0.086066	12
2	1.127160	25.431955	0.039321	0.887186	22.562866	0.044321	24
3	1.196681	39.336105	0.025422	0.835645	32.871016	0.030422	36
4	1.270489	54.097832	0.018485	0.787098	42.580318	0.023485	48
5	1.348850	69.770031	0.014333	0.741372	51.725561	0.019333	60
6	1.432044	86.408856	0.011573	0.698302	60.339514	0.016573	72
7	1.520370	104.073927	0.009609	0.657735	68.453042	0.014609	84
8	1.614143	122.828542	0.008141	0.619524	76.095218	0.013141	96

Months							Year
108	0.012006	83.293424	0.583533	0.007006	142.739900	1.713699	9
120	0.011102	90.073453	0.549633	0.006102	163.879347	1.819397	10
132	0.010367	96.459599	0.517702	0.005367	186.322629	1.931613	11
144	0.009759	102.474743	0.487626	0.004759	210.150163	2.050751	12
156	0.009247	108.140440	0.459298	0.004247	235.447328	2.177237	13
168	0.008812	113.476990	0.432615	0.003812	262.304766	2.311524	14
180	0.008439	118.503515	0.407482	0.003439	290.818712	2.454094	15
192	0.008114	123.238025	0.383810	0.003114	321.091337	2.605457	16
204	0.007831	127.697486	0.361513	0.002831	353.231110	2.766156	17
216	0.007582	131.897876	0.340511	0.002582	387.353194	2.936766	18
228	0.007361	135.854246	0.320729	0.002361	423.579854	3.117899	19
240	0.007164	139.580772	0.302096	0.002164	462.040895	3.310204	20
252	0.006989	143.090806	0.284546	0.001989	502.874129	3.514371	21
264	0.006831	146.396927	0.268015	0.001831	546.225867	3.731129	22
276	0.006688	149.510979	0.252445	0.001688	592.251446	3.961257	23
288	0.006560	152.444121	0.237779	0.001560	641.115782	4.205579	24
300	0.006443	155.206864	0.223966	0.001443	692.993962	4.464970	25
312	0.006337	157.809106	0.210954	0.001337	748.071876	4.740359	26
324	0.006240	160.260172	0.198699	0.001240	806.546875	5.032734	27
336	0.006151	162.568844	0.187156	0.001151	868.628484	5.343142	28
348	0.006070	164.743394	0.176283	0.001070	934.539150	5.672696	29
360	0.005996	166.791614	0.166042	0.000996	1004.515042	6.022575	30
372	0.005927	168.720844	0.156396	0.000927	1078.806895	6.394034	31
384	0.005864	170.537996	0.147310	0.000864	1157.680906	6.788405	32
396	0.005806	172.249581	0.138752	0.000806	1241.419693	7.207098	33
408	0.005752	173.861732	0.130691	0.000752	1330.323306	7.651617	34
420	0.005702	175.380226	0.123099	0.000702	1424.710299	8.123551	35
432	0.005656	176.810504	0.115947	0.000656	1524.918875	8.624594	36
444	0.005613	178.157690	0.109212	0.000613	1631.308097	9.156540	37
456	0.005573	179.426611	0.102867	0.000573	1744.259173	9.721296	38
468	0.005536	180.621815	0.096891	0.000536	1864.176824	10.320884	39
480	0.005502	181.747584	0.091262	0.000502	1991.490734	10.957454	40

MONTHLY COMPOUND INTEREST TABLES

8.00% ANNUAL INTEREST RATE

0.6667% MONTHLY EFFECTIVE INTEREST RATE

	1 FUTURE VALUE OF $1	2 FUTURE VALUE ANNUITY OF $1 PER MONTH	3 SINKING FUND FACTOR	4 PRESENT VALUE OF $1 (REVERSION)	5 PRESENT VALUE ANNUITY OF $1 PER MONTH	6 PAYMENT TO AMORTIZE $1	MONTHS
MONTHS							
1	1.006667	1.000000	1.000000	0.993377	0.993377	1.006667	1
2	1.013378	2.006667	0.498339	0.986799	1.980176	0.505006	2
3	1.020134	3.020044	0.331121	0.980264	2.960440	0.337788	3
4	1.026935	4.040178	0.247514	0.973772	3.934212	0.254181	4
5	1.033781	5.067113	0.197351	0.967323	4.901535	0.204018	5
6	1.040673	6.100893	0.163910	0.960917	5.862452	0.170577	6
7	1.047610	7.141566	0.140025	0.954553	6.817005	0.146692	7
8	1.054595	8.189176	0.122112	0.948232	7.765237	0.128779	8
9	1.061625	9.243771	0.108181	0.941952	8.707189	0.114848	9
10	1.068703	10.305396	0.097037	0.935714	9.642903	0.103703	10
11	1.075827	11.374099	0.087919	0.929517	10.572420	0.094586	11
12	1.083000	12.449926	0.080322	0.923361	11.495782	0.086988	12
YEARS							**MONTHS**
1	1.083000	12.449926	0.080322	0.923361	11.495782	0.086988	12
2	1.172888	25.933190	0.038561	0.852596	22.110544	0.045227	24
3	1.270237	40.535558	0.024670	0.787255	31.911806	0.031336	36
4	1.375666	56.349915	0.017746	0.726921	40.961913	0.024413	48
5	1.489846	73.476856	0.013610	0.671210	49.318433	0.020276	60
6	1.613502	92.025325	0.010867	0.619770	57.034522	0.017533	72
7	1.747422	112.113308	0.008920	0.572272	64.159261	0.015586	84
8	1.892457	133.868583	0.007470	0.528414	70.737970	0.014137	96

Year	Months						
9	108	0.013019	76.812497	0.487917	0.006352	157.429535	2.049530
10	120	0.012133	82.421481	0.450523	0.005466	182.946035	2.219640
11	132	0.011415	87.600600	0.415996	0.004749	210.580392	2.403869
12	144	0.010825	92.382800	0.384115	0.004158	240.508387	2.603389
13	156	0.010331	96.798498	0.354677	0.003664	272.920390	2.819469
14	168	0.009913	100.875784	0.327495	0.003247	308.022574	3.053484
15	180	0.009557	104.640592	0.302396	0.002890	346.038222	3.306921
16	192	0.009249	108.116871	0.279221	0.002583	387.209149	3.581394
17	204	0.008983	111.326733	0.257822	0.002316	431.797244	3.878648
18	216	0.008750	114.290596	0.238063	0.002083	480.086128	4.200574
19	228	0.008545	117.027313	0.219818	0.001878	532.382966	4.549220
20	240	0.008364	119.554292	0.202971	0.001698	589.020416	4.926803
21	252	0.008204	121.887606	0.187416	0.001538	650.358746	5.335725
22	264	0.008062	124.042099	0.173053	0.001395	716.788127	5.778588
23	276	0.007935	126.031475	0.159790	0.001268	788.731114	6.258207
24	288	0.007821	127.868388	0.147544	0.001154	866.645333	6.777636
25	300	0.007718	129.564523	0.136237	0.001051	951.026395	7.340176
26	312	0.007626	131.130668	0.125796	0.000959	1042.411042	7.949407
27	324	0.007543	132.576786	0.116155	0.000876	1141.380571	8.609204
28	336	0.007468	133.912076	0.107253	0.000801	1248.564521	9.323763
29	348	0.007399	135.145031	0.099033	0.000733	1364.644687	10.097631
30	360	0.007338	136.283494	0.091443	0.000671	1490.359449	10.935730
31	372	0.007281	137.334707	0.084435	0.000615	1626.508474	11.843390
32	384	0.007230	138.305357	0.077964	0.000564	1773.957801	12.826385
33	396	0.007184	139.201617	0.071989	0.000517	1933.645350	13.890969
34	408	0.007141	140.029190	0.066472	0.000475	2106.586886	15.043913
35	420	0.007103	140.793338	0.061378	0.000436	2293.882485	16.292550
36	432	0.007067	141.498923	0.056674	0.000401	2496.723526	17.644824
37	444	0.007035	142.150433	0.052330	0.000368	2716.400273	19.109335
38	456	0.007005	142.752013	0.048320	0.000338	2954.310082	20.695401
39	468	0.006978	143.307488	0.044617	0.000311	3211.966288	22.413109
40	480	0.006953	143.820392	0.041197	0.000286	3491.007831	24.273386

MONTHLY COMPOUND INTEREST TABLES

9.00% ANNUAL INTEREST RATE   0.7500% MONTHLY EFFECTIVE INTEREST RATE

	1 FUTURE VALUE OF $1	2 FUTURE VALUE ANNUITY OF $1 PER MONTH	3 SINKING FUND FACTOR	4 PRESENT VALUE OF $1 (REVERSION)	5 PRESENT VALUE ANNUITY OF $1 PER MONTH	6 PAYMENT TO AMORTIZE $1	MONTHS
MONTHS							
1	1.007500	1.000000	1.000000	0.992556	0.992556	1.007500	1
2	1.015056	2.007500	0.498132	0.985167	1.977723	0.505632	2
3	1.022669	3.022556	0.330846	0.977833	2.955556	0.338346	3
4	1.030339	4.045225	0.247205	0.970554	3.926110	0.254705	4
5	1.038067	5.075565	0.197022	0.963329	4.889440	0.204522	5
6	1.045852	6.113631	0.163569	0.956158	5.845598	0.171069	6
7	1.053696	7.159484	0.139675	0.949040	6.794638	0.147175	7
8	1.061599	8.213180	0.121756	0.941975	7.736613	0.129256	8
9	1.069561	9.274779	0.107819	0.934963	8.671576	0.115319	9
10	1.077583	10.344339	0.096671	0.928003	9.599580	0.104171	10
11	1.085664	11.421922	0.087551	0.921095	10.520675	0.095051	11
12	1.093807	12.507586	0.079951	0.914238	11.434913	0.087451	12
YEARS							**MONTHS**
1	1.093807	12.507586	0.079951	0.914238	11.434913	0.087451	12
2	1.196414	26.188471	0.038185	0.835831	21.889146	0.045685	24
3	1.308645	41.152716	0.024300	0.764149	31.446805	0.031800	36
4	1.431405	57.520711	0.017385	0.698614	40.184782	0.024885	48
5	1.565681	75.424137	0.013258	0.638700	48.173374	0.020758	60
6	1.712553	95.007028	0.010526	0.583924	55.476849	0.018026	72
7	1.873202	116.426928	0.008589	0.533845	62.153965	0.016089	84
8	2.048921	139.856164	0.007150	0.488062	68.258439	0.014650	96

9	2.241124	165.483223	0.006043	0.446205	73.839382	0.013543	108
10	2.451357	193.514277	0.005168	0.407937	78.941693	0.012668	120
11	2.681311	224.174837	0.004461	0.372952	83.606420	0.011961	132
12	2.932837	257.711570	0.003880	0.340967	87.871092	0.011380	144
13	3.207957	294.394279	0.003397	0.311725	91.770018	0.010897	156
14	3.508886	334.518079	0.002989	0.284991	95.334564	0.010489	168
15	3.838043	378.405769	0.002643	0.260549	98.593409	0.010143	180
16	4.198078	426.410427	0.002345	0.238204	101.572769	0.009845	192
17	4.591887	478.918252	0.002088	0.217775	104.296613	0.009588	204
18	5.022638	536.351674	0.001864	0.199099	106.786856	0.009364	216
19	5.493796	599.172747	0.001669	0.182024	109.063531	0.009169	228
20	6.009152	667.886870	0.001497	0.166413	111.144954	0.008997	240
21	6.572851	743.046852	0.001346	0.152141	113.047870	0.008846	252
22	7.189430	825.257358	0.001212	0.139093	114.787589	0.008712	264
23	7.863848	915.179777	0.001093	0.127164	116.378106	0.008593	276
24	8.601532	1013.537539	0.000987	0.116258	117.832218	0.008487	288
25	9.408415	1121.121937	0.000892	0.106288	119.161622	0.008392	300
26	10.290989	1238.798495	0.000807	0.097172	120.377014	0.008307	312
27	11.256354	1367.513924	0.000731	0.088839	121.488172	0.008231	324
28	12.312278	1508.303750	0.000663	0.081220	122.504035	0.008163	336
29	13.467255	1662.300631	0.000602	0.074254	123.432776	0.008102	348
30	14.730576	1830.743483	0.000546	0.067886	124.281866	0.008046	360
31	16.112406	2014.987436	0.000496	0.062064	125.058136	0.007996	372
32	17.623861	2216.514743	0.000451	0.056741	125.767832	0.007951	384
33	19.277100	2436.946701	0.000410	0.051875	126.416664	0.007910	396
34	21.085425	2678.056697	0.000373	0.047426	127.009850	0.007873	408
35	23.063384	2941.784474	0.000340	0.043359	127.552164	0.007840	420
36	25.226888	3230.251735	0.000310	0.039640	128.047967	0.007810	432
37	27.593344	3545.779215	0.000282	0.036241	128.501250	0.007782	444
38	30.181790	3890.905350	0.000257	0.033133	128.915659	0.007757	456
39	33.013050	4268.406696	0.000234	0.030291	129.294526	0.007734	468
40	36.109902	4681.320273	0.000214	0.027693	129.640902	0.007714	480

MONTHLY COMPOUND INTEREST TABLES

10.00% ANNUAL INTEREST RATE   0.833% MONTHLY EFFECTIVE INTEREST RATE

	1 FUTURE VALUE OF $1	2 FUTURE VALUE ANNUITY OF $1 PER MONTH	3 SINKING FUND FACTOR	4 PRESENT VALUE OF $1 (REVERSION)	5 PRESENT VALUE ANNUITY OF $1 PER MONTH	6 PAYMENT TO AMORTIZE $1	MONTHS
MONTHS							
1	1.008333	1.000000	1.000000	0.991736	0.991736	1.008333	1
2	1.016736	2.008333	0.497925	0.983539	1.975275	0.506259	2
3	1.025209	3.025069	0.330571	0.975411	2.950686	0.338904	3
4	1.033752	4.050278	0.246897	0.967350	3.918036	0.255230	4
5	1.042367	5.084031	0.196694	0.959355	4.877391	0.205028	5
6	1.051053	6.126398	0.163228	0.951427	5.828817	0.171561	6
7	1.059812	7.177451	0.139325	0.943563	6.772381	0.147659	7
8	1.068644	8.237263	0.121400	0.935765	7.708146	0.129733	8
9	1.077549	9.305907	0.107459	0.928032	8.636178	0.115792	9
10	1.086529	10.383456	0.096307	0.920362	9.556540	0.104640	10
11	1.095583	11.469985	0.087184	0.912756	10.469296	0.095517	11
12	1.104713	12.565568	0.079583	0.905212	11.374508	0.087916	12
YEARS							**MONTHS**
1	1.104713	12.565568	0.079583	0.905212	11.374508	0.087916	12
2	1.220391	26.446915	0.037812	0.819410	21.670855	0.046145	24
3	1.348182	41.781821	0.023934	0.741740	30.991236	0.032267	36
4	1.489354	58.722492	0.017029	0.671432	39.428160	0.025363	48
5	1.645309	77.437072	0.012914	0.607789	47.065369	0.021247	60
6	1.817594	98.111314	0.010193	0.550178	53.978665	0.018526	72
7	2.007920	120.950418	0.008268	0.498028	60.236667	0.016601	84
8	2.218176	146.181076	0.006841	0.450821	65.901488	0.015174	96

n							months
9	2.450448	174.053713	0.005745	0.408089	71.029355	0.014079	108
10	2.707041	204.844979	0.004882	0.369407	75.671163	0.013215	120
11	2.990504	238.860493	0.004187	0.334392	79.872986	0.012520	132
12	3.303649	276.437876	0.003617	0.302696	83.676528	0.011951	144
13	3.649584	317.950102	0.003145	0.274004	87.119542	0.011478	156
14	4.031743	363.809201	0.002749	0.248032	90.236201	0.011082	168
15	4.453920	414.470346	0.002413	0.224521	93.057439	0.010746	180
16	4.920303	470.436376	0.002126	0.203240	95.611259	0.010459	192
17	5.435523	532.262780	0.001879	0.183975	97.923008	0.010212	204
18	6.004693	600.563216	0.001665	0.166536	100.015633	0.009998	216
19	6.633463	676.015601	0.001479	0.150751	101.909902	0.009813	228
20	7.328074	759.368836	0.001317	0.136462	103.624619	0.009650	240
21	8.095419	851.450244	0.001174	0.123527	105.176801	0.009508	252
22	8.943115	953.173779	0.001049	0.111818	106.581856	0.009382	264
23	9.879576	1065.549097	0.000938	0.101219	107.853730	0.009272	276
24	10.914097	1189.691580	0.000841	0.091625	109.005045	0.009174	288
25	12.056945	1326.833403	0.000754	0.082940	110.047230	0.009087	300
26	13.319465	1478.335767	0.000676	0.075078	110.990629	0.009010	312
27	14.714187	1645.702407	0.000608	0.067962	111.844605	0.008941	324
28	16.254954	1830.594523	0.000546	0.061520	112.617635	0.008880	336
29	17.957060	2034.847258	0.000491	0.055688	113.317392	0.008825	348
30	19.837599	2260.487925	0.000442	0.050410	113.950820	0.008776	360
31	21.914634	2509.756117	0.000398	0.045632	114.524207	0.008732	372
32	24.209383	2785.125947	0.000359	0.041306	115.043244	0.008692	384
33	26.744422	3089.330596	0.000324	0.037391	115.513083	0.008657	396
34	29.544912	3425.389447	0.000292	0.033847	115.938387	0.008625	408
35	32.638650	3796.638052	0.000263	0.030639	116.323377	0.008597	420
36	36.056344	4206.761236	0.000238	0.027734	116.671876	0.008571	432
37	39.831914	4659.829677	0.000215	0.025105	116.987340	0.008548	444
38	44.002836	5160.340305	0.000194	0.022726	117.272903	0.008527	456
39	48.610508	5713.260935	0.000175	0.020572	117.531398	0.008508	468
40	53.700663	6324.079581	0.000158	0.018622	117.765391	0.008491	480

MONTHLY COMPOUND INTEREST TABLES

11.00% ANNUAL INTEREST RATE

0.9167% MONTHLY EFFECTIVE INTEREST RATE

	1 FUTURE VALUE OF $1	2 FUTURE VALUE ANNUITY OF $1 PER MONTH	3 SINKING FUND FACTOR	4 PRESENT VALUE OF $1 (REVERSION)	5 PRESENT VALUE ANNUITY OF $1 PER MONTH	6 PAYMENT TO AMORTIZE $1	MONTHS
MONTHS							
1	1.009167	1.000000	1.000000	0.990917	0.990917	1.009167	1
2	1.018417	2.009167	0.497719	0.981916	1.972832	0.506885	2
3	1.027753	3.027584	0.330296	0.972997	2.945829	0.339463	3
4	1.037174	4.055337	0.246589	0.964158	3.909987	0.255755	4
5	1.046681	5.092511	0.196367	0.955401	4.865388	0.205533	5
6	1.056276	6.139192	0.162888	0.946722	5.812110	0.172055	6
7	1.065958	7.195468	0.138976	0.938123	6.750233	0.148143	7
8	1.075730	8.261427	0.121044	0.929602	7.679835	0.130211	8
9	1.085591	9.337156	0.107099	0.921158	8.600992	0.116266	9
10	1.095542	10.422747	0.095944	0.912790	9.513783	0.105111	10
11	1.105584	11.518289	0.086818	0.904499	10.418282	0.095985	11
12	1.115719	12.623873	0.079215	0.896283	11.314565	0.088382	12
YEARS							**MONTHS**
1	1.115719	12.623873	0.079215	0.896283	11.314565	0.088382	12
2	1.244829	26.708566	0.037441	0.803323	21.455619	0.046608	24
3	1.388879	42.423123	0.023572	0.720005	30.544874	0.032739	36
4	1.549598	59.956151	0.016679	0.645329	38.691421	0.025846	48
5	1.728916	79.518080	0.012576	0.578397	45.993034	0.021742	60
6	1.928984	101.343692	0.009867	0.518408	52.537346	0.019034	72
7	2.152204	125.694940	0.007956	0.464640	58.402903	0.017122	84
8	2.401254	152.864085	0.006542	0.416449	63.660103	0.015708	96

n							n
108	0.014626	68.372043	0.373256	183.177212	0.005459	2.679124	9
120	0.013775	72.595275	0.334543	216.998139	0.004608	2.989150	10
132	0.013092	76.380487	0.299846	254.732784	0.003926	3.335051	11
144	0.012536	79.773109	0.268747	296.834038	0.003369	3.720979	12
156	0.012075	82.813859	0.240873	343.807200	0.002909	4.151566	13
168	0.011691	85.539231	0.215890	396.216042	0.002524	4.631980	14
180	0.011366	87.981937	0.193499	454.689575	0.002199	5.167988	15
192	0.011090	90.171293	0.173430	519.929596	0.001923	5.766021	16
204	0.010854	92.133576	0.155442	592.719117	0.001687	6.433259	17
216	0.010650	93.892337	0.139320	673.931757	0.001484	7.177708	18
228	0.010475	95.468685	0.124870	764.542228	0.001308	8.008304	19
240	0.010322	96.881539	0.111919	865.638038	0.001155	8.935015	20
252	0.010189	98.147856	0.100311	978.432537	0.001022	9.968965	21
264	0.010072	99.282835	0.089907	1104.279485	0.000906	11.122562	22
276	0.009970	100.300098	0.080582	1244.689295	0.000803	12.409652	23
288	0.009880	101.211853	0.072225	1401.347165	0.000714	13.845682	24
300	0.009801	102.029044	0.064734	1576.133301	0.000634	15.447889	25
312	0.009731	102.761478	0.058020	1771.145485	0.000565	17.235500	26
324	0.009670	103.417947	0.052002	1988.724252	0.000503	19.229972	27
336	0.009615	104.006328	0.046609	2231.480981	0.000448	21.455242	28
348	0.009566	104.533685	0.041775	2502.329236	0.000400	23.938018	29
360	0.009523	105.006346	0.037442	2804.519736	0.000357	26.708098	30
372	0.009485	105.429984	0.033558	3141.679369	0.000318	29.798728	31
384	0.009451	105.809684	0.030078	3517.854723	0.000284	33.247002	32
396	0.009421	106.150002	0.026958	3937.560650	0.000254	37.094306	33
408	0.009394	106.455024	0.024162	4405.834459	0.000227	41.386816	34
420	0.009370	106.728409	0.021656	4928.296368	0.000203	46.176050	35
432	0.009348	106.973440	0.019410	5511.216962	0.000181	51.519489	36
444	0.009329	107.193057	0.017397	6161.592447	0.000162	57.481264	37
456	0.009312	107.389897	0.015593	6887.228628	0.000145	64.132929	38
468	0.009297	107.566320	0.013975	7696.834582	0.000130	71.554317	39
480	0.009283	107.724446	0.012526	8600.127195	0.000116	79.834499	40

MONTHLY COMPOUND INTEREST TABLES

12.00% ANNUAL INTEREST RATE   1.0000% MONTHLY EFFECTIVE INTEREST RATE

	1 FUTURE VALUE OF $1	2 FUTURE VALUE ANNUITY OF $1 PER MONTH	3 SINKING FUND FACTOR	4 PRESENT VALUE OF $1 (REVERSION)	5 PRESENT VALUE ANNUITY OF $1 PER MONTH	6 PAYMENT TO AMORTIZE $1	
MONTHS							**MONTHS**
1	1.010000	1.000000	1.000000	0.990099	0.990099	1.010000	1
2	1.020100	2.010000	0.497512	0.980296	1.970395	0.507512	2
3	1.030301	3.030100	0.330022	0.970590	2.940985	0.340022	3
4	1.040604	4.060401	0.246281	0.960980	3.901966	0.256281	4
5	1.051010	5.101005	0.196040	0.951466	4.853431	0.206040	5
6	1.061520	6.152015	0.162548	0.942045	5.795476	0.172548	6
7	1.072135	7.213535	0.138628	0.932718	6.728195	0.148628	7
8	1.082857	8.285671	0.120690	0.923483	7.651678	0.130690	8
9	1.093685	9.368527	0.106740	0.914340	8.566018	0.116740	9
10	1.104622	10.462213	0.095582	0.905287	9.471305	0.105582	10
11	1.115668	11.566835	0.086454	0.896324	10.367628	0.096454	11
12	1.126825	12.682503	0.078849	0.887449	11.255077	0.088849	12
YEARS							**MONTHS**
1	1.126825	12.682503	0.078849	0.887449	11.255077	0.088849	12
2	1.269735	26.973465	0.037073	0.787566	21.243387	0.047073	24
3	1.430769	43.076878	0.023214	0.698925	30.107505	0.033214	36
4	1.612226	61.222608	0.016334	0.620260	37.973959	0.026334	48
5	1.816697	81.669670	0.012244	0.550450	44.955038	0.022244	60
6	2.047099	104.709931	0.009550	0.488496	51.150391	0.019550	72
7	2.306723	130.672274	0.007653	0.433515	56.648453	0.017653	84
8	2.599273	159.927293	0.006253	0.384723	61.527703	0.016253	96

Months						Years
108	0.015184	65.857790	0.341422	0.005184	192.892579	2.928926	9
120	0.014347	69.700522	0.302995	0.004347	230.038689	3.300387	10
132	0.013678	73.110752	0.268892	0.003678	271.895856	3.718959	11
144	0.013134	76.137157	0.238628	0.003134	319.061559	4.190616	12
156	0.012687	78.822939	0.211771	0.002687	372.209054	4.722091	13
168	0.012314	81.206434	0.187936	0.002314	432.096982	5.320970	14
180	0.012002	83.321664	0.166783	0.002002	499.580198	5.995802	15
192	0.011737	85.198824	0.148012	0.001737	575.621974	6.756220	16
204	0.011512	86.864707	0.131353	0.001512	661.307751	7.613078	17
216	0.011320	88.343095	0.116569	0.001320	757.860630	8.578606	18
228	0.011154	89.655089	0.103449	0.001154	866.658830	9.666588	19
240	0.011011	90.819416	0.091806	0.001011	989.255365	10.892554	20
252	0.010887	91.852698	0.081473	0.000887	1127.400210	12.274002	21
264	0.010779	92.769683	0.072303	0.000779	1283.065279	13.830653	22
276	0.010686	93.583461	0.064165	0.000686	1458.472574	15.584726	23
288	0.010604	94.305647	0.056944	0.000604	1656.125905	17.561259	24
300	0.010532	94.946551	0.050534	0.000532	1878.846626	19.788466	25
312	0.010470	95.515321	0.044847	0.000470	2129.813909	22.298139	26
324	0.010414	96.020075	0.039799	0.000414	2412.610125	25.126101	27
336	0.010366	96.468019	0.035320	0.000366	2731.271980	28.312720	28
348	0.010324	96.865546	0.031345	0.000324	3090.348134	31.903481	29
360	0.010286	97.218331	0.027817	0.000286	3494.964133	35.949641	30
372	0.010253	97.531410	0.024686	0.000253	3950.895567	40.508956	31
384	0.010224	97.809252	0.021907	0.000224	4464.650520	45.646505	32
396	0.010198	98.055822	0.019442	0.000198	5043.562459	51.435625	33
408	0.010176	98.274641	0.017254	0.000176	5695.894923	57.958949	34
420	0.010155	98.468831	0.015312	0.000155	6430.959471	65.309595	35
432	0.010138	98.641166	0.013588	0.000138	7259.248603	73.592486	36
444	0.010122	98.794103	0.012059	0.000122	8192.585529	82.925855	37
456	0.010108	98.929828	0.010702	0.000108	9244.292939	93.442929	38
468	0.010096	99.050277	0.009497	0.000096	10429.383172	105.293832	39
480	0.010085	99.157169	0.008428	0.000085	11764.772510	118.647725	40

MONTHLY COMPOUND INTEREST TABLES

13.00% ANNUAL INTEREST RATE | 1.0833% MONTHLY EFFECTIVE INTEREST RATE

	1 FUTURE VALUE OF $1	2 FUTURE VALUE ANNUITY OF $1 PER MONTH	3 SINKING FUND FACTOR	4 PRESENT VALUE OF $1 (REVERSION)	5 PRESENT VALUE ANNUITY OF $1 PER MONTH	6 PAYMENT TO AMORTIZE $1	MONTHS
MONTHS							
1	1.010833	1.000000	1.000000	0.989283	0.989283	1.010833	1
2	1.021784	2.010833	0.497306	0.978680	1.967963	0.508140	2
3	1.032853	3.032617	0.329748	0.968192	2.936155	0.340581	3
4	1.044043	4.065471	0.245974	0.957815	3.893970	0.256807	4
5	1.055353	5.109513	0.195713	0.947550	4.841520	0.206547	5
6	1.066786	6.164866	0.162210	0.937395	5.778915	0.173043	6
7	1.078343	7.231652	0.138281	0.927349	6.706264	0.149114	7
8	1.090025	8.309995	0.120337	0.917410	7.623674	0.131170	8
9	1.101834	9.400020	0.106383	0.907578	8.531253	0.117216	9
10	1.113770	10.501854	0.095221	0.897851	9.429104	0.106055	10
11	1.125836	11.615624	0.086091	0.888229	10.317333	0.096924	11
12	1.138032	12.741460	0.078484	0.878710	11.196042	0.089317	12
YEARS							**MONTHS**
1	1.138032	12.741460	0.078484	0.878710	11.196042	0.089517	12
2	1.295118	27.241655	0.036708	0.772130	21.034112	0.047542	24
3	1.473886	43.743348	0.022861	0.678478	29.678917	0.033694	36
4	1.677330	62.522811	0.015994	0.596185	37.275190	0.026827	48
5	1.908857	83.894449	0.011920	0.523874	43.950107	0.022753	60
6	2.172341	108.216068	0.009241	0.460333	49.815421	0.020074	72
7	2.472194	135.894861	0.007359	0.404499	54.969328	0.018192	84
8	2.813437	167.394225	0.005974	0.355437	59.498115	0.016807	96

n							n
9	3.201783	203.241525	0.004920	0.312326	63.477604	0.015754	108
10	3.643733	244.036917	0.004098	0.274444	66.974419	0.014931	120
11	4.146687	290.463399	0.003443	0.241156	70.047103	0.014276	132
12	4.719064	343.298242	0.002913	0.211906	72.747100	0.013746	144
13	5.370448	403.426010	0.002479	0.186204	75.119613	0.013312	156
14	6.111745	471.853363	0.002119	0.163619	77.204363	0.012953	168
15	6.955364	549.725914	0.001819	0.143774	79.036253	0.012652	180
16	7.915430	638.347406	0.001567	0.126336	80.645952	0.012400	192
17	9.008017	739.201542	0.001353	0.111012	82.060410	0.012186	204
18	10.251416	853.976825	0.001171	0.097548	83.303307	0.012004	216
19	11.666444	984.594826	0.001016	0.085716	84.395453	0.011849	228
20	13.276792	1133.242353	0.000882	0.075319	85.355132	0.011716	240
21	15.109421	1302.408067	0.000768	0.066184	86.198412	0.011601	252
22	17.195012	1494.924144	0.000669	0.058156	86.939409	0.011502	264
23	19.568482	1714.013694	0.000583	0.051103	87.590531	0.011417	276
24	22.269568	1963.344717	0.000509	0.044904	88.162677	0.011343	288
25	25.343491	2247.091520	0.000445	0.039458	88.665428	0.011278	300
26	28.841716	2570.004599	0.000389	0.034672	89.107200	0.011222	312
27	32.822810	2937.490172	0.000340	0.030467	89.495389	0.011174	324
28	37.353424	3355.700690	0.000298	0.026771	89.836495	0.011131	336
29	42.509410	3831.637843	0.000261	0.023524	90.136227	0.011094	348
30	48.377089	4373.269783	0.000229	0.020671	90.399605	0.011062	360
31	55.054699	4989.664524	0.000200	0.018164	90.631038	0.011034	372
32	62.654036	5691.141761	0.000176	0.015961	90.834400	0.011009	384
33	71.302328	6489.445641	0.000154	0.014025	91.013097	0.010987	396
34	81.144365	7397.941387	0.000135	0.012324	91.170119	0.010969	408
35	92.344923	8431.839055	0.000119	0.010829	91.308095	0.010952	420
36	105.091522	9608.448184	0.000104	0.009516	91.429337	0.010937	432
37	119.597566	10947.467591	0.000091	0.008361	91.555873	0.010925	444
38	136.105914	12471.315170	0.000080	0.007347	91.629487	0.010914	456
39	154.892951	14205.503212	0.000070	0.006456	91.711747	0.010904	468
40	176.273210	16179.065533	0.000062	0.005673	91.784030	0.010895	480

MONTHLY COMPOUND INTEREST TABLES

14.00% ANNUAL INTEREST RATE

1.1667% MONTHLY EFFECTIVE INTEREST RATE

	1 FUTURE VALUE OF $1	2 FUTURE VALUE ANNUITY OF $1 PER MONTH	3 SINKING FUND FACTOR	4 PRESENT VALUE OF $1 (REVERSION)	5 PRESENT VALUE ANNUITY OF $1 PER MONTH	6 PAYMENT TO AMORTIZE $1	MONTHS
MONTHS							
1	1.011667	1.000000	1.000000	0.988468	0.988468	1.011667	1
2	1.023469	2.011667	0.497100	0.977069	1.965537	0.508767	2
3	1.035410	3.035136	0.329475	0.965801	2.931338	0.341141	3
4	1.047490	4.070546	0.245667	0.954663	3.886001	0.257334	4
5	1.059710	5.118036	0.195387	0.943654	4.829655	0.207054	5
6	1.072074	6.177746	0.161871	0.932772	5.762427	0.173538	6
7	1.084581	7.249820	0.137934	0.922015	6.684442	0.149601	7
8	1.097235	8.334401	0.119985	0.911382	7.595824	0.131651	8
9	1.110036	9.431636	0.106026	0.900872	8.496696	0.117693	9
10	1.122986	10.541672	0.094862	0.890483	9.387178	0.106528	10
11	1.136088	11.664658	0.085729	0.880214	10.267392	0.097396	11
12	1.149342	12.800745	0.078120	0.870063	11.137455	0.089787	12
YEARS							**MONTHS**
1	1.149342	12.800745	0.078120	0.870063	11.137455	0.089787	12
2	1.320087	27.513180	0.036346	0.757010	20.827743	0.048013	24
3	1.518266	44.422800	0.022511	0.658646	29.258904	0.034178	36
4	1.745007	63.857736	0.015660	0.573064	36.594546	0.027326	48
5	2.005610	86.195125	0.011602	0.498601	42.977016	0.023268	60
6	2.305132	111.868425	0.008939	0.433815	48.530168	0.020606	72
7	2.649385	141.375828	0.007073	0.377446	53.361760	0.018740	84
8	3.045049	175.289927	0.005705	0.328402	57.565549	0.017372	96

n							months
9	3.499803	214.268826	0.004667	0.285730	61.223111	0.016334	108
10	4.022471	259.068912	0.003860	0.248603	64.405420	0.015527	120
11	4.623195	310.559534	0.003220	0.216301	67.174230	0.014887	132
12	5.313632	369.739871	0.002705	0.188195	69.583269	0.014371	144
13	6.107180	437.758319	0.002284	0.163742	71.679284	0.013951	156
14	7.019239	515.934780	0.001938	0.142466	73.502950	0.013605	168
15	8.067507	605.786272	0.001651	0.123954	75.089654	0.013317	180
16	9.272324	709.056369	0.001410	0.107848	76.470187	0.013077	192
17	10.657072	827.749031	0.001208	0.093834	77.671337	0.012875	204
18	12.248621	964.167496	0.001037	0.081642	78.716413	0.012704	216
19	14.077855	1120.958972	0.000892	0.071034	79.625696	0.012559	228
20	16.180270	1301.166005	0.000769	0.061804	80.416829	0.012435	240
21	18.596664	1508.285522	0.000663	0.053773	81.105164	0.012330	252
22	21.373928	1746.336688	0.000573	0.046786	81.704060	0.012239	264
23	24.565954	2019.938898	0.000495	0.040707	82.225136	0.012162	276
24	28.234683	2334.401417	0.000428	0.035417	82.678506	0.012095	288
25	32.451308	2695.826407	0.000371	0.030815	83.072966	0.012038	300
26	37.297652	3111.227338	0.000321	0.026811	83.416171	0.011988	312
27	42.867759	3588.665088	0.000279	0.023328	83.714781	0.011945	324
28	49.269718	4137.404359	0.000242	0.020296	83.974591	0.011908	336
29	56.627757	4768.093467	0.000210	0.017659	84.200641	0.011876	348
30	65.084661	5492.970967	0.000182	0.015365	84.397320	0.011849	360
31	74.804537	6326.103143	0.000158	0.013368	84.568442	0.011825	372
32	85.975998	7283.656968	0.000137	0.011631	84.717330	0.011804	384
33	98.815828	8384.213825	0.000119	0.010120	84.846871	0.011786	396
34	113.573184	9649.130077	0.000104	0.008805	84.959580	0.011770	408
35	130.534434	11102.951488	0.000090	0.007661	85.057645	0.011757	420
36	150.028711	12773.889538	0.000078	0.006665	85.142966	0.011745	432
37	172.434303	14694.368868	0.000068	0.005799	85.217202	0.011735	444
38	198.185992	16901.656478	0.000059	0.005046	85.281792	0.011726	456
39	227.783490	19438.584899	0.000051	0.004390	85.337989	0.011718	468
40	261.801139	22354.383358	0.000045	0.003820	85.386883	0.011711	480

MONTHLY COMPOUND INTEREST TABLES

15.00% ANNUAL INTEREST RATE

1.2500% MONTHLY EFFECTIVE INTEREST RATE

	1 FUTURE VALUE OF $1	2 FUTURE VALUE ANNUITY OF $1 PER MONTH	3 SINKING FUND FACTOR	4 PRESENT VALUE OF $1 (REVERSION)	5 PRESENT VALUE ANNUITY OF $1 PER MONTH	6 PAYMENT TO AMORTIZE $1	MONTHS
MONTHS							
1	1.012500	1.000000	1.000000	0.987654	0.987654	1.012500	1
2	1.025156	2.012500	0.496894	0.975461	1.963115	0.509394	2
3	1.037971	3.037656	0.329201	0.963418	2.926534	0.341701	3
4	1.050945	4.075627	0.245361	0.951524	3.878058	0.257861	4
5	1.064082	5.126572	0.195062	0.939777	4.817835	0.207562	5
6	1.077383	6.190654	0.161534	0.928175	5.746010	0.174034	6
7	1.090850	7.268038	0.137589	0.916716	6.662726	0.150089	7
8	1.104486	8.358888	0.119633	0.905398	7.568124	0.132133	8
9	1.118292	9.463374	0.105671	0.894221	8.462345	0.118171	9
10	1.132271	10.581666	0.094503	0.883181	9.345526	0.107003	10
11	1.146424	11.713937	0.085368	0.872277	10.217803	0.097868	11
12	1.160755	12.860361	0.077758	0.861509	11.079312	0.090258	12
YEARS							**MONTHS**
1	1.160755	12.860361	0.077758	0.861509	11.079312	0.090258	12
2	1.347351	27.788084	0.035987	0.742197	20.624235	0.048487	24
3	1.563944	45.115505	0.022165	0.639409	28.847267	0.034665	36
4	1.815355	65.228388	0.015331	0.550856	35.931481	0.027831	48
5	2.107181	88.574508	0.011290	0.474568	42.034592	0.023790	60
6	2.445920	115.673621	0.008645	0.408844	47.292474	0.021145	72
7	2.839113	147.129040	0.006797	0.352223	51.822185	0.019297	84
8	3.295513	183.641059	0.005445	0.303443	55.724570	0.017945	96

Months							Years
108	0.016924	59.086509	0.261419	0.004424	226.022551	3.825282	9
120	0.016133	61.982847	0.225214	0.003633	275.217058	4.440213	10
132	0.015509	64.478068	0.194024	0.003009	332.319805	5.153998	11
144	0.015009	66.627722	0.167153	0.002509	398.602077	5.982526	12
156	0.014603	68.479668	0.144004	0.002103	475.539523	6.944244	13
168	0.014270	70.075134	0.124061	0.001770	564.845011	8.060563	14
180	0.013996	71.449643	0.106879	0.001496	668.506759	9.356334	15
192	0.013768	72.633794	0.092078	0.001268	788.832603	10.860408	16
204	0.013577	73.653950	0.079326	0.001077	928.501369	12.606267	17
216	0.013417	74.532823	0.068340	0.000917	1090.622520	14.632781	18
228	0.013282	75.289980	0.058875	0.000782	1278.805378	16.985067	19
240	0.013168	75.942278	0.050722	0.000668	1497.239481	19.715494	20
252	0.013071	76.504237	0.043697	0.000571	1750.787854	22.884848	21
264	0.012989	76.983370	0.037645	0.000489	2045.095272	26.563691	22
276	0.012919	77.405455	0.032432	0.000419	2386.713938	30.833924	23
288	0.012859	77.764777	0.027940	0.000359	2783.249347	35.790617	24
300	0.012808	78.074336	0.024071	0.000308	3243.529615	41.544120	25
312	0.012765	78.341024	0.020737	0.000265	3777.802015	48.222525	26
324	0.012727	78.570778	0.017865	0.000227	4397.961118	55.974514	27
336	0.012695	78.768713	0.015391	0.000195	5117.813598	64.972670	28
348	0.012668	78.939236	0.013260	0.000168	5953.385616	75.417320	29
360	0.012644	79.086142	0.011423	0.000144	6923.279611	87.540995	30
372	0.012624	79.212704	0.009841	0.000124	8049.088447	101.613606	31
384	0.012607	79.321738	0.008478	0.000107	9355.876140	117.948452	32
396	0.012592	79.415671	0.007304	0.000092	10872.735858	136.909198	33
408	0.012579	79.496596	0.006293	0.000079	12633.437629	158.917970	34
420	0.012568	79.566313	0.005421	0.000068	14677.180163	184.464752	35
432	0.012559	79.626375	0.004670	0.000059	17049.463544	214.118294	36
444	0.012550	79.678119	0.004024	0.000050	19803.102194	248.538777	37
456	0.012543	79.722696	0.003466	0.000043	22999.400699	288.492509	38
468	0.012537	79.761101	0.002986	0.000037	26709.518627	334.868983	39
480	0.012532	79.794186	0.002573	0.000032	31016.054774	388.700685	40

MONTHLY COMPOUND INTEREST TABLES

16.00% ANNUAL INTEREST RATE

1.3333% MONTHLY EFFECTIVE INTEREST RATE

	1 FUTURE VALUE OF $1	2 FUTURE VALUE ANNUITY OF $1 PER MONTH	3 SINKING FUND FACTOR	4 PRESENT VALUE OF $1 (REVERSION)	5 PRESENT VALUE ANNUITY OF $1 PER MONTH	6 PAYMENT TO AMORTIZE $1	MONTHS
MONTHS							
1	1.013333	1.000000	1.000000	0.986842	0.986842	1.013333	1
2	1.026844	2.013333	0.496689	0.973857	1.960699	0.510022	2
3	1.040536	3.040178	0.328928	0.961043	2.921743	0.342261	3
4	1.054410	4.080713	0.245055	0.948398	3.870141	0.258389	4
5	1.068468	5.135123	0.194737	0.935919	4.806060	0.208071	5
6	1.082715	6.203591	0.161197	0.923604	5.729665	0.174530	6
7	1.097151	7.286306	0.137244	0.911452	6.641116	0.150577	7
8	1.111779	8.383457	0.119283	0.899459	7.540575	0.132616	8
9	1.126603	9.495236	0.105316	0.887624	8.428199	0.118649	9
10	1.141625	10.621839	0.094146	0.875945	9.304144	0.107479	10
11	1.156846	11.763464	0.085009	0.864419	10.168563	0.098342	11
12	1.172271	12.920310	0.077398	0.853045	11.021609	0.090731	12
YEARS							**MONTHS**
1	1.172271	12.920310	0.077398	0.853045	11.021609	0.090731	12
2	1.374219	28.066412	0.035630	0.727686	20.423539	0.048963	24
3	1.610957	45.821745	0.021824	0.620749	28.443811	0.035157	36
4	1.888477	66.635803	0.015007	0.529527	35.285465	0.028340	48
5	2.213807	91.035516	0.010985	0.451711	41.121706	0.024318	60
6	2.595181	119.638587	0.008359	0.385330	46.100283	0.021692	72
7	3.042255	153.169132	0.006529	0.328704	50.347235	0.019862	84
8	3.566347	192.476010	0.005195	0.280399	53.970077	0.018529	96

Year	Months						
9	108	0.017525	57.060524	0.239193	0.004192	238.554316	4.180724
10	120	0.016751	59.696816	0.204042	0.003418	292.570569	4.900941
11	132	0.016143	61.945692	0.174057	0.002810	355.892244	5.745230
12	144	0.015658	63.864085	0.148479	0.002325	430.122395	6.734965
13	156	0.015267	65.500561	0.126659	0.001934	517.140233	7.895203
14	168	0.014948	66.896549	0.108046	0.001615	619.148703	9.255316
15	180	0.014687	68.087390	0.092168	0.001354	738.730255	10.849737
16	192	0.014471	69.103231	0.078624	0.001138	878.912215	12.718830
17	204	0.014292	69.969789	0.067069	0.000959	1043.243434	14.909912
18	216	0.014142	70.709003	0.057213	0.000809	1235.884123	17.478455
19	228	0.014017	71.339585	0.048806	0.000684	1461.711177	20.489482
20	240	0.013913	71.877501	0.041633	0.000579	1726.441638	24.019222
21	252	0.013824	72.336367	0.035515	0.000491	2036.777427	28.157032
22	264	0.013750	72.727801	0.030296	0.000417	2400.575011	33.007667
23	276	0.013687	73.061711	0.025844	0.000354	2827.044294	38.693924
24	288	0.013634	73.346552	0.022046	0.000301	3326.981781	45.359757
25	300	0.013589	73.589534	0.018806	0.000256	3913.043898	53.173919
26	312	0.013551	73.796809	0.016043	0.000217	4600.067404	62.334232
27	324	0.013518	73.973623	0.013685	0.000185	5405.444997	73.072600
28	336	0.013491	74.124454	0.011674	0.000157	6349.565632	85.660875
29	348	0.013467	74.253120	0.009958	0.000134	7456.330682	100.417742
30	360	0.013448	74.362878	0.008495	0.000114	8753.759030	117.716787
31	372	0.013431	74.456506	0.007247	0.000097	10274.696396	137.995952
32	384	0.013416	74.536375	0.006182	0.000083	12057.646856	161.768625
33	396	0.013404	74.604507	0.005273	0.000071	14147.747615	189.636635
34	408	0.013394	74.662626	0.004498	0.000060	16597.911700	222.305489
35	420	0.013385	74.712205	0.003837	0.000051	19470.167508	260.602233
36	432	0.013377	74.754498	0.003273	0.000044	22837.229116	305.496388
37	444	0.013371	74.790576	0.002792	0.000037	26784.337116	358.124495
38	456	0.013365	74.821352	0.002382	0.000032	31411.416562	419.818887
39	468	0.013360	74.847605	0.002032	0.000027	36835.606677	492.141422
40	480	0.013356	74.870000	0.001733	0.000023	43194.226353	576.923018

MONTHLY COMPOUND INTEREST TABLES

17.00% ANNUAL INTEREST RATE   1.4167% MONTHLY EFFECTIVE INTEREST RATE

	1 FUTURE VALUE OF $1	2 FUTURE VALUE ANNUITY OF $1 PER MONTH	3 SINKING FUND FACTOR	4 PRESENT VALUE OF $1 (REVERSION)	5 PRESENT VALUE ANNUITY OF $1 PER MONTH	6 PAYMENT TO AMORTIZE $1	MONTHS
MONTHS							
1	1.014167	1.000000	1.000000	0.986031	0.986031	1.014167	1
2	1.028534	2.014167	0.496483	0.972258	1.958289	0.510650	2
3	1.043105	3.042701	0.328655	0.958676	2.916965	0.342822	3
4	1.057882	4.085806	0.244750	0.945285	3.862250	0.258916	4
5	1.072869	5.143688	0.194413	0.932080	4.794330	0.208580	5
6	1.088068	6.216557	0.160861	0.919060	5.713391	0.175027	6
7	1.103482	7.304625	0.136900	0.906222	6.619613	0.151066	7
8	1.119115	8.408107	0.118933	0.893563	7.513176	0.133100	8
9	1.134969	9.527222	0.104962	0.881081	8.394257	0.119129	9
10	1.151048	10.662191	0.093789	0.868774	9.263031	0.107956	10
11	1.167354	11.813238	0.084651	0.856638	10.119669	0.098817	11
12	1.183892	12.980593	0.077038	0.844672	10.964341	0.091205	12
YEARS							**MONTHS**
1	1.183892	12.980593	0.077038	0.844672	10.964341	0.091205	12
2	1.401600	28.348209	0.035276	0.713471	20.225611	0.049442	24
3	1.659342	46.541802	0.021486	0.602648	28.048345	0.035653	36
4	1.964482	68.081182	0.014688	0.509040	34.655988	0.028855	48
5	2.325733	93.581182	0.010686	0.429972	40.237278	0.024853	60
6	2.753417	123.770579	0.008079	0.363185	44.951636	0.022246	72
7	3.259747	159.511558	0.006269	0.306772	48.933722	0.020436	84
8	3.859188	201.825006	0.004955	0.259122	52.297278	0.019121	96

108	0.018136	55.138379	0.218873	0.003970	251.919548	4.568860	9
120	0.017380	57.538177	0.184876	0.003213	311.226062	5.409036	10
132	0.016788	59.565218	0.156159	0.002622	381.438553	6.403713	11
144	0.016319	61.277403	0.131903	0.002153	464.562540	7.581303	12
156	0.015943	62.723638	0.111415	0.001776	562.972341	8.975441	13
168	0.015638	63.945231	0.094109	0.001472	679.478890	10.625951	14
180	0.015390	64.977077	0.079491	0.001223	817.410030	12.579975	15
192	0.015186	65.848648	0.067144	0.001020	980.705566	14.893329	16
204	0.015018	66.584839	0.056715	0.000852	1174.029800	17.632089	17
216	0.014879	67.206679	0.047905	0.000713	1402.904761	20.874484	18
228	0.014764	67.731930	0.040464	0.000597	1673.867935	24.713129	19
240	0.014668	68.175595	0.034179	0.000501	1994.658995	29.257669	20
252	0.014588	68.550346	0.028870	0.000421	2374.440878	34.637912	21
264	0.014521	68.866887	0.024386	0.000354	2824.061507	41.007538	22
276	0.014465	69.134261	0.020598	0.000298	3356.363651	48.548485	23
288	0.014418	69.360104	0.017399	0.000251	3986.551756	57.476150	24
300	0.014378	69.550868	0.014696	0.000211	4732.626240	68.045538	25
312	0.014345	69.712000	0.012413	0.000178	5615.897651	80.558550	26
324	0.014317	69.848104	0.010485	0.000150	6661.595368	95.372601	27
336	0.014293	69.963067	0.008857	0.000127	7899.588246	112.910833	28
348	0.014273	70.060174	0.007481	0.000107	9365.237774	133.674202	29
360	0.014257	70.142196	0.006319	0.000090	11100.408126	158.255782	30
372	0.014243	70.211479	0.005337	0.000076	13154.661953	187.357711	31
384	0.014231	70.270000	0.004508	0.000064	15586.676066	221.811244	32
396	0.014221	70.319431	0.003808	0.000054	18465.917458	262.600497	33
408	0.014212	70.361184	0.003217	0.000046	21874.627526	310.890557	34
420	0.014205	70.396451	0.002717	0.000039	25910.171179	368.060758	35
432	0.014199	70.426241	0.002295	0.000033	30687.817929	435.744087	36
444	0.014194	70.451403	0.001938	0.000028	36344.034396	515.873821	37
456	0.014190	70.472657	0.001637	0.000023	43040.382285	610.738749	38
468	0.014186	70.490609	0.001383	0.000020	50968.133160	723.048553	39
480	0.014183	70.505773	0.001168	0.000017	60353.731845	856.011201	40

MONTHLY COMPOUND INTEREST TABLES

18.00% ANNUAL INTEREST RATE   1.5000% MONTHLY EFFECTIVE INTEREST RATE

	1 FUTURE VALUE OF $1	2 FUTURE VALUE ANNUITY OF $1 PER MONTH	3 SINKING FUND FACTOR	4 PRESENT VALUE OF $1 (REVERSION)	5 PRESENT VALUE ANNUITY OF $1 PER MONTH	6 PAYMENT TO AMORTIZE $1	
MONTHS							**MONTHS**
1	1.015000	1.000000	1.000000	0.985222	0.985222	1.015000	1
2	1.030225	2.015000	0.496278	0.970662	1.955883	0.511278	2
3	1.045678	3.045225	0.328383	0.956317	2.912200	0.343383	3
4	1.061364	4.090903	0.244445	0.942184	3.854385	0.259445	4
5	1.077284	5.152267	0.194089	0.928260	4.782645	0.209089	5
6	1.093443	6.229551	0.160525	0.914542	5.697187	0.175525	6
7	1.109845	7.322994	0.136556	0.901027	6.598214	0.151556	7
8	1.126493	8.432839	0.118584	0.887711	7.485925	0.133584	8
9	1.143390	9.559332	0.104610	0.874592	8.360517	0.119610	9
10	1.160541	10.702722	0.093434	0.861667	9.222185	0.108434	10
11	1.177949	11.863262	0.084294	0.848933	10.071118	0.099294	11
12	1.195618	13.041211	0.076680	0.836387	10.907505	0.091680	12
YEARS							**MONTHS**
1	1.195618	13.041211	0.076680	0.836387	10.907505	0.091680	12
2	1.429503	28.633521	0.034924	0.699544	20.030405	0.049924	24
3	1.709140	47.275969	0.021152	0.585090	27.660684	0.036152	36
4	2.043478	69.565219	0.014375	0.489362	34.042554	0.029375	48
5	2.443220	96.214652	0.010393	0.409296	39.380269	0.025393	60
6	2.921158	128.077197	0.007808	0.342330	43.844667	0.022808	72
7	3.492590	166.172636	0.006018	0.286321	47.578633	0.021018	84
8	4.175804	211.720235	0.004723	0.239475	50.701675	0.019723	96

MONTHS							YEARS
108	0.018757	53.313749	0.200294	0.003757	266.177777	4.992667	9
120	0.018019	55.498454	0.167523	0.003019	331.288191	5.969323	10
132	0.017444	57.325714	0.140114	0.002444	409.135393	7.137031	11
144	0.016991	58.854011	0.117190	0.001991	502.210922	8.533164	12
156	0.016630	60.132260	0.098016	0.001630	613.493716	10.202406	13
168	0.016340	61.201371	0.081979	0.001340	746.545446	12.198182	14
180	0.016104	62.095562	0.068567	0.001104	905.624513	14.584368	15
192	0.015913	62.843452	0.057348	0.000913	1095.822335	17.437335	16
204	0.015756	63.468978	0.047965	0.000756	1323.226308	20.848395	17
216	0.015627	63.992160	0.040118	0.000627	1595.114630	24.926719	18
228	0.015521	64.429743	0.033554	0.000521	1920.189249	29.802839	19
240	0.015433	64.795732	0.028064	0.000433	2308.854370	35.632816	20
252	0.015361	65.101841	0.023472	0.000361	2773.549452	42.603242	21
264	0.015300	65.357866	0.019632	0.000300	3329.147335	50.937210	22
276	0.015250	65.572002	0.016420	0.000250	3993.430261	60.901454	23
288	0.015209	65.751103	0.013733	0.000209	4787.658998	72.814885	24
300	0.015174	65.900901	0.011486	0.000174	5737.253308	87.058800	25
312	0.015146	66.026190	0.009607	0.000146	6872.605521	104.089083	26
324	0.015122	66.130980	0.008035	0.000122	8230.053258	124.450799	27
336	0.015101	66.218625	0.006721	0.000101	9853.042439	148.795637	28
348	0.015085	66.291930	0.005621	0.000085	11793.517795	177.902767	29
360	0.015071	66.353242	0.004701	0.000071	14113.585393	212.703781	30
372	0.015059	66.404522	0.003932	0.000059	16887.500372	254.312506	31
384	0.015049	66.447412	0.003289	0.000049	20204.043526	304.060653	32
396	0.015041	66.483285	0.002751	0.000041	24169.362788	363.540442	33
408	0.015035	66.513289	0.002301	0.000035	28910.370554	434.655558	34
420	0.015029	66.538383	0.001924	0.000029	34578.805589	519.682084	35
432	0.015024	66.559372	0.001609	0.000024	41356.089521	621.341343	36
444	0.015020	66.576927	0.001346	0.000020	49459.133344	742.887000	37
456	0.015017	66.591609	0.001126	0.000017	59147.279782	888.209197	38
468	0.015014	66.603890	0.000942	0.000014	70730.603711	1061.959056	39
480	0.015012	66.614161	0.000788	0.000012	84579.836287	1269.697544	40

MONTHLY COMPOUND INTEREST TABLES

19.00% ANNUAL INTEREST RATE

1.5833% MONTHLY EFFECTIVE INTEREST RATE

	1 FUTURE VALUE OF $1	2 FUTURE VALUE ANNUITY OF $1 PER MONTH	3 SINKING FUND FACTOR	4 PRESENT VALUE OF $1 (REVERSION)	5 PRESENT VALUE ANNUITY OF $1 PER MONTH	6 PAYMENT TO AMORTIZE $1	MONTHS
MONTHS							
1	1.015833	1.000000	1.000000	0.984413	0.984413	1.015833	1
2	1.031917	2.015833	0.496073	0.969070	1.953483	0.511906	2
3	1.048256	3.047751	0.328111	0.953965	2.907449	0.343944	3
4	1.064853	4.096007	0.244140	0.939096	3.846545	0.259974	4
5	1.081714	5.160860	0.193766	0.924459	4.771004	0.209599	5
6	1.098841	6.242574	0.160190	0.910050	5.681054	0.176024	6
7	1.116239	7.341415	0.136214	0.895865	6.576920	0.152047	7
8	1.133913	8.457654	0.118236	0.881902	7.458822	0.134069	8
9	1.151866	9.591566	0.104258	0.868156	8.326978	0.120092	9
10	1.170104	10.743433	0.093080	0.854625	9.181602	0.108913	10
11	1.188631	11.913537	0.083938	0.841304	10.022906	0.099771	11
12	1.207451	13.102168	0.076323	0.828191	10.851097	0.092157	12
YEARS							**MONTHS**
1	1.207451	13.102168	0.076323	0.828191	10.851097	0.092157	12
2	1.457938	28.922394	0.034575	0.685900	19.837878	0.050409	24
3	1.760389	48.024542	0.020823	0.568056	27.280649	0.036656	36
4	2.125583	71.089450	0.014067	0.470459	33.444684	0.029900	48
5	2.566537	98.939196	0.010107	0.389630	38.549682	0.025941	60
6	3.098968	132.566399	0.007543	0.322688	42.777596	0.023377	72
7	3.741852	173.169599	0.005775	0.267247	46.279115	0.021608	84
8	4.518103	222.195973	0.004501	0.221332	49.179042	0.020334	96

9	5.455388	281.392918	0.003554	0.183305	51.580735	0.019387	108
10	6.587114	352.870328	0.002834	0.151812	53.569796	0.018667	120
11	7.953617	439.175798	0.002277	0.125729	55.217118	0.018110	132
12	9.603603	543.385424	0.001840	0.104128	56.581415	0.017674	144
13	11.595879	669.213441	0.001494	0.086238	57.711314	0.017328	156
14	14.001456	821.144606	0.001218	0.071421	58.647086	0.017051	168
15	16.906072	1004.594042	0.000995	0.059150	59.422084	0.016829	180
16	20.413254	1226.100247	0.000816	0.048988	60.063930	0.016649	192
17	24.648004	1493.558135	0.000670	0.040571	60.595501	0.016503	204
18	29.761257	1816.500430	0.000551	0.033601	61.035743	0.016384	216
19	35.935259	2206.437425	0.000453	0.027828	61.400348	0.016287	228
20	43.390065	2677.267240	0.000374	0.023047	61.702310	0.016207	240
21	52.391377	3245.771169	0.000308	0.019087	61.952393	0.016141	252
22	63.260020	3932.211806	0.000254	0.015808	62.159509	0.016088	264
23	76.383375	4761.055238	0.000210	0.013092	62.331041	0.016043	276
24	92.229182	5761.843068	0.000174	0.010843	62.473102	0.016007	288
25	111.362218	6970.245332	0.000143	0.008980	62.590755	0.015977	300
26	134.464421	8429.331851	0.000119	0.007437	62.688195	0.015952	312
27	162.359199	10191.107326	0.000098	0.006159	62.768894	0.015931	324
28	196.040777	12318.364881	0.000081	0.005101	62.835728	0.015915	336
29	236.709632	14886.924139	0.000067	0.004225	62.891079	0.015901	348
30	285.815282	17988.333579	0.000056	0.003499	62.936920	0.015889	360
31	345.107947	21733.133503	0.000046	0.002898	62.974886	0.015879	372
32	416.700935	26254.795909	0.000038	0.002400	63.006328	0.015871	384
33	503.145960	31714.481694	0.000032	0.001987	63.032369	0.015865	396
34	607.524092	38306.784745	0.000026	0.001646	63.053935	0.015859	408
35	733.555571	46266.667644	0.000022	0.001363	63.071796	0.015855	420
36	885.732406	55877.836195	0.000018	0.001129	63.086589	0.015851	432
37	1069.478478	67482.851256	0.000015	0.000935	63.098840	0.015848	444
38	1291.342856	81495.338274	0.000012	0.000774	63.108986	0.015846	456
39	1559.233220	98414.729710	0.000010	0.000641	63.117389	0.015843	468
40	1882.697708	118844.065787	0.000008	0.000531	63.124348	0.015842	480

APPENDIX C

Online Resources

NOTE: These websites were compiled by and reprinted here with permission of the Indiana University Center for Real Estate Studies as examples of real estate sites that might be used to find information when valuing real estate income property. Websites continuously change and new ones are added. For a more complete and updated list of sites, please visit the website for this book at www.indiana.edu/~cres/books/valuation.htm.

Allen F. Hainge, Discounted Real Estate Software
Allen F. Hainge
www.leading.com/hainge/page4.html

Information about discounted real estate software packages including software for presentation, database, and financial management.

AllRegs Home Page
Mortgage Resource Center, Inc.
www.allregs.com

AllRegs is a comprehensive, accurate, and up-to-date database of residential mortgage lending guidelines. The home page offers a number of free and fee-based services.

ALLTEL Front End Systems and Mortgage Servicing Products
ALLTEL
www.alltelmd.com

Information on software for the mortgage banking industry.

ANSI
American National Standards Institute
www.ansi.org

Site for a private non-profit membership organization including standards-related information on activities and annual reports. Other topics include information on staff and directors of the organization, coming events, news, services, and a reference library.

Apex IV
Apex Software
www.APEXII.com

Information on software for appraisals targeted to fee appraisers, property assessors, and real estate professionals.

Appraisal Institute Home Page
Appraisal Institute, First Realty Advisors, Inc.
www.appraisalinstitute.org/

The Appraisal Institute's home page talks about who they are, what an appraisal is, careers in appraisal, leadership, the AI Forum, and the BBS.

Appraisal Institute of Canada - Courses
Appraisal Institute of Canada
www.aicanada.org/courses.htm

Information about courses, seminars, and workshops offered by the institution including a description of the course, prerequisites, schedules and contact names and phone numbers.

Appraisal Services Group
Shorett, Kidder, Mathews & Segner (KMS)
www.kmsoncor.com

Site for an organization offering appraisal, valuation, and consulting services for several types of properties. It includes an overview of its services, publications, and professional qualifications of the staff.

ARES Development Group
ARES Development Group, LLC
www.aresdg.com

Information on real estate software including product descriptions, access to downloads, download demonstrations, and sample reports.

ARES Home Page
American Real Estate Society
www.aresnet.org

ARES is a society of and for high-level practicing professionals and real estate professors at colleges and universities throughout the United States and the world. The society publishes several journals and newsletters, and was organized to deal with real estate industry research and education concerns.

AREUEA
American Real Estate and Urban Economics Association
www.areuea.org

Site of the real estate academic organization. Contains information about the organization and its journal: *Real Estate Economics*.

ARGUS Financial Software
ARGUS Financial Software
www.argussoftware.com

Research tool for analysis, valuations, due diligence, asset management, and budgeting.

Arthur Andersen Real Estate Services Group
Arthur Andersen
www.arthurandersen.com/bus_info/industry/resg/

Home page of the consulting firm including information about their real estate accounting and business advisory services and real estate valuation services. It also includes articles and links on location, development, investment, corporate real estate, strategic planning, hospitality and leisure issues, and industry trends.

AST
Advanced Software Technology
www.astsoft.com

Information on practice management software related to health care, real estate, and law. Real estate-related software includes property management, real estate sales, and lease management software.

ATS Training Services
ATS Training Services
www.atstraining.com

Information on the training offered on the fields of Real Estate Appraisal, Paralegal, Home Inspection, and Environmental Assessment including program description, number of hours and contact names and addresses.

Bank of America Home Page
BankAmerica Corporation
www.bankamerica.com

This website offers links to information that might be of interest to real estate professionals.

Bexar Appraisal District
Bexar Appraisal District
www.bcad.org

Site for a national appraisal organization. It includes property search and site index links.

Black's Guide
Black's Guide
www.blacksguide.com

Directory for commercial real estate services. Provides links to real estate associations.

BOMA International Home Page
Building Owners and Managers Association International
www.boma.org/

BOMA's home page offers numerous links on a variety of subjects, including BOMA information, joining BOMA, meetings and education, links, and government affairs.

BOMI Institute Home Page
BOMI Institute
www.bomi-edu.org/

BOMI Institute's home page details extensive offerings for educational opportunities within the commercial property industry.

Bureau of Economic Analysis Home Page
Bureau of Economic Analysis, U.S. Department of Commerce
www.bea.doc.gov

BEA is the nation's economic accountant, preparing estimates that illuminate key national, international, and regional aspects of the U.S. economy. The site provides this information, as well as news releases and BEA publications information.

Bureau of Labor Statistics
U.S. Department of Labor
http://stats.bls.gov/blshome.html

The site provides data, surveys and programs, publications and research papers, as well as links to other statistical sites.

CCIM Commercial Real Estate Network
Commercial Investment Real Estate Institute
www.ccim.com

A service of the Commercial Investment Real Estate Institute (CIREI), an affiliate member of the National Association of REALTORS®; it seeks to provide education opportunities in commercial investment real estate.

Chief Architect
Advanced Relational Technology
www.chiefarch.com

Information about architectural software for home design, plan creation, and 3D viewing of designs. It includes sales information and links to a technical support area.

CLR: Multifamily Property Management Software From Rent Roll
Rent Roll Inc.
www.clr.com/rentroll

RentRoll provides on-site multifamily property management software for property owners, fee managers, institutional investors, and REITs. Software includes accounting, executive information systems, applicant screening, affordable housing, budgeting, communications, facilities management, and property management.

CommCepts International
CommCepts International
www.commcepts.com

Provides education for real estate and mortgage lending through live seminars, computer based training, and web–based training for real estate counseling, mortgage loan origination, and the exchange of real estate.

CRES
IU Center for Real Estate Studies
http://www.indiana.edu/~cres

Contains information about the IU Center for Real Estate Studies, as well as links to many other valuable real estate sites.

DDT Table of Contents Page
Digital Data Technologies
www.MLS-INTERNET.com/toc.htm

Real estate links site.

Duke Realty Investments, Inc. Home Page
Duke Realty Investments, Inc.
www.dukereit.com

Duke Realty is a fully-integrated real estate company that owns interests in a diversified portfolio of industrial, office and retail properties across the Midwest. As one of the region's largest real estate companies, Duke provides leasing, property and asset management, acquisition, development, construction, build-to-suit and other related services.

Elliptus Software Solutions, Inc.
Elliptus Software Solutions, Inc.
www.gendata.com

Elliptus is a software development company that provides solutions for the title insurance industry and software for EDI transactions.

Ernst & Young - Real Estate Group
Ernst & Young
www.ey.com/realestate/

Site of the E&Y Kenneth Leventhal (EYKL) Real Estate Group including information about their audit, tax, real estate and hospitality services. It includes links to daily real estate and technology news, as well as, to websites of real estate trade associations and professional societies.

FAQ - Real Estate Appraisal
All Area Appraisal Ltd.
quickval.com/reafaq.htm

List of frequently asked questions related to real estate appraisals. It provides information about qualifications of appraisers and services provided by them, certification, and definitions of industry terms.

Federal Deposit Insurance Corporation
Federal Deposit Insurance Corporation--U.S. Government
www.fdic.gov

Banking news, public information, laws and regulations, consumer news, and asset sales information.

FedWorld Information Network Home Page
National Technical Information Service
www.fedworld.gov

The FedWorld Information Network page provides several search engines in various directories. It also provides substantial information and links to government information as well as a federal job listing service.

Geographic Information Systems - GIS
U.S. Geological Survey
http://info.er.usgs.gov/research/gis

Geographic information systems technology can be used for scientific investigations, resource management, and development planning. The site is information based for this technology.

Global Center
Global Center
www.globalcenter.net/

Company site including information about their Web publishing services and digital distribution solutions that ensure that Internet content is always on-line and easily accessible to internet users and website design services.

Glossary for WWW and NCSA Mosaic
The National Center for Supercomputing Applications - University of Illinois at Urbana-Champaign
www.ncsa.uiuc.edu/SDG/Software/Mosaic/Glossary/GlossaryDL.html

Glossary for the users of the Mosaic Software developed by the National Center for Supercomputing Applications and the World Wide Web in general. Includes definitions of terms such as anchor, browser, client, server, etc.

Government Information Sharing Project
Oregon State University
http://govinfo.kerr.orst.edu

Database providing demographic, education, and economic information, as well as links to other government websites.

Grubb & Ellis Home Page
Grub & Ellis Company
www.grubb-ellis.com

Grubb & Ellis is one of the nation's largest publicly traded commercial real estate services firms with over 4000 professionals and staff. Grubb & Ellis Company provides transaction services, management services, financial services, and strategic services to clients worldwide.

HCAD
Harris County Appraisal District
www.hcad.org

Site for a national appraisal organization. It includes general information and a search of property records by address, name, or account number.

Hillsborough County Property Appraiser
Hillsborough County Property Appraiser
www.propappr.co.hillsborough.fl.us

Site for a national appraisal organization based in Florida. It includes a search engine for its real estate database and links to related sites.

HomeNet Glossary of Real Estate Terms
Net Properties Corporation
www.homenet.com/gif/aditerms.html

Glossary of real estate terms.

HUD's Homes and Communities Home Page
U.S. Department of Housing and Urban Development
www.hud.gov

HUD's home page designed to "help people find homes and to help our Nation's communities develop and thrive." Visitors to the site can see consumer alerts, information on finding homes, and ways to become involved in their community.

Innkeepers Home Page
Innkeepers USA Trust
www.innkeepersusa.com

The page includes links to Inkeepers' hotels, stock quotes, SEC filings, press releases, and shareholder reports.

International Council of Shopping Centers Home Page
International Council of Shopping Centers
www.icsc.org/index.html

This is ICSC's home page. The site offers links to products and services, leasing opportunities, publications, forums, current news stories, and professional development.

Irvine Apartment Communities - Investments
Irvine Apartment Communities
www.iac-inv.com

Irvine Apartment Communities is an owner and operator of apartment communities on Southern California's world renowned Irvine Ranch. At this site you will find information about IAC, a publicly traded real estate investment trust traded on the New York and Pacific Stock Exchanges.

Korpacz Real Estate Source Directory
The Korpacz Company, Inc.
http://directory.korpacz.com

This directory is a database of original articles, descriptive information on data products and services, local government publications, productivity tools, books, and Internet resources for the real estate industry.

Marshall & Swift
Marshall & Swift, L.P.
www.marshallswift.com

The Marshall & Swift catalog provides building cost data, stand-alone software products, online services, and a reference library. It also provides an opportunity to acquire an array of real estate publications.

MBA of America Web Site
Mortgage Bankers Association of America
www.mbaa.org

MBA of America's website offers an array of services for its members, as well as numerous up-to-date additions of news for the public.

Meditrust Home Page
Meditrust
www.reit.com

This is Meditrust's home page (NYSE: MT), the nation's largest health care real estate investment trust REIT.

Michigan Environmental Law
Fink Zausmer
www.lawsite.com

Site for information regarding environmental law and regulation related to redevelopment of contaminated sites. It includes links to statutes, selected rules, guidance and model documents related to Michigan Environmental Law.

Mortgage Electronic Registration System, Inc. Home Page
Mortgage Electronic Registration System, Inc.
www.mersinc.org/

MERS, Inc.'s purpose is to enhance the efficiency of the real estate finance industry through electronic registration and tracking of mortgage ownership rights. This page provides greater detail on MERS services.

Municipal Code Corporation Home Page
Municipal Code Corporation
www.municode.com

Home page gives access to municipal codes, municipal list services, codification services, and more.

NAHB Home Page
National Association of Home Builders
www.nahb.com

Among other things, this page offers a daily news report, consumer and builder information, facts and figures, as well as information about the NAHB.

NAIOP Home Page
National Association of Industrial Office Properties
www.naiop.org

NAIOP is the national trade association for developers, owners, investors and managers of commercial real estate in the United States and Canada. The site gives information about seminars, conferences and awards, publications, government affairs, as well as chapter information.

NAREIT - Frequently Asked Questions
National Association of Real Estate Investment Trusts, Inc.
www.nareit.com/faqs.html

This page answers fundamental questions about REITs and is designed for investors, financial planners, stock brokers, the media, and the general public.

NAREIT - Research and Statistics
National Association of Real Estate Investment Trusts, Inc.
www.nareit.com/nareitrc.html

This is NAREIT's home page; it provides a good deal of information about its services and activities.

National Multi Housing Council Home Page
National Multi Housing Council
www.nmhc.inter.net/

This is NMHC's home page; it provides leadership for the apartment industry on legislative and regulatory matters, and promotes research and the exchange of information to enhance quality, and affordable apartment living.

NCREIF
National Council of Real Estate Investment Fiduciaries
http://www.ncreif.com

Information about the National Council of Real Estate Investment Fiduciaries (NCREIF), an association of institutional real estate professionals who share a common interest in their industry. Includes information about the NCREIF property index.

PikeNet Enhanced Links
PikeNet
www.pikenet.com/advertising/enhanced.html

Information about Enhanced Links, an offer of PikeNet to improve a company's link position on a Web site and display it toward the top of the page in bold type. The link would be ahead of other links that are not enhanced in order to make it more visible to the visitor, at a cost which depends on the number of market areas and categories.

PikeNet Question: How to Find Duff & Phelps, S&P and Moody's bond ratings.
PikeNet Directory of Commercial Real Estate
www.pikenet.com

Gives instructions on how to find Duff & Phelps, S&P and Moody's bond ratings.

PikeNet Question: Where to find information on synthetic leases at EYKL's site.
PikeNet Directory of Commercial Real Estate
www.pikenet.com

Gives instructions on how to find information on synthetic leases at EYKL's site.

PikeNet Question: Where to Find the CPI
PikeNet Directory of Commercial Real Estate
www.pikenet.com

Gives instructions on how to find the CPI (Consumer Price Index).

PikeNet Questions
National Facilities Group, Inc.
www.pikenet.com

Directory of commercial real estate and information on local tax and assessment records, finding property information and property tax rates.

Pinellas County Property Appraiser
Pinellas County Property Appraiser
pao.co.pinellas.fl.us

Site for a national appraisal organization, including information about services provided, how properties are valued, and taxing authorities. It also includes a searchable property database, frequently asked questions, and a glossary of terms.

REAL Estate Analysis Software
Roger Martin Company
www.teleport.com/~jrmartin/

Software for the financial analysis of investment real estate. Over 40 applications: rental survey, lease analysis, operating statements, cash flow analysis showing return rates "as if" sold each year, exchange structuring, installment sales, loan schedules and evaluations, and more.

Real Estate Appraisal Program
Bentley College
www.bentley.edu/admissions/dce/REALEST/reapp/REApp.htm

Site of the Real Estate Appraisal Program offered by Bentley College in coopera-
tion with the Massachusetts Board of Real Estate Appraisers. It includes links to
information about course offerings, faculty, course schedules, descriptions and
registration.

Real Estate Dictionary
Craig E. Buck, Attorney At Law
www.mortgageonline.com/html/terms.html

Real estate dictionary published by Mr. Buck.

Real Estate Software
Real Estate Center - Texas A & M University
recenter.tamu.edu/links/clresw.htm

List of links to information about varied real estate-related software.

Real Estate Software by RealData: Home Page
RealData, Inc.
www.realdata-inc.com

RealData's website for their real estate software and publications.

RECGA
Real Estate Counseling Group of America
http://www.recga.com

Site for a national appraisal organization.

Recommended Web Sites
Real Estate Information Work Group and Multi-Family Information Work Group
www.reiwg.com

Real estate and mortgage lending information and links to websites of councils and
associations which provide further information on standards, mortgage lending,
events, and publications.

REITNet
Evaluation Consultants, Inc.
www.reitnet.com

Information about REITs, including links to other REITs and a powerful search
engine to find articles about REITs and other real estate articles from over 15,000
articles in over 15 journals.

Storage Trust Realty Home Page
Storage Trust Realty
www.storagetrust.com

This page provides links to Storage Trust Realty information, such as its corporate profile, recent press releases, and annual reports.

Tanger Factory Outlet Centers Home Page
Tanger Outlet Centers
www.tangeroutlet.com

Tanger's home page provides links to its center locations, brand names, financial information, and more.

Texas Real Estate Commission License Requirements
Texas Real Estate Commission
www.sunscape.com/capital/license.html

Information about the requirements of the Texas Appraiser Licensing and Certification Board for obtaining licenses and recertifications for Salesman, Broker, Real Estate Inspector, Certified General Real Estate Appraiser, State Licensed Real Estate Appraiser and Appraiser Trainee.

The Appraisers Toolbox
Bradford and Robbins
www.AppraisersToolBox.com

Appraisal assistance site. Provides a number of its own software products to assist in the appraisal process, as well as provides links to several other appraisal sites.

The Complete Real Estate Software Catalog
Multimedia Ink Designs
www.mmink.com/realestate

Catalog for all types of real estate software (i.e., appraisal, building, legal, etc.).

The Counselors of Real Estate Home Page
National Association of REALTORS®
www.cre.org

CRE is an international group of seasoned real estate practitioners who provide advisory services to clients on property and land-related matters. This home page goes into greater depth describing their activities and services.

The Institute of Real Estate Management Home Page
Institute of Real Estate Management
www.irem.Inter.net

This page lists IREM courses, publications, designations, news, directories, links, and information about upcoming meetings and conventions.

U.S. Census Bureau Home Page
U.S. Census Bureau
www.census.gov

Census Bureau home page gives readers access to news, access tools, a variety of subjects, and a search engine.

U.S. Department of Labor
U.S. Department of Labor
www.dol.gov

Department of Labor home page has site links to minimum wage, divorce & pensions, pension search, welfare to work, America's job bank, as well as information about the Department itself.

U.S. Environmental Protection Agency's Homepage
U.S. E.P.A.
www.epa.gov

EPA homepage gives information access about the EPA, its laws and regulations, databases and software, projects and programs, and a local search drive.

Urban Land Institute Homepage
The Urban Land Institute
www.uli.org/homepage.cfm

This page offers information on ULI's many services, publications, and other links.

WEFA
WEFA, a subsidiary of Primark Corporation
www.wefa.com

WEFA's home page describes the company, and specializes in economic and business analysis for businesses around the world.

Wilshire Associates Incorporated
Wilshire Associates Incorporated
www.wilshire.com

The site offers information about Wilshire, who provides financial information services for institutional investors.

Glossary of Terms and Symbols

a. The symbol for *annualizer* in the general formula for a capitalization rate: $R = Y - \Delta a$.

absolute net lease. A lease in which the tenant pays all operating expenses usually with the exception of management fees.

absorption period. An estimate of the total time period over which a property can be successfully sold, leased, put into use or traded in its market area at prevailing prices or rentals.

access. A path of entry to a property or the physical and legal means of entrance. Most property owners have a right to access to their property from a public street that includes the right to unimpeded flow of light and air. Landlords also have rights to access a rented property under reasonable conditions.

accrued depreciation. The total deduction from cost new due to physical deterioration, functional obsolescence and/or external obsolescence. Accrued depreciation represents the total difference between an improvement's reproduction cost or replacement cost and its contributing value in the cost approach.

accumulated depreciation. The sum of the annual depreciation deductions taken by the investor to reduce taxable income.

accumulation of $1 per period. *See* future value annuity of $1 per period.

active income. Salaries, wages or fees for services and income from a trade or business in which the investor materially participates, by being involved in the operations of the activity on a regular, continuous and substantial basis. Rental real estate is *not* usually considered active income even if the investor materially participates in its operation.

adjustable rate mortgage (ARM). A mortgage loan in which the interest rate is adjusted periodically based on a specified index or formula. ARMs may include a limit on the amount that the interest rate can rise or fall in a given year as well as a limit on the total amount the rate can rise or fall over the life of the loan. Adjustable rate mortgages often have an initial interest rate that is lower than fixed rate mortgages because the risk of interest rate change is partially borne by the borrower with an adjustable rate loan. *See also* fixed rate mortgage.

adjusted basis. The original cost or purchase price of an investment (including land and improvements) plus any capital improvements made to the property less any accumulated depreciation taken to date. *See also* capital gain, accumulated depreciation.

adjusted internal rate of return (AIRR). An internal rate of return analysis in which different reinvestment and discount rates for both positive and negative cash flows have been specified. The adjusted internal rate applies a "safe rate" to all negative cash flows, discounts them to time period zero and adds them to the initial investment. The safe rate is the rate that could be earned on the funds until needed to cover negative cash flows. A market rate is applied to all positive cash flows, which are carried forward to the end of the investment holding period. The market rate is the rate that can be earned by investing the positive cash flows in other investments. The AIRR equals the internal rate of return (IRR) that equates the present value figure to the future value figure. The AIRR is usually less than the IRR for the same property because funds are assumed to be reinvested at a lower rate. Also called the modified internal rate of return. *See also* financial management rate of return, internal rate of return.

adjusted sales price. The estimated sales price of a comparable property after additions and/or subtractions have been made to the actual sales price to allow for differences between the comparable and the subject property transaction. This is what the comparable would have sold for if it had possessed all the characteristics of the subject property as of the effective date of the appraisal. *See also* adjustments, sales adjustment grid, direct sales comparison approach.

adjustments. The value changes added to or subtracted from the sales price of a comparable property to arrive at an indicated value for the property being appraised (subject property). Adjustments may be made by percentage changes or by specific dollar amounts. Real estate elements of comparison that are used to adjust the sales price of the comparable property include property rights, financing terms, conditions of sale, market conditions, location and physical characteristics. *See*

also direct sales comparison approach, percentage adjustments, sales adjustment grid.

administrative expenses. The expenses incurred in directing or conducting a business (including the construction process), as distinguished from the expense of manufacturing, selling and financing. The items included depend on the nature of the business, but usually encompass items such as salaries of officers, rent of offices, or office and general expenses. Also called general and administrative expenses or overhead expenses.

after-tax cash flow (ATCF). The cash flow (either from operations or at resale) that remains from net operating income and net resale proceeds after deduction for annual debt service, loan repayment and all ordinary income taxes applicable to each period. *See also* before-tax cash flow, debt service, net operating income, tax liability, taxable income.

after-tax equity yield rate. The annualized rate of return that discounts all expected after-tax cash flows (from operations and resale) to a present value equal to the original equity investment in the property. It represents the internal rate of return on equity after taxes. *See also* before-tax equity yield rate, equity yield rate.

after-tax IRR. *See* after-tax equity yield rate.

age-life approach. *See* economic age-life method.

Akerson format. An alternative way of writing the Ellwood formula; a series of calculations used to find an overall rate that is based on the mortgage equity analysis concept that allows for cash flow forecasts including the impact of financing. The process allows for a direct solution for value even though the loan amount is entered as a percentage of value, and any change in value (either appreciation or depreciation) may be entered as a percentage of value. *See also* Ellwood formula.

allocation. The division of the value of a property between land and improvements; an appraisal method in which the land value is found by deducting the value of improvements from the overall sales price of the property. The value of the improvements may be established by developing a typical ratio of site value to total property value and applying this ratio to the property to be appraised. Allocation is most frequently used in appraisals of vacant lots in which comparable sales of vacant lots cannot be found and improved sites must be used as comparables, e.g., in urban areas where few vacant lots exist or in rural areas where few sales exist. Also called abstraction or extraction method. *See also* land.

allowance for replacements. A noncash expense item included in many forecasted income and expense statements to compensate for the future replacement of building components that may wear out in the future, such as a new roof or replacement of heating, ventilation and air-conditioning (HVAC) equipment. The annual allowance for reserves should reflect the amount that must be set aside each year to have the funds required to replace the item at the time it must be replaced. Also called an allowance for reserves or a reserve for replacement.

amortization. (1) The process of retiring a debt through repayment of principal. It occurs when the payment on the debt exceeds the required interest payment for a particular time period. (2) Annual deductions allowed in the calculation of federal income taxes. For example, points paid on a loan on income property are amortized over the loan term.

amortization schedule. A table that shows the allocation of payments for principal and interest on a debt. Also referred to as a loan schedule. *See also* amortization.

amortization term. The length of time over which the periodic principal repayments are made to pay off a loan in its entirety. *See also* amortization, amortization schedule.

amount of $1 at compound interest. *See* future value of $1.

annualizer (a). A factor used in yield capitalization formulas to convert the total change in property value over a time period

to an annual rate of change; the value of (*a*) varies depending on the pattern of income flow. *See* yield capitalization formulas, sinking fund factor.

annuity in advance. A series of payments that occur at the beginning of each period. Also called an annuity due. *See also* ordinary annuity.

anticipation. The appraisal principle that states that value is created by the expectation of benefits to be received in the future.

appraisal. According to the Uniform Standards of Professional Appraisal Practice, (1) The act or process of estimating value; an estimate of value. (2) Pertains to appraising and related functions, e.g., appraisal practice, appraisal services. *See also* direct sales comparison approach, income capitalization approach, cost approach.

appraisal report. *See* report.

as if vacant. *See* highest and best use.

as improved. *See* highest and best use.

assessed value. The value or worth of a property according to tax rolls on which ad valorem taxes are based. *See also* property tax.

assumability. *See* assumable mortgage.

assumable mortgage. A mortgage that does not require approval from the lender to be transferred to a third party. The sales price of a property purchased with an assumable mortgage will probably have to be adjusted for the effects of financing. A property purchased with a below-market assumable mortgage will most likely sell at a higher price because of the lower mortgage payments assumed. *See also* mortgage.

assumptions. Specifications in an appraisal report that restrict the value estimate to be true only under certain conditions, e.g., no hazardous waste on the property. *See also* limiting conditions.

ATCF. *See* after-tax cash flow.

balance. The appraisal principle that states that property value is created and maintained when contrasting, opposing or interacting elements are in a state of equilibrium.

balloon payment. The remaining balance that is due at the end of a balloon mortgage. The final or balloon payment is substantially larger than the previous periodic payments. A balloon payment is necessary in mortgages in which the periodic payment does not fully amortize the principal balance over the life of the loan. Also called lump-sum payment.

band-of-investment technique. A method of estimating either overall capitalization rates or overall discount rates by calculating the weighted average of capitalization or discount rates for various components that make up a total property investment. *See also* debt coverage ratio, direct capitalization, income capitalization approach, overall capitalization rate, discount rate.

base rent. The minimum rent stipulated in a lease. It is typically associated with leases that also allow for overage rent. *See also* overage rent.

before-tax cash flow (BTCF). Income that remains from net operating income (NOI) after debt service is paid but before ordinary income tax on operations is deducted. Also called equity dividend or pre-tax cash flow. *See also* after-tax cash flow (ATCF), net operating income (NOI).

before-tax equity yield rate. The annualized rate of return that discounts all expected before-tax cash flows (either from operations or at resale) to a present value equal to the original equity investment in the property. It represents the internal rate of return on equity before taxes. *See also* after-tax equity yield rate, equity yield rate.

below-market interest rate. An interest rate typically associated with a mortgage that is below the current market rate (assuming the same amortization terms). The loan in this case would offer a benefit.

beneficial loan. A loan that contains favorable terms for the borrower compared to a typical loan for a particular property type. A beneficial loan may have a below-market interest rate, longer amortization term, assumability at resale or a higher loan-to-value ratio than a typical loan.

book value. The capital amount at which property is carried on the books of a company. It usually equals the original cost less reserves for depreciation plus any additions to capital. *See also* adjusted basis.

breakdown method. A method of estimating accrued depreciation by which each cause of depreciation is analyzed and measured separately. (The five causes measured include curable physical depreciation, incurable physical depreciation, curable functional obsolescence, incurable functional obsolescence and external obsolescence). The different types of depreciation are then summed to find the total depreciation. *See also* accrued depreciation, curable physical depreciation, incurable physical depreciation, curable functional obsolescence, incurable functional obsolescence and external obsolescence.

building capitalization rate (R_B). The capitalization rate that reflects the ratio of annual building income divided by the building value. Historically, the building capitalization rate was used to estimate building value in the building and land residual techniques. *See also* band-of-investment technique, building residual technique, land residual technique.

building cost. The estimated funds required to construct a building. Common methods of estimating building cost include the comparative unit-method, unit-in place-method and quantity survey method. *See also* direct costs, indirect costs, replacement cost, reproduction cost.

building permit. A document given to builders after a reviewing process that ensures adherence to zoning restrictions, compliance with building codes and adequate access to public facilities.

building residual technique. A method used to find total property value where the income attributable to the land is deducted from net operating income and the remainder is divided by the building capitalization rate to arrive at an estimate of the building value. The building value is then added to the land value to arrive at an estimate of the total property value. This appraisal method reflects buyer concerns and actions prior to the 1970s. *See also* residual techniques.

buildup method. A method of developing a discount rate whereby a riskless rate is used and then increased to adjust for types of risk such as management, financial and nonliquidity risks that are inherent in the property being analyzed. *See also* discount rate.

bundle of rights. An ownership concept that describes real property by the legal rights associated with owning the property. It specifies rights such as the rights to sell, lease, use, occupy, mortgage and trade the property, among others. These rights are typically purchased by the buyer in a sales transaction unless specifically noted or limited in the sale.

business value. The value resulting from business organization including such things as management skills, assembled work force, working capital, trade names, franchises, patents, trademarks, contracts, leases and operating agreements. Business value is an intangible asset that is distinct from the real property and tangible personal property. It is also referred to as enterprise value or business enterprise value. *See also* going-concern value.

capital gain. The amount of taxable gain that results from sale or disposition of an investment. A capital gain results from the sale of real estate if the net sale proceeds is greater than the property's adjusted basis. *See also* capital loss, adjusted basis.

capital loss. The amount of taxable loss that results from sale or disposition of an investment. A capital gain results from the sale of real estate if the net sale proceeds is less than the property's adjusted basis. *See also* capital gain, adjusted basis.

capital market. The market in which long-term or intermediate-term money instruments are traded by buyers and sellers.

capitalization. Any process of converting income into an estimate of value. *See also* capitalization rate, direct capitalization, ground rent capitalization, income

capitalization approach, yield capitalization, yield capitalization formulas.

capitalization in perpetuity. A capitalization procedure used to determine the value of a project in which an endless time period is considered. It provides for a return *on* investment, but not a return *of* investment.

capitalization of ground rental. *See* ground rent capitalization.

capitalization rate. A ratio that represents the relationship between a particular year's cash flow and the present value or the interest applicable to the cash flow. It is usually assumed to be an overall capitalization rate unless stated otherwise. In appraisal, the term is typically preceded by a description that identifies the applicable interest. For example, the capitalization rate found by dividing first-year net operating income by the overall property value is called the overall capitalization rate. Also called cap rate. *See also* building capitalization rate, equity capitalization rate, going-in capitalization rate, land capitalization rate, terminal capitalization rate, direct capitalization, yield capitalization, band-of-investment technique, mortgage capitalization rate.

capital market risk. Uncertainty due to changes in the market for debt or equity capital used to finance real estate investments.

cash equivalency adjustment. An adjustment made to a comparable sale that was financed in a manner atypical of the market. The adjustment eliminates the amount of the premium paid for beneficial financing. Once the adjustment is made, the adjusted sales price should reflect the price that would have been paid assuming financing typical of the market was used. The adjustment can be made through either the income capitalization approach or the direct sales comparison approach. *See also* direct sales comparison approach.

cash equivalent. A price expressed in terms of cash as distinguished from a price that is expressed all or partly in terms of the face or nominal amount of notes or other debt securities that cannot be sold on the market at their face amount. *See also* cash equivalency adjustment.

cash flow. The periodic income or loss arising from the operation and ultimate resale of an income-producing property. The cash flow could further be classified as either before-tax or after-tax cash flow and could also reflect the impact of financing. *See also* before-tax cash flow, after-tax cash flow, net operating income.

cash-flow ratio. *See* capitalization rate.

cash throw-off. *See* cash flow.

ceiling. Covering that may be attached directly to the floor above or may be placed in a suspension system. The covering may be made out of various materials, including fiber, wood, plaster, metal, etc.

certification. In an appraisal report, a certification of value that is signed, sealed and dated by the appraiser stating that the appraiser has personally conducted the appraisal in an unbiased and professional manner and that all assumptions and limiting conditions are set forth in the report.

change. An appraisal principle that recognizes the fact that a property and its environment are always in transition and are affected by economic and social forces that are constantly at work.

collection loss. Income that is lost when payment is not collected from tenants.

common areas. Land or building areas that are mutually used by and benefit all tenants or owners, including areas such as halls, elevators and playgrounds. Frequently found in condominiums and shopping centers.

comparable sales. *See* comparables.

comparables. Properties that have been recently sold or leased and are similar to a subject property. Sales prices of these properties are used to estimate a value for the subject property. Comparable properties need not be identical to the subject but should be similar and relatively easy to adjust for differences in order to arrive at an indicated value for the subject after adjustment. Also called comparable sales, comparable properties, comps. *See also* direct sales comparison approach.

comparative-unit method. A method used to estimate the cost of a building based on the values of comparable properties that were recently constructed and adjusted for time and physical differences. The total value is based on the sum of the value per square or cubic foot. Values may also be determined through a recognized cost service. *See also* building cost.

compound interest. Continuous and systematic additions to a principal sum over a series of time periods. The additions are based on a specific periodic interest rate with additions based on the total prior accumulation of interest and principal. *See also* amortization schedule, simple interest.

compound interest factor. *See* future value of $1.

condemnation. The exercise of the power of eminent domain by the government, i.e., the right of the government to take private property for public use. *See also* eminent domain, just compensation.

condition of sale. An element of comparison in the direct sales comparison approach that refers to the motivations of the buyer and seller in a sales transaction. Examples include the relationship between buyer and seller, financial needs of buyer and seller (a "quick" sale) and lack of exposure on the market. *See also* direct sales comparison approach.

conformity. An appraisal principle that states that the more a property is in harmony with its surroundings, the greater the contributory value.

consumer price index (CPI). A series of numbers released by the Bureau of Labor Statistics of the federal Department of Labor that represents the change in price levels of a predetermined mix of consumer goods and services. The CPI is often used to adjust rental payments in leases.

contract rent. The actual rental payment specified in a lease. Contract rent may be greater than, less than or equal to economic rent (market rent).

contractor's profit. The profit, above and beyond all construction costs, generally expressed as a percentage of direct construction costs, that is adequate to compensate a contractor for the time and effort required to construct an improvement; a component of direct costs in comparison to the developer's profit that is not part of direct costs.

contribution. An appraisal concept that states that the value of a particular component is equal to the amount it contributes to the property as a whole. The value of the component is not measured as its cost, but by the amount that its absence would detract from the entire property value.

conversion. The process of changing an income-producing property into another use.

cost. *See* building cost.

cost approach. One of the three traditional appraisal approaches to estimating value. In this approach, value is based on adding the contributing value of any improvements (after deduction for accrued depreciation) to the value of the land as if it were vacant, based on its highest and best use. If the interest appraised is other than fee simple, additional adjustments may be necessary for nonrealty interest and/or the impact of existing leases or contracts. *See also* appraisal, building cost, replacement cost, reproduction cost.

cost-benefit study. An analysis of the cost of creating an improvement versus the benefits that will be created by the improvement, including nonmonetary issues. A cost-benefit study is typically used by public agencies to make decisions concerning capital improvements.

curable functional obsolescence. A loss in value due to a defect in design, in which the cost to cure the item is less than or the same as the anticipated increase in value after the item is cured, e.g., flaws in materials or design or materials and design that have become obsolete over time. An element of accrued depreciation. Includes deficiencies requiring additions, substitutions or modernization and superadequacies.

curable physical depreciation. Items of deferred maintenance or in need of repair in which the cost to repair is reasonable and economically feasible, measured as the cost to restore the item to new or reasonably new condition. *See also* accrued depreciation.

curvilinear income pattern. An income pattern that is derived mathematically using compound interest factors. It is the income pattern implied by the use of a J factor to stabilize income. *See also* income stabilization factor, j factor.

date of agreement. Refers to the key dates in the negotiation of a lease. A key consideration in estimating the income to be collected under a lease. The key dates are the date of execution of the lease, the date the rental payments begin, the date the lease expires, the date of any renewal options and the date of notice.

debt coverage ratio (DCR). The ratio of annual net operating income (NOI) divided by the annual debt service. Lenders usually specify a minimum DCR (e.g., 1.2) that they require the property to meet during the first year of a loan term.

debt financing. The use of borrowed funds to acquire a capital investment, as opposed to investing one's own funds. In real estate, the property itself usually serves as the security for the debt.

debt service. The periodic payment specified in a loan contract that covers the repayment needed to amortize the outstanding debt. *See also* amortization.

deferred maintenance. Items that are in need of repair because upkeep and repairs have been delayed, the result of which is physical depreciation or loss in value of a building; a type of physical depreciation that is usually curable. *See* curable physical depreciation.

deficiency. An inadequate feature in a structure or one of its components. *See* functional obsolescence.

demographic characteristics. *See* demographic data.

demographic data. Information about the human population, especially in reference to changes in size, density, distribution and characteristics of the population in a specific area.

depreciation. The loss in property value due to age, wear and tear, any negative functional superadequacy or deficiencies and/or external forces. Also called cost recovery. *See also* accrued depreciation.

depreciation allowance. The amount of tax depreciation that is allowed by federal income tax law to be deducted as an expense in the calculation of taxable income. This is *not* related to any loss in property value due to physical depreciation, functional obsolescence or economic osbolescence.

development approach. A method of valuing residential, industrial or recreational land to be used for subdivision development. The analysis is typically used in feasibility studies and when comparable sales are scarce. The value of the land is estimated as the present value of the net cash flows considering absorption rates, development period and estimated sales prices of individual lots.

direct capitalization. The capitalization method whereby forecasted first-year net operating income is divided by an estimated overall capitalization rate in order to arrive at a value estimate for the total property. *See also* income capitalization approach, yield capitalization.

direct costs. Expenditures necessary for the labor and materials used in the construction of a new improvement, including contractor's overhead and profit. Also called hard costs. *See also* indirect costs.

direct sales comparison approach. *See* sales comparison approach.

discount rate. A general term representing a compound interest rate used to convert expected future cash flow into a present value estimate. In appraisal practice, the discount rate is the competitive rate of return applicable to the interest and cash flows analyzed and is identified by adding a descriptor to the rate. For example, the mortgage interest rate is the mortgage discount rate. *See also* yield rate.

discounted cash-flow analysis (DCF). In appraisal, any method whereby an appraiser prepares a cash-flow forecast (including income from operations and resale) for the interests appraised, selects a discount rate that reflects the return expected for the interest and uses the rate to calculate the present value of each of the cash-flows. The total present value of the cash becomes the value estimate for that interest. Sometimes the cash-flow forecast is based on an assumed pattern of change, e.g., compound growth. Also referred to as discounted cash flow. *See also* income capitalization approach, internal rate of return, net present value, present value, profitability index, yield capitalization.

discounting. The process of converting future income to a present value by mathematically reducing future cash flow by the implied interest that would have been earned assuming an initial investment, an interest rate and a specified period (possibly divided into shorter equal periodic increments). *See also* future value, income capitalization approach, present value.

disposition costs. The costs associated with selling a property. Selling costs must be subtracted from sales proceeds to determine the resale price when using the discounted cash-flow analysis or the yield capitalization analysis. *See also* discounted cash-flow analysis, yield capitalization

distressed property. A property that has problems due to factors such as an oversupplied market, poor design or improper location of the improvements, inadequate maintenance and poor management decisions.

dollar adjustments. An adjustment made to a comparable sale in the direct sales comparison approach of appraisal for a quantitative difference from the subject property. The adjustment is made in a lump-sum dollar figure, e.g., most of the ownership interests, cash equivalency, functional and economic obsolescence adjustments are made on a lump-sum dollar basis. *See also* direct sales comparison approach, percentage adjustments.

easement. A legal interest in real property that conveys use or enjoyment but not ownership of the property.

economic age-life method. A method used to estimate accrued depreciation by multiplying the reproduction or replacement cost by the ratio of effective age divided by total economic life. Curable and short-lived items are not estimated separately. *See also* accrued depreciation.

economic base. The industry in a geographic area that provides employment opportunities and allows it to attract income from outside its boundaries.

economic forces. In appraisal theory, one type of force that affects property value. It includes effects on value such as supply and demand, employment, wage levels, industrial expansion and availability of mortgage credit. *See also* forces.

economic life. The estimated time period during which an improvement yields a return over the economic rent attributable to the land itself; the estimated time period over which an improved property has value in excess of its salvage value. The economic life of an improvement is usually shorter than its actual physical life. *See also* remaining economic life, effective age.

economic obsolescence. A type of external obsolescence in which value loss is caused by an occurrence or situation that adversely affects the employment, quality of life or economics of an area, e.g., loss of a major employer, a high tax base or changes in zoning. *See also* external obsolescence.

economically feasible. Refers to a real estate project that is able to meet defined financial investment objectives, the ability of a project to produce sufficient cash flows to repay all of the expenses involved in creating and marketing the project plus provide a competitive return to the owner/developer. A criterion of highest and best use analysis. *See also* highest and best use.

effective age. The age of an improvement determined by its current condition and utility based on its design, location and current competitive market conditions. The effective age may be greater than or less than the actual age. *See also* economic life, remaining economic life.

effective annual rate. The annual interest rate equivalent to a nominal rate that is compounded more frequently than annually. For example, if the nominal rate is 10% compounded monthly, the effective annual rate is $(1 + (.10/12))^{12} - 1 = 10.47\%$.

effective date. In an appraisal report, the date for which the value is being estimated. The effective date is not necessarily the same as the date the report is written.

effective gross income (EGI). The anticipated income from the operation of a project after adjustment for vacancy and credit loss. The effective income can be further classified as actual, market and/or economic effective gross income depending on which rent levels were considered when making the calculation. *See also* effective gross income multiplier, net operating income, potential gross income.

effective gross income multiplier (EGIM). The ratio of the sales price, after adjustment for nonrealty interests and favorable financing divided by the projected first-year effective gross income. For income-producing properties, the EGIM can be derived from comparable sales as one method of estimating a property value in the direct sales comparison approach. *See also* effective gross income, potential gross income multiplier.

effective tax rate. (1) The ratio between a property's annual property tax and its market value; the tax rate times the assessed value divided by the market value; and the official tax rate times the assessment ratio. (2) A measure of the amount that the before-tax IRR is reduced due to the effect of federal income taxes. The effective tax rate is calculated by subtracting the after-tax IRR from the before-tax IRR and dividing the remainder by the before-tax IRR.

efficiency ratio. The ratio of the net leasable area of a building divided by the gross area.

electrical system. The wiring, circuit breakers, fuses, distribution box, wall switches, lighting fixtures and such necessary to provide sufficient electrical service to power all the electrical equipment in a building. Most wiring is armored cable. However plastic-coated wire and knob-and-tube wiring have also been used. Wire is typically made of copper, but aluminum wire was used frequently after the 1940s. Because of its lower resistance to fire, aluminum use is now prohibited in some areas.

elements of comparison. A categorization of property characteristics that causes real estate prices to vary, e.g., property rights, financing terms, conditions of sale, date of sale (or market conditions), location and physical characteristics. *See also* direct sales comparison approach, units of comparison.

Ellwood formula. An algebraic formula used to calculate an overall rate that is based on the mortgage equity analysis concept that allows for cash-flow forecasts including the impact of financing. The formula allows for a direct solution for value even though the loan amount is entered as a percentage of value and any change in value (either appreciation or depreciation) may be entered as a percentage of value.

eminent domain. The governmental right to take private property for public use upon the payment of just compensation. *See also* condemnation, just compensation.

entrepreneurial profit. The sum of money an entrepreneur expects to receive in addition to costs for the time and effort, coordination and risk bearing necessary to create a project. The portion associated with creation of the real estate by a developer is referred to as developer's profit. Properties that also include an operating business may include additional entrepreneurial profit that is reflected in the going-concern value of the property. *See also* going-concern value.

environmental conditions. The climate, topography, natural barriers, transportation systems and other factors of location that affect the value of a property.

environmental controls. Standards set by the Environmental Protection Agency to control air, water and noise pollution and other environmental conditions.

environmental forces. In appraisal theory, one of four categories of forces that affect property value; environmental forces include effects on value such as climate, location, topography, natural barriers and transportation systems. *See also* forces.

environmental impact study (EIS). An analysis of the impact of a proposed land use on its environment, including the direct and indirect effects of the project during all phases of use and their long-run implications.

environmental risk. Uncertainty due to changes in the property's environment that may affect the value of a property.

equity. The owner's capital investment in a property; the property value less the balance of any debt as of a particular point in time. Equity is equal to the property value if there is no debt on the property.

equity capitalization rate (R_E). The capitalization rate that reflects the relationship between a single year's before-tax cash flow and the equity investment in the property. The before-tax cash flow in this instance is the net operating income less the annual debt service payment, and the equity is the property value less any outstanding loan balance. The equity capitalization rate, when divided into the before-tax cash flows, gives an indication of the value of the equity. Also called cash-flow rate, cash on cash rate or equity dividend rate.

equity discount rate. *See* equity yield rate.

equity dividend. *See* before-tax cash flow.

equity dividend rate. *See* equity capitalization rate.

equity interest. *See* equity.

equity participation. An agreement by which a lender receives some share of the income and/or cash flow of a property based on the performance of that property. The participation might be based on a percentage of the net operating income, cash flow from operations and/or the gain from sale of the property. The equity participation results in an additional return to the lender above the interest rate charged on the loan.

equity residual technique. An appraisal technique for solving for value by which the first year's before-tax cash flow (net operating income minus annual debt service) is capitalized by the equity capitalization rate (equity dividend) to arrive at an estimate of the equity value. The equity value is then added to the loan balance to arrive at an estimate for the total property. *See also* residual techniques.

equity yield rate (Y_E). A rate of return on the equity capital; the equity investor's internal rate of return based on expected before-tax cash flows and the investor's original equity; used as the discount rate in a discounted cash-flow analysis to estimate the present value of the before-tax cash flows (from operation and resale) to arrive at a value estimate for the equity. The equity yield rate reflects the effect of financing on the investor's rate of return. *See also* after-tax equity yield rate, before-tax equity yield rate, yield capitalization.

escheat. The governmental right to transfer property ownership to the state when the owner dies without a will or any ascertainable heirs.

excess land. On an unimproved site, land that is not needed to accommodate a site's highest and best use. On an improved site, excess land is the surplus land that is not needed to serve or support the existing improvement.

excess rent. The amount by which contract rent exceeds market rent due to unfavorable lease terms. The additional rent could be a result of market changes, sales overage clauses and/or poor negotiating skills on the part of the tenant.

expected return. The return found by weighing possible returns by their respective probabilities.

expense passthrough. *See* passthrough.

expense ratio. *See* operating expense ratio.

expense stop. In a lease, a dollar amount (usually expressed on a per square foot basis) above which the tenant agrees to pay operating expenses. An expense stop is used to help protect the lessor from unexpected increases in expenses from inflation or other factors. The amount paid by the tenant is said to "pass through" to the tenant. *See also* passthrough.

exterior wall. In construction, any outer wall, except a common wall, that encloses a building.

external depreciation. *See* external obsolescence.

external obsolescence. A loss in property value resulting from negative influence outside the property itself. An element of accrued depreciation. External obsolescence is generally incurable and can be further defined as either economic obsolescence or locational obsolescence. *See also* accrued depreciation, economic obsolescence, locational obsolescence.

extraction method. *See* allocation.

feasibility analysis. According to the Uniform Standards of Professional Appraisal Practice, a study of the cost-benefit relationship of an economic endeavor. *See also* marketability study, market analysis.

feasibility rent. The level of rent that is necessary for it to be feasible to construct a new building.

feasibility study. *See* feasibility analysis.

Federal Home Loan Bank Board (FHLBB). An entity created by the Federal Home Loan Bank Act of 1932 to regulate federal savings and loan associations. The FHLBB sets credit policies, administers reserve and liquidity requirements, and controls lending practices of member associations.

Federal Home Loan Mortgage Corporation (FHLMC). An agency directed by the Federal Home Loan Bank Board for the purpose of increasing the availability of mortgage funds and providing greater flexibility for mortgage investors. The FHLMC purchases single-family and condominium mortgages from approved financial institutions and resells its mortgage inventories. Also called Freddie Mac.

Federal National Mortgage Association (FNMA). An independent agency that purchases mortgages from the primary markets and issues long-term debentures and short-term discount notes. Also called Fannie Mae.

fee simple estate. Absolute ownership of real estate that is unencumbered by any other interest or estate and is subject to the limitations of eminent domain, escheat, police power and taxation. A fee simple estate can be valuated by the present value of market rents. *See also* leased fee estate, leasehold estate.

fee simple interest. *See* fee simple estate.

fee simple value. The value of a fee simple estate. *See* fee simple estate.

financial leverage. *See* leverage, positive leverage, negative leverage, zero leverage.

financial management rate of return (FMRR). Similar in concept to the adjusted internal rate of return. Negative cash flows are discounted at a safe rate, and positive cash flows are compounded forward to the end of the holding period at a reinvestment rate. If negative cash flows occur after a positive cash flow, the negative cash flow is discounted back and netted against the positive cash flow. The net remaining is either discounted back (if negative) or compounded forward (if positive). *See also* adjusted internal rate of return, internal rate of return.

financial risk. Uncertainty that results from the use of debt to finance an investment.

financially feasible. A requirement of highest and best use; refers to a project that satisfies the economic objectives of the investor. *See also* highest and best use.

financing premium. An incremental amount paid for a property that is purchased with favorable financing, e.g., assumption of a below-market interest rate loan. *See also* cash equivalency adjustment.

fixed expense. An operating expense that does not vary with the occupancy level of a

property, e.g., property taxes, insurance, repairs and maintenance, advertising and promotions. *See also* variable expense.

fixed rate mortgage. A loan in which the interest rate is constant over the term of the loan. *See also* adjustable rate mortgage.

flood plain. A geographic area close to a river or stream that is subject to flooding. In some areas, flood plains are mapped by the Federal Emergency Management Agency so that they may be covered by the National Flood Insurance Plan.

floodway. Ground area that is usually covered annually by water.

floor cover. Covering over the subflooring. It may be made of various types of material, including carpeting, terrazzo, vinyl, wood, brick or various types of tile. The quality of the floor covering material is generally directly related to the quality of the building.

floor structure. Typically, in commercial or industrial buildings, a reinforced concrete slab on the ground floor and metal joists covered by metal decking and a concrete slab for above-ground floors. Apartments may have wooden joists covered by wooden subflooring. Some industrial buildings have raised floors to facilitate the loading and unloading of trucks.

forces. In appraisal theory, any of four dynamic and changing powers and their interactions that affect the value of real property. Includes social forces (population trends), economic forces (employment, wage levels, supply and demand), governmental forces (zoning, fiscal policies, legislation) and environmental forces (climate, topography, transportation). *See also* economic forces, environmental forces, governmental forces, social forces.

forecasting. The process of assimilating past information and compiling the data for the purpose of drawing conclusions as to the probable happenings or conditions in the future.

foundation. The base on which something is built; the part of a structure on which the superstructure is erected; the part of a building that is below the surface of the ground and on which the superstructure rests. Includes all construction that transmits the loads of the superstructure to the earth.

frame. The load-bearing skeleton of a building.

frontage. The length of a property that abuts the street line or other landmark such as a body of water. Frontage differs from width, which may vary from the front of the lot to the back.

functional depreciation. *See* functional obsolescence.

functional obsolescence. A loss in the value of real estate improvements owing to functional inadequacies or subadequacies owing to poor design and/or change in market standards or requirements for building components. *See also* curable functional obsolescence, incurable functional obsolescence.

functional utility. The extent to which a property is able to be used for the purpose that it was intended. Functional utility includes factors such as current trends in tastes and styles, architectural style, design and layout and traffic patterns.

future value. The worth of a property at some later date. See also future value of $1, future value annuity of $1 per period.

future value annuity of $1 per period ($S_{\overline{n}}$). A compound interest factor that represents the sum to which a constant periodic investment of $1 per period will grow, assuming compound growth at a specific rate of return for a specific number of compounding periods. It is shown in column two of the compound interest tables. In an appraisal, these payments are generally assumed to be made at the end of each period. Also called accumulation of $1 per period. *See also* six functions of $1.

future value of $1 ($S^n$). The amount to which an investment of $1 grows with compound interest after a specified number of years at a specified interest rate. It is shown in column one of the compound interest tables. Also called the amount of $1, future value

interest factor, future worth of one dollar. *See also* six functions of $1.

future worth of $1 per period. *See* future value annuity of $1 per period.

general market area. A geographic area or political jurisdiction in which similar property types compete on an economic basis for potential buyers, users or patrons.

going-concern value. The value of a property that includes the value due to a successful operating business enterprise that is expected to continue. Going-concern value results from the process of assembling the land, building, labor, equipment and marketing operation and includes consideration of the efficiency of plant, the know-how of management and the sufficiency of capital. The portion of going-concern value that exceeds that of the real property and tangible personal property is an intangible value that is referred to as business value. *See also* business value.

going-in capitalization rate. The overall capitalization rate found by dividing first year's net operating income by the present value of the property. When the term capitalization rate is used without a prefix, it is assumed to be a going-in capitalization rate. *See also* capitalization rate, terminal capitalization rate.

governmental forces. In appraisal theory, one of four forces thought to affect real estate value, e.g., governmental controls and regulations, public services, fiscal policies, and zoning and building codes. *See also* forces.

government regulations. *See* governmental forces.

graphic analysis. A method of analyzing comparable sales using Ellwood Graphic Analysis whereby a range of expectation with regard to the relationship between expected yield rates and associated changes in cash-flow forecasts are projected using sensitivity analysis that, if required by an investor, would have resulted in the price paid for the comparable property. The technique is used to support the inputs in a discounted cash-flow approach. *See also* discounted cash-flow analysis, yield capitalization, Ellwood formula.

gross building area (GBA). The total floor area of a building measured in square feet from the external walls, excluding unenclosed areas. Unlike gross living area measurements, GBA does include basement areas.

gross lease. A lease that specifies that the landlord is responsible for the payment of all operating expenses. The lease, however, may contain expense increase passthrough provisions. *See also* expense stop, net lease.

gross sale price. Cash or other property received in payment for the property sold plus any liabilities against the property assumed by the buyer. *See also* net sale proceeds.

ground lease. A lease for the use and occupancy of land only. Also called land lease.

ground rent. Rent paid for the right to use and occupy land; a percentage of total rent designated for land use and occupancy.

ground rent capitalization. A method of estimating land value by either dividing a first-year land lease payment by an appropriate land capitalization rate or by discounting a series of land lease payments by an appropriate land discount rate. *See also* land.

heating, ventilation and air-conditioning system (HVAC). A system that provides consistent regulation and distribution of heat and fresh air throughout a building.

highest and best use (HBU). The reasonable and probable use that results in the highest present value of the land after considering all legally permissible, physically possible and economically feasible uses. Capitalization rates or discount rates for each feasible use should reflect typical returns expected in the market. Highest and best use is usually determined under two different premises: as if the site was vacant and could be improved in the optimal manner or as the site is currently improved.

In the latter premise, the highest and best use of the site will either be to keep the existing building or demolish the building and develop a building that is the highest and best use. In general, it is not feasible to demolish an existing building as long as it contributes to the value of the site.

highest and best use of land. *See* highest and best use.

highest and best use of improved site. *See* highest and best use.

holding period. The term of ownership or expected ownership of an investment. In appraisal, the holding period used reflects the appraiser's estimate as to what the typical expected holding period would be for a particular property.

Hoskold premise. An appraisal theory that was designed to value the income stream of a wasting asset. Two separate interest rates are used: a speculative rate, representing a fair rate of return on capital, and a safe rate for a sinking fund designed to return all the invested capital in a lump sum at the termination of the investment. The Hoskold premise assumes that a portion of the net operating income is reinvested at a safe rate to replace the investment. *See also* Ellwood formula, yield capitalization.

improvements. Structures or buildings that are permanently attached to the land.

income approach. *See* income capitalization approach.

income capitalization approach. One of the three traditional appraisal approaches to estimating value. In this approach, value is based on the present value of future benefits of property ownership. In direct capitalization, a single year's income is converted to a value indication using a capitalization rate. In yield capitalization, future cash flows are estimated and discounted to a present value using a capitalization rate. *See also* appraisal, capitalization rate, yield rate.

income multiplier. First-year ratios calculated by dividing the value of the property by either the potential gross income, effective gross income or net operating income. *See also* after-tax cash flow, effective gross income, net operating income, potential gross income.

income. *See* net operating income.

income property. A property that is held in anticipation of receiving income; e.g., residential properties that are typically rented, such as apartments, and nonresidential properties that are typically leased, such as office buildings, shopping centers and hotels.

income rate. *See* capitalization rate.

income stabilization factor. A constant that is used to convert any irregular income pattern into its level equivalent annuity that has the same present value at a specified discount rate. *See also* j factor, k factor.

incurable functional obsolescence. A defect caused by a deficiency or superadequacy in the structure, materials or design of a structure. The defect is deemed incurable if the cost to cure the defect is greater than the anticipated increase in value after the defect is cured. A component of accrued depreciation. *See also* accrued depreciation, breakdown method, deficiency, superadequacy.

incurable physical depreciation. A defect caused by physical wear and tear on the building that is unreasonable or uneconomical to correct. An element of accrued depreciation. Incurable physical depreciation can be further classified as long lived or short lived. Long-lived items are expected to have a remaining economic life that equals the remaining economic life of the structure. Short-lived items are expected to have a remaining economic life that is less than the remaining economic life of the structure. *See also* accrued depreciation, breakdown method.

indirect costs. Construction expenses for items other than labor and materials, e.g., financing costs, taxes, administrative costs, contractor's overhead and profit, legal fees, interest payments, insurance costs during construction and lease-up costs. Also called soft costs. *See also* direct costs.

inflation risk. Uncertainty due to unexpected inflation that could cause cash flows from a property to lose purchasing power.

installment to amortize $1. *See* payment to amortize $1.

insulation. In construction, material such as plasterboard, asbestos, compressed wood-wool or fiberboard placed between inner and outer surfaces that reduces the transfer of heat, cold or sound by dissipating air currents.

insurable value. The value of the destructible parts of a property. This value is used to determine the amount of insurance carried on the property.

interest. Money paid for the use of money over time; a return on capital. Interest payments are deductible for income tax purposes, although payments of principal are not. *See also* amortization schedule, effective annual rate.

interest rate. The ratio of the cost of using money divided by the money advanced. *See also* interest.

interest only mortgage. A nonamortizing loan in which payments of interest are made at specified times throughout the life of the loan and the principal is paid in a lump sum at the maturity of the loan.

interim use. A temporary use for a property when the highest and best use of the property is different from the highest and best use of the land as if vacant.

internal rate of return (IRR). A rate of return that discounts all expected future cash flows to a present value that is equal to the original investment. An IRR can be calculated for any defined cash flows, e.g., for the whole property or for just the equity position. Also called yield rate. *See also* adjusted internal rate of return, discounted cash-flow analysis.

investment analysis. According to the Uniform Standards of Professional Appraisal Practice, a study that reflects the relationship between acquisition price and anticipated future benefits of a real estate investment.

investment value. The value of a property to a particular investor. *See also* investment analysis.

Inwood annuity factor. *See* present value annuity of $1 per period.

Inwood premise. An appraisal theory used to value an income stream of equal payments in which the present value of the income stream is based on a single discount figure; the basis for the present value of an ordinary annuity factor in compound interest tables. *See* present value annuity of $1 per period.

j factor. An income stabilization factor used to convert a curvilinear income stream into its level equivalent annuity. *See also* income stabilization factor, k factor.

just compensation. Fair and reasonable compensation to a private owner of property when the property is taken for public use through condemnation. *See also* condemnation, eminent domain.

k factor. An income stabilization factor used to convert an income stream that is changing at a compound rate into its level equivalent annuity. *See also* income stabilization factor, j factor.

land. The earth's surface including the solid surface of the earth, water and anything attached to it; natural resources in their original state, e.g., mineral deposits, timber, soil. In law, land is considered to be the solid surface of the earth and does not include water.

land capitalization rate (R_L). The rate that reflects the first-year land lease payment divided by the value of the land. *See also* band-of-investment technique, building residual technique, land residual technique.

land density. The ratio of building units or occupants divided by a unit of land area (acre, square mile).

land lease. *See* ground lease.

land residual technique. A technique used to find the value of a property by subtracting income attributable to the building from the net operating income and valuing the residual land income, e.g., by dividing the land income by a land capitalization rate to arrive at a land value indication. The land value is then added to the building value to arrive at an estimate of value for the total property. The land residual technique is one way of evaluating the highest and best use of a site. Under its highest and best use, the building value should equal its development cost and the highest land value will result for this use. *See also* land, residual techniques.

land utilization study. An analysis of the potential uses of a parcel of land and a determination of the highest and best use for that parcel; a complete inventory of the parcels in a given community or other area classified by type of use, plus (in some cases) an analysis of the spatial patterns of use revealed by this inventory. Land utilization studies do not embody the viewpoint of any particular investor nor do they focus on any one parcel. Furthermore, no consideration of markets and feasibility is normally included.

leased fee estate. An ownership interest in the real estate held by a landlord who has transferred the right of occupancy to a property through the execution of a lease. The leased fee estate can be valued as the present value of the lease income plus the right to the reversion at the end of the lease. *See also* fee simple estate, leasehold estate.

leased fee interest. *See* leased fee estate.

leased fee value. The value of a leased fee estate. *See* leased fee estate.

leasehold estate. An ownership interest in real estate held by a tenant during the term of a lease. The leasehold estate can be valued as the present value of the difference between the market rent and the rent specified by the lease. *See also* fee simple estate, leased fee estate.

leasehold interest. *See* leasehold estate.

leasehold value. The value of a leasehold estate. *See* leasehold estate.

legally permitted. Required in highest and best use; that which is allowable by law. To be the highest and best use of a site, the use must be legally permissible. *See also* highest and best use.

legislative risk. Uncertainty due to changes in laws and regulations.

lender participation. *See* equity participation.

lessee. A person or entity that has been granted the right to use and occupy a property as the result of the execution of a lease agreement; a tenant. *See also* leasehold estate.

lessor. The owner of a property who transfers the right to use and occupy the property to a tenant as the result of the execution of a lease agreement; a landlord. *See also* leased fee estate.

level-payment mortgage. A mortgage in which equal, periodic payments are made over the life of the loan that cover both interest and principal. Payments are credited first against interest on the declining balance and then against principal, so that the amount of money credited to principal gradually increases over the life of the loan, while that credited to interest gradually decreases.

leverage. The use of borrowed funds in the purchase of an investment. If the addition of the mortgage increases the return to the equity (equity dividend rate or equity yield rate), the addition of the mortgage has resulted in positive leverage. If the addition of the mortgage decreases the return to the equity, the addition of the mortgage has resulted in negative leverage. *See also* negative leverage, positive leverage, zero leverage.

lighting costs. Costs that allow for the service distribution, light fixtures and light receptacles. Typically, the cost of lighting components are directly related to the overall quality of the structure itself.

limiting conditions. Specifications in an appraisal report that restrict the assumptions in the report to certain situations, e.g., date and use of the appraisal, definition of value, identification of real estate and property rights being valued, definition of surveys used or not used.

liquidation value. The price that results from the sale of the property without allowing for a reasonable time on the market. The liquidation price may be less than market value, depending on the degree of interest in the property at the time it is liquidated.

liquidity. The ease with which an asset may be sold for cash at a price close to its true value.

liquidity risk. Uncertainty caused by the lack of a ready, organized real estate market and the length of time required to find a buyer. *See also* risk.

loan constant. *See* mortgage capitalization rate.

loan constraints. Typically, one of two methods of selecting the level of funds to be advanced to a property owner. The methods are loan-to-value ratio (M) or the first-year debt service coverage ratio (DCR). *See also* debt coverage ratio, loan-to-value ratio.

loan participation. *See* equity participation.

loan-to-value ratio (M). The ratio of the outstanding loan balance divided by the total property value.

locational attributes. Characteristics of the area surrounding a property. Probably the most important locational factor is current neighborhood land use and potential patterns of change.

locational obsolescence. A type of external obsolescence in which value loss is caused by a negative influence outside the property due to its location. *See also* external obsolescence.

management risk. Uncertainty caused by the quality of the management operating the property. *See also* risk.

market analysis. According to the Uniform Standards of Professional Appraisal Practice, a study of real estate market conditions for a specific type of property.

market area. *See* general market area.

market extraction method. A method used to estimate depreciation in which depreciation is measured by extracting the percentage loss from market sales of similar properties.

market price. The amount actually paid, or to be paid, for a property in a particular transaction. Market price differs from market value; it is an accomplished historical fact, whereas market value is and remains an estimate. Market price involves no assumption of information or prudent conduct by the parties or absence of undue stimulus or of any other condition basic to the market value concept. *See also* market value.

market rent. The rental income that a property would command if exposed for lease in a competitive market.

market rent equivalency adjustment. The adjustment that reflects the impact of any existing below-market leases on the market value of a property. It represents the difference between the fee simple interest and the leased fee interest, unless the leased fee interest is greater than the fee simple interest. In that case, the difference would be a nonrealty interest known as the rent premium.

market segmentation. (1) The process of classifying consumers or buyers into relatively homogeneous groups based on their economic, demographic and/or psychographic characteristics (such as attitudes, habits and life-styles). (2) The process of differentiating the potential users of the subject property from the general population, according to defined consumer characteristics.

market study. *See* market analysis.

market value. According to the Uniform Standards of Professional Appraisal Practice, market value is the major focus of most real property appraisal assignments. Both economic and legal definitions of market value have been developed and refined. A current economic definition agreed upon by federal financial institutions in the United States is:

The most probable price a property should bring in a competitive and open market under all conditions requisite to a fair sale, the buyer and seller each acting prudently and knowledgeably, and assuming the price is not affected by undue stimulus. Implicit in this definition is the consummation of a sale as of a specified date and the passing of title from seller to buyer under conditions whereby:

1. buyer and seller are typically motivated;
2. both parties are well informed or well advised, and acting in what they consider their best interests;
3. a reasonable time is allowed for exposure in the open market;
4. payment is made in terms of cash in United States dollars or in terms of financial arrangements comparable thereto; and
5. the price represents the normal consideration for the property sold unaffected by special or creative financing or sales concessions granted by anyone associated with the sale.

Substitution of another currency for United States dollars in the fourth condition is appropriate in other countries or in reports addressed to clients from other countries.

Persons performing appraisal services that may be subject to litigation are cautioned to seek the exact legal definition of market value in the jurisdiction in which the services are being performed.

market value (of a loan). The value of a loan considering current market rates. The market value is determined by discounting the loan payments and any final balance at the current market rate for similar loans.

marketability study. A real estate analysis of a specific property that addresses the ability of the property to be absorbed, sold or leased under current and anticipated market conditions.

marketing period. The time period beginning when an owner decides to begin actively selling a property to when the sale is actually closed. The marketing period is typically an observable fact. If a marketing period that is shorter than typical is assumed in an analysis, the value found would be considered a forced, or liquidation, value rather than market value.

maximally productive. One of four criteria in highest and best use analysis. It states that a use is the highest and best use if it produces the highest value or price. *See also* highest and best use.

minimum rent. *See* base rent.

modified internal rate of return. *See* adjusted internal rate of return.

mortgage. A legal document in which real estate is named under certain conditions as the security or collateral for the repayment of a loan.

mortgage capitalization rate (R_M). The mortgage capitalization rate that is the ratio of the first-year debt payment divided by the beginning loan balance. In some instances, the ratio may be calculated using one month's payment, but typically it is the total of the loan payment for an entire year. Also called mortgage constant.

mortgage constant. *See* mortgage capitalization rate.

mortgage interest. Money paid for the use of borrowed money through a mortgage. The rate can be fixed or variable.

mortgage loan value (V_M). The benchmark on which lenders base mortgage investments in real estate. Typically, market value and mortgage value would be identical. A lender, however, may introduce restrictions in underwriting policy that may alter this relationship.

mortgage residual technique. An appraisal technique for solving for value when the amount of available equity is known but the mortgage value is unknown. The mortgage value is found by subtracting income to equity from the net operating income and capitalizing this amount by the mortgage capitalization rate. The mortgage value is then added to the equity value to find the total property value. *See also* residual techniques.

mortgage yield rate (Y_M). The discount rate that equates the present value of the loan payments with the principal borrowed. *See also* effective annual rate, mortgage interest.

negative amortization. The difference between the loan payment and the amount of interest charged when the loan payment is less than the interest charged per period. In effect, the loan balance increases each period by the amount of interest unpaid. This generally occurs in mortgages with initially low payments that increase at some point in time. Mortgages with negative amortization usually require higher interest rates or larger down payments. *See also* amortization schedule.

negative leverage. A situation in which the rate paid on a mortgage is greater than the rate generated by an investment on an unleveraged basis. *See also* leverage, positive leverage, zero leverage.

neighborhood. A geographical area delineated by geographical or political boundaries that is characterized by having complementary land uses.

neighborhood analysis. The objective analysis of observable and/or quantifiable data indicating discernible patterns of urban growth, structure and change that may detract from or enhance property values.

neighborhood life cycle. The changes that occur in a neighborhood over time. The cycle is defined by four stages: growth, stability, decline and revitalization. Gentrification is not part of the natural neighborhood life cycle.

net income multiplier (NIM). The ratio of the price or value of a property divided by its net operating income; the reciprocal of the overall rate.

net leasable area. Floor space that can be rented to tenants; may include common areas.

net lease. A lease in which the tenant pays expenses such as property taxes, insurance and maintenance. Sometimes referred to as a net-net-net lease. *See also* gross lease.

net operating income (NOI). The actual or anticipated income remaining during a year after deducting operating expenses from effective gross income but before any deductions for debt service payment or income taxes.

net present value (NPV). The discounted value of all future cash flows minus the initial cash outlay. A net present value greater than or equal to zero is acceptable. *See also* discounted cash-flow analysis, internal rate of return, present value.

net sale proceeds. The gross sale price less selling expenses, e.g., legal fees, recording fees, brokerage fees.

net usable area. Floor space that can be occupied by tenants. *See also* net leasable area.

nominal discount rate. A discount rate that includes a premium for expected inflation.

nonrealty interests. Property rights that might be purchased with real estate, land, buildings and fixtures that are either tangible or intangible personal property such as furniture in a hotel or the franchise (business) value of the hotel.

nonresidential property. Property that is not used as a permanent dwelling, including property types such as office, industrial, retail, hotel and special purpose properties.

occupancy obsolescence. The loss in value due to an above average vacancy rate in a distressed property.

on-site improvements. Physical improvements that are constructed within the boundaries of a parcel of land.

operating expense ratio (OER). The ratio of total operating expenses divided by effective gross income.

operating expenses. Expenditures necessary to maintain the real property and continue the production of income. Includes both fixed expenses and variable expenses, but does not include debt service, depreciation or capital expenditures. *See also* fixed expense, variable expense.

opportunity cost. The cost of options forgone or opportunities not chosen.

ordinary annuity. A series of level payments that are made at the end of a series of equal time periods; the type of annuity assumed in compound interest tables. *See also* annuity in advance.

overage rent. A rent paid in addition to a fixed base rent. It is usually based on a variable figure such as a percentage of sales or an index. Because it is less certain than the fixed base rent, it is usually discounted at a higher rate.

overall capitalization rate (R_O). A single year's cash-flow ratio that is calculated by dividing the net operating income (NOI) by the total value of the property. When calculated, using NOI for the first year of operations, it is sometimes referred to as a "current yield." However, it is *not* a yield rate that considers NOI over the entire holding period, nor does it consider resale proceeds. Thus it should not be confused with an overall yield rate. Frequently used to find the value of a property by dividing the first year's net operating income by the overall capitalization rate. The inverse of the overall capitalization rate is the net income multiplier. Also called overall cap rate. *See also* band-of-investment technique, yield

capitalization formulas, capitalization rate, direct capitalization, income capitalization approach, net income multiplier and overall yield rate.

overall yield rate (Y_O). The discount rate that equates the present value of the net operating income and resale proceeds with the purchase price. Sometimes referred to as a free and clear yield because it does not consider financing. *See also* internal rate of return, equity yield rate.

overhead. *See* administrative expenses.

overimprovement. *See* superadequacy.

ownership interest. *See* fee simple estate, leased fee estate, leasehold estate.

paired sales analysis. A procedure used in the sales comparison approach to estimate adjustments by comparing properties that are very similar in all but one element of comparison.

parties to the lease. *See* lessee, lessor.

partitioning the IRR. Using the internal rate of return for an investment to determine the proportion of the present value that comes from different sources of cash flow.

passive income. Income or loss from a trade or business where the investor does not materially participate in the management or operation of the property by being involved in the operations of the activity on a regular, continuous and substantial basis. Income from real estate investment is generally classified as passive income.

passthrough. Expenses charged to a tenant as a result of expense stop provisions in a lease. *See also* expense stop.

payback period. The time required for cumulative income from an investment to equal the amount initially invested. Usually calculated to the next whole year. It does not consider the time value of money and, therefore, is not a discounted cash-flow analysis technique. *See also* discounted cash-flow analysis.

payment to amortize \$1 ($1/a_{\overline{n}|}$). The periodic payment necessary to repay a \$1 loan with interest paid at a specified rate over a specified time on the outstanding loan balance; column six of the compound interest tables. *See also* six functions of $1.

percentage adjustments. The adjustment of the price of a comparable property when the amount of adjustment is based on a percentage of either the price of the subject property or a percentage of the price of the comparable property.

percentage rent. A type of rent that is based on a percentage of sales from the property, usually associated with a guaranteed base rent. *See also* base rent, overage rent.

permeability. The ability of soil to absorb water.

perpetuity. (1) The state of existing forever. (2) An ordinary annuity that continues forever. *See also* capitalization in perpetuity.

personal property. According to the Uniform Standards of Professional Appraisal Practice, identifiable, portable and tangible objects that are considered by the general public as being personal, e.g., furnishings, artwork, antiques, gems and jewelry, collectibles, machinery and equipment; all property that is not classified as real estate.

physical characteristics. The tangible aspects of real estate.

physical deterioration. Physical depreciation. *See* curable physical deterioration, incurable physical deterioration.

physical factors. Tangible aspects of a community that may affect a property's value. Examples of physical factors include location, natural geographic boundaries, topography, soil conditions, climate, natural resources, water availability and transportation.

physical incurable depreciation. *See* incurable physical depreciation.

physically possible. One of four criteria in highest and best use analysis. For a use to be the highest and best use, the size, shape and terrain of the property must be able to accommodate the use. *See also* highest and best use.

plottage. An increment of value that results when extra utility is created by combining two or more sites under a single ownership.

plumbing system. The piping and fixtures necessary to carry water, wastes and other fluids to and from a building. Piping consists of a large part of the cost of the plumbing system and may or may not be constructed to last for the life of the building. Water is carried under pressure through pipes, whereas waste pipes depend on gravity.

police power. The governmental right to regulate property for the purpose of protecting public safety, health and general welfare, e.g., condemnation, rent control, zoning.

portfolio income. Interest and dividend income from stocks, bonds and some categories of real estate that are classified as capital assets.

positive leverage. A situation in which the rate paid on a mortgage is less than the rate generated by an investment on an unleveraged basis. *See also* leverage, negative leverage, zero leverage.

potential gross income (PGI). The amount of theoretical income a property could potentially generate assuming 100% occupancy at market rental rates. *See also* after-tax cash flow, before-tax cash flow, effective gross income, net operating income.

potential gross income multiplier (PGIM). The ratio calculated by dividing the sales price of a property by its potential gross income. *See also* potential gross income.

present value (PV). The current value of a payment or series of future payments found by discounting the expected payments by a desired rate of return in order to compensate for the time value of money. *See also* discounted cash-flow analysis, internal rate of return, net present value, yield capitalization.

present value annuity of $1 per period ($a_{\overline{n}}$). A compound interest factor typically calculated for an annual interest rate that is used to discount a series of equal future cash flows in order to arrive at a current present value of the total stream of income; column five of the compound interest tables. *See also* six functions of $1.

present value of $1 ($1/S^n$). A compound interest factor typically calculated for an annual interest rate that is used to discount an expected future cash flow in order to arrive at its current present value. It is found in column four of the compound interest tables. Also called present value of one dollar, present value of one factor, present value interest factor, present worth of $1. *See also* six functions of $1.

preservation of capital. *See* return of capital.

pre-tax cash flow (PTCF). *See* before-tax cash flow.

price index. *See* consumer price index (CPI).

price per square foot. A unit of comparison in the direct sales comparison approach. Gives a good indication of the value of a subject property only after ensuring that each sale represents the same ownership interests and that adjustments have been made for differences in the locational and physical characteristics of the subject and the comparable properties. *See also* direct sales comparison approach, sales adjustment grid, units of comparison.

primary data. Information gathered by the appraiser that is not available in a published source. *See also* secondary data.

primary mortgage market. The interaction of lenders who originate loans with borrowers seeking mortgage loans to purchase or refinance a property. *See also* secondary mortgage market.

principal (loan). The amount of capital borrowed or remaining to be paid on an investment. Also refers to that portion of a loan payment that reduces the balance of the loan.

proceeds of resale. *See* reversion.

profitability index (PI). The ratio of the present value of future cash flows at a specified discount rate divided by the initial cash outlay. It is similar to the net present value except that the initial cash outlay is divided into the present value of future cash flows instead of subtracted from the present value of future cash flows. A profitability

index greater than one is acceptable. *See also* net present value, discounted cash-flow analysis.

property tax. An ad valorem levy issued by the government based on the assessed value of privately owned property.

property value (V). The monetary worth of interests held in real estate arising from property ownership. A property may have several different values depending on the interest or use involved. Common methods of estimating property value include the cost approach, direct sales comparison approach and income approach.

property yield rate. *See* overall yield rate.

prospective value. An estimate of the value of a property at a future point in time. *See also* value on reaching stabilized occupancy, value on completion but prior to rentup.

quantity survey method. The most comprehensive method of estimating building construction or reproduction costs in which the quantity and quality of all materials and labor are estimated on a current unit cost basis to arrive at a total cost estimate. It duplicates the contractor's method of developing a bid. Also called builder's breakdown method, price take-off method. *See also* building cost.

rate extraction. *See* graphic analysis.

ratio extraction. In the direct sales comparison approach, a process in the adjustment process in which different appraisal ratios are calculated for comparable properties. The ratios serve as a check on the comparableness of the properties. *See also* direct sales comparison approach, sales adjustment grid.

real discount rate. A discount rate that does *not* include a premium for expected inflation. *See also* nominal discount rate.

real estate. According to the Uniform Standards of Professional Appraisal Practice, an identified parcel or tract of land, including improvements, if any. *See also* real property, personal property.

real property. According to the Uniform Standards of Professional Appraisal Practice, the interests, benefits and rights inherent in the ownership of real estate. *See also* real estate, personal property.

Comment: In some jurisdictions, the terms *real estate* and *real property* have the same legal meaning. The separate definitions recognize the traditional distinction between the two concepts in appraisal theory.

reconciliation. In the appraisal process, the analysis of value indications from different appraisal approaches to arrive at a final value estimate.

reinvestment rate. An interest rate used to modify interim cash flows in a cash-flow analysis to arrive at a future value estimate when calculating an adjusted interest rate of return. *See* adjusted internal rate of return, financial management rate of return.

remaining economic life. The time period over which an improvement is expected to add value above the value of the land as if vacant and valued at its highest and best use. *See also* economic life, effective age.

replacement cost. The cost of constructing a building today with a structure having the same functional utility as a structure being appraised. The cost includes construction using modern materials and modern techniques. *See also* reproduction cost, building cost.

report. According to the Uniform Standards of Professional Appraisal Practice, any communication, written or oral, of an appraisal, review or analysis; the document that is transmitted to the client upon completion of an assignment. *See also* appraisal.

Comment: Most reports are written, and most clients mandate written reports. Oral report guidelines (see Standards Rule 2-4) and restrictions (see Ethics Provision: Record Keeping) are included to cover court testimony and other oral communications of an appraisal, review or consulting service.

reproduction cost. The cost of constructing a building today with an exact duplicate or replica of a structure being appraised, including all deficiencies, superadequacies and obsolescence that are in the current building. *See also* replacement cost, building cost.

resale. Sale of a property at the termination of the holding period. The resale price can be estimated by a growth rate or by a terminal cap rate applied to the net operating income occurring the year following the holding period.

resale proceeds. *See* reversionary value.

resale value. *See* reversionary value.

reserve for replacement. *See* allowance for replacements.

residential property. Vacant sites or land improved with buildings devoted to or available for use for human habitation, e.g., single-family houses, rental apartments, residential condominium units and rooming houses, but not hotels or motels.

residual techniques. Valuation techniques in which one component of value (e.g., land or mortgage) is assumed to be known. Income is estimated for the known component and subtracted from net operating income to estimate values for the unknown component. *See also* building residual technique, equity residual technique, land residual technique, mortgage residual technique.

return of capital. The recovery of the original investment either through operating income cash flows or proceeds from resale. Also called capital recovery.

return on capital. An annual rate of return that results when income received is greater than the invested capital.

reversion. The lump-sum payment received by an investor at resale of the investment. *See also* after-tax cash flow, before-tax cash flow.

reversionary value (V_R). The value of a property at resale. Also called resale value. *See also* resale.

risk. Uncertainty arising from the probability that events will not occur as expected. *See also* financial risk, liquidity risk, management risk, capital market risk, space market risk, environmental risk, inflation risk, legislative risk.

roof. The top of a structure. The frame of the roof is designed to support its own roof and is determined by the type of roof being built. Common roof types include: flat, gable, gambrel, hip, mansard, shed and salt box.

safe rate. The rate of return that can be obtained on a risk-free or relatively risk-free investment, e.g., the rate on U.S. treasury bills. *See also* adjusted internal rate of return, financial management rate of return, speculative rate.

sales adjustment grid. A grid used in the direct sales comparison approach, in which the elements of comparison are listed by line for the subject property and comparable properties. A sales adjustment grid allows comparison of different properties for adjustment to find the value of the subject property. *See also* direct sales comparison approach.

sales and marketing expenses. Costs incurred by the developer to sell a property, e.g., sales commission, advertising and promotional material.

sales comparison approach. One of the three traditional appraisal approaches to estimating value. Value is estimated by comparing similar properties that have sold recently to the subject property. Formerly referred to as the "market approach." *See also* adjustments, appraisal, comparables, land, sales adjustment grid.

salvage value. The value of any improvements assuming they are moved from the site and sold for scrap.

scenarios. Alternative assumptions as to how a property may perform in the future.

secondary data. Data that are obtained from published sources and have not been collected by the appraiser, e.g., census information, demographic information and published interest rates. *See also* primary data.

secondary mortgage market. The interaction of buyers and sellers of existing mortgages. Created by government and private agencies, the secondary mortgage market provides greater liquidity for the mortgage market. *See also* Federal National Mortgage

Association, Federal Home Loan Mortgage Corporation.

segmented market. *See* market segmentation.

segregated cost method. A method of estimating building costs in which total building cost is estimated by summing prices for various building components as installed, based on specific units of use such as square footage or cubic footage. Also called the unit costs method. *See also* building cost.

sensitivity analysis. Evaluating how a change in assumptions affects the performance of a property.

simple interest. Interest that is based only on the principal amount and not on accrued interest. *See also* compound interest.

sinking fund factor ($1/S_{\overline{n}}$). A compound interest factor that represents the level payment percentage required to be periodically invested and compounded at a specific interest rate in order to grow to an amount equal to $1 over a specified time period; column three of the compound interest tables. *See also* six functions of $1.

site. A plot of land improved for a specific purpose.

site development cost. Direct and indirect costs incurred to prepare a site for use, e.g., clearing, grading, installing utilities, etc.

site improvements. *See* on-site improvements.

site preparation. Activities required to bring a site to the condition needed to add improvements, e.g., excavation and grading.

six functions of $1. The six compound interest factors that are used in the mathematics of finance in order to adjust present or future payments for the time value of money. Includes future value of $1 ($S^n$), future value annuity of $1 per period ($S_{\overline{n}}$), sinking fund factor ($1/S_{\overline{n}}$), present value of $1 ($1/S^n$), present value annuity of $1 per period ($a_{\overline{n}}$) and the payment to amortize $1 ($1/a_{\overline{n}}$).

social characteristics. *See* social forces.

social factors. *See* social forces.

social forces. In appraisal theory, one of four forces thought to influence property value; refers to population characteristics such as population age and distribution. *See also* forces.

space market risk. Uncertainty arising from changes in the market for space that is leased to tenants.

speculative rate. The rate that typically could be earned on comparable real estate investments. *See also* adjusted internal rate of return, financial management rate of return, safe rate.

sprinkler system. A fire protection system installed in buildings that consists of an overhead system of pipes that contain pressurized water and are fitted with valves, or sprinkler heads, that open automatically at certain temperatures.

standard deviation. The square root of the variance. *See also* variance.

straight-line capitalization. *See* yield capitalization formulas.

substitution. The appraisal principle that states that a buyer will pay no more for a property than the cost of obtaining an equally desirable substitute. If several similar goods are supplied, the good with the lowest price will produce the greatest demand and quantity sold. Substitution is one of the key principles for both the direct sales comparison approach and the cost approach to appraisal.

superadequacy. A type of functional obsolescence that is caused by a structural component that is too large or of a higher quality than what is needed for the highest and best use of the property; an item in which its cost exceeds its value; an overimprovement (e.g., high ceilings in an office, built-in bookshelves in a building to be used as a restaurant). *See also* curable functional obsolescence, incurable functional obsolescence.

supply and demand. An appraisal principle that states that the value of a property depends on the quantity and price of the property type available in the market and on the number of market participants and the price that they are willing to pay.

tax liability. The dollar amount of taxes owed for a specific time period. The tax liability from operations equals the taxable income multiplied by the appropriate marginal ordinary income tax rate. The tax liability from sale of a property equals the capital gain multiplied by the appropriate marginal ordinary income tax rate. *See also* after-tax cash flow, taxable income.

taxable income. Income that is taxable by law; calculated as the net operating income minus interest and depreciation. Taxable income from sale of a property equals the capital gain. *See also* after-tax cash flow.

taxation. A governmental right to raise income for use of public property and projects by assessing goods and services.

terminal capitalization rate. An overall capitalization rate used to forecast a reversionary value in a discounted cash-flow analysis. It is calculated by dividing the projected net operating income (NOI) for the year of sale by the selected rate. Sometimes the projected NOI for the year *after* the sale is used because this is the NOI that the buyer will receive for the first year. The terminal capitalization rate is typically forecast to be higher than the going-in cap rate due to a higher risk associated with estimating NOI at the time of the sale. *See also* capitalization rate, going-in capitalization rate.

time value of money. A financial principle based on the assumption that a positive interest can be earned on an investment and, therefore, that money received today is more valuable than money received in the future. *See also* discounted cash-flow analysis.

topography. The features and contour of the land.

total economic life. *See* economic life.

troubled property. *See* distressed property.

underimprovement. An improvement whose highest and best use does not match the highest and best use of the land as if vacant or whose size is not optimal for the site size. *See also* superadequacy.

underwriter's method. A method used to estimate property value by calculating the overall cap rate as a function of the loan-to-value ratio, debt coverage ratio and mortgage capitalization rate.

unit-in-place method. *See* building cost.

unit sales income. In the development approach to valuing sites, the estimated income from sales of individual lots. *See also* development approach.

units of comparison. A physical or economic measure that can be divided into the property's price to provide a more standardized comparison of the properties. The measure should be one that accounts for differences in the price typically paid for the properties such as price per square foot (office building), price per seat (theater) or price per gallon of gas pumped (gas station). Income can also be a unit of comparison such as when price is divided by effective gross income to obtain an effective gross income multiplier. *See also* elements of comparison, direct sales comparison approach.

usable area. *See* net leasable area.

utility. In economics, the enjoyment gained from a good in relationship to its risk and return.

vacancy allowance. In the income approach, a deduction from potential income for current or expected future space not rented due to tenant turnover. *See also* collection loss, potential gross income, effective gross income.

vacancy and collection loss. *See* vacancy allowance, collection loss.

value as is. The value of a property based on the land and any existing improvements on the site at the date of the appraisal. *See also* prospective value.

value in use. The value of a property or space to a specific user. Sometimes more particularly the value of a property designed or adapted to fit the specific requirements of the user.

value on completion but prior to rentup. An estimate of the value of a proposed project after construction is complete but before the building is occupied.

value on reaching stabilized occupancy. An estimate of what a proposed property will be worth after it is constructed and leased up to a stabilized occupancy.

variable expense. An operating expense that varies with the occupancy level or intensity of use of a property, e.g., utilities, management, and maintenance. *See also* fixed expense.

variable interest rate. An interest rate on a mortgage that changes throughout the term of the mortgage and is usually tied to an index, e.g., treasury bills, prime rate.

variable rate mortgage. *See* adjustable rate mortgage.

variance. A measure of the uncertainty or risk associated with an investment.

visibility. The ability of a site and/or improvements to be seen, usually from a transportation thoroughfare. The importance of having visibility depends on the property type.

yield capitalization. A method of estimating property value by discounting all expected future cash flows to a present value by a rate typical for investors in the marketplace for the interest being valued. The approach may or may not explicitly include financing. Algebraic formulas have been developed to discount future cash flows; however, these are no longer needed with the availability of computer spreadsheets. *See also* yield capitalization formulas, Hoskold premise, Inwood premise, Ellwood formula, Akerson format, discounted cash-flow analysis.

yield capitalization formulas. Formulas that are used to calculate an overall rate (R_O) for a property. These formulas were developed as shortcut techniques for estimating value with a discounted cash-flow analysis based on the yield rate (Y_O) for the property. These formulas express the overall rate as being equal to the yield rate plus or minus a term, which accounts for assumptions as to how the property's income and value are projected to change over the holding period. This term will differ for different income patterns.

yield rate (Y). The return on an investment, which considers income received over time;

the discount rate that equates the present value of future cash flows with the initial investment. Same as internal rate of return. *See also* equity yield rate, overall yield rate.

zero leverage. The use of borrowed funds at a rate equal to the equity yield rate. *See also* leverage.

zoning. An application of police power by a local government that provides a legal mechanism for the government to regulate land use and density of development for privately owned real property. Zoning establishes areas with uniform restrictions regarding property characteristics such as property use (residential, commercial, etc.), improvement height, specifications for signs and billboards, and density of development.

SYMBOLS AND ABBREVIATIONS

a	annualizer
AIRR	adjusted internal rate of return
$a_{\overline{n}}$	present value annuity of $1 per period
$1/a_{\overline{n}}$	payment to amortize $1
ARM	adjustable rate mortgage
ATCF	after-tax cash flow
BTCF	before-tax cash flow
CPI	consumer price index
Δ_O	change in property value
CR	annual compound percentage change in value
DCF	discounted cash-flow analysis
DCR	debt coverage ratio
E	equity ratio
EGI	effective gross income
EGIM	effective gross income multiplier
EIS	environmental impact study
FHLBB	Federal Home Loan Bank Board
FHLMC	Federal Home Loan Mortgage Corporation
FMRR	financial management rate of return

FNMA	Federal National Mortgage Association
FV	future value
GBA	gross building area
HBU	highest and best use
HVAC	heating, ventilation and air-conditioning system
i	interest rate
IRR	internal rate of return
M	loan-to-value ratio
NIM	net income multiplier
NOI	net operating income
NPV	net present value
OER	operating expense ratio
P	percent of loan paid off during holding period
PGI	potential gross income
PGIM	potential gross income multiplier
PI	profitability index
PTCF	pre-tax cash flow
PV	present value
R_B	building capitalization rate
R_E	equity capitalization rate
R_L	land capitalization rate
R_M	mortgage capitalization rate
R_O	overall (capitalization) rate
R_T	terminal capitalization rate
S^n	future value of $1
$S_{\overline{n}}$	future value annuity of $1 per period
$1/S_{\overline{n}}$	sinking fund factor
$1/S^n$	present value of $1
V	property value
V_B	value of the building
V_E	value of the equity
V_L	value of the land
V_M	mortgage loan value
V_R	reversionary value
Y	yield rate
Y_E	equity yield rate
Y_M	mortgage yield rate
Y_O	overall yield rate

Index